THE BLOOMSBURY HANDBOOK
OF SOCRATES

Also available from Bloomsbury

Andrea Cesalpino and Renaissance Aristotelianism, edited by Fabrizio Baldassarri and Craig Martin

Cooperative Flourishing in Plato's 'Republic', by Carolina Araújo

Socrates On Trial, by Nigel Tubbs

The Bloomsbury Handbook of Plato (2nd edition), edited by Gerald A. Press and Mateo Duque

The Bloomsbury Handbook of Ethics (2nd edition), edited by Christian B. Miller

THE BLOOMSBURY HANDBOOK OF SOCRATES

Second Edition

Edited by Russell E. Jones, Ravi Sharma and Nicholas D. Smith

BLOOMSBURY ACADEMIC
LONDON • NEW YORK • OXFORD • NEW DELHI • SYDNEY

BLOOMSBURY ACADEMIC
Bloomsbury Publishing Plc
50 Bedford Square, London, WC1B 3DP, UK
1385 Broadway, New York, NY 10018, USA
29 Earlsfort Terrace, Dublin 2, Ireland

BLOOMSBURY, BLOOMSBURY ACADEMIC and the Diana logo are trademarks of
Bloomsbury Publishing Plc

First published in Great Britain 2012
This edition published 2024

Copyright © Russell E. Jones, Ravi Sharma, Nicholas D. Smith and Contributors, 2024

Russell E. Jones, Ravi Sharma and Nicholas D. Smith have asserted their right under the
Copyright, Designs and Patents Act, 1988, to be identified as Editors of this work.

Cover image: Socrates statue against blue sky
(© Nikos Pavlakis / Alamy Stock Photo)

All rights reserved. No part of this publication may be reproduced or transmitted in any form or by
any means, electronic or mechanical, including photocopying, recording, or any information
storage or retrieval system, without prior permission in writing from the publishers.

Bloomsbury Publishing Plc does not have any control over, or responsibility for, any third-party
websites referred to or in this book. All internet addresses given in this book were correct at the time
of going to press. The author and publisher regret any inconvenience caused if addresses have
changed or sites have ceased to exist, but can accept no responsibility for any such changes.

A catalogue record for this book is available from the British Library.

A catalog record for this book is available from the Library of Congress.

ISBN: HB: 978-1-3501-8567-8
        ePDF: 978-1-3501-8568-5
        eBook: 978-1-3501-8569-2

Series: Bloomsbury Handbooks

Typeset by RefineCatch Limited, Bungay, Suffolk

To find out more about our authors and books visit www.bloomsbury.com
and sign up for our newsletters.

CONTENTS

List of Contributors		vii
Preface		viii
List of Abbreviations		ix
1	Socrates in Old Comedy *Alessandro Stavru*	1
2	Xenophon's Socrates on Teaching and Learning *Russell E. Jones and Ravi Sharma*	23
3	Socratic Methods *Eric Brown*	45
4	Socrates and the Forms *William J. Prior*	63
5	Socratic Ignorance *Keith McPartland*	85
6	The Priority of Definition *Hugh H. Benson*	127
7	Socratic Virtue Intellectualism *Justin C. Clark*	153
8	Socratic Eudaimonism *Paul Woodruff*	179
9	Socratic Motivational Intellectualism *Freya Möbus*	205
10	Socrates on Love *Suzanne Obdrzalek*	229
11	Socrates on Emotions *Irina Deretić*	255
12	Socrates' Political Philosophy *Curtis N. Johnson*	275
13	Socratic Theology and Piety *Mark L. McPherran*	299

| 14 Socrates on Death and the Afterlife | 323 |
| Emily A. Austin | |

15 The Trial of Socrates — 343
Nicholas D. Smith

BIBLIOGRAPHY — 367
INDEX — 395

LIST OF CONTRIBUTORS

Emily A. Austin
Wake Forest University
USA

Hugh H. Benson
University of Oklahoma
USA

Eric Brown
Washington University in St Louis
USA

Justin C. Clark
Hamilton College
USA

Irina Deretić
University of Belgrade
Serbia

Curtis N. Johnson
Lewis & Clark College
USA

Russell E. Jones
University of Oklahoma
USA

Keith McPartland
Williams College
USA

Mark L. McPherran
Simon Fraser University
Canada

Freya Möbus
Loyola University Chicago
USA

Suzanne Obdrzalek
Claremont McKenna College
USA

William J. Prior
Santa Clara University
USA

Ravi Sharma
Clark University
USA

Nicholas D. Smith
Lewis & Clark College
USA

Alessandro Stavru
University of Verona
Italy

Paul Woodruff
The University of Texas at Austin
USA

PREFACE

This second edition of *The Bloomsbury Companion to Socrates* has the same aim as the first: to provide a comprehensive guide to the main issues in the philosophy of Socrates, primarily as presented in the shorter dialogues of Plato, but with attention also to Socratic thought in the writings of other ancient authors. This edition goes further than the first by including two chapters primarily devoted to authors other than Plato: one centred on Socrates as he appears in Aristophanes and another on Socratic thought as portrayed by Xenophon. Among the other chapters, some are newly commissioned and the rest are revised to varying degrees from the first edition. Our decisions about whether to commission new chapters or revisions were largely guided by our sense of how much the state of scholarship on individual topics has changed since the appearance of the first edition. To fit our sense of the focus of recent scholarship we also made some changes to the weight given various topics. For example, the second edition contains somewhat less focus on religion, and somewhat more on moral psychology. In all these decisions, we were guided by a substantial set of referee reports collected by the press, and we are grateful to the scholars involved for their expert advice.

In general, the production of the second edition was motivated by the recognition that Socratic studies continues to be a dynamic field of scholarship. Our authors were instructed to give up-to-date and comprehensive analyses of their assigned topics. If they also wished to present their own views, we encouraged them to do so. The result, however, is that the editors do not always agree with the positive views put forward in these chapters.

We are grateful to Layla Williams for her excellent work as a research assistant and to the University of Oklahoma for making this assistance possible. It has been easy to work with the expert editorial team at Bloomsbury; our thanks especially to Jade Grogan, Suzie Nash and Lucy Harper.

The Editors
Russell E. Jones
Ravi Sharma
Nicholas D. Smith

LIST OF ABBREVIATIONS

Ael. *VH*	Aelian's *Varia Historia*
Alc. I	*Alcibiades* I
Alex.	Alexis
Amm. Marc. *Res gest.*	Ammianus Marcellinus' *Res Gestae*
Ap.	Plato's *Apology*
Apol.	Xenophon's *Apology*
Arist.	Aristotle
Aristoph.	Aristophanes
Ath.	Athenaeus' *Deipnosophistae*
Chrm.	*Charmides*
Cr.	*Crito*
Cyr.	*Cyropaedia*
Dio *Or.*	Dio Chrysostom's *Orationes*
DK	H. Diels and W. Kranz, *Fragmente der Vorsokratiker*, 6th ed.
DL	Diogenes Laertius
Epigr.	*Epigrams*
Eu.	*Euthyphro*
Euthd.	*Euthydemus*
Gnom. Vat.	*Gnomologium Vaticanum*
Grg.	*Gorgias*
Hier. *Adv. Jov.*	St Jerome's *Against Jovinian*
Hi.Ma.	*Hippias Major*
Hi.Mi.	*Hippias Minor*
Iul. *Orat.*	Julian's *Orationes*
KA	R. Kassel and C. Austin, *Poetae Comici Graeci*
La.	*Laches*
Ly.	*Lysis*

M.	*Meno*
Math.	*Adversus Mathematicos*
MM	*Magna Moralia*
Mem.	*Memorabilia*
Metaph.	*Metaphysics*
NE	*Nicomachean Ethics*
Oec.	*Oeconomicus*
Phd.	*Phaedo*
Phdr.	*Phaedrus*
Phlb.	*Philebus*
Piscat.	*The Fisher*
Plat.	Plato
Plt.	*Statesman*
Prt.	*Protagoras*
Pyth.	Alexis' *The Pythagorean Woman*
Pythag.	Aristophon's *The Pythagorean Man*
Rep.	*Republic*
Sph.	*Sophist*
SSR	*Socratis et Socraticorum Reliquiae*
Sym.	Xenophon's *Symposium*
Symp.	Plato's *Symposium*
Theod. *graec. aff. cur.*	Theodoretus' *Cure of the Greek Maladies*
Thesm.	*Thesmophoriazusae*
Thg.	*Theages*
Tht.	*Theaetetus*
Xen.	Xenophon

CHAPTER ONE

Socrates in Old Comedy

ALESSANDRO STAVRU

I. INTRODUCTION

The earliest surviving evidence on Socrates goes back to the Athenian comedies of the fifth century BCE.[1] In plays performed between the 430s and 405, Socrates is lampooned as a pretentious charlatan, and his teaching activity as futile, absurd and morally reprehensible. These comedies were staged in city theatres before large audiences. We must assume, therefore, that Socrates would have become a household name during this period, and indeed a well-known personality.

Socrates features in three extant comedies by Aristophanes, the major playwright of Old Comedy, namely *Clouds II* (420–417), *Birds* (414) and *Frogs* (405). These are the sole extant texts about Socrates that date to his own lifetime. Information about Socrates and other intellectuals of the fifth century can also be found in texts attributed to other comedians, such as Cratinus, Teleclides, Callias, Eupolis, Ameipsias and Plato Comicus. Fragments of their plays have been preserved through quotations by later authors, but it is not always clear to which plays these texts belong, making it difficult to provide a chronological order of them. Another difficulty in dealing with ancient Comedy lies in its conventional features: the comic distortions and exaggerations, a highly allusive language, the wide use of sexual and sadomasochistic innuendo, political satire and *ad hominem* attacks against a variety of historical figures (some of whom are unknown to the modern reader), all of which make it hard to assess – or even to grasp – each humorous twist and turn occurring in the plays. This problem is especially pertinent in the use of ancient Comedy as a resource for uncovering genuine information about Socrates' life and thought. Comic texts provide such information within a satiric context, through the deforming lens of ridicule. It is important to note that Comedy was not conceived to provide a reliable portrait of Socrates: On the contrary, its aim was to lampoon public persons of various kinds – including Socrates. This caveat should always be kept in mind when reading these texts. On the other hand, one should also be aware that the comic effect of these texts could only be achieved if the characters targeted by the playwrights were realistic, i.e., *recognisable to the audience*.[2] Despite all exaggerations and distortions, the comic evidence on Socrates must have had a solid foothold in reality.[3] Hence the value of these texts to reconstruct not only the cultural context of Socrates' activity, but – and even more importantly – to understand how this activity was perceived by his contemporaries.

Unlike Plato, Xenophon and the other Socratics, who portray Socrates years after his death, the comedians stage him in the midst of his activity. Another major difference lies in the fact that the Socratics describe their master as an ethical and philosophical model, while the comedians heavily attack him, his pupils and every aspect of his activity. Moreover, the image of Socrates put forward by his followers mirrors the standpoint of just a small group of people (i.e., his associates and friends), while that of Old Comedy reflects the playwrights' views, which hence became widely known in Athens thanks to their representation on stage. For all of these reasons, the testimony provided by Old Comedy is of utmost importance – notwithstanding the unavoidable difficulties linked to its use.

II. THE NEW WISDOM

Several comedies staged in the 430s and 420s deal with 'education' (*paideia*). It has been rightly observed that these plays form a 'subgenre' of Old Comedy.[4] At least seven plays by six comedians (Cratinus, Telecleides, Callias, Eupolis, Ameipsias and Plato Comicus) target 'wisdom' (*sophia*) and those who teach or acquire it, the 'sophists' or 'thinkers' (*sophistai* or *phrontistai*).[5] Such intellectuals, or followers of them, form the choirs of five comedies that centre around the matter of teaching and acquiring a new kind of wisdom.[6] Such wisdom is ridiculed by the comedians as bizarre and foolish. It consists of four distinct subjects that were not encompassed in traditional *paideia*, namely:

A) The study of nature;

B) Non-official religiosity and scepticism about traditional religion;

C) Fraudulent lyrical and rhetorical skills;

D) Asceticism and poverty.

We will see that all of these four subjects are core features of Aristophanes' portrayal of Socrates. All other playwrights discuss A) without any reference to Socrates and his pupils. Callias is the only other comedian who indirectly relates B) to Socrates. C) and D), on the contrary, appear to be unique features of Socrates, not only according to Aristophanes but also according to all of the abovementioned comedians.

A) The Study of Nature

One of the first comedies mocking 'intellectuals' is Cratinus' *All-Seers* (*Panoptai*), a play first performed in Athens sometime between 435 and 430.[7] Here, the natural philosopher Hippon of Samos, nicknamed 'the Atheist', is ridiculed for comparing the sky to an oven-cover (*pnigeus*).[8] This joke would be later exploited by Aristophanes in connection with Socrates: One of the first things we are told about him and his entourage in *Clouds* is that 'they convince other people that the sky is an oven-cover' (96).[9] It is important to note that analogies of this kind, between 'macro-scale' naturalistic phenomena and 'micro-scale' objects of daily use, are typical of pre-Socratic thought.[10] Cratinus and Aristophanes lampoon the *pnigeus* analogy as both futile and atheistic, its immediate consequence being that divine efficacy is substituted by natural necessity, and that, as a corollary, traditional gods turn out to be useless.[11]

A similar context seems to arise in a fragment drawn from Eupolis' *Flatterers* (*Kolakes*), a play rehearsed in 421. Here, Protagoras is attacked for being a 'plague who boasts about celestial matters'.[12] As we have seen in Cratinus, an atheistic background is also likely in this case. Protagoras was known for his agnosticism, which eventually resulted in a condemnation for atheism.[13] The fragment is important because it confirms what is

SOCRATES IN OLD COMEDY

known from other sources, namely that Protagoras had interests that went far beyond the art of discourse.[14] In his case, it is particularly evident that the definition of 'sophist' encompasses the same study of 'heavenly things' (*meteōra*) that Socrates is devoted to in Aristophanes' *Clouds*;[15] hence his boastful attitude (*alazonei*) Eupolis mocks at. It should be noted that this is one of the first occurrences of *alazoneia*, which is a typical feature of the 'sophists' in Old Comedy. The term appears for the first time in Cratinus, and it is an important characteristic of Socrates and his pupils in Aristophanes' *Clouds*.[16]

B) Non-official Religiosity and Scepticism about Traditional Religion

In Old Comedy, the decline of the traditional gods is matched by the emergence of a new class of seers, oracle mongers and charlatans of various kinds.[17] Among the comedians, the most popular figure of this sort is the seer Lampon, an authority on religious matters. Lampon was a close associate of Pericles. He signed the Peace of Nicias in 421 and played an important role in the foundation of Thurii in southern Italy in 444. Cratinus attacks him in *Fleeing Women* (*Drapetides*), a comedy written after 444, for being gluttonous.[18] A quality typical of characters such as Lampon is 'haughtiness' (*semnotēs*), a characteristic that other comedians also apply to Socrates.[19] In Callias' *Men In Shackles* (*Pedetai*), a play probably staged in 431,[20] the playwright Euripides (probably dressed as a woman) is asked: 'Why are you so haughty and why are your thoughts so deep?' Euripides responds: 'Because I can afford it: Socrates is the author.'[21] The banter mocks the 'sophist' Euripides,[22] who is so fond of having Socrates as a ghost-writer of his plays that he has no problem in admitting it. If anything, he is even boastful about it: Thanks to Socrates he 'thinks deeply' and is 'holy' like a charismatic religious leader. The text suggests that Euripides imitates these attitudes of Socrates. This implies that Callias attributes the qualities of 'haughtiness' and 'deep thinking' to Socrates more so than to Euripides, thus anticipating two core features of Socrates that will be brought on stage later by Aristophanes, in both *Clouds* and *Frogs*.[23]

C) Fraudulent Lyrical and Rhetorical Skills

The collaboration between Euripides and Socrates is also mocked in two unattributed fragments by Teleclides. In the first fragment, Mnesilochos, Euripides' father-in-law, 'fries a new play for Euripides, and Socrates provides the wood for frying'.[24] The second fragment consists of just two words, namely 'Euripides . . . [your plays are] built of socratic rods'.[25] Both texts, although brief and fragmentary, are clear in stating that Euripides owes his literary production to Socrates. This confirms what we saw in Callias, that Socrates is the ghost-writer of Euripidean tragedy. A close link between Socrates and Euripides is also evident in Aristophanes: According to *Clouds I*, Socrates is the author of Euripides' tragedies; in *Clouds II*, Euripides is mentioned twice, while in *Frogs* he is ridiculed for spending his time chatting with Socrates.[26] A late anecdote reported by Aelian provides the background for this alleged liaison between the two: Apparently, Socrates did not attend public theatres, except when new tragedies by Euripides were rehearsed. For instance, this reportedly happened when Euripides was participating in a contest in the Piraeus: Apparently, Socrates went there because 'he loved the man for his wisdom as well as for the sweetness of his verse'.[27]

Socrates' poetical skills are also ridiculed by Eupolis, who portrays him at a symposium, receiving a wine cup and singing a poem by Stesichorus to the accompaniment of the lyre,[28] when, quite unexpectedly, he purloins the wine decanter. Not only does this fragment claim that Socrates is able to inspire one of the greatest playwrights of his time, Euripides, but that he is also keen on reciting the songs of one of the most revered poets of the past, Stesichorus, in order to distract his audience and steal the wine-jug. These parodies are typical of a series of comedies which ridicule poetry. Among these plays are also Cratinus' *Hesiods* and *Archilochuses* (probably written in the 430s), Plato Comicus' *Sophists* (date unknown), Phrinicus' *Muses* and Aristophanes' *Frogs* (the latter two rehearsed in 405).

It is interesting to note that Telecleides, Callias and Eupolis each hint at Socrates as possessing highly developed lyrical skills. However, nothing in their fragments suggests that Socrates wrote poetry himself, although it seems that he would have been perfectly able to. There is, therefore, no contradiction between these texts and a much-discussed passage from Plato's *Phaedo*, according to which Socrates never wrote anything, except during the last days of his life when he was in prison waiting to be executed: He apparently composed a hymn to Apollo and verse retellings of Aesop's fables.[29] Late authors confirm Plato's account: Diogenes Laertius retains the beginnings of both texts Plato hints at. Athenaeus quotes a fragment of an elegiac distich he believes to be from Socrates, and Ammianus Marcellinus reports that Socrates endeavoured to learn a poem by Stesichorus while in prison.[30]

The fact that Socrates' lyrical skills are portrayed in plays by four comedians of his time (Callias, Telecleides, Eupolis and Aristophanes) suggests that such skills were widely acknowledged in Athens during the last quarter of the fifth century. Plato's account of the *Phaedo*, which was written many years after Socrates' death, might well rely on these texts: Socrates must have had poetical abilities which he used repeatedly, but he did not put anything to paper until the very last days of his life.

Socrates' poetic abilities are likely connected to another quality similarly lampooned by the comedians in their plays, namely his rhetorical skill. Aristophanes and Eupolis ridicule this skill as a form of vain 'chatter' (*adoleskhein, perilalein*) that Socrates teaches to his pupils. In a fragment from Eupolis, likely deriving from his play *Flatterers* (staged in 421), Socrates is ridiculed as a 'chattering beggar' (*ptokhon adoleskhen*), whose main activity is to 'think' (*pephrontiken*).[31] From the same period comes another fragment stemming from the play *Autolycus* (also rehearsed in 421). Here, an unknown character urges a 'sophist' to teach another unknown character to chatter.[32] It is likely that the 'sophist' mentioned here is Socrates since *adoleskhein* is related to Socrates and his teaching, not only in the previous fragment by Eupolis but also in the dramatic final scene of Aristophanes' *Clouds*.[33] *Adoleskhein* is, therefore, a core feature of Aristophanes' and Eupolis' descriptions of Socrates. Both Plato and Xenophon refer to it as a distinctive feature of the comic Socrates.[34]

D) Asceticism and Poverty

Ameipsias, Eupolis and Aristophanes provide detailed reports about the ascetic features of Socrates and his companions. Socrates' extreme poverty is ridiculed by their pointing out that: 1) he and his pupils have very little to eat and are, as a consequence, on the verge of starving; 2) Socrates must invent ruses and commit petty thefts in order to scrape together the money he needs for his and his associates' maintenance; 3) Socrates' clothing is inadequate, especially during the cold season.

At the same festival in which Aristophanes rehearsed his *Clouds*, that is, the Great Dionysia of 423, another comedy was devoted to Socrates. A contemporary of

SOCRATES IN OLD COMEDY

Aristophanes, the playwright Ameipsias, staged *Connus*, a comedy in which he ridiculed a core aspect of Socrates' asceticism, namely his 'endurance' (*karteria*).[35] Socrates is described as wearing neither a proper coat nor shoes. He does not get enough food, which makes him so weak that he is not even able to flatter (*kolakein*). A fragment of Eupolis' *Flatterers* provides a clue to understanding the meaning of this fragment. Socrates earns his living by 'flattering': he praises whatever people say in order to receive a pittance from them, with which he then buys himself his daily meal.[36] The problem is that since he does not get enough food, he is too weak to praise people. Therefore, he is unable to get the amount of money he needs in order to provide the food he needs. This, in turn, makes him weaker and less able to flatter others, thus giving way to a vicious circle from which there is no escape.

We have already seen that Eupolis mocks Socrates as a 'chattering beggar' who 'thinks about everything except how to get something to eat'.[37] This fits well with the other abovementioned fragment by Eupolis in which Socrates sings a poem by Stesichorus.[38] It seems likely that both fragments belong to the play *Flatterers*, which might have had the following plot: Socrates spends his time chatting nonsense with his pupils; at some point hunger drives him to praise people in order to scrape some money together, both for himself and his associates; but he is too weak to succeed; he then goes to a symposium, where he distracts the other diners by singing a poem by Stesichorus; thereupon, he attempts to steal a wine decanter; but again he does not succeed, since the decanter is too bulky to go unnoticed.[39] This plot strongly brings to mind a much-discussed episode in Aristophanes' *Clouds*, in which Socrates once again resorts to thefts in order to get something for himself and his associates to eat: in that case, he purloins Strepsiades' cloak and shoes.[40] Another passage in *Clouds* suggests that thefts of this kind were regular; indeed, all those who wanted to become associates of Socrates were forced to enter his school naked, leaving their cloak and all of their clothes outside.[41]

This explains why Socrates himself is described as wearing a threadbare cloak and going around barefoot, and the Socratics as suffering from hunger and thirst. The comic distortion is evident: The ascetic techniques practised by Socrates and his pupils are mocked by the comedians as senseless hardships, which everyone sees as strange and futile – except Socrates and his associates, who instead see in their training a reason for boasting about their superiority over anyone else.[42] This dichotomy was perpetuated after Socrates' death, both by his associates and his enemies. The comic image of the ascetic Socrates was picked up by the Socratics, and especially by the Cynics, who turned it into a positive image. Socrates' cloak and bare feet thus became a sort of 'uniform' – i.e., a symbol of the status of the philosopher.[43] On the other hand, this very image was re-used for its negative aspects in Middle Comedy. The Pythagoreans of the fourth century BC were portrayed in the same way as Socrates and the Socratics were one century before, i.e., as dirty, wearing a threadbare cloak and enduring hunger, hot and cold weather.[44]

III. SOCRATES ON STAGE: CHRONOLOGY AND DRAMATIC SETTING

The evidence discussed thus far suggests that the comedians focused on Socrates since the 430s. Socrates' supposed role in helping Euripides write his plays was perceived by the comedians as crucial, since it questioned the authorship of Euripides' work as a whole. The issue was debated in the earliest datable comedy in which Socrates is mentioned: Callias' *Men in Shackles* (431), as well as in Telecleides.[45] It should be noted, however, that none of these texts implies a portrayal of Socrates on stage. Nor is there any evidence that the first comedy written by Aristophanes, the *Banqueters* (dated 427), featured any character playing Socrates. It is very likely that Socrates became a dramatic persona for the first time at the Dionysian festival in 423, when two of the three comedies rehearsed dealt with Socratic education. By then, Socrates was already a popular figure due to the deeds he had performed in two military campaigns: the siege of Potidaea (in 432) and the retreat from Delium (in 424).[46] Socrates was a hero in both campaigns: In Potidaea, he saved his friend and associate Alcibiades, who would then become a prominent Athenian general and play a crucial role in the Peloponnesian War; in Delium, Socrates showed more self-control than the general Laches, keeping his calm during the retreat.

Neither of the two plays won first prize. Out of the three comedies rehearsed, Aristophanes' *Clouds* was placed last, whereas Ameipisas' *Connus*, a piece named after Socrates' music teacher and dealing with Socrates' own education in music, took second place. First place was awarded to Cratinus' last play, the *Wine Flask* (*Pytine*), a comedy in which Cratinus joked with his own habit of excessive drinking. We know from Diogenes Laertius that Ameipsas' *Connus* staged a barefooted Socrates dressed in a threadbare cloak. He was ridiculed because of his *karteria* – the same quality he had displayed the previous year in Potidaea and Delium. Plato reports on both episodes. At Potidaea, Socrates 'took the hardships (*karterēseis*) better than anyone in the army': he was able to resist hunger, cold and even alcohol.[47] He stood thinking for a whole night and day without going to sleep, and he saved Alcibiades' life during a battle.[48] During the retreat from Delium, when the Athenian army was on the run, he showed both bravery and self-control.[49]

In Aristophanes' *Clouds* (869–870), Socrates was probably represented wearing the same threadbare cloak (*tribōn*) of Ameipsias' *Connus*.[50] His character's first appearance saw him hitched up to a crane-like device (*mēkhanē*) that made him fly through the air – probably a comic allusion to Socrates' collaboration with Euripides, who was renowned for his use of this device. It was due to this apparition *ex machina* that Socrates' arrival on the scene soon became memorable: Many years later, Plato would recall *Clouds* as the comedy that had 'introduced one Socrates swinging about and saying that he is skywalking'.[51] After 423, Aristophanes depicted Socrates on stage once again in *Clouds II*, but not in *Birds* (414) nor in *Frogs* (405).

The only playwright who apparently represented Socrates on stage after Aristophanes' *Clouds* was Eupolis. According to Lucian's *Fishermen*, '[Aristophanes and] Eupolis brought Socrates on stage to ridicule him, writing all kinds of comedies about him'.[52] This means that Socrates was indeed a character in Eupolis' plays. A scholium to *Clouds* specifies that although 'Eupolis mentioned Socrates a few times, he attacked him more than Aristophanes in the whole of *Clouds*'.[53] As discussed above, we know of two such instances: In both *Flatterers* and *Autolycus* Socrates is lampooned for his chattering.

Toward 415, Socrates must have become a widely known personality. This is clear from Aristophanes' *Birds* (rehearsed in 414), in which those who 'behave like Socrates' are defined using a newly coined verb, *sokratan*, which unmistakably proves how Socratic lifestyle had become a benchmark for a well-defined group of people.[54] Another new, similar verb, *sokratizein*, may have occurred in Eupolis' *Demes* (staged in 412). In this case, the meaning is slightly different, namely 'doing Socratic things' – which again implies that both Aristophanes and Eupolis had a clear-cut idea about what their audience considered to be 'Socratic' and what they did not.

Much of Socrates' fame during the last decades of the fifth century came as a result of the look he was given on stage. Unfortunately, the surviving comic texts make very little reference to his physiognomy, providing just a few details. We have seen that Ameipsias focuses on his threadbare cloak and bare feet. Aristophanes also mentions his cloak, and repeatedly describes the inhabitants of the thinkery as 'pale'.[55] As to the mask the character of Socrates wore on stage, there is no scholarly consensus as to what it looked like. A passage of *Knights* (performed in 424, one year before *Clouds I*) informs us that mask-makers were able to create portrait-masks of public personalities.[56] This suggests that in the 420s characters playing public figures wore masks depicting individual physiognomic traits. The 3rd century Roman writer Aelian recalls that during the comedies Socrates 'could be spotted among the actors, since the costumists portrayed him as well as they possibly could'. But Socrates 'stood for the whole duration of the comedy', in order to be identified by the foreigners who were attending the rehearsal and did not know him. This suggests that, *despite the costumists' efforts*, the actor playing Socrates was so unlike him that the real Socrates, by standing all the time, could show the difference between himself and its character.[57]

According to an ancient scholium, the Socrates of *Clouds* looked like a Silenus,[58] implying that he wore a Silenus-like mask in that comedy.[59] This Silenic feature could also be corroborated by an unattributed comic fragment that describes Socrates as *dimorphos*, 'two-formed', that is, half human and half goat/horse like a satyr.[60] It may well be, therefore, that the Silenic Socrates portrayed decades later by Plato and Xenophon drew on a comic avatar, reinterpreting it as a philosophical icon.[61]

IV. ARISTOPHANES

Among Aristophanes' eleven extant comedies, only *Clouds* is entirely devoted to Socratic education.[62] The comedy was staged in 423 (= *Clouds I*), but the version that has come down to us is a reworking dating to the years 420–417 (= *Clouds II*). In two other plays (*Birds*, of 414, and *Frogs*, of 405), Socrates appears only briefly, albeit in sections that are crucial for the plots of both comedies. Socratic education seems to have played an important role in Aristophanes' first play, the *Banqueters* (*Daitaleis*, rehearsed in 427).

This evidence attests to Aristophanes' interest for Socrates in a period that stretches over two decades: From 427 to 405 he continuously deals with issues linked to Socrates or Socratic education and lifestyle. During these twenty years, two distinct periods can be identified: the period prior to 423 (see below, section IV.1.), where the focus is already on Socratic education; and 423–405 (section IV.II.), in which Aristophanes works on *Clouds* (versions I and II), as well as on the descriptions of Socrates and the Socratic lifestyle in *Birds* (v. 1553–1564 and 1280–1283) and *Frogs* (v. 1491–1499).

IV.I. *Before 423:* Banqueters

The first comedy written by Aristophanes, *Banqueters* (*Daitaleis*), was produced by Callistratus, and took second prize at the Great Dionysia of 427.[63] Socrates did not appear on stage, but scholars have long noticed that one of the main characters of the comedy, the 'teacher' (*didaskalos*), has markedly 'sophistic' – if not altogether 'Socratic' – traits.[64] He imparts lessons in the same subjects that were ridiculed by other comedians, namely: A) the study of nature (astronomy: fr. 227 KA); B) non-official religiosity (necromancy:

205);[65] C) fraudulent lyrical and rhetorical skills (Homeric glosses: 233; language and rhetoric: 233; and the invention of new words: 205); and D) asceticism and poverty (cold baths: 247; Laconian habits: 225; and the poor and dishonest character Lysimachus: 205). The plot centres around the activity of the teacher. The teacher has two brothers as pupils: One of them is 'chaste' (*sōphrōn*), the other 'lascivious' (*katapugōn*). The chaste boy has been educated according to a traditional curriculum (music and gymnastics), and will eventually flee from his teacher; the lascivious boy, on the contrary, has been educated in new sophistic wisdom and is a fervent admirer of the teacher. At some point, the elderly father of the two boys complains about the degeneracy of his lascivious son (225).[66] The lascivious boy then goes so far as to insult his father (205), thus anticipating the plot of *Clouds II*.[67] The father summons Alcibiades and Thrasymachus, holding them responsible for the wickedness of his son, but his son defends them because he deems them 'men who cultivate beauty and goodness'.[68]

The new wisdom displayed by the lascivious boy has a Socratic provenance. This can be drawn from the fact that two of Socrates' closest associates, namely Aristodemus (242) and a young Alcibiades (244), are also among the lascivious pupils who receive lessons from the teacher.[69] In fact, we know from Plato that both of them were Socrates' 'lovers' (*erastai*).[70] The sexual language used by Aristophanes to describe them is explicit: *Katapugōn* literally stands for 'up the ass', and Alcibiades is 'born for his phallus'.[71] Aristophanes is the first comedian to describe Socratic education by employing such a detailed description of sexual debauchery.[72] Wrong education is not only ethically reprehensible; it also leads to a wicked sexuality. This will become evident in *Clouds II*, where the contest between the Stronger and the Weaker Argument is also a contest between two opposing models of sexuality: the former relying on *sophrōsunē*, i.e., restraint from physical sex; the latter urged by the 'needs of nature', and thus *euruprōktosunē*, a wanton consumption of sex.[73]

IV.II. From 423 to 405: Clouds, Birds and Frogs

The similarities between *Banqueters* and *Clouds* have long been noted. According to several scholars, *Clouds* should be understood as an evolution of *Banqueters*.[74] Both comedies are centred on 'new' education – the same sort of education (A–D) seen in other comedies. The plots of *Banqueters* and *Clouds* are indeed similar: The new education is imparted by a 'bad teacher'; an old father is concerned about the negative effects of such teaching on his lascivious son; the son uses this education to turn against the father.

In 423, Aristophanes staged a version of *Clouds* (*Clouds I*) that has not come down to us.[75] This version was preserved in antiquity up until the Hellenistic age. It is very likely that a copy of *Clouds I* was in the library of Alexandria since Alexandrian scholiasts refer to it, comparing it with *Clouds II*.[76] Thanks to these scholars we know that *Clouds II* was very similar to *Clouds I*, except for the parabasis of the chorus (v. 518–562), the *agōn* of the two discourses (889–1104) and the burning of Socrates' school (1483–1511), all of which were added in the second version.[77] In the parabasis of *Clouds II*, Aristophanes polemically refers to the vulgar jokes used by other comedians of his time (553–560). He promises he will not use any of them in his own comedy. These jokes are about big leather phalluses, bald men, indecent dances, old men who talk and beat others up with a stick, torches, and cries of desperation (537–543). All of these jokes are indeed used in *Clouds II*.[78] This suggests that by introducing lowbrow humour – despite denying doing so – Aristophanes is actually making fun of the public that had rejected *Clouds I*. If this

SOCRATES IN OLD COMEDY

reconstruction is correct, the sections devoted to the above-mentioned jokes in *Clouds II* would have been absent in *Clouds I*.[79]

A few years after 423, Aristophanes reworked *Clouds* with the view to restaging it at a Dionysian festival.[80] The reworking was apparently not granted a chorus by the archons responsible for selecting the plays to be performed at the Dionysia.[81] Moreover, two prefaces and a scholium from the Alexandrian age seem to suggest that the reworking was never restaged.[82] This is certainly true for the two central dramatic competitions staged in Athens, namely the Dionysia and the Lenaia.[83] But there is strong evidence to suggest that the play was restaged in other dramatic Athenian or non-Athenian festivals, or in non-competitive events.[84] In *Apology*, a text written some decades after 423, Plato recalls that the 'first accusers' of Socrates 'got hold of the Athenians since childhood', so as to make them believe that 'there is a certain Socrates, a wise man, who investigates all things in the sky and below the earth, who makes the worse argument the stronger'.[85] The first accusers of Socrates were both 'dangerous' and 'numerous', since they 'were making their accusations over a long period of time'. They were able to do so because they took advantage of the fact that the Athenians, by virtue of their young age, were inclined to believe their slander. Therefore, they 'won their case by default, as there was no defence'. Plato is explicit about the fact that *Clouds* exerted a disruptive effect on those Athenians who, at the time of the play's first performance in 423, were *young*, and, more importantly, that this disruptive effect was only possible *because it occurred over a long period of time*.[86] These claims perfectly make sense if we surmise that *Clouds* did not just circulate in its written form, but was staged repeatedly in the years that followed 423.[87] Such repeated theatrical performances would explain how the Socrates who deals with heavenly things and makes the worse argument the stronger could become part of the Athenians' collective imagination in the years after 423.

Another argument supporting the restaging of *Clouds* is the circumstance that it is the only comedy to which Plato explicitly refers in his dialogues.[88] By contrast, other comedies dealing with Socrates, such as those of Callias and Telecleides, or even plays in which Socrates was represented on stage, such as Ameipsias' *Connus*, or Eupolis's *Flatterers* and *Autolycus*, are never mentioned.[89] Particularly odd is the case of Ameipsias' *Connus*, a comedy Plato appears to ignore completely despite doing better than *Clouds* in 423. The reason for this silence must have been the popularity *Clouds* had achieved by the end of the fifth century BC – most likely due to its repeated restaging, which we must surmise did not occur for the other comedies.[90]

One major feature of *Clouds* is its ending, which is atypical for Old Comedy. The protagonist of the play, Strepsiades, sets the thinkery on fire, causing Socrates and his pupils, who were inside the building (1476–1510), to be burnt alive. Strepsiades performs this act out of rage: He has just been deceived by Socrates and beaten up by his son Pheidippides. However, Strepsiades is not the victim here. On the contrary, the whole plot centres around his own 'outrageousness' (*hubris*). His aim is to learn the Weaker Argument in order to outwit his creditors so as to defraud them. Indeed, one important feature of the Weaker Argument is precisely *hubris* (1068). But Strepsiades never gets to learn the Weaker Argument; instead, only his son Pheidippides will be permitted to do so (886–887). Nonetheless, Strepsiades eventually succeeds in warding off his creditors thanks to the sophistry he has learned from Socrates (1214–1302). Specifically, he flogs the second creditor, thus committing *hubris* (1299).[91] The Chorus in *Clouds* prophesies to Strepsiades that he will soon pay for his 'love for evil deeds' (1303–1310). The punishment is exacted by Pheidippides, who beats his father up (1321–1443), then

10 THE BLOOMSBURY HANDBOOK OF SOCRATES

justifies the beating through the eristic arguments of the Weaker Argument (1444–1446). The leader of the Chorus intervenes and tells Strepsiades: 'This is what we do each time we see someone who falls in love with evil deeds: we hurl him into misery, so that he may learn to fear the gods' (1458–1461). Strepsiades admits his guilt, since he should have repaid the money he had borrowed (1462–1463). On the other hand, he wants to take revenge on Socrates and Chaerephon for having deceived him (1465–1466). Strepsiades asks the god Hermes for forgiveness: Hermes advises him to burn the thinkery down. The last words Strepsiades utters to the burning philosophers are that 'they commit *hubris* against the gods' (1506).

It has rightly been observed that these passages of *Clouds* have a 'paratragic' flavour.[92] Not only is the ending of the comedy disruptive, the references to *hubris* are also unmistakably tragic since they all entail violent punishments. Strepsiades is neither a comic nor a tragic hero. At best, he is a caricature of both: contrary to comic heroes, he does not succeed in defeating the evil. He burns the thinkery down, but this does not solve the problem since the *hubris* of the Weaker Argument survives in his son. Nor is he a proper tragic hero since he both commits and punishes *hubris*, but without any effect. Contrary to tragic heroes, he evokes neither pity nor fear since he is not a virtuous man. His most important feature entails from his name, which derives from *strephein*, meaning 'twist', 'turn', or 'deviate'.[93] Throughout the comedy, Strepsiades' aim is to evade his creditors by 'twisting' all legal verdicts in his favour (*strepsodikēsai*, 434), and thus to become a 'twister' (*strophis*). And although he does not succeed in learning 'to twist his words around' (*glottostrophein*, 792), he eventually manages to defraud his creditors. And after Pheidippides has beaten him up, he is reproached by the leader of the Chorus: 'you alone are responsible for this, since you turned (*strepsas*) to wicked things' (1455).[94]

In fact, all of Strepsiades' actions represent a 'deviation' from traditional moral values.[95] He is a farmer, used to hard work, but contrary to other heroes of Aristophanes (such as Dicaeopolis in *Acharnians*, and Trygaeus in *Peace*), he does not stick to the age-old values of country life. Instead, he betrays them, preferring the prototype of urban culture, namely the 'new wisdom' taught by Socrates. He is old and forgetful, but he joins the young and pretends to learn the most difficult topic imparted in the thinkery: the Weaker Argument. Moreover, Strepsiades is clear about the fact that *this is the only topic he wants to learn*.[96] Socrates, on the contrary, urges him to stick to a strict course of study, which entails a gradual approach to the different topics taught in the thinkery.[97] These topics are the same as those previously staged in comedies by other playwrights, namely: (A) the study of nature; (B) non-official religiosity and scepticism about traditional religion; (C) fraudulent lyrical and rhetorical skills; (D) asceticism and poverty.

In *Clouds*, it quickly becomes clear that each of these topics is linked to the others, making it impossible to selectively learn one of them without mastering all of the others. Rhetorics, eristics and the two Arguments (= C) are the very last subjects taught at Socrates' school, whereas asceticism and poverty (= D) are taught in parallel to A–C. As it turns out, Strepsiades will be rejected from Socrates' school just before the teaching of the two Arguments. Pheidippides will then take his place and complete the regular course of study.

A) The study of nature The study at the thinkery begins with natural phenomena. The first pupil Strepsiades encounters tells him about experiments involving tiny animals, such as fleas, gnats and geckos (143–173). Then, Strepsiades meets other disciples who investigate the subterranean world down to its most abyssal regions, Tartarus and Erebus

SOCRATES IN OLD COMEDY

(186–192), as well as astronomy, geometry and geography (193–202). Another disciple shows him instruments by which it is possible to measure and map the earth, but Strepsiades has difficulties in telling apart the locations indicated on the map from the real locations they correspond to (203–216). Socrates then appears, floating in the air in a basket (218–225). He tells Strepsiades that he needs to be in the sky so as to correctly study the heavens: Socrates claims that thinking is only possible in a rarefied atmosphere, since the earth draws moist thoughts down (227–233).[98] The idea that thought and air are of the same kind, and, accordingly, that air becomes intelligence when breathed, goes back to Diogenes of Apollonia.[99] The dichotomy between dry air and moist earth is common among pre-Socratic philosophers: Aristophanes is mocking a set of cosmological theories variously attributed to Anaximander, Xenophanes and Heraclitus.[100] It is noteworthy that none of these names appear in *Clouds*.[101] On the other hand, Thales is mentioned just once, as a philosopher 'worthy of admiration' (180).[102]

B) Non-official religiosity and scepticism about traditional religion Socrates presents himself as 'looking down upon the gods' (226), thus introducing the second major topic tackled in his school: that of non-official religiosity. All teachings imparted within the thinkery call the Mysteries to mind; hence their secrecy (140–143). First, Socrates proceeds with Strepsiades' initiation (254–261). It soon turns out that he is a religious leader (a *hiereus*, 359; see also 296–297). He then invokes the new divinities: Air, Aether and the Clouds (262–265).[103] The latter's protegees are the *sophistai*, a strange bunch of fellows: prophetic seers from Thurii, medical artificers, lazy long-haired types with onyx seal rings,[104] poets who produce twisted choral music for dithyrambic songs, men with airy minds (331–334). It can be noticed that these 'sophists' encompass the same variety of 'wise men' we have already noted in other comedies: seers (such as Lampon, who participated in the foundation of Thurii), healers (such as Empedocles, or even Pythagoras), shaman-like persons (again Empedocles and Pythagoras come to mind) and hyper-modern poets (such as Euripides).[105] The Clouds have a metamorphic ability: They can assume any shape, and thus reveal the true nature of any man (346–355). The Clouds are also the patron divinities of the *meteōrosophistai*, the 'wise men who study the heavens', such as Prodicus and Socrates, as well as their associates. The Clouds provide them with thought, reasoning and intelligence (316–318 and 358–363). Socrates is explicit about the fact that 'only the Clouds are goddesses' (365), and that 'Zeus does not exist' (367).[106] Rain and thunder do not originate from Zeus, but from the Clouds and the Vortex (369–384).

The atheistic basis of these statements is quite evident.[107] The theory of the Vortex had been propounded in Athens by the famous atheist Anaxagoras, who had been charged with impiety back in 450.[108] Other divinities of Socrates' pantheon are Chaos and Tongue (423). Socrates makes clear that all of these divinities want to be worshipped instead of the official gods (424–426) – another unambiguous claim that implies impiety. It is important to note that at this stage the Clouds approve Strepsiades' plan to outwit his creditors (429–436). They even go so far as to promise him eternal glory and beatitude (458–460). As we have seen, this will change completely once Strepsiades carries out his plan (1302–1320 and 1454–1461).[109]

C) Fraudulent lyrical and rhetorical skills The next topic that Socrates teaches Strepsiades is lyrical and rhetorical skills. In concise fashion, he starts posing him questions about ordinary matters; such as, how would Strepsiades react if he were beaten? Strepsiades is unable to provide a convincing answer (493–496). Socrates gets impatient and switches to yet another subject: that of poetry. He tries to explain to Strepsiades the rhetorical use of poetic measures, verses and rhythms, but again his elderly interlocutor seems lost (636–653). The same applies to matters of grammar, namely the masculine and feminine genera. All of these topics were widely studied among sophists such as Protagoras and Hippias.[110] Strepsiades is just too dumb to grasp the meaning of Socrates' lecture (659–693). The next lesson addresses 'thought' (*gnōmē*) and the 'method of division' (*diairēsis*): Socrates urges Strepsiades to 'find ideas' and 'divide up' his own thoughts (727–745). This time Strepsiades manages to contrive two arguments that prove to be effective for outwitting creditors (747–772). Socrates is enthusiastic (773).[111] He then asks Strepsiades how he would behave in a trial without witnesses. This time Strepsiades' answer irritates Socrates to the point that he dumps his elderly pupil for good (776–790). As we have seen, Pheidippides will take over and complete the course by attending the contest of the Stronger and the Weaker Argument.

D) Asceticism and poverty Asceticism and poverty are omnipresent within the regular course of study imparted in the thinkery. In fact, each of the subjects taught within Socrates' school (A–C) appears to be linked with specific ascetic practices. Without the endurance that can be acquired through these practices, it is impossible to (A) study natural phenomena, (B) worship the new divinities or (C) learn rhetorical and eristic skills. Socrates and his associates are so poor that they hardly get anything to eat (175, 186, 416, 441). In order to pay for the dinner of his community, Socrates regularly makes off with cloaks and other pieces of clothing from the thinkery or public places (176–179; see also 497–500, 856–859 and 1498).[112] Socrates even charges his students a fee (98, 245, 810, 1146), but this must have been small, since he himself cannot afford proper clothing: we have already seen that he wears a worn-out cloak (869–870) and goes barefoot (103 and 363). Hygienic conditions within the thinkery are poor (834–838): Socrates and his pupils are plagued by insects (fleas, gnats and bugs). It appears that Socrates' closest students are those able to endure these insects so much that they become experts in entomology (such as Chaerephon, 145–158 and 831). Strepsiades, on the contrary, is unable to endure the bugs' bites (634–725), and, as we know, he is eventually rejected by Socrates.

The disciplines taught within the thinkery can be learned only through strenuous endurance. The Socratics care about their souls, not about their physique: hence their pale complexions and skinny bodies (102–104, 1015–1017). Their frugal lifestyle makes them appear as Homeric *psuchai*, 'ghosts of the dead'.[113] Aristophanes ridicules Socrates' school as the 'thinkery of wise ghosts' (94), and the Socratics' abstention from food as a 'care' (*epimeleia*), which leads to a gradual deterioration of the body (501). This shows that Aristophanes is aware of what in the fourth century will be presented as one of the main tenets of Socrates' teaching, namely his 'care for the soul' (*epimeleia tēs psuchēs*).[114] It also shows that the ascetic features described by Aristophanes largely match those attributed to Socrates by both Plato and Xenophon: abstinence from food, alcohol and sleep and enduring the cold.[115] The most disciplined of Socrates' associates is Chaerephon, whose frugal lifestyle makes him look 'half-dead' (*hēmithnēs*, 504).

In *Birds*, rehearsed in 414, we learn more about this lifestyle: Socrates and his associates not only endure corporal fatigues such as abstaining from food, they do not shave or anoint themselves, nor do they wash themselves (1282–1283). These behaviours are defined as 'craziness for Spartan ways' (*elakōnomanoun*, 1281), a feature that clearly identifies the Socratics as philo-Laconian – i.e., as anti-patriotic – amid the Peloponnesian

SOCRATES IN OLD COMEDY   13

War. Socrates is described as a 'summoner of souls' (1554) and Chaerephon as an 'infernal bat' (1564). In this comedy Chaerephon's transformation is more advanced than in *Clouds*: Chaerephon is portrayed as 'rising up from below' (1563), i.e., as normally dwelling in the deepest regions of the underworld, but still being able to reach the upperworld.[116] Socrates is a necromancer, who has the ability to summon souls – even those who descend to the underworld, as in the case of Chaerephon.

The motif of the descent to the netherworld also occurs a decade later in *Frogs*, where Dionysus travels to Hades to bring Euripides back from the dead. As we have already seen in Callias and Telecleides, Euripides is portrayed here as closely linked to Socrates: The Chorus accuses him of forgetting the true skills of tragic poetry because he wastes time 'sitting and chatting with Socrates' (1492). It is due to Socrates that Euripides' plays are full of 'haughty discourses' and 'petty quibbles' (1496–1497). Euripides 'idly spends his time', as 'men who are not able to think' do (1498–1499). The verb used here, '*paraphroneō*', reminds us of the thinkery of *Clouds*. Socrates' petty thoughts have an influence on Euripides' dramatic production, which aims to convey sophistic ideas instead of sticking to the age-old aesthetic values of tragic poetry. For this reason, Dionysus will eventually change his mind: Instead of bringing back Euripides, as planned, he will save Aeschylus.

CONCLUSION

It appears that Aristophanes' Socrates deals with the same topics that were being debated by other comedians during the 430s and 420s, namely A) the study of nature, B) non-official religiosity and scepticism about traditional religion, C) fraudulent lyrical and rhetorical skills, and D) asceticism and poverty. *Clouds* (both *I* and *II*) clearly shows that Socratic education consists of a coherent course of study: Topics A–D are propaedeutic one to each other and, therefore, reciprocally interconnected. This implies that Aristophanes' picture of Socrates is far from inconsistent, as several scholars have claimed.[117] The wide variety of topics Socrates teaches, his religious beliefs and his ascetic lifestyle are not heterogeneous parts of an inextricable jumble: On the contrary, they form a unity which the plot of *Clouds* gradually unfolds.

NOTES

1. I am thankful to Nicholas Smith and Ravi Sharma for their insightful comments, which greatly helped me improve this chapter. For a general overview of Old Comedy before Aristophanes, see Geissler 1969 and Bonanno 1979; on Socrates in Old Comedy (outside Aristophanes' *Clouds*), see Weiher 1913; Dover 1968, xxxii–lvii; Gallo 1983; Guthrie 1971, 39–57; Patzer 1994; Souto Delibes 1997; Imperio 1998a; Carey 2000; Bromberg 2018.

2. As David Konstan rightly observes, 'parody, if it is to be effective, must have some basis in reality' (Konstan 2011, 76).

3. As A. E. Taylor has put it, 'a successful burlesque must be founded on notorious fact, or what is believed as such. It must be a distortion, for comic effect, of something which is not the mere invention of the caricaturist' (Taylor 1933, 18–19).

4. Bromberg 2018. On this genre, see Galy 1979; Imperio 1998a; Carey 2000; Edmunds 2006; Tell 2011, 26.

5. Namely: Cratinus' *All-Seers* (*Panoptai*, rehearsed between 435 and 430); Eupolis' *Nanny Goats* (*Aiges*, 424), *Flatterers* (*Kolakes*, 421) and *Autolycus* (421); Ameipsias' *Konnos* (of 423), and Plato Comicus' *Sophists* (*Sophistai*). It is very likely that other comedies also dealt with matters related to education: e.g., Phrynicus' *Kolakes*. On the wide range of meanings encompassed by the word *sophistēs*, see Untersteiner 1967, xvi–xxiii; and Guthrie 1977, 27–34.

6. In Eupolis' *Kolakes*, the flatterers: Napolitano 2012, 105–110; in Ameipsias' *Konnos*, the chorus consisted of twenty-four 'thinkers': Orth 2013, 213–222; in Cratinus' *Panoptai*, the all-seers: Grey 1896, 11–13; Pieters 1946, 163–164; Rosen 1988, 61–62; Carey 2000, 426–427; Storey 2011, 341–345; in Aristophanes' *Daitaleis*, the *Banqueters*: Cassio 1977: 29–31; Segoloni 1994, 148–169; MacDowell 1995, 27–29; Rusten 2011, 301–307; in the *Clouds*, the clouds: Pucci 1960, 41–42; Segal 1969; Saetta Cottone 2013, 73–77; in Plato Comicus' *Sophistai*, the chorus was formed by sophists (perhaps also including 'Spartans' and 'poets'): Pirrotta 2009: 162–164, 284–285.

7. On *Panoptai*, see Grey 1896, 11–13; Pieters 1946, 163–164; Rosen 1988, 61–62; Carey 2000, 426–427; Storey 2011, 341–345. Rusten 2011, 197. Regarding the date of *All-Seers*, see Geissler 1969, 23; Rosen 1988, 62; Grey 1896, 11.

8. KA 167 (cp. A2 DK). As Olson points out, 'Ἁ πνιγεύς . . . is a hemispherical terracotta baking-shell roughly similar to a modern Weber grill, which was placed over burning charcoal . . . to get it hot enough for baking' (Olson 2021, 78). On Hippon's atheism, see A4, 8 and 9 DK.

9. The *pnigeus*-joke also occurs in Aristophanes' *Birds* (1000–1001), where the astronomer Meton claims that 'the entirety of the air is very much like an oven-cover in shape'.

10. See, e.g., Thales A12 and 14 DK ('the earth floats on water as a piece of wood floats on a pond'); Xenophanes A38 DK ('celestial bodies are similar to burning coals'); Anaximenes B2 DK and Diogenes of Apollonia B2 DK (analogy between the human breath and the air); Empedocles B84 DK (analogy between the eye and the lantern) and B100 DK (analogy between respiration and the functioning of a clepsydra or pipette). On the use of analogy in Presocratic thought, see Lloyd 1966 and Barnes 1979, 40–42 (who goes so far as to claim that 'examples [of such analogies] can be found in every early Greek thinker').

11. The vast majority of scholars agree in establishing a close connection between the *pnigeus*-analogy and Hippon's atheism: See Taillardat 1965, 33; O'Regan 1992, 28–29; Guidorizzi and Del Corno 1996, 200. For a different reading, see Picot 2013, 119, who claims that 'the *pnigeus* does not imply the absence of the Olympian gods . . . on the contrary, it presupposes them'.

12. Eupolis 157 KA. On Eupolis' representation of Socrates, see Storey 2003, 194-197 and 321-327.

13. According to DL 9.53, Protagoras was forced into exile upon having been condemned for atheism: See Gigon 1946, 9 n. 7; Lenfant 2002; Demont 2012, 1704. Plato's report at *Meno* 91d-e seems however to rule out that a trial against Protagoras ever took place: See Burnet 1928, 111–112; Dover 1976, 34–35; Schiappa 1991, 144–145; Wallace 1994, 135; and Bolonyai 2007, 249–251.

14. For example, Protagoras wrote about mathematics, geometry and physics; see B7 DK. On the link between the sophists' art of discourse and the study of nature, see most importantly Mondolfo 1956.

SOCRATES IN OLD COMEDY

15. For *meteōra* in Aristophanes' *Clouds*, see 228, 264, 266, 333, 490 and 1284. For *meteōrosophistēs*, see 360.

16. The first occurrence of *alazoneia* is in an unassigned fragment by Cratinus (380 KA). For *alazoneia* in *Clouds* (at v. 102, 449, 1127, 1492), see Major 2006.

17. For a thorough overview on religious leaders in Old Comedy (mostly in Aristophanes), see Smith 1989.

18. Cratinus 62 KA. Lampon is a common target in Old Comedy; see also Cratinus fr. 57, 58, 62; Callias fr. 14 and 20; and Aristoph. *Birds* 521 and 988. In *Clouds* (331), Aristophanes refers to 'seers of Thurii' (*Thouriomanteis*), an expression which very likely includes Lampon. In *Peace*, 1046–1126, Aristophanes strongly attacks the seers (*manteis*) for being deceitful impostors.

19. See n. 23.

20. On the date of *Pedetai*, see Storey 1988 and Imperio 1998b, 196–197.

21. Callias 15 KA (*Pedetai*): [A.] τί δὴ σὺ σεμνὴ καὶ φρονεῖς οὕτω μέγα; / [B.] ἔξεστι γάρ μοι· Σωκράτης γὰρ αἴτιος. On this fragment, see Raines 1934, 341; Patzer 1994: 56; Revermann 2006, 191; and Bagordo 2014, *ad loc*. On the meaning of Euripides' disguise as a woman, see Stob. 3.12: 'You were wrong at reproaching me for my weakness and my female body shape. If I can think well, this gives me more strength than a mighty arm.' Other explanations of the fragment depend on how to read the phrase τί δὴ σὺ σεμνή, which might also refer to the Muse of Euripides' poetry (as in *Frogs* 1305–1308; see Bagordo 2018, 480), to the wife of Euripides (Gallo 1983), or to a female character in one of his plays (Arrighetti 1994, 40), or even to Aspasia (Imperio 1998b, 225). On the liaison between Socrates and Euripides, see Feugère 1874; Snell 1948; Moline 1975; Irwin 1983; Patzer 1998; Egli 2003, 157–163; Alesse 2004; Schorn 2004, 227–240; Wildberg 2006; Lefkowitz 2016; Bromberg 2019, 58–67.

22. On Euripides as the 'archetypal sophist', see Carey 2000, 429. In *Archilochuses* (2 KA), Cratinus uses the word *sophistes* to define poets. Diogenes Laertius, who quotes the passage, clarifies that 'also poets may be sophists, as Cratinus in *Archilochuses* calls Homer and Hesiod, using the term as a compliment' (2.13).

23. On Socrates' 'haughtiness' (*semnotes*), see *Clouds* 363 and *Frogs* 1496 (but also the passage in *Birds*, 1553–1564. *Semnotes* also applies to the divinities worshipped by Socrates, namely the Clouds, 315, Earth, 364, and Aether, 570). On Socrates' 'thinking' (*phronein*), see 155, 225–233 and 266.

24. Telecleides 41 KA: Μνησίλοχός ἐστ' ἐκεῖνος ⟨ὃς⟩ φρύγει τι δρᾶμα καινὸν / Εὐριπίδῃ, καὶ Σωκράτης τὰ φρύγαν' ὑποτίθησιν.

25. Telecleides 42 KA: Εὐριπίδης σωκρατογόμφους.

26. Aristoph. *Clouds I*, 392 KA (= DL 2.18), *Clouds II*, 891 and 922; *Frogs* 1491–1499.

27. Ael. *VH* 2.13. The only author who apparently contradicts the comic evidence is Diogenes Laertius (DL 2.33), who depicts Socrates as criticising a verse of Euripides' lost tragedy *Auge* (TGF 437 Nauck). The play was staged somewhere between 414 and 406.

28. Eupolis 395 KA (the fragment derives possibly from *Flatterers*, rehearsed in 421): δεξάμενος δὲ Σωκράτης τὴν ἐπίδεξι' ἄιδων Στησιχόρου.

29. Plat. *Phd.* 60c–d.

30. See DL 2.42, Ath. 14.628f, and Amm. Marc. *Res gest.* 28.4.14. On these passages, see Patzer 1994, 70 and Segoloni 2003, 303–304. The issue is complicated by an early tradition going back to the second-generation Socratic Menedemus of Eretria. According to him, Socrates wrote seven dialogues. After his death his wife Xanthippe passed them on to Aeschines (DL 2.60, also reported by Ath. 13.611d-e, who draws on the Epicurean Idomeneus of Lampsacus).

31. Eupolis 386 KA.

32. Eupolis 388 KA. On the other verb used in old Comedy for indicating Socrates' 'chatter', i.e., *(peri)lalein*, see Aristoph. *Frogs*, 1491–1499.

33. See Aristoph. *Clouds*, 1479 and 1485. On the attribution of 388 KA to Socrates, see the convincing arguments by Patzer 1994, 74–75.

34. Cp. Plat. *Phd.* 70c and Xen. *Oec.* 11.3. In only two instances, *adoleskheia* is attributed not to Socrates, but to other philosophers such as Prodicus (Aristoph. *Frogs*, 506) and Plato (Alex. 185 KA).

35. On Ameipsias' *Connus*, see Orth 2013: 213–222. *Karteria* is of utmost importance for three major Socratics, namely Antisthenes, Aristippus and Xenophon. For Antisthenes, see DL 6.7 (= *SSR* V A 90), Dio *Or.* 3, 83–85 (= *SSR* V A 126), Theod. *Graec. aff. cur.* III 53 (= *SSR* V A 53). For Aristippus, DL 2.67 (= *SSR* IV A 36), DL 2.74–75 (= *SSR* IV A 96), Gnom. Vat. 34 (= *SSR* IV A 124). For Xenophon, see I 2, 1–5, I 6, 6–8, II 1, 18–20, II 6, 22, IV 5, 8–9; *Sym.* 8, 8; *Apol.* 25; *Oec.* V 4. For an overview on Socratic endurance, see Rossetti (2008); Redfield (2010); Boys-Stones and Rowe 2013, 66, 72–75, and 105–110; Dorion (2013), 93–122; and Stavru 2016.

36. Eupolis (*Kolakes*) 172 KA.

37. Eupolis 386 KA. On the fragment, see Olson 2007, 234–235.

38. Eupolis 395 KA. On the fragment, see Patzer 1994, 70–71 and Olson 2007, 235.

39. For a reconstruction of the theft of the decanter in 395 KA, see Patzer 1994, 70–71.

40. The cloak theft happens in *Clouds*, 177–179, and is recalled at 856–857 and 1498. On this episode, see Gelzer 1956, 68–69; and Meynersen 1993.

41. *Clouds*, 497–500. As Nicholas Smith pointed out to me, the connection between poverty and thievery shows the trickiness of using comic tropes to gain insights about the 'historical Socrates': Socrates' followers consistently confirm the first trait (poverty), but they remain silent about the latter (thievery).

42. The connection between ascetic practices and a boastful attitude is evident in *Clouds*, 361–362, where a barefoot Socrates is ridiculed as 'haughtily stalking like a pelican in the streets and casting his eyes from side to side'. Plato quotes these verses in *Symp.* 221b to describe Socrates' behaviour at the battle of Delium (424). While all other Athenians flee in panic, Socrates keeps his calm and stays in full control of the situation. On Plato's reuse of the pelican-image, see Stavru 2018, 231.

43. For Plato, see esp. *Symp.* 220b, and *Phdr.* 229a. For Antisthenes: Hier. *Adv. Jov.* 2.14 (= *SSR* V A 12). For Diogenes of Sinope: DL 6.22-23 (*SSR* V B 174). For Xenophon: *Mem.* 1.6.2. For an overview on these passages, see Edmunds 2004, 196–197; and Stavru 2020, 50–54.

44. See, e.g., Alexis (*Pyth.*) 196 KA and Aristophon (*Pythag.*) 9 KA.

45. Callias 15 KA and Telecleides 41–42 KA.

SOCRATES IN OLD COMEDY 17

46. Plato deals with both campaigns at *Ap.* 28e (where the campaign at Amphipolis in 422 is also mentioned), *La.* 181b and *Symp.* 219e–221c.

47. Plat. *Symp.* 219e–220a.

48. Plat. *Symp.* 220c–e.

49. Plat. *Symp.* 221a–c and *La.* 181a–b.

50. The *tribōn* did not protect from cold, heat, sun or rain, since it was 'wrapped around the upper torso twice, thus keeping the chest, waist, and groin warm while leaving legs and arms exposed to the elements' (Desmond 2008, 79).

51. Plat, *Ap.* 19c.

52. Lucian, *Piscat.* 25.

53. Scholium to *Clouds*, 96 (see Iul. *Orat.* 12.24): see also Storey 2003, 322.

54. *Birds*, 1282. Patzer 2012 convincingly argues that the imperfect *esōkratōn* derives from the verb *sokrataō* (inf. *sokratān*). As other contract verbs in *-aō*, it denotes a condition of mental or physical illness (especially in Aristophanes: see Willi 2003, 84–85). In this case the meaning is likely 'to be crazy like Socrates'. This fits with the other verb attributed to the Socratics in the previous line, *elakōnomanoun*, 'to be mad on Spartan ways' (v. 1281).

55. See *ōkhroi*, *khrōma*, and *khroia* at 102–104, 120, 186, 1015–1017 and 1112.

56. *Knights*, 231–233. Kenneth Dover thinks that these masks were not exact replicas. Specific facial traits were exaggerated so as to make them identifiable from a distance (i.e., the shape of hair, beard and colour): see Dover 1967.

57. Ael. *VH* 2.13. On the passage see Dover 1968, xxxiii and Lapatin 2006, 111.

58. See Σ223. As noted by Dover 1968, 125–126, this scholium seems to be confirmed by scholium Σ^V, according to which Pindar has the Silenus Marsyas uttering at the musician Olympus the words 'O miserable, ephemeral being' (fr. 157 Maehler). Capra 2018, 72, aptly points out the similarity with Arist. *Eudemus* fr. 44.27–29 Rose, where Silenus says: 'Ephemeral seed of painful destiny, why do you force me to speak?'

59. According to Dover 1968, 126, the identification of Socrates with Silenus is 'far-fetched'. Catoni and Giuliani 2019, 704, are 'fairly sure . . . that the mask could *not* have been a satyr mask'. Dupréel 1922, 324; C. W. Marshall 1999, 194; Revermann 2006, 190; McLean 2007; Charalabopoulos 2012, 176; Telò 2016, 139; and Capra 2016 and 2018 all believe that Socrates wore a satyr mask.

60. On Socrates *dimorphos* (= Adesp. 940 KA = SSR I A 17) see J. M. Edmonds 1957 vol. IIIa; Bühler 1999, 110; McLean 2002, 47–51; Stavru 2011, 100–105.

61. See Stavru 2018, 209–210.

62. According to ancient testimonies (Aristophanes 1, 59–61; 2ab, 10–11; 4, 10–11 KA), Aristophanes authored forty-four plays, four of which have been attributed to Archippus.

63. On *Banqueters*, see Dover 1968, ad 528; Cassio 1977; Segoloni 1994, 111–193; MacDowell 1995, 27–29; Papageorgiou 2004; Rusten 2011, 301–307.

64. Segoloni's identification of Socrates as the *didaskalos* certainly makes sense (1994, 120), although one should ask oneself why Socrates' name never occurs in *Daitaleis*. One possible explanation is that the parts of the comedy in which he was mentioned became lost: 'per quanto riguarda Socrate nei *Banchettanti*, non escluderei del tutto una sua presenza sulla scena quale personaggio o forse come membro del coro' (Segoloni 1994,

122). This is, of course, possible, but, in this case, it would be strange to have Socrates both as a *didaskalos* and as another character. The safest explanation for the absence of Socrates is that Aristophanes deliberately chose not to refer to him in *Daitaleis*.

65. As Segoloni 1994, 155, notes, the coinage *sorellē* ('old mummy') should be understood as a hybrid of *soros* ('coffin') and *torellē* ('conjurer of funerary images').

66. See 225 KA: 'He did not learn these things when I sent him to school, but rather drinking, then bad singing, Syracusan food, Sybaritic feasting, Chian wine from Spartan bowls.'

67. See esp. Aristoph. *Clouds II*, 1444–1468.

68. 225 KA: *andras kalokagathein askountas*.

69. In 427, Alcibiades was in his early twenties, but he was already a common character in Old Comedy. For a survey on the extant evidence, see Littman 1970 and Vickers 1993.

70. For Aristodemus, see Cratinus' *All-Seers* (160 KA) and Plat. *Symp.* 173b (and Brisson 1989b; Nails 2002, 52–53). For Alcibiades, see Plat. *Symp.* 218c–219d (and Brisson 1989a; and Nails 2002, 10–17).

71. 44 KA: *epi phaliniou gegenēsthai*. In Aristophanes' *Acharnians* (425 BCE), Alcibiades is said to be both *euruprōktos* and *lalos* at v. 716. I owe this point to Nicholas Smith.

72. For more on sexuality in Old Comedy, see esp. Henderson 1991 and (for iconographic evidence) Keuls 1993.

73. See esp. Aristoph. *Clouds II*, 1068 for a *sophrōsunē* that is too weak to sustain the temptation of unlawful sex, and is thus forced to convert into its opposite condition, *euruprōktosunē*, the wanton fulfilment of sexual needs (1060–1082). On the contest between the Stronger and the Weaker Argument, see Erbse 1954, 391–402; Strauss 1966, 29–39; Dover 1968, lvii–lxvi; Nussbaum 1980, lvii–lxvi; Casanova 2007; and Cerri 2012.

74. See Nestle 1940, 464; Murray 1993, 85; and Segoloni 1994, 119–135.

75. The fragments going back to *Clouds I* are 392–401 KA. On the plot of *Clouds I*, see Heidhues 1897, 14–25; Gelzer 1960, 138–140; Dover 1968, lxxx–xcviii; Hubbard 1986; Tarrant 1991.

76. The Hypotheses V and VI Wilson (= I and II Dover) make statements that seem to derive from a comparison of two divergent versions. The same applies to the scholia at Σ^E 520 and Σ^{VE} 543. The scholium Σ^{Vb3} 1115 (by Heliodorus) even suggests that an ancient commentary to *Clouds I* may have existed. See Dover 1968, lxxxv: 'the evidence for the survival of the first version into Hellenistic times is overwhelming'.

77. See Hypothesis IV Wilson (= Hypothesis I Dover).

78. I follow the reconstruction of Hubbard 1986, 189, who claims that Aristophanes 'clearly does utilize every single one of [these jokes] in the present version of the play'.

79. Leather phalluses seem to appear at 196–197, 653–654, and 734; the bald man is probably Socrates: see the allusions at 146–147 and 171–173; wild dances: 439–456, 540, and 1201–1213; the old man striking others with a stick is Strepsiades, who chases off the second creditor at 1296–1302; the torches are those employed by Strepsiades to burn down the school of Socrates at 1491–1493, and the cries of desperation are those uttered both at the very beginning of the play by Strepsiades (1) and by Socrates' pupil in the final scene of the comedy (1493).

80. The extant version of *Clouds* was intended for a Dionysian festival, as entailed by v. 520–533, where Aristophanes addresses the same public who had turned down the first

SOCRATES IN OLD COMEDY

19

version of the comedy (which was rehearsed in the theatre of Dionysus). See esp. v. 528, where the adverb of place *enthade* clearly hints at the theatre of Dionysus, as well as v. 609, where Aristophanes greets 'the Athenians and their allies': We know that among the dramatic festivals of Athens, foreigners used to attend only the Dionysian ones.

81. See Russo 1962, 169.

82. See Hypotheses V and VI Wilson (= II and I Dover), respectively, and the scholium in *Clouds*, 553. The vast majority of scholars rely on this evidence to claim that *Clouds II* was never restaged: see e.g. Dover 1968, lxxxi–xcviii; Storey 1993, 73–74, and Rosen 1997, 401.

83. Hypothesis V Wilson (= II Dover) claims that *Clouds* was restaged under the archonship of Aminias (422), 'but the outcome was even worse, and thereafter [Aristophanes] did not restage the reworking'. This claim cannot apply to the Dionysia and the Lenaia, since in the didascalic records of these two festivals there is no entry for a reperformance of *Clouds* after 423.

84. H. R. Marshall 2012, 70, provides arguments to claim that *Clouds* 'was . . . being performed several years after its debut at the Dionysia'.

85. Plat. *Ap.* 18b–c. On the date of Plato's *Apology*, see de Strycker and Slings 1994, 16–21.

86. See also 19a: 'the slander you made over a long time' (τὴν διαβολὴν ἣν ὑμεῖς ἐν πολλῷ χρόνῳ ἔσχετε), and especially 19c: 'you have been seeing (ἑωρᾶτε) this yourself in the comedy of Aristophanes, a Socrates swinging about there, saying he was walking on air and talking a lot of other nonsense'. As W. J. M. Starkie poignantly observes, the imperfect ἑωρᾶτε implies repeated performances of the play (Starkie 1911, liv n. 3). Starkie believes that 'the first edition was acted more than once (perhaps in the theatre in the Piraeus)' and that 'Plato's reference is to that edition'.

87. A scholium at v. 591 says that Aristophanes reworked *Clouds* several times. The textual problems of *Clouds II* (on which see Hubbard 1986, 184, fn 11) may reflect the stratification of such reworkings. It is tempting to think that each of these reworkings corresponded to a reperformance.

88. In addition to the passages of the *Apology* (18b and 19b–c), see the quotation at v. 362–363 in *Symp.* 221b. Aristophanes is the only playwright who also appears as a character in Plato's *Symposium*, where he holds one of the most memorable speeches of the whole dialogue. On Plato's personal admiration for Aristophanes, see esp. the epigram he composed for him: 'The Graces, seeking for themselves a shrine that would not fall, found the soul of Aristophanes.' (Quoted after Plat. *Epigr.* 18, in Cooper 1997, 1745.)

89. Although Plato does not mention these plays, his dialogues are clearly influenced by them. See, e.g., the strong influence of Eupolis' *Flatterers* on *Protagoras*: Kerferd 1981, 39; Nightingale 1995, 186–187; Capra 2001, ch. 1–3; Tylawski 2002, 44–47; Notomi 2013, 14–18 and n. 10; Storey 2003, 184–185; Arieti and Barrus 2011, 8–13; Charalabopoulos 2012, 70 and n. 105; and Bromberg 2018, 40–41.

90. It should be noted, however, that *Clouds* was not the only comedy to circulate in distinct versions. Therefore, it is unlikely to be the only comedy that was reworked but not restaged: see Aristophanes' *Frogs* (two revisions), *Aeolosicon*, *Thesmophoriants*, *Peace*, and *Wealth*; Magnes' *Dionysus*; Diocles' *Thyestes*; and Eupolis' *Autolycus* (on the reperformances of these plays, see H. R. Marshall 2012, 66; on restaging in tragedy, see Butrica 2001, 56–58, and Lamari 2017).

91. The last words of the second creditor to be flogged by Strepsiades are: 'is this [what you are doing to me] not a *hubris*?' (1299).

92. See Newiger 1957, 67–68; Rau 1967, 173–175; Silk 1993, 498–504; Guidorizzi and Del Corno 1996, 348–351; Belardinelli 2013; and Saetta Cottone and Buarque de Holanda 2020–2021.

93. The first attestation of Στρεψιάδης occurs in Pindar I. 7.21. On Strepsiades, see Marzullo 1953; Silk 1993, 500; and Judet de La Combe 2006. On 'speaking names' in Aristophanes, see Kanavou 2011 (on Strepsiades, see 67–70).

94. See also the occurrences in which *streph-* cognates are referred to Strepsiades by other characters: 36 (Pheidippides asks Strepsiades why he has been 'tossing and turning' in bed all night long), 701 (the leader of the Chorus asks Strepsiades to 'turn and toss his mind'), 776 (Socrates asks Strepsiades how he would 'twist away' when launching a counter-suit in a trial); also 88 (Strepsiades urges Pheidippides to immediately 'turn his life upside down' and to enrol with him at the thinkery.

95. Indeed, the whole of *Clouds* is about *strephein*, i.e., about 'subverting' specific divinities, figures, and institutions: Zeus is substituted by other gods such as Vortex, the Clouds, and Thunder; the Stronger Argument must surrender to the Weaker; the father Strepsiades is beaten up by the son Pheidippides; the urban thinkery, inhabited by the bright Socratics, is destroyed by the most ignorant and stupid of its pupils, the rural Strepsiades.

96. On Strepsiades' impatience to learn nothing but the Weaker Argument, see 112–116, 129–130, 239–246, 425–434, and 657. Upon his failure, the only wish of Strepsiades is that his son Pheidippides should eventually learn the Weaker Argument: see 882–885, 1148, and 1229.

97. The existence of a specific order in which the topics are to be taught is clear at 657–658. Socrates is imparting lessons to Strepsiades, who is, however, impatient as he only wants to learn 'the most unjust of all arguments'. Socrates reproaches him: 'you need to learn other matters *before that*!' (my italics).

98. As Saetta Cottone 2013 notes, the 'rarefied atmosphere' (λεπτὴν. . ἀέρα) recalls the 'subtleness of thoughts' at 153 (λεπτότης τῶν φρενῶν), as well as the 'subtle talking' at 320 (λεπτολογεῖν).

99. See Diogenes of Apollonia B4–5 DK, which Vander Waerdt 1994, 66–75, and others compare with Plato's account of the 'first sailing' at *Phaedo* 96a–99d. Betegh 2013 argues that this theory might as well derive from Archelaus, who in Socrates' youth was his teacher. On the relationship between Socrates and Archelaus, see Patzer 2006, 163–212.

100. Anaximander: A7 DK; Xenophanes: A27 DK; Heraclitus: A15, B36 and B77 DK.

101. Except maybe for Xenophanes. Alexander Mourelatos 2013 claims that the 'son of Xenophanes' (Ξενοφάντου) at 349 refers to Xenophanes of Colophon, and that the verses 348–350 imply an 'astrophysics of Clouds'.

102. Thales is invoked as an intellectual genius also in *Birds*, at 1009.

103. This invocation reminds of Pythagoras (DL 8.6: οὐ μὰ τὸν ἀέρα τὸν ἀναπνέω), who seems to be hinted at also at 219 (αὐτὸς [ἔφα]) and 225 (ἀεροβατεῖν).

104. Olson 2021, 109 provides the following definition: 'wealthy people who have possessions valuable enough to keep under seal and those whose nails are unbroken because they do no hard physical labour'.

105. On Empedocles in *Clouds* see Saetta Cottone 2013, who claims that the Chorus implies an Empedoclean cosmology.

SOCRATES IN OLD COMEDY

21

106. The non-existence of Zeus and the genera of nouns are among the few topics Strepsiades retains from his lessons with Socrates. He teaches both to his son Pheidippides (828–831 and 837–853).

107. It has long been noticed that the reference to 'Socrates the Melian' at 830 hints at Diagoras of Melos, a famous atheist (on whom see Woodbury 1965; Guthrie 1977, 235-237; Patzer 1993, 32). As Mario Montuori and others point out, this reference implies that Aristophanes sees Socrates as an atheist (Montuori 1966, 37 and Patzer 1993, 32).

108. On the charge of impiety, see DL 2.12–14. For discussion, see Woodbury 1981; Curd 2007, 136, 209; Tsamalikos 2016, 489–491. For discussion of all trials against impiety that took place in Athens since the decree of Diopeithes (probably issued in 430 to convict Anaxagoras), see Derenne 1930.

109. This about-face of the Clouds is another instance of the *strephein* that characterises the comedy. On this crucial issue, see van Leeuwen 1898 ad v. 1458–1461; Newiger 1957, 68–69; Whitman 1964, 129; Dover 1968, lxvi–lxviii; Segal 1969; Ambrosino 1983, 43–45; Saetta Cottone 2013, 73–75.

110. For Protagoras, see A25, 29; for Hippias, see B6 and A11.

111. I believe that until this point *Clouds I* and *II* followed approximately the same plot. After v. 773 *Clouds I* most likely continued at v. 1214 (Strepsiades successfully wards off the creditors), while *Clouds II* presents a new section, which includes the contest between the Stronger and the Weaker Argument.

112. On the stolen-cloak routine in *Clouds*, see Compton-Engle 2015, 64–65. On the theft of clothes, see *Thesm.*, 26, 40 and 275. On the crime of 'clothing theft' (λωποδυσία) in ancient Athens, see Cohen 1983, 80–82.

113. On this identification, see Burnet 1916, 256; Havelock 1972, 15–16; and Sarri 1975, 115–117. The frugal lifestyle of the Socratics entails the ability to 'suffer within the soul' (τὸ ταλαίπωρον ἔνεστιν ἐν τῇ ψυχῇ) and to endure a set of physical deprivations (see the passage quoted above, *Clouds*, 412–417).

114. On the 'care for the soul', see, in Plato, *Ap.* 29d–e, 30a–b, 31b, 36b–c; *Alc.* I, 127e–133c; *Cr.* 47b–48b; *Prt.* 313a–c; *Grg.* 464b, 480a–b, 523a–527e; *Phd.* 114d–115c; in Xenophon: *Mem.* I, 4, 13–14; III, 10, 1–8; IV, 3, 13–15; *Cyr.* VIII, 7, 17–21.

115. Plato's portrait of Socrates in *Symposium* seems to hint at *Clouds*: See 220a (abstinence from food and alcohol), 220c (sleep), 220a (enduring the cold). The verse Plato quotes at 221b2–3 (362: βρενθυόμενος καὶ τὠφθαλμὼ παραβάλλων) immediately precedes that on Socrates's endurance at walking barefoot (361). This makes it likely that Plato's portrait of a Socrates *karterikos* hints at *Clouds*: see Stavru 2016, 350–351. On Xenophon and other Socratics, see the occurrences of *enkrateia* and *karteria* listed in n. 35.

116. It should be noted that, at 414, Chaerephon was still alive. By staging him as an infernal bat, Aristophanes probably hints at his hybrid status: Chaerephon has been a pupil of Socrates for so long that he has almost been transformed into an underwordly *psuchē*, and is, therefore, able to dwell in both the upperworld and the netherworld. On Chaerephon, see Brisson 1994, 304–305; Nails 2002, 86–87; and Moore 2013, 284–285 and 296.

117. See e.g. Grote 1849, VI, 136–138; Starkie 1911, xxx–xxxvii; Pucci 1960, 120; Dover 1968, xxxii–lvi; and Gelzer 1970, 1441–1444.

CHAPTER TWO

Xenophon's Socrates on Teaching and Learning[*]

RUSSELL E. JONES AND RAVI SHARMA

I. SETTING THE CONTEXT

Readers of Plato are sometimes hard-pressed to remember that there is another Socratic from whom we have full works. The reasons are not far to seek. For much of the history of modern scholarship – especially since Joël 1893/1901 – Xenophon has been compared unfavourably to Plato as an intellectual and has been judged as being of little or no value as an independent source for Socratic thought.[1] It is no wonder that generations of scholars, presented with this portrait of an inferior and derivative thinker, have focused their energies elsewhere.

That portrait has been challenged. The early 1970s featured the appearance of two monographs by Strauss (1970, 1972), who had long held a positive view of Xenophon.[2] In non-Straussian circles, serious reappraisal of Xenophon was still more than a decade away, but recent years have seen a revival of interest. Some highlights include the pioneering work of Morrison (for instance his 1987, 1994 and 1995) and Gray (especially her 1998), the thorough three-part commentary on the *Memorabilia* by Dorion (with a new text by Bandini: Bandini and Dorion 2010 [2000], 2011a, 2011b) and another by Bevilacqua (2010), Dorion's collected essays (2013) and book-length studies by Danzig (2010) and Johnson (2021). This trend has brought welcome reassessments, but detailed work is still in its early stages and is largely confined to a generous handful of scholars. The scholarly energy expended on Xenophon's Socratic works is still but a tiny fraction of that devoted to the Platonic dialogues usually considered 'Socratic'.

Because the revival of interest in Xenophon has been relatively recent, close comparative studies of Xenophon's Socrates and Plato's are also in their early stages. Indeed, there is as yet no agreement on the broad contours of the philosophical relationship between the two authors; and scholarly judgments have correspondingly varied widely regarding the solubility of the 'Socratic Problem' of whether and, if so, how the views of the historical Socrates can be recovered from the representations of him in ancient literature. In several influential publications, Dorion has argued that there is a host of basic doctrinal divergences between Xenophon's Socrates and Plato's, and that as a result the Socratic Problem must be deemed insoluble.[3] That judgment has been widely accepted, though the acceptance has not been universal. In his 2021 book on Xenophon's Socrates, Johnson qualifies a number of Dorion's judgments concerning a doctrinal divergence and, as a result, remains open to further discussion of the Socratic Problem.[4]

In what follows, we look closely at a theme in Xenophon's Socratic writings that bears centrally on the question of the fit between Xenophon's Socrates and Plato's: in what way, if any, Xenophon's Socrates may be considered to have knowledge of virtue and to teach what he knows to others. Scholars have tended to think that the evidence from Xenophon is internally contradictory, and that several of the core texts diverge sharply from Plato's portrayal of Socrates, thereby undermining any attempt to effect a *rapprochement* between the two authors. In re-examining the relevant passages of Xenophon's *Memorabilia* and *Apology*, we resist those judgments. The passages in fact allow for a unified reading, one that makes a form of epistemic modesty central to the outlook of Xenophon's Socrates, and thereby acknowledges a family resemblance between Xenophon's portrayal of Socrates and Plato's. This suggests that the doctrinal gulf between the two authors is not nearly so wide as it has been made out to be and may even be largely a scholarly mirage – a conclusion that we think could be bolstered by looking anew at other areas in which a fundamental divergence has been posited. (For one such reexamination see Jones and Sharma 2019.)

At least two things follow: (i) The Socratic question may prove much more tractable than has generally been supposed; (ii) While a closeness between the two authors does not mean that Xenophon develops the overlapping themes with the theoretical sophistication found in Plato's dialogues, it does suggest that Xenophon's Socratic writings may be valuable to consult in sorting some of the interpretive debates about Plato's Socratic works: Xenophon's writings may map Socrates' core commitments and their interrelations in a way that matches Plato's work, or may at least provide a useful foil for interrogating the philosophical moves made by Plato.

II. INTELLECTUALISM

Mem. 3.9.4–5 states bluntly a core Socratic commitment:[5]

> **(T1)** [3.9.4] [Socrates] did not differentiate wisdom and moderation (*sōphrosunē*) . . . [3.9.5] He said that justice and the whole rest of virtue is wisdom. After all, he said, just actions and all actions done from virtue are estimable (*kala te kai agatha*).[6] Those knowing what's estimable would never select anything else in preference to it, and those ignorant of it are incapable of doing it. Even if they try, they fail.

Minimally, (T1) asserts that Socrates considered virtue to be wisdom.[7] That is to say, (T1) casts Socrates as a virtue intellectualist, someone who holds that virtue is a type of wisdom or knowledge. Given the common expectation that virtue will be manifested in appropriate behaviour, one might expect a behavioural link to be made; and Xenophon's narrator[8] duly makes it with the observation that knowers of what is estimable will always choose the virtuous course. The precise nature of the link between knowledge and behaviour is beyond the scope of our discussion here; but for our treatment of it, see Jones and Sharma 2018 and 2020.[9]

The view that virtue is knowledge is confirmed, sometimes in less direct terms, in other passages. Hence in the first chapter of the *Memorabilia*, the narrator says:

> **(T2)** Socrates constantly discussed human affairs, looking into what is pious, and what impious; what is admirable, what shameful; what is just, what unjust; what is sound-mindedness (*sōphrosunē*),[10] what madness; what is courage, what cowardice; what is a city-state, what a politician; what is rule over people, and what a ruler of people. He

thought that knowing those and other like things made people estimable, while those ignorant of them are rightly called slavish.

– *Mem.* 1.1.16

The key point at present is the final sentence: Socrates holds that knowledge of matters moral and political makes people estimable or virtuous, while ignorance of the same matters leaves them slavish. Hence in *Memorabilia* 4.6, where we see Socrates taking up some of the topics from the list in (T2), the discussion is continually brought around to knowledge: The pious person is the one who knows what is 'lawful' when it comes to dealing with the gods (4.6.2–4), the just person the one who knows what is 'lawful' when it comes to dealing with people (4.6.5–6), and so forth.

The upshot is that the Socratic ethical project of becoming a virtuous person is at once an epistemological project. Questions of the nature of moral knowledge, and of the methods to be used in discovering and communicating it, are urgent for Socrates because of the supreme importance of becoming estimable. And interpreters of Socratic epistemology and methodology can expect to find much of their data in specifically ethical contexts: Discussions of how to become good are at once discussions of how to become wise.

III. SOCRATES, KNOWER AND TEACHER

So far, Xenophon's Socrates seems closely aligned with Plato's.[11] Yet if we look at their respective portraits of Socrates' epistemic and moral achievements, there seems to be a sharp divergence. Plato's Socrates readily and repeatedly disclaims knowledge, and thereby virtue. Xenophon's Socrates claims virtue, and thereby knowledge. Consider a self-description to Hermogenes in the *Apology*:

(T3) Don't you know that up to this point there is no human being I would grant to have lived better than I? I had the sweetest thing of all: awareness (*ēdein*) of having lived my whole life piously and justly. Respecting myself deeply for that, I found my associates forming the same judgment about me.

– *Apol.* 5

Consider, too, the closing statement of the *Apology*:

(T4) When I reflect on the wisdom (*sophian*) and nobility of the man, I am able neither to put him out of my mind nor in recalling him to withhold my praise. If anyone who longs for virtue has had dealings with a person more beneficial than Socrates, I consider that man worthy of being deemed most blessed.

– *Apol.* 34

The narrator of the *Memorabilia* echoes and amplifies that judgment at the work's close:

(T5) As far as I'm concerned, he was just the sort of person I've described. He was so pious that he would do nothing without the input of the gods. He was so just that he would harm no one in even a small way and would confer the greatest benefits on those who had dealings with him. He was so self-controlled that he would never choose the more pleasant in preference to the better. And he was so shrewd (*phronimos*) that he never went completely astray in judging the better and the worse, needing the direction of another, but was self-reliant in his thinking about those things, capable of expressing and delimiting them in his reasoning and likewise capable of putting other people to the test, refuting them when they went wrong and provoking them to pursue virtue and an estimable character. To me, he seemed just the kind of man that the best and happiest would be. But if those qualities seem insufficient to anyone, let that person set the character of others beside them and then render judgment.

– Mem. 4.8.11

That is a summary assessment, one based on the evidence presented throughout the *Memorabilia.* For the moment, let's highlight one aspect of it, the contention that Socrates was 'capable of expressing and delimiting [the better and the worse] in his reasoning'. Exactly what one should make of this claim depends on how one reads the passage on which it most directly depends – *Memorabilia* 4.6, which we treat below. But it is clear, at least, that the narrator is praising Socrates not only for his behaviour but also for his reasoning.

If Socrates has knowledge of what virtue is, one would expect an affirmation that he can teach others. And there are indeed several passages where Socrates affirms that he is a teacher. Consider a comment of his to Antiphon:

(T6) An analogous point holds for wisdom [as for offering one's body to another]: people disparage as sophists those who sell it for money, while the person who recognizes someone of good nature and makes a friend by teaching any good thing he knows, him we deem to be doing what befits an estimable citizen. . . . [A]nd if I know of anything good, I teach it, and I introduce [my friends] to others from whom I think they will benefit morally.

– Mem. 1.6.13–14

In discussing that text, Morrison leans heavily on the 'if' in Socrates' last remark, saying, '[W]e have a typical example of Xenophontic subtlety. Socrates describes what he would do *if* he could teach, but the whole thing remains hypothetical: he never affirms that he can.' (1987: 20 n.8) Yet Socrates is here describing his desire for friends who are good, something he has said he wants more strongly than others want a good horse or dog or bird. Indeed he goes on in what immediately follows (T6) to describe how he joins his friends in reading and discussing the words of wise writers of former times. If in the midst of all this he were to indicate subtly that he has nothing to teach, he would be undercutting his central point, saying in effect, 'I so much want friends who are good that I'd be willing to teach them any good thing I knew; but since I know of none, I supply my prospective friends with no benefits of the sort I am describing.' We think it more likely that this is an affirmation that Socrates is indeed a teacher to his friends.[12]

Socrates' final remark to the jury is similar:

(T7) I know the time past and the time to come will bear witness in my case too [like that of Palamedes] that I never did anyone any wrong and did not ever make anyone more wicked. Instead I was a benefactor to those who conversed with me, teaching them for free any good of which I was capable.

– Apol. 26

Just earlier in the *Apology* (17), Socrates noted that many Athenians and foreigners who desire virtue have flocked to him, that many are eager to give him gifts though they know he has little capacity to make a return, and that many consider themselves in his debt. The clear implication is that, to those who value virtue and pursue Socrates' company, Socrates provides something of great value. What could it be except progress in virtue?[13]

XENOPHON'S SOCRATES ON TEACHING AND LEARNING   27

The narrator concurs in this judgment. In *Memorabilia* 1.2, he addresses the criticism that Socrates taught two men, Alcibiades and Critias, who did enormous harm to Athens. He doesn't deny that Socrates taught them but says:

> (T8) Someone might respond that Socrates should not have taught his associates political skills before he taught moderation (*sōphronein*). I'm not disputing that. But I observe that all teachers show their pupils how they themselves practice what they teach in addition to persuading them by their words. I know that Socrates showed his associates that he himself was an estimable man and conversed most finely with them about virtue and the rest of the human condition.
>
> – *Mem.* 1.2.17

Late in the *Memorabilia*, the narrator makes a comment akin to what Socrates says in (T6):

> (T9) That Socrates revealed his thoughts plainly to his associates is clear, I think, from what has been said. That he was also concerned for them to be self-sufficient in the activities to which they were suited, I'll now state. More than anyone else of whom I'm aware, he was intent on finding out what one or another of his companions might be said to understand. As for what it befits an estimable man to know, he was more eager than anyone else to teach any knowledge he might have; and on whatever he was relatively inexperienced, he brought them to those who did understand it. He also taught them the extent to which the properly educated person should be familiar with each subject.
>
> – *Mem.* 4.7.1–2

Those passages collectively reveal that neither Xenophon's Socrates nor the narrator refrain from attributing knowledge to Socrates, and each passage affirms his eagerness to teach what he knows to others.

IV. PROBLEMATISING SOCRATES AS KNOWER AND TEACHER

However, things are not nearly so straightforward as they appear from the above passages. The narrator, in the very chapter in which he seems to allow that Socrates taught Critias and Alcibiades, also denies that Socrates professed to teach at all:

> (T10) Being the sort of person he was, how could he make others impious or lawless or gluttonous or lustful or too delicate for hard work? He *saved* many from those conditions by making them desire virtue and by supplying them the hope that if they took care of themselves they would be estimable. But not one single time did he profess to be a teacher of that. Instead, by obviously being such a person himself he inspired the hope that those who spent their time with him and imitated him would turn out to be people of the same sort.
>
> – *Mem.* 1.2.2–3

The apparent implication of the passage is that Socrates *did not teach*; or at least, insofar as he might be thought a teacher, it is only because people observed his behaviour, admired him for it, and so emulated him.

Moreover, despite Socrates' high degree of self-praise in (T3) ('there is no human being I would grant to have lived better than I'), he holds back at a crucial moment later in the *Apology*. The context is worth recalling. The opening of the work charges that in dealing with the trial other writers have failed to explain Socrates' haughtiness. The proper explanation, we are told, is that Socrates was ready to die and that he considered the trial a gift from the gods in reward for his life-long concern with virtue. The gift will allow him to exit life at the right time, in an easy manner, and in a way that will best foster a longing for him and his mode of life in the hearts of his friends.

What Socrates then does at his trial is to provoke the jury by giving them an unvarnished depiction of his concern for virtue and his consequent superiority over his fellows. The culmination of that approach is the oracle story. In response to an unspecified question from Chaerephon, Apollo is said to have declared, before many witnesses, that no person is freer or more just or more moderate (*sōphronesteros*, *Apol.* 14). As if that isn't provocative enough, Socrates digs the spur deeper by declaring with mock humility that the god judged him to be far superior only to the *rest of humankind* and did not deliberate – as he did in the case of Lycurgus – whether to address Socrates as god or man! Socrates then bids the jury to join him in reflecting on the ascribed virtues one by one. The result? Socrates may be considered more moderate insofar as no one is less enslaved to bodily desire than he. He is among the freest insofar as he has never bound himself to anyone by taking payment for his services. And the mark of his unsurpassed justice is that his desires are so in harmony with his resources that he has zero motive to cheat others out of what they have.

So far, everything seems to be in line with the view of Xenophon's Socrates as a paragon of virtue. But notice an important wrinkle at the end of Socrates' celebration of his virtue. Unprompted by the god's oracle, he slips in a comment on his wisdom:

> (T11) And how could someone reasonably fail to call me wise when, beginning from the time I could understand what was being said, I have never stopped seeking and learning whatever good thing I could.

– Apol. 16[14]

What's striking about that remark is its modesty. It comes at the rhetorical climax of Socrates' self-praise. He is intent on goading the jury to kill him, though he will not lie about himself. In discussing his wisdom, he stresses only his *effort* to learn good things. To be sure, he says he has never stopped seeking *and learning*, and immediately maintains that his effort 'has not been in vain' (*Apol.* 17). But the emphasis is firmly on his (efficacious) efforts continually to improve, as opposed to his arrival at some state of 'wisdom'. Socrates here makes a relatively modest (and indefinite) claim, stopping far short of an assertion that he has acquired knowledge of virtue and thus achieved as much as any human being could hope for. Indeed, if one looks back at Socrates' description of his virtues, one can see they are all about his restrained appetites and not directly a function of superior intellectual achievement. If this is all Socrates will here say regarding his condition, it must be all there is to be said.

V. A PROPOSED SOLUTION

How should one respond to this seeming contradiction in the way Socrates is depicted in Xenophon's writings? Vlastos takes the view that although Xenophon chiefly means to depict Socrates as having extensive moral knowledge, he also allows in a trace of the epistemic modesty that Vlastos takes genuinely to characterise the historical Socrates. The example of the latter on which Vlastos comments is at *Memorabilia* 4.4.9, where the sophist Hippias complains that Socrates is always questioning others and never states his own views. Vlastos remarks: 'That Xenophon should have painted this into his portrait of Socrates in this single paragraph of the *Memorabilia* is his tribute – all the more impressive for having been doubtless inadvertent – to the truth suppressed throughout that work' (1991: 105, cf. 31–2). However, that judgment fails to reckon with the fact that the evidence in Xenophon for Socrates' epistemic modesty goes well beyond a one-time slip.

Cooper (1999: 21–2) saves Xenophon's coherence at the expense of denying him intellectual depth: Xenophon's Socrates 'never formally professed to *teach* virtue', but nevertheless was constantly offering informal instruction. 'Clearly, Xenophon has no idea that Socrates had any deep reason for denying that he was a teacher of virtue, and if that term should be understood appropriately in an ordinary and undemanding sense of giving good advice and encouragement about how to live, what to prefer and what to value less, and so on, he is content to be regarded as a teacher of virtue.' So, Socrates never advertised himself as a teacher, but he was nevertheless constantly teaching, and Xenophon never understood that Socrates' disavowal of teaching might be motivated by deeper philosophical commitments. Once again, such an interpretation does questionable justice to the complex evidence for Socrates' epistemic modesty.

Acknowledging that evidence offers a path toward a more coherent portrait and one with greater intellectual depth. It also brings Xenophon's portrayal of Socrates much closer to Plato's on this issue – a convergence that has scarcely been noted in modern scholarship. In this section, we want to highlight a feature of the texts earlier cited that should incline one toward a solution. Even in the passages we cited as evidence that Socrates is a knower or teacher, each of them can be read as stopping just short of an affirmation that Socrates knows or teaches *what virtue is*. Yet that does not imply that Socrates is a teacher only in the mundane sense advocated by Cooper. He is a dedicated seeker of knowledge, and that intellectual orientation is the key to his usefulness to those who associate with him.

Let us frame our discussion by returning to what seems an especially difficult passage, namely (T5). It was a central piece of evidence for the judgment that Socrates is a knower, and it represents the narrator's most extreme praise of Socrates. According to the passage, Socrates 'never went completely astray in judging the better and the worse, needing the direction of another, but was self-reliant in his thinking about those things'. That may initially seem a strong affirmation of Socrates' epistemic successes; but note the relative modesty of the remark that he 'never went completely astray (*mē diamartanein*)'. We take it to signal only that he never made gross intellectual errors of a sort that would compromise one's thinking and require someone else's correction[15] – for instance, by equating goodness and pleasure (cf. *Mem.* 4.5.6).[16] In light of that, his self-reliance can readily be interpreted as an ability to make progress under his own power. Nothing here need be taken to imply that Socrates knows what virtue is.

To be sure, the narrator goes on to say that Socrates was 'capable of expressing and delimiting [the virtues] in his reasoning (*logōi eipein te kai diorisasthai*)'. That could easily be read as an acknowledgment of Socrates' definitional abilities. Here too, though, we take it to signal something weaker, as is shown by the related discussion in *Memorabilia* 4.6, which offers a sample of the way Socrates delimited (*diōrizeto*, 4.6.1) the virtues. Socrates seems to offer several sample definitions, but caution is in order as to what they are meant to provide. The chapter begins, for example, with the virtue of piety. Rather than offer any account of essence, Socrates is content simply to emphasise that the virtue turns on knowledge of what is 'lawful' concerning the gods. So too for the discussions of the other virtues (justice, wisdom, courage) and the related evaluative ideas: Instead of giving a specification of their content, Socrates repeatedly emphasises the importance of knowledge. The overall effect is to suggest that Socrates' powers of delimitation were geared toward focusing attention on the *type* of answer that would prove adequate but stopped short of being able to generate definitions.[17]

That is fully in keeping with Socratic intellectualism: Socrates is urging upon his friends the importance of cultivating moral knowledge. But this does little to show that Socrates possesses or can convey to others the *content* of that knowledge. If one were to press Socrates to say what exactly the pious person or just person knows, or what qualities make something lawful with respect to gods or people, he may not yet have anything precise to say. Consider an analogous skill: Socrates may well be able to give a convincing argument that medicine is the knowledge of human health, but it hardly follows that he could produce health, successfully predict what a skilled physician might do, or say what constitutes a healthy condition of the body. In support of that judgment, note that the description of Socrates' piety, justice, and self-control at the beginning of (T5) is squarely about Socrates' practice and stops short of attributing to him knowledge of what those virtues are.

In this connection, consider also the end of *Memorabilia* 4.5 and the beginning of 4.6. *Memorabilia* 4.5 recounts a conversation between Socrates and Euthydemus on the value of self-control (*enkrateia*). Much of the discussion is occupied with emphasising that licentiousness (*akrasia*) leads to intellectual misjudgment about the nature of what is good and even about the true sources of pleasure. The capstone of the whole discussion is 4.5.11–4.6.1:

> (T12) [4.5.11–12, Socrates is speaking]: 'Only the self-controlled (*tois enkratesi*) can investigate the weightiest matters (*ta kratista*) and, by dividing them (*dialegontas*) after their kind in speech and in action, choose what's good and avoid what's evil.'
>
> That, [Socrates] said, is how men become best and happiest and most capable of conversing (*dialegesthai*). He said it was in fact called 'conversing' (*to dialegesthai*) after the practice of coming together to deliberate in common by dividing matters (*dialegontas*) after their kind . . . .
>
> [4.6.1] That he made his associates more dialectically skilled I shall now try to document. Socrates thought that those who know what any given thing is could also expound it to everyone else. As for those who don't know, he said it's no surprise that they themselves go wrong and make others go wrong. For that reason, he never stopped investigating together with his companions what any given thing is.

The beginning of the passage (4.5.11–12) sets out an ideal, one whereby the self-controlled are capable of making relevant distinctions in dialectical discussion and, thereby, of achieving insight into the good. Yet the final paragraph, the opening of 4.6, is importantly ambiguous as to where Socrates stands with respect to the ideal. The narrator clearly considers knowledge to involve the ability to articulate and defend a position in dialectical exchange. But all that is said of Socrates specifically is that he improved the skills of his associates and that he was unflagging in his inquiries. The passage could certainly be read as consistent with the idea that Socrates has knowledge of what the virtues are, since the emphasis on his eagerness for inquiry could be read as an eagerness *to instruct* those who do not have such knowledge. But the passage need not be so read and is most straightforwardly understood to suggest that the inquiries are Socrates' own, not simply ones to which he incites his companions.[18] In light of what follows in 4.6, we take

XENOPHON'S SOCRATES ON TEACHING AND LEARNING

Xenophon's narrator to be self-consciously positioning Socrates as someone who had impressive dialectical abilities, though he had not yet achieved knowledge of the essences of the virtues.

If we return now to (T5) and consider Socrates' role as teacher, we can see that the passage contrasts two fundamental ways in which Socrates typically engaged with others: On the one hand, as we have already seen, Socrates was able to delimit the virtues and thereby put others on the track to investigating them properly along with him; and on the other, he was able to test others' claims to knowledge, refute their errors (*hamartanontas elenxai*) and thereby turn them toward a concern for virtue. The division here can be mapped onto the similar one in another well-known and much-discussed passage in Book One of the *Memorabilia*:

> (T13) If there are those who believe what some have expressed in their conversation and writings[19] – judging Socrates to have been most effective at encouraging people to pursue virtue but inadequate in advancing them toward it – then let them gauge whether he was adequate at making his associates better after considering not merely the refutations (*ēlengchen*) he gave by way of correction, when he asked questions of those who thought they knew everything, but *also* what he said when he passed his days with those who spent their time with him.
>
> – *Mem.* 1.4.1

We take it that two forms of activity are being contrasted in (T13). First, there are the refutations that proceed by question-and-answer exchange. Socrates used them to disabuse people of false conceptions of value (the 'correction' he administered), and it is those conversations to which his critics point in saying that his abilities are limited to protreptic. Second, there are the daily conversations in which Socrates engaged with his associates.[20] Nothing precise is said here about the character of those conversations; but given the parallel between this passage and (T5), we take them to include the dialectical practice discussed there and at 4.6.1 (in T12).[21]

To be clear about what is at issue, we do not consider the contrast here to involve fundamentally distinct philosophical methods. Xenophon uses the verb '*elenchein*' generally for the practice of exposing the errors or the failings of others.[22] When used specifically of Socratic conversation, the term does not signal any precise method, and the interlocutor need not even concede defeat for an *elenchus* to be successful. What is crucial is simply that Socrates makes plain, whether to the interlocutor or to the audience, an error in the interlocutor's way of thinking.[23] Since the exposure and correction of error is presumably also a central feature of the activity of establishing proper divisions through question-and-answer exchange, phases of Socrates' dialectical engagement may resemble closely what he does in his refutational conversations. The difference between the activities lies in their contrasting goals and in the different audiences for which those different goals are appropriate.[24]

In neither case does Socrates' activity presuppose that he himself have knowledge of the essences of the virtues. Note that the common but misguided criticism of Socrates mentioned in (T13) is not that he failed to make his students virtuous but, instead, that he failed to advance (*proagagein*) his students toward virtue; and the narrator can respond without presuming that Socrates is capable of supplying the students with knowledge of virtue. Hence, none of the aforementioned passages on Socrates' conversational practice actually requires one to suppose that Socrates has the knowledge that the text elsewhere stops short of affirming. And while they all cast him as being more dialectically skilled than his companions, nothing in them forces one to suppose that he has the maximum of such skill. Of course, the narrator says in (T5): 'To me, he seemed just the kind of man that the best and happiest would be.' But that judgment is speculative, and the narrator clearly refrains from asserting that he has any acquaintance with the best and happiest of people. Indeed, in the next sentence – the final one of the *Memorabilia* – he invites anyone who disagrees to make a case for a competing view. What he means in comparing Socrates to the 'best and happiest' sort of person is just to maintain that Socrates' mode of life, with its dominating focus on virtue, is exactly the mode of life that the best person would choose.

Such an interpretation fits the other passages affirming that Socrates is a teacher. (T6), (T7) and (T9) all declare that he teaches any good thing he knows. As will be explained below, that can be understood as an assertion that he gives his students valuable insights without yet amounting to a contention that he was able to impart knowledge of what virtue is. But what of a passage like (T3), which seems to affirm Socrates' virtue and hence, given his intellectualism, his knowledge? ('I knew that I had lived my whole life piously and justly.') Here again, there is no overt claim that Socrates knows what virtue is, and considering the other evidence we think such a claim is not implicit here, either. That leaves two broad approaches to accounting for this passage.

First, one might posit a type of knowledge corresponding to Socrates' virtue – a type of knowledge that does not include in its content a grasp of the essences of the virtues. What exactly this might be is unclear; but perhaps Socrates has something like a conviction bolstered by plausible reasons that nonetheless falls short of what he would acknowledge to be a complete dialectical defence of the definitions of the virtue-terms. If so, one could make sense of the idea that Socrates is virtuous and knowledgeable in some way, or to some degree, but also striving continually to become even more so. The difficulty here is that Xenophon never provides the kind of sustained epistemological discussion that would ground this approach and allow us to determine what the central features of such knowledge would be. Still, if one is comfortable with importing a good deal of theoretical apparatus into the discussion, the approach may be feasible.[25]

Yet we prefer a second approach, one that we think is rooted more directly in Xenophon's presentation of Socrates. It links knowledge of virtue tightly to a grasp of essences and so denies Socrates any type of knowledge of virtue. On that approach, (T3) must be read so as to stop short of attributing such knowledge to Socrates. The simplest way of doing so is to take Socrates to be speaking loosely there: All he means to say is that he lived with *a constant concern* to act piously or justly. Admittedly, however, Socrates doesn't say as much explicitly, and when (T3) is considered in isolation such a reading may well seem implausible.

Yet there is in fact support for that reading in a further passage of Xenophon's Socratic writings. The bulk of *Memorabilia* 4.8 overlaps with central parts of *Apology* and contains a variation on (T3), one that is interesting for its divergences.

> **(T14)** Don't you know that up to this point there is no human being I would grant to have lived better or more pleasantly than I? I think they live best who take the best care to become as good as possible, and most pleasantly who are most keenly aware that they are becoming better. Up to this point I have been aware that those things were true of me; and encountering everyone else and comparing myself with them I have only persisted in that judgment of myself. Not only do I do so, but my friends also persist in being so disposed toward me – not out of friendship for me, since in that case

XENOPHON'S SOCRATES ON TEACHING AND LEARNING

one who befriends anyone else would also be so disposed toward his friend – but because they also think that by associating with me they will turn out best.

– Mem. 4.8.6–7

There are several interesting divergences here from (T3). One is that here there is an emphasis on his friends' desire for self-improvement, a point not evident in (T3). But the crucial change for what is presently of concern is that in (T14) the judgment that Socrates' life is at least as good and pleasant as anyone else's is said to be founded *on his constant pursuit of virtue*, and not simply on the possession of virtue throughout his life. As in (T11), Socrates' claim centres on his continuous improvement rather than the achievement of some desirable condition.

Most commentators assume that (T14) is the later text, and we too consider that most likely.[26] In that case, (T14) is a rewrite of (T3), one designed to emphasise more clearly the limits of Socrates' ability. Yet we need not presuppose any view about relative dates in order to make our interpretative point. What is telling is simply the existence of a different version of the thought of (T3) that pulls back from the idea that Socrates was virtuous in a thoroughgoing sense. In light of it, we are prepared to interpret the passing remark of (T3) about justice and piety along the lines of our earlier suggestion: Socrates is aware that he has never strayed from his concern about trying to live as justly and piously as he possibly can.[27]

(T14) also sheds light on the earlier part of (T5), where the narrator discusses Socrates' virtue. At the outset of (T5) he speaks, for instance, of Socrates as 'so just that he would harm no one in even a small way and would confer the greatest benefits on those who had dealings with him'. Here, we take it, the narrator is talking about Socrates' behavioural tendencies, and is not going so far as to assert that Socrates in fact had knowledge or made no wrong decisions at any point in his life.[28]

On this approach, then, Socrates has a deep, life-long commitment to cultivating virtue. Since he takes virtue to be a matter of knowledge, his life is largely centred on an epistemological project. But the project is ongoing: Socrates has not yet achieved the knowledge he seeks because he lacks answers to questions of the form '*What is X?*', where the values of X range over the evaluative (or implicitly evaluative) notions discussed in (T2). Answers to such questions are precisely the ones he is described as pursuing in (T12). What Socrates securely possesses is a set of dialectical tools that enable him to make progress himself and to encourage and assist others in progressing. As a result of his ongoing inquiry, he also has definite ideas about human affairs, ideas that are well-grounded in argument and are expressed at numerous points in Xenophon's Socratic works. But he does not claim to have knowledge of the essences of the virtues or of other human matters.[29]

Since this more restrictive interpretation, whereby Socrates would have some well-founded views about human affairs, though not knowledge of them, cuts against most general interpretations of Xenophon's Socratic writings, let us emphasise just how infrequent are the direct attributions of knowledge to Socrates in Xenophon's *corpus*. So far as we are aware, we have quoted every one of them above.[30] In (T3) Socrates claims 'knowledge of having lived my whole life piously and justly', and (T5) describes him as 'so shrewd (*phronimos*) that he never went completely astray in judging the better and the worse'. Both of those passages, we have argued, admit of readings that fall short of knowledge-attributions. (T4) does speak directly of Socrates' wisdom (*sophia*), but the interpretation of that passage should be constrained both by what precedes in the *Apology* and by the similar but more expansive remarks in (T5). We are thus inclined to read (T4) as high praise of Socrates' intellectual achievements without thereby attributing to him knowledge of virtue. The wisdom there attributed to him may be continuous with the knowledge attributed to him in (T6) ('[A]nd if I know of anything good, I teach it'), (T7) ('I was a benefactor to those who conversed with me, teaching them for free any good of which I was capable'), and (T9) ('He was more eager than anyone else to teach any knowledge he might have'). We argued above that such passages do imply that Socrates knows some good things to teach: It is not an empty boast (though the force of (T7) is limited by its context, and particularly by (T11)). How, on the more restrictive reading, should we understand those claims?

What we propose is that the good things Socrates teaches do not amount to making him a teacher *of virtue* but instead involve imparting positions that Socrates takes to be crucial to dedicating one's life to the pursuit of such knowledge. For instance, in *Mem.* 1.4, Socrates confronts Aristodemus over his neglect of sacrifice, prayer and divination. Aristodemus doubts that the gods concern themselves with him; hence his neglect of them. Socrates mounts an argument from design – the first of its kind on record – aimed at establishing the benevolent concern of the gods for humans. None of this amounts to a comprehensive view of what the human good consists in, nor does it imply knowledge of virtue. But it is nonetheless relevant to the pursuit insofar as it shows that we do not live in an indifferent universe where virtue will go unrewarded.[31]

Such a passage can be seen as representative of the kind of advice Xenophon represents Socrates as giving. It allows one to view Socrates as a valued associate to his friends, and even as a teacher of sorts; but when it comes to understanding what virtue is, all Socrates can offer his friends is that they join him in his dialectical pursuits.

While we favour this more restricted reading of the sense in which Socrates is knower and teacher to the view that Socrates has a degree, but not the highest degree, of knowledge, we grant that no text unambiguously secures that reading. Strikingly, either interpretation makes clear that some form of epistemic modesty is a robust part of Xenophon's portrayal of Socrates. It is often rightly observed that the *Memorabilia* has an apologetic aim and that Xenophon's Socratic writings are centrally concerned to present Socrates as a benefactor to those around him. Xenophon thus has every motivation to cast Socrates as wise. The fact that he holds back suggests to our minds that some form of epistemic modesty was indeed a prominent characteristic of the historical Socrates, one that Xenophon was concerned to find room for despite the slight tension it produces for the way he aims to memorialise Socrates. Yet we leave that for future discussions of the Socratic Problem.

VI. A CASE STUDY: CRITIAS AND ALCIBIADES

With this general picture in mind, let's take a closer look at *Memorabilia* 1.2, the context of both (T10), where the narrator denies that Socrates was a teacher, and (T8), where, instead of simply denying that Socrates taught Critias and Alcibiades, the narrator launches into a lengthy discussion aimed at demonstrating how they could turn out badly despite Socrates' beneficial instruction. *Memorabilia* 1.2 explicitly addresses the accusation that Socrates corrupted the youth, one of the formal charges for which Socrates was tried, and is particularly concerned with the idea that Socrates made his associates violent. It is in this context that Critias and Alcibiades play a prominent role:

XENOPHON'S SOCRATES ON TEACHING AND LEARNING

(T15) For Critias proved, of all those who took part in the oligarchy, the greediest and most violent and murderous, while Alcibiades in turn proved the most licentious and insolent and violent of all those who took part in the democracy.

– Mem. 1.2.12[32]

We needn't rehearse their histories beyond noting that Critias was centrally involved in the brutality that the so-called Thirty Tyrants displayed toward a broad cross-section of Athenian society, and that Alcibiades actively abetted the enemies of Athens during the Peloponnesian War, most consequentially during the catastrophic campaign in Sicily. If Socrates bore any responsibility for those disastrous episodes, it would indeed be a mark against him.

The narrator's strategy is to demonstrate how thoroughly the behaviour of Critias and Alcibiades was shaped by their ambition for power. Indeed, it was this ambition that drew them to Socrates in the first place, because they thought he could help them be more effective in the political arena. And their political ambitions, as the narrator describes them, were effectively boundless (*Mem.* 1.2.14–15). They recognised three prominent characteristics of Socrates: his extreme self-sufficiency despite having little money, his mastery (*enkratestaton onta*) of every kind of pleasure and his ability 'to deal with his conversation partners however he wanted' (1.2.14). Clearly, says the narrator, what they wanted from Socrates was not at all 'his life and his moderation (*sōphrosunē*)', but rather they sought to become 'most capable in speech and action' – a stock phrase in the Athenian context meaning 'politically proficient' (1.2.15).[33]

This raises an obvious objection: 'Socrates should not have taught his associates political skills before he taught moderation' (1.2.17, see (T8) above). In response, the narrator insists that Socrates *did* teach them to behave moderately, both by example and by argument. And he did so with some success, such that 'even those two behaved moderately (*sōphronounte*) as long as they were with Socrates' (1.2.18; cf. 1.2.24, 26). This leaves open one aspect of the objection: Perhaps Socrates should have waited to begin teaching them politics – i.e., the ability to achieve success in debate – until their commitment to moderation was robust enough to guarantee that they would use any political skill for good rather than ill. The narrator doesn't address that objection directly here, an omission that is striking since he elsewhere attributes a relevant position to Socrates:

(T16) Socrates was not intent on pushing his students to become skilled at speaking and acting or resourceful; rather, he thought they first needed to develop moderation (*sōphrosunē*). He considered people who had a facility for those things but who lacked moderation (*sōphronein*) to be more unjust and to have a greater capacity for wrongdoing.

– Mem. 4.3.1

An objector, then, need only point to Socrates' own convictions: Why wouldn't Socrates ensure that Critias and Alcibiades were sufficiently moderate before even beginning to teach them political skills?

Though the narrator does not avail himself of them directly, we think there are resources available in the *Memorabilia* to construct a response. To insist on a clean division between teaching moderation and teaching politics is fundamentally to misunderstand the nature of Socrates' instruction. As we saw in (T12), Socrates teaches his students a set of dialectical skills that allow them to inquire together with him into the nature of human affairs, including moderation. Those are precisely the skills that attracted Critias and

Alcibiades to Socrates in the first place, not because they longed for moderation but because the same skills could be turned to political ends. So, while Socrates is indeed committed to teaching them moderation first and foremost and to holding them back from political activity during this process, there is in practice no way to foster it without, to some extent, fostering the skills of intellectual debate generally. Students who pick up dialectical skills from Socrates may, with Socrates' encouragement, use those skills for moral inquiry and the cultivation of virtue; but Socrates cannot stop the politically ambitious from acting against his advice and using their dialectical skills for political advancement to the exclusion of moral progress. (T16) clearly articulates Socrates' priorities. Coupled with (T12), it also highlights the inherent risks of Socratic pedagogy. To manage those risks, Socrates must attempt to channel the energies of his students toward the most appropriate uses of their developing skills. In the early stages, politics is to be put aside in favour of a single-minded focus on developing virtue.

One can appreciate here why Xenophon might have hesitated, in the context of an attempted exoneration of Socrates, to have his narrator comment explicitly on the risks of Socratic pedagogy. Instead, he chooses to emphasise a salient feature of Socrates' association with Critias and Alcibiades, which is that despite their long-standing political ambitions they were strongly influenced by Socrates, so much so that they believed at that time that behaving moderately was the best thing to do. But as we'll discuss shortly, even their brief commitment to moderation was circumscribed by their political ambitions and far less reflectively grounded than one would hope. And in the end, their political ambitions won out: The narrator describes an Alcibiades who left Socrates as soon as he thought himself better than the leading politicians, and a Critias who eventually became so opposed to Socrates in thought and conduct that after the fall of Athens they were in open conflict.

That account of the dynamic between Socrates and his troubled associates goes some way toward exonerating Socrates for their conduct. But the narrator then imagines being confronted with a further objection by 'many of those who claim to engage in philosophy': *How can Alcibiades and Critias have gained some virtue from Socrates and then lost it? Virtue is knowledge, and knowledge isn't the sort of thing to be gained and then lost: Once you gain it, you have it.* In response, the narrator swiftly confirms that he, too, is an intellectualist. But he denies the second thought: Knowledge can in fact be gained and lost. The narrator explains by arguing that intellectual abilities operate the same way as physical ones: They must be exercised to be maintained.

> (T17) I observe that just as those who do not train their bodies are unable to perform tasks appropriate to the body, so too those who do not train their souls are unable to perform tasks appropriate to the soul. They are unable, that is, to do or to refrain from what they should.

> – *Mem.* 1.2.19

Shortly afterward, the narrator explains the circumstances which lead to regression in virtue:

> (T18) I observe that, just as those who fail to practice are forgetful of poetic verses, so too forgetfulness becomes the condition of those who neglect instructional discourse. And whenever someone forgets words of advice, *he also has forgotten the state the soul was in when it desired moderation (sōphrosunē)*; and in his forgetfulness of that, it is no surprise that he would likewise forget the moderation (*sōphrosunē*).

> – *Mem.* 1.2.21

Here we note a divergence between our translation and Marchant's rendering in the Loeb edition. Marchant translates the underlined clause as: '[he] forget[s] the experiences that prompted the soul to desire self-control'.[34] He thus takes the narrator to be suggesting some causal relation between certain life-experiences and the instruction one has received. On our reading, the point is that there is a tight connection between understanding the reasons for moderation and desiring to be moderate. To interpret the passage this way is to commit Xenophon's narrator, and presumably his Socrates as well, not just to virtue intellectualism but to at least a qualified form of motivational intellectualism. When grasped, the reasons for acting naturally produce in one an affective condition: the desire to pursue moderation. Correlatively, to neglect those reasons is to lose one's sense of why moderation matters, and so to lose one's motivation for pursuing it.[35] Looking back to the remark in (T17) about those who fail to train the soul, the point is not about their desire swamping their sense of what is right, but about a distortion in their thinking that produces the wrong affective state. People go wrong because they have failed properly to cultivate and maintain an understanding of why they should or shouldn't act in certain ways, and so they fail to see the right sorts of action as good or bad.[36]

The idea that one may regress as well as progress with respect to virtue allows us to make some sense of Critias' and Alcibiades' association with Socrates. Surely, Critias and Alcibiades never achieved knowledge of the essences of moderation and the other virtues – knowledge that Socrates would have been unable to provide them if it is true that he too lacked it. If one adopts the view that knowledge of virtue comes in degrees, one could say that what they achieved was some measure of knowledge, but a measure falling far short of Socrates' own (still-incomplete) knowledge. Thus, whereas Socrates' knowledge was sufficient to sustain his strong commitment to a life of virtue, whatever weak commitment to virtue they had was soon fully supplanted by political ambition.

Our preferred reading, on which even Socrates lacks knowledge of virtue, also allows one to make sense of their case. Surely the narrator's point about knowledge can be applied to states of lesser cognitive insight. A straightforward way of developing the narrator's point would then be to suppose that Socrates led Alcibiades and Critias to achieve some measure of insight, which affected their behaviour, but that the insight and the corresponding behaviour were not robust enough to prove lasting in the face of contrary influences.

Either way, the narrator's position here makes sense of his insistence that Alcibiades and Critias were really committed to moderation for a time:

> (T19) I know that even [Critias and Alcibiades] behaved moderately (*sōphronounte*) as long as they were with Socrates, not because they feared that he would fine them or beat them, but because at the time they thought it best to act that way.
>
> – *Mem.* 1.2.18

What enabled them to behave as they did was the persuasiveness of his argument coupled with the power of his example. The narrator emphasises again later that Socrates' presence in their lives was crucial:

> (T20) So long as they were with Socrates, Critias and Alcibiades were able, using him as an ally, to control (*kratein*) their not-so-admirable desires; but when they got away from him [they became much worse people].
>
> – *Mem.* 1.2.24

There are, however, weaknesses in such a reading of Socrates' influence. One significant question goes unanswered: If Socrates had such a beneficial impact on Critias and Alcibiades, what precisely explains how they were pulled away from him? It is tempting to suggest, as we just did, that that their progress toward virtue under Socrates was so incomplete that other temptations proved strong enough to abandon him. Had they had more time with him and continued to advance, eventually they could have avoided such backsliding. Yet that story seems hard to square with the narrator's repeated emphasis on just how out of step with Socrates they were. They came to him with a deep revulsion at the thought of living like him, so much so that the narrator speculates they would rather have died than be like Socrates (1.2.16). They chafed when questioned by Socrates about their mistakes (1.2.47), and they sprang away from Socrates the moment they took their political abilities to be sufficient for their ambitions (1.2.16, 1.2.47). They were thus unsympathetic to Socrates *from start to finish*:

> (T21) I would maintain that no one gets any education from someone who is distasteful to them. And Critias and Alcibiades found Socrates distasteful the whole time they associated with him. Right from the start they set out to lead the city. Witness the fact that even while with Socrates they would try most of all to talk with those who were especially engaged in politics.

> – *Mem.* 1.2.39

All this sounds like they were eagerly awaiting the moment when they could dispense with Socrates' company, rather than that they became attracted to his life and teachings, but not so strongly that they resisted all alternatives.

There is thus some tension in Xenophon's account of Socrates' influence on Alcibiades and Critias. This is perhaps unsurprising: Xenophon's narrator is attempting to walk a tightrope by insisting that Alcibiades and Critias benefitted from Socrates, but were not so influenced by him that he bears any responsibility for their later misdeeds. The result is a defence of Socrates that is only partly satisfying. There is, however, a way of understanding the narrator's position which resolves some, though perhaps not all, of the tension – namely, by severely circumscribing the sense in which Critias and Alcibiades were committed to moderation while with Socrates: Their *entire* engagement with Socrates was shaped by their consuming political ambitions. Having been attracted to Socrates for his argumentative skill, they became impressed by Socrates' self-mastery, recognising how his focus and discipline allowed him to concentrate on what mattered to him. They thus valued an aspect of moderation – discipline – without adopting the governing values central to true moderation. Indeed, the lure of politics alienated them from Socrates' modest lifestyle, and their pride made them resistant to his attempts at correction. Hence they emulated Socrates only in limited fashion, using him as inspiration for channelling their own energies in the pursuit of different ambitions. This is the sense in which they could simultaneously be attracted to Socrates because of his commitment to moderation and be repelled by the Socratic lifestyle that resulted from that commitment.

Their great failing, then, was that they always subordinated the importance of moderation to their larger aims, and never managed to see how properly valuing moderation would require them to allow it to *shape* their ambitions rather than merely *serve* them. And even that partial lesson was only temporary. Once outside of Socrates' sphere, having attained from him what they came for, pride and ambition led both men to forget their lessons and to lose even what share of moderation they had attained. Eventually, their excesses would be their downfalls, but for some time natural talents

XENOPHON'S SOCRATES ON TEACHING AND LEARNING

and social advantages allowed each to 'succeed' – at least by their own standards of success.

Such an account has a cost: It leaves Socrates open to the charge that the skills he taught Critias and Alcibiades were eventually used to harm Athens. Perhaps Critias and Alcibiades would have been less dangerous if Socrates had left them alone. Yet it may be reasonable to respond that for Socrates to have washed his hands of them from the start would have been for him to resign himself to looking on while they marched down the path of corruption. After all, the relevant 'political' skills could also have been acquired from other, unscrupulous teachers; and at least a longshot bid to turn them toward a better life had some chance of success. But it must be said that such an account leaves little room to praise Socrates for anything except his effort and motives. And in that case one should consider forced the narrator's suggestion (1.2.26–27) that Socrates deserves praise for holding them back at the age when they would naturally be most foolish and licentious, and all the more praise for supplying them with moderation for a time given how bad they later turned out.

In any event, Socrates stands in sharp contrast to Critias and Alcibiades. They had *at most* a weak and attenuated grasp of the power of virtue to enhance their lives, while Socrates is committed, as the central tenet of his life, to virtue and the continual exercise required for its effective pursuit. Socrates' commitment is secure: He has progressed far enough to recognise that any meaningful life must give virtue pride of place, and his recognition of how far he has yet to travel down the path toward virtue drives him to be unflagging in his pursuit of it through dialectical investigations. Even if that latter theme – the ways Socrates has yet to achieve fully the ideal condition – is not front and centre in Xenophon's Socratic works, it emerges as an important part of a well-rounded portrait of Socrates as knower and teacher in Xenophon. It is in recognition of this life-defining project of continual improvement that the narrator makes his final remark about Socrates in the *Memorabilia* [(T5)]: 'To me, he seemed just the kind of man that the best and happiest would be.'

NOTES

* We are grateful to audiences at the 2017 and 2018 Tahoe Workshop in Ancient Philosophy, and the 2020 Central Division Meeting of the American Philosophical Association, for feedback on antecedents to this essay; to the members of the History of Philosophy Roundtable at the University of California, San Diego for a stimulating discussion at a late stage; and to Nick Smith and Hugh Benson for written comments on the penultimate draft.

1. Influential negative appraisals were also published at the beginning of the twentieth century by Robin (1910), Burnet (1911) and Maier (1913). In one of the few mid-twentieth-century monographs on Xenophon's Socratic works, Chroust (1957) seasons his chapters liberally with insults to Xenophon's feeble intellect. For further discussion of the history of scholarship, see especially Dorion 2011.

2. We won't be discussing the tradition of Straussian interpretation here, but for consideration of it, see Dorion 2010 and Johnson 2012. For a recent comprehensive interpretation of Xenophon's Socratic works along Straussian lines, see Pangle 2018 and 2020.

3. See especially Dorion 2006 and 2011.

4. See e.g. Johnson 2021: 4, 6–7, 283.

5. All translations are our own and are drawn, in the case of the *Memorabilia*, from Bandini's Budé text (see Bandini and Dorion 2010, 2011a & b) or, in the case of other works, from Marchant's Oxford Classical Texts edition.

6. The expression '*kala (te) k'agatha*' (or, as here, '*kala te kai agatha*') is the counterpart of the personal '*kalos k'agathos*', which often has class overtones: 'gentlemanly' or 'gentleman' in the Victorian sense of elite, leisured and decent. In Xenophon's works the expressions are often used in a predominantly moral sense, one grounded in the ready moral connotations of the component adjectives, 'noble (*kalos*)' and 'good (*agathos*)'. We translate as 'estimable' to capture that moral sense while also marking the fact that Xenophon's usage represents a transformational appropriation of the class-based idea.

7. We say 'minimally' because there are various interpretations of *Mem.* 3.9.4–5 that include the basic assertion that virtue is wisdom. There is, on the one hand, a question of the relation of the virtues to one another. Some think that the individual virtues are here identified with one another and with wisdom (see e.g. Irwin 1974: 412, Vander Waerdt 1993: 42); others that moderation is the general virtue, and justice and the others its parts (Morrison 2010: 228–229); and others still that each virtue is a form of wisdom, not wholly disconnected from the others but not identical to them either (Dorion in Bandini and Dorion 2011a: 344 n.13). On the other hand, there is a question whether all there is to say about virtue is that it is wisdom. 'Virtue is wisdom' might be thought to indicate that virtue just is wisdom, with no remainder; or one might offer an interpretation whereby wisdom is the core of virtue, guaranteeing the possession of any other aspects of virtue (such as the appropriate affective states). None of our arguments in this essay turns on any of these interpretative choices, and so we shall speak of 'virtue intellectualism' or the claim that 'virtue is knowledge/wisdom' in a way meant to be inclusive of the full range of interpretations.

8. We use this way of speaking because we do not think the narrator of the *Memorabilia* (or for that matter, the *Symposium* or *Oeconomicus*) should be identified with the author Xenophon. The narrator is instead an ideal Socratic, someone who has been able to observe Socrates closely in a wide range of situations and to understand the force of his words. Accepting that position on the literary character of the work is not essential for understanding the arguments to follow.

9. On the nature of the wisdom that is virtue and its connection to choosing well, with special attention to *Mem.* 3.9.5, see now also Bjelde 2021.

10. '*Sōphrosunē*' and cognates have a semantic range that doesn't neatly match any English expression. Often in Xenophon's discussions of Socrates, it is used so as to contrast primarily with self-indulgence or licentiousness. At other times (only in (T2) among the texts we quote) the contrast is primarily with unsound thinking. Sometimes as well, neither contrast is obviously the more prominent. Here in (T2) we translate 'sound-mindedness', and elsewhere we have translated 'moderation', always marking its use in quoted passages. To recognise these two different cases is not to deny that self-indulgence is closely connected to wrong thinking: The self-indulgent are also deeply misguided about what contributes to their own welfare. '*Sōphrosunē*' is, moreover, closely related to '*enkrateia*', a term of narrower scope that we translate as 'self-control'. We discuss these and related terms in Jones and Sharma 2018, especially in connection to (T1). For a comprehensive review of the uses of '*sōphrosunē*' in Xenophon, see North 1966: 123–132.

11. For discussion of intellectualism in Plato, see Clark's contribution to this volume.

12. Xenophon's narrator seems to think so, remarking at the close of the discussion (1.6.14), 'When I heard those remarks I thought him a blessed fellow, one leading his hearers toward an estimable character.' Cf. *Mem.* 4.7.1 [(T9) below], where the context likewise makes a conditional reading improbable.

13. (T7) is no offhand remark: It is Socrates' final statement to the jury that would shortly sentence him to death. It would hardly do to defend Socrates here as Morrison proposed for (T6), by saying that (T7) is a disguised conditional that would not be rendered false even if Socrates knew of nothing good. To take that line would be to put Socrates in the camp of another suspect character once described by Bertrand Russell, the atheist running for public office who takes advantage of a certain analysis of statements to affirm that he does not think it false to say, 'The Ruler of the Universe is wise'.

14. As Stokes 2012 notes, von Arnim (1923: 87) and Hackforth (1933: 8 n.2, which also refers to a concurring view by Gomperz) would prefer to emend the text of the oracle's report so as to include wisdom. Their position is rebutted by Stokes (2012: 254): Socrates does not take himself to be in *superlative* possession of wisdom, as would be demanded if the oracle had actually included wisdom among his virtues. But since Socrates is an intellectualist about virtue, Stokes' rebuttal falls short: Socrates should have a comparable judgment about his wisdom as he does of his other virtues. Still, we think it significant that in remarking on his wisdom, Socrates does not make comparative judgments to the wisdom of others. That suggests to us that Socrates is not here trying to justify a statement of the oracle but is adding an observation of his own.

15. The phrase μὴ διαμαρτάνειν is commonly translated so as to suggest that Socrates was always correct in his judgments – for instance by Marchant in Marchant, Todd and Henderson 2013 [1923] ('unerring'); Dorion in Bandini and Dorion 2011b ('ne pas se tromper'); and Johnson 2021: 47 ('never made a mistake'), 175 ('never erred about the right thing to do'). But the verbal prefix δια- is here intensive, emphasising the totality of the mistakes in question, while its negation need signal only that Socrates was not altogether wrong.

16. Some have argued, wrongly in our view, that a moderate hedonism is in fact acceptable to Xenophon's Socrates. See e.g. Gosling and Taylor 1982: 37–40, Sedley 2007: 81–82, and Johnson 2021: 151–161. Even on such a reading, though, an *unnuanced* equation of goodness and pleasure might be just the sort of serious error that could undermine the goodness of one's life.

17. That *Mem.* 4.6 supplies definitions of virtues is a common scholarly judgment. For example, Cooper holds (1999: 25): 'In IV 6, as noted above, Socrates is presented working out in question-and-answer discussion definitions of several virtues. Piety is knowledge of what is lawful (*nomimon*) in connection with the gods. . .'. Johnson maintains (2021: 10) that Xenophon's Socrates defines every item from (T2) somewhere in the *Mem.*, including several of them in 4.6. (Compare further the judgments of two prominent Platonic scholars, Vlastos (1991: 298) and Irwin (1974: 411–12), who contrast sharply the supposed facility of Xenophon's Socrates with ethical definitions to the lack of ability so familiar from Plato's portrayal.) Such statements are insufficiently nuanced: The 'definitions' Socrates offers are not the sort of thing Socrates is after when he pursues moral knowledge. They constitute only a framework for such a pursuit. The reliable provision of such a framework is, we take it, precisely what the narrator has in mind in saying (T5) that Socrates did not go completely astray.

18. Compare also (T2), which describes Socrates' interest in investigating 'definitional' questions without referring directly to his role as a teacher. Indeed, the contrast there with those who inquire into natural science strongly suggests that the investigations represent Socrates' own intellectual endeavours.

19. The opening of the sentence has commonly been thought to require emendation. All of the mss. read: Εἰ δέ τινες Σωκράτην νομίζουσιν, ὡς ἔνιοι γράφουσί τε καὶ λέγουσι περὶ αὐτοῦ τεκμαιρόμενοι . . . . In their edition of the text, Bandini and Dorion follow a number of earlier scholars in thinking that ὡς should be altered to οἷς. The emendation was first proposed by Jacobs in 1818; see here Bandini and Dorion 2010: 137 n. 226, and cf. cxxxiii–iv. Marchant rejected the emendation, noting in the preface to the second edition of his Oxford Classical Texts volume of Xenophon's Socratic works that a papyrus fragment of the third or fourth century CE preserves the reading of the mss. (The Loeb edition by Marchant, Todd and Henderson relies on Sauppe's earlier text and records the emendation.) If one reads the text of the mss., Xenophon's narrator would be reporting a judgment about Socrates that accords with the one explicitly made by certain other writers and speakers. According to the emendation, he would be reporting a judgment made by unspecified parties *based (inferentially) on* some written or spoken representations of Socrates – perhaps including the writings of Plato or other Socratics.

    The linguistic argument for altering the text is that Xenophon elsewhere does not use τεκμαίρεσθαι without complements. Instead, he uses the verb only with the dative or with prepositions followed by the genitive. That is to say, he otherwise consistently uses the verb along with a specification of the means by which, or the basis upon which, a given judgment has been reached. However, there is no reason why an author who standardly uses the verb with such specifications might not on occasion use it without them. Indeed, the complete sentence at 1.4.1 makes abundantly clear the basis for the judgment in question – namely, that the relevant parties have only a partial view of Socrates' activity. Hence the typical complements are here unnecessary. (Slings (1999: 77 n.142) likewise rejects the emendation, noting simply that other authors comfortably use τεκμαίρεσθαι without any complement.)

20. Some interpreters (e.g. Slings 1999: 78 n.145, 80–81) consider there to be *three* types of conversation at issue in this passage: protreptic, refutative argument and daily conversation with associates. For counterargument, see Dorion's discussion in Bandini and Dorion 2010: cxxvii–cxxxiii.

21. Contrary to what is suggested by Dorion (Bandini and Dorion 2010: cxxv–cxxvi, Bandini and Dorion 2011b: 228–229 n. 7), there is no conflict between (T13) and (T5). Dorion understands what is said in (T5) ('provoking them to pursue virtue and an estimable character') as an indication that Socrates was effective at protreptic *but unable to make others virtuous*; and he takes that to conflict with the import of (T13). (Cf. also Danzig 2017: 298–299, which agrees that there is a tension of the sort Dorion describes and ventures the solution that in (T13) Xenophon is intentionally promising a positive defence of Socrates that he cannot deliver, as part of a process of distracting the reader from more negative accusations that Socrates' conversation humiliated and harmed his interlocutors.) However, as mentioned previously, (T5) notes that Socrates was skilled in refutations, and thereby in protreptic, but it *also* discusses his ability to delimit the virtues in conversation. That fits neatly with the idea sounded in (T13), which is that Socrates was capable of advancing (*proagagein*) others toward virtue. As we read it, the latter remark stops short of an affirmation that Socrates rendered others virtuous and instead only stresses his value to them in the pursuit.

22. For fuller discussion, see Bandini and Dorion 2010: cxxi–cxxv (with a full list of the verb's uses in Xenophon at cxxi n.2).

23. See here Danzig 2017: 301–304, which is presented as a correction to Bandini and Dorion 2010: cxliv ff.

24. In cases where an interlocutor can satisfy both descriptions to some extent, a reader would expect a mix of both refutation and positive conversation. Most scholars consider the conversation between Socrates and the young Euthydemus in *Mem.* 4.2 to be a paradigm example of a Xenophontic *elenchus*; but in fact, it is *both* refutation and a conversation able to advance an interlocutor nearer to virtue, as we argue in Jones and Sharma 2020. Socrates regards Euthydemus as eminently capable of being a close associate, and he thus treats him to a refutation that contains the seeds of positive Socratic teaching. For development of a similar point with respect to other Socratic conversations in Xenophon, see Johnson 2005: 42–43.

25. A similar limitation applies to an approach that tempted us when we presented some of the central ideas of this chapter at the 2018 Tahoe Workshop in Ancient Philosophy and the 2020 Central Division Meeting of the American Philosophical Association: explicating Socrates' knowledge in terms of craft-knowledge. The idea of treating virtue as a craft is familiar from Plato, and there are significant resources in the Platonic corpus for constructing a theory of craft-knowledge as coming in degrees, as evidenced by Smith's (2021) monograph on the topic. It is tempting to import these ideas into Xenophon and to say that Socrates has achieved a degree of the knowledge that is virtue but not the fullest degree. But this would be an importation, and therefore speculative: Xenophon's corpus simply does not contain the rich reflection on craft-knowledge that would allow us to construct the theory internally. That is not to say that there aren't some tantalising passages. When Critias orders Socrates to stop talking of shoemakers and carpenters and smiths, joking (though menacingly) that he must have exhausted them by now, Socrates follows up by asking if he must therefore cease discussion of 'what follows upon these – the just, the holy, and the other such things' (*Mem.* 1.2.37). The joke works only if Socrates really is constantly talking about craftspeople, and the prohibition matters only if he really is using them to explain moral virtue. Maybe comments like these are sufficient to open the door to the centrality of craft-knowledge in Xenophon's Socrates, but virtually all the heavy lifting will have to be done by Plato. Since our primary focus in this essay is what we can get from close examination of Xenophon's Socratic works, we leave to one side the possibility of making craft-knowledge the linchpin of an interpretation.

26. For discussion of the relations between the works, see the treatments and further references in Bandini and Dorion 2011b: 243–250 and Johnson 2021: 120–122. We do not subscribe to the common idea that the priority of *Apol.* is shown by its apparent lack of awareness of the anti-Socratic work of Polycrates, which *Mem.* 1.2 supposedly addresses. Even leaving aside the question of whether it is safe to assume that *Mem.* 1.2 and 4.8 share the same relative date with regard to *Apol.*, we are inclined to reject the thesis that Polycrates is behind *Mem.* 1.2, notwithstanding Smith's argument for that thesis in his contribution to this volume. We also do not subscribe to the idea that *Apol.* does a poorer job of defending Socrates than *Mem.* 1.1–2. Defending Socrates is not the primary intention of the former work. (Cf. here Bandini and Dorion 2011b: 243–244, Johnson 2021: 120–121.) Instead, any decision as to relative dates must be made solely on interpretative grounds; and since we consider *Mem.* 4.8 the more careful elaboration, we think it likely later.

27. Johnson would explain the differences between the passages solely in terms of Socrates' different purposes in *Apol.* and *Mem.* 4.8. Specifically, he suggests, *Apol.* is oriented around Socrates' boasting, and one might thus expect it to make stronger claims for him (2021: 121). Ultimately, however, the appeal to contextual purpose does not take one as far as Johnson's observation may suggest: Since Socrates does not otherwise go so far as to lie about himself in *Apol.*, the reader is still faced with the task of reconciling what is said in the two passages.

28. Had he wanted to make that point specifically, he would surely have used the indicative with ὥστε rather than the infinitive.

29. On this approach, then, Xenophon's Socrates might hold something akin to the *priority of definition principle* often attributed to Plato's Socrates (on which see Benson's chapter in this volume), although, again, there is little explicit theorising on the matter to be found in Xenophon.

30. Two additional texts are relevant, though they don't contain direct attributions of knowledge. At *Apol.* 20–21, Socrates responds to the charge that he corrupts the youth not by denying that he is involved in their education, but by noting that it is appropriate for them to follow him rather than their parents in such matters if they judge him superior when it comes to education. And *Mem.* 1.2.49–55 is similar, though more expansive. Both texts are readily assimilable to the analysis we are proposing.

31. On *Mem.* 1.4 and the related 4.3, see DeFilippo and Mitsis 1994, McPherran 1996: 272–291, Viano 2001, Sedley 2007: 78–86 and Sedley 2008, as well as the relevant notes in Bandini and Dorion 2010 and 2011b.

32. Marchant prefers a different reading in his Oxford Classical Texts edition. It may be translated: 'For Critias proved, of all those who took part in the oligarchy, the greediest and most violent, while Alcibiades in turn proved the most licentious and insolent of all those who took part in the democracy.'

33. So, when introducing Pericles before the crucial foreign policy speech that determined Athenian strategy in the lead-up to and the early years of the Peloponnesian War, Thucydides says simply that he was the 'leading man' in Athens of that time and was 'most capable in speaking and acting'; i.e., Pericles was the preeminent and finest Athenian politician of his day (1.139.4; cf. 1.127.3).

34. The Greek for the underlined clause is: ἐπιλέλησται καὶ ὧν ἡ ψυχὴ πάσχουσα τῆς σωφροσύνης ἐπεθύμει. By contrast to Marchant, we think the imperfect ἐπεθύμει leans rather to a description of the condition of the soul, where the coordinate πάσχουσα refers to accompanying affective states.

35. Dorion renders (Bandini and Dorion 2010 *ad loc.*): 'When one has forgotten the discourses proper to exhortation, one also forgets the impressions thanks to which the soul was aspiring to moderation'. ('Quand on a oublié les discours propre à exhorter, on oublie aussi les impressions grâce auxquelles l'âme aspirait à la modération'.) That seems also to attribute a form of motivational intellectualism to the passage, though in a manner slightly different from our translation.

36. Compare *Mem.* 4.5.6.

CHAPTER THREE

Socratic Methods*

ERIC BROWN

'THE SOCRATIC METHOD'

Socrates is famous in large part for *how* he philosophised. Some of what he did, especially involving his trial and death, earned him press. So did some of what he said, even if it is difficult for us to be confident which of the sayings attributed to him were genuinely said by him. But his most enduring fame and perhaps his earliest publicity owe more to the distinctive *way* in which he practiced philosophy. As Plato famously portrays him, Socrates regularly asked questions and then tested the answers with additional questions. This is what we think of, broadly, as 'the Socratic method'. Plato advertises it as a distinctive form of intellectual activity, and the hypothesis that Socrates philosophised in a novel way helps to explain the proliferation of Socratic literature (*Sōkratikoi logoi*) in the fourth century BCE.

Readers of the surviving *Sōkratikoi logoi* are still attracted to and puzzled by the way in which Socrates philosophises. Scholars have sought to characterise more exactly Socrates' method, and to distinguish it from other ways of intellectual inquiry. As a result, there are debates about how exactly to characterise Socrates' method and even about whether he has a method at all. This chapter offers an opinionated and selective guide to these debates, insofar as they are focused on Plato's Socratic dialogues, and it starts with the scholars who say that there is no Socratic method, to clarify what is at issue when we talk about Socrates' method.

DOES SOCRATES HAVE A METHOD?

Scholars have argued that Socrates has no method in two ways that together might seem to pose a dilemma. Either a method is something technical, requiring some worked-out theory or expertise, or it is just any patterned way of proceeding. If the former, one might argue that Socrates lacks a method on the grounds that he possesses no theory about what he is doing and no relevant expertise (*technē*). And if the latter, one might argue that there is no distinctive Socratic method on the grounds that Socrates exhibits many patterns in his philosophising. But each of these arguments is contestable, and the dilemma itself leaves room for other characterisations of method.

Brickhouse and Smith (1994: 3–10) and Wolfsdorf (2003a) argue that Socrates lacks a method on the grounds that he possesses no theory about what he is doing and no relevant expertise (*technē*). Wolfsdorf (2003a) emphasises that Socrates does not explicitly articulate any theory about how to philosophise. That is true, but can we infer that he has no theory to offer? It is certainly not as though he has *nothing* to say about how he proceeds and why he does so. He regularly and explicitly favors a question-and-answer format, with short answers (*Prt.* 347c–348a, *Grg.* 447b–449d, *Hi.Mi.* 369b–d), and he frequently demands that the answerer state their own beliefs (*Cr.* 49c–d, *Prt.* 331c, *Grg.* 500b, *Rep.* I 346a). Moreover, Socrates has things to say about what *kind* of answer he is looking for when he asks 'What is F?', especially in the *Euthyphro* (6d–e) and *Meno* (72a–76a). But on Wolfsdorf's (2003a: esp. 293) interpretation, Socrates' account of how he proceeds and why he does so remains 'theoretically and methodologically naïve', because he does not investigate the metaphysical and epistemological questions that he would need to answer to have an account that is not naïve. Moreover, Wolfsdorf (2003a: 293) takes Socrates to be *aware* of this limitation, as he thinks it best explains Socrates' disavowals of knowledge.

Brickhouse and Smith (1994: 3–10) also tie Socrates' lack of a method to his ignorance, by arguing that Socrates lacks expertise (*technē*). One might think that Socrates cannot possess any expertise because expertise confers wisdom (*Ap.* 22d) and he disavows all wisdom, great and small (*Ap.* 22b). But Socrates qualifies this sweeping disavowal when he acknowledges that he has human wisdom, the grasp that he lacks wisdom about 'the biggest things', that is, about how to live (*Ap.* 23a–b).[1] One might also think that Socrates cannot possess any expertise because he sharply distinguishes himself from the 'craftsmen' or experts (*Ap.* 22c–d). But in this passage he actually distinguishes himself from the *manual* craftsmen, which leaves the door open for him to possess non-manual expertise (*cf. Grg.* 450a–e).

Brickhouse and Smith (1994: 3–10) have a more promising way of arguing that Socrates lacks expertise, in two steps. Step one extracts from Socrates' various remarks about cobblers, medical doctors, horse trainers and such seven requirements for expertise (Brickhouse and Smith 1994: 6–7). First, expertise is exercised in an orderly fashion, not by guesswork or at random. Second, expertise is teachable: Experts transmit their mastery to apprentices. Third, experts can explain what they do by giving an account of their expertise's object and its causes (*Grg.* 465a, 500e–501b). Fourth, the expert's work and judgments (about their expertise) are free from error. Fifth, the expert stands out from other people in possessing their expertise: Others lack the expert's knowledge and cannot do what the expert does without much greater chance of failure. Sixth, every expertise is defined by its own subject matter. And seventh, the expert has knowledge and wisdom insofar as they are an expert.[2]

In step two, Brickhouse and Smith (1994: 7–8) argue that Socrates falls short of these standards. True, he does not proceed randomly or by pure guesswork (requirement 1). But they insist that a *technē* must have not only an orderly procedure but also an orderly outcome (*Grg.* 503d–504e), and they find the predictable outcome of Socratic questioning – perplexity (*aporia*) – to be disorderly (*Eu.* 11b–e, *M.* 79e–80b, *Hi.Mi.* 372a–e and 376b–c). In reply, one might suggest that perplexity is not the ultimate outcome of Socrates' questioning, but that human wisdom is. If human wisdom is not just a passing or isolated awareness of one's perplexity but a deeper kind of self-knowledge – the developed ability to examine one's commitments and to find them falling short of divine wisdom[3] – then the goal of Socratic examination would be the ability to exercise Socratic examination, which is itself orderly. But then Brickhouse and Smith (1994: 8) would surely note that human wisdom, so understood, is *not* the regular outcome of Socratic examination, since so many of Socrates' interlocutors, including especially Charmides, Critias and Alcibiades, turned out badly (Nails 2002). So how could Socrates be said to be an expert in Socratic examination if he does not regularly

SOCRATIC METHODS

achieve the goal of Socratic examination? This is not exactly the inerrancy of expertise (requirement 4).

The defender of Socrates' expertise might answer with two points. First, Socrates' examinations *do* regularly have the outcome of human wisdom *in the case of Socrates himself*. He says that he examines himself when he examines others (*Ap.* 28e, *Chrm.* 166c–d, *Prt.* 348c–e, *Grg.* 505e–506a), and we might take him at his word and infer that when he examines others, he also exercises his ability to sustain his human wisdom.[4] Second, we should not demand inerrancy of a would-be expert without regard to the question of whether they have the necessary materials to do their work. We cannot require the cobbler to make good sandals from wool or the shipwright to make good ships from cardboard. So, if many of Socrates' interlocutors prove unable to continue practising the examinations they begin with him – because they lack the courage (*La.* 194a with *La.* 187c–188d; *M.* 81d, 86b–c) or because they have other desires that pull them away[5] – perhaps this should be explained not as a defect in Socrates' expertise but as a defect in the materials with which – with *whom* – he works.[6]

But even if Socratic questioning proceeds in an orderly fashion toward an orderly outcome and even if his failures do not count against his expertise, Brickhouse and Smith (1994: 7–8) have five other requirements to consider. They take up two of them directly. They say that Socrates is unwise, because he disavows knowledge of the subjects of his inquiries (requirement 3), and they say that his examinations do not appear to have a distinct subject matter, since he uses them to investigate not only questions about virtue but also questions about Ion's activity as a rhapsode (requirement 6). But these points do not distinguish between expertise in examination by question and answer and expertise in the subject matter examined. Socrates could be an expert examiner over many subjects, though he lacks any subject-matter expertise.[7] Socrates could, that is, disavow knowledge of virtue and of how to live while suggesting that he is an expert in conversations that test his own and his interlocutor's knowledge of virtue and of how to live.

Socrates does in fact suggest that he is an expert at examination by question and answer, what he sometimes just calls 'conversing' (*dialegesthai*).[8] He explicitly tells Euthyphro that he uses expertise in their conversation (*Eu.* 11d), and explicitly tells Polus that he *knows* how to 'produce one witness' for the points he makes (*Grg.* 474a–b).[9] Moreover, he notes that the ability to converse in question-and-answer mode (*dialegesthai*) can be cultivated or neglected, just as speech-giving can, and he chastises Polus for neglecting it (*Grg.* 471d, *cf.* 448d).[10] Socrates has surely cultivated this ability, and he acknowledges having a 'customary manner' of putting words together (*Ap.* 27b2). Finally, he claims some knowledge that would seem to be part of the examinational expertise, including the distinction between correct opinion and knowledge (*M.* 98b) and what would follow from what (*Prt.* 360e–361a).[11]

To show that Socrates is wrong to suggest that he is an expert in his customary question-and-answer conversation, Brickhouse and Smith could turn to the requirement that expertise be distinctive, since Socrates wants many others to do what he does (requirement 5). But Socrates plainly does not think that many others already possess expertise in examination. Indeed, if we construe the expertise of Socratic examination as the ability to induce and sustain one's own human wisdom, then the rarity of human wisdom entails the rarity of Socratic expertise.[12]

Still, Brickhouse and Smith can appeal to the two remaining requirements for expertise: Experts can explain what they do (requirement 3), and experts can teach others their expertise (requirement 2). Socrates does not explain how he examines others to test their claims to knowledge and he does not obviously take on apprentices to teach them what he does. But should we infer that he *cannot* explain how he does what he does or that he *cannot* teach others? In the *Apology*, he says that his followers imitate what he does, and will continue to do so, even more vigorously, after he dies (*Ap.* 39c–d, *cf.* 23c, 37d). This looks like transmission of the ability to do Socratic examination, and it might even strike the reader of the *Apology* as a piece of advertising that Plato has inserted for himself as Socrates' most successful pupil.[13] But it must be admitted that Plato does not depict Socrates being examined about how he does what he does, so there is room for uncertainty about whether Socrates is or is not fully an expert at what he does.[14]

In addition to these doubts about the arguments that Wolfsdorf (2003a) and Brickhouse and Smith (1994) advance, one might question their assumption that Socrates cannot have a method without a theory or expertise. Socrates himself nowhere limits methods to experts or theoreticians. He does not say, for instance, that Gorgias lacks a method of persuading audiences when he argues that Gorgias lacks expertise. In fact, he effectively concedes that Gorgias persuades audiences by using some techniques that he has learned from experience (*empeiria*), and he does not deny that Gorgias can pass these techniques on to his pupils. Instead, Socrates argues that Gorgias lacks expertise because he cannot provide an account (*logos*) of the causes by which he persuades (*Grg.* 465a). That is, Socrates highlights Gorgias' theoretical deficiencies but not any deficiencies of method or practice when he distinguishes between Gorgias' skill and genuine expertise. This supports Brickhouse and Smith's insistence that *expertise* requires some theory, but it does not show that Socrates requires theory or expertise for the possession of a *method*.

At this point, the scholarly disagreement over whether Socrates possesses a method seems to turn on what counts as a method, perhaps as opposed to a mere 'customary manner' (*cf.* Wolfsdorf 2003a: 302). Plato's Socrates does not help here, since Plato does not use the word *methodos* in the *Gorgias* or any other Socratic dialogue.[15] This might seem to be grist for Wolfsdorf's (2003a) mill, since Socrates' lack of an explicit account of what a method is might tell against his possessing a method. But Plato does use the word *methodos* in other dialogues, and he typically uses the word to describe a self-conscious, orderly manner of inquiry, whether it is used by someone who is an expert (as, for instance, Hippocrates [*Phdr.* 270c]) or by someone who is seeking to become an expert (*Phdr.* 270d; *cf. Phd.* 79e4, *Rep.* X 596a). In fact, so far as I can tell, Plato's dialogues nowhere insist that a method belongs exclusively to those who possess a theory or expertise, and their use of the term *methodos* matches easily Socrates' own 'customary manner' of putting words together (*Ap.* 27b2).

But one might still doubt that Socrates has a method, because one might think that he does not have a *single* self-conscious, orderly manner of inquiry. Carpenter and Polansky (2002) and Brickhouse and Smith (2002a) make a case for this conclusion by pointing to the plurality of ways in which Socrates conducts question-and-answer conversations. Carpenter and Polansky (2002) suggest that Socrates is typically engaged in examination to refute something his interlocutor has said, but they point to 'much variety in the sorts of things Socrates sets out to refute and some variety in the ways in which he sets out to refute them' (Carpenter and Polansky 2002, 90; *cf.* Brickhouse and Smith 2002a: 147). This argument, too, threatens to devolve into a debate about what *we* think, for we might well disagree about how to individuate methods. Does a sculptor who sculpts in wood and stone use two different methods, or the same method in different materials? Does a sculptor who sculpts horses use the same method as the one who sculpts humans? Socrates says he has 'a customary manner' of putting words together (*Ap.* 27b2), but we can easily

SOCRATIC METHODS 49

draw some distinctions among the ways in which he does this. Should we say that Socrates is wrong to say he has a customary manner? Should he have said that he has customary manners of putting words together? We do not have to do that. We could just think of his 'customary manner' as a general method that is employed in several different ways, or as a general superordinate method with some specific, subordinate methods.

We surely should not doubt that Socrates has a method on the grounds that his orderly way of proceeding is not *self-conscious*. For Socrates is perfectly self-conscious in possessing a customary manner, perfectly self-conscious in rejecting long speeches (*Prt.* 347c–348a, *Grg.* 447b–449d, *Hi.Mi.* 369b–d) and majority rule (*Cr.* 46d–47d, *La.* 184d–e, *Grg.* 473e–474b), in favour of short question-and-answer, in the pursuit of truth. Carpenter and Polansky (2002: 90) suggest that these methodological remarks 'tend to be restricted to the immediate context of the present argument with a particular interlocutor', so that 'an embracing reflection upon all elenctic [that is, refutative] discussion does not appear' (quoted favourably by Brickhouse and Smith 2002a: 152). But in the *Apology*, Socrates *does* offer some 'embracing reflections' on what he does when he converses in his 'customary manner' and philosophises. He thinks his accusers misunderstand him because they think of all philosophers as atheistic nature-theorists and sophistical rhetoricians (*Ap.* 23d, *cf.* 19b–c). In response, Socrates identifies his philosophising with examining people (*Ap.* 28d-29a) – that is, testing to see whether they have knowledge about how to live (*Ap.* 21e–23b, 29e) – and with exhorting people to care less for their possessions and social status and more for their soul (*Ap.* 29d–30b).[16]

In sum, in the Socratic dialogues, Socrates reverts again and again to question-and-answer conversation, as opposed to other means of inquiring, and in the *Apology*, he presents himself as conversing in his 'customary manner' for general aims, to induce in himself and others the concern for human wisdom, in particular, and the right values, more generally. We might doubt that he has a rich enough theoretical grasp of what he is doing to count as having a method, or we might doubt that his various ways of leading conversations manifest just one general method. But there is room to make good on the widespread assumption that Socrates' 'customary manner' of putting words together is a distinctive method. To do so, we need to look more closely at Socratic conversations, and in particular at how he examines and how he exhorts.

SOCRATIC EXAMINATION

Socrates' examinations have prompted scholarly debate about two broad questions: his aim and his results. First, does Socrates examine merely to refute his conversational partner – that is, to show that they lack knowledge – or to establish the true answer to the questions he asks, or somehow both? Second, whatever his aim, does Socrates have a method or manner of examination that succeeds in achieving that aim?

That Socrates aims to refute his interlocutor has long seemed obvious to many readers. Their point is not merely that Socrates confesses to this aim on occasion (*Chrm.* 166c–e; *Rep.* I 348a). Rather, he announces this as his *general* aim. In the *Apology*, he says he converses with people to test whether they know how to live, and he says he has found everyone wanting. Moreover, the conversations that Plato records in his Socratic dialogues largely fit this characterisation. Socrates regularly argues against some interlocutor's claim, often a definition, and the regular results of these conversations is perplexity (*aporia*) and the interlocutor's failure. Unsurprisingly, then, there is a long tradition, going back to Grote 1865 and Campbell 1867, of referring to Socrates' method of 'the elenchus', after the Greek word *elenchos*, which applies to tests or refutations and is one of the terms used most often by Plato to refer to Socrates' 'customary manner' of conversation.[17]

The basic pattern of Socrates' refutations has also long seemed clear. Robinson (1953, 7) articulates the simple schema: Socrates (1) targets an interlocutor's claim for testing or refutation, (2) elicits some further premises, and then (3) shows that these premises entail the contradictory of the targeted claim.[18] Vlastos (1983a/1994a) adds to this schema the insistence that Socrates also (4) takes the conclusion drawn from the elicited premises to be true and thus infers that its contradictory, the targeted claim, is false. But this fourth element of the refutations, says Vlastos, is problematic, because Socrates' reasoning shows only that the targeted claim is inconsistent with the elicited premises, and not that the elicited premises or what follows from them is true.

In this way, Vlastos (1994a: 3–4 and 21) claims to discover '*the* problem of the elenchus', but he also proposes that Socrates has a solution, built of three points. First, for every false belief that Socrates might target, the interlocutor who believes that claim *also* believes further claims that can be elicited as premises that entail the contradictory. So if the interlocutor were to try to save the targeted claim from refutation by rejecting one of the elicited premises, Socrates would just generate another set of elicited premises that contradict the targeted claim. Second, the premises that Socrates elicits in his elenctic arguments are acceptable not only to the interlocutor but also to Socrates himself. Third, as a result of his long experience with elenctic arguments, Socrates possesses a consistent set of beliefs. Given that Socrates' beliefs are consistent (point three), they must be all true, as every false belief is accompanied by a set of beliefs that contradict it (point one). But if Socrates' beliefs are all true, and if he elicits only those premises he agrees with (point two), then he can be justified in taking what follows from these elicited premises to be true, and their contradictory, the targeted claim, to be false.

Vlastos' account has generated a flurry of responses that engage more specific versions of our two main questions about Socratic examinations. First, is Vlastos right to insist that Socratic refutations aim to establish truths? Second, is he right to propose the solution that he does? Some scholars have agreed with Vlastos about '*the* problem of the elenchus' but have proposed alternative solutions. Other scholars have criticised all the proposed solutions to '*the* problem of the elenchus' but have urged that there is no such problem because Vlastos was wrong to insist that Socratic refutations aim to establish truths. Still other scholars have been sceptical about how much Vlastos' schematic account of Socratic refutations captures of Socrates' customary way of leading question-and-answer conversations.[19]

If Socratic refutations are to establish truths, and not merely contradictions, then the elicited premises must have some status superior to that of the targeted claim, a status that warrants the conclusion that what follows from the elicited premises should be accepted as true and its contradictory, the targeted claim, should be rejected as false. Perhaps, then, the elicited premises are supposed to be more obvious (e.g., Reeve 1989: 165), or more 'reputable' because more widely held or held by the wise (Polansky 1985), or more deeply held (*cf.* Brickhouse and Smith 1991) than the targeted claim.

Aristotle seems to have thought that some of the premises in Socratic refutation have privileged status. He credits Socrates with originating not only 'universal definition' in his 'What is F?' questions but also 'inductive argument' (Aristotle, *Metaph.* XIII 4.1078b27–29). By 'inductive argument', Aristotle has in mind Socratic reasoning from, say, the

SOCRATIC METHODS

carpenter does such-and-such, the medical doctor does such-and-such and the cobbler does such-and-such to experts do such-and-such. Socrates' examinations offer this kind of reasoning from time to time, and then they use a general premise like 'experts do such-and-such' in the set of elicited premises that entails a contradiction with the interlocutor's targeted claim. But Socratic 'induction' does not always work like that. Sometimes, Socrates skips the general premise that 'experts do such-and-such' and moves directly from a string of individual kinds of experts to another kind of expert (as, for instance, the expert in bravery). And sometimes, Socrates uses 'induction' not to generate a premise in the set of elicited premises, but to establish the contradictory of the targeted claim (e.g., *Hi.Mi.* 373c–375d).

Socratic 'induction' – sometimes called Socratic *epagōgē* – is an important part of his method or manner of conversing, and there are questions about how exactly it is supposed to work. Robinson (1953: 33–48 at 35) frames one central question as whether Socrates and his interlocutor take their 'induction' to involve (a) the intuition of the universal in the instances, (b) the certain inference of the universal from a complete enumeration of instances, or (c) the probabilistic, defeasible inference of the universal from the instances. Strangely, Robinson (1953: 36) finds in the Socratic dialogues (b) more than (a) or (c): He thinks that Socrates 'vaguely supposes that he has gone through all the cases'. Vlastos (1991: 267–269) maintains that these 'inductions' are not inductive inferences at all, because they certainly do not involve (c). On his view, Socrates introduces the instances just to get at what the universal means, almost as if (a) were right and the 'induction' were just the intuition of the universal in the instances. McPherran (2007) offers the fullest reckoning, and he argues that Aristotle was right to attribute genuinely inductive arguments to Socrates, as Socrates does occasionally make probabilistic inferences from instances to a universal claim. *Charmides* 159b–160d is McPherran's star evidence, and it also serves as a plain example of rational support for a premise in a refutation of an interlocutor's targeted claim.

Still, it is not tenable that *all* the elicited premises in Socrates' refutations have higher status than the targeted claim. Euthyphro's claim that the gods argue with each other (*Eu.* 7b), for instance, is surely not viewed as having higher status by Socrates (*Eu.* 6a, 7d, 8e). So it is difficult to maintain that the refutations are methodically designed to establish the *falsity* of the targeted claim by inferring its contradictory from the elicited premises. Accordingly, it is available to maintain, as Benson (1987; 1995; 2000: 32–56; 2002; 2011) has, that Socratic refutations are *not* designed to establish any truth or falsehood but are designed only to show that the interlocutor lacks knowledge. Benson concedes that *some* of the elicited premises in Socratic refutations are more plausible than others, that Socrates accepts some of them and even that some of them are supported. But according to Benson (2011: 186), the only requirement that *must* be met by an elicited premise is that the interlocutor accept it, and he calls this – Vlastos' (1994a: 7) 'say what you believe' requirement – the 'doxastic constraint'.

One problem for Benson's interpretation is that the 'doxastic constraint' seems not to be a requirement of every elicited premise in every Socratic refutation. In fact, Brickhouse and Smith (2002a: 147–149) argue that if genuine Socratic refutations require clear evidence that the interlocutor believes the elicited premises, then very few Socratic conversations will count as genuine Socratic refutations. For one thing, while Socrates occasionally insists that his interlocutor state what they believe (*Cr.* 49c–d, *Prt.* 331c, *Grg.* 500b, *Rep.* I 346a), he also occasionally allows an interlocutor to go along with the argument without explicit agreement (*Prt.* 333c, *Grg.* 505d–507a, *Rep.* I 350d–e). For another, when Socrates presses an interlocutor from one definition to another, any evidence that the interlocutor believes one of these definitions is evidence that the interlocutor does *not* believe the others.

But these objections do not undo Benson's interpretation. His point is that Socratic refutations aim to show that the interlocutor is inconsistent and thus does not have knowledge. If Socrates has shown this before he lets Protagoras, Callicles and Thrasymachus save face a bit, then he has not failed to refute them. And if he continues to articulate their inconsistencies without forcing them to own up publicly to them, is this any the less obviously a refutation? Also, if Socrates shows that each of an interlocutor's several definitions conflicts with other things the interlocutor believes, does it really matter that it is unclear which, if any, of these definitions the interlocutor really believes? The conversation has started from the interlocutor's beliefs, and it has shown that the interlocutor does not have knowledge.

The more serious problem for Benson's interpretation is that it severs Socrates' refutations from the pursuit of the truth. This is not the worry that Socrates has no way of pursuing the truth, for Benson correctly insists that refutations can be just one of several tricks in Socrates' bag. But if Socrates' refutations do not pursue the truth, then what distinguishes his refutations from those of Dionysodorus and Euthydemus, the experts at disputation (*eristikē*) who refute their interlocutors for sport? We cannot now say that Socrates' refutations, unlike theirs, pursue the truth (Brickhouse and Smith 2002a: 153–154). Benson (1989) responds by arguing that disputatious or eristic debaters focus merely on *verbal* contradictions and not, as Socrates does, on contradictions in *beliefs*. But one might still worry about severing Socratic refutations from the truth. If Socrates' refutations do not pursue the truth, why does Socrates at least occasionally advertise them as truth-seeking (*Eu.* 7a, *Ly.* 218c, *Rep.* I 339b)?[20]

The difficulties facing those who have tried to characterise Socratic refutations on the simple schema of Robinson (1953) and Vlastos (1983a/1994a) have led some scholars to seek a slightly more complicated schema. Wolfsdorf (2003a), for instance, focuses on how Socrates tests definitions, in particular, and he distinguishes between two kinds of elicited premise that Socrates uses to do so. Some of the premises articulate a fundamental condition that the definition must meet and others articulate how the definition fails to meet that condition. On Wolfsdorf's (2003a: 275–278) analysis, Socrates almost always agrees with the condition that must be met, while he does not nearly so often agree to the premises used to show that the definition fails to meet the condition. But because Socrates regularly concentrates on the conditions that he accepts, Wolfsdorf argues, Socrates' intention is plainly to cooperate with his interlocutor and to make progress toward an acceptable definition. Wolfsdorf (2003a: 299–302) concludes that Socrates' conversations are not refutative ('elenctic') at all because they are not adversarial. They are, instead, shared inquiries.[21]

With this move, Wolfsdorf severs Socrates' use of refutation in the search for definitions from his stated goal, in the *Apology*, to help the god by eliminating the false conceit of knowledge. Wolfsdorf (2003a: 306) suggests that Plato has particular aims for the *Apology* that distort its picture of Socratic activity. But we do not have to think that Socrates' conversations are either adversarial refutations or cooperative inquiries. They can be both. Socrates can be showing that his interlocutors lack knowledge, that their definitions (and other targeted claims) do not agree with their other beliefs, while he also seeks truth, including true definitions, by building on premises that he himself accepts. Wolfsdorf might be right that Socrates' examinations are not best characterised as *adversarial*, since

SOCRATIC METHODS

he aims for common goods (*e.g.*, *Chrm.* 166d, *Grg.* 505e). But the common goods include being shown that one does not know (*e.g.*, *Grg.* 505e–506a), and even if Socrates does not undertake this out of hostility, it can *feel* hostile to those being examined. This, as we will see, is one way in which Socratic examination poses a special challenge to Socratic exhortation.

But before we proceed to Socratic exhortation, there are two other ways of complicating the schema for Socratic examination. Robinson (1953) and Vlastos (1983a/1994a) define an episode of Socratic refutation narrowly: One argument against one targeted claim counts as one iteration of the Socratic method of refutation. By this reckoning, Plato shows Socrates regularly going through multiple iterations of refutation with each interlocutor. But perhaps the natural unit for the Socratic method of conversing in question-and-answer is not given by our logic, but by Socrates' conversations. That is, perhaps we should count a single conversation with an interlocutor as a single iteration of the Socratic method of refutation. This allows one iteration of the method to test and refute several claims, which makes it easier to see how the method aims *both* at refutation *and* at pursuing the truth. For some individual arguments are clearly less helpful for truth-seeking than others, and one individual argument refuting one individual claim is unlikely to shake many interlocutors' confidence that they know.

But this broadened schema of Socrates' method might not be broad enough. Socrates converses in his 'customary manner' not just for the sake of examining his interlocutor but also for the sake of examining himself (*Ap.* 28e, *Chrm.* 166c–d, *Prt.* 348c–e, *Grg.* 505e–506a), and nothing limits Socrates' methodical work of examining himself to just one conversation.[22] Even if an individual conversation does not contain enough elicited premises of privileged status to infer anything of interest, the conversation still offers Socrates some evidence about where inconsistencies arise. After he has conversed with many people over a long period of time, he has a very large body of evidence about what premises cohere and which introduce inconsistency. Brickhouse and Smith (1994: 10–29), Gentzler (1994) and Irwin (1995: 17–30) have independently argued that Socratic refutations successfully pursue the truth by some induction from this larger body of evidence. McPherran (2002) carefully analyses how this works in one case, when Socrates infers what the oracle means from a large set of refutations (*Ap.* 21b–23b). McPherran's point is not that Socrates *proves* what the oracle means, but that he arrives at a plausible, inductively supported interpretation by testing multiple interpretations through a large number of conversations. Similarly, Brickhouse and Smith, Gentzler and Irwin would explain Socrates' confidence that (for instance) it is better to suffer injustice than to do injustice to be grounded in his repeated showings that alternatives to this claim meet with contradiction.[23]

Socratic examination turns out not to be simple, especially if we take him at his word when he says he examines to find the truth. Even when Socrates is targeting a claim for refutation, eliciting premises, and showing that these premises entail the contradictory of the targeted claim, he is not merely doing that. So he *is* arguing *ad hominem*, using premises his interlocutor accepts, but not merely that. This refutation is part of a larger conversation, and in any given conversation, some arguments are more constructive than others, drawing on premises that Socrates himself accepts and not merely on premises that his interlocutor accepts. But the conversation, too, is part of a larger pattern of inquiry for Socrates. To understand Socrates' 'customary manner' and to uncover whatever method he might have requires these broader perspectives in addition to the careful focus on each individual argument.

SOCRATIC EXHORTATION

In the *Apology*, Socrates characterises his philosophising not only as examination but also as exhortation. He not only tests people to see whether they know how to live; he also encourages them to care less about social and material resources and to care more for their soul. This is a project of conversion. Socrates sees a sharp divide between his cares – justice and wisdom – and those of his fellow Athenians, and he recognises no common ground (*Cr.* 49d; *cf. Ap.* 31d–32a). He seeks to persuade people who care about money and status and who eagerly devote themselves to the affairs of their household and city to turn away from those concerns and to turn toward being just and pursuing wisdom. One might distinguish here between a broad project to convert toward virtue and a narrow project to convert toward philosophy (Slings 1999: 59–60), but Socrates sees no distinction between these. But how does Socrates exhort others? How does he seek to convert others to the life that loves justice and wisdom above all else?

Socrates appears to answer these questions in the *Apology*, but his answers puzzle many readers. He explains that he exhorts the Athenians by

> saying in my customary way, 'Best of men, since you are a citizen of Athens, the greatest city and a city most famous for wisdom and power, aren't you ashamed to care to get as much money, reputation, and honor as you can, while you do not care for or think about wisdom and truth and the best condition of your soul?'
>
> – *Ap.* 29d–e

This is puzzling because Plato does not regularly show Socrates speaking like this. And the puzzlement deepens when Socrates proceeds to say,

> I go around doing *nothing other* than persuading the younger and older among you not to care for your bodies or money before or as intently as the best condition of your soul, by saying 'Virtue does not come to be from money, but from virtue money and all other things become good for human beings, both individually and collectively'.
>
> – *Ap.* 30a–b, emphasis added

Plato's portrait of Socrates is dominated by Socrates' examinations of others, and not by Socrates making speeches about the superior importance of the soul over the body.

There are at least three ways of dissolving this puzzle. First, one might suppose that in the *Apology* Socrates is exaggerating his exhortations, or even misrepresenting what he does. After all, he is on trial, and the rhetorical needs of this occasion are quite different from those of the other Socratic dialogues (*cf.* Wolfsdorf 2003a: 306, as mentioned above). Second, one might suppose that Socrates' characterisations in the *Apology* are only slightly exaggerated, and the discrepancy with the other Socratic dialogues is to be explained by Plato's particular interests. Perhaps Plato was more interested in Socratic examinations than in Socratic exhortations, and thus he largely suppresses the hortatory aspect of Socrates' philosophising. If Slings (1999) is right that Plato wrote the *Clitophon*, but wrong to say that Clitophon's quotations of Socrates (esp. 407a–e) are a parody of another author's portrayal of Socratic exhortation, then the *Clitophon* shows that Plato did not entirely suppress Socrates' hortatory speeches. But still, one might be eager to explain the differences between Plato's Socrates and Xenophon's in part by their different attitudes toward explicit exhortation and advice. Perhaps, however, there is no real misfit between the *Apology* and the other dialogues to be explained away. Socrates might be exactly right that he does *nothing more* than exhort others, even though he does spend a

SOCRATIC METHODS

lot of time examining them. He might be exactly right because his examinations are *also* exhortations, as Irwin (1995: 19) and many other scholars insist.

These scholars have explored how Socratic examinations implicitly and explicitly exhort others to virtue and wisdom. Implicitly, the examinations are supposed both to show the examinee that they lack knowledge, which removes an obstacle to the pursuit of wisdom, and to stimulate the desire to continue examining, both to pursue a better understanding of how to live and to sustain human wisdom. One way in which Socratic examination can stimulate the examinee's desire to examine is by the examinee's experience of perplexity (Robinson 1953: 11–12; Matthews 1999; Belfiore 2012: 68–74). The inability to answer questions one would like to answer can stimulate the desire to continue searching for an answer. Socrates explicitly offers this explanation in the *Meno* (84a–d), and it fits with his discussions of desire in the *Lysis* and *Symposium*, since those discussions suggest that we all desire what we both lack and perceive to be good for us.[24] Another way in which Socratic examination can stimulate the examinee's desire to examine is by making the examinee feel shame at their lack of knowledge (Brickhouse and Smith 1994: 25). Nicias seems to refer to this in the *Laches*, when he explains that Socratic examination inevitably targets the life of the examinee and 'brings to [their] attention what [they] have done or are doing wrong' (187e–188c, quoting 188a–b; *cf. Sph.* 230c–d).[25]

Stump (2020) argues that these mechanisms by which examination stimulates the desire to examine are not enough to explain how examination counts as exhortation, because they are not enough to explain the conversion of the examinee from their prior values to the philosophic values that prize the examined life. He proposes that what converts the examinee into a committed examiner, in love with examination, is the pleasure of examining. But while Socrates mentions that his examinations bring pleasure to onlookers, who then take pleasure in imitating him (*Ap.* 23c, 33c), he also sees that the refutations offered by the disputatious, unphilosophical Dionysodorus and Euthydemus bring pleasure to the audience (*Euthd.* 276b–c). So the pleasure of examination cannot *by itself* explain the conversion to philosophy, either. It is, at best, a supplement to the curiosity or shame that drives the examinee to satisfy their curiosity or remove their shame.

There is a deeper problem with the implicit hortatory mechanisms of Socratic examination. The perplexity and shame induced by Socratic examination often stimulate not the desire to examine further but despair or hostility toward Socrates and his examinations. Alcibiades describes his own despair as a common response to Socratic examination (*Symp.* 215d–216b), and many characters, including especially Socrates' accuser Anytus (*M.* 89e–95a), manifest hostility, as Socrates well knows (*Ap.* 21e, 22e–23a, 24a–b). So whereas Socratic examination is supposed to encourage examination, it can in fact induce 'misology', hatred of inquiry (*cf. Phd.* 89c–91c). This makes Socratic examination a risky way of implicitly exhorting people to care about virtue and wisdom (*cf. Rep.* VII 537d–539d, *Phlb.* 15d–16a).

But Socratic examination also *explicitly* exhorts examinees to care about virtue and wisdom. The most obvious way Socrates does this is by steering the conversation toward certain questions. In the *Laches*, for instance, two fathers want to know how to train their sons, and Socrates argues that they need to find an expert in the virtue that they want that training to produce, which leads to an inquiry about what courage is. And while Laches, one of the generals consulted by the fathers, is quick to think of courage in behavioural terms, Socratic examination leads to the thought that courage should be defined in psychological terms. So the fathers are given reasons to focus on the state of their sons' souls. This Socratic two-step, from an ordinary, worldly concern to a question about what virtue is, and from an ordinary, behavioural account of virtue to a psychological one, is common in Socratic dialogues. Socrates does not simply examine his interlocutors on whatever topic they happen to care about. He steers the examination until it focuses on the state of their souls.

In addition, Socrates weaves explicit exhortation into his conversations, sometimes as part of an examination and sometimes as a distinct incitement. He does this most often by attempting to shame his interlocutor away from non-philosophical commitments and toward philosophical ones, just as he advertises in the *Apology* (29d–e, quoted above). So, for instance, he explicitly tries to shame Callicles out of his hedonism (*Grg.* 494c–e), and to shame Meno into being 'manly' (or courageous, *andreios*) enough to continue examining (*M.* 81d, 86b). But he also sometimes joins these shaming incitements to some strange, mythical stories. For Callicles, Socrates compares pleasure-seeking souls with leaky jars, drawing on stories he attributes to wise people in Sicily or Italy, and he offers these images to 'make clear what I want to persuade you to change your mind about if I can' (*Grg.* 492e–494a). For Meno, Socrates appeals to another story from 'wise men and women', this one a tale of the soul's existence before birth, when it learns all things (*M.* 81a–e). He offers this story to give Meno some reason to suppose that he has the correct answer somewhere within him and that he therefore can inquire successfully.

These mythical appeals, which are absent in many Socratic dialogues but appear in the *Meno* and *Gorgias*, and again in the *Phaedo* and *Republic*, might not fit Socrates as Plato initially characterised him, and might have been grafted on to Socrates after Plato visited Sicily and heard such stories. Schofield (2008), for instance, offers this plausible speculation. But even if these parts of Plato's portrait of Socrates are clearly indebted to sources other than the historical Socrates, Plato manifestly sees no difficulty in adding them to Socrates' set of hortatory tools. The mythical story just adds a layer to the straightforward exhortation that Socrates needs to offer, because Plato's Socrates is committed to exhortation and is not limited to exhorting by examining.

Socrates' concern for exhortation also manifests itself in the *Euthydemus*, where he asks Dionysodorus and Euthydemus for a display of exhortation (274e–275b, 278d, 282d) and then twice provides the brothers a model of the sort of display he wants (278d–282d, 288c–293a). Socrates wants and models what he calls 'exhortative or protreptic speeches' (*protreptikoi logoi*, 282d6), and it might sound as though he is referring to a special kind of speech or argument, or even a special literary genre.[26] Socrates' first model of exhortative argument differs from his 'customary manner' of examination, since it does not target a claim for refutation and leave Cleinias in perplexity, but instead leads Cleinias from the premise that everyone wants to do well to the positive conclusion that wisdom is the only good thing for a human being (*Euthd.* 281e, *cf.* 292b), *via* the thought that only wisdom has the power to cause a person to do well, since other things benefit us only when they are used wisely and harm us when they are used foolishly.[27] So this protreptic argument does not exhort Cleinias to a life of examination indirectly, by refuting him, but rather gives him a direct case in favour of pursuing wisdom. Socrates' second model of exhortative argument picks up where the first leaves off and seeks to identify the wisdom that Cleinias is newly motivated to pursue, but this part of the discussion ends in perplexity.

Two other Socratic dialogues, possibly not written by Plato, appear to comment on the *Euthydemus* and its protreptic arguments, and thus further complicate our picture of

Socrates' ways of exhortation. In the *Alcibiades I*, Socrates offers another protreptic argument, with a positive conclusion that Alcibiades ought to pursue virtue (135b). But this argument starts not with a premise that applies to everyone – everyone wants to do well – but with a premise particular to Alcibiades – Alcibiades wants supreme power over people (105b–c). Perhaps Plato really wrote the *Alcibiades I*, in part to portray direct protreptic arguments as an important part of Socratic exhortation.[28]

Finally, in the *Clitophon*, Clitophon praises Socrates for successfully turning people toward the pursuit of virtue, but criticises him as unable to say what virtue is and help anyone with that pursuit. This seems to mirror the success and failure of Socrates' two protreptic models in the *Euthydemus*,[29] except the hortatory speeches that Clitophon praises are not protreptic *arguments*, but direct admonitions that seek to turn people away from their concern for wealth, say, and toward virtue. Slings (1999) might be right that the *Clitophon* offers a parody of Socratic protreptic, and not a straight presentation of how Plato's Socrates exhorts. Or Slings might be wrong in concluding that the *Clitophon* was written by Plato. But it is also possible that Plato really wrote the *Clitophon* and is signaling that Socrates' ways of exhorting others were much broader than some protreptic arguments and a lot of examinations woven together with some shaming. Plato's *Sophist* contrasts two ways of teaching, one that encourages and admonishes, as parents do with children, and the other that examines and refutes (229d–230e). Perhaps both of these are in the toolkit of Plato's Socrates.

However that may be, Socrates' attempts to convert others to the examined life and the pursuit of virtue and wisdom are not limited to his examinations. So he has some resources with which to mitigate the risks and limitations of his exhortations *via* examination. But we should not think that Socrates' expanded toolkit gives him regular success in converting others. Plato reminds us of these failures, by drawing attention to interlocutors such as Alcibiades, Charmides and Critias who later did very bad things, and in the *Gorgias*, he dramatises at least one failure, when Callicles withdraws from Socratic examination without having been persuaded or brought to perplexity.[30]

In the *Euthydemus*, Socrates comments shrewdly on the difficulty of converting someone to the pursuit of wisdom and virtue. After Dionysodorus and Euthydemus have claimed to be able to teach virtue and make their pupils good, Socrates asks, 'Are you able to make good only a man who is already persuaded that he should learn from you, or can you also make good that one who is not yet persuaded, either because he thinks generally that this thing, virtue, cannot be taught, or because he thinks that you two are not its teachers?' (*Euthd.* 274d–e) In other words, Socrates notices that conversion requires openness to being converted, and some disposition to think that the would-be converter is worth taking seriously. It is striking, then, that the youngster Socrates tries to convert in the *Euthydemus*, Cleinias, goes straight to Socrates to sit beside him (*Euthd.* 273a–b). Perhaps even here, when Plato is flagging the difficulty of conversion, he is also making room for another means at Socrates' disposal, as his character attracts admiration that makes others more likely to be converted by him.

THE SOCRATIC METHOD

Much of what Plato's Socrates does is not especially distinctive. He shares refutations with disputatious sophists, such as Dionysodorus and Euthydemus in the *Euthydemus*, and as Ausland (2002) argues, he even shares refutations as examinations aiming at the truth with forensic practices in the law-courts (*cf. Grg.* 471e). The exhortations to virtue and a distinctively philosophic way of life were likely to be found in other Socratic texts, but also in Isocrates' work, as Nightingale (1995) and Collins (2015) show. What marks Plato's Socrates' philosophising as so distinctive is his *combination* of these activities: He refutes and he exhorts, often in the same conversation. He weaves his examinations and exhortations together with the aim of inducing himself and others to continue to examine, so that these continued examinations might keep them aware of their lack of wisdom and bring them a better grasp on truths about how to live.

To really appreciate Socrates' customary manner of philosophising, one needs to study his full conversations, and some of the best scholarship on 'the Socratic method' in recent years has done just this, abjuring sweeping investigations that draw on evidence from a wide range of dialogues (as this chapter does) and focusing on one full dialogue at a time.[31] When one studies full conversations, one will see ways in which his refutations do and do not exhort, ways in which they do and do not pursue the truth, and how he weaves in other forms of exhortation. Sometimes, the whole conversation seems to succeed, and at least for a time, Socrates' interlocutor seems to be interested in more examination and in pursuing wisdom. But aside from Socrates himself and Plato, it is not clear how many people Socrates turned to the examined life.

Perhaps this checkered track record defies what one expects of a method, or at least what one expects of an expert's method. Or perhaps the wide variety of turns that Socratic conversation takes defies the tidy patterns one expects of a method. But the expert cobbler will vary their techniques to make different sorts of shoes, or to work on different materials, and no expert cobbler can turn the weakest materials into strong sandals or the hardest materials into comfortable footwear. The medical doctor's art is still more complicated, and we should not expect the expert physician to treat every patient, no matter their condition, in the same ways or to have the same results. So there is room for a complicated expertise of Socratic conversation, too, a mastery of a method that includes a flexible range of tools and techniques. But as we enrich and complicate our account of Socrates' customary manner of conversation to account for the many things he does in the conversations Plato depicts, there is also the risk that Socrates' mastery of Socratic conversation becomes nothing more than his mastery of being himself. Perhaps there is no Socratic method detachable from its one and only practitioner, but only imitations of it.

NOTES

*   I thank the editors for their invitation and for their encouragement and help. Their patience and efficiency have been exemplary.

1.   Here and throughout the translations are mine, with heavy borrowing from those in Cooper (1997).

2.   One might compare Reeve 1989, 37–45, Roochnik 1996 and Hardy 2010.

3.   Socrates explicitly conceives of knowledge as an ability (*dunamis*) in the *Republic* – see especially *Rep.* V 476d–480a with Smith 2000 – but his use of expertise as a model for knowledge and wisdom in the Socratic dialogues already ties knowledge to ability, as expertise is practical mastery. One might contrast the idea of knowing that one is not wise as an ability with knowing that one is not wise as a piece of knowledge, akin to knowing a friend's sister's name or knowing how to tie a bowline knot. A piece of knowledge can be gained and lost easily (*Symp.* 207d–208a). But abilities, especially expert abilities, require robust development and are then sustained by regular practice.

SOCRATIC METHODS

59

4. Occasionally, Socrates might examine his own views when his interlocutor puts them forward (*La.* 194c–d), and in the *Lysis* and *Hippias Major*, Socrates tests several views that he has introduced, once it is clear that his interlocutors are not up to the task of either testing or putting forward views worth testing. But there is no reason to think that these are the only occasions on which Socrates is examining himself.

5. For instance: In the *Apology*, Socrates records that responsibilities to one's household or polis can conflict with one's commitment to examination (*Ap.* 23b), and in the *Gorgias* and *Euthydemus,* he records how one might be led by greed to develop rhetorical abilities or eristic skill that does not constitute genuine expertise in examination (*cf. Phd.* 90b–c).

6. In the *Gorgias*, Socrates argues that if a politician is prosecuted by his own citizens unjustly, he has failed to be a political expert, because political expertise is the art of making citizens live well, which requires making them just (517a–519d). In this argument, Socrates makes no allowance for defective materials. But political expertise is not supposed to be the same as expertise in Socratic question-and-answer conversation. The political expert has broader responsibility for the citizens' well-being than the conversational expert has for their interlocutors' human wisdom because the political expert has power over the education of citizens that the expert examiner lacks. So there is no inconsistency in maintaining that Socrates lacks political expertise but possesses some conversational expertise, despite the failures of Socrates' interlocutors.

7. In the *Phaedrus*, Socrates suggests that experts in rhetoric must also be experts in the subject matter about which they speak (269d–274a, with Brown 2003). But the expertise of rhetoric might well be much more demanding than the art of Socratic examination, just as the political expertise is (see the previous note). Indeed, the expertise of rhetoric might count as part of the political expertise (*Grg.* 517a with 502d–504e, *cf. Plt.* 303e–304a). Of course, if the expertise in Socratic examination does *not* require expertise about the subject matters under examination, then Socrates is committed to the possibility of knowing whether someone knows this or that without knowing this or that oneself. In the *Charmides*, he raises puzzles about such second-order knowledge, but we need not think that these puzzles are insuperable. See LaBarge 1997, Carone 1998, Benson 2003 and Tuozzo 2011.

8. The word 'dialectic' transliterates the Greek word *dialektikē*, which is, etymologically, expertise in conversation (*dialegesthai*). So if Socrates is an expert at question-and-answer conversation, then it would not be inapt to say that he is an expert in dialectic. But caution is required. Although Socrates does make a claim about how to proceed in a way that befits *dialektikē* in *Meno* 75d, he does not use the word *dialektikē* to describe his own abilities in the Socratic dialogues, and there might well be differences between Socrates' question-and-answer conversations and the various conceptions of dialectic that can be found in the *Phaedrus* (262d with 259e–274b) and *Republic* (VI 506c–e with VII 531d–535a, 537c), let alone the *Sophist* and *Statesman* and Aristotle's *Topics*. For a start on Platonic conceptions of dialectic, see Benson 2015 and Broadie 2021.

9. Socrates also calls himself an expert in erotic love (*Symp.* 177d; *cf. Ly.* 204c, *Phdr.* 257a) and an expert at midwifery (*Tht.* 149a). These might be related to his suggestion in the *Euthyphro* that he is an expert in examination, for he might claim erotic expertise on the grounds that he is expert in desiring truth and wisdom (or, punning on the similar Greek words for eros and for questions, that he is expert in asking questions) and he might claim midwifery on the grounds that he is expert in testing the fruits of such desire. See also Reeve 2006 and Belfiore 2012 for Socrates as an expert on love and Burnyeat 1977 and Sedley 2004 for Socratic midwifery.

10. *Cf.* 508a, where Socrates chastises Callicles for neglecting geometry. Perhaps we do not all need to be *experts* in geometry, but we should not entirely neglect it, either.

11. Wolfsdorf (2003: 293n92) cites *Charmides* 175e6 as evidence that Socrates does not think he is an expert inquirer, but I doubt that Socrates is being entirely serious. The dialogue is coming to a close, and he is exhorting Charmides to continue to inquire, and not to despair that he lacks temperance. To do so, he blames himself for the failures of their inquiry he has shared with Charmides and Critias. If there were a time for Socrates to fudge the truth, it would be when he is exhorting others to (continue to) examine.

12. In addition, although Socrates occasionally reasons from the rarity of this or that expertise (*e.g.*, *Ap.* 24c–25b), he is not obviously committed to the thought that every expertise is necessarily rare. A political community's need for a diverse range of products and services suffices to explain why there are many different kinds of expertise (*cf. Rep.* II 369b–371e), and given that there are many different kinds of expertise and each expertise requires a considerable investment of time and effort to obtain, it is inevitable that most expertises will be held by a small portion of the community. But this reasoning does not establish that expertise *as such* must be rare, or that expertise in Socratic examination must be. For all this reasoning says, if there were an expertise needed to live well, we might all share that expertise. (Do many share the expertise of arithmetic? *Cf.* the previous note.) We do not all need to be cobblers to live well, and in fact, if we all spent the time and energy needed to become cobblers, it would be harder for us to *also* provide for clothes, shelter, food, education and health care.

13. In the *Apology*, Socrates issues a blanket denial that he is a teacher (*Ap.* 33a–b); arguably he is not denying that he teaches anything in any way, but only that he teaches by conferring beliefs about what is valuable to pupils who otherwise would have lacked those beliefs. For discussion, see Kraut 1984: 294–304; Reeve 1989: 160–169; Nehamas 1992; G.A. Scott 2000.

14. Scholars often call Socrates an expert examiner without confronting the grounds for doubt. LaBarge (2005: 32–34) is exceptional in this regard, but more work is needed. I thank Jeremy Henry for helpful discussion of Socrates as an expert.

15. Unless one thinks of the *Theaetetus* as Socratic (see Sedley 2004). '*Methodos*' occurs in the *Laws* (638e4, 965c6), *Phaedo* (79e4, 97b6), *Phaedrus* (269d8, 270c4, 270d9), *Republic* (435d1, 510b8, 510c5, 531c10, 533b2, 533c8, 596a6), *Sophist* (218d5, 219a1, 227a8, 235c7, 243d7, 265a2), *Statesman* (260e9, 266d7, 286d9), and *Theaetetus* (183c2).

16. Here and at a few other points in this chapter, I am drawing on Brown (2022), which concerns Socrates' conception of philosophising in the *Apology*.

17. Tarrant (2002) helpfully studies how Plato uses *elenchos*, related words and a range of other terms for Socrates' customary manner of conversation.

18. Robinson (1953, 23) further distinguishes Socrates' 'direct' and 'indirect' refutations, where the 'indirect' ones 'deduce' an 'obvious falsehood' from the targeted claim itself. On this view, some of Socrates' refutations aim to show that an interlocutor's claim is in some way self-contradictory. This interpretation has not won many supporters, but Forster (2006a) makes a case for it, which depends upon a broad view of what follows from a given claim.

19. In the interests of space, for the material in the other sections of this chapter, I will pass over much of this literature in silence. Benson (2011) and Wolfsdorf (2013) offer fuller and more detailed surveys.

SOCRATIC METHODS
61

20. Vlastos (1983a/1994a) originally leaned hard on evidence from the *Gorgias* for the claim that Socratic refutations were truth-seeking, but this left an opening for others to think that the *Gorgias* was an outlier of sorts. But there is clear evidence outside the *Gorgias* that Socrates presents his refutations as truth-seeking.

21. Compare Tarrant 2002.

22. Some of Socrates' conversations also address an audience that is not currently participating in the conversation. Sometimes this is indirect: In the *Lysis*, for instance, Socrates' conversation with Lysis and Menexenus about friendship *also* provides Hippothales with a model of wooing to compare with his own. But sometimes the audience members are being invited to examine themselves in just the way that the conversation-partner is. In the *Gorgias*, for instance, Socrates' deflationary account of rhetoric as a mere knack for flattery arises in his conversation with Polus but is clearly aimed at Gorgias, as well. At the margins of Socrates' conversations, Socrates is offering many people some *potential* examination, and in this way inviting them to examine themselves. See the next section on the exhortation of the audience.

23. Vlastos (1983a/1994a), too, has Socrates' confidence rest on his long experience. But for Vlastos, that confidence is embedded in sweeping assumptions that convert each of his refutations into truth-seeking a demonstration. The other scholars considered here do not take Socrates to suppose that his beliefs are entirely consistent or that every false belief is accompanied by beliefs that contradict it, and they do not claim that every refutation is a demonstration of truth and falsehood.

24. See Obdrzalek, 'Socrates on Love', Chapter 10 in this volume.

25. This effect of Socratic examination shows again how important the 'say what you believe' requirement or 'doxastic constraint' is.

26. Scholars agree that by the third century BCE, there was a special literary genre of 'protreptic', with Aristotle's *Protrepticus* as the genre's paradigm. (For the reconstruction of Aristotle's lost *Protrepticus*, see Hutchinson and Johnson 2005.) There is, however, some dispute about when this genre of exhortations to the philosophical life arose. Gaiser (1959) locates the origins in sophistic discourse of the fifth century, which combined the advice prominent in some earlier poetry and encomiums to construct an exhortation to a life of virtue, or a specific way of living. Slings (1999) and Collins (2015) both criticise Gaiser's speculative account, but disagree about the genre's subsequent origins. Slings finds the genre in Socratic discourse of the fourth century, whereas Collins (2015) sees the genre as still in embryonic form at that point. Part of their dispute concerns what a genre is: Slings (1999) and Collins (2015) draw on competing theories of genre, Slings from Cairns (1972) and Collins from Bakhtin (1981, 1984, 1986). Another part of their dispute rests on what to make of some evidence of missing fourth-century work. Slings eagerly collects fourth-century texts and passages that plainly involve some exhorting or something called exhorting, combines them with later reckonings of what protreptic is, and builds from these some characteristics of 'protreptic' that fit the fourth-century scraps. Collins charges Slings with finding what he was looking for and with failing to give due credit to how flexible and unsettled the fourth-century cases of broadly exhortative literature are. So, for instance, later antiquity might have seen some fourth-century works as protreptics, such as the lost works by Antisthenes and Aristippus called *Protrepticus*, but these titles might not accurately reflect their authors' original conception of the works.

27. For this argument, see Dimas (2002) and Jones (2013a). Jones and some others would say that I am misrepresenting Socrates' conclusion, and that he really concludes only that

wisdom is the only independent or unconditional good, since he allows that some other things, such as health and wealth, are beneficial when used wisely. But these other things are no more conditional goods than they are conditional bads, and Socrates consistently prescinds from calling them good things of any sort and even offers an alternative label of 'intermediates' (*ta metaxu*) for them in *Gorgias* 467e–468a.

28. For the dispute over the authenticity of the *Alcibiades I*, see Denyer (2001: 14–26) and Jirsa (2009) for, and Joyal (2003) and Smith (2004) against.

29. The success I attribute to the first model can be questioned; Collins (2015: 97) argues that Cleinias is ambiguous in his commitment to philosophising at *Euthd.* 282d.

30. See Woolf 2000.

31. Consider, for some instances, Kahn 1983 and Woolf 2000 on the *Gorgias*, Weiss 2001 and Scott 2006 on the *Meno*, and Miller 1996 and Harte 1999 on the *Crito*. The dialogue-by-dialogue approach is also clear in some broader studies, such as Peterson 2011.

CHAPTER FOUR

Socrates and the Forms

WILLIAM J. PRIOR

INTRODUCTION

The question I shall deal with in this chapter is whether there is a version of the theory of forms in the *Euthyphro* and several other early Platonic dialogues. I argue that there is such a theory, that it is stated in *Eu.* 5c–d and 6d–e and mentioned again at 11a–b. In this I follow R. E. Allen, whose work on the early theory of forms remains today, fifty years after its first publication, the most thorough defence of an early theory of forms in Plato (Allen 1970, 1971). I also argue, again following Allen, that the early theory of forms differs from the version of the theory developed in five middle period dialogues – in alphabetical order, the *Cratylus, Phaedo, Phaedrus, Republic* V–VII and X and *Symposium* – and criticised in the first part of the *Parmenides*. The difference between the early theory of forms and the middle period theory is that the middle period forms are said to exist *separately* from their phenomenal participants, whereas the early forms are not explicitly said to exist separately. Having stated the view that there is an early theory of forms that differs in this one salient respect from the middle period theory, I deal with two sets of objections to these claims. First, I consider the views of several scholars who deny that there is a theory of forms in the early dialogues. Second, I consider the views of two scholars who argue that there is a theory of forms in the early dialogues, but who deny that it is different from the middle period theory of forms.

Interpreters customarily divide Plato's dialogues into three chronologically distinct groups: the early, middle and late dialogues. This chapter will be concerned only with the first two of these three groups. This grouping originates with studies of Plato's style beginning in the late nineteenth century, referred to collectively as 'stylometry' (for a discussion see Brandwood 1992 and Kahn 2002). Over the course of the twentieth century the membership of the middle group of dialogues was modified by interpreters to include all of those dialogues that refer to separately existing forms mentioned above. Charles Kahn notes this modification with disapproval (Kahn 1996: 44–45; 2002: 94–97), but even Kahn follows the practice of talking about 'early' and 'middle' dialogues. I shall use the terms 'early' and 'middle' in this chapter in the way they are used by all the interpreters whose views I shall discuss below. It follows from this usage that the early dialogues do not refer explicitly to separately existing forms, whereas at least some of the middle dialogues do.

Interpreters of Plato's thought in the past century have generally assumed that it developed over time: that the early dialogues represent a phase of Plato's thought that is most influenced by his mentor Socrates, that the middle dialogues give the reader Plato's own views (though expressed by the character Socrates), and that the late dialogues contain further developments

64 THE BLOOMSBURY HANDBOOK OF SOCRATES

in Plato's thought, partly in response to the critique of the middle period theory of separate forms presented in the *Parmenides*. This interpretation is known simply as 'developmentalism'. Developmentalism comes in many varieties. Some interpreters, such as Gregory Vlastos (1988, 1991), argue that the early phase of Plato's thought is an accurate reflection of the views of the historical Socrates; others do not assert this. Some interpreters deny that the early phase of Plato's thought contains any version of a theory of forms; I shall refer to this view as 'radical developmentalism'. Others, including myself, believe that the early dialogues contain an early version of the theory of forms; I refer to this view as 'moderate developmentalism'. A third view, known as 'unitarianism', generally rejects the developmental framework in favour of one that stresses the unity of Plato's thought. One way of stating the issue to be discussed in this chapter is: Is Plato to be understood developmentally, and if so, is his development of the radical or the moderate variety?

THE *EUTHYPHRO* AND THE EARLY THEORY OF FORMS: ALLEN

The dialogue that most explicitly supports the case for an early theory of forms is the *Euthyphro*. In this dialogue Socrates encounters the religious prophet Euthyphro at the porch of the King Archon, where Socrates has gone for a preliminary hearing before his trial. Euthyphro is prosecuting his father on a charge of impiety; Socrates, surprised, states that Euthyphro must be 'far advanced in wisdom' (4b) if he would dare to do this. Euthyphro agrees that he is wise, whereupon Socrates offers to become his pupil, in order to be able to answer the charges against him. As is typical of Socrates in Plato's early dialogues, he begins by asking Euthyphro for a definition of piety:

> (T1) So tell me now, by Zeus, what you just now maintained you clearly knew: what kind of thing do you say that godliness and ungodliness are, both as regards murder and other things; or is the pious not the same and alike in every action, and the impious the opposite of all that is pious and like itself, and everything that is to be impious presents us with one form . . . in so far as it is impious?
>
> – 5c–d; Grube, trans.

When Euthyphro fails to understand this request, Socrates repeats it:

> (T2) SOCRATES: Bear in mind then that I did not bid you tell me one or two of the many pious actions but that form itself that makes all pious actions pious, for you agreed that all impious actions are impious and all pious actions pious through one form, or don't you remember?
> EUTHYPHRO: I do.
> SOCRATES: Tell me then, what this form itself is, so that I may look upon it, and using it as a paradigm,[1] say that any action of yours or another's that is of that kind is pious, and if it is not that it is not.
>
> – 6d–e

Later in the dialogue, after Euthyphro has attempted to define piety as what all the gods love, and Socrates has shown him that this definition may be true of piety but does not define it, Socrates sums up his critique of Euthyphro's definition by saying:

> (T3) I'm afraid, Euthyphro, that when you were asked what piety is, you did not wish to make its nature clear to me, but you told me an affect or quality of it, that the pious

SOCRATES AND THE FORMS

has the quality of being loved by all the gods, but you have not yet told me what the pious is.

– 11a–b

These three passages make several claims about piety, the object of Socrates' search:

1. The first is that piety is an *idea* (5d4, 6d11, 6e3), an *eidos* (6d11). These are two of the most common terms Plato uses in the middle dialogues for his forms; Grube translates both as 'form'.

2. The second is that the form of piety is what philosophers call a *universal*, a 'one over many': something that is 'the same . . . in every (pious) action' (5d1–2). Whatever is impious, also, 'has one single form with respect to impiety' (5d3–4; my translation). A universal is an entity which retains its identity though it has multiple instances.

3. The third is that piety is that *by* which all pious things are pious (6d11); as Socrates reminds Euthyphro, 'you said that it is by a single idea that all the impious things are impious and all the pious things pious (6d11–e1; my translation). This "by" is an instrumental dative in Greek, and it indicates that the form of piety is somehow responsible for the piety of pious things. In other words, the form is the *cause* of the corresponding characteristic in things. It is not clear in precisely what sense the form is a cause; it is only said that it is that by which pious things are pious.

4. The fourth is that Socrates wants something that he can use as a *paradeigma*, a paradigm or standard, to judge the piety of allegedly pious things. (Grube translates 'model', which has the connotation of a particular that plays a certain role in the application of a term. I prefer 'standard', which does not have that connotation.) It is not entirely clear, from these passages, how the form of piety is to function as a paradigm. Somehow it is to aid one in judging the piety or impiety of particular acts. In the context of this dialogue, Socrates wants a paradigm that he can use to determine whether Euthyphro's prosecution of his father is pious or impious.

The first two passages from the *Euthyphro*, (T1) and (T2), tell us four basic things about piety, then: that it is a form, that it is a universal, that it is a cause and that it is a paradigm or standard. Allen summarises these points as follows:

> The words *eidos* and *idea* . . . have a range of ordinary meanings: sort or kind, figure, including the human figure, the nature of a thing . . . its *species* or outward appearance. But the words here are used in a special way. The *eidos* or *idea* of holiness is a universal, the same in all its instances, and something its instances have; it appears to be a condition for the existence of holy things, that *by which* – the dative is instrumental – holy things are holy; and it is a standard or *paradeigma* for determining what things are holy and what are not. In short, the words *eidos* and *idea* here carry freight they do not ordinarily bear, and for that reason, commentators have often translated them as 'Idea' or 'Form'.

– Allen 1971: 321

The third passage, (T3), though brief, clarifies the object of Socrates' search considerably. It tells us that Socrates is seeking to understand the nature, the essence (*ousia*: 11a7) of piety; he is seeking to understand *what piety is* (*hoti pot' estin*, 11a7). In Aristotle's terminology, Socrates is seeking the *definition* of piety: as Aristotle says in the *Metaphysics*:

> (T4) Socrates, . . . was busying himself about ethical matters and neglecting the world of nature as a whole but seeking the universal in these ethical matters, and fixed thought for the first time on definitions.
>
> – A.6, 987b1–4

> (T5) Socrates occupied himself with the excellences of character, and in connection with them became the first to raise the problem of universal definitions . . . It was natural that Socrates should seek the essence. For he was seeking to deduce, and the essence is the starting-point of deductions . . . Two things may fairly be ascribed [to][2] Socrates – inductive arguments and universal definition.
>
> – M.4, 1078b17–19, 23–25, 27–29; Barnes, trans.

The phrase that Barnes translates 'essence' is *to ti estin*, literally, 'the what it is', or 'the what is it?' When Aristotle says that Socrates wants to know the universal definition of the essence of piety, the nature of piety, he wants to know what piety is. That is what Socrates wants from Euthyphro, a universal definition that is true of every instance of piety, a definition that he can use as a standard to explain the very nature of piety. The reason Socrates cannot tell Euthyphro precisely what he wants is that Socrates lacks the word for definition (*diorismos*; an Aristotelian technical term). What Socrates wants is a verbal formula that will express the nature of piety.

According to Aristotle, then, the early theory of forms is a theory of definition, but definition of a particular kind. Philosophers generally distinguish two sorts of definitions: nominal and real. A nominal definition explains the meaning of a word or phrase in terms of another word or phrase. The traditional example is 'bachelor', defined nominally as 'an unmarried man'. Real definitions, in contrast, explain the nature of something in the world that is defined by a particular word or phrase. Consider for example the chemical definition of water as H_2O. This definition states, in chemical shorthand, that water is a molecule composed of two atoms of hydrogen bonded with a single atom of oxygen. A real definition is a verbal formula, but its referent is the nature, the essence, of a thing in the world. It is crucial to the early theory of forms that Socrates is searching for real definitions. The notion of a real definition embraces both a verbal formula and the non-verbal, real thing defined by that formula. Socrates wants a verbal formula that explains the essence of something real; he wants the *logos tēs ousias*, the verbal explanation or account of the essence of the real thing he is seeking to understand. In the *Euthyphro*, he wants a verbal account of the essence of piety. For this search to succeed, piety must be a real thing, a universal, a nature or essence. The early theory of forms is committed to the existence of real essences, as well as to verbal formulas that explain their natures. Socrates' examination of Euthyphro in the *Euthyphro* shows Socrates committed to the existence of a verbal formula for the essence of piety. Quoting Allen again:

> The important thing is that the definition in view is real and not nominal. It is analysis of essence, rather than stipulation as to how words shall be used or a report as to how they are in fact used . . . An essence . . . is the nature of something which is. And *real definition, in the early dialogues, is analysis of essence.*
>
> – Allen 1971: 327–328; my italics

SOCRATES AND THE FORMS

The fact that forms are characterised by Socrates as universals, causes, paradigms and essences, the objects of real definition, 'seems to imply', according to Allen, something which is properly called a 'Theory of Forms' (Allen 1971: 328). This theory of forms is

> 'in the first place, a technical theory, a body of rules governing the practice . . . of dialectic . . . But it is also a metaphysical theory. It assumes the existence of Forms, as universals, standards and essences . . . As essences, Forms do not, so to speak, just sit there. They do honest work. They affect the career of the world, being that by which things are what they are'.
>
> – Allen 1971: 328–329

This claim, that the early theory of forms is a metaphysical theory, is one that critics of the early theory of forms wish to deny. Though the early theory of forms is metaphysical, it is 'continuous with common sense' (Allen 1971: 330). Socrates' interlocutors, intellectuals and ordinary people alike, accept the existence of forms such as justice and piety without question. Although the existence of forms is a matter of common sense, Socrates' conception of forms goes beyond common sense:

> His question is hardly one which common sense, left to its own devices, will ask. But it is a question to which common sense may certainly be led . . . The progress of dialectic involves passage from the naïve existence claim that 'there is such a thing as holiness' to the highly sophisticated existence claim that there is an essence of holiness, and that it can be defined . . . [T]he commitment to essence is then latent in the common sense use of words. The essence of holiness is what we mean by the word 'holiness' – when we fully understand our meaning.
>
> – Allen 1971: 331

It is in this sense that the theory of forms is a theory of meaning. The theory of meaning is a referential one: The meaning of a term is the characteristic to which it refers, which is a form (Allen 1970: 125). Allen allows that not every use of a term is ontologically significant:

> the Muses may inspire a poet, made drunk by their presence, to compare the redness of a rare sunset to the redness of a rare beefsteak; they do not, or do not thereby, inspire him with the belief that he has added redness along with sunsets and beefsteaks to his ontology. But if that same poet, in more sober mood, were to ask what redness is, explaining that he wished to be told the nature of a characteristic . . . and if he went on to add that when he learned what it is, he expected to use it as a standard for distinguishing what is really red from what isn't; and that he expected it to state its *ousia*, its nature and reality . . . if, in short, he laid down rules for real definition and followed them in his inquiry, we should begin to suspect that the inspiration the Muses had visited upon him was metaphysical rather than poetical, and that he now came equipped with a view of the way the world is, and what it contains, which goes considerably beyond anything which ordinary language or common sense can show.
>
> – Allen 1971: 329–330

This connection between common sense and metaphysics is essential to Allen's view that the early theory of forms is a metaphysical theory.

Allen insists that the theory of forms in the early dialogues is *a* theory of forms, not *the* theory of forms:

68   THE BLOOMSBURY HANDBOOK OF SOCRATES

> [T]hat theory of the choir of heaven and the furniture of earth found in the *Phaedo*, *Republic* and other middle dialogues . . . The philosophy of the middle dialogues is a nest of contrasts: Being and Becoming, Appearance and Reality, Permanence and Flux, Reason and Sense, Body and Soul, Flesh and the Spirit. Those contrasts are rooted in an ontology of two Worlds, separated by a gulf of deficiency . . . This is 'separation', and it is possible to fix with some precision the kind of separation it is. It assumes both that sensible instances of Forms are deficient resemblances of Forms, and that they are less real than Forms. There is no trace of either of these claims in early dialogues such as the *Euthyphro*.

– Allen 1971: 332–333

The term 'separation' may be used in different ways, with different implications. When Allen uses the term in the passage just quoted, he connects it with the being-becoming distinction that is developed in Plato's *Republic*. When I speak of 'separation' in this chapter, it is this notion of separation that I have in mind. Plato's middle period forms are separate in that they are inhabitants of the realm of being, whereas their phenomenal participants are inhabitants of the realm of becoming. The forms in the early dialogues are not, or at least are not said to be, separate in this sense.

Allen summarises his view of the early theory of forms thus:

> This is metaphysics, but not the metaphysics of the middle dialogues. The middle dialogues do not abandon the 'What is it?' question. They pursue it in the light of a new ontology. That ontology rests on two principles, the immortality and divinity of the rational soul, and the complete reality and eternity of the objects of knowledge. These principles, in F. M. Cornford's phrase, are the pillars of Platonism, and their architrave is the doctrine of Recollection, the doctrine that the truth of things is always in the soul. The foundation on which this lofty structure rests is a theory of Forms which implies the diminished reality and deficiency of resemblance of sensible objects. None of this is found in the early dialogues.

– Allen 1971: 334

The reason for the change, Allen says, is that

> Plato's account in the middle dialogues is conditioned by problems in epistemology which the early dialogues had not faced. Those problems arose over scepticism and *a priori* knowledge. They arose not *in* Socratic dialectic but *about* it; specifically, they arose when Plato turned to deal with the question of how Socratic dialectic, as a search for forms or essences, is possible.

– Allen 1970: 157

These problems arise in the *Meno*, which Allen describes as an 'early middle' or 'boundary' dialogue, connecting the early dialogues with the middle dialogues, in particular the *Phaedo*. The scepticism of Meno's paradox is answered by the doctrine of recollection. In the *Phaedo* this doctrine is connected to the theory of separate forms. Sceptical doubts about the possibility of Socratic inquiry thus led to a doctrine of the deficiency of sensibles to forms, developed into a full-blown doctrine of two worlds, and a new conception of separation. This conception is not found in the early dialogues because scepticism about Socratic inquiry is not present there. What does this say about the relation between the ontology of the early dialogues and that of the middle dialogues? Allen concludes his article with an answer to this question: 'the theory of Forms in the middle dialogues, then,

SOCRATES AND THE FORMS

is neither the same theory as that of the early dialogues, nor a different one. Not different because it contains the earlier theory as a part. Not the same because it is directed toward issues which the early dialogues do not raise' (Allen 1971: 334; cf. Allen 1970: 163–164).

RADICAL DEVELOPMENTALISM AND THE CRITIQUE OF THE EARLY THEORY OF FORMS: VLASTOS, DANCY AND WOODRUFF

Radical developmentalism, as I have defined it above, claims that there is no theory of forms in Plato's early dialogues. Radical developmentalists hold that there is only one theory of forms, the Platonic theory of separate forms, and that this theory is confined to the middle dialogues. Radical developmentalists do not disagree with moderate developmentalists such as Allen and myself on the content of passages (T1–T3) in the *Euthyphro*, but they offer interpretations of those passages that deny they contain a metaphysical theory. In this section I shall examine the views of three radical developmentalists, Gregory Vlastos, Russell Dancy and Paul Woodruff, with special attention to their critique of the early theory of forms.

The most influential proponent of radical developmentalism is Gregory Vlastos, and his view is most fully stated in his (1991). Vlastos' project is, first, to distinguish the Socrates of Plato's early dialogues, whom he calls 'Socrates$_E$', from the Socrates of the middle dialogues, whom he labels 'Socrates$_M$', and second, to argue that Socrates$_E$ represents the historical Socrates while Socrates$_M$ represents Plato. Vlastos' view is that Plato operated in the first part of his career as a Socratic philosopher. His early dialogues are not re-creations of historical Socratic conversations, but original philosophical creations that are based on Socratic principles. (The exception is Plato's *Apology*, which Vlastos takes to be a more or less accurate report of what Socrates said in his own defence at his trial.) Vlastos states the first part of his view as follows: 'I have been speaking of *a* Socrates in Plato. There are two of them. In different segments of Plato's corpus two philosophers bear that name. But in different sets of dialogues he pursues philosophies so different that they could not have been depicted as inhabiting the same brain throughout unless it had been the brain of a schizophrenic' (Vlastos 1991: 45–46).

Vlastos distinguishes Socrates$_E$ from Socrates$_M$ on the basis of ten 'Theses', of which only the first two will concern us. The first thesis is that 'Socrates$_E$ is exclusively a moral philosopher', whereas 'Socrates$_M$ is a moral philosopher *and* metaphysician *and* epistemologist *and* philosopher of science *and* philosopher of language *and* philosopher of religion *and* philosopher of education *and* philosopher of art. The whole encyclopedia of philosophical science is his domain' (Vlastos 1991: 47–48). As he puts the matter in his (1988), 'in the whole history of Western thought no philosophy has had a wider range than SM's or a narrower one than SE's' (139). Vlastos' second thesis is that 'Socrates$_M$ had a grandiose metaphysical theory of "separately existing" Forms and of a separable soul which learns by "recollecting" pieces of its pre-natal fund of knowledge' whereas 'Socrates$_E$ has no such theory' (Vlastos 1991: 48). Vlastos describes this second thesis as 'the most powerful of the ten', and adds that *'the irreconcilable difference between Socrates$_E$ and Socrates$_M$ could have been established by this criterion even if it had stood alone'* (Vlastos 1991: 53; italics in the original). For the purposes of this chapter I shall set aside the part of thesis two that is concerned with the epistemological doctrine of recollection and focus exclusively on the metaphysical theory of separately existing forms.

Vlastos' statements of the differences between Socrates$_E$ and Socrates$_M$ are carefully formulated. Thesis one states that Socrates$_E$ is 'exclusively a moral philosopher' and not a metaphysician. As he puts it a little later, 'he is a moralist and nothing more – no metaphysician, no ontologist' (Vlastos 1991: 58). Thesis two states that Socrates$_M$ has a theory of 'separately existing' forms; there is no consideration of forms that may not exist separately from their phenomenal participants. The reason for his care is this: Ideally, radical developmentalism should deny that Socrates$_E$ has any metaphysical view, any ontology at all, but Vlastos cannot admit that. His Socrates$_E$ is concerned with definitions, and definitions must meet two conditions: First, 'the definiens must be true of all cases falling under the definiendum' (Vlastos 1991: 56), and second, 'the definiens must disclose the reason why anything is an instance of the definiendum' (Vlastos 1991: 57). In support of his first condition of a successful definition he cites *Euthyphro* 5d: 'Is not the pious the same as itself in every [pious] action? And the impious, in turn, is it not opposite to all that is pious but similar to itself, everything which is to be impious having a certain single character (*idean*) with respect to impiety?' In support of his second condition he cites *Euthyphro* 6d–e: 'recall that I did not ask you to teach me one or two of the many pious [actions] but that form itself because of which all the pious [actions] are pious. For you said that it is because of a single character that impious [actions] are impious and pious ones are pious. Or don't you remember?'

These two passages from the *Euthyphro* provide the strongest textual evidence from the early dialogues that Socrates$_E$ in fact possesses an ontology containing forms. This is a point that Vlastos concedes:

> In assuming that these two conditions can be met S$_E$ is making a substantial ontological commitment. He is implying that what there is contains not only spatio-temporal items, like individuals and events, but also entities of another sort whose identity conditions are strikingly different since they are 'the same' in persons and in actions which are not the same: justice here and justice there and again elsewhere, the same in different individuals and occurrences, real in each of them, but real in a way that is different from that in which they are real, its own reality evidenced just in the fact that it can be instantiated self-identically in happenings scattered widely over space and time, so that if justice has been correctly defined for even a single instance, the definiens will be true of every instance of justice that ever was or ever will be anywhere – in Greece or Persia, on earth or on Olympus or in Hades.

> – Vlastos 1991: 57–58

Without using the term, Vlastos in this passage describes what philosophers mean when they talk about universals, 'ones over many': entities whose identity conditions are such that they are one and the same in many instances. Vlastos goes on to say, 'that there are things which meet this strong condition is a piece of ontology that is fixed in Socrates$_E$'s speech and thought. He *has* this ontology' (Vlastos 1991: 58). I would remind the reader that the main question of this chapter is: 'Does Socrates, the character in Plato's early dialogues, possess a version of Plato's theory of forms?' Vlastos is clearly talking about the character in Plato's early dialogues and he clearly says that this Socrates is committed to, *has* (his italics), an ontology containing universals, which he labels 'forms'. So the answer Vlastos gives to the question would seem clearly to be 'yes'.)

SOCRATES AND THE FORMS

Vlastos, however, has three qualifications to his admission that Socrates$_E$ has an ontology containing universal forms. The first is that the terms *eidos* and *idea*, Plato's terms for 'form', do 'strictly definitional work' (Vlastos 1991: 56). This is an important point: It connects Socrates$_E$'s ontology with his interest in definition. Even if this is true, however, this does not disqualify them as terms in Socrates$_E$'s ontology, as Vlastos admits. Vlastos' second qualification is that, though Socrates$_E$ has an ontology, he is not an ontologist, a metaphysician, for he never makes ontology

> an object of reflective investigation . . . He never asks what sort of things forms must be if their identity conditions can be so different from those of spatio-temporal individuals and events that the identical form can be 'in' non-identical individuals and events . . . He asks: What is the form piety? What is the form beauty? And so forth. What is form? he never asks.
>
> – Vlastos 1991: 58

His third qualification is that the commitment to an ontology of forms in the early dialogues is not a commitment to a *theory*: 'it is gratuitous to credit him . . . with a theory of forms. His belief in their reality is no more evidence of his having such a *theory* than is the man in the street's belief in the reality of physical objects evidence of his having a theory of physical objects. A belief is not a theory if everyone's agreement with it can be presumed as a matter of course' (Vlastos 1991: 59). So Socrates has an ontology of universal forms, but he is not an ontologist, and his ontology is not a theory. I shall consider these points in my discussion of my (2004) below.

A second radical developmentalist is Russell Dancy, who presented his view in a book (2004) and a chapter in a collection (2006). In one respect, Dancy's position is more extreme than Vlastos': Dancy does not admit that the character Socrates in the early Platonic dialogues has an ontology, a metaphysics. According to Dancy, 'where Socrates is concerned with definitions, he is not concerned with metaphysics at all' (Dancy 2006: 71). This makes for a sharp distinction between Plato's early and middle dialogues: The early dialogues are not concerned with ontology, with metaphysics, at all, but with definition, whereas the middle dialogues are – they contain the theory of separate forms. On the other hand, as Dancy describes the kind of definitions that the Socrates of Plato's early dialogues is concerned with, he ascribes to them three requirements: the Substitutivity Requirement, the Explanatory Requirement and the Paradigm requirement, and he states that 'the latter two especially will feed into the Theory of Forms' (Dancy 2006: 71). At the end of his (2006) Dancy states that the 'heritage' of the theory of forms 'is pretty clearly Socrates' quest for definitions' (83). So a fair summary of Dancy's view would seem to be that, although the early Platonic dialogues do not contain an ontology, and specifically not the theory of forms, they contain constraints on definition that will, in the middle dialogues, give rise to that ontology. Thus, Dancy's denial that there is a theory of forms in the early dialogues is not as radical as it might seem to be at first sight.

Dancy's 'Substitutivity Requirement' and his 'Explanatory Requirement' are the same as the two requirements Vlastos placed on definitions in his (1991). His 'Paradigm Requirement' states that the '*definiens* must give a paradigm or standard by comparison with which cases of its *definiendum* may be determined' (Dancy 2006: 73). The textual basis of this requirement is *Euthyphro* 6e, the latter part of my (T2), the continuation of the passage Vlastos quoted, which has Socrates asking, 'then teach me this idea, what it is, so that looking to it and using it as a paradigm, whatever is such as it is among the things either you or anyone else does, I shall say is pious, and whatever is not such, I shall say

[is] not' (Dancy 2006: 75). Dancy does not commit himself on the difficult question of what is meant by saying that the form must be a paradigm, but he does assert that the paradigm of *F*, where *F* is the referent of a general term, is *F* and in no way not-*F* (Dancy 2006: 76). This leads Dancy to an argument that he believes marks the presence of the theory of forms in the middle Platonic dialogues: what he calls the 'Argument from Relativity'. This argument states that, whereas the form of *F* is unequivocally, absolutely *F*, and not in any respect not-*F*, ordinary *F* things are only relatively *F* and are in some respects not-*F*; from which it follows that the form of *F* is not identical with any ordinary *F* thing (Dancy states this argument using the example of the form of the beautiful in Dancy 2006: 71). This argument, Dancy claims, is missing from the early dialogues, but he admits there is an argument that anticipates it in the *Hippias Major* (289a–d). Hippias has proposed to define the beautiful as a beautiful girl: Socrates responds that although there is such a thing as the beautiful, any beautiful girl is also ugly, whereas the beautiful can never be ugly; therefore the beautiful is not the same as any beautiful girl (Dancy 2006: 79). Dancy remarks: 'This is not quite the Argument from Relativity, for that requires a generalisation Socrates does not give us in the *Hippias Major*, to the effect that (arG) is not just true of girls, horses, or lyres, but of any mundane beautiful thing whatever' (Dancy 2006: 79; [arG] is the premise that any beautiful girl is also ugly).

Plato's departure from the Socratic search for definitions begins in the *Meno*, where, as Dancy states, 'there is a massive shifting of gears' (Dancy 2006: 79). The *Meno* introduces the doctrine of recollection and the method of hypothesis, and abandons what Dancy calls the 'Intellectualist Assumption', what others have called the 'priority of definition principle' or the 'Socratic fallacy': the view that one cannot know any of the properties of something, or identify cases of it, until one can define what it is. (For a discussion see Chapter 6 in this volume.) Socrates also refers to forms as the objects of definition, but 'this is a far cry from an explicit Theory of Forms', says Dancy; 'we must wait for the *Phaedo* for that' (Dancy 2006: 80). Still, 'it looks very much as if, in the *Meno*, we have Plato striking out on his own' (Dancy 2006: 81). The *Meno*, that is, marks the end of the Socratic period of Plato's writing and the beginning of the Platonic period.

Dancy refers to the forms that appear in the early dialogues as 'forms' and the forms that appear in the middle dialogues as 'Forms', and he states that it is in the *Phaedo* that 'we first encounter the Forms' (Dancy 2006: 81). He notes that the introduction of 'Forms' is accompanied by the 'Argument from Relativity', when Socrates distinguishes 'the equal itself', which is absolutely equal, from equal sticks and stones, which are only relatively equal (*Phd.* 74a–c). Diotima makes the same point using 'beautiful' as her example in the *Symposium* (210e–211b). This passage describes the form of the beautiful as a paradigmatically beautiful thing, meeting the 'Paradigm Requirement' of the Socratic theory of definition. The 'Explanatory Requirement' is also satisfied in *Phd.* 100c, where Socrates accepts the form of beauty as the sole cause of the beauty of beautiful things. It is because the theory of forms meets these two definitional requirements that Dancy says the 'heritage' of the theory 'is pretty clearly Socrates' quest for definitions' (Dancy 2006: 83). So Dancy's view is that, though the early Platonic dialogues do not contain the theory of separate forms, or indeed any ontology, they pave the way for that theory in the middle dialogues.

The strictest and in that sense the most radical of the radical developmentalists I shall discuss is Paul Woodruff. Whereas Vlastos allows that the Socrates of the early dialogues has an ontology, and Dancy admits that the legacy of Socrates' theory of definitions is an ontology, the most that Woodruff will admit is that some passages of the early dialogues

SOCRATES AND THE FORMS

'invite' ontology. The first of his works that I shall discuss is an article published in 1978. I shall also discuss a chapter of his 1982 book on the *Hippias Major* and a 2019 article on the passages from the *Euthyphro* I have quoted above. These three works are consistent in their denial that Plato's early dialogues contain an ontology. In his (1978) he states that 'the Socrates of Plato's early dialogues did not dabble in ontology'. Such ontology as there is in the early dialogues comes from 'the boasting or otherwise arrogant behaviour of his interlocutor' (Woodruff 1978: 101). This is a theme of Woodruff's critique; it returns in his (2019). Woodruff sees Socrates as 'an asker of questions', who is not committed to his questions being answerable. 'Socrates' inquiries do not and need not require him to engage in metaphysical speculation. The early dialogues ... are thus innocent of metaphysics' (Woodruff 1978: 101–102). They may tempt one to provide an ontology for them, but they are compatible both with 'Plato's lavish ontology and ... Aristotle's more austere one' (Woodruff 1978: 102). Woodruff discusses two claims of the *Hippias Major*, that certain forms exist (including the fine, *to kalon*) and that things derive their qualities from these forms, and offers 'ontologically neutral' readings of these claims. Throughout his analysis he is concerned to show that the passages in which these claims are discussed do not establish the existence of *separate forms* (see Woodruff 1978: 105). It is Plato who makes the ontological turn by separating the forms (Woodruff 1978: 113–114). 'The earlier Socratic *distinction* between a form and its instances is a forerunner of that separation, but innocent ... of a theory committed to the separate existence of the forms' (Woodruff 1978: 114). As in the case of Vlastos and Dancy, the concept of separation seems to be for Woodruff the mark of a metaphysical theory. For Woodruff, as for Vlastos and Dancy, the theory of separate forms is the only theory of forms that Plato accepts, and it is Plato's theory and not Socrates'.

Again in his (1982) Woodruff claims that 'we do not need to attribute any ontological theory to Socrates, either in the *Hippias Major* or in any other dialogue of search' (Woodruff 1982: 161). What Socrates says 'invites' ontology but does not require it. As in his (1978) Woodruff is concerned with the theory of separate forms, a theory that includes the distinctions between being and becoming and knowledge and opinion, and that attributes to the forms the attributes of independence, priority and transcendence (Woodruff 1982: 162–163). He regards ontology as 'a distinctively philosophical matter ... not every question about what there is is ontological' (Woodruff 1982: 163). In particular, he denies that existence claims such as those found in the *Protagoras* are ontological: 'any discussion presupposes the existence of the subjects it discusses; but few discussions commit themselves to an ontological theory about their subjects' (Woodruff 1982: 164). Only if the philosopher is committed to such claims as that justice and piety are universals is the philosopher committed to an ontology. Woodruff admits that there are 'traces of the doctrines of the one-over-many (1), logical causation (2), and self-predication (3) ... in early Plato' (Woodruff 1982: 165), but no doctrines that entail the separate existence of forms. The early dialogues do not place the forms in a distinct ontological category (Woodruff 1982: 167). There is no general theory of definition or ontology in the early dialogues (Woodruff 1982: 170).

In his (2019) Woodruff criticises the view that there is an early theory of forms in the *Euthyphro*. In this article he responds to the view of Allen, but also to views that I shall state later in this chapter defending an early theory of forms. He initially states that 'there is no Socratic or Platonic theory of forms in the *Euthyphro*' (Woodruff 2019: 118); Socrates might well have had such a theory, but the text of the *Euthyphro* does not show that he did (Woodruff 2019: 128). He attributes the view that there is a paradigm form of piety not to Socrates but to Euthyphro. He understands a paradigm of piety to be an 'action type that is untainted by impiety' (Woodruff 2019: 125), that is purely pious and in no way impious, and he denies that there is any such paradigm. Euthyphro needs such an action type if he is to justify prosecuting his father, but Socrates' demand for a paradigm does not require that such a paradigm exist, or that Socrates believes it does. Woodruff describes what Socrates is looking for as a 'visible form' (Woodruff 2019: 124), and he calls visible forms and paradigms 'Euthyphronian entities' (Woodruff 2019: 126). Woodruff notes that 'we might reasonably attribute to him [i.e., Socrates] a belief in the existence of essences' but 'we cannot attribute to him any interest in the ontological status of essences' (Woodruff 2019: 128). This is similar to Vlastos' view that Socrates has an ontology of forms but is not interested in the ontological status of those forms. As was stated previously, Woodruff's Socrates is an inquirer, a man aware of his own ignorance, not a metaphysical theorist. For Woodruff, it is not easy to see how he might be both.

CRITIQUE OF THE CRITICS (I)

In this section I shall subject some of the salient views of the three radical developmentalists whose views I have discussed to criticism. I shall begin with general comments that I believe apply to all three of the interpreters I discussed above and move on to critical comments about the individual views of each of the three writers. The strategy of the radical developmentalist is to draw as sharp a contrast as is possible between Plato's early dialogues and his middle dialogues, to make the difference between the Socrates of the early dialogues and the Socrates of the middle dialogues as clear as possible. The aim of this strategy is to isolate a Socrates in the early Platonic dialogues who accurately reflects the views of the historical Socrates. This aim, however, is explicitly a part only of Vlastos' interpretive project. Other radical developmentalists claim only to distinguish two portraits of Socrates in Plato. One wonders, however, whether the quest for the historical Socrates does not lie behind this interpretive project. There are certainly differences in tone as well as in content between dialogues such as the *Protagoras* and dialogues such as the *Phaedo*. Again, however, one wonders whether these differences are as sharp as the radical developmentalist requires. One also wonders whether the early dialogues share a set of distinctive features that distinguish them categorically from the middle dialogues in the way required by the radical developmentalist. One wonders why it is so important to the radical developmentalist that the Socrates of the early dialogues should have no ontological theory, that these dialogues should be a 'metaphysics-free' zone.

All three of the radical developmentalists I have considered take the question of whether the early dialogues contain the theory of forms to be a question about whether Socrates professes in those dialogues a theory of *separate* forms. Vlastos admits that his Socrates$_E$ has an ontology of universal characteristics, but he insists that this is not the theory of forms. The other two do not admit as much as Vlastos. None of the three, however, takes the early dialogues to contain separate forms. It would seem as though these three interpreters regard the theory of separate forms as an ontological theory, but anything less than that as not an ontological theory. How is this point justified? Unfortunately, none of the three tells us what he means by a metaphysics or an ontology. (Neither, I must admit, do proponents of an early theory of forms.) In this context I find Vlastos' admission that Socrates has an ontology of universals significant. I would say that anyone who puts forward an ontology of universal characteristics is engaged in metaphysics. Metaphysics, and ontology in particular, is the investigation of questions of

SOCRATES AND THE FORMS

a fundamental nature about the make-up of the world, and an ontology of universal characteristics is certainly an answer to such questions.

All three of the interpreters I have discussed emphasise the difference between the early and middle dialogues. There certainly are differences in content and tone between the two groups of dialogues, but there are also similarities. Vlastos admits that Socrates$_E$ has an ontology of forms; Dancy admits that Socrates' constraints on definition give rise to the theory of forms; even Woodruff admits that what Socrates says about forms in the early dialogues invites ontological speculation. One wonders whether this is a sufficient acknowledgment of what Socrates says about forms in the *Euthyphro* as well as in other early dialogues, such as the *Protagoras*, *Hippias Major* and *Meno*. The major question for radical developmentalism is whether it can take adequate account of passages such as (T1–T3). Proponents of an early theory of forms would argue that it cannot.

Each of the three radical developmentalists I have discussed has problems specific to his own formulation of his view. None of them presents an absolutely pure distinction between the early and middle dialogues, not even Woodruff. The view that has attracted the most attention is that of Vlastos. Shortly after the publication of Vlastos' (1991) Gail Fine wrote an article critical of his distinction between Socratic and Platonic forms (1993a).[3] In this article she criticises Vlastos' view that Socrates does not have a *theory* of forms, because he takes the existence of forms to be unproblematic. She argues that the existence of forms is not unproblematic for everyone in the dialogues as Vlastos believes. Vlastos seems to think that the existence of forms in the Socratic dialogues is uncontroversial because no one challenges it, but she notes that there are other controversial Socratic claims that go unchallenged in the Socratic dialogues. 'The man in the street, for example, doesn't explicitly believe that virtue is some one thing, the same in all cases; but this is a belief that Socrates explicitly holds and often relies on' (Fine 1993a: 71).

Vlastos says that both Platonic and Socratic forms are unobservable and unchangeable; Fine thinks that Socrates is not committed to either view. Finally, Vlastos believes that although Platonic forms are separate, 'Socrates rejects separation'. Fine notes that people 'understand separation in different ways', and that Vlastos in his (1991) 'takes separation to be independent existence . . . On this account, forms can be both separate and also the properties of particulars' (Fine 1993a: 76; this is a different sense of 'separation' from that which I adopt in this chapter). Again, Fine does not think that Socrates takes a position on the question of the separate existence of forms: 'the most we can say is that Socrates is uncommitted about separation, one way or another' (Fine 1993a: 78). Fine does not believe that Plato is explicitly committed to separation before the *Timaeus*. 'Perhaps Plato accepts separation all along; certainly the tenor of the middle dialogues is congenial to separation. But if he accepts it, he doesn't tell us that he does so: he never says that forms are separate' (Fine 1993a: 83).

In 2004 I published 'Socrates Metaphysician', a critique of Vlastos' claim that Socrates was 'exclusively a moral philosopher'. In this article I held that the dichotomy Vlastos drew between the moral philosopher of the early dialogues and the metaphysician of the middle dialogues is a false one, and that, though Socrates$_E$ does not hold the 'grandiose' theory of 'separately existing' forms that Socrates$_M$ holds, he does hold a theory of forms and this is a metaphysical theory. I argued that the view presented by Allen was essentially correct. Plato was not schizophrenic for holding both metaphysical views, though he did not hold both simultaneously. One developed out of the other. The early version of the theory of forms is not a theory of *separate* forms. It is, however, a theory of universals

(Prior 2004: 3–4). As a believer in the existence of universals, Socrates$_E$ holds a metaphysical view.

Vlastos admits that Socrates has an ontology of universals. His objections are that

a) This ontology is not a *theory*, and

b) Socrates is not an *ontologist* for holding it.

Vlastos' reason for claiming that Plato's ontology in the early dialogues does not constitute a theory is, as we have seen, that 'a belief is not a theory if everyone's agreement with it can be presumed as a matter of course' (Vlastos 1991: 59). Like Fine, I argued that Vlastos was mistaken about this. It is true that neither Socrates nor his interlocutors regard the existence of forms as problematic. Vlastos is correct to say that this was a difference between the early and middle dialogues. Does this mean that the early theory of forms is not a theory? I held that it does not, for three reasons. First, It seems clear to me that a view's having widespread or even universal acceptance does not disqualify it as a theory. I cited the heliocentric theory of the solar system as an example. The ontology of physical objects may not be a theory to the average New Yorker, as Vlastos states, but it is a theoretical claim for philosophers who take scepticism about the external world seriously.

Second, whether something is a theory, as these examples show, does not depend on the statements contained in it as much as on the person who holds it. The existence of universal moral characteristics may be taken for granted by people such as Euthyphro and even Protagoras, but this matter of common sense may lead to abstract metaphysical theorising in the hands of a philosopher such as Socrates. I claimed that what Vlastos was attempting to show in his 'The Socratic Elenchus' (Vlastos 1983a: 27–58), was that the elenchus is 'an attempt to make the interlocutors aware of the theoretical, i.e. philosophical, depth and significance of the apparently ordinary, non-theoretical, non-philosophical statements they are inclined, unreflectively, to make about moral matters' (Prior 2004: 11). The early theory of forms may begin with an interlocutor's unreflective acceptance of what seems to be a matter of common sense, but it does not end there.

Third, I argued, in agreement with Fine, that Vlastos seriously misrepresented the uncontroversial nature of Socrates' ontology. I noted three features of Socrates' arguments. First, he is careful to get explicit assent from his interlocutors about his existence claims. Second, his interlocutors often show that they do not really understand these claims even when they have assented to them. Hippias and Euthyphro find the idea of a common character intellectually daunting, and it takes much subsequent discussion to sort matters out. Third and most important, not every character in the dialogues takes the existence and definition of a common character to be unproblematic. For example, Meno does not; he rejects Socrates' comparison between virtue and bees, or health, size and strength. Subsequent discussion not only fails to define virtue but also leads to Meno's famous paradox of inquiry. The idea that virtue is a common character is hardly unproblematic for Meno (Prior 2004, 12–13).

Vlastos' second objection is that Socrates is not an ontologist because he holds his view unreflectively. Specifically, Socrates does not ask, 'What is form?' (Vlastos 1991: 58). Vlastos believes that Socrates asks the 'what is form' question in the middle dialogues, where the existence of forms becomes a highly contestable hypothesis instead of a generally accepted fact, and where Plato distinguishes four 'categorical' features of the forms: their inaccessibility to the senses, their changelessness, their incorporeal nature and their existence 'themselves in themselves'. In 2004 I responded to this objection in

SOCRATES AND THE FORMS

two ways. First, I said that Vlastos' requirement was too restrictive. True, Socrates does not explicitly ask the question, 'What is form?' in the early dialogues, but neither does he ask it explicitly in the middle dialogues. Only in the first part of the *Parmenides* does Parmenides raise for the young Socrates explicit questions about the nature of forms and their relation to their participants. I argued that it was not necessary for Socrates to raise explicitly the 'What is X?' question about something for him to maintain the existence of forms in a serious philosophical manner. Not all philosophical questions, I said, were questions of definition, and Socrates never says that only when he is engaging in questions of definition is he engaging in philosophical thought. Second, even if we were to accept Vlastos' principle that to engage in serious inquiry one must ask the 'What is X?' question, it does not follow that Socrates does not ask that question about form. The definitions Socrates sought were identity statements, and when Socrates investigates the nature of piety he is investigating the nature of a form. For Socrates, moral inquiry and metaphysical inquiry are inseparable: 'if Socrates is a moral philosopher of the sort described in the elenctic dialogues, then, he cannot be *exclusively* a moral philosopher, for his moral philosophy presupposes a metaphysical theory, a theory of common properties. Without this metaphysical underpinning, Socratic moral enquiry cannot take place' (Prior 2004: 10).

Writing today, I am not altogether happy with this answer, and I would supplement it in the following way. I would say that, although Socrates does not explicitly ask the question, 'What is form?' in the middle dialogues, he does answer it, at least in part. He does attempt to describe the essential nature of forms, and these categorical features are part of that description. If we were to grant that Socrates does attempt to answer the question, 'What is form?' in the middle dialogues, by stating categorical features of the forms, however, we must say that he tries to answer it in the early dialogues as well. If Socrates had said only that forms exist in the early dialogues, but had left their nature a complete mystery, Vlastos might be justified in saying that Socrates did not attempt to answer the 'What is form?' question. Allen would agree. But he does not: He characterises the forms as universals, as causes, as paradigms and as essences. If Socrates attempts to explain the nature of form in the middle dialogues, we must admit that he does so in the early dialogues too. If this is what makes someone a metaphysician, an ontologist, and not someone with merely an uncritically held ontology, then Socrates in the early dialogues is surely a metaphysician.

Another critique of Vlastos has been provided by Nicholas Smith (2014). Smith focuses on Vlastos' assertion that, although Socrates has an ontology of forms in the early dialogues, he is not an ontologist, because he does not ask the second-order question, 'what is Form?' Smith notes my criticism that Vlastos' criterion is too restrictive, but says that he believes Socrates 'both asks *and answers* the second-order question in Plato's early dialogues' (Smith 2014: 426). He argues that Socrates discusses forms in two ways that he believes distinguish the early theory of forms from Plato's middle period theory, ways that he believes are different from those posited by previous interpreters. The first is that forms in the early dialogues, but not in the middle dialogues, participate in part-whole relationships. The second is that Socrates in the early dialogues believes that virtue forms are *constituted* by knowledge, whereas the forms of the middle dialogues are not, though they are *objects* of knowledge. Smith writes,

If the virtue forms (the only ones discussed *as* forms in the early dialogues) are actually constituted by knowledge, then there is an obvious way that they are not separate from the entities they characterize: if piety is a kind of knowledge, then piety will be no more separable from the one who *is* pious than one's *knowledge* would be separable from the one who knows. On the other hand, if the object of knowledge is itself separate from the knower (as Plato certainly seemed to believe), then insofar as piety, as a form, is an object of knowledge, it will be separate, in nature, from the one who is pious. So Socrates did not, and Plato did 'separate' the forms.

– Smith 2014: 432

Turning from the critique of Vlastos to that of Dancy, I would first note that Dancy provides an interesting account of definition in the Socratic dialogues, and of the development of the theory of forms in the *Phaedo* and *Symposium*. What he fails to show, however, is that the account of definitions in the Socratic dialogues is not metaphysical in nature. Dancy shows, like Vlastos, that the theory of definition is not equivalent to the theory of separate forms of the middle dialogues, but he does not show that it is not a precursor to it. In fact, he insists that the 'heritage' of the theory of forms is the Socratic quest for definitions. He claims that it is a metaphysically innocent precursor, but he does not show this, for he does not offer an account of what makes a theory metaphysically innocent. Dancy (like Vlastos and Woodruff) seems to identify having a metaphysical view with having what Vlastos calls 'a grandiose theory of separately existing Forms'. He does not consider the more modest theory of immanent forms in the Socratic dialogues to be a metaphysical theory, but he does not explain the basis for the distinction between metaphysical and non-metaphysical views. As Donald Zeyl states in criticising Dancy, 'I worry about the lack of attention given to the question as to what counts as a metaphysical theory, and what distinguishes such a theory from one that isn't metaphysical. That distinction is crucial to Dancy's overall argument, yet it seems assumed without much support' (Zeyl 2006). Zeyl states that Dancy 'does not . . . explicitly identify and defend criteria that distinguish non-metaphysical talk from metaphysics; he appears to think that if a claim is intelligible to philosophically naïve interlocutors and accepted by them as obviously true it is not metaphysical' (Zeyl 2006). However, as he later adds, 'Why, one might wonder, should a philosophically naïve interlocutor be incapable of understanding a metaphysical proposition' (Zeyl 2006).

If I were to suggest an explanation as to why Dancy does not regard the references to the forms in the Socratic dialogues as metaphysical, it would be that he may believe a metaphysical theory must be based on the postulation of entities not recognised by common sense. Another way of putting this would be to say that Dancy may believe that a metaphysical theory must appeal to the existence of another world beyond the ordinary world of our experience. I think, however, that such a conception of metaphysics is too restrictive. Metaphysics deals with questions that arise from our ordinary experience, as Allen notes. There can be a 'metaphysics of ordinary experience', and the early theory of forms looks like such a metaphysics, at least to me.

Dancy holds that the origin of the theory of forms lies in Socrates' understanding of definitions. I agree. He also wants to hold, however, that Socratic definitions are not metaphysical. This would be true if Socrates were not seeking *real* definitions, but as we have seen, Allen argues that he is. He also argues that the argument about the beautiful girl in the *Hippias Major* is a large step from the argument from relativity in the middle dialogues. For me the step is a small one, and the generalisation is almost inevitable when one realises that there is nothing special about the example of a girl, that she is simply an example of the deficiency of entities in the phenomenal world. Dancy distinguishes several metaphysical features of forms in the early dialogues, and notes that they do not individually entail the theory of forms. He does not, however, consider whether the whole package of metaphysical distinctions – the claims that forms are ones over many, causes, self-predicational paradigms and essences – do not together constitute a metaphysical theory. I think they do.

Paul Woodruff's denial that the character Socrates in Plato's early dialogues is an ontologist stems from two assertions with which I disagree: The assertion that ontology is an activity for philosophers alone and the denial that existence claims, such as the claim in the *Protagoras* and elsewhere that 'justice is something,' are matters of ontology. These two assertions are related: Woodruff's denial that 'justice is something' is an instance of ontology reflects his view that ontology is a matter for philosophers. I accept Allen's view that ontology begins in common sense, though it does not end there. I believe that someone who accepts the assertion that justice exists accepts an ontology of universals. This does not necessarily make that person an ontologist. Vlastos is correct on this point: Not everyone who has an ontology is an ontologist. Whether one is an ontologist depends on the use to which he or she puts this existence claim. If Socrates in the dialogues had merely claimed that justice was something and did not go on to characterise justice as a one over many (a universal), a cause, a paradigm and an essence, it could be argued that he was not an ontologist. Woodruff believes that if someone asserts justice exists that person is not engaging in ontology, but if someone asserts that justice is a universal, he or she is. It may be that Protagoras, Euthyphro and others do not initially see the ontological implications of their naïve existence claims. Socrates, however, treats this sort of existence claim as the first step in the postulation of universal paradigmatic causes, essences, and this shows that he regards the existence claim as the beginning of an ontological inquiry. When Socrates states at *Euthyphro* 6d that it is by one form that all pious things are made pious he describes piety as a one over many, a universal, and that makes the claim ontological, even on Woodruff's account. Socrates' interlocutors are led by Socrates into the realm of ontology, just as the young Socrates is led by Parmenides into an ontological inquiry in the first part of the *Parmenides*. As Allen puts it, the interlocutors are led from a common-sense existence claim to a highly sophisticated existence claim; and that is a matter of ontology. Woodruff shows that Socrates did not accept what he calls the 'mature' theory of forms, what I have been calling the theory of separate forms, but that is because he does not accept the thesis of separation. He does not show that Socrates does not accept an ontology of universal, paradigmatic causes. An ontology of forms without the thesis of separation is still an ontology; or so I would claim.

I do not accept Woodruff's view that Euthyphro, and not Socrates, is the proponent of the view that piety is a paradigm. I believe that Euthyphro has little or no idea of what he means until Socrates clarifies it for him by his questions. I think he is one of Socrates' interlocutors who is least able to engage in metaphysical inquiry. I do not accept Woodruff's characterisation of a paradigm as an action type that is not qualified by its opposite. I think that Socrates' paradigms are essences, the objects of real definitions. When Socrates says he wants a paradigm he wants the principle that enables us to characterise any alleged case of a quality as a genuine case. He wants to know the nature of the form he is attempting to define. I think that Woodruff's characterisation of form as 'visible' is tendentious. It is true that the etymology of *idea* has its roots in visual experience, but Socratic forms, like Platonic ones, are intelligible objects. They may be grasped by intuition, but it is intellectual, not sensory intuition.

THE UNITARIAN ALTERNATIVE: KAHN AND FRONTEROTTA

The radical and the moderate interpreter agree on a general interpretive approach to Plato's dialogues: They agree that the dialogues show development over time. They disagree on the nature of the development, but both moderate and radical developmentalists would agree that the early dialogues are in some sense 'Socratic' in spirit, whereas the middle dialogues are 'Platonic'. There is a sense in which the disagreement between the radical and the moderate developmentalist is a family quarrel. Another school of interpretation, the unitarian, rejects this common assumption of developmentalism. The unitarian interpreter holds that the dialogues reflect a single philosophy, that of Plato, and that this can be found in the early as well as in later dialogues. It is difficult to find a pure unitarian among modern interpreters of Plato. Paul Shorey perhaps comes closest. Shorey holds that 'Plato's philosophy and his conception of life had taken shape at the age of thirty or thirty-five, and that his extant works, though not of course a predetermined systematic exposition, are the naturally varied reflection of a homogeneous body of opinion, and of a consistent attitude in the interpretation and criticism of contemporary life' (Shorey 1903: 4–5). According to this view, when Plato wrote the *Euthyphro* and other early dialogues that make reference to forms, he already conceived of the forms as separate from their participants. He did not state this view, but he can't be criticised for unfolding his conception of forms gradually over the course of the dialogues. Now it is difficult, if not impossible, to know what Plato was thinking at a particular point in his writing career, apart from what he tells us; so the question for the interpreter becomes, does Plato tell us things about the forms in the early dialogues that are incompatible with their separation, or is he merely silent about separation in those dialogues?

Two recent interpreters, Charles Kahn and Francesco Fronterotta, follow the unitarian program to some extent, though neither is a strict unitarian. What each denies is that the early period forms differ from the middle period forms on the matter of separation. Kahn's critique of the early theory is found in his (1996). Kahn is critical of the developmental view that there is a significant difference between the Socratic view of the early dialogues and the Platonic view of the middle dialogues. Though he believes that a few of the early dialogues represent an early stage of Plato's thought, he thinks that a group of ten dialogues, including seven he calls 'threshold dialogues' (*Laches, Charmides, Euthyphro, Protagoras, Meno, Lysis* and *Euthydemus*), express the same philosophical view. 'The reading of these seven dialogues,' he states, are 'deliberate philosophical preparation for the views to be presented in the *Symposium, Phaedo* and *Republic*' (Kahn 1996: 42). He describes the interpretation of the seven threshold dialogues as 'proleptic' or 'ingressive' (Kahn 1996: 48). 'I assume that Plato did not change his thought in any fundamental way between the *Laches* and *Protagoras*, on the one hand, and the *Phaedo* and *Republic*, on the other' (Kahn 1996: 59). Rather, 'the seven threshold dialogues are designed to prepare the reader for the views expounded in the *Symposium, Phaedo*, and *Republic*' (Kahn 1996: 59–60). These views include the theory of forms. For Kahn, the theory of forms is the theory of transcendent, separately existing forms of the middle dialogues. As he states near the end of his exposition of the theory, 'at least half a dozen dialogues, from the *Laches* and *Euthyphro* to the *Republic* and *Phaedrus*, can be read as the progressive exposition of a single, complex view of essential Forms, a view different aspects of which are displayed in different contexts' (Kahn 1996: 367–368). Kahn describes his interpretation of the theory of forms as unitarian (Kahn 1996: 363). This

SOCRATES AND THE FORMS

makes it sound as if he understands the forms of the *Euthyphro* as separate forms, and I believe that this is his position. He has to admit, however, that Plato does not insist on the separate existence of the forms until the middle dialogues. In fact, Kahn presents an account of the gradual revelation of the theory of forms in the threshold dialogues that does not differ in most important respects from the developmental account. He describes what he calls the 'raw material' for the theory of forms, several linguistic practices of ordinary Greek, that do not constitute a theory of forms but that nonetheless provide the backdrop for it. He describes the search for essences in the early, Socratic dialogues, but he says that 'the metaphysical status of such essences is left unspecified' (Kahn 1996: 337). The description of these essences given in the *Euthyphro* could 'be satisfied equally well by Aristotelian essences or Platonic Forms' (Kahn 1996: 337); and yet, 'when he comes in the *Phaedo* to specify the metaphysical and epistemic status of his Forms, he takes pains to remind the careful reader that these are the *same* essences that are under discussion in the dialogues of definition' (Kahn 1996: 337). 'The author of the *Phaedo*, then, carefully marks the continuity between the metaphysical Forms of this dialogue and the metaphysically indeterminate essences of the *Meno* and the *Euthyphro*' (Kahn 1996: 338). He reserves the *Symposium* for the explicit revelation of the theory of separate forms, but 'any reader acquainted with the terms *eidos* and *idea* for essences in the dialogues of definition must come gradually to see that these new metaphysical entities announced in the *Symposium*, and identified in the *Phaedo* as objects of prenatal, supersensible cognition, are after all what was being sought for all along in the request for definitions' (Kahn 1996: 354). Socratic essences are, after all, Platonic separate forms; Plato just revealed this identity slowly, over the course of several dialogues.

Kahn raises several objections to treating these essences as the immanent universals of the early theory of forms, including an objection to the 'very notion of immanent universals,' which he states is 'philosophically problematic' and the claim that 'to speak of universals, particulars, and instances is to resort to a vocabulary much more technical and theory-laden than anything we actually find in Plato's text' (Kahn 1996: 336).

Kahn's unitarianism is limited to ten dialogues: the seven threshold dialogues and three middle dialogues, the *Phaedo*, *Symposium* and *Republic*. An interpreter who comes closer to being a pure unitarian than Kahn (though he prefers the term 'anti-developmentalist') is Francesco Fronterotta. Fronterotta wrote a response, published in 2007, to my critique of Vlastos, stating that my article 'undermines almost three decades of quasi unity in the English speaking world on a certain interpretation of Plato's theory of Ideas with regard to the relationship between Plato and Socrates' (Fronterotta 2007: 37). Fronterotta's criticism is that I did not go far enough in my critique: The forms I posited were immanent in things rather than separate. Fronterotta believes that Vlastos' view of the early dialogues was the result of his concern for the Socratic question; that is, he believes that Vlastos interprets Plato's theory of forms in light of his quest to discover in the dialogues the historical Socrates. He urges that the dialogues be studied without that question in mind.

Fronterotta distinguishes three aspects of agreement sought in the Socratic search for definition: linguistic agreement, agreement based on knowledge of the subject to be defined, and agreement

> which depends on the ontological status of the definiendum. In this case it is no longer sufficient to know the universal semantic extension of 'X', but it is necessary to grasp directly the very nature or proper being of 'X', its unchangeable Form or Idea that is

always identical to itself throughout the particular circumstances, actions or things in which it is present.

– Fronterotta 2007: 48

The question raised in the definitional dialogues, emphasizing the need for a definition, leads to positing Ideas as the real beings one has to know beforehand, in themselves and in their relationship with the multiplicity of things or instances in which they are present, in order to put forward an appropriate definition: on these terms, it seems to me beyond doubt that one can legitimately speak of a 'theory of Ideas' in Plato's early dialogues.

– Fronterotta 2007: 49

'Socrates clearly requires a real definition', Fronterotta notes, citing Allen, 'one that shows the very nature of the object to be defined, and that results from an immediate and objective knowledge of it' (Fronterotta 2007: 52). The forms are said to be causes, which must be distinct from the effects they produce. The form is not the property as it is found in its many instances, Fronterotta states; rather, it is what produces the property. 'The Ideas therefore exist independently of the logical and intellectual act of definition and knowledge by a subject, by being distinct, autonomous, and prior to the multiplicity of particular things of which they represent the proper being' (Fronterotta 2007: 54); that is, they exist *separately* from their instances.

The developmentalist interpreter insists that the forms in the early dialogues are immanent in the things they characterise, whereas forms in the middle dialogues are separate entities, 'transcendent and self-sufficient' (Fronterotta 2007: 54). Fronterotta responds that 'at least up to the *Parmenides* Plato does not take a clear stand on the modalities of participation, and one is forced to admit that the problem is left unsolved even in middle and late dialogues' (Fronterotta 2007: 56). The developmentalist insists that only in the middle dialogues does Plato divide forms and phenomena into two worlds, and that 'only in these dialogues are Ideas finally conceived as properly metaphysical objects'. Fronterotta responds that the status of forms as eternal, unchanging objects is a consequence of the status they have in the early dialogues as 'self-identical, universal, and perfectly accomplished entities' (Fronterotta 2007: 56), and the status of phenomena as ever-changing entities is likewise established in the early dialogues. He describes the being-becoming distinction as 'mythical' and as 'a narrative change at most, consisting in the enlargement of the same epistemological and ontological hierarchy of beings from a "geographical" point of view, which does not actually change Plato's philosophical perspective' (Fronterotta 2007: 57); in other words, a metaphor. For Fronterotta, the forms of the early dialogues are as separate as are those of the middle dialogues.

Fronterotta attributes the attempts to distinguish the two theories of forms to the Socratic problem, and in particular the attempt to read separate forms out of the early dialogues as part of an attempt 'to make a clean cut between the early and middle dialogues' (Fronterotta 2007: 58). Fronterotta's response is that 'the theory of Ideas progressively arises, starting from the definitional dialogues ... in a uniform and consistent form, without any symptom of a clean break or a radical shift in Plato's thought ... I believe that Plato already inaugurates an original philosophical trend from the early dialogues, especially regarding the onto-epistemological framework of the theory of Ideas' (Fronterotta 2007: 59). He concludes that 'the only constant factor it [the anti-developmentalist perspective] supposes ... is a certain onto-epistemological principle,

SOCRATES AND THE FORMS

which in my view does actually seem unfailingly present in Plato's thought' (Fronterotta 2007: 61).

CRITIQUE OF THE CRITICS (II)

The basic difference between unitarian and developmentalist interpreters comes down to the question of whether we are allowed to attribute to Plato in certain dialogues a view that he does not explicitly state there. The unitarian might argue that, as Plato uses the terms *eidos*, *idea* and *paradeigma* in the *Euthyphro* to state what he is looking for, and as these are the terms he most commonly uses in the middle dialogues as names of the forms, we ought to presume that he is talking about the same entities, namely separate forms, in both places. The argument in favour of the unitarian interpretation lies in its simplicity. On the other hand, the developmentalist interpreter can argue that it is wrong to attribute to Plato in a given dialogue a position he takes explicitly only in another. The developmentalist may state that this principle is strengthened if the two dialogues date from different periods of Plato's career. (One must be careful here, however: As Kahn has pointed out, the modern formulation of the difference between the early and middle dialogues has been constructed with the developmentalist framework in mind, which suggests that the appeal to different periods may be question-begging.) It is difficult to decide between these two large-scale interpretive positions; after all, as Kahn admits, 'we cannot read Plato's mind' (Kahn 1996: 338).

I do not find Kahn's objections to the language of immanent universals persuasive. I do not think that interpreters are required to mean more by this language than that the forms of the *Euthyphro* are described as 'the same and alike in every pious action' (*Eu.* 5d1–2). I do not think that the interpreter's use of such terms is particularly technical or esoteric. Socrates speaks in the language of the ordinary Greek, and Plato in general eschews a technical vocabulary. His claims that forms are 'ones over many', universals, which are 'in' many things that possess them, do not require a knowledge of philosophical logic to be understood by the reader. The question that Kahn's interpretation raises is whether there are decisive reasons for regarding Plato's remarks about forms in such early dialogues as the *Euthyphro* as part of a single literary project which extends through the *Republic*. I would argue that there are not, but I must admit that Kahn's proleptic reading of the early theory of forms is an interesting alternative to the developmentalist framework.

Interpreters such as Allen and I can appreciate much that Fronterotta says, especially his claim that the Socratic quest presupposes an ontological principle, not merely a linguistic one (real, as opposed to merely nominal definition; see Fronterotta 2007: 52). The one point on which Fronterotta and I are at odds is his diminution of the significance of the being-becoming distinction and its epistemological corollary, the distinction between knowledge and belief. I think that the introduction of these distinctions reflects a real change in Plato's view. It may result from Plato's Heracliteanism, as Aristotle said, or from the new focus on a response to scepticism about moral inquiry, as Allen indicates, but I think that it results in Plato's reconfiguration of forms from common characters to separately existing abstract objects. I think this requires us to posit a development between the early and middle period theory of forms. Fronterotta, on the other hand, diminishes the significance of the language of being and becoming. Again, we would seem to come down to our inability to read Plato's mind, to determine the nature of his project at any given point in his career.

CONCLUSION

I have argued in this chapter for a certain interpretation of three passages in Plato's *Euthyphro* and in similar passages in other early Platonic dialogues. That interpretation is that Plato's character Socrates accepts and urges his interlocutors to accept an ontology of universal characteristics, which he calls forms, and which he treats as paradigms, causes and essences. I believe that this is a metaphysical theory, the precursor of the theory of separate forms in the middle dialogues but not identical to that theory. I agree with the critics of an early theory of forms in Plato that Socrates' belief in forms is grounded in his search for definitions, but I think that the fact Socrates is seeking real definitions means that he is engaged in metaphysical inquiry. I believe that this interpretation is more faithful to the sense of Plato's text than rival accounts, which either deny the existence of a metaphysical theory in the early dialogues or which claim that the early theory of forms is in fact identical to the middle period theory. The former account of these passages seems strained to me, and to be based on a Procrustean conception of a Socrates without metaphysical commitments that I believe is imposed on the text. The latter account requires the interpreter to attribute propositions to Socrates in the *Euthyphro* that he does not assert until later. My account, like that of some other interpreters, is developmentalist in nature, but the development it attributes to Plato is moderate rather than radical. I believe that the beginnings of Plato's theory of separately existing forms are to be found in Plato's earliest work, and may go back to the thought of the historical Socrates. It is rare in scholarship that one interpretation actually refutes its rivals, and I am certain that proponents of these rival views will find reasons to dispute my analysis. I can only say in anticipation of their response that I find the early theory of forms a more plausible reading of the text than its rivals.

NOTES

1. *Paradeigma*; Grube translates, 'model'.

2. Barnes has 'by'.

3. Fine also includes a discussion of the Socratic theory of forms in her (1993b). I considered this discussion in my (2013). I refer the reader to that essay for an account of that view.

CHAPTER FIVE

Socratic Ignorance

KEITH MCPARTLAND

I. INTRODUCTION

Socrates denies that he is wise. He denies that he has the kind of knowledge of virtue and the virtues that serves as the goal of his philosophical inquiries. Socrates takes this ignorance to matter. Without such knowledge he questions whether anyone counts as virtuous. When it comes to virtue, Socrates claims that the best of his fellow citizens stand to the person with knowledge as the shades in Hades stand to living human beings (*M.* 100a).

Socrates, however, is not a sceptic when it comes to first-order ethical claims. He expresses little uncertainty about how he ought to conduct his own life. He is completely confident that he must devote his life to his philosophical mission and that he must avoid vice at all costs. He regularly defends his own ethical views and attacks those of his opponents with carefully reasoned arguments, and clearly thinks that his positions fare better in these exchanges. Socrates also claims that he is able to avoid harmful actions by following the advice of an infallible divine voice. In short, Socrates takes himself to have true beliefs supported by evidence – at times stunningly strong evidence – that he takes to rule out alternatives to his own views. On at least a few occasions, Socrates is willing to ascribe ethical knowledge to himself, and on other occasions makes claims that are naturally taken to imply that he takes himself to have such knowledge.

Many commentators have been struck by a tension that results when Socrates' disavowals of knowledge are read alongside his claims to know various things. While there has been widespread agreement that this tension *can* be resolved, there has been less agreement about exactly *how* this resolution is to be achieved.

One way to dissolve the tension, forcefully presented in Wolfsdorf (2004a), reminds us to keep in mind that Plato's Socrates is a literary character in a number of different dialogues. Rather than treating Socrates as a philosopher in his own right whose views we find by examining a number of statements in the so-called 'early dialogues', we need to look at the point that Plato is trying to make in each particular work by having a character named 'Socrates' make certain utterances. Once we keep in mind the fact that Plato can have a consistent philosophical position without this character's utterances across different works being consistent, there is no mystery presented by Socrates' inconsistent utterances.

Another sort of solution, endorsed by Kraut (1984), is developmentalist. The tension results from the fact that Plato's Socrates changes his mind about whether knowledge of the essential nature of virtue is required for all ethical knowledge. The passages in which Socrates claims to have ethical knowledge are from earlier dialogues in which Plato (and

Socrates) are not yet committed to the claim that definitional knowledge is required for all ethical knowledge. However, in later early dialogues, Socrates accepts a principle of definitional knowledge according to which all knowledge requires knowledge of definitions.

There is no doubt a good deal that can be said for and against each of these attempts to resolve the problem of Socratic ignorance. I will, however, say very little about either sort of solution in this chapter. Instead, I will make a few assumptions for the purposes of this chapter, which is an exercise in 'Socratic Studies' as understood and defended by Brickhouse and Smith (2010). I assume that there is a series of philosophical positions espoused by Socrates in a subset of Plato's dialogues, that these positions differ in critical ways from those that we find in other Platonic dialogues, and that there is some intellectual merit in the attempt to find a coherent and defensible interpretation of the Socratic position.

II. TWO QUESTIONS

When we ask whether Socrates takes himself to have any knowledge or wisdom, we should be careful to distinguish two questions. First, we might be asking whether Socrates takes himself to be in a state that he does or should use his own epistemic terminology to ascribe. This question is complicated by the fact that the English word 'know' and its cognates are plausible translations of several different Greek terms. In the *Apology* alone, Socrates uses the verbs *'epaiein'*, *'suneidenai'*, *'eidenai'*, *'epistasthai'* and *'gignōskein'*. It is typical to use these verbs to ascribe knowledge of a particular fact to someone. This use is nicely captured by the use of 'that'-clauses in English. We can think of such knowledge as involving a relation to a particular proposition or fact.

Socrates also talks about *epistēmē* (knowledge) and *sophia* (wisdom). When he denies that he is wise, he is talking about a state very closely related to possessing *epistēmē*. Being wise, however, is not simply a matter of being related to a single proposition. Socrates commonly thinks of being wise and possessing *epistēmē* in terms of the possession of a *technē* (art or craft), where this seems to be a matter of mastery over a whole field of enquiry or action. So we need to be careful about moving too quickly from Socrates' denial that he possesses *epistēmē* to the denial that he has any knowledge of particular facts.

In order to answer our first question, we need to look at two things. First, we need to look at how Socrates uses his epistemic vocabulary in talking about himself. Second, we need to look at Socrates' commitments given his other statements about the phenomena that he uses his epistemic vocabulary to talk about. When Socrates characterises wisdom (*sophia*) and knowledge (*epistēmē*), he indicates that he has in mind an extraordinarily high-grade cognitive achievement. The wise person or the person who has *epistēmē* grasps the definitional nature of the subjects she knows about, and possesses an explanatory account of the truths she believes concerning these subjects. The possession of *epistēmē* makes the wise person an expert, and endows her with sophisticated recognitional, inferential and practical capacities. A person with *epistēmē* concerning piety, for example, will never misclassify an impious action as pious or *vice versa*. Her decisions about how best to pursue piety will invariably be correct, and she will also be endowed with the ability to teach what she knows to others. Finally, wisdom yields a remarkable degree of doxastic stability. The wise person's beliefs are unshakeable and will survive any attempt at refutation. It is clear that Socrates does not take himself to meet these requirements for

SOCRATIC IGNORANCE

wisdom or expertise.[1] Furthermore, we will see that sometimes Socrates moves from his failure to possess wisdom or expertise to an unwillingness to credit himself with knowledge (i.e. the state that he uses his own epistemic vocabulary to describe) of various propositions.

We might, however, ask a second question. We can ask whether Socrates takes himself to be in a state that *we* would describe as knowing something. If we are asking whether Socrates has or commits himself to having what we would call 'knowledge', a lot depends on what we take knowledge to be. The requirements for knowledge, however, have always been controversial. People who disagree about what is needed for knowledge might also disagree about whether the states that Socrates takes himself to be in should count as knowledge. I do not know whether there is a proper analysis of knowledge and I certainly don't know what it is. When I talk about what *we* mean by 'knowledge', I intend some sort of *justified (or warranted) true belief* account of knowledge strengthened to deal with Gettier-style counterexamples (Gettier 1963). In what follows, I will sometimes refer to this as 'weak knowledge' or 'knowledge$_w$', and say that a person has weak knowledge when she has a true belief based on evidence sufficient for full rational commitment to what she believes. In addition, I allow for the possibility that Socrates can take himself to be in a state that counts as knowing$_w$ something, even if Socrates has no term or concept that represents knowledge$_w$. The question that I am interested in is the question of whether Socrates has a certain tacit or explicit *de re* belief. Does Socrates ever take himself to be in a state or condition that he would count as believing something true on the basis of evidence sufficient for full rational commitment? With respect to this second question, I will argue that Socrates does sometimes take himself to be in such a state. Furthermore, in cases where Socrates does claim that he possesses ethical knowledge, it is likely that he has something like knowledge$_w$ in mind, rather than the kind of knowledge possible only for the completely wise person whose knowledge proceeds from a comprehensive grasp of ethical natures.

III. SOCRATES' DISAVOWALS

I turn now to some texts in which Socrates claims that he lacks wisdom and knowledge. I begin by examining evidence from the *Apology* in which Socrates' disavowal of wisdom plays a particularly central role. Afterwards, I turn to some other Socratic texts.

III.I Disavowal in the Apology

In the course of his defence in the *Apology*, Socrates' disavowals of knowledge and wisdom are at times quite sweeping. He claims at the outset of his defence that he has been wrongly thought of as a natural philosopher, and recounts the charge against him as follows.

> (AP1) It goes something like this: Socrates is guilty of wrongdoing in that he busies himself studying things in the sky and below the earth; he makes the worse into the stronger argument, and he teaches these same things to others. You have seen this yourself in the comedy of Aristophanes, a Socrates swinging about there, saying he was walking on air and talking a lot of other nonsense about things of which I know (*epaiein*) nothing at all. I do not speak in contempt of such knowledge (*epistēmē*), if someone is wise (*sophos*) in these things – lest Meletus bring more cases against me – but, gentlemen, I have no part in it, and on this point I call upon the majority of you as witnesses.
>
> – *Ap.* 19b–c[2]

88   THE BLOOMSBURY HANDBOOK OF SOCRATES

Socrates also claims that he has been incorrectly lumped in with sophists such as Gorgias, Hippias, Prodicus and Evenus who claim to be able to teach young people to be virtuous. These people pride themselves in possessing knowledge (*epistēmē*) or a craft (*technē*) of how to make young people excellent or virtuous (*aretē*). As Socrates notes about Evenus:

> (AP2) I thought Evenus a happy man, if he really possesses this art (*technē*), and teaches for so moderate a fee. Certainly I would pride and preen myself if I knew (*epistasthai*) these things, but I do not know (*epistasthai*) them, gentlemen.

> – *Ap.* 20b–c

While Socrates claims that his reputation as a teacher of virtue is misleading and undeserved, he nevertheless claims that the source of this reputation is his possession of a kind of wisdom.

> (AP3) What has caused my reputation is none other than a certain kind of wisdom (*sophia*). What kind of wisdom? Human wisdom (*anthrōpinē sophia*), perhaps. It may be that I really possess this, while those whom I mentioned just now are wise with a wisdom more than human; else I cannot explain it, for I certainly do not possess it, and whoever says I do is lying and speaks to slander me.

> – *Ap.* 20d–e

We should note the tight connection between greater than human wisdom (*sophia*) and knowledge (*epistēmē*) suggested in (A1)–(A3). It is precisely because Socrates thinks that he lacks certain kinds of knowledge (*epistēmē*) that he denies the possession of any wisdom beyond human wisdom. He allows that others could have the knowledge of natural philosophy that he lacks, and allows that Evenus might possess a greater than human wisdom, provided the latter really does have the sort of knowledge that he claims to have. We end up with a tight connection between certain kinds of knowledge and having higher grade wisdom: The wise person will possess knowledge, and the person who possesses (at least some kinds) of knowledge will count as wise.

Socrates goes on to explain what he means in claiming to possess human wisdom while denying any wisdom beyond human. He begins by alluding to a striking pronouncement that the oracle of Delphi once made to his friend Chaerephon.

> (AP4) He went to Delphi at one time and ventured to ask the oracle – as I say, gentlemen, do not create a disturbance – he asked if any man was wiser than I, and the Pythian replied that no one was wiser.

> – *Ap.* 21a

Socrates claims to have been shocked by the oracle's reply.

> (AP5) When I heard of this reply I asked myself: 'Whatever does the god mean? What is his riddle? I am very conscious that I am not wise at all; what then does he mean by saying that I am the wisest? For surely he does not lie; it is not legitimate for him to do so.'

> – *Ap.* 21b

Notice that in (AP4) the Pythia claims only that no one is wiser than Socrates, which strictly speaking does not imply that Socrates is wise. Socrates, however, takes the god to have said through the Pythia that he is the wisest of men. Socrates' disavowal of wisdom in (AP5) is very general. In Grube's translation, Socrates says, 'I am very conscious

SOCRATIC IGNORANCE

89

(*suneidenai*) that I am not wise at all.' An alternative translation of this sentence would be, 'I know (*suneidenai*) myself to be wise (*sophos*) concerning neither great nor small things.'[3]

In response to the oracle's statement and his own puzzlement about it, Socrates begins to examine various people reputed to be wise. In each case where Socrates examines a person with a reputation for wisdom, he soon learns that the person is not wise at all. Socrates reports his reaction after one such examination.

> (AP6) So I withdrew and thought to myself: 'I am wiser (*sophoteron*) than this man; it is likely that neither of us knows (*eidenai*) anything worthwhile, but he thinks he knows something when he does not, whereas when I do not know, neither do I think I know; so I am likely to be wiser than he to this small extent, that I do not think I know what I do not know.'
>
> *– Ap.* 21d

What Socrates disavows in (AP6) is that he knows (*eidenai*) anything '*kalon kagathon*'. The phrase '*kalon kagathon*', translated by Grube as 'worthwhile', is a conjunction of two terms: '*kalos*', meaning beautiful, noble or fine, and '*agathos*', meaning good. This conjunction can be used as an idiomatic formula to describe anything taken to be valuable by the speaker, and Grube's 'worthwhile' captures this use of the phrase nicely. Socrates' disavowal of knowledge seems to have a very wide scope on this construal of '*kalon kagathon*'. Any knowledge that Socrates allows himself on this reading is knowledge of something trivial or worthless.

I incline, however, toward a somewhat more inflationary reading of the phrase. The elenctic investigations on the basis of which Socrates comes to believe that a person lacks knowledge focus on centrally important subjects in ethics, and the people he investigates are shown not to know what virtue or a particular virtue is. In addition, knowing something *kalon kagathon* seems both necessary and sufficient for possessing greater than human wisdom. Even the craftspeople, whom Socrates grants a sort of wisdom, apparently do not count as knowing anything *kalon kagathon*.

From his continued examination of the politicians, poets and craftsmen in Athens, Socrates claims that he came to the conclusion that those with the greatest reputation were most lacking in wisdom, while those thought to be inferior were actually superior in wisdom (*phronēsis*). Unlike the poets who create without wisdom, and the politicians who don't have any knowledge on which they base their political practice, Socrates takes craftsmen to have knowledge and to possess a kind of wisdom. The craftsmen, however, go wrong when they think themselves wise in matters that go beyond their crafts.

> (AP7) Finally I went to the craftsmen, for I was conscious (*suneidenai*) of knowing (*epistasthai*) practically nothing, and I knew (*eidenai*) that I would find that they had knowledge (*epistasthai*) of many fine (*kala*) things. In this I was not mistaken; they knew (*epistasthai*) things I did not know (*epistasthai*), and to that extent they were wiser (*sophōteron*) than I. But, men of Athens, the good craftsmen seemed to me to have the same fault as the poets: each of them, because of his success at his craft (*technē*), thought himself very wise (*sophōtatos*) in other most important pursuits, and this error of theirs overshadowed the wisdom they had, so that I asked myself, on behalf of the oracle, whether I should prefer to be as I am, with neither their wisdom (*sophia*) nor their ignorance (*amathia*), or to have both. The answer I gave myself and the oracle was that it was to my advantage to be as I am.
>
> *– Ap.* 22c–e

Socrates' disavowal of knowledge in (AP7) seems to have a somewhat narrower scope than his disavowal in (AP5), and he here claims that he is conscious or knows (*suneidenai*) that he knows (*epistasthai*) practically nothing, or 'nothing so to speak' (*ouden hōs epos eipein*). We again see a tight connection between knowledge (*epistēmē*) and wisdom (*sophia*). Possessing certain kinds of knowledge suffices for wisdom, and because Socrates allows that the craftsmen have knowledge of many fine or noble (*kala*) things he claims that they are wiser than he is. Furthermore, Socrates never retracts either the claim that the craftsmen have knowledge or the claim that this knowledge makes them wise *pro tanto*. What he claims instead is that the wisdom the craftsmen possess with respect to their crafts is overshadowed by the ignorance that they have with respect to other greater matters.

The word translated as 'ignorance' in (AP7) is '*amathia*'. However, we should distinguish ignorance as a mere lack of knowledge from *amathia*. The former might be a wholly passive state, while the latter involves active epistemic overreach. The *amathēs* person takes himself to know what he does not really know. Because of his own epistemic modesty, Socrates takes himself to be better off than the craftsmen despite the fact that they possess some knowledge that he does not.

Later in the dialogue, Socrates describes taking oneself to know what one does not know as the 'most blameworthy ignorance'. Once again, he suggests that his avoidance of this sort of *amathia* concerning what happens after death distinguishes Socrates from many of his contemporaries.

> (AP8) To fear death, gentlemen, is no other than to think oneself wise when one is not, to think one knows what one does not know. No one knows whether death may not be the greatest of all blessings for a man, yet men fear it as if they knew that it is the greatest of evils. And surely it is the most blameworthy ignorance to believe that one knows what one does not know. It is perhaps on this point and in this respect, gentlemen, that I differ from the majority of men, and if I were to claim that I am wiser than anyone in anything, it would be in this, that, as I have no adequate knowledge of things in the underworld, so I do not think I have.
>
> – *Ap.* 29a–b

In (AP8) Socrates claims that fear of death implies taking oneself to know (*eidenai*) that death is a great evil. Socrates claims that his superiority in wisdom is a result of his epistemic modesty about what happens after death. Once again, he is wiser because he does not think that he knows something that he does not know.

As a result of his failure to find anyone wiser than himself in Athens, Socrates comes to understand the oracle's statement to Chaerephon as a claim about the worthlessness of human wisdom.

> (AP9) What is probable, gentlemen, is that in fact the god is wise and that his oracular response meant that human wisdom (*anthrōpinē sophia*) is worth little or nothing, and that when he says this man, Socrates, he is using my name as an example, as if he said: 'This man among you, mortals, is wisest who, like Socrates, understands (*gignōskein*) that his wisdom is worthless'.
>
> – *Ap.* 23a–b

In (AP9) Socrates comes back to the human wisdom (*anthrōpinē sophia*) he claimed to possess at 20d–e. He contrasts being wise in fact (*tōi onti*) with having human wisdom, and claims that the latter is worth little or nothing. He strengthens the claim at 23b2–4, an

SOCRATIC IGNORANCE

alternative translation of which might be, 'The one among you, human beings, is wisest who like Socrates knows (*gignōskein*) that he is in truth worth nothing with respect to wisdom.'

We have seen several texts in the *Apology* where Socrates disavows knowledge and wisdom. In some cases, these disavowals are quite sweeping. Socrates claims that he is wise with respect to neither great nor small matters, and claims to be worth nothing with respect to wisdom. He claims to have no knowledge of natural science, and to know (*eidenai*) nothing *kalon kagathon*. However, Socrates also claims that he possesses human wisdom and is wiser than the politicians, poets and craftsmen that he has examined. On a strong reading of 23b2–4, according to which the god is addressing all possible human beings, Socrates implies that his situation is pretty much as good as it gets for human beings when it comes to wisdom.

To avoid inconsistency, we need to distinguish the wisdom that Socrates thinks he has from the wisdom he thinks he lacks. We have already seen that Socrates takes the possession of wisdom with respect to something to be strongly connected to the possession of knowledge (*epistēmē*) about that thing. The wisdom that Socrates claims he lacks is the kind of greater-than-human wisdom about important matters that would involve knowing something *kalon kagathon*. This sort of wisdom would also make a person truly worth something with respect to wisdom. Neither Socrates nor anyone he has investigated turns out to have this kind of wisdom, which would involve a positive epistemic achievement that is perhaps possible only for a god.

Socrates' human wisdom, on the other hand, is primarily negative and consists in his not taking himself to know what he does not know. For example, he does not take himself to know what things are like in the underworld. Human wisdom is not *purely* negative. A dog does not think that it knows what things are like in the underworld, but does not possess human wisdom. The key difference between Socrates and the dog lies in the former's awareness that he lacks a certain kind of knowledge or wisdom. Socrates is able to represent his lack of knowledge to himself in a way that the dog does not. In fact, Socrates is willing to use the verb '*gignōskein*', which can be translated as 'to know', to talk about his own condition. The god claims that Socrates is the wisest person because he *knows* that he is, in truth, worthless with respect to wisdom. Charity demands that we take Socrates to think that knowing (*gignōskein*) that he is worthless with respect to wisdom is a possible state. Therefore, knowing (*gignōskein*) something should not imply that a person possesses genuine wisdom.

Socrates distinguishes the real wisdom of the god from human wisdom possession of which does not, in truth, make Socrates worth anything with respect to wisdom. Furthermore, at least in the *Apology*, Socrates takes himself to be wiser than others because of his recognition of his own limitations rather than because of a superiority in positive ethical knowledge. We will see that the story becomes more complicated when we turn to other passages below.

III.II Disavowals in Other Works

I turn now to some disavowals of knowledge in works other than the *Apology*. In these works, Socrates is concerned mainly to deny that he has knowledge concerning ethical subjects. We do not see Socrates spend time thinking about problems of natural philosophy, nor does he raise sceptical problems about the reliability of his senses, memory or other faculties. (For further discussion of the relation between Socrates and scepticism, see Benson 2000; Brickhouse and Smith 1994, 1996, 2000; Wolfsdorf 2004a.)

92   THE BLOOMSBURY HANDBOOK OF SOCRATES

We can distinguish three sorts of ethical knowledge that Socrates denies having. First, Socrates denies that he has definitional knowledge. He claims not to know what virtue itself is, and denies knowing the nature of particular virtues such as piety, courage, justice and moderation. He claims that he does not know the nature of the beautiful or fine, and that he does not know what a friend is. In each of these cases Socrates denies that he knows something that would count as *kalon kagathon*. Furthermore, his recognition that neither he nor his interlocutors possess definitional knowledge causes him to raise doubts about whether they possess any ethical knowledge at all, and leads to a second sort of disavowal of ethical knowledge. He worries that a person who does not know what some virtue is can know neither what features that virtue possesses nor whether or not that virtue properly characterises particular actions or sorts of actions. Finally, Socrates denies that he possesses knowledge of how to make people better. Just as he does in the *Apology*, Socrates denies that he has the sort of expertise that would qualify him as a teacher of virtue. It will be helpful to look a few examples of each sort of denial.

In the *Euthyphro*, Socrates offers to become Euthyphro's student in order to learn what piety is (*Eu.* 5a). He claims that receiving an account of the nature of piety will provide him with a model (*paradeigma*) that he will be able to look at in deciding whether various actions are pious or impious. At the close of the dialogue, Socrates complains that Euthyphro is departing without having taught him the nature of piety. While Socrates' interactions with Euthyphro are characterised by a good deal of irony, his claim not to know the nature of the pious and impious and to lack wisdom about the divine are just what we would expect given his claims in the *Apology*. Socrates further indicates that had he received a proper account of the pious from Euthyphro, he both would have become wise and would stop making errors due to his own lack of wisdom.

> (EU1) SOCRATES: What a thing to do, my friend! By going you have cast me down from a great hope I had, that I would learn from you the nature of the pious and the impious and so escape Meletus' indictment by showing him that I had acquired wisdom in divine matters from Euthyphro, and my ignorance would no longer cause me to be careless and inventive about such things, and that I would be better for the rest of my life.
>
> – *Eu.* 15e–16a

In the *Charmides*, Critias attempts to define *sōphrosunē* (temperance or self-control) in terms of the Delphic Oracle's command to know oneself. He tells Socrates that he will elaborate on this proposed definition, if Socrates does not agree that to be temperate is to know oneself. In response, Socrates claims that he cannot simply choose to agree with Critias, because he does not know what *sōphrosunē* is.

> (CH1) Socrates: 'But Critias,' I replied, 'you are talking to me as though I professed to know (*eidenai*) the answers to my own questions and as though I could agree with you if I really wished. This is not the case – rather, because of my own ignorance (*dia to mē autos eidenai*), I am continually investigating in your company whatever is put forward'.
>
> – *Chrm.* 165b–c

Socrates does not take himself to know the nature of *sōphrosunē* and to engage in elenchus simply to trip others up. Rather he is actively trying to figure out what *sōphrosunē* is. Furthermore, Socrates does not seek to refute his interlocutor merely out of competitive zeal.

SOCRATIC IGNORANCE

(CH2) 'Oh come', I said, 'how could you possibly think that even if I were to refute everything you say, I would be doing it for any other reasons than the one I would give for a thorough investigation of my own statements – the fear of unconsciously thinking I know (*eidenai*) something when I do not know it. And this is what I claim to be doing now, examining the argument for my own sake primarily, but perhaps also for the sake of my friends. Or don't you believe it to be for the common good, or for that of most men, that the state of each existing thing should become clear?'

– *Chrm.* 166c–d

Socrates claims that his primary purpose in refuting someone else is to avoid thinking that he knows something when he does not. Elenchus thus serves as a way to avoid the sort of blameworthy *amathia* that Socrates talks about in the *Apology*. In addition to preserving our epistemic modesty, however, Socrates implies that his investigations might serve a positive role in making clear how each thing is.

At the outset of the *Meno*, in response to Meno's question about whether virtue is teachable, Socrates denies that he knows what virtue is and suggests that failure to know what virtue is counts as an obstacle to knowing what sorts of features virtue possesses. Furthermore, Socrates claims that he has never met anyone who did know the nature of virtue.

(M1) Socrates: If then you want to ask one of us [Athenians] that sort of question [whether virtue is teachable], everyone will laugh and say: 'Good stranger, you must think me happy indeed if you think I know (*eidenai*) whether virtue can be taught or how it comes to be; I am so far from knowing whether virtue can be taught or not that I do not even have any knowledge (*eidenai*) of what virtue itself is'. I myself, Meno, am as poor as my fellow citizens in this matter, and I blame myself for not knowing (*eidenai*) at all about virtue. If I do not know (*eidenai*) what something is, how could I know (*eidenai*) what qualities it possesses?

– *M.* 71a–b

When Meno claims to have learned what virtue is from Gorgias, Socrates begins to question him about the nature of virtue. After being examined Meno claims that he used to know what virtue was but has now been led into perplexity by Socrates, who has the same effect as the numbing torpedo fish. In his response to Meno, Socrates again insists that he is equally perplexed about the nature of virtue.

(M2) Now if the torpedo fish is itself numb and so makes others numb, then I resemble it, but not otherwise, for I myself do not have the answer when I perplex others, but I am more perplexed than anyone when I cause perplexity in others. So now I do not know (*eidenai*) what virtue is; perhaps you knew before you contacted me, but now you are certainly like one who does not know.

– *M.* 80c–d

Socrates similarly denies that he knows what a friend is, what the beautiful is, and what justice is. The following passages occur at the end of the *Lysis*, the *Hippias Major* and Book I of the *Republic*:

(LY1) These people will go away saying that we are friends of one another – for I count myself in with you – but what a friend is we have not yet been able to discover.

– *Ly.* 223b

(HM1) But when I'm convinced by you and say what you say, that it's much the most excellent thing to be able to present a speech well and finely, and get things done in court or any other gathering, I hear every insult from that man (among others around here) who has always been refuting me. He happens to be a close relative of mine, and he lives in the same house. So when I go home to my own place and he hears me saying those things, he asks if I'm not ashamed that I dare discuss fine activities when I've been so plainly refuted about the fine, and it's clear I don't even know (*eidenai*) at all what *that* is itself! 'Look', he'll say. 'How will you know whose speech – or any other action – is finely presented or not, when you are ignorant of the fine? And when you're in a state like that, do you think it's any better for you to live than die?'

– *Hi. Ma.* 304c–d

(R1) Before finding the answer to our first inquiry about what justice is, I let that go and turned to investigate whether it is a kind of vice and ignorance or a kind of wisdom and virtue. Then an argument came up about injustice being more profitable than justice, and I couldn't refrain from abandoning the previous one and following up on that. Hence the result of the discussion, as far as I'm concerned, is that I know (*eidenai*) nothing, for when I don't know what justice is, I'll hardly know whether it is a kind of virtue or not, or whether a person who has it is happy or unhappy.

– *Rep.* I 354b–c

In each of these cases, Socrates makes a point of concluding his conversation with an interlocutor by insisting that he lacks definitional knowledge about the main topic of that conversation. Furthermore, Socrates takes his lack of definitional knowledge to undermine other claims to knowledge that he might make. Just as his failure to know what virtue is undermines any claim to know whether virtue is teachable (M1), his failure to know what justice is undermines any claim to know whether the just person is happy (R1), and his failure to know what the fine is undermines any claim to know whether a particular speech or action is fine (H1).[4]

In the *Euthyphro* Socrates suggests that a definition of piety would allow a person to judge whether any given action is pious, and implicitly chastises Euthyphro for prosecuting his father in the absence of such knowledge.

(EU2) If you had no clear knowledge (*eidenai*) of piety and impiety you would never have ventured to prosecute your old father for murder on behalf of a servant. For fear of the gods you would have been afraid to take the risk lest you should not be acting rightly, and would have been ashamed before men, but now I know well that you believe you have clear knowledge of piety and impiety.

– *Eu.* 15d

Taken together, the foregoing passages suggest that Socrates takes the failure to have definitional knowledge to imply a failure to possess at least some other sorts of knowledge. Whether Socrates accepts a full-fledged version of the *Principle of Priority of Definitional Knowledge* (PD) is more controversial. I here follow Benson's formulation of the principle (Benson 2000: 112–113).

(PD) If A fails to know what F-ness is then A fails to know anything about F-ness.[5]

As Benson notes, we can distinguish two theses within (PD). The first concerns the dependence of particular knowledge on knowledge of definitions.

SOCRATIC IGNORANCE

(P) If A fails to know what F-ness is, then A fails to know, for any x, whether x is F.

The second principle involves the dependence of knowledge about the features of properties on definitional knowledge about those properties.

(D) If A fails to know what F-ness is, then A fails to know, for any G, whether F-ness is G.

The passages quoted above indicate that Socrates sometimes accepts something like (PD). In the absence of definitional knowledge concerning a property, Socrates is inclined to deny that he knows various facts about the distribution and features of that property. However, matters here are somewhat tricky. Socrates is sometimes willing to credit himself with some forms of knowledge even in the absence of definitional knowledge. In the *Meno*, for example, Socrates takes himself to know that knowledge differs from right opinion even while denying that he knows precisely how knowledge differs from right opinion.

> (M3) SOCRATES: . . . That is why knowledge (*epistēmē*) is prized higher than correct opinion, and knowledge differs from correct opinion in being tied down.
> MENO: Yes, by Zeus, Socrates, it seems to be something like that.
> SOCRATES: Indeed, I too speak as one who does not have knowledge (*hōs ouk eidōs legō*) but is guessing. However, I certainly do not think I am guessing that right opinion is a different thing from knowledge. If I claim to know *eidenai* anything else – and I would make that claim about few things – I would put this down as one of the things I know.
>
> – M. 98a–b

A completely universal application of (PD) to all of Socrates' uses of his own epistemic terminology would render what he says here inconsistent.[6] Furthermore, we will see below that Socrates sometimes makes other knowledge claims in cases where he takes himself to lack definitional knowledge. Before turning to these passages, however, it will be useful to look at a third sort of knowledge that Socrates disavows.

Socrates denies that he has knowledge of the art of making people better, and connects this ignorance to his ignorance about the nature of virtue and the individual virtues. We have already seen that Socrates denies having this sort of knowledge in the *Apology*, and he makes a similar denial in the *Laches* where he denies knowing or ever having learned the art of improving people's souls (*Laches* 186c). Because Socrates takes himself to be as ignorant as his interlocutors, he denies that he has any special ability to help them raise their sons.

> (LA1) LYSIMACHUS: . . . What do you say, Socrates? Will you comply with our request and take an active part with us in helping the young men to become as good as possible?
> SOCRATES: Well, it would be a terrible thing, Lysimachus, to be unwilling to join in assisting any man to become as good as possible. If in the conversations we have just had I had seemed to know (*eidenai*) and the other two not to know, then it would be right to issue a special invitation to me to perform this task; but as the matter stands, we were all in the same difficulty. Why then should anybody choose one of us in preference to another? What I think is that he ought to choose none of us. But as things are, see whether the suggestion I am about to make may not be a good one: what I say we ought to do, my friends – since this is just between ourselves – is to join in searching for the best possible teacher . . .
>
> – La. 200d–201a

96 THE BLOOMSBURY HANDBOOK OF SOCRATES

Socrates takes his inability to teach others to be virtuous to follow from his own lack of knowledge or wisdom. In the *Meno* as well, Socrates insists that the inability to teach others to be excellent shows that a person lacks knowledge or wisdom.

(M4) Socrates: So it is not by some kind of wisdom (*sophia*), or by being wise (*sophos*), that such men lead their cities, those such as Themistocles and those mentioned by Anytus just now? That is the reason why they cannot make others be like themselves, because it is not knowledge (*epistēmē*) which makes them what they are.

– M. 99b

(M5) Socrates: Therefore, if it is not through knowledge (*epistēmē*), the only alternative is that it is through right opinion that statesmen follow the right course for their cities. As regards knowledge, they are no different from soothsayers and prophets. They too say many true things when inspired, but they have no knowledge of what they are saying ... And so, Meno, is it right to call divine these men who, without any understanding, are right in much that is of importance in what they say and do?

– M. 99b–c

If there are people who truly possess virtue but are unable to teach others to be virtuous, then, Socrates concludes virtue cannot be knowledge. Nevertheless, Socrates holds that those who possess virtue without knowledge are markedly inferior to a virtuous person with the ability to teach others. Such a person would be 'as Tiresias among the dead' and would be a 'as a true reality compared with shadows' (M. 99e). Socrates counts himself among the inferior folk who are without understanding (*nous*) when it comes to virtue.

Since the inability to teach implies a lack of *epistēmē*, Socrates concludes that the successful statesmen of the past possessed correct or true opinion without knowledge. Correct opinion in any individual case will lead to the same sort of success as knowledge, but Socrates claims that knowledge has the advantage of being secured by an explanatory account.

(M6) For true opinions (*doxai alētheis*), as long as they remain, are a fine thing and all they do is good, but they are not willing to remain long, and they escape from a man's mind, so that they are not worth much until one ties them down by (giving) an account of the reason why (*aitias logismō*). And that, Meno, my friend, is recollection, as we previously agreed. After they are tied down, in the first place they become knowledge, and then they remain in place. That is why knowledge is prized higher than correct opinion, and knowledge differs from correct opinion in being tied down.

– M. 97e–98a

In order to possess knowledge that something is the case, a person needs to grasp an account of why it is the case, and finding this explanatory account will involve recollection. In the discussion of recollection earlier in the *Meno*, Socrates suggested that recollection was also the means by which a person could find the answer to the question of what virtue is. There is a strong suggestion, therefore, that what is needed for someone to have knowledge rather than true belief about what is virtuous is an account of the nature of virtue. In the absence of such definitional knowledge, the statesman with true beliefs cannot teach others to be virtuous. The person who possessed this sort of knowledge would be a person who knew something *kalon kagathon* and would count as having significant worth with respect to wisdom.

SOCRATIC IGNORANCE

We have seen that Socrates disavows three interrelated sorts of knowledge in the ethical sphere. He denies that he has definitional knowledge concerning ethical matters. Without definitional knowledge of the nature of virtue, Socrates fails to possess the explanatory account of virtue required for knowledge rather than true belief. In the absence of such explanatory definitional knowledge, Socrates worries that he lacks ethical knowledge altogether. Finally, Socrates denies he is in a position to teach others to be virtuous in the absence of definitional knowledge.

IV. SOCRATIC KNOWLEDGE

IV.I *Some Direct Avowals of Knowledge by Socrates*

Socrates' disavowals of knowledge and wisdom are widespread. Socrates consistently denies the kind of definitional knowledge that would allow him to answer questions about the nature of various virtues. Furthermore, he seems to doubt that other kinds of ethical knowledge are possible in the absence of definitional knowledge. Nevertheless, Socrates does sometimes claim to have knowledge about particular actions. Furthermore, for a person who takes himself to have no knowledge, Socrates exhibits a surprising degree of confidence in his beliefs. In this section, I begin by examining some of Socrates' direct avowals of knowledge. I then turn to some indirect evidence that Socrates takes himself to possess something that we could justifiably consider knowledge.

In the *Euthydemus*, Socrates claims that he knows many trivial things but that he fails to know other things.

> (ED1) Then come answer me this, he [Euthydemus] said: Is there anything you know (*epistasthai*)?
> Oh, yes, I [Socrates] said, many things, though trivial ones.
> That will serve the purpose, he said. Now do you suppose it possible for any existing thing not to be what it is?
> Heavens no, not I.
> And do you know something? he said.
> Yes, I do.
> Then you are knowing, if you really know?
> Of course, as far as concerns that particular thing.
> That doesn't matter, because mustn't you necessarily know everything, if you are knowing?
> How in heaven's name can that be, said I, when there are many other things I don't know?
>
> – *Euthd.* 293b–c

This discussion occurs immediately after Socrates raises some difficulties involved in discovering what sort of knowledge makes human beings happy (*Euthd.* 292e), after which Euthydemus attempts to show that it is impossible to know anything without knowing everything. For our purposes, what is important in this passage is the fact that Socrates readily admits that he knows some things. There is no suggestion, however, that Socrates takes himself to possess the sort of definitional knowledge mentioned in (PD).

In the *Euthyphro* as well, Socrates distinguishes questions that are easily settled from problematic ethical questions.

THE BLOOMSBURY HANDBOOK OF SOCRATES

(EU3) SOC: What are the subjects of difference that cause hatred and anger? Let us look at it this way. If you and I were to differ about numbers as to which is the greater, would this difference make us enemies and angry with each other, or would we proceed to count and soon resolve our difference about this?
EUTH: We would certainly do so.
SOC: Again, if we differed about the larger and the smaller, we would turn to measurement and soon cease to differ.
EUTH: That is so.
SOC: And about the heavier and the lighter, we would resort to weighing and be reconciled.
EUTH: Of course.

– Eu. 7b–c

(EU3) suggests that it is possible to settle ordinary empirical questions by observation and measurement. It is plausible to count the answers to these questions as among the many trivial things that Socrates claims that he knows in (ED1). These easily settled questions are contrasted with questions about the just and unjust, the beautiful and ugly, and the good and bad (*Euthyphro* 7c–d). Socrates draws a distinction between ethical knowledge and knowledge of the ordinary empirical features of things, and allows that the latter is fairly easy to acquire. Since Socrates' disavowals of knowledge mainly concern ethical matters, the kinds of knowledge that he implies he has in (EU3) and (ED1) need not worry us too much.

However, Socrates also claims to have some ethical knowledge. In the *Apology*, Socrates seeks to contrast his ignorance of what happens after death with his knowledge that it would be wrong for him to disobey the god. (AP8) quoted above is immediately followed by the below passage.[7]

(AP10) It is perhaps on this point and in this respect, gentlemen, that I differ from the majority of men, and if I were to claim that I am wiser than anyone in anything, it would be in this, that, as I have no adequate knowledge (*ouk eidōs hikanōs*) of things in the underworld, so I do not think I have. I do know (*eidenai*), however, that it is wicked and shameful to do wrong (*adikein*), to disobey one's superior, be he god or man. I shall never fear or avoid things of which I do not know whether they may not be good rather than things that I know to be bad.

– Ap. 29b

Socrates here claims to know that it is wicked and shameful to do wrong or to disobey his superior. He goes on to note that for him to abandon his philosophical mission would amount to such disobedience. What does Socrates mean when he talks about a superior? If Socrates means to indicate someone who has the right to give him an order, which is suggested by his example of obedience to a military commander at 28d–e, then he is claiming knowledge of a substantive and controversial moral fact. He is claiming to know that it is always wicked to disobey the command of someone who is in a legitimate position to issue that command. In the absence of definitional knowledge of wickedness, Socrates' knowledge claim is inconsistent with (PD).

However in talking about someone who is *beltiōn*, Socrates might mean to indicate a moral superior, in which case what he says here does not amount to a very substantive ethical claim. He claims simply that it would be vicious for him to disobey virtuous demands, which we might take to be a simple truism.[8] Even on this interpretation of

SOCRATIC IGNORANCE

'*beltiōn*', however, what Socrates says seems to be incompatible with a fully universal application of (PD). Even if the general claim that injustice and disobedience to a moral superior is vicious borders on tautologous, Socrates needs to apply this knowledge to particular situations. But this application seems to require the ability to recognise a moral superior, and (PD) seems to rule out this ability in the absence of definitional moral knowledge.

Later in the *Apology*, Socrates claims to know that imprisonment or exile would be bad, and that it would be irrational to choose these punishments in preference to death since he does not know whether death is good or bad.

> (AP11) I am convinced (*peithesthai*) that I never willingly wrong anyone, but I am not convincing you of this, for we have talked together but a short time. If it were the law with us, as it is elsewhere, that a trial for life should not last one but many days, you would be convinced, but now it is not easy to dispel great slanders in a short time. Since I am convinced that I wrong no one, I am not likely to wrong myself, to say that I deserve some evil and to make some such assessment against myself. What should I fear? That I should suffer the penalty Meletus has assessed against me, of which I say I do not know (*ouk eidenai*) whether it is good or bad? Am I then to choose in preference to this something that I know very well (*eu oida*) to be an evil and assess the penalty at that?
>
> – *Ap.* 37a–b

Socrates here makes another knowledge claim that is incompatible with (PD), on the assumption that he lacks definitional knowledge about badness. Furthermore, at two points in (AP11), Socrates claims to be convinced that he has never wronged, or at least never willingly wronged, anyone. He holds that given more time he could convince the jurors of this fact as well. Socrates seems to take his conviction that he has never willingly wronged anyone to be based on evidence and reasoned argument, and thinks that he could convince the jury by presenting his reasoning and evidence. Assume for a moment that Socrates has never willingly harmed everyone, and that his evidence is strong enough to convince others of this fact. On these assumptions, Socrates takes himself to have a true belief on the basis of evidence sufficient for conviction. Socrates, therefore, seems to take himself to satisfy the conditions for weak knowledge. We might claim, nevertheless, that Socrates takes himself to have a rationally grounded true belief that he has never willingly harmed anyone, but deny he takes himself to *know* that he has never done so.

Whatever we are inclined to say about (A11), however, Socrates makes an even stronger claim – that he *knows* that anyone who attempts to prosecute him will be a wicked person – in the *Gorgias*. When Callicles suggests that Socrates lives in danger of being brought to court and deprived of his property or life, Socrates acknowledges this possibility.

> (G1) SOCRATES: In that case I really am a fool, Callicles, if I don't suppose that anything might happen to anybody in this city. But I know this well (*eu oida*): that if I do come into court involved in one of those perils which you mention, the man who brings me in will be a wicked man – for no good man would bring in a man who is not a wrongdoer – and it wouldn't be at all strange if I were to be put to death.
>
> – *Grg.* 521c–d

In (G1) Socrates takes himself to know that anyone who attempts to prosecute him will be a wicked person. Furthermore, he claims to know this fact on the basis of an argument. The argument contains as one premise a general moral claim, that no good person prosecutes anyone who is not a wrongdoer. The argument also requires a particular claim, that Socrates has never wronged anyone. On the assumption that we cannot know the conclusion of an argument on the basis of that argument without also knowing the premises, Socrates takes himself to know that prosecution of innocent folks is wrong and that he is innocent. Once again, given his avowed lack of definitional knowledge, what Socrates commits himself to in (G1) cannot be made consistent with (PD). There is some textual evidence, therefore, that Socrates takes himself to have some ethical knowledge. From other things that Socrates says, I believe that there are also indirect arguments that he takes himself to be in a state or condition that counts as weak knowledge of ethical truths.

IV.II Indirect Arguments that Socrates takes Himself to Have Knowledge

We have seen a few passages in which Socrates directly claims to know an ethical truth, despite the fact that he does not think he has the kind of definitional knowledge and grasp of explanations that he requires for *epistēmē* in the *Meno*. Other things that Socrates says give us some indirect indication that he takes himself to possess true beliefs on the basis of a warrant sufficient for that belief. Socrates is willing to make various ethical assertions and expresses a good deal of confidence in his ethical beliefs. In fact, he is confident enough in his ethical beliefs to die in their defence. Clearly a person can have a high degree of confidence in a belief and can be willing to assert the content of these beliefs without having knowledge. Confidence and willingness to assert do not entail knowledge. However, I take the problem of Socratic ignorance to be a problem concerning the consistency of Socrates' commitments. While a person can assert and have confidence in things that she does not know, it is far from obvious that a person can consistently assert and confidently believe things that she does not take herself to know, or, worse, things that she takes herself not to know. In being fully confident in his ethical beliefs, and in being willing to make unhedged moral assertions, I suggest that Socrates implies he takes himself to have weak knowledge.

The problems at issue here are related to views about assertion, belief and knowledge that can be traced back to G. E. Moore (1962: 277). *Moore's Paradox* is commonly stated in terms of belief:

(MPB) It is raining outside, but I do not believe that it is raining outside.

The proposition that is expressed by (MPB) is not contradictory. There are all sorts of things that are true about the world that I fail to believe. However, it is paradoxical for a person to utter an instance of (MPB). According to Moore, when I say, 'It is raining outside', I do not assert but I do imply that I believe it is raining outside. When I go on to say, 'I do not believe that it is raining outside', I contradict what I implied in the first clause of (MPB).[9] Moore (1962), along with many subsequent philosophers, finds the following sentence problematic as well:

(MPK) It is raining outside, but I do not know that it is raining outside.[10]

While I am inclined to hear any utterance of (MPB) as completely inapt, my reaction to (MPK) is somewhat more complicated. The complication is due to an unusual feature of the word 'know'. 'Know' is a perfectly ordinary English word frequently used in non-philosophical contexts. However, 'know' is also a technical term, the analysis of which has long been an object of dispute.

SOCRATIC IGNORANCE

101

With respect to everyday non-philosophical uses of 'know', I am strongly inclined to take an utterance of (MPK) to be inapt.[11] When a person denies that he knows it is raining outside, it is natural to take him to be less than fully committed to the claim that it is raining outside. However, when a person makes the unhedged assertion that is raining outside, it is natural to take him to be fully committed to the content of his assertion. When a person utters (MPK) the implications of the two clauses diverge, and inconsistency ensues.

However, when we consider (MPK) with a philosophical theory of knowledge in mind, our views about inaptness seem to depend on details about the theory of knowledge. For example, any utterance of (MPK1) strikes me as inapt:

(MPK1) It is raining but I do not have a true belief that it is raining based upon evidence sufficient to rule out alternatives to the claim that it is raining.

(MPK1) seems especially inapt in contexts where we are not considering various sorts of sceptical scenarios to be relevant alternative possibilities. Even in contexts where such scenarios are relevant, however, a person who thinks that he has failed to rule out the sceptical possibilities should refrain from the unhedged assertion that it is raining. Both being entitled to make an assertion and being sufficiently warranted in believing the content of that assertion might be context-sensitive. If so, however, they seem context-sensitive in the same way. In any context, a person should not take herself to be entitled to assert what she does not take herself to have sufficient warrant to believe.

On the other hand, consider:

(MPK2) It is raining, but I do not have an account of what rain is by reference to which I can give an account of the cause of the fact that it is raining.

(MPK2) does not seem inapt. There are plenty of situations in which we take a person to be entitled to make an assertion despite the fact that she is fully aware she lacks an explanatory account for the content of her assertion. A person who accepts (MPK2) as capturing the content of (MPK) has an extraordinarily demanding conception of knowledge. In general, as our philosophical account of knowledge becomes more demanding, we will tend to find an utterance of (MPK) less inapt.

It is important to recognise that Socrates often refrains from making unhedged assertions. In the ordinary case of elenchus, Socrates usually asks questions of an interlocutor rather than making assertions of his own. Sometimes what superficially seem to be assertions by Socrates are held up to an interlocutor for assent or dissent, and need not be taken to represent any commitment of Socrates. In other cases, what syntactically seems to be an assertion is really a matter of drawing out the logical consequences of other things that an interlocutor has said, and not a view that Socrates endorses. Finally, Socrates often hedges his assertions by using locutions like 'it seems' (*eikos*). In none of these cases does it seem right to take Socrates to make an unhedged assertion expressing his own commitment.

In some cases, however, Socrates does make unhedged assertions. Here are three examples taken from the *Apology*.

(AP12) You are wrong, sir, if you think that a man who is any good at all should take into account the risk of life or death; he should look to this only in his actions, whether what he does is right or wrong, whether he is acting like a good or a bad man.

– *Ap.* 28b

(AP13) This is the truth of the matter, men of Athens: wherever a man has taken a position that he believes to be best, or has been placed by his commander, there he must I think remain and face danger, without a thought for death or anything else, rather than disgrace.

– *Ap.* 28d

(AP14) Be sure (*eu iste*) that this is what the god orders me to do, and I think there is no greater blessing for the city than my service to the god. For I go around doing nothing but persuading both young and old among you not to care for your body or your wealth in preference to or as strongly as for the best possible state of your soul, as I say to you: 'Wealth does not bring about excellence, but excellence makes wealth and everything else good for men, both individually and collectively'.

– *Ap.* 30a–b[12]

In each of these cases it would be troubling for Socrates to claim that he lacks a true belief based on evidence sufficient to rule out the alternatives to what he asserts. Imagine Socrates making the following utterance:

(S1) Excellence makes wealth good, but I do not have evidence sufficient to rule out the possibility that it is not the case that excellence makes wealth good.

An utterance of (S1) would exhibit the problems that we see in other cases of Moore's Paradox. In asserting the first conjunct, Socrates recommends that his listener believe that excellence makes wealth good. In the second conjunct, Socrates undermines his entitlement to make this recommendation. If Socrates does not take himself to have a warrant to believe what he asserts that is strong enough to rule out alternatives, he should not make an unhedged assertion. Insofar as he thinks that his evidence leaves open the possibility of his being mistaken, Socrates ought to hedge his assertion somehow. Socrates' willingness to make these sorts of assertions is evidence, therefore, that he takes himself to have warrant for the corresponding beliefs strong enough to rule out contextually relevant alternatives. When Socrates makes an unhedged assertion, we should hold that he takes himself to have a sufficiently warranted true belief that what he asserts is the case. Insofar as we are inclined to think that having have a sufficiently warranted true belief is enough for knowledge, we should think that Socrates takes himself to be in a state that many of us would be willing to call 'knowledge'.

I suggested above that when Socrates talks about 'having been convinced' (*peithesthai*) in (AP11) he indicates that he comes to have some of the beliefs that he does on the basis of rational inquiry and argument. Socrates makes similar points in both the *Crito* and the *Gorgias*. At *Crito* 46b–c, Socrates claims that in deciding how to act he is always convinced (*peithesthai*) by the argument or reason (*logos*) that seems best to him on rational consideration (*logizesthai*). In the absence of a compelling counterargument, Socrates endorses and acts on what he rationally considers to be the best reasons.

In the *Gorgias* Socrates claims that the position he has been maintaining against Callicles – that it is better to suffer injustice than to commit it – is well supported by argument.

(G2) These conclusions, at which we arrived earlier in our previous discussions are, I'd say, held down and bound by arguments of iron and adamant, even if it's rather rude to say so. So it would seem, anyhow. And if you or someone more forceful than you won't undo them, then anyone who says anything other than what I'm now saying

SOCRATIC IGNORANCE

cannot be speaking well. And yet for my part, my account is ever the same: I don't know how these things are, but no one I've ever met, as in this case, can say anything else without being ridiculous. So once more I set it down that these things are so.

– *Grg.* 508e–509b

Socrates' initial claim in (G2) is particularly emphatic. His belief is tied down by arguments of iron and adamant, and no one has been able to maintain the opposite without being made to look foolish. Socrates expresses no doubt that he has sufficient warrant for his belief, and takes all the reasons he considers to support his belief. Insofar as we are willing to count true beliefs with ironbound reasons as knowledge, it seems that Socrates takes himself to be in a state that we would count as knowledge. However, in the midst of this very passage, Socrates states that he does not *know how these things are* (*egō tauta ouk oida hopōs echei*), despite the fact that he takes himself to have such strong warrant for his belief. (G2) is an absolutely essential passage in thinking through the problem of Socratic ignorance, and we will see below how various commentators treat the passage. For now, however, it is important simply to note that Socrates uses his own knowledge terminology in such a way that he does not seem to take the following statement to be inapt:

(S2) It is better to suffer injustice than to commit injustice, but I do not know how these things are.

I have argued, however, that the following statement would be inapt:

(S3) It is better to suffer injustice than to commit injustice, but I do not have evidence sufficient to rule out the possibility that committing injustice is better than suffering it.

It follows that whenever Socrates claims not to know how things are, he is not denying that he has a true belief based on evidence that warrants full commitment to his belief that suffering injustice is better than committing it.

It can also be instructive to look at the beliefs that Socrates has on the basis of testimony from his *daimonion*. Socrates claims initially that he does not fear death because he does not know sufficiently what things are like in the underworld, or take himself to know what things are like in the underworld. Later, however, Socrates comments on the fact that his mantic sign did not warn him not to act in a way that would bring about his death. On the basis of his belief that his *daimonion* always warns him to avoid what is bad, Socrates concludes that death is not something bad.

(AP15) At all previous times my familiar prophetic power, my spiritual manifestation, frequently opposed me, even in small matters, when I was about to do something wrong, but now that, as you can see for yourselves, I was faced with what one might think, and what is generally thought to be, the worst of evils, my divine sign has not opposed me, either when I left home at dawn, or when I came into court, or at any time that I was about to say something during my speech. Yet in other talks it often held me back in the middle of my speaking, but now it has opposed no word or deed of mine. What do I think is the reason for this? I will tell you. What has happened to me may well be a good thing, and those of us who believe death to be an evil are certainly mistaken. I have convincing proof (*mega tekmērion*) of this, for it is impossible that my familiar sign did not oppose me if I was not about to do what was right.

– *Ap.* 40a–c

In (AP15) Socrates claims that he has a great proof or a sure sign (*mega tekmērion*) that death is not an evil, and claims that it would not be possible for his sign to fail to oppose his actions unless he was about to do the right thing. Socrates' claim would be inappropriate if he took his evidence to leave open the possibility that death was something evil. So he takes himself to have a true belief based on evidence that rules out alternatives to that belief. Socrates, therefore, takes himself to be in a condition that is plausibly taken to count as weak knowledge that facing death is better than abandoning his philosophical mission.

My claim here should be taken as a conditionalised *de re* claim. Socrates takes himself, at least tacitly, to be in a state that *would* count as an instance of knowledge were his belief true and were he to have the reasons he takes himself to have. Assume that Socrates' belief that giving up his philosophical mission would be worse than death is true. Socrates has this belief in part on the basis of his belief that he has received divine testimony. Even if we do not grant that Socrates is receiving divine testimony and do not think that he can have knowledge on the basis of his evidence, we should be willing to grant that divine testimony would count as very good evidence for a belief.

Imagine Socrates making the following utterance:

(S4) Death is not something bad, but I do not have definitional knowledge of the nature of death and badness in terms of which I can explain why death is not bad.

(S4) is not an instance of Moore's Paradox. Socrates could be entitled to assert the first conjunct even in the absence of definitional knowledge of badness. Similarly, Socrates can have a warrant sufficient to assert that death is something good on the basis of divine testimony without knowing precisely what happens after death. While Socrates' confidence in his assertions suggests that he takes himself to be in a state that is plausibly considered weak knowledge, this confidence does not imply that Socrates has the explanatory account and definitional knowledge that characterises the knowledge and wisdom he claims he lacks. Furthermore, (G2) gives us strong evidence that Socrates sometimes uses his knowledge words to indicate something that goes beyond true belief based on a sufficient warrant.

Socrates' discussion of death in the *Apology* provides further indirect evidence that he takes himself to have some kind of knowledge. In (AP8) Socrates claims, 'To fear death, gentlemen, is no other than to think oneself wise when one is not, to think one knows what one does not know.' On the face of it, this claim is extremely problematic. People often fear things without taking themselves to have knowledge about precisely what those things are like. In fact, uncertainty about what happens after death seems to be part of the reason people are afraid of death. Socrates' intellectualist moral psychology can go some way toward explaining his claim about fear and knowledge. In what follows, I will assume without argument that Socrates takes a person's desiring that P to entail that she believes that P is good, and that he takes a person's believing that P is good to entail that she believes that P conduces to her happiness. (For more complete discussions of Socratic moral psychology, see Brickhouse and Smith 2010, as well as Chapter 9 in this volume.)

Parity of reasoning about aversion can get us to the claim that aversion is tightly connected to the belief that something is bad and contrary to one's happiness. Since fear is one sort of aversive psychological state, if a person fears something she believes that thing to be contrary to her happiness.

All that Socrates is entitled to so far, however, is the claim that the person who fears death *believes* that death will detract from her happiness. However, he claims that the

SOCRATIC IGNORANCE

person who fears death takes herself to be *wise* and to *know* that what follows death will be something bad. Unless Socrates thinks that there is something special going on in the case of death, he is committed to claiming that whenever a person fears anything, she takes herself to know that what she fears is something bad. Similarly, whenever somebody desires anything, she takes herself to know that the thing is question is something good. Since Socrates has various aversions and desires, he will be committed to the claim that he takes himself to know that various things are good or bad.

What sort of knowledge must someone take himself to have when he fears or desires something? Here is a sketch of how we might try to make Socrates' claim about fear and knowledge somewhat more plausible. According to the intellectualist, fear and desire follow belief. What we need is a way to get taking oneself to know something to follow from believing that it is the case. Perhaps Socrates can claim that belief is essentially an attitude that is responsive to what a person takes to be her evidence. In ordinary circumstances, a rational person who believes that something is bad rather than good will take herself to have evidence that is strong enough to commit to the claim that the thing in question is bad rather than good. If she takes her evidence to be insufficient to rule out the possibility that the thing in question is good or neutral, then she will not (and ought not) fully commit to the belief that the thing in question is bad. If fear requires fully committal belief, then the rational person who does not take herself to have sufficient evidence in favour of the claim that something is bad will not fear that thing. It follows that the person who does fear something takes herself to have a true and sufficiently warranted belief that the thing in question is bad.

This argument assumes, perhaps implausibly, that Socrates holds that it is not possible for a rational person to form and maintain beliefs other than as a response to what she counts as evidence. Notice that Socrates can still maintain that a person might count something as evidence when she is afraid that she would not count it as evidence upon sufficient reflection. On the view that I am suggesting, Socrates will hold that once a person realises she lacks good evidence for believing that something is bad, she will stop having the belief and as a result will stop being afraid. On this line of reasoning, Socrates might maintain the position that fear entails taking oneself to have knowledge in the sense of thinking that she has a sufficiently warranted true belief. Socrates' claim about fear and knowledge could be taken as a claim that a person who fears death takes herself to have weak knowledge that death is something bad. Socrates, on the other hand, takes himself to have weak knowledge on the basis of divine testimony that death is not bad, and that his death may turn out to be a good thing for him.

V. RESTATEMENT OF THE PROBLEM OF SOCRATIC IGNORANCE AND A SURVEY OF PROPOSED SOLUTIONS

V.I Restatement

We have seen a number of passages in which Socrates denies that he possesses wisdom. The strongest disavowals are extremely wide-ranging. I have reviewed evidence that seems to suggest each of the following claims.

(1) Socrates believes that he is not wise with respect to any subject matter.

Socrates takes his lack of wisdom to be equivalent to his failure to know (*eidenai*) anything *kalon kagathon*, and claims that he knows (*epistasthai*) practically nothing. It is tempting, on the basis of passages in the *Apology*, to attribute to Socrates the belief that knowing anything implies being wise with respect to some subject matter.

(2) Socrates believes that any person who knows anything possesses wisdom with respect to some subject matter.

However, as we saw in passage (ED1) above, Socrates is willing to claim that he knows (*episthasthai*) many trivial things. What Socrates is most concerned to deny is knowledge or wisdom concerning ethical subjects. Restricting (1) and (2) to ethical subjects, and working with a very minimal notion of proposition, we get the following:

(3) Socrates believes that he is not wise with respect to any ethical subject matter.
(4) Socrates believes that anyone who possesses knowledge of an ethical proposition is wise with respect to some ethical subject matter.

On the assumption that Socrates believes, at least in this case, the obvious logical consequences of what he believes, we get:

(5) Socrates believes that there are not any ethical propositions that he knows.
However, we have seen a number of cases in which Socrates claims or implies that he does take himself to have some ethical knowledge.
(6) Socrates believes that there are some ethical propositions that he knows.

The problem of Socratic ignorance stems from the fact that, at least on the face of things, (5) and (6) commit Socrates to inconsistent beliefs. I am assuming that a resolution of the problem should show that Socrates does not have inconsistent beliefs. An acceptable resolution, therefore, must deny (5), deny (6), or show that, despite initial appearances, (5) and (6) can be true without committing Socrates to inconsistent beliefs. Furthermore, in order to deny (5), a solution must deny either (3) or (4).

So, there are four basic strategies for resolving the problem of Socratic ignorance, as well as strategies that combine two or more of these basic strategies. We can deny (3), and hold that Socrates does take himself to be wise. We can deny (4), and hold that Socrates allows for the possibility of some ethical knowledge without wisdom. We can deny (6), and hold that Socrates does not take himself to have any ethical knowledge. Finally, we can claim that 'know' does not occur univocally in (5) and (6), in which case we need to distinguish what Socrates believes he lacks in (5) from what he believes he possesses in (6).

VI.II *Solutions that Deny (6)*

Perhaps Socrates really takes himself to lack knowledge of any ethical proposition. There are not many texts in which Socrates directly claims to know any ethical proposition. If (6) causes us to attribute contradictory beliefs to Socrates, and we have only a few texts in favour of (6), it might be best to claim that those texts are outliers or that despite appearances Socrates does not really claim to have knowledge in those texts. Terence Irwin, for example, claims that Socrates does not take himself to have knowledge (Irwin 1979, 1995). Rather Socrates thinks that he has stable and rationally defensible moral convictions that are practically reliable and which merit great confidence. Irwin is a *constructivist* and takes Socrates' justification for his beliefs to arise, at least in part, from his elenctic practice. However, because Socrates holds (PD), he has the further belief that his moral convictions do not count as knowledge (Irwin 1995: 29). As Wolfsdorf (2004a) points out, Irwin must hold that Socrates sometimes uses knowledge words not to ascribe

SOCRATIC IGNORANCE

knowledge to himself, but to ascribe to himself a different state (Wolfsdorf 2004a: 114). Just as Socrates distinguishes the human wisdom that he possesses from the true wisdom that he lacks, Irwin holds that Socrates distinguishes his elenctically justified ethical beliefs from true knowledge.

Hugh Benson similarly claims that when Socrates uses knowledge words to describe his own condition, he does not mean to claim that he possesses knowledge in the strict philosophical sense treated in the early dialogues. Rather, Socrates is speaking with the vulgar when he ascribes knowledge to himself (Benson 2000: 236). Unlike Irwin, Benson is a *nonconstructivist* and denies that Socrates uses the elenchus to establish or justify any positive position (Benson 1995, 2000: ch. 2–3). Like Irwin, however, Benson grants that Socrates takes himself to have some rational basis for the things that, speaking with the vulgar, he claims to know. Socrates' commitment to (PD), however, rules out his taking himself to have knowledge. What Socrates lacks, and takes to be necessary for ethical knowledge, is a systematic understanding of ethical phenomena and their connections to one another, in virtue of which he can provide explanatory accounts for the contents of his true ethical beliefs, and in virtue of which he can provide proper answers to definitional questions (Benson 2000: 205–215).

I argued above that Socrates' confidence in his beliefs and his willingness to make unhedged assertions should count as evidence that he takes himself to have sufficiently warranted true beliefs. I also suggested that someone in this state is typically counted to have at least weak knowledge. However, it is clear that a person could take herself to have a sufficiently warranted true belief without taking herself to have the sort of definitional knowledge and systematic understanding that Benson or Irwin take to be necessary for Socratic knowledge. It is crucial to notice that the kind of systematic understanding that is necessary for ethical knowledge on this account goes well beyond the possession of a sufficient warrant for a single ethical belief, and requires a wide-ranging grasp of ethics as a whole. The sort of justification needed to have wisdom or to have *epistēmē* concerning a proposition will require a large system of beliefs that cohere with and mutually support one another. For more on the holistic or coherentist aspects of Socratic and Platonic epistemology, see Benson 2000 and Fine 1979, 2003. Benson is even willing to grant that there might be some lower-level epistemic state or power that Socrates sometimes uses his knowledge words to ascribe to himself or others, but he emphasises that Socrates nowhere sets out to give a detailed account of this low-level knowledge (Benson 2000: 236–238).

As we will see below, interpretations that attempt to resolve the problem of Socratic ignorance by holding that there are different senses of 'know' involved in (5) and (6) rely on a distinction between two sorts of knowledge that is quite similar to the distinction that Irwin and Benson want to draw between rationally supported true belief and knowledge. In some ways, I suspect that the disagreement between solutions that deny (6) and solutions that posit an ambiguity in the use of 'know' in (5) and (6) will turn out to be more terminological than substantial. There is widespread agreement that Socrates takes himself to lack definitional knowledge and a grasp of explanatory accounts, and that he takes these to be of paramount importance in many of his discussions of knowledge. There is also agreement that Socrates takes himself to have reached the bar for a lower-level cognitive achievement, and that he thinks his having done so does not constitute possession of the wisdom that he denies having. There is disagreement about whether Socrates does or should take this lower-level achievement to count as knowledge.

With this in mind, I turn to solutions that deny (5) and solutions holding that 'know' is used equivocally in (5) and (6).

V.III. *Solutions that Deny (3)*

One way to deny (5) is by denying (3). While Socrates claims that he lacks wisdom and knowledge, Socrates in notoriously ironic. (For some interpretations denying that Socrates is sincere in his disavowals of knowledge, see Gulley 1968: 69ff; Teloh 1981: 61–64, 1986: 30–32; Versenyi 1963: 120–124, 1982: 31–32). In Book I of the *Republic*, for example, Thrasymachus responds to Socrates' denial that he knows what justice is by claiming that Socrates is using his customary irony (*hē eiōthumia eirōneia*) to avoid having to answer the questions of others. The word '*eirōneia*' in Greek has the connotation of deception or pretence. According to Thrasymachus, Socrates is so averse to answering questions posed by others that he pretends to be ignorant when he does not really take himself to be ignorant

Aristotle discusses irony in the course of his own discussion of the virtue of truthfulness, and points to Socrates as an example.

> Ironic people (*hoi eirōnes*) appear more elegant in character by underestimating themselves in what they say. They do not speak to gain profit but to avoid bombast. They especially deny what is esteemed as, for example, Socrates used to do.
>
> – *Nicomachean Ethics* 1127b22–26

The ironic person is given to self-deprecation. When she really takes herself to have the admirable qualities that she denies having she fails to be completely truthful. Furthermore, she runs the risk of falling into the vice of false-modesty. If Socrates really does think that he has the knowledge he denies having, then Thrasymachus' charge is a just one.

If Socrates is practicing false-modesty and merely pretending to be ignorant, why is he doing so? Socrates might feign ignorance for pedagogical purposes, because he thinks that his interlocutor will best learn the truth by working things out for himself. When Socrates questions the slave in the *Meno*, we see this sort of pedagogy in action. By asking the slave questions and showing where his answers lead to absurdity, Socrates is able to lead him toward an understanding of how to double the square.

Notice, however, that Socrates' conversations about ethical matters are unlike his conversation with the slave in important respects. Socrates does not succeed in leading his interlocutors to a positive grasp of ethical truths that he claims to know. At best, Socrates gets his interlocutors to realise that they do not have the knowledge they claimed to have. In many cases, Socrates does not even succeed in getting the interlocutor to recognise his own ignorance. We can understand the difference between what happens with the slave and what happens with the ethical interlocutors, on the assumption that Socrates' claims to be ignorant are sincere.

Socrates presumably does understand how to double a square, and this understanding guides him in his questioning of the slave. Since Socrates knows where he wants the slave to end up, he is able to craft his questions to lead him to the right conclusion. If Socrates really does possess the ethical knowledge that he denies possessing, he should be able to lead an interlocutor to a conclusion that Socrates would be willing to claim he knows. But we don't see him lead his ethical interlocutors to such conclusions. A plausible explanation for this failure is that Socrates really does take himself to lack the knowledge he says he lacks. If Socrates' ignorance is a pretence for pedagogical purposes, it is surprising that we do not see him succeed in bringing his interlocutor to a conclusion that Socrates is willing to assert he knows to be true.

SOCRATIC IGNORANCE

Socrates' disavowals of knowledge are so frequent and so insistent, that I find it hard to think they are merely pretence. This does not mean, however, that Socrates is completely innocent of false-modesty. In *Euthyphro*, *Meno* and *Republic* I, Socrates does not merely claim that he lacks knowledge. He also rather elaborately suggests that his interlocutors might be wiser than he is. When he claims that he hopes to learn important ethical truths from Euthyphro or Thrasymachus, it seems obvious that Socrates is not being completely sincere. However, this comparative false modesty is compatible with Socrates being sincere when he denies that he possesses any genuine wisdom. If Socrates is sincere, then (3) is true and we need to look elsewhere for a solution to the problem of Socratic ignorance.

V.IV Ambiguity Solutions and Solutions Denying (4)

In this section, I discuss a number of solutions that deny (4). There are two sorts of solutions that we should consider. First, we could take Socrates to use his knowledge terms univocally and take him to deny (4) outright. According to this sort of solution, we need to be careful about the scope of Socrates' disavowals of ethical knowledge and wisdom. Socrates denies that he knows general or fundamental truths about ethical matters, but still takes himself to know many ordinary and particular ethical truths. To deny (4), this sort of solution must deny (PD), especially (P). A second sort of solution holds that Socrates uses his knowledge terms equivocally. He denies that he possesses a high-grade epistemic state that involves certainty, expertise or systematic explanatory understanding, but does think that he has knowledge of another sort. Furthermore, on this sort of view, (PD) is generally taken to govern the higher-grade but not the lower-grade kind of knowledge.

The most natural place to begin a discussion of these sorts of solutions to the problem of Socratic ignorance is with Gregory Vlastos' paper 'Socrates' Disavowal of Knowledge' (Vlastos 1994b). Vlastos presents his solution as an attempt to avoid both Irwin's denial that Socrates takes himself to have any knowledge (Irwin 1977) and Gulley's claim that Socrates' disavowals of knowledge are merely ironic (Gulley 1968: 62–73). Vlastos proposes to solve the problem of Socratic ignorance by distinguishing a weak form of knowledge, which he calls 'elenctic knowledge' or 'knowledge$_E$' from a stronger form of knowledge requiring certainty, 'knowledge$_C$'. According to Vlastos, Socrates takes himself to possess the former sort of knowledge while denying that he possesses the latter.

In order to have knowledge$_C$, a person must have true belief on the basis of evidence that entails the truth of the belief (Vlastos 1994b: 55). It is important to note that Vlastos is working with an internalist conception of evidence according to which perfect intrinsic psychological duplicates will possess exactly the same evidence independently of the state of the external world. For example, on the assumption that 'to see' is factive, were my evidence for a belief allowed to include the fact that I *see* something, my evidence would entail the truth of my perceptual beliefs. Knowledge$_C$ would then be too easy to come by to serve Vlastos' purposes.

Instead, my evidence can include only the fact that I have a certain visual impression as of P's being the case. Since someone in a world where P is not the case could have this visual impression, my evidence will not entail the truth of my belief. A person will know$_C$ that P only if all her possible internal psychological duplicates will have a true belief that P. Furthermore, in order to know$_C$ that P, a person must possess knowledge$_C$ of her evidence for believing that P. On Vlastos's view some propositions are known$_C$ through themselves and immediately, and all other knowledge$_C$ involves deductive inference from the immediately known$_C$ propositions. A hallmark of knowledge$_C$ is infallibility (Vlastos 1994b: 52–55).

Knowledge$_C$ is contrasted with 'fallible knowledge', which a person has if she has a true belief on the basis of reasonable evidence that fails to entail the truth of her belief (Vlastos 1994b: 51). One type of fallible knowledge is 'elenctic knowledge' or 'knowledge$_E$', in which a person's evidence for her belief is the result of her elenctic investigation. Socrates' knowledge$_E$ that an ethical proposition is true is based on reasonable evidence that fails to entail the truth of his belief. According to Vlastos, Socrates' knowledge$_E$ that P is based on evidence given in the two-part schema [Q] (Vlastos 1994b: 56):

Q[a] P is entailed by beliefs held by anyone who denies P.
Q[b] not-P is not entailed by beliefs held by Socrates who affirms P.

Vlastos takes knowledge$_E$ to be fallible in a few ways. First of all, Vlastos denies that the truth of Q is sufficient to entail the truth of P. It is consistent with the evidence available to Socrates that both P and the interlocutors' beliefs entailing P are false.

A second problem with Q[a] on Vlastos' view has to do with the grounds that someone has for believing Q[a]. I cannot know$_C$ that P on the basis of Q, unless I know$_C$ that Q. According to Vlastos, however, Socrates can have only inductive evidence that Q[a] is the case. The fact that every interlocutor so far has been committed to P does not suffice to show that every possible interlocutor is committed to P.

Vlastos also denies that Socrates has immediate access to all the entailments of his many beliefs. So his confidence that Q[b] holds – that he is not committed to not-P – can be based only on the fact that he has not yet been shown to be committed to not-P. Since Socrates' evidence for both Q[a] and Q[b] turns out to be inductive, his evidence does not entail the truth of Q. Since Socrates does not know$_C$ that Q, he can have no knowledge$_C$ on the basis of Q. Any knowledge$_E$ that Socrates has on the basis of Q will be fallible knowledge.

With these distinctions in mind, we can restate (4) and (6) in terms of knowledge$_C$ and in terms of knowledge$_E$.

(4_C) Socrates believes that for any ethical proposition, P, if a person knows$_C$ that P then she has wisdom with respect to some ethical subject matter.
(4_E) Socrates believes that for any ethical proposition, P, if a person knows$_E$ that P then she has wisdom with respect to some ethical subject matter.

According to Vlastos, (4_C) is true but (4_E) is false. In order for Socrates to have knowledge$_C$ of any ethical proposition, he would need to be able to derive that proposition from known$_C$ ethical first principles. But knowledge$_C$ of these ethical first principles would count as exactly the sort of wisdom that Socrates disavows. Nevertheless, Vlastos holds that Socrates can have knowledge$_E$ of any number of ethical facts without possessing this sort of wisdom. Furthermore, on Vlastos' view, Socrates takes knowledge$_C$, but not knowledge$_E$, to be governed by (PD).

We can also distinguish two different ways of taking (6):

(6_C) Socrates believes that there are some ethical propositions that he knows$_C$.
(6_E) Socrates believes that there are some ethical propositions that he knows$_E$.

According to Vlastos, (6_E) is true while (6_C) is false. Socrates believes that he has fallible knowledge$_E$, but denies that he has knowledge$_C$.

SOCRATIC IGNORANCE

Vlastos is most concerned to distinguish knowledge$_E$ from knowledge$_C$. Knowledge$_E$, however, is just one sort of fallible knowledge, and Vlastos does not spend much time thinking about whether Socrates has fallible knowledge on the basis of something other than elenchus. We might wonder whether Socrates takes himself to have fallible knowledge on the basis of something weaker than [Q]. It seems possible for Socrates to satisfy the conditions on weak knowledge discussed above without being in a position to be confident that [Q] is the case. A person could take himself to have a reason for his belief strong enough to warrant full confidence in that belief, but not have any commitments at all about whether every possible set of beliefs entails his belief. There is also a problem posed by Socrates' *daimonion*. I have argued that Socrates takes himself to have weak knowledge on the basis of divine testimony, but there is little reason to think that he will have knowledge$_E$ in such a case.

James Lesher worries that Vlastos illegitimately multiplies senses of 'knowledge' (Lesher 1987). According to Lesher, Socrates endorses a position of 'semantic monism' according to which 'whenever we employ a word, there is a single quality designated by that term which, once properly identified, can serve as a distinguishing mark for all the things designated by that term' (Lesher 1987: 278).

Lesher's own solution to the problem of Socratic ignorance holds that there is a single sense of 'knowledge', that (4) is simply false while (6) is true. Socrates thinks that it is possible to have knowledge of some ethical propositions without being wise, although knowledge of some other ethical proposition might require wisdom. On Lesher's view, Socrates takes himself to have knowledge concerning the moral character of particular cases. In denying that he has wisdom or knows anything *kalon kagathon*, Socrates does not mean to suggest that he lacks knowledge of particular ethical propositions, but only to deny that he possesses knowledge of the essence of virtue. Lesher writes:

> Further, lacking knowledge about the essence of virtue, [Socrates] would reasonably claim not to know the truth of various propositions *about virtue* (how to acquire it, whether it is better to suffer injustice than to commit it, whether virtue guarantees happiness), matters about which he holds firm convictions, but not *knowledge*.
>
> – Lesher 1987: 284

Lesher seems to agree that Socrates accepts principle (D) in (PD), but argues that Socrates can know the ethical character of particular actions without definitional knowledge. Socrates must then deny principle (P) in (PD). Lesher must interpret passages such as (EU2) and (HM1) as allowing for knowledge of the ethical character of particular actions in the absence of definitional knowledge. Judgments about the plausibility of Lesher's interpretation, therefore, will depend on the depth of one's commitment to (P).

Furthermore, Lesher does not provide a very precise characterisation of just what is involved in the single knowledge relation that Socrates bears to particular ethical propositions but that he fails to bear to propositions about virtue. We need to know more about just what Socrates takes himself to lack when he has a firm conviction about virtue but does not take himself to have knowledge.

In addition, we might wonder on what basis Socrates can legitimately claim to have knowledge of the ethical character of a particular action without having knowledge *about* the corresponding virtue. There is a distinction between failing to have definitional knowledge concerning an ethical property, and lacking all general knowledge about that property. If Lesher means to deny that Socrates has any general knowledge about virtue or the virtues, it is difficult to see what counts as the basis for Socrates' knowledge about the ethical character of particulars. Lesher will not be able to claim that Socrates has knowledge of the ethical character of a particular action by recognising some feature of that action and inferring its ethical character from its possession of that feature and a general ethical truth. If Socrates cannot *know* the general ethical truth, he cannot claim to *know* the particular ethical truth on the basis of this kind of argument. However, Socrates sometimes supports his convictions about particular cases by reference to general ethical principles. In the *Crito*, for example, his conviction that it would be wrong for him to escape prison is justified by reference to the general claim that it is always wrong to return harm for harm or to break your agreements.

Furthermore, in the *Apology*, Socrates does not claim to know merely that a particular disobedient action is wrong. Rather, Socrates makes a general claim that it is always wrong to disobey a superior, and then applies this general ethical rule to his own case. If Socrates knows that it is always wrong to disobey a superior, then he would seem to be in a position to know something general about virtue and disobedience. While it is possible to maintain that Socrates lacks definitional knowledge about virtue, it seems too strong to say that he completely lacks general knowledge *about virtue*. Nevertheless, a more restricted version of Lesher's interpretation seems plausible, according to which Socrates takes himself to possess certain sorts of ethical knowledge even while denying that he has knowledge of the ethical definitions or essences.

For Vlastos the wise person and person who lacks wisdom will bear different epistemic relations to the same propositional content. On Lesher's account there is a single epistemic relation involved, but the wise and non-wise person bear this relation to different ranges of propositions. Both the wise person and the non-wise person can bear the very same knowledge relation to a particular ethical proposition. The superiority of the wise person consists in the fact that she has something in addition to knowledge that a particular ethical proposition is true. She has knowledge of a broader range of propositions which includes definitional propositions.

Notice, however, that on Lesher's view, a person with knowledge of the essence of virtue will have evidence for her particular ethical beliefs that the person without wisdom is not in a position to have. While both the wise person and Socrates will know that a particular action is unjust, the wise person will be in a position to give a justification of his belief that the non-wise person is not in a position to give. This is because the wise person can justify his belief about a particular action by reference to ethical definitions that he knows to be true. While it might seem somewhat artificial to do so, we can now introduce a relation, knowledge*. For example, A person knows* that a particular action is just if and only if she knows that the action is just in Lesher's single sense of 'know', she knows the essence of justice, and she knows that the particular action is just because it possesses the essential features of justice. The person who knows* that a particular action is just would seem to be in a superior epistemic situation to the person who simply knows that that action is unjust. The point here is that some of the distinctions Vlastos draws by recognising different knowledge relations can be recast in terms of different ranges of a single knowledge relation.

This brings us to an additional feature of Vlastos' view. Vlastos takes Socrates' quest for definitional knowledge to be driven by a quest for certainty. As long as Socrates lacks definitional knowledge, there remains a possibility that his beliefs will turn out to be false. Furthermore, as long as this possibility remains, Socrates will not have reached the end of enquiry. It should be noted that Socrates does express uncertainty about his own views. When Socrates engages in elenchus with an interlocutor, he represents himself as open to the possibility that the interlocutor's belief will survive examination. Even in passage (G2), despite the great confidence that Socrates expresses in his own view, there remains in the background a worry that some interlocutor might come along with the ability to defend a position contrary to Socrates' own position. Were there such an interlocutor, Socrates' claim to have iron-bound arguments would be undermined and his confidence in his own beliefs could be shaken.

Socrates, therefore, finds himself in a tricky epistemic situation. He takes all the evidence that he has to support his belief, and does not think that there is evidence in favour of the contrary belief of his interlocutor. If Socrates really thinks that the questions he is investigating are settled, why does he continue his investigations?

One possibility is that Socrates is simply trying to teach others what he takes himself to know already, and that his representation of himself as open to the possibility that he is mistaken is simply a pose. A second possibility is that Socrates takes himself to lack something that he would need to settle his questions once and for all. He has confidence in his beliefs and no confidence in any alternative, and takes himself to have evidence sufficient to warrant his confidence. However, he also takes himself to be unable to rule out the possibility that he has overlooked something in his investigations. The search for definitions is essential on this view, because it is only when he possesses knowledge$_C$ of the proper definitional facts that Socrates will be in a position to end inquiry with complete confidence. Only at this point will Socrates be able to possess absolute and unshakeable confidence in his beliefs.

The quest for definitional knowledge, therefore, seems to be motivated by something like sceptical doubt. Socrates, however, does not exhibit many of the concerns that we expect in an epistemologist whose goal is anti-sceptical. He does not express doubts about the reliability of his perceptual or cognitive faculties, and he seems quite willing to make the kinds of ordinary empirical knowledge claims that sceptics often worry about. He shows no tendency at all to seek a higher degree of certainty about these ordinary matters. Socrates also has great confidence in a cognitive resource that he does not share with other people. He seems to have no doubt at all that his *daimonion* is right in all its pronouncements, and never worries that he might be hallucinating. On the internalist conception of evidence that Vlastos is working with, however, Socrates could have exactly the same evidence in a world where his senses were faulty and where no *daimonion* exists. So Socrates' evidence does not entail the truth of his belief. If Socrates has general sceptical worries, it is somewhat surprising that they do not extend to his senses or to the voice in his head.

If Socrates is not motivated to search for definitions because of sceptical worries, then why does he continue to search for definitions? One promising possibility is that Socrates is looking for explanatory understanding rather than certainty. Robert Bolton, for example, draws a close parallel between Aristotle's views in the *Posterior Analytics*, and Socrates' understanding of *epistēmē* (Bolton 1993). Knowledge *that* something is the case needs to be distinguished from knowledge of *why* it is the case. For Aristotle, we do not possess *epistēmē* about something unless we know why it is the case. In a similar way, as we saw above in the passages from the *Meno*, Socrates denies that anyone has *epistēmē* or *sophia* with respect to virtue without an explanatory account proceeding from definitional knowledge about virtue. The person who possesses definitional knowledge is in a superior epistemic position to the person who lacks definitional knowledge, even if both of them know *that* some ethical fact is the case.

On Bolton's view, Socrates adopts a similar view to Aristotle about the source of ordinary knowledge *that* something is the case. Many of the things that Socrates takes himself and others to know are known as a result of ordinary and widely available experience of the world (Bolton 1993: 151). In some cases, such as *Crito* 47d–e, Socrates suggests that he has knowledge of controversial claims as a result of arguments. Even in these cases, however, the arguments rely on premises that are known as a matter of ordinary experience. Bolton is a constructivist about elenchus, and holds that, insofar as elenctic investigation is able to confirm Socrates' views or disconfirm the views of his opponent, Socrates and his opponent must possess some knowledge of ordinary facts based on experience (Bolton 1993: 147). Socrates' inquiry into the nature of virtue begins from ordinary knowledge that some particular acts or types of acts are virtuous and others are vicious. Socrates takes himself to have such ordinary knowledge, which I take to be equivalent to weak knowledge. Such knowledge can arise from a number of different sources and does not require definitional knowledge. The goal of the inquiry is knowledge of the essential nature of virtue, which will allow us to explain why such acts are virtuous or vicious. This is the sort of knowledge involved in wisdom and the sort of knowledge that Socrates denies possessing.

The person with explanatory knowledge arising from a proper grasp of essences is in a superior epistemic position to the person who lacks this sort of knowledge. We need to be somewhat careful, however, in thinking through just what is involved in this epistemic superiority. The person who possesses definitional knowledge and an explanatory account will be able to offer a form of justification for her beliefs that is unavailable to the person without such knowledge.[13] We can call this *superiority in justification*. In some cases, superiority in justification will lead to a greater level of warranted confidence in a particular claim. Perhaps, we are dealing with a very difficult case in which a grasp of essences will allow us to answer questions that we were otherwise unable to answer. However, it does not seem that this increased level of warranted confidence always accompanies knowledge of essences. For example, I take myself to be completely warranted in my belief that sticking my hand in the fire is painful. When I learn about the physiology of the nervous system or the chemistry of combustion, I do gain the ability to give additional reasons for my belief that sticking my hand in the fire is painful. I do not think, however, that my level of confidence in my belief that sticking my hand in the fire is painful increases. I've suggested that weak knowledge is closely related to the degree of confidence in a belief warranted by our evidence.

There is a second sort of epistemic superiority that characterises the person with definitional knowledge, however, which we might call *superiority in understanding*. Benson (2000) holds that the epistemic superiority of the person with definitional knowledge consists not primarily in her having a superior level of warranted confidence to the person without definitional knowledge, but in her having a kind of understanding of what she knows that the other person lacks (Benson 2000: 212–221).[14] The person who possesses *sophia* or *epistēmē* does not simply know isolated propositions, rather she possesses understanding. As Fine puts it, such understanding consists in 'a deep, synoptic, explanatory grasp of a domain' (Fine 2008b: 70).

A person can have a true belief that something is the case on the basis of evidence sufficient for full confidence even in the absence of this type of understanding. We have already seen that there is a good deal of controversy about whether Socrates would describe a person in this state as possessing knowledge. Some commentators, such as Irwin (1979, 1995), Fine (2008b) and Benson (2000), take Socrates to deny that a person without understanding possesses genuine knowledge. Even on these views, however, Socrates allows that such a person possesses well-justified moral convictions. Other

SOCRATIC IGNORANCE   115

commentators think Socrates counts a person in this state to have knowledge of a kind, e.g. weak knowledge, knowledge *that* or fallible knowledge, while denying that the person has full explanatory understanding. What is common among interpreters, however, is that Socrates does recognise the distinction between the person with understanding and the person with a well-grounded belief who lacks understanding. Furthermore, Socrates often takes himself to be in the latter condition but consistently denies that he is in the former.

The wise person with ethical understanding has an explanatory grasp of an entire domain of inquiry, not isolated knowledge of particular ethical facts. In short, she is an ethical expert. Paul Woodruff distinguishes 'expert knowledge', which only the wise person has, from 'common knowledge' (Woodruff 1990). Common knowledge is 'a common property of ordinary people' rather than an exceptional cognitive achievement (Woodruff 1990: 79).

The ethical expert, on the other hand, has the ability to give an account of the nature of the various goods that he claims expertise about. As Socrates' many examples of craftspeople reveal, the sort of ethical expertise that he is trying to confirm or disconfirm by elenctic testing has much in common with the craft-knowledge (*technē*) possessed by a master craftsperson. A master of a craft is a reliable guide with respect to the quality of products of that craft. Furthermore, a master craftsperson has a systematic understanding of the way to bring about the goods at which he aims, and has the ability to teach his craft to others. We have seen texts from both the *Apology* and the *Meno* in which Socrates connects wisdom and *epistēmē* about virtue with the ability to teach others to be virtuous.

Woodruff also draws a distinction between subordinate *technai* and *technai* in the strict sense. Most of the examples of *technai* discussed by Socrates are subordinate *technai*. Possession of a subordinate *technē* requires only that the technician can choose the correct means to ends that are taken as given. The ethical expert or master of the political *technē* must possess a *technē* in the strict sense, which requires something beyond instrumental proficiency. The strict technician must not only able to choose the right means to reach a given end, but must have an understanding of why the ends of his craft count as genuine goods. This understanding of the goodness of the ends of his craft requires the technician in the strict sense to be able to give an appropriate account of the ends of his craft and an appropriate account of *goodness*, from which he can demonstrate the genuine goodness of his ends. In order to accomplish this task, the genuine technician must possess the sort of definitional knowledge that Socrates is seeking in the early dialogues. Anyone who proves unable to produce a proper definition is not a technician in the strict sense and lacks expert knowledge. (PD) then holds with respect to expert knowledge, but does not hold with respect to common knowledge.

On Woodruff's view, practicing elenchus is not sufficient for arriving at expert knowledge. Woodruff goes farther and claims the purpose of elenchus is not even to provide justification for claims to common knowledge. Rather the point of elenchus is to show a person that he does not really believe what he initially claims to believe (Woodruff 1990: 79–80). Any disagreement between Socrates and his interlocutors is merely apparent, and elenchus reveals to a person what she actually believes. According to Woodruff:

Socrates holds that, in the last analysis, you believe the consequences of whatever views you are left with after elenchus has done its work. The elenchus thus exposes what you believe in the last analysis, and simply treats this sort of belief, without apology, as non-expert knowledge.

– Woodruff 1990: 81

In support of his view, Woodruff points to the interchange between Socrates and Polus at *Gorgias* 474–481. At *Gorgias* 474b, Socrates claims that Polus and everyone else holds or believes (*hēgeisthai*) that doing injustice is worse than suffering it. Polus claims that no one, including Socrates, holds this position. Socrates begins an elenctic investigation of Polus, and at 479d–e Polus is forced to admit that Socrates has proven his point. Woodruff suggests that Socrates takes himself to have shown Polus what he really believed all along. Furthermore, while the elenchus plays a role in discovering what he really believes, it cannot play a role in the justification of that belief.

There are problems with each of Woodruff's claims. The claim that Polus along with everyone else holds that committing injustice is worse than suffering it is somewhat ambiguous. Socrates might mean that Polus is committed to this claim by other things that he believes, and that careful attention to the implications of his various beliefs will reveal this commitment. On the other hand, Socrates might mean that the belief that committing injustice is worse really already has some kind of psychological reality in Polus. I do not think that a belief has to be explicit or introspectively accessible for it to have psychological reality. Nevertheless the belief should play some role in how a subject speaks, thinks and acts. Even after the elenchus, let alone before the elenchus, there is no evidence that Polus would choose to suffer injustice rather than commit it. Furthermore, Polus does not even wholeheartedly assent to Socrates' claim after the elenchus. He claims that what Socrates says 'appears' to be true, or that it is the case 'according to the argument'.

Socrates does reveal to Polus that his initial claim is inconsistent with other positions that Polus holds, but he does not show that the belief that committing injustice is worse has any psychological reality for Polus. I take knowledge, even weak knowledge, to require some kind of psychologically real belief. Elenchus cannot result in any kind of knowledge unless the interlocutor comes to have a psychologically real belief.

A second problem with Woodruff's understanding of common knowledge is that it threatens to erode any distinction between mere belief and non-expert knowledge. While I have some inclination to allow that fully believing something and *taking oneself to have knowledge* go hand in hand, it seems deeply problematic to hold that all belief counts as knowledge. Even non-expert knowledge would seem to require truth.

Finally, Woodruff allows no justificatory role for elenchus. Assume that as a result of my continued discussions with Socrates, I do come to believe that it is better to suffer injustice than to commit injustice. This belief is psychologically real and I come to assent sincerely to the claim that committing injustice is worse and to deny the opposite claim. I claim that I have changed my mind about the relation between injustice and happiness. When you ask me why I changed my mind, I claim that Socrates convinced me through elenchus that my former belief was incompatible with too many of my other beliefs. When I give you this answer, I do not seem to be telling you something about a causal process by which I discovered what I already believed. Rather, I seem to be providing reasons for my having changed my mind. In at least some cases, then, elenchus plays a justificatory role.

We can hold on to Woodruff's distinction between expertise and common knowledge, as well as his observations about the relation between expert knowledge and craft knowledge, while allowing a justificatory role for elenchus. C. D. C. Reeve's solution to

SOCRATIC IGNORANCE 117

the problem of Socratic ignorance, for example, relies on a distinction between expert and non-expert knowledge that is similar to Woodruff's, but allows that elenchus plays a justificatory role with respect to non-expert knowledge (Reeve 1989: 37–62). The fact that a person's beliefs survive elenctic investigation, while those who maintain the opposite of her beliefs are refuted, provides evidence in favour of her beliefs. On the basis of this sort of evidence, and probably on the basis of other sorts of evidence as well, she can possess non-expert knowledge.

Nevertheless, this evidence cannot rise to the level needed for expert knowledge, which Reeve also understands in terms of craft knowledge (*technē*). Expert knowledge requires the knowledge of definitions and the possession of an explanatory account. 'Expert knowledge seems to be craft-knowledge, then: that is to say, it is explanatory, teachable, luck-independent, elenchus-proof, certain knowledge' (Reeve 1989: 45).

Woodruff and Reeve are both in a position to claim that there is one kind of knowledge that requires wisdom and another kind that does not. In other words, (4) is true for expert knowledge but false for ordinary knowledge. They also claim that Socrates takes himself to have ordinary knowledge but to lack expert knowledge. In other words, (6) is true for ordinary knowledge but false for expert knowledge. Socrates does not believe that he has expert knowledge concerning any ethical proposition.

How exactly we should characterise the distinction between expert and non-expert knowledge is somewhat tricky. At a minimum, it seems that the expert can be distinguished from the non-expert in terms of the range of her knowledge and in terms of the sort of explanatory understanding that she possesses. She knows some things that the non-expert does not know and she is a position to justify and explain her claims by reference to her own correct grasp of essences. Whether we need to go further and say that that there are two fundamentally distinct knowledge relations is a different question. I'm not sure how we should go here. It seems possible, however, to distinguish the expert from the non-expert without introducing two distinct knowledge relations. The expert and the non-expert can both know that P in the same sense of 'know', but the expert possesses a whole lot of stuff in addition to knowledge that P.[15] Alternatively, we could say that the possession of this additional stuff changes the nature of the relation between the expert and the proposition in question.

I want to discuss one more interpretation that relies on the distinction between expert and non-expert knowledge in resolving the problem of Socratic ignorance. The interpretation offered by Brickhouse and Smith (1994, 2000) resembles others we have already examined. There is a distinction between the person who possesses ethical expertise and the person who has ordinary knowledge that a certain ethical claim is true. In this way, their interpretation is similar to that of Woodruff and Reeve. Socrates can freely allow that people possess sufficiently warranted true beliefs about ethical matters, but this sort of knowledge is not of much interest to Socrates. Instead, when Socrates discusses knowledge and wisdom, he is interested in a kind of ethical expertise akin to the craft knowledge possessed by master craftspeople. In addition to knowledge that an ethical proposition is true, the expert knows why or how it is the case that the proposition in question is true. Brickhouse and Smith distinguish knowledge that P is true from knowledge of why P is true or knowledge of how it is the case that P is true (Brickhouse and Smith 1994: 39; Brickhouse and Smith 2000: 105–109). The latter sort of knowledge requires a grasp of definitions and explanatory accounts, and is what Socrates disavows.

Brickhouse and Smith pay special attention to *Gorgias* 508e–509b ((G2) above). After claiming that his conclusions are held down and bound with arguments of iron and adamant, Socrates says, 'I do not know how these things are' (*egō tauta ouk oida hopōs echei*). What Socrates disavows, according to Brickhouse and Smith, is not knowledge that various ethical propositions are true. In fact, Brickhouse and Smith hold that what Socrates says in (G2) is fully compatible with his taking himself to have a fully warranted true belief that it is better to suffer injustice than to commit injustice. Rather, in claiming that he does not know 'how these things are,' Socrates is denying ethical expertise. He is denying that he possesses the kind of definitional knowledge which would allow him to explain precisely why suffering injustice is preferable to committing it (Brickhouse and Smith 1994: 38–39; 2000: 108–109).[16]

So far Brickhouse and Smith's interpretation is quite similar to Bolton's distinction between knowledge that and knowledge why. Like Woodruff and Reeve, however, Brickhouse and Smith stress the central importance of craft knowledge (*technē*) and the practical abilities involved in exercising that craft knowledge to Socrates' conception of expert knowledge. On Bolton's view, the kind of ethical knowledge that Socrates is searching for looks a lot like scientific or theoretical knowledge.

However, Brickhouse and Smith place particular emphasis on the practical dimension of expertise. They write:

> We cannot stress enough how completely Socrates' epistemology is suffused with a concern for action, and how little concerned he is with pure theory . . . For Socrates, because the only knowledge that concerns him is knowledge that has consequences for how we should live, his conception of knowledge cannot simply be understood as knowing *that* something or other is true, for it plainly also has an one of its components that the knower knows *how* to do something or other.

> – Brickhouse and Smith 1994: 43–44

Brickhouse and Smith distinguish knowledge that something is the case not only from knowledge why something is the case, but also from the sort of expertise that involves practical know-how. While the master craftsperson will possess explanatory knowledge and will be able to answer definitional questions concerning her craft, what is even more important is the fact that she will possess practical know-how. She will be able to perform certain actions or make certain products. We need to distinguish the knowledge of the expert from propositional knowledge, where this is thought of as 'a cognitive *state* that consists in the knower standing in a relation to some *proposition* or some *information*' (Brickhouse and Smith 2000: 105). Ordinary non-expert knowledge that something is the case is propositional knowledge. We might also analyse knowledge why something is the case in terms of propositional knowledge: I know why the *explanandum* is the case if and only if I know that the *explanans* is the case and I know that the *explanans* provides the correct explanation for the *explanandum*.

The person who has *sophia* or *epistēmē* concerning virtue has an explanatory account of her true beliefs that proceeds from her definitional knowledge. This state of expertise partially consists in propositional knowledge that she possesses. Brickhouse and Smith, however, deny that *sophia* or *epistēmē* can be completely analysed in terms of propositional knowledge.[17] In addition to possessing a good deal of propositional knowledge, the person with *sophia* or *epistēmē* must possesses various practical abilities.

> [W]e would expect any adequate analysis to feature some conditions that required the one with know-how to have the right sorts of abilities or capacities to *do* and to *produce* the right sorts of things. It is not clear that *any* sort of propositional knowledge

SOCRATIC IGNORANCE

would suffice to guarantee the satisfaction of such requirements. For example, just because one knows *that* a certain tool is for cutting, it does not follow that one knows *how* to cut with the tool in question; just because one knows *that* a certain kind of wood is best for making chariot wheels, it does not follow that one would know *how* to make good chariot wheels from such wood, and so on.

– Brickhouse and Smith 2000: 106–107

Brickhouse and Smith identify know-how with the possession of certain practical or productive abilities. There is a good deal in this view that seems right, and it is worth examining the notion of know-how or expertise in some detail.[18] First, we should draw a distinction between knowing how to do something and having the ability to do it. For example, a former concert pianist with advanced arthritis might no longer have the ability to play the piano. However, she might still have all the knowledge that she used to have concerning how to play the piano. She might be able to explain step by step how she would go about playing a particular piece of music if she didn't have arthritis. Such a person might still possess expertise even though she is no longer in a position to exercise her expertise.

The expert's knowledge that a certain sequence of actions constitutes playing a piece of music might be understood in terms of propositional knowledge. The same can be said with respect to using cutting tools and building chariot wheels. Is there anything else involved in knowing how to play a piece of music, i.e. in the possession of the relevant expertise? Imagine a person who has read an instruction manual or watched a video about making chariot wheels. This person might be able to accurately describe the process of building a chariot wheel and we might credit her with a kind of knowledge that a certain sequence of actions constitutes wheel building. However, we might balk at saying that such a person knows how to build a wheel, and we certainly balk at attributing to her the expertise of the wheelwright.

Compare this case to an expert jazz pianist who is playing an old standard with a group of musicians she has never met. It seems clear that an expert piano player has a number of perceptual and cognitive abilities in addition to her propositional knowledge that a specific sequence of actions constitutes playing a piece of music. First of all, she has certain recognitional abilities that a non-expert typically lacks. The expert attends to the epistemologically and practically relevant features of her environment. She is sensitive to these features and has a stable disposition to make the right sorts of inferences in response to them. As a result of these dispositions, the expert forms different beliefs about her environment than the non-expert. She will recognise that the hammers on the piano are slightly worn, or that the drummer is playing a bit slowly. Furthermore, the expert pianist adjusts her behaviour in accordance with her beliefs about her situation. She makes all kinds of correct practical inferences. If the hammers in the piano are worn, she hits the keys harder to get the proper sound. If the drummer is playing a bit slowly, she adjusts the tempo at which she plays, et cetera. She grasps various salient features of her situation in a way that informs and guides her actions. Even bracketing the physical ability to play the piano, there seems to be more involved in expertise than mere knowledge that a certain sequence of actions is required to accomplish a task.

Presumably a good deal of the perception, inference and decision that go on in piano playing is not explicit. Given the subtle adjustments involved in any complex task, it is unclear that all of the information being processed by the expert could be verbalised. In many cases, however, we do expect an expert to be able to give some account of why she made a certain judgment or undertook a certain course of action. In these cases, her explanation will look like a bit of theoretical or practical reasoning involving propositional attitudes: 'I realized that the drummer was playing a bit slowly, and I wanted to stay in time with the drummer. I knew that I could do this by slowing down a bit. So, I adjusted the tempo at which I was playing.' Socrates' requirement that a person with wisdom be able to teach what she knows to others requires that the expert be able to make the reasons for her beliefs and actions explicit to her students. Someone who possesses a great deal of skill in performing an activity but who is unable to give an account of why she is doing what she is doing won't possess the sort of wisdom that Socrates seeks.

The person with *sophia* concerning ethics attends to the correct features of her situation and is disposed to form the proper ethical beliefs about that situation. For example, the person who knows what piety is not only has the ability to make definitional statements about piety that will survive attempts at refutation. In addition, as we see in the *Euthyphro*, she will be authoritative about whether particular actions are pious or impious. In fact, Socrates goes so far as to claim that the person with expertise will invariably be correct in her judgments about particular cases. (See Brickhouse and Smith 2000: 109–111; also see Reeve 1989: 43–45.)

In addition to her ability to recognise the ethical character of her situation, the wise person will correctly judge the way in which her ends are to be pursued in whatever situation she is in. At *Euthydemus* 280a–b, Socrates insists that the possession of wisdom renders any other good fortune otiose. In her decisions about how to pursue her ends, the wise person is infallible (see Brickhouse and Smith 2000: 107; Reeve 1989: 43–45). It is highly implausible to take the kind of infallibility that characterises the wise person as a guarantee that her actions will always result in the desired outcome. However, the expert will adjust her aims to fit her situation and will invariably choose the best means to these ends. Her reasoning will be flawless even if her actions do not always succeed.

Given the cognitive abilities that it requires, Brickhouse and Smith deny that expertise can be flatly identified with a body of propositional knowledge. Like Woodruff and Reeve, Brickhouse and Smith resolve the problem of Socratic ignorance by denying (4). A person can possess ordinary propositional knowledge – i.e. sufficiently justified true belief – concerning ethical subjects even in the absence of wisdom or ethical expertise (Brickhouse and Smith 2000: 106). Socrates is willing to say that he does have some propositional knowledge even while denying that he has fully-developed expertise.

Brickhouse and Smith draw a contrast between having propositional knowledge and having *expertise*. 'Expertise' is not a propositional attitude term. 'Expertise' is a fine translation of '*sophia*', which is not used as a propositional attitude term. Similarly, there are many uses of '*epistēmē*' that do not take a propositional complement, for which 'expertise' works nicely. There are, however, uses of both the noun '*epistēmē*' and the verb '*epistasthai*' that do take a propositional complement. Furthermore, this is the use that seems especially relevant when Socrates draws the distinction between '*epistēmē*' and true opinion at *Meno* 97e–98a. True opinions seem to be propositional attitudes. They seem to be beliefs *that* various things are the case. But Socrates claims that these true beliefs become instances of knowledge (Socrates uses the plural '*epistēmai*', 'knowledges') when tied down by an explanatory account. These instances of knowledge, therefore, do seem to be propositional attitudes. Furthermore, Socrates seems to take the possession of an explanatory account to be a necessary condition to have *epistēmē* that something is the case. Socrates explicitly denies that he has much of this sort of knowledge. This denial

SOCRATIC IGNORANCE

seems to go further than mere denial of expertise; Socrates seems to be denying that he has much propositional *epistēmē*.

Brickhouse and Smith hold that possession of *epistēmē* is supposed to suffice for expertise. Their denial that propositional knowledge can suffice for expertise leads them to conclude that *epistēmē* should not be identified with propositional knowledge. Knowledge that P, where 'P' is replaced by a definitional formula, does not seem to suffice for all of the cognitive abilities that characterise an expert. Even the ability to apply a definition correctly in particular cases seems to require something more than knowing that some definitional statement is true. For example, I might know on the basis of expert testimony that piety is the part of justice concerned with service to the gods in bringing about the good. However, in order to use this definition to make correct judgments about individual actions I need a great deal in addition to propositional knowledge of the definition.

We should note that it is possible to drive this wedge between propositional knowledge of definitions and expertise only if we recognise a kind of propositional knowledge that a non-expert could possess. It is possible, however, to deny this possibility. For example, Irwin (1979, 1995), Fine (1979, 2003, 2008b) and Benson (2000) are far more demanding about the conditions under which a person has propositional knowledge. Only a person who has a synoptic and explanatory grasp of a field of inquiry will turn out to possess any propositional knowledge at all. On this view, whatever the non-expert possesses simply fails to count as propositional *knowledge*. A person who has a true belief about proper definitions on the basis of expert testimony simply does not have propositional knowledge of the definition or of any proposition whose explanation requires propositional knowledge of the definition.

If the conditions on propositional knowledge become this demanding, then only an expert in a field will have any propositional knowledge concerning that field. Since Socrates denies ethical expertise, the result would seem to be that Socrates must deny that he has any propositional knowledge concerning ethical subjects. In other words, we are back to a position that solves the problem of Socratic ignorance by denying (6). However, even someone who denies (6) needs to hold that Socrates takes himself to have true beliefs based on a warrant sufficient for unhedged assertion and full confidence in his beliefs. In other words, Socrates takes himself to possess something that many of us would recognise as a kind of knowledge that falls short of expertise.[19]

By this point, we should recognise a kind of emerging consensus among various attempts to resolve the problem of Socratic ignorance. In all cases, we can distinguish two sorts of cognitive achievement. One sort of cognitive achievement – true belief with warrant sufficient for unhedged assertion and full confidence – is significantly less demanding than the other and corresponds to weak knowledge. I have argued that Socrates sometimes takes himself to be in a state that satisfies these conditions. The second sort of cognitive achievement is extremely hard to come by. The person who manages such an achievement is an expert about a field of inquiry. She possesses definitional knowledge and has an explanatory account of what she knows. She possesses a host of recognitional and inferential abilities. Her judgments in her field of expertise are authoritative and inerrant, and she has the ability to teach her expertise to others. Socrates consistently denies that he has this kind of expertise. Socrates can be wholly consistent in taking himself (either tacitly or explicitly) to have reached the lower level of cognitive achievement even while denying that he has reached the higher level. While there remain differences over how best to interpret Socrates' epistemic vocabulary and over many other issues in Socratic epistemology, we can see a kind of emerging consensus when it comes to the question: Does Socrates take himself to have any knowledge?

The answer is a firm 'In a way, yes. In a way, no.'

NOTES

1. At least when it comes to fully realised knowledge or wisdom. Whether there is a lower-grade cognitive achievement that counts as genuine *sophia* or *epistēmē* is a difficult question. For an argument that wisdom, knowledge and craft (*technē*) should be thought of as gradable, see Smith 2021: ix–xi. Smith's suggestion is that Socrates thinks that a person can have knowledge and be wise without being fully wise in just the way that a good but imperfect woodworker can possess the *technē* of carpentry. There are three difficult questions arising from Smith's observation that deserve more attention than I can give them here. First, does Socrates recognise a genuine type of ethical wisdom that falls short of perfect ethical wisdom? Second, what is the level of cognitive achievement needed to count as genuinely ethically wise? Third, does Socrates think that he or anyone he has met meets the conditions for such imperfect genuine wisdom? For more on these questions, see Smith 2016 and Jones 2016.

2. All translations are from Cooper 1997, sometimes slightly modified.

3. As Fine (2008b) points out, we should be careful about taking this passage to commit Socrates to the paradoxical claim that he knows that he knows nothing. While Socrates takes the possession of *epistēmē* to imply wisdom, we need not think that knowing (*suneidenai*) something is sufficient for having *epistēmē* of that thing. It is possible, therefore, that a person is aware (*suneidenai*) of something without being wise.

4. Gareth Matthews (2006: 107–111) suggests that we can take Socrates' question at (H1) to be a genuine expression of perplexity. On Matthews' view, Socrates does not mean to commit himself to the claim that one cannot know that a speech is finely done without knowing the nature of the fine. Rather, Socrates takes knowledge of the nature of the fine to provide one way in which knowledge of the fineness of a particular action is possible, and wonders whether there are other ways of knowing available as well. Matthews' reading of (H1) strikes me as possible. However, (R1) does not seem open to the same kind of *aporetic* reading. In that passage, Socrates denies that he will be able to know whether the just person is happy without first knowing what justice is. The *Meno* is somewhat complicated. In (M1) and the passages immediately around it, Socrates indicates that his failure to know what virtue is renders him unable to answer Meno's question. Later in the dialogue (*M. 86d–87c*), however, Socrates indicates a hypothetical method for trying to determine whether or not virtue is teachable. This method does not seem to require knowledge of the nature of virtue. However, it is unclear whether the results of the hypothetical method truly count as coming to possess *epistēmē* about the teachability of virtue. On the view that I'm suggesting, Socrates does think that definitional knowledge is necessary for the possession of full-blown *epistēmē* concerning ethical subjects. However, a person might count as having the sort of warranted true belief needed for knowledge$_w$ in the absence of definitional knowledge.

5. We might wonder what precisely counts as knowing something about F-ness in (PD). Does knowing that there is such a thing as justice count as knowing something about justice? Does knowing that justice is identical to itself or distinct from injustice count as knowing something about justice? What about knowing that if there are such things as justice and

SOCRATIC IGNORANCE

123

injustice, then these are each self-identical and distinct from one another? If we take the 'x' in (P) to range over properties as well as individuals and are liberal about what substitution instances of 'F-ness' and 'G-ness' are admissible, then (P) and (D) will yield a very strong version of (PD). For example, without knowing what justice is, a person will be unable to know whether justice exists or that if there is justice then it is some one thing in each of its instances. On this construal of (PD) Socrates will fail to know (in the relevant sense of 'know') facts about existence and facts that seem to follow from logic alone.

6. Presumably if Socrates did have definitional knowledge concerning knowledge, he would know the precise way in which knowledge differs from true opinion. As Benson (2000: 142–156) puts it, Socrates holds that a person with definitional knowledge about F-ness will be able to answer a host of questions about the nature and distribution of the property. Since Socrates does not know the precise nature of the difference between knowledge and true opinion, he does not have definitional knowledge about knowledge. Nevertheless, he claims that he does *know* that knowledge and true opinion are distinct. Socrates cannot accept both (PD) and (SD) and claim to know that knowledge and true opinion differ, unless he is using his knowledge vocabulary equivocally.

7. My discussion of Socrates' avowals of knowledge in this section owes a great deal to Wolfsdorf 2004a, which contains a thorough discussion of several other passages in which Socrates seemingly claims to have knowledge. Wolfsdorf gives a number of compelling arguments against taking a number of passages as direct avowals of knowledge by Socrates.

8. Vasiliou (2008) holds that Socrates is talking about a moral superior. Brickhouse and Smith (1994, 2000, 2013a) hold that the context makes clear that Socrates is referring to someone with the legal authority to issue a command.

9. If (a) assertion implies belief; (b) the assertion of a conjunction implies the assertion of each conjunct; and (c) belief is transparent, we can get to a formal contradiction from an utterance of (MPB) in short order. In this context, to claim that belief is transparent is to claim that a person does believe whatever she believes that she believes, and that she does not believe whatever she believes that she does not believe. See Adler and Armour-Garb 2007: 147–149 for a fuller discussion of arguments deriving a formal contradiction from these assumptions.

10. Williamson (1996, 2000: Ch. 11) points out that in response to an assertion, we often ask someone how he knows what he has asserted.

> A: It's raining outside.
> B: How do you know that it's raining outside?
> A: I don't know that it's raining.

In response to A's denying knowledge, I am torn between two reactions. The first reaction is to think that A should not have asserted that it is raining. The second is to think that A is using 'know' for a very high-grade epistemic state. In the latter case, I might expect to hear some indication in A's tone of voice.

11. Fine (2008b) briefly considers whether Williamson's knowledge norm of assertion – (KNA) a speaker is entitled to assert that P if and only if she knows that P – should be accepted and applied in interpreting Socrates. (KNA) requires that a person with a well-justified false belief is not entitled to assert the content of that belief. For my purposes here, only a weaker norm is needed. I have some inclination to accept:

(WNA) A speaker is entitled to assert that P only if she takes herself to know that P.

We might worry, however, about possible cases in which a person has knowledge but does not have beliefs about her knowledge, in which case she is not entitled to assert what she knows according to (WNA). In what follows, I will assume that Socrates (at least tacitly) believes he knows whatever he does know. With this proviso in mind, I will argue that (WNA) is true concerning weak knowledge. When Socrates makes an unhedged assertion that P, he (at least tacitly) takes himself to be in a state where he has a true belief that P on the basis of a warrant sufficient for fully believing that P. When he makes an unhedged assertion, Socrates takes himself to be in a state that would count as weak knowledge under the right conditions. If fact, I think that an even weaker norm than (WNA) will generate a problem concerning Socrates' commitments:

(WNA*) If a person believes that she does not know that P, then she is not entitled to assert that P.

Socrates violates (WNA*) if he asserts something that he takes himself not to know. As long as we are talking about weak knowledge, (WNA*) seems to be a fairly minimal norm governing assertion.

12. We might translate the '*eu iste* . . .', which Socrates uses on other occasions as well, as 'know well that . . .'. Wolfsdorf is right that his uses of '*eu iste*' need not be taken to be cases of Socrates' ascribing knowledge to himself. However, they do seem to be cases of emphatic unhedged assertion.

13. This ability seems to be independent of whether definitional knowledge meets the conditions on knowledge$_C$ suggested by Vlastos. Whether Socrates requires definitional knowledge to be self-evident is a difficult question that I want to set aside. The requirement of self-evidence generally goes along with a foundationalist epistemology taking certainty to be the hallmark of knowledge. We might, however, deny that Socrates has a foundationalist epistemology on which definitional claims are self-evident, and hold that even definitional beliefs are justified by their evidentiary and inferential relations to other beliefs. One advocate of this sort of coherentist picture of Socratic and Platonic epistemology is Gail Fine (See Fine 1979; Fine 2003: Introduction). The fact that certain evidentiary and inferential relations hold between beliefs does not entail that any of those beliefs are true. So even definitional knowledge, on this kind of view, will not count as knowledge$_C$ in Vlastos' sense. Nevertheless, such definitional knowledge can play a crucial justificatory and explanatory role for the person who has it. Fine (2008b) is inclined to deny that anyone who lacks definitional knowledge counts as having any knowledge at all, and would attempt to solve the problem of Socratic ignorance by denying (6). Socrates takes himself to have rationally justified true belief without taking himself to have knowledge. We can follow Fine's lead in denying that definitional knowledge satisfies the entailment condition, however, without denying that Socrates takes himself to have some kind of knowledge even in the absence of definitional knowledge. We can also grant that a person with definitional knowledge is in an epistemically superior position to a person who has knowledge of some ethical fact without definitional knowledge.

14. Other commentators who emphasise the role of understanding in Socratic knowledge include Moravcsik 1979; Fine 1979, 2008b; Prior 1998; A. Smith 1998; and Wolfsdorf 2004a.

15. Reeve distinguishes ordinary knowledge, which is something like justified true belief, from expertise. The latter state is infallible, elenchus-proof and requires knowledge of definitions, while the former is fallible, elenchus-resistant, and does not require knowledge of definitions. Wolfsdorf (2004a: 111–112) claims that Reeve must think that Socrates uses

SOCRATIC IGNORANCE
125

knowledge words equivocally – using the term for expert knowledge in his disavowals and for ordinary knowledge in his avowals. It might be possible, however, for Reeve to hold that Socrates accepts only a single type of knowledge. I will have ordinary knowledge that P if and only if I know that P. I will have expert knowledge that P if and only if I know that P, and my justification for believing that P renders me infallible, immune to elenchus, et cetera. There is still a sense in which Socrates uses his knowledge terms equivocally – sometimes he denies ordinary knowledge + high-grade and explanatory justification, sometimes he claims or implies that he has ordinary knowledge. Understood in this way, however, I am not sure that the equivocation is particularly philosophically problematic. There is, however, an interpretative difficulty when we ask what Socrates means to deny when he affirms or denies his possession of *epistēmē*. Is he affirming/denying that he has sufficiently justified true belief? Or is he affirming/denying that he has sufficiently justified true belief plus an explanatory grasp? On each of the views that we have looked at, Socrates sometimes takes himself to have the first but to lack the second. I suspect that Socrates is not generally concerned with the notion of sufficiently justified true belief. However, part of what I am arguing in the chapter is that Socrates' disavowals of *epistēmē* are not disavowals of properly justified true belief.

16. For criticisms of Brickhouse and Smith's reading of (G2), see Wolfsdorf 2004a: 108–110.

17. It is useful to keep in mind a way in which the Greek uses of the verb '*epistasthai*' and the noun '*sophia*' are coordinate with English uses of 'to know' and 'wisdom'. The verb can accept a propositional complement, a person can know (*epistathai*) *that* something is the case. On the other hand neither 'wisdom' nor '*sophia*' naturally take such a complement. I do not have wisdom (*sophia*) that something is the case. I can have wisdom (*sophia*) and knowledge or expertise (*epistēmē*) concerning a subject, which will consist, at least in part, in knowing *that* various things are the case. As we will see, however, fully realised *epistēmē* and *sophia* requires a good deal in addition.

18. For a detailed discussion of expertise and the role of expertise in Socrates' thought, see A. Smith 1998.

19. Some recent work, especially N. Smith 2021, has suggested that Socrates can take himself to possess some level of expertise even while denying that he has fully developed expertise. If we think of expertise along the lines of craft-knowledge and craft-knowledge comes in degrees, then a possibility is opened for a person with some craft-knowledge that fails to reach the craft-knowledge of the master craftsperson. The result would be that Socrates can take himself to have some low-level expertise. I am not sure what to think about this suggestion. For additional discussion, see A. Smith 1998; N. Smith 2016, 2021; and Jones 2016.

CHAPTER SIX

The Priority of Definition

HUGH H. BENSON

I. INTRODUCTION

One thing we seem to know about Socrates[1] is that he was preoccupied with questions of the form 'What is F-ness?'.[2] Aristotle famously tells us that

> Socrates busied himself concerning the ethical virtues and was the first to seek to define them universally . . . He was reasonable in seeking the what it is; for he sought to syllogize, and the what it is is the starting point of syllogisms . . . For Socrates may be fairly attributed two things, epagogic arguments and defining the universal . . .
>
> – *Metaphysics* 1078b17– 29, Ross trans.; see also *Metaphysics* 987b1–4

According to Xenophon

> [Socrates'] own conversation was ever of human things. The problems he discussed were, What is godly, what is ungodly; what is beautiful, what is ugly; what is just, what is unjust; what is prudence, what is madness; what is courage, what is cowardice; what is a state, what is a statesman; what is government, and what is a governor; – these and others like them, of which the knowledge made a 'gentleman,' in his estimation, while ignorance should involve the reproach of 'slavishness.'
>
> – *Memorabilia* 1.1.16; Marchant trans.

And of course, the Socratic dialogues[3] of Plato abound in such questions. Socrates and his interlocutor(s) focus on the question 'What is piety (or holiness)?' in the *Euthyphro*, 'What is temperance (or moderation)?' in the *Charmides*, 'What is courage (or bravery)?' in the *Laches*, 'What is fineness (or beauty)?' in the *Hippias Major*, 'What is a friend?' in the *Lysis*,[4] 'What is justice?' in *Republic* I, 'What is a sophist?' in part of the *Protagoras*, 'What is rhetoric?' in part of the *Gorgias*, and 'What is virtue?' in the first third of the *Meno*.

Given this preoccupation one is immediately led to wonder what Socrates would count as adequate answers to such questions. An immediate response is that Socrates is searching for definitions. Indeed, this preoccupation is often characterised as a search for definitions, following Aristotle. But appealing to definitions here is problematic for at least two reasons. First, pointing out that in asking these sorts of questions Socrates is looking for definitions of the relevant F-nesses (piety, courage, temperance, et cetera) only pushes the question back. One wants to know what features are required for definitions of the relevant F-nesses.[5] Second, talk of definitions is potentially misleading since it is likely to carry with it anachronistic connotations concerning the nature of definition. Indeed, it is noteworthy that Plato never uses Aristotle's favoured term for definition (*horismos*), and rarely (at least in the Socratic dialogues) uses Aristotle's other technical terms (*horos* and *horizein*) in the sense of definition.[6] Nevertheless, Socrates' concern to raise questions of the form 'What is F-ness?' is clear whether or not providing an answer to such questions amounts to providing a definition.

I propose to leave the question concerning what amounts to adequate answers to Socrates' 'What is F-ness?' questions to one side, to the extent that I can.[7] Instead I will focus on another related question concerning Socrates' preoccupation with 'What is F-ness?' questions: What motivates this preoccupation? What, that is, is so valuable about the answers to these questions that Socrates is so devoted to asking them? I suspect that a number of considerations motivate his preoccupation, but a fairly traditional answer (and one with which I am in general agreement) is that Socrates takes such answers to have a special epistemic status.[8] Knowledge of these answers is in some way epistemically prior to other sorts of knowledge, and given Socrates' commitment to knowledge, it is natural for and incumbent upon him to pursue what is epistemically prior. It is the task of this chapter to examine more closely this alleged motivation for Socrates' preoccupation with 'What is F-ness?' questions.

I begin with a sketch of the nature of this alleged motivation. The motivation depends on Socrates' endorsement of an epistemic priority principle which I will call henceforth 'the priority of definition principle' (keeping in mind the flaws of using the word 'definition').[9] I will then run through the primary evidence for and against attributing such a principle to the Socrates of Plato's Socratic dialogues. We will see that the evidence appears to cut both ways. I then conclude the chapter by rehearsing the various ways in which scholars have attempted to resolve this interpretive tension. In the end, I hope the reader will see that anything like a confident stance with respect to Socrates' endorsement of the priority of definition principle will depend on one's interpretation of many more features of Socratic philosophy than we can consider here.

II. THE PRINCIPLE

Let us begin by stating the principle in its most general form.

(PD) If A fails to know what F-ness is, then A fails to know anything about F-ness.

So stated, the principle requires a variety of qualifications and comments.

First, I will simply stipulate that for Socrates to know what F-ness is is to know the answer to his 'What is F-ness?' question. Of course, what it is to know the answer to the 'What is F-ness?' question cannot be fixed in light of my earlier decision to leave unexplored the adequacy conditions of a successful answer to the 'What is F-ness?' question. But suffice it to say that to know the answer to a 'What is F-ness?' question is at least to be able to survive a Socratic examination or elenchus. Again, what precisely is required in order to survive a Socratic elenchus is a long and controversial story,[10] but suffice it to say that surviving a Socratic elenchus at least requires the ability to state an answer to the 'What is F-ness?' question that coheres with one's other F-ness related[11] beliefs. Consequently, we need to distinguish the priority of definition principle from two related but distinct principles concerning the nature of knowledge of what F-ness is, viz., the verbalisation requirement and the coherence requirement:

(V) If A fails to be able to state an answer to the 'What is F-ness?' question, then A fails to know what F-ness is.[12]

THE PRIORITY OF DEFINITION

(C) If A's F-ness related beliefs fail to cohere, then A fails to know what F-ness is.

When these two principles are conjoined to (PD), we get the result that being unable to coherently answer a 'What is F-ness?' question entails that one lacks any knowledge of F-ness. Such a result may or may not receive Socratic endorsement, but its Socratic endorsement is distinct from the Socratic endorsement of (PD). It is (PD) that is the focus of this chapter.

Second, as the preceding discussion indicates, (PD) is a principle regarding the priority of *knowledge*. (PD) requires definitional *knowledge* of F-ness (whatever that amounts to) for any other *knowledge* regarding F-ness. It should not be confused with the view that stating an answer to the 'What is F-ness?' question is prior to knowledge of anything else about F-ness; that is the conjunction of (PD) and (V). Nor should it be confused with the view that knowledge of what F-ness is is prior to the ability to state or assert that something is F or that F-ness has some property or other. To arrive at that sort of view from (PD) requires commitment to something like the following assertability requirement:

(A) If A asserts something about F-ness, then A knows what A has asserted.

Again such a principle may or may not receive Socratic endorsement, but whether it does is not the focus of this chapter. Our focus is on (PD), the claim that *knowledge* of what F-ness is is prior to any other *knowledge* regarding F-ness.

Third, (PD) is a conjunction of two principles which have often been discussed separately in the literature. The first maintains that knowledge of what F-ness is is prior to knowledge that anything is F. For example, one cannot know that Socrates is virtuous, if one fails to know what virtue is. The second maintains that knowledge of what F-ness is is prior to knowledge of any of the properties of F-ness. For example, one cannot know that virtue is beneficial, if one fails to know what virtue is. Put only a bit more formally, (PD) is the conjunction of

(P) If A fails to know what F-ness is, then A fails to know, for any x, that x is F,

And

(D) If A fails to know what F-ness is, then A fails to know, for any G, that F-ness is G.

Finally, (PD) should not be confused with what might be called the sufficiency of definition principle. As the name implies, the sufficiency principle maintains that knowledge of what F-ness is is sufficient for knowing anything about F-ness. For example, if one knows what virtue is, then one knows that Socrates is virtuous. Again, whether or not Socrates would endorse such a principle (or more plausible versions of it),[13] this principle is distinct from (PD). (PD) maintains that knowledge of what F-ness is is necessary for any other knowledge involving F-ness, while the sufficiency principle maintains that such definitional knowledge is sufficient.

In conclusion, the priority of definition principle (PD), is the conjunction of two principles (P) and (D), each asserting the *necessity* of *knowledge* of what F-ness is for *knowledge* of other things about F-ness. According to (P), knowledge of what F-ness is is necessary for knowledge of which things are F, and according to (D), knowledge of what F-ness is is necessary for knowledge of which properties F-ness has. It is important to note that (PD) on its own only asserts the necessity of knowledge of what F-ness is for *knowledge* of other things about F-ness. It is silent about whether such knowledge is necessary for belief, assertion, action or anything else. It is also important to note that

130   THE BLOOMSBURY HANDBOOK OF SOCRATES

(PD) as here discussed is *fully general*. According to (PD), knowledge of what *any* F-ness is is necessary for *anyone* to know *anything else* about that F-ness. Certainly, if Socrates does endorse (PD) in the Socratic dialogues we can understand why he is so preoccupied with trying to acquire knowledge of the answers to his 'What is F-ness?' questions. The question, of course, is whether he endorses such a principle.

III. SOCRATES' ENDORSEMENT OF (PD)?

Given this sketch of the priority of definition principle, both what it is and what it is not, we need to examine the evidence concerning Socrates' endorsement of this principle. I will begin by looking at the evidence which appears to support Socrates' endorsement, first by looking at the evidence for (P) and then the evidence for (D). Then, I will turn to the evidence which appears to argue against this endorsement.

III.I Evidence That Socrates Endorses (PD)

The strongest evidence for Socrates' endorsement of (P), the principle, that if one fails to know what F-ness is, then one fails to know for any x that x is F, comes from two passages in Plato's *Hippias Major*.[14] Early on in the dialogue Socrates relates an imagined exchange he had with someone[15] concerning his critique of various parts of speeches he had heard.

> (a) Not long ago, someone caused me to be at a loss when I was finding fault with things in some speeches as being foul and praising others as being fine; he questioned me in the following very rude way. (b) 'How do you know what sort of things are fine and foul? Come now, can you say what the fine is?' (c) I was at a loss because of my worthlessness and was not able to answer appropriately. Going away from the gathering I was angry at myself and reproached myself, and resolved that the first time I met one of you wise men I would listen and learn and study and then go back to the questioner and fight the argument again.
>
>   – *Hi.Ma.* 286c–d[16]

And again at the conclusion of the dialogue, Socrates reverts to the same theme, saying

> (a) He asks me if I am not ashamed daring to talk about fine practices, when I have clearly been refuted concerning the fine, to the effect that I do not know what the thing itself is. (b) 'And yet', he will say, 'how do you know whether someone has spoken finely or not, or done any other thing whatsoever, when you do not know the fine? (c) Being in such a state, do you think it is better for you to be alive than dead?'
>
>   – *Hi.Ma.* 304d–e

Between these two passages Socrates professes to want to learn from Hippias the knowledge of what fineness is (*Hi.Ma.* 286d–e), which Hippias professes to have (*Hi.Ma.* 286e). Hippias proposes seven different answers to the 'What is fineness?' question, all of which are found wanting by Socrates, in much the same way presumably as Socrates' own attempt to answer this question was found wanting by his imagined interlocutor. The key for our purposes is noticing that the (b) portion of both passages contains a nearly identical question that has led many commentators to take Socrates to be committed to the view that Socrates (or anyone else) cannot know which speeches are fine, if he fails to know what fineness is. But such a commitment is simply a substitution instance of the more

THE PRIORITY OF DEFINITION   131

general principle (P), with 'fineness' substituted for 'F-ness' and individual unnamed speeches substituted for 'x'.

Of course, some commentators have focused on the fact that the (b) portions contain questions, not assertions, and have suggested that these questions are not meant to be rhetorical, but are genuine (see, for example, Lesher 1987: 285). Socrates is not affirming that one cannot know which speeches are fine without knowing what fineness is. Rather Socrates is genuinely wondering how it is possible (assuming that it is possible) to know that a given speech is fine when one fails to know what fineness is. But this is difficult to square with the context. Socrates does not follow up the first question by looking for an alternative explanation for his knowledge of fine speeches, but with attempting to acquire the knowledge that the question in (b) indicates is necessary. In the second passage Socrates has no reason to be ashamed at lacking the knowledge of what fineness is if there are other ways he might have known that some speeches were fine. Rather the questions in the (b) portions of these two passages from the *Hippias Major* provide rather strong *prima facie* evidence that Socrates endorses a substitution instance of (P).[17]

Socrates appears to endorse a similar substitution instance near the beginning of the *Euthyphro* in the following passage.

> EUTH: (a) [My relatives say] that it is impious for a son to prosecute his father for murder, knowing poorly, Socrates, how the gods view the pious and the impious.
> SOC: (b) Euthyphro, do you think that you have such accurate knowledge concerning divine affairs, and concerning pious things and impious things that, the situation being as you say, you do not fear that by prosecuting your father you may be doing something impious?
> EUTH: (c) Socrates, I would be useless and no different than the average man, if I did not know accurately all such things.
>
> . . .
>
> SOC: (d) Tell me, then, what you just now asserted you knew clearly, what sorts of things you say the pious and the impious are in the case of murder and all other actions.
>
> – *Eu.* 4d–5d

In the (a) portion of this passage Euthyphro explains that his relatives think he is making a mistake by prosecuting his father for murder on the grounds that doing so is impious. In the (b) portion Socrates is surprised that Euthyphro is not afraid that perhaps his relatives are right and supposes that Euthyphro must think that he knows 'concerning divine affairs, and concerning pious things and impious things'. Socrates suggests here that knowledge that prosecuting his father is pious is required either for doing what Euthyphro is doing or for not being afraid that what he is doing is impious. In either case, in (c) Euthyphro boasts that he has the requisite knowledge, leading Socrates in (d) to ask Euthyphro to tell him what he had just claimed to know – what piety and impiety are. The movement in this passage goes from not being afraid to prosecute one's father for murder to knowing that prosecuting one's father for murder is pious, to knowing concerning divine affairs and concerning pious and impious things, to knowing what piety and impiety are. Whatever one thinks about the details of this movement, it appears to indicate a Socratic endorsement of the following substitution instance of (P): If Euthyphro knows that prosecuting his father for murder is pious, then he knows what piety is. Lest we miss this endorsement, Plato wraps up the dialogue with Euthyphro as follows:

For if you did not know clearly the holy and the unholy, it is not possible that you would attempt to prosecute your aged father for murder on behalf of a hired labourer, but you would have feared the gods, risking that you did not do this correctly, and would have been ashamed before men; now, I know well that you think you know clearly the holy and the not holy.

– *Eu.* 15d–e[18]

In addition to these passages, Socrates concludes other dialogues with what appear to be substitution instances of (P). Near the end of the *Charmides*, following a series of failed attempts to answer the 'What is temperance?' question, Socrates urges Charmides to see whether he is temperate, and if he is to ignore Socrates' babbling. Charmides responds

But good heavens, Socrates, I don't know whether I have it or whether I don't – because how would I know the nature of a thing when neither you nor Critias is able to discover it, as you say?

– *Chrm.* 176a–b

Here Charmides explains that he fails to know whether he is temperate because he fails to know what temperance is, suggesting another substitution instance of (P). It is true that this is Charmides and not Socrates,[19] but the context of this passage provides no reason to think that Socrates would not endorse Charmides' sentiment.

Finally, again following a series of failed attempts to answer the 'What is a friend?' question, Socrates concludes the *Lysis* as follows:

We have been ridiculous . . . For the ones going away will say that we think that we are friends with each other and yet we have not been able to discover what a friend is.

– *Ly.* 223b

Here Socrates finds fault with himself and his interlocutors, Lysis and Menexenus, for thinking they are friends when they fail to know what friendship is. Of course, Socrates cannot mean by this that it is impossible for Menexenus to think or believe that he is a friend to Lysis when he fails to know what a friend is (as he does). Counter-examples to that sort of principle are abundant.[20] Indeed, Socrates, Lysis and Menexenus are counter-examples themselves.[21] Instead, Socrates must have in mind something like his criticism of Euthyphro to the effect that the three friends are unjustified, unwarranted, unreliable or in some other way epistemically at fault in thinking they are friends. They fail to know that they are friends. And the evidence for this is that they fail to know what a friend is. But this indicates yet another substitution instance of (P).

Similar evidence can be cited for (D).[22] Following Meno's introduction of his eponymous dialogue by asking how virtue is acquired, Socrates responds as follows.

(a) Good stranger, you must think me happy indeed if you think I know whether virtue can be taught or how it comes to be; I am so far from knowing whether virtue can be taught or not that I do not know at all what virtue itself is. . . . (b) If I do not know what something is, how could I know what qualities it possesses? (c) Or do you think that someone who does not know at all who Meno is could know whether he is good-looking or rich or well-born, or the opposite of these? Do you think that is possible?

– *M.* 71a–b; adapted from Grube trans.

THE PRIORITY OF DEFINITION

The (a) and (c) portions indicate substitution instances of (D), viz., if Socrates fails to know what virtue is, then Socrates fails to know that virtue is teachable, and if Socrates fails to know who Meno is, then Socrates fails to know that Meno is good-looking, or that Meno is rich, or that Meno is well-born. But in between we find the most explicit evidence for the general principle that one could plausibly expect, viz., if someone fails to know what something (F-ness) is, then one fails to know what qualities (G-nesses) it possesses.[23] Additional passages in the *Meno* suggest a similar commitment (see *Meno* 79c, 86d–e and 100b), but none so explicitly as (b).

Socrates appears to endorse additional substitution instances of (D) in the *Laches*. In pursuing the same investigation as that posed at the beginning of the *Meno*, Socrates says in the *Laches*:

> Then isn't this necessary for us to begin, to know what virtue is? For if we do not know at all what virtue happens to be, how would we become advisors to anyone regarding how it might best be attained?
>
> *– La.* 190b–c

Here again, Socrates appears committed to the view that if one fails to know what virtue is, then one fails to know how it is acquired. Of course, one might object that this passage does not explicitly require knowledge of the nature of virtue for *knowledge* of how it is to be acquired, but rather for becoming an (appropriate?) advisor for how it is acquired. And we might imagine that Socrates envisions the requirements for being a virtue-acquisition advisor to exceed the requirements for knowledge of how virtue is acquired. But in an earlier passage that serves as a sort of epagogic inference to 190b–c, Socrates avers:

> For if we happen to know concerning anything whatever that its being added to something makes that thing to which it is added better and further we are able to cause that thing to be added to it, then it is clear that we know that thing itself concerning which we advise how someone might best and most easily attain it . . . If we happen to know that sight added to the eyes makes them better and further we are able to cause it to be added to the eyes, then it is clear that we know what sight is concerning which we advise how someone might best attain it. For if we did not know what sight is or what hearing is, we would hardly be advisors or doctors worthy of attention concerning eyes and ears, how someone might best attain hearing and sight.
>
> *– La.* 189e–190b

Two features about this passage are noteworthy. First, Socrates is explicit that knowledge of the nature of F-ness is a requirement for *knowledge* of how F-ness is acquired, not simply advice concerning how F-ness is acquired. And second, while the passage continues to indicate a restriction to qualities (G-nesses) associated with the acquisition of F-nesses, it testifies to a broader principle than one restricted to virtue. Something like the following substitution instance of (D) is indicated: If one fails to know what F-ness is, then one fails to know that F-ness is G (for G-nesses associated with the manner in which F-ness is best acquired).

Two other dialogues testify to additional substitution instances of (D). In the introductory dialogue between Socrates and Hippocrates in the *Protagoras*, Socrates indicates that if Hippocrates fails to know what a sophist is, then he fails to know that a sophist is good (312b-c).[24] And Socrates concludes the first book of the *Republic* as follows:

Hence the result of the discussion, as far as I'm concerned, is that I know nothing, for when I don't know what justice is, I'll hardly know whether it is a kind of virtue or not, or whether a person who has it is happy or unhappy.

– Rep. 354d–c

Once again, we appear to be presented with a substitution instance of (D) to the effect that failing to know what justice is entails failing to know that justice is a virtue or that justice is happiness-conducive. Indeed, Socrates' initial suggestion that the result of the dialogue so far is that he knows *nothing* may even be taken as indicating a more general principle to the effect that failing to know what justice is entails failing to know anything about justice. Indeed, when this is conjoined with the second passage from the *Laches*, something very close to the general statement in the (b) portion of the passage from the *Meno* is indicated.

If this were the end of the matter we would have little reason to rest content with Robinson's 'vague impression' that the Socrates of Plato's Socratic dialogues is committed to the priority of definition principle, i.e., (PD).[25] The evidence is considerably stronger than a vague impression. While Socrates never explicitly states (PD) in its full generality, he does appear to state (D) in its full generality, as well as endorsing at least six different substitution instances. In the case of (P), the general claim is never explicitly stated, but the manner in which the substitution instance of it is introduced in the *Hippias Major* does not suggest any restrictions are in the offing, and again at least three more substitution instances appear in surrounding dialogues. When the passages on behalf of (D) are combined with those on behalf of (P), it is difficult to imagine that we have stronger evidence for any other alleged Socratic thesis than we have for his commitment to the priority of definition principle,[26] *if*, as I say, this were the end of the matter. But as the qualification suggests, this is not the end of the matter. For in addition to the abundant evidence on behalf of Socrates' endorsement of (PD) there appear to be strong considerations that tell against his endorsement. Let us turn to those considerations now.

III.II *Evidence That Socrates Does Not Endorse (PD)*

The considerations offered against Socrates' endorsement of (PD) fall roughly into two categories: textual considerations and philosophical considerations. The textual considerations themselves follow three main lines of argument. According to the first, it is maintained that Socrates' method of searching for knowledge is inconsistent with a commitment to (PD). This method of inquiry, it is averred, depends on possessing knowledge of things that are F and of properties of F-ness in an attempt to come to know what F-ness is. As such Socrates' method of inquiry presupposes that Socrates does not endorse (PD), for it presupposes knowledge about F-ness (its instances and its properties) prior to knowledge of what F-ness is.[27]

For example, in the *Laches* Socrates proposes that Laches search out the answer to the 'What is courage?' question by searching for what various examples of courageous behaviour have in common at 191c–e.[28] Similarly, at *Euthyphro* 6d–e, Socrates appears to encourage Euthyphro to answer the 'What is piety?' question by examining a variety of pious actions and indicating the form itself by virtue of which those pious actions are pious. In the *Charmides*, after Socrates rejects Charmides' first answer to the 'What is temperance?' question, Socrates encourages Charmides to re-examine himself, an apparent example of a temperate individual, in order to try to answer again the 'What is temperance?' question.[29] These and other examples, throughout the Socratic dialogues,

THE PRIORITY OF DEFINITION

indicate that Socrates is committed to the possibility that one can know particular actions or individuals are courageous, pious or temperate while failing to know the answer to the relevant 'What is F-ness?' question. But that provides rather compelling evidence that Socrates would not endorse the view that one who fails to know what F-ness is cannot know which actions or individuals are F, viz., (P).

According to a second line of argument based on the text, Socrates tests proposed answers to his 'What is F-ness?' questions by appealing to examples and properties of the relevant F-ness. Indeed, Socrates frequently objects to proposed answers by citing counter-examples. Thus, Socrates objects to Laches' initial answer to the 'What is courage?' question that courage is remaining in the ranks and facing one's enemy by citing the courageous flight of the Scythian cavalry and of the Spartan hoplites at Plataea. In the *Charmides*, Socrates objects to the answer that temperance is quietness by appealing to various activities that are temperate but not quiet. And, in *Republic* I, Socrates famously objects to Cephalus' answer that justice is giving to each his due by noting the injustice of returning a sword to a madman. Once again Socrates' method indicates that he thinks one can know various things are F while failing to know what F-ness is, contrary to (P). Moreover, on those occasions in which Socrates does not appeal to a counter-example in opposition to a proposed answer, he appeals to properties of the definiendum which the definiens fails to have or vice versa. For example, in opposition to Charmides' second answer to the 'What is temperance?' question that temperance is modesty, Socrates points out that while temperance is always fine, modesty is not. Again, in opposition to Nicias' answer that courage is the knowledge of fearful and daring things, Socrates points out that while courage is a part of virtue, knowledge of fearful and daring things is the whole of virtue. These and numerous other examples[30] indicate that Socrates thinks one can know a variety of properties of courage or temperance, for example, while failing to know what courage or temperance is. In these cases, we appear to have rather straightforward evidence that Socrates does not endorse (D), and when these passages are combined with the counter-example passages, any suggestion that Socrates endorses (PD) looks hopeless.

A third line of argument connected to the text is independent of Socrates' characteristic method of searching for and examining answers to his 'What is F-ness?' questions. According to this line of argument, Socrates frequently professes knowledge of various things about F-nesses, while at the same time professing ignorance of what those F-nesses are.[31] The frequency of these Socratic professions of knowledge is a matter of some dispute,[32] but not that Socrates does sometimes profess to know things. Two such professions are well-known from the *Apology*.

> I do know, however, that it is bad and shameful to do wrong, to disobey one's superior, be he god or man. I shall never fear or avoid things of which I do not know, whether they may not be good rather than things that I know to be bad.
>
> *– Ap.* 29b; adapted from Grube trans.

> Am I then to choose in preference to this something that I know very well to be an evil and assess the penalty at that?
>
> *– Ap.* 37b

In the first passage Socrates explicitly professes to know that disobeying a superior is bad and shameful, while in the second passage he professes to know that saying he deserves some punishment other than death would be among the bad things. If Socrates endorses

(PD), or more specifically (P), he should profess to know what badness is and what shamefulness is, since he professes to know instances of badness and shamefulness. But while Socrates never to my knowledge explicitly professes ignorance of what badness or what goodness is in the Socratic dialogues,[33] it is difficult to believe in light of his general professions of ignorance that he would profess to know this. Moreover, as we saw in the *Hippias Major*, Socrates does maintain his ignorance of what fineness is and so presumably his ignorance of what shamefulness is.[34] Consequently, given Socrates' professions of knowledge of instances of badness and shamefulness and yet the strong presumption, if not explicit expression, of his ignorance of what badness is and shamefulness is, we have good reason to conclude that Socrates does not endorse (PD), or at least (P).[35]

In addition to these textual considerations on behalf of denying Socrates' endorsement of (PD), there is a philosophical consideration. (PD) is simply too implausible to be charitably attributed to anyone approaching Socrates' philosophical acumen. What is philosophically implausible about (PD) is perhaps best captured by Peter Geach, who following Wittgenstein, writes the following: 'We know heaps of things without being able to define the terms in which we express our knowledge.'[36] Indeed, Geach finds this principle so implausible that, in perhaps a momentary lack of interpretive generosity, he dubbed it 'the Socratic Fallacy' and blamed Socrates for a style of mistaken thinking more damaging to the progress of philosophy than Plato's theory of forms.[37] Perhaps the obvious falsity of the principle would have led a more generous interpreter to doubt Socrates' commitment to (PD), as it has a variety of scholars since Geach's influential paper. Indeed, I suspect that Geach's forceful repudiation of the principle was partially responsible for rediscovering the texts that argue against Socrates' endorsement.

IV. THE LANDSCAPE OF INTERPRETATIONS[38]

Thus, we face an interpretive tension in the Socratic dialogues, not uncommon in the history of philosophy. On the one hand, considerable evidence indicates that Socrates endorses the priority of definition principle (PD). While precious little textual evidence indicates the general principle, numerous passages testify to a commitment to various substitution instances of (PD). If there were not evidence to the contrary, we would have rather compelling evidence for Socrates' endorsement of (PD). But, on the other hand, there does appear to be considerable evidence to the contrary. His method of searching for and testing answers to his 'What is F-ness?' questions appears to presuppose that Socrates does not accept (PD). Moreover, various Socratic professions of ignorance and knowledge are contrary to an endorsement of (PD), and of course, (PD) is philosophically implausible. How then are we to resolve this interpretive tension?

As one might expect there are three general approaches to this tension in the literature. Some interpreters simply accept the tension and, à la Geach, proclaim so much the worse for Socrates. I will call this 'the embrace the tension approach'. Some interpreters re-examine the alleged textual evidence *on behalf* of (PD) and explain it away. I will call this 'the reject (PD) approach'. And some interpreters re-examine the alleged textual evidence *against* (PD), explain it away, and offer a philosophically respectable understanding of the principle. I will call this 'the embrace (PD) approach'. Let us look more closely at each of these three general approaches.

THE PRIORITY OF DEFINITION

IV.I Embrace the Tension

Geach may perhaps be the most famous representative of those interpreters who appear happy to embrace this tension in Socratic thought. Indeed, Geach is so happy to attribute to Socrates a principle that Geach considers obviously fallacious that he never even considers the evidence to the effect that Socrates does not endorse (PD). But another, perhaps more generous, representative of this sort of interpretation can be found in Russell Dancy's recent book (2004).[39] Dancy spends considerable time responding to those interpreters who attempt to explain away the passages which appear to testify to Socrates' endorsement of (PD).[40] None of their attempts, Dancy maintains, are compelling. Nevertheless, Dancy does not deny that Socrates' endorsement of (PD) is incompatible with his method of searching for and examining purported answers to his 'What is F-ness?' questions (see Dancy 2004: 39–41). Indeed, he even agrees that the principle is false (Dancy 2004: 37–38). According to Dancy:

> Various attempts have been made to read the dialogues in a way that gets around the apparent conflict between Socrates' claims and his practice. The way I'm going to read them, the conflict is there, and is one of the driving forces tending toward the theory of recollection we find in the *Meno*. Attempts to make Socrates come out smelling like roses will be dealt with along the way. But a Socrates who is inconsistent on this score strikes me as more interesting than these consistent ones.
>
> – Dancy 2004: 41

Notice that Dancy's interpretation is motivated by two considerations. First, he rejects a strong form of the principle of charity as a guiding principle in interpreting philosophical texts.[41] According to Dancy, we should not assume that philosophers, even great ones, fail to make mistakes, even big ones, or are always consistent. Indeed, the reverse is more likely to be true. An interpretation according to which Socrates is mistaken and/or inconsistent is not only likely to be more plausible, but also, according to Dancy, more philosophically interesting. Second, the thesis of Dancy's book is to defend 'a developmental view [of Plato's dialogues] with an analytic emphasis' (Dancy 2004: 1). Part of his defence of this developmental interpretation is seeing Plato as attempting to resolve this tension between Socrates' commitment to (PD) and Socrates' (or any reasonable) philosophical method. As Dancy sees it, at least by the time of the composition of the *Meno*, Plato recognises this tension in Socratic philosophy and resolves it by rejecting (PD) by means of the theory of recollection.[42] So, in the end, while Socrates may not 'come out smelling like roses', Plato does, or at least in a sense.[43]

IV.II Reject (PD)

By far the most popular approach in recent years to the interpretive tension surrounding Socrates' endorsement of (PD) involves explaining away the alleged evidence offered on behalf of his endorsement. According to this reject (PD) approach, the passages we cited above on behalf of Socrates' endorsement of (PD) are understood in one of three ways. [1] Either they fail to testify to any principle at all and are contextually explained away;[44] or [2] they testify to some other less general or weaker principle or principles which are compatible with his method of searching for and testing answers to his 'What is F-ness?' questions and his professions of knowledge and ignorance, and are philosophically respectable (or at least more respectable than (PD)); or [3] they fail to testify to Socratic, as opposed to Platonic views.[45] Various combinations and applications of these three ways of dealing with the passages which suggest Socratic endorsement of (PD) lead to roughly four distinct versions of this general approach.

The first version of the reject (PD) approach is represented by Gregory Vlastos and John Beversluis.[46] It is characterised by two features. First, some of the passages we cited above, for example, *Hippias Major* 286c–d and 304d–e for (P) and *Meno* 71a–b for (D), do indeed testify to an endorsement of (PD). But they do not testify to a Socratic endorsement. Rather they testify to a Platonic endorsement. According to Vlastos and Beversluis, the *Hippias Major*, *Lysis*, *Euthydemus* and *Meno* are transitional dialogues. They were composed by Plato between the dialogues that represent the philosophy of Socrates and the middle dialogues that represent a distinctly new and different Platonic philosophy. As such these transitional dialogues contain elements of the older Socratic view (in particular its moral doctrines) and elements of the emerging Platonic view (in particular a new emerging methodology borrowed from Plato's new interest in mathematics). Far from being at odds with the new emerging methodology of these dialogues (as (PD) is with the methodology of the earlier dialogues), (PD) is rather an essential component of the methodology of the middle dialogues. Consequently, according to Vlastos and Beversluis, (PD) can be found in the *Hippias Major*, *Meno* and *Lysis* passages,[47] but these passages testify to Plato's endorsement of (PD), and not to Socrates'.

Second, according to Vlastos and Beversluis, the remaining passages that allegedly indicate a Socratic endorsement of (PD) do not indicate anything as general (and hence as implausible) as (PD). For example, while they do not explicitly discuss *Euthyphro* 4d–5d, they evidently take it to indicate a commitment to a more restricted and hence more plausible principle roughly to the effect that if an individual fails to know what piety is (perhaps what any F-ness is), then that individual fails to know controversial and/or borderline instances of piety (like whether prosecuting one's father for murdering a murderous slave is pious).[48] Since Socrates does not (and does not need to) appeal to controversial or borderline cases of F-ness in order to search for and test answers to his 'What is F-ness?' questions, this more restricted principle is compatible with the method of the Socratic dialogues and moreover is philosophically plausible. Similarly, they take the *Laches* passages as testifying only to something like the following principle: If one fails to know what F-ness is, then one fails to know how F-ness is best acquired.[49] Once again this principle is not as general as (PD) (or even (D)) and so does not rule out knowing various properties of F-ness (other than how F-ness may best be acquired) prior to knowing what F-ness is. Knowledge that F-ness possesses these properties then can be appealed to in searching for and testing answers to his 'What is F-ness?' questions. Thus, according to Vlastos and Beversluis, we can avoid the interpretive tension associated with (PD) by taking those passages which are most indicative of (PD) as attributable to Plato and his new methodology, and the remaining passages as either not indicating any principle at all or as indicating a variety of less general and so more plausible principles and, moreover, ones perfectly compatible with Socratic method and professions of knowledge.[50]

The second version of this general approach, represented by Alexander Nehamas, does not resort to the distinction between Socratic and transitional dialogues in order to address the interpretive tension. Rather, Nehamas takes all of the passages cited above to testify to Socratic views, but he maintains that they testify to more restricted principles than (PD). Thus, like Vlastos and Beversluis, Nehamas takes *Euthyphro* 4d–5d to testify to Socrates' endorsement of the principle that one cannot know whether controversial and borderline cases of piety (like Euthyphro's prosecution of his father for murdering a

THE PRIORITY OF DEFINITION   139

murderous slave) are pious unless one knows what piety is (Nehamas 1987: 278). But, unlike Vlastos and Beversluis, who take the *Hippias Major* passages as evidence of Plato's endorsement of (PD) in full generality, Nehamas maintains that these passages testify to the principle that one cannot know *in general* which things are fine, if one fails to know what fine-ness is. Thus, the *Hippias Major* passages permit knowledge of uncontroversial examples of fine-ness, but not knowledge of fine things in general, when one fails to know what fine-ness is (Nehamas 1987: 287).

In the case of *Meno* 71a–b, Nehamas maintains that, while the (b) portion of the passage does appear to be fully general, the examples on either side importantly circumscribe the principle. Nehamas points out that the properties of being good-looking, being rich, and being well-born are thought (in the culture at the time) to be essential properties of an individual. So, in claiming that one cannot know whether Meno is good-looking, rich or well-born, unless one knows who Meno is, all that Socrates means to be endorsing is that one cannot know *essential* properties of a thing, unless one knows what that thing is. He is not maintaining that one cannot know *any* of the properties of the thing. Similarly, being teachable (or not) is plausibly thought to be an essential property of virtue, and so in maintaining that one cannot know whether virtue is teachable unless one knows what virtue is, Socrates is again only endorsing the restricted principle.

Nehamas deals with the concluding passage of *Republic* I in a similar way. He points out that being a virtue and being happiness-conducive are plausibly thought to be essential properties of justice, and so in maintaining that one cannot know whether justice possesses these properties unless one knows what justice is, Socrates is only endorsing the restricted principle that if one fails to know what justice is, then one fails to know whether justice is G (where 'G' is a variable for essential or controversial properties of justice).[51]

Nehamas concludes his discussion of the passages offered in support of Socrates' endorsement of (PD) as follows:

> Socrates' insistence on the priority of definition is therefore very narrowly circumscribed. First, it seems to concern primarily the virtues and not every thing or every term, ... Second, it seems to apply only to specific issues, and not to all the features of virtue, ... Socrates seems to believe that we need to know the definition of a virtue in order to decide whether certain disputable features (either traditionally disputed, like teachability, or disputed on particular occasions, like its benefits in the case of Thrasymachus) are or are not true of it. We also need to know it in order to discourse generally about it, that is, in order to present ourselves, as Hippias does, in the guise of experts in this regard. None of this amounts to a fallacy and none of it requires a broad methodological response.[52]

                                                             – Nehamas 1987: 290–291

Notice that Nehamas' version of the reject (PD) approach proceeds primarily[53] by restricting the application of the variables in (PD). Recall that (PD), as we introduced it at the beginning of this essay, is a fully general conjunction of (P) and (D) and so can be represented as follows:

> (PD) For any A, and for any F-ness, if A fails to know what F-ness is, then A fails to know, for any x, that x is F, and, for any G, that F-ness is G.

While Nehamas leaves unrestricted the application of 'A' (the principles Nehamas attributes to Socrates apply to everyone), he takes Socrates to restrict the application of 'F-ness' to 'primarily the virtues', and the application of the 'x' and 'G' to controversial or disputable instances and properties of F-ness or instances and properties in some way connected to the essence of F-ness. I mention this here because the third version of the reject (PD) approach has much in common with Nehamas' approach in that it does not take any of the passages to require a Socratic or Platonic endorsement of (PD) but only of weaker and less general principles, but it does so, not by restricting the application of the variables but by distinguishing between distinct types of knowledge.

Thomas Brickhouse and Nicholas Smith represent this third version of the reject (PD) approach (Brickhouse and Smith 1994: 45–60).[54] They are unique in addressing each and every one of the passages cited above on behalf of Socrates' endorsement of (PD). But they do not treat all these passages in the same way. Rather they appear to see the passages as falling roughly into three groups.

They understand some of the passages as simply failing to testify to Socrates' endorsement of any very general substantive epistemic principle at all. This is, for example, how I understand their reading of *Lysis* 223b, *Meno* 71a–b, *Charmides* 176a–b and *Protagoras* 312c. For example, after considering a variety of ways of understanding *Meno* 71a–b that fall short of (PD) in its full generality, they appear to settle on the idea that the question in the (b) portion is rhetorical and it is Meno who commits to the impossibility of knowledge of what properties F-ness has, when one is ignorant of what F-ness is (Brickhouse and Smith 1994: 52).[55] Brickhouse and Smith take Socrates to be maintaining in the *Lysis* simply that Menexenus and Lysis look ridiculous in failing 'to understand what they take themselves so plainly to instantiate' (Brickhouse and Smith 1994: 51), i.e., a friend. And in the *Protagoras*, they take Socrates to indicate only that 'one ordinarily does not go to a carpenter [or any other expert] for some assistance without some fairly clear idea of what the carpenter is skilled at doing, unless, of course, one has some other, very exceptional ground for doing so' (Brickhouse and Smith 1994: 53). In none of these passages, then, according to Brickhouse and Smith, does Socrates endorse an exceptionless epistemic principle on the order of (PD).

A second group of passages, according to Brickhouse and Smith, testify to Socrates' endorsement of something like the following principle:

(BS) If A fails to know what F-ness is, then A fails to know *clearly* anything about F-ness.

Thus, Brickhouse and Smith understand *Laches* 189e–190b, as well as the passages from the *Euthyphro* and *Hippias Major*, as testifying to Socrates' endorsement of the view that failing to know what F-ness is entails failing to know in general what things are F. According to Brickhouse and Smith, Socrates distinguishes between two types of knowledge, a kind that is constitutive of wisdom (expert or clear knowledge) and a kind that is not (ordinary or unclear knowledge) (see Brickhouse and Smith 1994: 30–45). The former kind of knowledge requires knowing how or why something is the case; the latter sort of knowledge requires knowing simply that something is the case. It is only the former sort of knowledge that allows one to know in general what things are F, and the *Laches*, *Euthyphro* and *Hippias Major* passages indicate that according to Socrates, knowing in general what things are F requires knowledge of what F-ness is. Consequently, they indicate a Socratic commitment to (BS). But given Brickhouse and Smith's distinction between two types of knowledge we should not confuse (BS) with:

(BW) If A fails to know what F-ness is, then A fails to know in the ordinary way anything about F-ness.

THE PRIORITY OF DEFINITION   141

Whatever plausibility that accrues to (BS) in virtue of the nature of clear knowledge is absent from (BW).

According to Brickhouse and Smith, Socrates does not need to appeal to knowledge of how or why specific actions are pious in order to search for an answer to his 'What is piety?' question. Nor does Socrates need to know why the Spartans were courageous at Plataea in order to accept it as a counter-example to Laches' answer that courage is remaining in one's ranks. Moreover, Socrates' own professions of knowledge should not be understood as the sort of knowledge that constitutes wisdom, i.e., as knowledge of how or why it is bad to disobey one's superior. On the contrary, given Socrates' repeated expressions of his failure to be wise, we should understand Socrates' professions of knowledge to be knowledge of the ordinary sort. Finally, while it is philosophically implausible to think one needs to know what virtue is in order to know in an ordinary way *that* Meno is virtuous, it is not so implausible to so suppose that one might need this definitional knowledge in order to know *why* Meno is virtuous. Thus, the evidence against (PD) which we discussed above tells against (BW), but the *Laches*, *Euthyphro* and *Hippias Major* passages only commit Socrates to (BS).

The final group of passages (*La.* 190b–c, *M.* 100b and *Rep.* 354d–c), according to Brickhouse and Smith, fail to testify to an *epistemological* principle at all. Rather, according to Brickhouse and Smith, they testify to a *procedural* priority principle. For example, when at the end of the *Meno* Socrates says:

> We shall have clear knowledge of this when, before we investigate how it comes to be present in men, we first try to find out what virtue in itself is.
>
> > – M. 100b

he is not simply testifying to his commitment to (BS), the principle according to which *clear* knowledge of how virtue comes to be acquired requires knowledge of what virtue is, he is also endorsing a particular procedure which can lead to the acquisition of *unclear* knowledge of how virtue comes to be acquired. The idea is that seeking to come to know what virtue is would enable one to acquire *clear* knowledge of how virtue comes to be acquired, if one's inquiry were to succeed in coming to know what virtue is.[56] But proceeding to inquire what virtue is will also enable one to acquire *unclear* knowledge of how virtue comes to be acquired, without succeeding in knowing what virtue is. Brickhouse and Smith maintain that one of the ways one can acquire *unclear* knowledge according to Socrates is by means of repeated elenctic episodes devoted to an inquiry concerning what some F-ness is. Thus, when Socrates encourages an inquiry concerning what virtue is at the end of the *Meno*, this is not because Socrates thinks knowledge of the nature of virtue is necessary for *unclear* knowledge concerning how virtues come to be acquired, but because he wants to encourage a kind of inquiry which has the potential to lead to the acquisition of *unclear* knowledge over the long run. Even so, Brickhouse and Smith are quick to point out, Socrates recognises other methods of acquiring *unclear* knowledge besides searching for answers to his 'What is F-ness?' questions, through dreams, divinations or the like.

A fourth and final version of the reject (PD) approach appears in a recent paper by Michael Forster. Forster argues against what he maintains is the orthodox interpretation of Socratic definitions, which consists of the following three claims:

> First, Socrates' motive in demanding ethical definitions was a desire to attain them in order to achieve ethical knowledge in and through them. Second, Socrates expected

142   THE BLOOMSBURY HANDBOOK OF SOCRATES

these definitions to provide substantive explanations of the qualities referred to by the
definienda, and accordingly to be scientifically abstruse and complex in character (not
the sort of definitions that it would be reasonable to expect the ordinary man to have
at his fingertips). Third, and relatedly, Socrates expected these definitions to be more
than mere statements of the meanings of the definienda, more than mere statements of
what anyone must know in order to understand the definienda (in the everyday
semantic sense of 'understand').

– Forster 2006b: 3

As part of his argument against the third claim, that Socrates expected more than mere
statements of meaning in response to his 'What is F-ness?' questions, Forster cites what at
first blush appears to be Socrates' endorsement of (PD), but more precisely, turns out to
be Socrates' endorsement of a considerably weaker version of (PD).[57] According to
Forster, we should understand the passages that have been cited as evidence for (PD),
instead as evidence for

(MF) If A fails to understand 'the meaning that the word 'F-ness' bears',[58] then A fails
to know anything else about F-ness.

If we do, then we can understand why Socrates takes this principle to be so self-evident
as not to need argument, at least on a plausible construal.[59] For example, according to
Forster, one cannot plausibly think one knows that Helen is beautiful (i.e., that Helen has
beauty) if one fails to understand the meaning that the word 'beauty' bears. In this way,
Forster avoids the philosophical objection to Socrates' commitment to (PD). (MF), at
least on one construal, is simply not philosophically implausible. On the contrary, it is
self-evidently true, at least according to Forster. Consequently, all of the passages that
testify to (MF) testify to understanding Socrates as taking answers to his 'What is F-ness?'
questions as merely amounting to statements of meaning. For the best explanation of
those passages is a Socratic endorsement of (MF), since an explanation that commits
Socrates to (PD) would be uncharitable; and an endorsement of (MF) indicates a
commitment to taking answers to 'What is F-ness?' questions as merely amounting to
statements of meaning.

Unfortunately, Forster cites, but does not discuss, the passages that he takes as evidence
for (MF) (see Forster 2006b: nn. 81 and 82).[60] He does, however, have a way of countering
the textual evidence that has been cited against Socrates' commitment to (PD), now
understood as (MF). Forster maintains that the view that Socrates has a method for
searching for knowledge is at odds with Socrates' view that knowledge is beyond a
human's ken (see Forster 2006b: 6–22). Consequently, Forster rejects the evidence against
Socrates' endorsement of (PD)/(MF) based on his method of searching for and testing
answers to his 'What is F-ness?' questions. Since knowledge of such answers is beyond a
human's ken; according to Forster, Socrates' method should not be seen as searching for
such knowledge. Rather, Socrates' method is aimed simply at refuting his interlocutors'
pretensions to wisdom, and Socrates can accomplish this aim, without professing to know
examples and properties. This is because on Forster's account most of the interesting
Socratic refutations are aimed at uncovering internal inconsistencies in the interlocutors'
answers, while true belief concerning those examples and properties suffices for the
remaining refutations found in the text (see Forster 2006a).[61]

Finally, Forster explains how (MF) fails to conflict with Socrates' alleged professions of
knowledge of examples and properties of F-ness whose definition he professes not to

THE PRIORITY OF DEFINITION

143

know. Forster simply denies that any such Socratic professions of knowledge are to be found in the text of the so-called Socratic dialogues. According to Forster, Socrates' and his interlocutors' ethical insights (insofar as they have them) are 'at bottom an acceptance of [i.e., belief in] uncomprehended true sentences' (Forster 2007: 18 n. 27; see also Forster 2006b: 14–16). Forster appears somewhat uncomfortable with this consequence, but not enough apparently to overthrow the evidence on behalf of (MF).[62]

IV.III Embrace (PD)

With Forster's interpretation we come exceptionally close to the third and final general approach to the interpretive tension surrounding Socrates' endorsement of (PD). According to this approach Socrates endorses (PD), the passages allegedly in conflict with this endorsement can be explained away, and (PD) is not as philosophically implausible as it has been supposed.

Let us begin with the version of this approach which Vlastos proclaimed in 1985 to be 'now widely regarded to be the right solution to the [tension]' (Vlastos 1985a: 23 n. 52) and which he dubbed 'the sufficiency of true belief' interpretation, or STB for short.[63] As the name implies, the key to the STB interpretation is that the evidence cited against Socrates' endorsement of (PD) does not require that individuals possess knowledge of instances and properties of F-ness prior to knowledge of what F-ness is. Rather it only requires that individuals possess true belief of instances and properties of F-ness.

For example, according to the STB interpretation, it suffices to refute Laches' definition that courage is remaining in the ranks and facing one's enemies to believe correctly that the Spartans were courageous in their retreat at Plataea. One does not need to *know* that the Spartans were courageous. Again, one does not need to know whether Charmides is an example of a temperate individual to begin one's search for the nature of temperance by looking at him. Rather it suffices to believe correctly that Charmides is temperate. Nor does one need to know that temperance is fine and good to reject Charmides' definition that temperance is modesty. And finally, those passages in which Socrates expresses strong positive convictions concerning various F-nesses, whose 'What is F-ness?' questions he professes not to be able to answer, should not be read as knowledge claims, but rather professions of true belief (see Irwin 1995: 29 and Fine 2008b: 72 and n. 40). Those who endorse STB point out, however, that (PD) does not prevent the possibility of true belief concerning the examples and properties of an F-ness when one fails to know what F-ness is. Rather, (PD) only prohibits *knowledge* of those examples and properties when one fails to know what F-ness is. Consequently, the alleged textual tension disappears. (PD) only prohibits *knowledge* of examples and properties prior to knowledge of what F-ness is. And the evidence of the text only requires *true belief* of examples and properties prior to knowledge of what F-ness is.

Unfortunately, advocates of the STB interpretation devote very little time responding to the philosophical implausibility of (PD). Indeed, Irwin argues that Socrates must think true belief of examples and properties is sufficient for inquiry into what F-ness is, since such an inquiry would be impossible if he did not, given his endorsement of (PD). And, Irwin takes Socrates' endorsement of (PD) as the best philosophical explanation of Socrates' view that failure in an elenchus is evidence of an interlocutor's lack of knowledge (see, for example, Irwin 1995: 20–21 and 27–29). Nevertheless, the alleged philosophical implausibility of supposing one can acquire knowledge of what F-ness is or reject answers to Socratic 'What is F-ness?' questions on the basis of examples and properties without knowledge of those examples and properties is at least open to debate (see Fine 1992: 212, *pace* White 2008: 43–44 n. 13). But Geach's charge that 'we know heaps of things without being able to define the terms in which we express our knowledge' goes explicitly unaddressed, at least as far as I have been able to determine.

I have reserved to the end my own response to the interpretive tension surrounding Socrates' endorsement of (PD).[64] Like the supporters of the STB interpretation, I embrace Socrates' commitment to (PD). I take the evidence cited on behalf of Socrates' endorsement as providing a compellingly strong inference to the best explanation. I concede that no single passage requires a Socratic endorsement of (PD),[65] but the variety of passages which indicate substitution instances of (PD) or something very much like it provides good reason to maintain that the best explanation of all of those texts is Socrates' endorsement of (PD). Of course, an inference to the best explanation is especially susceptible to counter-evidence, and so just as the defenders of STB needed to explain away the counter-evidence we rehearsed above, so do I.

Perhaps the most significant difference between my version of the embrace (PD) approach and the STB version is the way I respond to the first two textual considerations. Recall that the first two textual considerations concerned Socrates' method of seeking to come to know answers to his 'What is F-ness?' questions and testing the answers offered by his various interlocutors. It was maintained that Socrates sought and tested those answers by appealing to examples and properties of F-ness. The defenders of the STB interpretation agree, but deny that doing so requires knowledge, as opposed to true belief, of those examples and properties of F-ness. I, however, maintain that supposing Socrates to be seeking to come to know answers to his 'What is F-ness?' questions and to be refuting (i.e., showing to be false) answers to his 'What is F-ness?' questions is to misunderstand the nature of Socratic method, or at least a unique and prevalent aspect of it – the Socratic elenchus. I defend an interpretation of the Socratic elenchus according to which Socrates does not aim to come to know an answer to his 'What is F-ness?' questions nor refute the answers that he has been offered. Rather Socrates aims to test the knowledge claims of his interlocutors. And that Socrates can and does do that by examining the coherence of his interlocutors' F-ness related beliefs.[66] But to examine and test the coherence of his interlocutors' beliefs Socrates neither needs to know nor correctly believe that the examples and properties cited in the course of an elenchus are examples and properties of F-ness.

In the case of the texts in which Socrates professes to know examples and properties of F-ness despite disavowing knowledge of the relevant F-ness, I am sympathetic to the STB interpretation. I maintain that the alleged Socratic professions of knowledge are much less frequent than they have sometimes been taken to be, but that nevertheless a few such professions remain. In the cases that remain we should either understand Socrates to be professing a weaker sort of knowledge than the robust sort referred to in (PD), roughly along the lines of Brickhouse and Smith's distinction between ordinary knowledge and clear knowledge, or we should understand those Socratic professions as misstatements made in the heat of the moment or in the manner of the vulgar.[67] Neither of these alternatives are entirely satisfactory, but it is noteworthy that this difficulty is not unique to those who embrace Socrates' endorsement of (PD). Anyone who takes seriously Socrates' professions of ignorance must opt for one or the other of these alternatives.[68]

Finally, I want to turn to the philosophical implausibility of (PD), because I believe it is this objection that has driven the debate concerning Socrates' endorsement of (PD)

THE PRIORITY OF DEFINITION

145

more than any other. Indeed, I suspect that it was Geach's philosophical attack on Socrates that led many Socratic scholars to become uneasy with Robinson's 'vague impression' that Socrates endorses (PD).[69] This led them to re-examine the text, perhaps more carefully, and predictably texts were 'discovered' that testified against Socrates' endorsement.[70] But I wonder how genuinely implausible (PD) is. Consider, for example, Geach's assertion that 'We know heaps of things without being able to define the terms in which we express our knowledge.' Would Socrates agree that we know heaps of things about the good, virtue, justice, piety, courage, temperance, friendship, et cetera? One fairly clear lesson Socrates learned from the Delphic Oracle story in the *Apology* is that most, if not all, of us (including Geach presumably) think we know a great deal more than we do in fact know. So Socrates would not find the results of his commitment to (PD) to be as implausible as Geach (and apparently most contemporary philosophers) would. But how are we to understand this difference? We can either think that Socrates is just mistaken in denying that we know the heaps of things we think we know, or we can think that Socrates has in mind a more robust sort of knowledge than the sort that Geach and others do. In the latter case Socrates is not denying that we know – in the ordinary, justified true belief sense of knowledge – the heaps of things that we think we do; rather he is denying that we know those things in a more robust way. If this is so, then (PD) does not require knowledge of what F-ness is in order to know – in the ordinary, justified true belief way – examples and properties of F-ness. Rather it only requires knowledge of what F-ness is in order to know – in the robust way – examples and properties of F-ness. But understood in this latter way, (PD) loses whatever implausibility it may have had understood in the former way.[71] I maintain that it is not only the textual evidence on behalf of (PD) that indicates this latter way of understanding (PD) (based on a moderate principle of charity),[72] but also a variety of other evidence – independently of one's interpretation of Socrates' endorsement of (PD) – indicates Socrates' endorsement of such a robust understanding of knowledge.[73] This latter evidence, however, serves to reinforce the textual evidence on behalf of Socrates' endorsement of (PD).

V. CONCLUSION

In the end, I hope it is clear that the question of Socrates' endorsement of some sort of epistemic priority of answers to his 'What is F-ness?' questions remains open and hotly disputed. The textual evidence appears to cut in both directions, as do the philosophical considerations. Moreover, attempts to address this interpretive tension involve a variety of other (equally controversial) features of Socratic and Platonic philosophy, including, but not limited to, the compositional order of the dialogues, the nature (if any) of Plato's philosophical development, the nature of Socratic knowledge, the nature of Socrates' professions of ignorance and knowledge, the nature of Socrates' distinction between knowledge and true belief, the nature of Socratic definition, the nature of the Socratic elenchus and, more generally, the nature of Socrates' philosophical mission and method. It also involves numerous philosophical questions, ranging from the nature of knowledge to the nature of the philosophical method. This, of course, should not surprise us. It is not unique to the question of Socrates' endorsement of (PD), but likely applies to every interesting question concerning Socratic philosophy. Indeed, it testifies to the depth and fertility of Socrates' philosophy and the texts of his most famous student.

NOTES

1. My concern in this chapter will be primarily with the character Socrates in Plato's so-called Socratic dialogues. I begin with Aristotle and Xenophon, however, to indicate the likelihood that the feature of Socratic dialogues (and indeed of the Platonic dialogues a whole) concerned with 'What is F-ness?' questions may have been a feature of the historical Socrates' philosophical perspective. By the 'Socratic dialogues' I mean (in alphabetical order) *Ap.*, *Chrm.*, *Cr.*, *Euthyd.*, *Euthphr.*, *Grg.*, *Hi.Ma.*, *Hi.Mi.*, *Ion*, *La.*, *Ly.*, *M.*, *Prt.* and *Rep.* I. As we will see below, the scholarly debate concerning Socrates' preoccupation with 'What is F-ness?' involves, among other things, which of these dialogues should be included on this list. I begin, however, by being inclusive. Those who are less inclusive will be discussed below.

2. My reasons for using the inelegant 'F-ness' can be found in Benson 1990a: 125 n. 2.

3. See n. 1 above.

4. See Sedley 1989 for a different understanding of the Ly.

5. It is at this point that the debate concerning whether Socrates is pursuing nominal or real definitions arises; see, for example, Locke, *Essay*, III 3.13–17, Vlastos 1965: 156 n. 26, Penner 1992a: 141–144, Fine 1992: 202, Irwin 1995: 25–26, Fine 2004: 54 n. 36 and 62 n. 58 and Forster 2006b: 25–33.

6. See Dancy 2004: 23–24, who points out that only one of the six occurrences of '*horos*' (*Rep.* 331d), and only two of the fifteen occurrences of '*horizein*' (*Chrm.* 173a and *La.* 194c) in the Socratic dialogues, are best translated as 'definition'. In Benson 2011 I mistakenly claimed that Socrates does sometimes use '*horismos*' in the Socratic dialogues. To the best of my knowledge he does not.

7. For important discussions see, for example, Nehamas 1975, Vlastos 1981b, Woodruff 1982: ch. 4, Benson 1990a, Wolfsdorf 2003b, Forster 2006b, Charles 2006 and Fine 2010.

8. See, for example, Ross 1951: 16. See Forster 2006b: 35–39 for a different, but related, motivation.

9. The principle has gone by a number of names, perhaps most famously by 'the Socratic fallacy'. Dancy 2004: 35–64 calls it the Intellectualist Assumption (AI). (See Nehamas 1987: 275–277, who takes Socrates' alleged commitment to this principle as a component of 'Socratic intellectualism'.) I prefer the priority of definitional knowledge, but I will not ride my hobby horse here.

10. See Chapter 3 and, esp., Vlastos 1983a, Kraut 1983, Brickhouse and Smith 1984, Polansky 1985, Benson 1987, Brickhouse and Smith 1994a: ch. 1, Benson 1995, Adams 1998, the essays in Scott 2002, Forster 2006a, Young 2006, White 2008 and Benson 2011.

11. For the notion of F-ness related beliefs, see my brief remarks concerning 'appropriate related beliefs' at Benson 2000: 161–162. For the notion of doxastic coherence as opposed to consistent beliefs, see Benson 2011.

12. See, for example, Irwin 1995: 27 and Dancy 2004: 37–38 for this requirement.

13. See Benson 2000: 142–160 for a defence of a Socratic endorsement of a more plausible version of the sufficiency principle.

14. Concerning Plato's authorship of the *Hi.Ma.*, see Woodruff 1982 and Kahn 1985. Its relative compositional date will be an issue below.

15. By the end of the dialogue it has become fairly clear that this is Socrates' alter ego.

THE PRIORITY OF DEFINITION

16. All translations are my own unless otherwise noted, in which case they are found in Cooper 1997.

17. For a longer discussion of this passage along roughly the same lines see Wolfsdorf 2004c: 42–45.

18. For a longer discussion of the first *Eu.* passage along similar lines see Dancy 2004: 41–47.

19. See Santas 1972: 138 who takes this to be the most explicit text for (P), but denies that Socrates is committed to it since it is put in the mouth of Charmides.

20. Nearly every interlocutor in the Socratic dialogues professes to believe something about a relevant F-ness whose ignorance of which is subsequently revealed in the same dialogue.

21. See Brickhouse and Smith 1994: 51 for this general line of criticism.

22. Lesher 1987 takes the evidence for (D) to be persuasive, but not the evidence for (P).

23. To be fair the (b) portion of this passage restricts the principle to Socrates, but the (c) portion makes clear that this is not philosophically salient.

24. See also *Grg.* 462c–d and 463c for a similar suggestion concerning rhetoric, although the *Grg.* passages may be more suggestive of a procedural priority principle. For the procedural principle see also *M.* 86d–e, and my discussion of Brickhouse and Smith 1994, which follows.

25. See Robinson 1953: 51, who was taken to task by Beversluis 1987: 211 for resting content with a 'vague impression'.

26. In addition to this textual evidence, Irwin (1995: 27–28) offers an argument that Socrates must have been committed to (PD) in order to plausibly take failure in an elenchus as evidence for an individual's general lack of knowledge.

27. In addition to Beversluis 1987 and Vlastos 1990, who cite specific instances of this tension, see Santas 1979: 116, Brickhouse and Smith 1984b: 128, Nehamas 1987: 292 and Woodruff 1988: 22, who make the point somewhat more generally. To describe this and the following consideration as 'textual considerations' is a bit imprecise. The claim that Socrates employs a method of inquiry and of testing answers to his 'What is F-ness?' questions that depends on *examining* examples and properties of F-ness is a *textual* consideration. The further claim that such a method of inquiry and of testing depends on *knowledge* of those examples and properties of F-ness is a *philosophical* consideration, one which, as we will see below, is denied by those who defend the sufficiency of true belief interpretation. See pp. 143–144 below.

28. Cited by Beversluis 1987: 212 and Vlastos 1990: 6 as evidence against Socrates' commitment to (PD). See also Socrates' example of how to answer the 'What is swiftness?' question at *La.* 192a–b.

29. Beversluis 1987: 212–213 cites the examples from the *Eu.* and *Chrm.*

30. See Beversluis 1987: 222 n. 17, who cites in addition the following passages against (D): *Chrm.* 160e and *La.* 192c, 192c and 192d. He also cites the following passages against both (P) and (D); *Cr.* 54d, *Grg.* 474b, *Prt.* 329e–333b and *Grg.* 470d. But, in fact, the number of passages in which Socrates appeals to a property of the definiendum in the course of examining an interlocutor's answer are nearly too numerous to list.

31. For perhaps the clearest statement of this line of argument, see Brickhouse and Smith 1994: 45.

32. For more detailed accounts of Socrates' various knowledge avowals and disavowals see Vlastos 1985a, Brickhouse and Smith 1994: 30–72, Benson 2000: 223–38, Forster 2007, Wolfsdorf 2004a, Fine 2008b and Wolfsdorf 2008: 131–145.

33. He does, of course, profess ignorance of the form of the good at *Rep.* 506b–c.

34. It is noteworthy that the *Hi.Ma.* passage appears to indicate that knowledge of what fineness is is necessary not only for knowledge that something is fine, but also that something is shameful. This may be connected to the general Greek commitment to knowledge of opposites. See, for example, *Phd.* 97c–d.

35. Arguably less explicit professions of knowledge together with corresponding professions of ignorance of answers to 'What is F-ness?' questions provide similar evidence against Socrates' commitment to (D), as well as (P). See, e.g., *Prt.* 357d–e, *Rep.* 351a and *Euthd.* 296e–297a.

36. Geach 1966: 371. Geach follows this by indicating the philosophical implausibility of successful inquiry given a commitment to (PD). See White 2008: 33 and n. 31 above. But it seems clear that Geach's main objection is the one quoted above.

37. See Brickhouse and Smith 1994: 51 n. 34, who suggest that I am alone in attempting to deny (PD)'s implausibility. For some potential fellow travellers see Penner 1992a: 168 n. 78 and Prior 1998.

38. The taxonomy of interpretations is an imprecise and subjective business, and nothing of philosophical importance hangs on the way I have chosen to carve up the interpretations. My hope is simply that it may help the reader see the various options for responding to the interpretative tension. See n. 57 below.

39. Other scholars who might be placed in this general category of interpreters include Charles 2006: 125 and Wolfsdorf 2004c: esp. 67. But neither of them is as explicit as Dancy nor do they maintain a longer term resolution of the tension as Dancy does. To this extent Charles and Wolfsdorf may be closer to Geach. See also Irwin 1995: 358 n. 32, which concedes this possibility.

40. Dancy dubs this principle the Intellectualist Assumption; Dancy 2004: 36 n. 40. For Dancy's defence of Socrates' endorsement of (PD), with which I am in substantial agreement, see Dancy 2004: 42–64; see also Wolfsdorf 2004c: 40–55.

41. Dancy is not rejecting the principle of charity completely. He would endorse the principle that one should not understand a philosopher in such a way that he or she is inconsistent 'if there are viable alternatives. The trouble', according to Dancy 'is that here no alternatives seem to me really viable' (Dancy 2004: 41).

42. That Plato abandoned (PD) in the so-called middle and late dialogues is a matter of some dispute. For some passages which might be cited for his continued commitment, see *Rep.* 336c, 354b–c, 402b–c, 462c, 505a–506a, *Symp.* 199c–d, *Tht.* 147b, 196d–e, 210a, *Sph.* 260d–261a and *Phlb.* 12c–d. Of course, each of these passages needs individual examination and can be interpreted otherwise, just as in the Socratic dialogues. It is interesting to note that the Vlastos-Beversluis interpretation discussed below takes the opposite approach. It denies that Socrates endorsed (PD) in the Socratic dialogues, but concedes that Plato endorsed it in the post-Socratic dialogues. See also Kahn 1996: esp. 163, who, though rejecting Dancy's developmentalism, agrees that the tension can be found in dialogues like the *Laches* and resolved in dialogues like the *Phd.* in virtue of the introduction of the theory of recollection and theory of forms. But Kahn does not think that Plato abandons (PD).

43. I doubt that Dancy thinks the theory of recollection smells like roses.

44. This is how, for example, Vlastos understands *Chrm.* 176a–b and how Brickhouse and Smith understand *Ly.* 223b.

THE PRIORITY OF DEFINITION

149

45. For perhaps the earliest version of this general approach in the recent literature, see Santas 1972.

46. The interpretation is presented in the following essays: Vlastos 1985a, Beversluis 1987, and Vlastos 1990. The dependence on each other is clear from the notes (see esp. Beversluis 1987: 223 n. 29 and Vlastos 1990: 13 n. 1), although the direction of influence is more difficult to determine. Such differences as there are between these two scholars on this issue will be for the most part set aside for our purposes. A more recent version of this general approach can be found in Ferejohn 2013: 21–63, though the way he understands the change in the *Meno* is different.

47. They consider *Rep. I* to be a Socratic dialogue, but they take the concluding passage of this book, which contains the evidence for (PD), to be tacked on to facilitate the book's new role as the introduction to Plato's *magnum opus*. See, for example, Vlastos 1990: 15 n. 31.

48. See Beversluis 1987: 214. Somewhat surprisingly neither Vlastos nor Beversluis discuss *Eu.* 4d–5d. They do, however, rightly point out that *Eu.* 6d–e, cited by Geach on behalf of (P), testifies not to the necessity of definitional knowledge, but rather to its sufficiency. (See also Santas 1972: 136.) They maintain that *Eu.* 15d–e is a 'spin-off' of 6d–e (Vlastos 1985a: 23 n. 54 and Beversluis 1987: 215). But reading *Eu.* 15d–e in this way is difficult to understand; see Dancy 2004: 47 n. 68.

49. Beversluis 1987: 215 only cites *La.* 190b–c and takes it to testify to the view that 'if you do not know the nature of virtue, you cannot usefully advise anyone about how best to achieve it', but as we saw above, *La.* 189e–190b requires something more. Vlastos 1985a: 23 n. 54, who does cite *La.* 189e–190b, only says that it does not assert (PD) in full generality. Vlastos says the same thing about *Chrm.* 176a–b, and neither of them says anything about the *Prt.* passage.

50. See Vlastos 1985a for how Socrates' professions of knowledge are to be understood on this approach.

51. Nehamas 1987: 290. The connection between a property being essential (or nearly so: see Nehamas 1987: 284–285) and being controversial is brought out by Nehamas' suggestion that the essential properties of F-ness are in as much dispute as the nature of F-ness itself. See Nehamas 1987: 284 and 292.

52. Nehamas does not explicitly discuss *Euthphr.* 15d–e, *Chrm.* 176a–b, *La.* 189e–190b or *Prt.* 312b–c, but one suspects he would deal with them similarly.

53. I say 'primarily' because Nehamas' talk of discoursing generally may have inspired Brickhouse and Smith's distinction between expert and ordinary knowledge below. See Brickhouse and Smith 1994: 60 n. 41, where they explicitly acknowledge the influence of Nehamas 1987.

54. See also Woodruff 1988, who at times appears to offer a similar resolution based on a distinction between expert and non-expert or ordinary knowledge, as opposed to Brickhouse and Smith's distinction between clear and unclear knowledge or knowledge how (or why) and knowledge that; see Woodruff 1988: 80, 85 and 92, and McPherran 1988: esp. 126, who prefers Brickhouse and Smith's version of this resolution to Woodruff's. At other times Woodruff's view resembles Nehamas' approach; see Woodruff 1988: 104. See n. 38. Brickhouse and Smith's discussion is more extensive and so I will focus on their account. See also Brickhouse and Smith 1984b for an earlier version of their resolution.

55. Similarly, they appear to maintain that it is Charmides, not Socrates, who endorses (P) at *Chrm.* 176a–b; Brickhouse and Smith 1994: 59 n. 40.

56. According to Brickhouse and Smith, Socrates takes such knowledge to be impossible for mere humans to acquire.

57. It is, of course, somewhat arbitrary whether we consider Forster as maintaining 'a reject (PD) view' or as 'an embrace (PD) view'. I have located Forster's view in the former because he denies that Socrates endorses (PD) under the orthodox construal of Socratic definition. Nevertheless, the view that I endorse also attempts to explain away the evidence against (PD) in part by recommending a non-orthodox understanding of (PD), and yet I categorise it as 'an embrace (PD) view'. Indeed, one might take Forster's view to be an attempt to explain away the evidence against (PD) by endorsing a weakened version of (PD), while I attempt to explain away the same evidence by endorsing a strengthened version of (PD). Understood in this way, one would assume that Forster's and my approach ought to fall within the same taxonomical genus. What this shows, of course, is simply that taxonomies of interpretations are arbitrary and typically reflect the taxonomist's interests and prejudices. Nothing of philosophical importance hangs on whether Forster's view should be seen as rejecting Socrates' endorsement of (PD) or my view should be seen as embracing Socrates' endorsement of (PD). See n. 38 above.

58. Forster 2006b: 34–35: 'though not necessarily that the word ['F-ness'] bears it, since, for instance, you might happen not to know English . . .'

59. Unfortunately, according to Forster, the plausible construal is not Socrates'. Forster maintains that according to Socrates in order to understand 'the meaning that the word "F-ness" bears" one must be able to give an informative synonym of that word. (See Forster 2006b: 27.) But such an assumption is false and has very damaging consequences for Socrates' project (Forster 2006b: 45–46). For the inability of Socrates' interlocutors to give an informative synonym does not show that they lack an understanding of 'the meaning that the word "F-ness" bears' and so does not show that they fail to know anything else about F-ness. Thus, in the end, Forster agrees with Geach and Dancy that Socrates' position is 'fatally flawed' (Forster 2007: 32–33), but it is not because of Socrates' commitment to (MF), rather because of Socrates' commitment to a particular version of the verbalisation requirement. See (V) above.

60. Forster generously cites Benson 1990b as having 'convincingly refuted' those who would reject Socrates' commitment to (PD). I fear, however, Forster's generosity considerably overestimates the results of my essay.

61. For the claim that true belief suffices for the remaining refutations, see Forster 2006a: 19 n. 25.

62. Politis 2015 offers an extended version of the reject (PD) approach. As I understand it, he maintains that definitional knowledge (knowledge of the answer to a *ti esti* question) is required only for knowledge of answers to whether-or-not questions which have generated *aporia*. He also provides a complex theory of whether-or-not questions and the *aporia* they can generate.

63. To my knowledge there is no sustained defence of this approach in the literature. Various scholars appear to endorse it, but with varying degrees of enthusiasm. Woodruff 1982: 140 appeared to endorse it, but then appears to abandon it in Woodruff 1988. STB is not the main focus of Burnyeat 1977, although he appears to endorse it, and Irwin 1977: 40–41 only devotes a couple of pages to the issue. See also Irwin 1995: 27–28 and Santas 1979:

THE PRIORITY OF DEFINITION

151

115–126. Perhaps the most sustained defence is provided by Gail Fine, given her defence of a sufficiency of true belief interpretation of Meno's paradox. Since she thinks Socrates endorses (PD), which she labels [PKW] (Fine 2004: 57 and 75), and she thinks the paradox depends upon (PD) (Fine 1992: 201–204), her defence of her interpretation of how Plato/Socrates avoids the paradox amounts to a defence of Socrates/Plato's endorsement of (PD). More recently, see Fine 2014: 31–42. It should be noted, however, that she does not offer a detailed review of the evidence that creates the tension we have been trying to resolve.

64. See Benson 1990b, Benson 2000: ch. 6 and most recently Benson 2011. See also Prior 1998 and perhaps Scott 2006: 86–90 and n. 25, although since Scott is only concerned with the views endorsed in the *M.* he does not respond to the contrary evidence in the Socratic dialogues. Scott does appear to endorse something like my response to the philosophical objection.

65. Although *M.* 71b comes very close to requiring a Socratic endorsement of (D), at least in my view.

66. See Benson 1987, Benson 1995, Benson 2000: ch. 2–4 and most recently Benson 2011. I do not, however, deny that Socrates seeks to come to know answers to his 'What is F-ness?' questions in the elenctic dialogues. I simply deny that he does so by employing his elenchus, at least in the way it is typically understood. Rather, he seeks to come to know answers to his 'What is F-ness?' questions by finding someone who knows what F-ness is and learning from him or her. See, for example, *Hi.Mi.* 369d–e. I hint at this view in Benson 2003: 9 and n. 12. I develop this view at length in Benson 2002. Thus, unlike Forster, who would agree that, at least in the interesting cases, Socrates' elenctic method aims at uncovering an incoherence in the interlocutors' beliefs, I concede that Socrates is seeking knowledge of answers to his 'What is F-ness?' questions. Rather, I deny that the method by which he seeks this knowledge, as well as the method by which he tests others' purported knowledge of these answers, requires that Socrates know (or even truly believe) examples and properties of F-ness whose nature he fails to know, at least according to Socrates' own lights.

67. See Benson 2000: 223–238 for longer discussion of these passages. See also Irwin 1995: 29, Fine 2008b: 72 and n. 40 and Forster 2006b: 14–16 cited above.

68. This is true even if one does not take Socrates to be professing universal ignorance, as I do not. At *Ap.* 23b Socrates professes ignorance of important things, and it is difficult not to take the knowledge professions made at *Ap.* 29b and 37b to be about important things. See Benson 2000: 231–233 for why I do not think Vlastos' distinction between elenctic and certain knowledge can resolve this difficulty.

69. See n. 25 above.

70. I do not mean in any way to be critical here. This is how the history of philosophy makes progress. See Vlastos 1983a: 46–47 for the idea of 'discovering' a text one has read numerous times before.

71. See Brickhouse and Smith's view (BS) above.

72. See n. 41 above.

73. See, for example, Benson 2000: ch. 9, Fine 2008b and Wolfsdorf 2008: ch. 3.

CHAPTER SEVEN

Socratic Virtue Intellectualism

JUSTIN C. CLARK

INTRODUCTION: SOCRATIC INTELLECTUALISM

In Plato's *Apology*, Socrates describes his mission in life to his fellow Athenians as follows: 'I was always concerned with each of you, approaching you like a father or an elder brother to persuade you to care for virtue (*aretē*)' (31b).[1] 'Virtue' refers collectively to the various excellences in human character. For Socrates, the virtues are five – piety, courage, temperance, justice and wisdom – and 'caring for virtue' means cultivating 'the very best state of one's soul'. Thus, Socrates goes around urging his fellow Athenians to prioritise virtue above the more common concerns of personal wealth and reputation (30b), and questioning them about the nature of the virtues.[2] In the *Euthyphro*, he investigates the nature of piety with a self-proclaimed expert on divine matters. In the *Laches*, he investigates courage with two proven generals. In the *Charmides*, he investigates temperance with a promising youth recognised for temperate behaviour. In the *Meno*, he investigates virtue with a student of rhetoric who claims to have 'given many fine speeches to large audiences' concerning virtue (80b). In each of these dialogues, we find traces of Socratic intellectualism. The label 'Socratic intellectualism', however, is ambiguous. For Socrates holds intellectualist positions with regard to both human motivation and human excellence. In the case of motivation, Socrates holds that every agent seeks to pursue the human good (*eu prattein*), and to avoid the bad. This can be interpreted (most plausibly) to mean that every agent wants what is *actually* good for them.[3] In any case, Socrates holds that anyone who has the opportunity to do what they believe to be best will always do it. Scholars refer to this as **motivational intellectualism**.[4] To subscribe to motivational intellectualism is to deny the possibility of *akrasia* – the phenomenon of acting against one's better judgment. For Socrates, all actions are the result of an agent's *beliefs* about what's best (at the moment of action). This implies that all moral error is the result of false beliefs about what's best (ignorance). At the same time, to subscribe to intellectualism is also to accept that 'doing what is best' requires true belief, or perhaps *knowledge*, about what's best. Socrates takes the virtues to be *stable* dispositions to do what's best; and only knowledge has the necessary stability. Thus, for Socrates, the virtues are constituted by a certain kind of knowledge. Scholars refer to this as Socrates' **virtue intellectualism**. For Socrates, however, not only are the virtues identified with a certain kind of knowledge, they also form a *unity* of some kind. This additional thesis is referred to as the 'the unity thesis'. The goal of this chapter is to provide a general survey of the literature concerning virtue intellectualism and the unity thesis.

Our first reaction to virtue intellectualism might be one of astonishment. Isn't virtue more than simply a matter of knowing? Socrates is aware that his intellectualist position runs contrary to what most people think. Responding to 'the Many' in the *Protagoras*, he sets out to demonstrate that all wrongdoing comes from false belief, and that knowledge is far too strong to be overcome by the presence of other things (pleasure, pain, fear, appetite, et cetera). Apparently, Aristotle was unconvinced. According to Aristotle, Socrates was wrong to conclude that the virtues are 'all of them a form of knowledge'. The Socratic view, he writes, is 'obviously contrary to the empirical evidence' (*Nicomachean Ethics* 1144b–45b). The *Magna Moralia* adds:

> Socrates spoke better and more fully [than did Pythagoras] about these matters [the moral virtues]. But neither did he speak correctly. For he made the virtues forms of knowledge, and this is impossible. All forms of knowledge are activities of reason, and reason arises in the intellectual part of the soul; so in his view all virtues arise in the reasoning part of the soul. In consequence, by making the virtues forms of knowledge, he does away with the irrational part of the soul. And in doing this, he does away with both passion and moral character. This is why he does not treat the virtues correctly. But afterwards Plato divided the soul correctly into rational and non-rational parts and assigned to each its appropriate virtues.
>
> – *Magna Moralia* 1182a.[5]

Plato eventually departs from virtue intellectualism in Book IV of the *Republic*.[6] For both Plato and Aristotle, the development of virtue requires much more than the acquisition of knowledge. Virtue requires an entire process of perfecting the emotions and desires, of improving non-cognitive factors through habituation in order to prevent them from interfering with knowledge and reasoning. The main criticism of Socratic intellectualism, then, is that it leads to an overly simplified view of the soul. But the Socratic view of virtue is far more complex than it initially appears. Throughout the early dialogues, Socrates compares virtue to the *expertise* involved in a technical skill or craft (*technē*). The development of 'craft-knowledge' requires its own process of training and experience; the knowledge involved can be quite complex. Thus, the analogy with *technē* adds a significant layer of complexity to the Socratic position. The plausibility of virtue intellectualism may well depend on how we understand Socrates' use of this analogy. Scholarly debates concerning the craft-analogy will be discussed in the final section. I begin here by introducing textual evidence suggesting that virtue intellectualism is a Socratic view. I then outline competing interpretations of virtue intellectualism and the unity thesis.

SOCRATIC VIRTUE THEORY

Evidence for virtue intellectualism can be found in the *Protagoras*, where Socrates explicitly defends the thesis that virtue is knowledge. In the dialogue's conclusion, Socrates imagines how an onlooker might summarise the investigation:

> If virtue is anything other than knowledge (*epistēmē*), as Protagoras has been trying to say, then it would clearly not be teachable. But if virtue turns out to be wholly knowledge, as you now urge, Socrates, it would be very surprising indeed if virtue could not be taught.
>
> – *Protagoras* 361b

SOCRATIC VIRTUE INTELLECTUALISM 155

Socrates defends a version of virtue intellectualism in the *Protagoras*. He also defends the unity of the virtues. Much like virtue intellectualism, the unity thesis is alluded to in many of Plato's early dialogues. But the strongest evidence is found here in the *Protagoras*. At 329c–d, Socrates initiates a discussion about the nature of virtue by asking Protagoras how the individual virtues are related to the whole.

> Is virtue a single thing, with justice and temperance and piety its parts (*moria*), or are the things I have just listed all names for one and the same thing?
>
> *– Protagoras 329c–d*

Socrates presents his interlocutor with two options. He asks Protagoras whether (1) wisdom, temperance, courage, justice and piety are all *parts of a single whole*, or whether (2) they are all names for *one and the same thing* (329c–d). When Protagoras opts for the former, (1), he is immediately confronted with a further question about how the parts are related.

> Do you mean in the way that the parts of a face, the mouth, eyes, and ears, are parts of a whole, I asked, or like parts of gold, none of which differs from any of the others or from the whole, except in greatness or smallness?
>
> *– Protagoras 329d*

Socrates presents another pair of options. He asks whether (1a) their relation resembles the parts of a face, each part possessing a distinct power, or whether (1b) their relation resembles the parts of a piece of gold, which do not differ from one another, or from the whole, except in size. Protagoras argues that the different virtues constitute a whole just as the parts of a face constitute a whole, (1a). It is a matter of controversy which position Socrates endorses. Some scholars think he agrees with Protagoras about (1), but disagrees about (1a). Other scholars contend that Socrates disagrees with Protagoras on both counts, and that Socrates endorses (2) instead. This question shapes much of the literature concerning virtue intellectualism in Plato's early dialogues.

One thing is clear: Socrates rejects the face analogy, (1a), which is accepted by Protagoras. Yet the notion that the virtues are distinct 'parts of a single whole' arises in connection with Socrates throughout the early dialogues. Let's call this the **part-whole doctrine**. In attempting to uncover Socrates' theory of virtue, therefore, we must consider three distinct theses:

> **virtue intellectualism**: virtue is knowledge (each virtue is constituted by a certain kind of knowledge)
>
> **the unity thesis**: the virtues are 'one and the same thing' (the virtues form a unity)
>
> **the part-whole doctrine**: the virtues are 'parts of a single whole' (each virtue is a distinct part of the whole)

Socrates hints at each of these doctrines on multiple occasions in the early dialogues, but it is unclear what exactly Socrates means to do with them. Commentators agree that virtue intellectualism is central to Socrates' position. Yet virtue intellectualism has been subjected to a wide variety of interpretations in light of the other doctrines. The part-whole doctrine appears to be inconsistent with the unity thesis, at least when the unity thesis is understood as an explicit *identity* claim (per [2]). Something X cannot be *identical* to Y and also a proper *part* of Y. Thus, if we are to reach an understanding of the Socratic position concerning virtue, we must either find a way to resolve the tension, or resort to a more pessimistic interpretation. Friedländer (1964) concludes that Socrates has staked out a hopelessly indefensible position; Devereux (1992) concludes that the relevant texts on this issue are inconsistent. It is also possible that Plato's Socrates had no positive view to defend in these dialogues (Grote 1865: 292–299). Yet there are four *positive* lines of interpretation to consider. The identity interpretation attempts to resolve the tension by claiming that Socrates rejects the part-whole doctrine. The bi-conditional interpretation attempts to resolve the tension by understanding the unity thesis as something weaker than identity. The developmentalist interpretation suggests that Socrates' position concerning virtue is a work in progress: His position changes from one dialogue to the next. And lastly, various reconciliation interpretations maintain that there is one sense in which Socrates endorses a strong version of the unity thesis, and another compatible sense in which he endorses the part-whole doctrine.

THE PENNER-VLASTOS DEBATE

Let us begin with a well-known debate between two leading interpretations. According to the **identity interpretation** defended by Penner (1973), Socrates simply rejects the part-whole doctrine. Socrates is said to endorse the view that the individual virtues are actually 'one and the same thing'. Thus, the unity thesis is understood as an explicit identity. Socrates identifies all human excellence (piety, courage, temperance, justice and wisdom) with a single kind of knowledge – the knowledge of good and bad. There is ample reason for selecting the knowledge of good and bad here. After all, the knowledge of good and bad makes a noteworthy appearance in multiple dialogues and is often introduced at crucial moments.[7] Thus, according to the identity interpretation, Socrates would have opted for (2) had he been confronted with the same question as Protagoras. The knowledge of good and bad is the single thing comprising the whole of virtue. It is responsible for all virtuous action. This interpretation was originally put forward as an alternative to a rival interpretation, the bi-conditional interpretation defended by Vlastos (1972).

According to the **bi-conditional interpretation**, Socrates is deeply committed to the part-whole doctrine. The virtues are distinct parts of a single whole. On this reading, each virtue requires its own separate definition. The thesis that 'virtue is knowledge' is understood to imply that each virtue is knowledge of a different kind (so that courage is knowledge of P, temperance knowledge of Q, justice knowledge of R and so forth). The virtues form a unity simply because they are inseparable – an agent will possess one virtue *if and only if* she possesses them all. In this way, the bi-conditional reading retains virtue intellectualism alongside the unity thesis, while the unity thesis is understood as an equivalence rather than an explicit identity.[8] The extent to which the bi-conditional reading is able to retain the part-whole doctrine is not exactly clear. As we shall see, understanding the relation between the virtues in terms of biconditionality may prove unproblematic in *some* dialogues where the part-whole doctrine appears (e.g. *Laches* and *Meno*). But the bi-conditional interpretation encounters a problem with a passage in the *Euthyphro* to be discussed later. For now, the main takeaway is that the bi-conditional interpretation depicts the virtue-names as definitionally distinct, yet inseparable within an agent.

Thus, one important question concerns the part-whole doctrine, and whether Socrates is committed to it. Vlastos (1972: 25) argues persuasively that the part-whole doctrine is 'standard Socratic doctrine'. He cites passages from the *Laches* and *Meno* in defence of this conclusion. In these dialogues, Socrates introduces the part-whole doctrine unprompted. In the *Laches*, for example, Socrates guides the discussion deliberately,

SOCRATIC VIRTUE INTELLECTUALISM

suggesting to Nicias and Laches that they begin their investigation by examining a *part* of virtue, rather than the whole of it:

> Let us not, O best of men, begin straightaway with an investigation of the *whole* of virtue – that would perhaps be too great a task – but let us first see if we have a sufficient knowledge of some *part (merous tinos)* of it. Then it is likely that the investigation will be easier for us.
>
> *– Laches* 190c

A similar passage occurs in the *Meno*, where Socrates introduces the part-whole doctrine again. Meno suggests that virtue is a desire for good things and the power to acquire them. Socrates responds that it matters how these 'good things' are acquired, whether justly or unjustly.

> It seems then that the acquisition must be accompanied by justice or temperance or piety or some other part (*allo ti morion*) of virtue; If not, it will not be virtue, even though it provides good things.
>
> *– Meno* 78d–e

It was not necessary for Socrates to introduce the part-whole doctrine here. Yet he introduces the doctrine of his own accord. Just moments later, at 79b–c, Socrates reinforces the part-whole doctrine. With such passages in mind, therefore, Vlastos argues that Socrates would have opted for (1) were he confronted with the same question as Protagoras. Vlastos adds that the two alternatives provided by Socrates in response to Protagoras' answer, (1a) and (1b), seem to indicate that (2) cannot be the unity relation that Socrates has in mind.

Vlastos may be overstating the case. It is common in the early dialogues for Socrates to proceed with questioning using only those premises granted by his interlocutor, and this may be the case in the *Protagoras* – the alternatives Socrates presents to his interlocutor, (1a) and (1b), may not reflect his own view at all. Nevertheless, Vlastos is correct about one thing. There are passages in the *Laches*, *Meno* and *Euthyphro* that present problems for the identity reading. Those who defend the identity interpretation will have to explain such passages away. Penner goes so far as to dismiss entire dialogues. He suggests that the *Euthyphro* and *Meno* entertain merely 'demotic' virtues – virtues as conventionally conceived.[9] Of course, this suggestion will seem *ad hoc* to those who hold a different view.

At the same time, if we leave other dialogues aside for a moment, a careful reading of the *Protagoras* will suggest that Penner is probably right. Socrates does appear to endorse the identity view (2) in the *Protagoras*. For instance, at 331b, Socrates states his own position as follows:

> On my own behalf, I would answer both that justice *is* pious and that piety *is* just . . . that justice is *the same thing as* piety or as similar as possible . . .
>
> *– Protagoras* 331b, emphasis mine

In this passage, Socrates indicates that he has a personal stake in one of the alternatives presented to Protagoras. He is not merely conducting a dialectical procedure.[10] In fact, at 333c, Socrates says he is 'examining equally both [himself] and the one answering'. This follows an argument to the effect that temperance and wisdom are the same thing (331a–b). Socrates gets Protagoras to agree that folly is opposite to both wisdom and temperance. He then draws the conclusion that wisdom and temperance are the same thing, since a single thing can only have one opposite. Thus, Socrates appears to have a position, and he appears to favour (2) rather than (1). This constitutes evidence in favour of the identity interpretation, and poses a problem for those who would reject the identity reading.

Vlastos attempts to disarm the apparent sense of these passages. Such assertions involve what he calls 'Pauline' predication, rather than claims about identity. By claiming that 'justice is pious', or 'wisdom is courage' (350c), in other words, Socrates is not claiming that justice and piety are 'one and the same thing', nor is he claiming that wisdom and courage are identical. According to Vlastos, Socrates is merely claiming that the *instances* of justice can be described as pious, and the *instances* of wisdom can be described as courageous. After all, if the virtues are inseparable within an agent, as the bi-conditional interpretation purports, then the justice of a just individual will necessarily be accompanied by piety. It will be *a pious sort of justice*. And the wisdom of a wise individual will necessarily be accompanied by courage. It will be *a courageous sort of wisdom*. In fact, any instance of one virtue will necessarily be attended by the others. In this way, Vlastos responds to the threatening appearance of such passages by suggesting that the virtue-names are inter-predicable of those who are virtuous.

Vlastos argues admirably. But there are problems with his reading of the *Protagoras*. When Socrates reaches the conclusion that temperance and wisdom are the same thing, both Socrates and Protagoras understand this conclusion to be problematic for Protagoras' answer (1) that the virtues are parts of a whole. Throughout the dialogue, Protagoras takes Socrates to be defending position (2), the position that the virtues are different names for 'one and the same thing'. This observation alone lends significant support to the identity interpretation of the *Protagoras*. It brings us to an impasse. The bi-conditional interpretation faces serious problems in the *Protagoras*, while the identity interpretation faces serious problems outside the *Protagoras*.

THE DEVEREUX DISCREPANCY

Devereux (1992) was instrumental in shedding light on these interpretive complications. According to Devereux, there is a discrepancy between the *Protagoras* and the *Laches*. Socrates is committed to the identity view (2) in the *Protagoras*; yet he endorses the part-whole doctrine (1) in the *Laches*. The part-whole doctrine, as it appears in the *Laches*, is compatible with the bi-conditional interpretation. But we would be wrong to assume that the appearance of the part-whole doctrine in any dialogue provides positive *support* for the bi-conditional interpretation. There are two reasons for this. First, as the part-whole doctrine is depicted in the *Euthyphro*, the doctrine is entirely *incompatible* with the bi-conditional interpretation. And second, even if we grant (in accordance with the part-whole doctrine) that the individual virtues are distinct 'parts of a single whole', this would not entail that an agent with one virtue will possess them all. Nor does it entail that the virtues will be constituted by different kinds of knowledge.[11] There is plenty of interpretive work left to be done with regard to the *Laches*, and how exactly the *Laches* connects with these competing interpretations of virtue intellectualism.

In the *Laches*, as we have seen, Socrates suggests that he and his interlocutors begin by considering a *part* of virtue first (190c). He remains loyal to the part-whole doctrine throughout. In fact, he turns down Nicias' suggestion (194e) that courage is a kind of knowledge – the knowledge of what is to be feared and dared – a knowledge which turns out to be identical to the knowledge of good and bad. In the *Laches*, the knowledge of good and bad embodies the whole of virtue. Socrates asks,

SOCRATIC VIRTUE INTELLECTUALISM

> Then does a man with this kind of knowledge [the knowledge of good and bad] seem to depart from virtue in any respect if he really knows in the cases of all goods whatsoever, what they are and will be and have been, and similarly in the case of bad things? And do you regard that man as lacking in temperance or justice and piety to whom alone belongs the ability to deal circumspectly with both gods and men with respect to both the fearful and the hopeful, and to provide himself with good things through his knowledge of how to associate with them correctly?
>
> – *Laches* 199e

Socrates goes on to insist that 'the knowledge of what is to be feared and dared' cannot define the *part* of virtue they are pursuing (courage). After all, the knowledge of what is to be feared and dared is identical to the knowledge of good and bad, and the knowledge of good and bad constitutes the *whole* of virtue, not the part.[12] The upshot of the entire investigation, therefore, is that Nicias must either reject the notion that courage is a *part* of virtue (the part-whole doctrine) or he must give up his definition of courage as a kind of knowledge (the knowledge of what is to be feared and dared) identical to the whole itself. This dilemma generates the dialogue's aporetic ending.

Perhaps Nicias could have resolved the dilemma by remaining committed to his definition (Penner 1992b; 1997: 100). Courage is the knowledge of what is to be feared and dared. Of course, this would have meant rejecting the part-whole doctrine, and accepting that courage is identical to the knowledge of good and bad (the whole of virtue), thus aligning with the identity interpretation. According to the identity reading, therefore, it is Nicias who fails to avail himself of the proper conclusion. Nicias fails to accept that the individual virtues are names for 'one and the same thing'.

Within the context of the *Laches*, the identity interpretation has some appeal. But there are at least two problems. First, on this reading of the *Laches*, Socrates would be introducing a false premise (the part-whole doctrine) merely as a way to trip Nicias up. Those who accept the identity view may need to provide additional support for the claim that Socrates operates with trickery of this kind. That the Socrates of these early dialogues conducts his business in this fashion, by wilfully introducing false premises to refute his interlocutors, is controversial.[13] Second, Socrates appears to *retreat* from the identity conclusion himself, in order to re-emphasise the part-whole doctrine. According to Devereux, if Socrates were still committed to the identity view, as he was previously in the *Protagoras*, then he would have availed himself of Nicias' definition. Instead, he retreats from Nicias' definition. Thus, it appears Socrates has changed his position since the *Protagoras*. This line of reasoning creates space for a **developmentalist interpretation** concerning virtue intellectualism. On this interpretation, Socrates changes his view from one dialogue to the next. Socrates' view concerning the virtues may well be a work in progress, and his position in the *Laches* might differ significantly from his position in the *Protagoras* (Devereux 1992).[14]

Importantly, Devereux rejects a bi-conditional reading of the *Laches* as well. Even if we were to adopt a bi-conditional interpretation, Socrates' position in the *Laches* would remain incompatible with his position in the *Protagoras*. A bi-conditional reading of the *Protagoras* will suggest that each virtue carries equal status as a *part*. Piety, courage, justice, temperance and wisdom are each considered distinct parts of a single whole.[15] In the *Laches*, however, Socrates treats four of the virtues (justice, courage, temperance and piety) as parts, while wisdom is said to be the elite virtue that constitutes the whole. In the *Laches*, wisdom (*phronēsis*) is equated with the knowledge of good and bad, the whole of virtue. This discrepancy leads Devereux (1992: 788) to conclude that, in the *Laches*, 'Plato . . . articulates a more coherent doctrine . . . he drops the claim that the virtues are identical . . . and develops and refines the idea that the virtues are parts of a whole, and that wisdom is the key to their unity.'

The *Laches* therefore introduces a new set of questions for interpreters. If the individual virtues are each distinct parts, and wisdom somehow binds them together in representing the whole, how are we to differentiate them? What would a successful definition of one 'part' look like? Devereux carves out new territory in the debate over virtue intellectualism by proposing an answer to this question. At 192b, Laches suggests that courage is a sort of 'endurance of the soul'. When Socrates responds by distinguishing between foolish endurance and wise endurance (193c), Laches admits that courage cannot be the same thing as endurance. Devereux pays close attention to Socrates' response:

> So, if you are willing, let us hold our ground in the search and let us endure, so that courage itself won't make fun of us for not searching for it courageously, when this very endurance might turn out to be courage after all.
>
> – *Laches* 194a

According to Devereux (1992: 776), this would be a strange thing to say 'for someone who believes that endurance has no part in the definition of courage'. From here, it is a short step to Devereux's conclusion. Since the knowledge of good and bad (wisdom) constitutes the whole of virtue, courage must be the knowledge of good and bad *accompanied by* the quality of endurance. Courage is, in other words, a *wise* sort of endurance. On this interpretation, each virtue involves knowledge of good and bad. But the knowledge of good and bad (wisdom) is accompanied by various non-cognitive qualities, which serve to differentiate the individual virtues. The inclusion of *non-cognitive* qualities in the definitions for individual virtues might seem to create new complications for Socrates' position. After all, an interpretation of this kind dilutes the intellectualist component of Socrates' position. Virtue, on this interpretation, is more than just knowledge – the virtues consist of *cognitive* and *non-cognitive* elements. In response to this concern, however, one might suggest that the non-cognitive qualities simply arise as a by-product of the cognitive, or the knowledge of good and bad (Devereux 1992: 784). Thus, the Socratic position can retain its intellectualist character, while simultaneously allowing non-cognitive qualities to individuate the virtues. An important feature of this interpretation is that it allows each virtue a distinct definition.

There is something to be said for Devereux's solution. Often, Socrates appears to be searching for a characteristic *unique* to each individual virtue. But Devereux's interpretation would have us accept that Socrates' position in the *Protagoras* is at odds with his position in closely-related dialogues. Many readers have come to expect more stringent consistency from a writer as careful as Plato. The prospect of an interpretation that makes sense of Plato's Socrates without positing such inconsistency might therefore carry some advantage.

SOCRATIC DEFINITION: THE 'WHAT IS F-NESS?' QUESTION

Let us return to our original problem from the *Protagoras*, in order to entertain another question. Might there be a sense in which Socrates accepts (1), that each of the individual virtues are 'parts of a single whole', and another *compatible* sense in which Socrates accepts

SOCRATIC VIRTUE INTELLECTUALISM

an identity reading of (2), that the virtues are all names for 'one and the same thing'? Some interpreters suspect that there is (Woodruff 1976; Ferejohn 1982, 1984; Brickhouse and Smith 1997a, 2010; Clark 2015). On this reading, once the proper *senses* of (1) and (2) have been made clear, the part-whole doctrine is entirely compatible with an identity reading of the unity thesis. But how can this be? In order to explain, Ferejohn (1982, 1984) and Clark (2015, 2018b, 2022) both find it useful to pay closer attention to Socrates' pursuit of definitions. It would be useful, in other words, to know what type of answer Socrates wants in response to the 'What is F-ness?' question, or what constitutes a successful definition.[16] Following Devereux's interpretation would require that we speculate about non-cognitive qualities that serve to distinguish the many virtues. Unfortunately, this suggestion may encounter problems with Socrates' criteria for definition. In searching for an answer to his 'What is F-ness?' question, Socrates demands the *essence* (*ousia*) of F-ness.[17] Since courage is a *part* of virtue, the essence of virtue (the whole) should encompass the essence of courage. For Devereux, however, the knowledge of good and bad (the whole of virtue) contains *less* content than do the individual virtues. For the individual virtues consist in the knowledge of good and bad *plus* an additional non-cognitive quality. And yet, if that non-cognitive quality (endurance) is indeed *essential* to the individual virtue (courage), then shouldn't that non-cognitive quality also occupy a place *within* the definition of virtue as a whole? The whole should contain the part, in other words, not the other way around. Thus, it is odd for Devereux's position to imply that the knowledge of good and bad contains *less* content than do the individual virtues. Technically, the *whole*, on Devereux's picture, would seem to be the knowledge of good and bad *together with* a comprehensive array of non-cognitive qualities. But, of course, it would have been even more implausible for Devereux to suggest that the definition of virtue as a whole, on Socrates' view, includes a list of non-cognitive qualities like endurance.[18] If these non-cognitive qualities turn out to be *essential* to virtue as a whole, we may need to revisit the question of whether Socrates' position is truly intellectualist. And we may need to ask whether the depiction of Socrates in *Magna Moralia*, for instance, is somehow misleading. More likely than not, for Socrates, non-cognitive qualities are *accidental* features of the virtues at best.

This observation brings us closer to another noteworthy interpretation of the unity thesis. Paul Woodruff (1976) argues that the virtues share the same definition, the same essence. Yet the virtues are still *distinguishable* by means of their accidental features. For instance, we might distinguish between the *substance of gold*, which is 'the same thing' in every case, and *distinct pieces of gold* when they are separated into ingots. In this analogy, the substance represents the essence, while the distinct form of each bar represents an accidental feature. In much the same way, then, the virtues might share a single substance (knowledge), while being formed somehow into separate parts. Woodruff (1976) represents our first **reconciliation interpretation**. There is one sense in which Socrates endorses an identity reading of the unity thesis (one and the same substance), and another sense in which Socrates endorses the part-whole doctrine (separate pieces). Unfortunately, this reading doesn't shed light on the *Laches* (Rudebusch 2017: 334), where Socrates appears to distinguish courage (one *part* of virtue) sharply from wisdom (the *whole* of virtue). Nor does it explain how the relevant 'pieces' might be inseparable within the agent.

Socrates typically begins an investigation by raising a question of the form 'What is F-ness?' In the *Euthyphro*, Socrates raises the question 'What is piety?' In the *Laches*, he raises the question 'What is courage?' and so on. Understanding the 'What is F-ness?' question is crucial to understanding Socratic philosophy. Unfortunately, there is disagreement

162   THE BLOOMSBURY HANDBOOK OF SOCRATES

about what Socrates wants in response. Vlastos assumes that Socrates wants the *meaning* of the concept 'F-ness'. Scholars refer to this as the **meaning view**. The meaning view happens to shed light on Vlastos' bi-conditional interpretation and corresponding rejection of the identity interpretation. After all, once we assume the meaning view of the 'What is F-ness?' question, accepting that the virtues are 'one and the same thing' will be tantamount to accepting that the virtue-names are *synonymous*. Yet the virtue-names are not synonymous; they have distinct meanings.[19] Thus, for Vlastos, there is good reason to reject the identity interpretation. The identity interpretation appears to attribute an absurdity to Socrates.

Of course, Penner holds a different view of the 'What is F-ness?' question. Socrates is not requesting the *meanings* of various virtue-terms. Instead, when Socrates raises the 'What is F-ness?' question, he is raising the 'general's question'. An army general would want to know *what it is* within a person that makes them courageous, what characteristic *causes* courageous behaviour on the battlefield.

> . . .that question is not a request for the *meaning* of the word . . ., but rather a request for a psychological account (explanation) of what it is in men's psyches that makes them brave. For the 'What is F?' question is often put {by Socrates} as 'What is that single thing by virtue of which (with or by which) the many F things are F?'; and I will be arguing that that too is a *causal* or explanatory question rather than an epistemological or semantic one'.
>
>   – 1973: 56–57

This is referred to as the **causal view**. On the causal view of the 'What is F-ness?' question, Socrates is requesting an account of the psychological state, or the 'motive force' internal to a virtuous person. Penner identifies this 'motive force' as the power (*dunamis*) associated with virtue. On this reading, Socrates wants an account of the specific *power* that causes virtuous behaviour.[20]

Socrates and Protagoras both accept that virtue involves a power (*dunamis*). When Protagoras asserts that the individual virtues are related just as the parts of a face are related, (1a), he commits himself to the view that each virtue has a separate power. Thus, Socrates asks:

> And does each have its own separate power (*dunamis*)? In the analogy to the parts of a face, the eye is not like the ear, nor is its power the same, and this applies to the other parts as well: they are not like each other in power or in any other way. Is this how it is with the parts of virtue? Are they unlike each other both in themselves and in the power of each?
>
>   – *Protagoras* 330a–b

Of course, Socrates does not accept the face analogy. For Socrates, the individual virtues are constituted by a *single* unifying power (*dunamis*) represented by the knowledge of good and bad. This is precisely what Penner maintains. Rudebusch (2017) agrees, as do others (Taylor 1976; Irwin 1977: 86–90; Schofield 1984). In any event, it should be clear how the causal view of the 'What is F-ness?' question informs the identity interpretation.

In rather subtle ways, then, competing views of the 'What is F-ness?' question tend to inform different interpretations of virtue intellectualism. Scholars have offered many views of the 'What is F-ness?' question. Kraut (1984: 282, fn. 57) argues that Socrates is requesting something closer to a full-blown ethical theory in asking this question. After all, Socrates expects an adequate answer to serve as a standard (*paradeigma*) for determining right action (*Euthyphro* 6d-e).[21] Wolfsdorf (2005) argues that Socrates is searching for the *identity* of F-ness, which always implies a *metaphysical* search – a search either for the power of F-ness, or for the metaphysical Form of F-ness. Allen (1970) supports the latter. He argues that the 'What is F-ness?' question is always a search for the Form of F-ness. After all, the vocabulary used by Socrates (*ousia, eidos, paradeigma*) in seeking definitions is the same vocabulary used in reference to the theory of forms in later dialogues. In keeping with this focus on technical vocabulary, however, I have argued (2015, 2018b, 2022) that the 'What is F-ness?' question has a dual function. Scholars have been wrong to assume that Socrates is looking for a single type of answer. The 'What is F-ness?' question is *not* asked univocally across dialogues. Instead, it serves as a springboard for two distinct types of investigation into F-ness. In some dialogues, the 'What is F-ness?' question is framed as a request for the essence (*ousia*) of F-ness, thus prompting an investigation into the *meaning* of F-ness. In other dialogues, however, the 'What is F-ness?' question is framed as a request for the power (*dunamis*) of F-ness, thus prompting an investigation into the motive-force (or causal power) responsible for virtuous behaviour. The **dual-function view** therefore makes use of the meaning view *and* the causal view. The key to understanding any given dialogue is to determine which type of investigation is being conducted. This can be done by attending to the technical vocabulary of each search (e.g. *ousia, eidos, paradeigma* as opposed to *dunamis, pragma, pephuke* et cetera). The dual-function view of the 'What is F-ness?' question provides support for the following family of reconciliation readings, and is indebted to them.

RECONCILIATION INTERPRETATIONS

Ferejohn was the first to examine the 'What is F-ness?' question as part of a **reconciliation interpretation**. He wanted to show that Socrates endorses *both* the part-whole doctrine *and* an identity reading of the unity thesis. While Ferejohn (1982: 17) appears to accept the meaning view, he also maintains that Socrates is not looking for a synonymous expression.

> ... the view I wish to propose is that even though the 'meaning view' is correct, Socrates does regard all the special virtues as identical with one single power, and that it is this single power he is referring to when he identifies virtue with 'knowledge of goods and evils' ...
>
> – Ferejohn 1982: 15

For Ferejohn, the knowledge of good and bad is the sole object of Socratic inquiry. And yet, this knowledge also happens to admit various *descriptions*. That's what the individual virtue-names provide. The individual virtue-names provide non-synonymous descriptions of a single unifying power (*dunamis*) – namely, the power to discern goods and bads. Thus, Ferejohn goes on to add 'it is quite possible (and even not uncommon) for there to be distinct and non-synonymous descriptions of a single power' (1982: 17). Importantly, Nicias' definition of courage as the 'knowledge of what is to be feared and dared' is considered one of these descriptions. Ferejohn accepts this definition, and perhaps for good reason. Nicias makes a significant announcement when he proposes this definition. At 194d, Nicias claims that he has heard Socrates provide similar answers before.

> **Nicias:** I have been thinking for some time that you are not defining courage in the right way, Socrates. And you are not employing an excellent observation I have heard

164 THE BLOOMSBURY HANDBOOK OF SOCRATES

you make before now . . . I have often heard you say that every one of us is good with respect to that in which he is wise and bad in respect to that in which he is ignorant –

Soc: By heaven, you are right, Nicias.

Nicias: Therefore, if in fact the courageous man is good, then he is clearly wise

– 194c–d

This exchange culminates in our definition of courage as the 'knowledge of what is to be feared and dared'. The very same definition is recommended by Socrates in the *Protagoras* (360c–d). If we connect the dots, therefore, we might conclude that this constitutes a 'Socratic' definition. Ferejohn (1984) concludes that it is one relevant *description* of the knowledge of good and bad. This suggestion puts us in a position to see how the conflict between the identity interpretation and the bi-conditional interpretation can be resolved. Socrates holds simultaneously that the virtue-names refer to 'one and the same' power (the power to discern goods and bads), and that the virtues represent distinct 'parts of a single whole'. The virtues are distinct *parts*, because each virtue-name describes a *sub-class* of goods and bads to be discerned. Courage, for example, characterises the power to discern *future* good and *future* bad (*Laches* 198a–d). Meanwhile, in keeping with the bi-conditional reading, the possession of one 'part' of virtue will imply the possession of the other 'parts'. After all, they are descriptions of the same power.[22]

Ferejohn's ground-breaking effort to reconcile an identity reading of the *Protagoras* with the part-whole doctrine from *Laches* and *Meno* has paved the way for a host of similar reconciliation projects, some of which mark significant improvements upon Ferejohn's initial attempt. This family of reconciliation interpretations is characterised by the shared view that the virtues are unified under a single power (*dunamis*) – the knowledge of good and bad. Yet authors differ in their explanations as to how the individual virtues should be *defined*, and how the individual virtues should be understood as *parts*. Brickhouse and Smith (1997a, 2010) produce an influential interpretation. They focus on a passage from the *Euthyphro*. At 12d, when the investigation begins to founder, Socrates highlights the unique relationship between piety and justice.

> . . . the odd is a part of number. So it is not true that where there is number there is also oddness. But where there is oddness, there is also number . . . this is the type of thing I was asking before, when I asked whether where there is piety there is also justice, but where there is justice there is not always piety, for the pious is a part (*moria*) of justice . . . we must, it seems, find out what part of justice piety is.

– *Euthyphro* 12d

In this passage, Socrates suggests that piety (one part of virtue) is also a part of justice (another part of virtue). Moreover, piety is a part of justice in the same way oddness is a part of number. While all pious things are just, not all just things are pious. This analogy poses a problem for every interpretation we have encountered thus far. It is problematic from the perspective of the identity interpretation, since the identity interpretation rejects the part-whole doctrine. It is problematic from the perspective of the bi-conditional interpretation, since 'odd' and 'number' are not extensionally equivalent (thus, piety and justice cannot possibly be related bi-conditionally, since some things that count as just will not count as pious).[23] It is problematic for Devereux's interpretation, since the analogy cannot be explained by additional non-cognitive qualities. Brickhouse and Smith explain this passage by reference to one of the options presented to Protagoras. When considering

SOCRATIC VIRTUE INTELLECTUALISM

virtues as 'parts of a single whole', Socrates presented two options – either the virtues are related as the parts of a face (1a), or the virtues are related as the parts of a piece of gold (1b). Protagoras opted for (1a). Brickhouse and Smith (1997a) contend that Socrates would have chosen (1b). For Socrates, the relation among virtues resembles the parts of a piece of gold. In keeping with Woodruff's previous example (1976), therefore, the analogy would suggest that the virtues are made of the same basic substance, yet still distinct in terms of 'greatness or smallness'. But what exactly are we to make of this analogy? If the knowledge of good and bad is the single power (*dunamis*) representing the 'whole' of virtue, then the individual virtues will need to be distinguished on account of something else, something that would represent a difference in size, so to speak.

Socrates often characterises virtue as a craft (*technē*). The Greek word *technē* is typically rendered 'craft', or 'art'. But the word also carries the connotation of 'skill' or 'expertise'. It is sometimes even translated as 'science'. Whatever else it may be, a craft (*technē*) involves technical knowledge (*epistēmē*). And the knowledge involved in a craft constitutes the power (*dunamis*) of the craft. But this type of knowledge involves another feature. In the early dialogues, as soon as a branch of knowledge has been identified, Socrates inquires into the *result* (*ergon*) it produces. This is what happens in the *Euthyphro*. As soon as piety has been identified as a branch of knowledge, Socrates inquires: 'And what result (*ergon*) would the knowledge that provides service to the gods ultimately accomplish?' (12e). Different areas of expertise are distinguished from one another by reference to two things – a subject matter and a result. Medicine, as a branch of knowledge, concerns the body. But the medical art (*technē*) aims to produce *health*.[24] This is the productive result (*ergon*) of medicine. According to Brickhouse and Smith, some branches of knowledge are even more complex, since they involve distinct *applications* as well. Medical knowledge, for instance, might be applied either to *human* bodies, or to *non-human* animals. This difference in *application* generates a further distinction between physician and veterinarian. According to Brickhouse and Smith, the knowledge of good and bad is complex in this way. The individual virtues represent different *applications* of the same knowledge (the knowledge of good and bad). Moreover, these applications might be distinguished by their results.

This is a promising account of how to individuate the virtues. It explains how the individual virtues can be considered 'one and the same thing', while also being understood as distinct 'parts', thus reconciling claims (1) and (2) above. But some details remain unclear. For example, how are we to understand the virtues as distinct *applications*? How are we to explain justice and piety? And what exactly are the distinctive *results* (*erga*) of each virtue?

SUB-DISCIPLINES AND APPLICATIONS

Richard Kraut (1984: 261) suggests that the individual virtues are related to the whole as *sub-disciplines* are related to a general discipline. He uses the example of economics. Economics can be broken down into further *sub-disciplines* like welfare economics and micro-economics. One problem with Kraut's suggestion is that there are no principles unique to the discipline of economics as a whole (Brickhouse and Smith 1997a: 320). Rather, the general discipline, in this case, seems to be nothing more than the collection of sub-disciplines. In the case of economics, moreover, one could master one sub-discipline without thereby mastering the others. Socrates would never accept such a claim about the virtues. Thus, perhaps we need a different example to illustrate Socrates' position. Brickhouse and Smith suggest the knowledge of triangulation.

It is easy enough to see how a single and unitary sort of knowledge could be sorted into different kinds of application . . . The knowledge of triangulation just is the knowledge that allows surveyors to determine property borders and such. The knowledge of triangulation is also the very knowledge that is used in various kinds of navigation – for example, coastal or harbor navigation. Of course, there are obvious differences between surveying and navigation, and no one with any knowledge of these skills would fail to notice the differences.

– Brickhouse and Smith 2010: 164

Triangulation can be divided into more specialised *applications*, such as coastal navigation and surveying. These are not sub-disciplines. They are *applications* of the same general knowledge. Thus, in the case of triangulation, there is a single expertise that can be applied to different areas (or domains). Having the knowledge for one of these applications is identical to having the knowledge for the other applications. And we might interpret the virtues in a similar way. Brickhouse and Smith use this example to illustrate how some applications can be considered *parts* of others. Coastal navigation, for instance, happens to encompass harbour navigation, since harbour navigation is narrower in scope – the harbour is *part* of the larger coast. We might explain piety as a species of justice in a similar way. Justice (as an application) covers a larger territory, thereby encompassing piety. In this way, piety and justice will differ in terms of 'greatness or smallness' like the parts of a piece of gold.

This example has explanatory power as a parallel for Socratic virtue. McPherran (2000) offers a similar example. He considers the skill of drawing as a model for understanding the virtues.

Wisdom – conceived of as the knowledge of good and evil – is then analogous to a general technical skill such as 'the drawing skill', a skill which can be applied in various situations to produce different products which in turn lend different skill-names to those activities, such as 'drafting' or 'landscape-drawing'.

– McPherran 2000: 314

On both interpretations, the virtues are described as distinct *applications* of a single craft-knowledge. Rudebusch (2017) argues against these solutions. He claims that each application will necessarily involve some knowledge in addition to the knowledge that is supposed to unify them. Thus, once again, one could master one 'application' without thereby mastering the others. Rudebusch's argument, while strictly true, may be beside the point. The kind of knowledge that unifies the virtues is *craft*-knowledge. That craft-knowledge is the same in each virtue. The kind of knowledge Rudebusch is talking about are little bits of fact-knowledge, which are independent of (and do not constitute) the craft. It may be the case, therefore, that Rudebusch's argument turns on an equivocation involving 'knowledge'.[25]

THE RESULTS OF PIETY AND JUSTICE

Brickhouse and Smith suggest that the virtues (understood as distinct applications) might be distinguishable by means of their characteristic activities or results (2010: 163). They cite the *Euthyphro* in support of this suggestion. After all, the search for piety breaks down precisely where Euthyphro fails to identify the result of piety (13e). In fact, Socrates appears to lead Euthyphro into thinking about piety *as a part of justice* in terms of 'some distinctive result that [piety] produces'. Unfortunately, the result of piety is never disclosed. It may be tempting to suggest that virtue produces *benefit*, while justice produces *benefit to others*, piety produces *benefit to the gods* and so on. Ferejohn (1982: 17; 1984: 384) comes close to suggesting something along these lines. Unfortunately, at 13a–b, this suggestion is abandoned by Socrates. According to Socrates, piety will *not* produce benefit to the gods. The gods are self-sufficient, which means they are not in need of anything. Without having any needs, they are not open to receiving benefit. And so, the distinctive result of piety remains undisclosed.

It is one thing to differentiate the virtues as distinct applications of a single knowledge. It is another thing to distinguish the virtues by means of their results (*erga*). We might wonder whether it is necessary to do both. Of course, the investigation of the *Euthyphro* collapses where Euthyphro fails to identify the productive result. But this collapse may not constitute a failure to distinguish piety *as a part of justice*. At 12e, Euthyphro offers an interesting answer about piety as a part of justice. Euthyphro says that piety is 'the part of justice concerned specifically with *service to the gods* [rather than human beings]'. Socrates applauds Euthyphro's answer, saying that the answer is 'very well-put'. Euthyphro's answer distinguishes the virtues by means of their applications alone, without reference to their results. After this exchange, Socrates no longer questions Euthyphro about piety *as a part of justice*.

Should we conclude that Socrates is satisfied with this answer concerning the relation between piety and justice? It's hard to tell from the text. At 13e, Socrates continues to demand the 'all-noble result' of piety (*pagkalon ergon*). When we learn that piety does *not* produce benefit to the gods, we are left to consider what piety does produce. One plausible answer is that piety produces benefit to *human beings*. Serving the gods might require benefitting other people. Of course, this productive result overlaps with that of justice.[26] As McPherran (2000: 303) explains, 'it is likely that the only or most important component of the god's chief product is virtue; and hence, our primary service to the gods . . . is to help produce virtue *via* . . . the improvement of the human *psyche*'. Even if piety and justice happen to produce the same thing, they still apply to distinct *relational categories*.[27] Piety concerns our relationship *to the gods*, justice concerns our relationship *to others*. And so, perhaps it is not necessary to distinguish the virtues by means of their results.[28]

More should be said about the relation between piety and justice, however. I have suggested that, for Socrates, the individual virtues can be distinguished by means of their *applications* alone. Justice is the knowledge of good and bad applied in relation to *others*. Piety is the same knowledge as applied in relation to *the gods*. However, we have learned that the gods cannot be benefitted – the gods require only that we benefit other human beings. But let's suppose that I can fulfil my duty to the gods merely by acting well (i.e. justly) toward others. In this case, we might wonder what *real* difference there is between the two virtues. After all, piety and justice would require the same behaviour from me as an agent. I want to suggest, however, that there *is* a real difference. To be sure, knowing what is good and bad in relation to the gods (piety) requires acting well in relation to others; but it requires this (namely, just action) specifically *in the service of the gods*. As a disposition (and as an *intention*), this is significantly different, say, from acting in the same way *in spite of the gods*, or performing those same actions in a state of dogmatic disbelief concerning them. In this way, we might make sense of the idea that all pious activity is just, but not all just activity is pious.

The virtues might also be understood in terms of some contribution they make to the *health* of souls (Kahn 1996: 130). In the *Gorgias*, Socrates makes an important distinction between sciences (*technai*) and knacks (*empeiriai*). The procedure of a science can be explained, since the procedure is based on a knowledge of its object, and aims at some good (465a, see Anton 1980). Some sciences aim at the improvement of the body or the soul. By contrast, knacks (like cookery or rhetoric) aim at gratification or pleasure, through the use of flattery and imitation (rather than knowledge). Among the *sciences* that produce healthy bodies, Socrates places both medicine and physical training. Among the sciences that produce healthy *souls*, Socrates places both justice and legislation. Dodds (1959: 226) suggests that medicine and justice are paired together by virtue of being 'corrective' sciences – sciences that remove a bad condition in the body or the soul. Meanwhile, legislation and physical training are paired together by virtue of being 'regulative' sciences – sciences that sustain a good condition. Temperance presents itself as a major theme as well:

> I think the name for the states of organization of the body is 'healthy', as a result of which health and the rest of bodily excellence comes into being in it . . . and the name for the states of organization and order of the soul is 'lawful' and 'law' (*nomimon te kai nomos*) which lead people to become law-abiding and orderly, and these are justice and temperance.
>
> – *Gorgias* 504c–d

The 'true politician', says Socrates, is one who applies the science of caring for souls, thus giving attention to how justice and temperance and every other virtue may 'come to exist in the souls of his fellow citizens'. Socrates suggests that he practices this 'ruling craft' (*politikē technē*) himself through the use of his method (Moss 2007: 237), since 'the things he says on each occasion do not aim at gratification, but at what's best, not at what's most pleasant' (521d–e).

Most reconciliation interpretations find a way to express that there are several *relational categories* toward which the knowledge of good and bad might be applied. Justice, for instance, involves one's relationship to others, temperance involves one's relationship to oneself, piety involves one's relationship to the gods, and so on. Courage, it seems, involves one's relation toward an uncertain future. The virtues may diverge simply because they apply the knowledge of good and bad to different relational categories. Since no distinctive result is ever disclosed for any virtue, it is possible that the individual virtues share a single result. This seems to be the implication of certain passages in the *Euthydemus* and *Charmides*.[29] The knowledge of good and bad is said to produce happiness (*eudaimonia*). On this view, the 'all-noble result' of piety (as with any virtue) is simply the production of good and happy lives.

This proposal may face problems of its own. The task of identifying the characteristic activity or result (*ergon*) of any virtue is complicated. But there is at least one thing we learn from this exploration. Regardless of how we individuate the virtues in our interpretation of Socrates, there is real potential for *reconciling* the claim that the virtues are 'one and the same' thing with the claim that they are also 'parts of a single whole'.

VIRTUE AND *EUDAIMONIA*

The knowledge of good and bad is a recurring theme in the early dialogues. It is often associated with *eudaimonia* – faring well and being happy. In the *Charmides*, during an investigation into temperance, Socrates tells of a dream he once had (173a–e) depicting a

SOCRATIC VIRTUE INTELLECTUALISM

situation in which all things are done with expertise, always in accordance with knowledge (*epistēmē*). In the dream, mankind falls short of faring well, despite the expertise of doctors and so many others. The medical art, even when accompanied by other branches of knowledge, falls short of producing real benefit. There is but one knowledge (*epistēmē*) that can produce *benefit* in the sense of making people live well and be happy. In the *Charmides*, this knowledge is identified as the knowledge of good and bad (174b), the only knowledge that can produce *eudaimonia*. No real benefit will come to mankind from all the other branches of knowledge combined, so long as this knowledge is absent.[30]

In the *Protagoras*, the knowledge of good and bad is equated with wisdom (*phronēsis*) and depicted as a 'craft of measurement'. Socrates argues that knowledge (*epistēmē*) is the most powerful 'of all human things' (352a–d). As such, it cannot be overcome by pleasure, fear or anger. The knowledge of good and bad, as a power (*dunamis*) in the soul, guarantees that all decisions and actions will remain sound. Of course, Socrates reminds us that things aren't always as they appear. Visually speaking, things *appear* much larger when they are near (spatially near), even though they are not actually larger on account of proximity. In a similar way, pleasures and pains *appear* much greater when they are near (temporally near), even though they are not actually greater on account of their proximity either. This phenomenon is referred to as the 'power of appearance'. It is a significant obstacle to correct choice. As a craft (*technē*), however, the knowledge of good and bad serves to *counteract* the power of appearance. It does this by means of measurement.[31]

> So like an expert in weighing, put pleasures and pains together, place both near and distant into the scales, and say which is the greater quantity . . . Wasn't it the power of appearance that caused us to go astray . . . as we kept taking the same things differently and changing our minds in our actions and choices of large and small? Wouldn't the art of measurement (*metrētikē technē*), by contrast, have nullified the effect of appearance? Wouldn't this have caused our soul to remain calm and to stand by what was true? Wouldn't this have saved our lives?
>
> – 356b–e

In short, the knowledge of good and bad is construed as wisdom (*phronēsis*). It is a power in the soul that safeguards an agent from being carried away by the power of appearance, and enables an agent to stand firm in her measurements concerning pleasures and pains. According to Socrates, this power alone will 'save us' (*sōsein*) by allowing us to live well (*eu prattein*) and be happy (*eudaimonein*).

In some ways, this conclusion resembles that of the *Charmides*. Yet there is a hedonistic tone that will strike many readers as uncharacteristic of Socrates. At 351b, Socrates allows Protagoras to supply an account of goodness and badness. Protagoras settles on a hedonistic answer – pleasure is the good, pain is the bad (354c). Socrates does provide Protagoras with an opportunity to revise this answer (355a), but Protagoras declines. In the end, Socrates develops a striking account of wisdom as a 'craft of measurement' using the hedonistic values supplied by Protagoras. Commentators disagree about whether Socrates endorses these values. Irwin (1995: 82) concludes that Socrates accepts them; other commentators draw the opposite conclusion (Vlastos 1969; Zeyl 1980; Kahn 1996). There is textual evidence from other dialogues suggesting that Socrates rejects a purely hedonistic value system.[32] Rudebusch (1999) argues that Socrates rejects one form of hedonism and accepts another, as do Gosling and Taylor (1982).

Regardless of where we stand on Socrates' attitude toward hedonism, there may be reason to accept the account of wisdom as a 'craft of measurement'. As a result, one important question for interpreters involves the *set of values* this craft is meant to weigh (Rudebusch 1999: 89–96). Vlastos (1985b: 184) contends that Socrates endorses a principle called the **sovereignty of virtue**. According to this principle, the main consideration for any course of action is whether it instantiates a specific virtue, like justice. This standard appears decisive for Socrates, quite regardless of any unpleasantness that might result. In both *Apology* and *Crito*, Socrates explains his conduct using this standard; the language of measurement is noticeably present:

> You don't speak well, if you believe that a man worth anything at all would give *countervailing weight* (*hypologizesthai*) to danger in life or death, instead of considering only this when he acts: whether his action is just or unjust, the action of a good or bad man . . . he should remain, giving no countervailing weight to death *or to anything else* when the alternative is to act basely.
>
> *– Apology* 28b–d

> But for us, since the argument thus compels us the only thing we should consider is whether we would be acting justly . . . or, in truth, unjustly . . . And if it should become evident that this action is unjust, then the fact that by staying here I would die or suffer anything else whatever should be given no *countervailing weight* when the alternative is to act unjustly.
>
> *– Crito* 48c–d[33]

In the *Crito*, Socrates considers escaping from prison. He weighs this course of action against the alternative – awaiting a death sentence – and we are given a glimpse into Socrates' deliberation process as he weighs competing goods. Socrates insists that virtue is always decisive, and this happens to fit well with his general message. Socrates consistently urges his fellow citizens to prioritise virtue above all other considerations (*Apology* 30b). Vlastos sums this up well:

> Socrates is confronting that fatality of our lives which forces us to choose between competing values or, in the more down-to-earth language he uses himself, between competing 'goods' (*agatha*). He would recognize (cf. *Euthydemus* 279a–b) a wide variety of such *agatha*. Physical goods, to begin with: bodily health and strength, good looks; life itself as a biological fact – living as distinct from living well. Next on his list would come those social and intellectual goods which Socrates takes to be morally neutral, seeing no moral merit in their possession or stigma in their dispossession. Such he thinks wealth, social connections, good reputation and prestige, success in politics or war . . . Over against all these he sets the moral goods, his five canonical virtues, all of which stand or fall together: whatever stake any of them has in a given choice, each of the other four has the same.
>
> *– Vlastos 1985b: 184*

Along with the introduction of conventional 'goods', however, the sovereignty of virtue tends to deepen the puzzle for interpreters. As we have seen, Socrates equates virtue with the knowledge of good and bad, and he understands the knowledge of good and bad as a *craft*. In the final section, we will explore further possibilities concerning its result (*ergon*).

THE RESULT OF VIRTUE AS A CRAFT

Interpreters come to different conclusions regarding the result (*ergon*) of virtue. The Greek *ergon* refers either to a characteristic activity or to a productive result (Wolfsdorf 2005). It is possible that Socrates never intended the craft analogy as an adequate model for understanding virtue, in which case, the project of determining the result is mistaken (Klosko 1981). It is also possible that Socrates understands virtue as a purely *theoretical* activity. Socrates does acknowledge the possibility of theoretical crafts in the *Charmides* (165e). Theoretical crafts, like geometry or astronomy, do not produce any tangible results (Roochnik 1986). But suppose instead we take the craft analogy at face value. If virtue is supposed to be analogous to a productive craft, one possible reading is that each virtue produces a separate result. We have considered this possibility already, with the prospect of distinct *benefits* associated with each virtue, but the details of such a reading could be filled in variously. A second possibility is that virtue (as a whole) produces *eudaimonia* as a result. On this interpretation, however, we may have to revise our understanding of the *value* of virtue. For Socrates, crafts (*technai*) derive their value from the things they produce. If *eudaimonia* is the productive result (*ergon*) of virtue, then virtue itself will appear to have a purely instrumental value. This implication doesn't cohere with the sovereignty of virtue.[34] Nor does it cohere with Socrates' stance in the *Republic*, where justice is said to have both intrinsic and instrumental value (357d–358a).

Of course, this last point assumes that virtue produces *eudaimonia* as a separate result (a result alien to the performance of the craft). It is possible, instead, that virtue is *constitutive* of *eudaimonia*, or that a good and happy life is (at least partially) *constituted* by the very performance of the craft. Along these lines, several commentators interpret Socrates as suggesting that the possession of virtue is itself *sufficient* for a good life. On this reading, whoever is virtuous is happy (Annas 1999; Dimas 2002; McPherran 2005; Russell 2005). This is often referred to as the **sufficiency thesis**. In defending the sufficiency thesis, Irwin (1995) contends that virtue is sufficient *as a means* for securing the pleasant life as a separate result. Vlastos defends a different version of the thesis. For Vlastos (1985b, 1991: 224–232) virtue is the main *constituent* of happiness. There are other goods (*agatha*) that might make us happier by their presence, but the virtuous person can be happy without them.[35] Other commentators maintain an even stronger view of this relation. On **the identity view**, Socrates holds that virtue and happiness are *identical* – virtue and happiness are two different names for the same thing (Annas 2002; Rudebusch 1999: 123–128). The identity view manages to retain the sovereignty of virtue, but it creates problems of a different kind. For suppose virtue, wisdom and happiness are all considered 'one and the same thing'. This widespread equivalence is not only unintuitive, it also happens to confuse the aforementioned possibility that *eudaimonia* is the productive result (*ergon*). In order to accept the identity view, therefore, we may have to adjust our understanding of virtue as a craft (*technē*). Virtue will no longer produce a result distinct from itself.[36] In fact, on this reading, it is unclear what virtue *does*. Brickhouse and Smith (2010: 179) suggest that the possession of virtue equips an agent to play a key role in making other people virtuous, which explains Socrates' preoccupation with education. Parry (2003) suggests that virtue empowers an agent to *rule* wisely, which explains Socrates' characterisation of virtue as a 'ruling craft' (*politikē technē*).[37] Along the same lines, it has been suggested that the virtuous person's character is *itself* a result (Graham 1991: 15; McPherran 2000). In one way or another, then, the productive result of virtue

172　　　　　　　　　THE BLOOMSBURY HANDBOOK OF SOCRATES

as a craft may turn out to be virtue itself. Virtue might be understood in this scenario as equivalent to happiness (*eudaimonia*) as well.

In the *Euthydemus*, Socrates suggests that wisdom produces good fortune or success (*eutuchia*).[38] For Socrates, wisdom constitutes the whole of virtue. Thus, the *Euthydemus* may contain additional clues regarding virtue's result. It is assumed that human beings wish to do well (*eu prattein*) and be happy (*eudaimōn*). The main question of the dialogue, therefore, is how to go about achieving this end. Cleinias provides a list of 'goods' (*agatha*) that help make one's life happy, including wealth, health, good looks, noble birth, public honours, virtues and success (*eutuchia*). These goods contribute to happiness through some benefit they offer. But the main passage of the dialogue (278e–282d) develops the thesis that wisdom is valuable in a different way. Wisdom puts these other 'goods' to correct use. Conventional goods, in other words, serve as material for wisdom to work on.[39]

But this is just the beginning; Socrates proceeds to remove *eutuchia* from the list of goods. With wisdom already included among the good things in life, Socrates suggests that the inclusion of success (*eutuchia*) is redundant. The Greek word *eutuchia* has connotations of 'luck', 'chance', 'good fortune' and 'success'. Dimas (2002: 4) and Jones (2013a) understand this passage to mean that wisdom produces a certain kind of success. A reading of this kind comes close to interpreting success (*eutuchia*) as a productive result. In order to make this answer viable, however, it will be necessary to settle upon a suitable notion of 'success' (*eutuchia*). Jones (2013a: 9) makes a useful distinction between 'internal-success', which is a matter of how one plays the game, and 'outcome-success', which is a matter of winning the game, so to speak. Outcome-success is what's at issue in the *Euthydemus*, since *eudaimonia* is assumed to be the end (and appears to be a matter of outcome-success). Importantly, however, outcome-success (winning the game) can be influenced by both luck and skill. Naomi Reshotko (1992: 157) draws a useful distinction between 'luck of the draw' and 'luck of the play'. She has us consider a card game (e.g. bridge), where even the most experienced players have no control over the cards they are dealt – this is simply 'luck of the draw'. Nevertheless, players who have converted experience into expertise (*technē*) have better odds. They have a better chance to come away with 'good fortune' (*eutuchia*). This represents 'luck of the play'. In this sense, crafts tend to produce success, and we can apply the same observation to wisdom. Wisdom (as a craft) cannot improve 'luck of the draw'. Some circumstances in life are beyond our control. However, the possession of wisdom increases our odds of constructing a good and happy life, even despite bad consequences. It is unclear whether this can explain Socrates' puzzling claim (280a) that wisdom 'necessarily acts correctly and succeeds'. Commentators often struggle to make sense of Socrates' bold claims about wisdom. Reshotko (2006: 158) has suggested that wisdom itself, for Socrates, is a kind of omniscience. Daniel Graham (1991: 10) gives a different explanation:

> The crafts represent the great hope for the future subjection of all chance to order and rationality. For the crafts are practices in which rationality prevails over chance as established procedures are applied systematically to obtain the desired outcomes. The crafts are interesting to Socrates precisely because of the promise they hold out of replacing random actions with rational planning and execution in pursuit of desired ends.
>
> – Graham 1991: 10

The possession of a craft (*technē*) improves one's chance of securing a good outcome. Thus, in general, a skilled pilot will have better success (*eutuchia*) navigating passengers

SOCRATIC VIRTUE INTELLECTUALISM

173

safely to shore, and a skilled doctor will have better success curing her patients. In the same way, the possession of wisdom will improve one's chances at securing a good life.

At the same time, it seems unrealistic to suggest that a skilled doctor will *always* cure her patient, or that a skilled pilot will *always* bring passengers safely to shore. The same reasoning applies to wisdom. It seems unrealistic to suggest that wisdom will *always* bring happiness. Some authors reject the sufficiency thesis (Jones 2013a) for this reason. As Brickhouse and Smith (2010: 183) put it, Socrates is suggesting that wisdom produces success (*eutuchia*) in a more limited sense. In any area of expertise, unlucky circumstances (poor materials) will place limits on the value of the product. An expert shoemaker will be limited by poor materials for shoemaking, just as an expert card player will be limited by a bad hand. And yet, despite these limitations, the true expert will be able to make the most of the materials available to her. The final product will therefore be the *best result possible* from human action, even if better materials would have led to a better product. In an analogous way, Socrates may hold that wisdom guarantees the best life possible given the circumstances of the agent. Of course, the resulting life might fall short of *eudaimonia* whenever the agent's circumstances fall below a certain threshold (see Jones 2013a: 9–12).

At 281a–d, Socrates develops the thesis that conventional 'goods' (health, wealth, status, et cetera) do not benefit by their mere presence. Conventional 'goods' have *conditional* value. Suppose we possess conventional goods, but we do not put them to use. In this case, they fail to contribute to the quality of our lives. Suppose instead that we *use* them, but we use them in a foolish way. In this case, they will detract from the quality of our lives. But if we use conventional goods, and we use them *correctly*, they will increase the quality of our lives. For Socrates, in the *Euthydemus*, this is exactly what wisdom does. Wisdom *makes proper use* of other things. At 281e, however, Socrates carries this line of reasoning one step further. He suggests that conventional 'goods' have no value whatsoever *in themselves*.[40]

> It seems likely that with regard to all the things we called good in the beginning, the correct account is not that they are in themselves by nature goods, but rather as follows: If ignorance leads them they are greater evils than their opposites, to the extent that they are more able to serve an evil leader. But if understanding and wisdom lead them, they are greater goods, but in themselves none of these is of any value.
>
> – *Euthydemus* 281d–e

This argument is often understood as a precursor to the Stoic view. Virtue is the only constituent of happiness; all other things are neither good nor bad (Annas 1994).[41] According to Brickhouse and Smith (2010: 173), we can interpret Socratic wisdom either as *evaluative*, or as *productive*. This distinction can be clarified by asking whether wisdom makes other things good, or whether wisdom makes good things. If Socrates understands virtue as *evaluative*, then virtue gives to other things a value they didn't have before. This may indicate something important about virtue as a craft. Virtue may produce value in things, or draw benefit from them, or bring goodness into the world in some other way. On the other hand, if we understand virtue as *productive*, then virtue will produce things that are in some way good already.[42] In other words, virtue will *produce* goods (*agatha*) like health, wealth, friendship, et cetera. Of course, this result can seem unintuitive as a reading of Socratic philosophy. Burnyeat (2003) and Vlastos (1991: 220, n.73) have resisted the productive reading. But consider the following passage from the *Apology*:

174   THE BLOOMSBURY HANDBOOK OF SOCRATES

I go about doing nothing else than prevailing upon you, young and old, not to care for your bodies or for wealth more than the perfection of your souls, or even so much; and I tell you that virtue does not come from wealth, but from virtue come wealth and all other good things for human beings.

– Apology 30a–b

Brickhouse and Smith (2010) take this passage to mean that virtue plays a role in bringing conventionally good things into existence. Virtue need not play a *direct* role in producing such things, of course.[43] But on this reading, virtue plays some role in generating conventional goods. At the same time, insofar as these things are considered 'good', they may need to be *accompanied* by virtue; they may also need to be produced in a way (or to a degree) that they remain beneficial to the agent.[44] But this marks another possible way of understanding Socratic virtue as *productive*, provided that we understand the passage as Brickhouse and Smith understand it. On the other hand, Burnyeat (2003) rejects this way of reading the passage. He favours Burnet's (1924) translation instead, which reads 'it is goodness that makes money and everything else good for men'. This is another plausible reading of the passage at 30b2–4.[45] This way of reading the passage would suggest *not* that virtue helps one to produce a good income, for instance, but that virtue simply gives value to the money one already happens to have.

Needless to say, the result of virtue remains somewhat blurred by the text. Socrates probably understands virtue as productive. And most likely, he understands the result (*ergon*) of virtue as beneficial due to some relation it bears with *eudaimonia*. But what exactly this relation is, and how the productive result of virtue should be characterised, is a subject for further research.

NOTES

1. All translations of Plato in this chapter are from (or adapted from) Cooper 1997, unless otherwise noted.

2. In this chapter, I focus exclusively on the character Socrates in the set of dialogues generally considered to have been written early in Plato's career: *Apology, Charmides, Crito, Euthydemus, Euthyphro, Gorgias, Hippias Major, Hippias Minor, Ion, Laches, Lysis, Meno, Protagoras* and *Republic I*.

3. This is the interpretation of Penner and Rowe (1994: 1–25), according to which one never desires bad things, even when one takes them to be good. The *real* good is always the object of one's desire. Thus, whenever an agent has a false belief about what is best for them, they do not (strictly speaking) desire to perform the action they perform as a result of the mistaken belief. On the other side of the debate is Gerasimos Santas (1979), who holds that bad things are sometimes desired by those who think they are good, even though bad things themselves are never the intended objects of their desires.

4. For motivational intellectualism, see Chapter 9 of this volume.

5. This translation and other translations of Aristotle are my own, adapted from Jonathan Barnes (1984). Another important critique of Socratic virtue intellectualism can be found at *Eudemian Ethics* 1216b.

6. I endorse the notion that the views of Plato are expressed in the *Republic* (esp. Books II–X) through the character of Socrates. Book IV contains a tripartite account of the virtues that departs from Socratic Intellectualism as described here.

SOCRATIC VIRTUE INTELLECTUALISM

7. See *Laches* (199b–e), *Charmides* (174b–c), *Protagoras* (351b–357c). For commentary, see Santas (1969).

8. The identity interpretation understands the unity thesis as endorsing the strong relation (piety = courage = temperance = justice = wisdom); the bi-conditional interpretation understands the unity thesis as endorsing the weaker relation (pious ↔ courageous ↔ temperate ↔ just ↔ wise).

9. For a useful commentary on this issue as it pertains to the *Euthyphro*, see Weiss (1994).

10. O'Brien (2003) suggests that Socrates leaves both views (2) and (1b) open in opposition to Protagoras' answer here, since Socrates is mainly concerned with refuting Protagoras' position. Thus, he thinks 311b is inconclusive due to the disjunction. See also Manuwald (2005) on this topic.

11. Of course, Vlastos constructs his position in such a way that Socrates' position in the *Laches* is informed by further content from the *Protagoras*. But since Vlastos' reading of the *Protagoras* has been shown problematic, and since the part-whole doctrine poses further problems for his view once we get to the *Euthyphro*, we might question how much support the *Laches* can offer to the bi-conditional interpretation.

12. This glosses over a few crucial steps in the argument. Devereux formulates the full argument quite helpfully:

    1. Courage is a part of virtue;
    2. Courage = knowledge of what is to be feared and dared (proposed by Nicias);
    3. Things to be feared and dared are merely future evils and future goods;
    4. Therefore, courage = knowledge of future goods and future evils;
    5. Knowledge of future goods and evils = knowledge of all goods and evils;
    6. So, courage = knowledge of good and bad;
    7. Knowledge of good and bad = the whole of virtue;
    8. Courage is therefore not a part of virtue, it is the whole;
    9. But courage was agreed to be only a part of virtue;
    10. Thus it seems the definition in (2) cannot be right.
    (Devereux 2006: 328)

13. I owe this observation to Nicholas Smith, who brought it to my attention during the preparation of this chapter. For a good discussion, see Vlastos (1991: 132–156). Guthrie (1975: 246) and Kahn (1983: 93), for instance, argue that Socrates does go about his business in this way, introducing false premises to 'cheat' his way to refutation. Such a tactic, however, would reveal Socrates as ready to violate the 'say what you believe' rule of elenctic argument.

14. Devereux considers this a 'Platonic innovation' (2006: 335). Devereux's reasoning commits him to a certain chronology among dialogues; the *Protagoras* was composed prior to the *Laches*. Moreover, *Laches* was composed prior to *Euthyphro*, since the *Euthyphro* clearly endorses the part-whole doctrine.

15. O'Brien (2003) argues instead that the two dialogues are mostly compatible when it comes to wisdom as a whole.

16. Ferejohn (1984) describes Socratic inquiry merely in terms of answers to the 'What is F-ness?' question. He has reservations about describing the object of Socratic inquiry in terms of definition.

17. *Euthyphro* 11a–b; *Meno* 72b.

18. Of course, I am depicting the part-whole relation here as a composite containing constituents, so that the essence of the whole will *contain* (or 'encompass') the essence of each part. There may be alternative ways of depicting the part-whole relation when it comes to essences. Soldiers are certainly *parts* of an army, for example, but the essence of an army may not contain the essence of each individual soldier. We might wonder whether something similar can be said for the virtues. I am grateful to Ravi Sharma for bringing this to my attention. However, when it comes to virtue, Devereux appears to posit a much closer relation between essences. In his view, the essence of each individual part is said to consist of the essence of the whole (the knowledge of good and bad) *together with* additional non-cognitive qualities. Thus, for Devereux, the essence of the whole is contained within (the essence of) each part. What then? Does it follow that the relation must run the other direction? Does it follow that the essence of the whole (of virtue) must somehow contain the essences of the individual parts? Perhaps not; there may be a way to disarm the objection. But some clarification is required, at least. If (as we said before) the non-cognitive qualities that differentiate the individual virtues necessarily accompany the knowledge of good and bad as byproducts, then they are already *entailed by* the knowledge of good and bad. What, then, is the explanation as to why the essence of the whole excludes those non-cognitive qualities? Why are they essential to the parts, but not the whole?

19. For Vlastos, determining the meaning of 'F' involves an analysis of the concept named by the word, rather than a 'lexicographical inquiry into contemporary Greek usage' (Vlastos 1976: 411, fn. 3). Vlastos explains that such an analysis may lead to a 'radical revision of the meaning which attaches to those words in unreflective current usage'. After examining the concept of courage, in other words, we might come to learn that the concept applies much more broadly than its ordinary usage would seem to suggest. In response to this, one might complain that Vlastos is equivocating in his objection to the causal view. The objection to the causal view, which says that 'the virtue names are not synonymous' depends on a claim about ordinary usage, whereas Vlastos uses 'meaning' in a way that is divorced from ordinary usage. I owe these observations to Ravi Sharma, who brought them to my attention during the editing process in preparing this chapter. Commentators often fail to see that a vital connection to ordinary usage should be preserved, if the objection at issue here is to be sustained.

20. Presumably, Socrates wants to know this 'power' in order to develop it in himself, and in order to teach or impart it to others.

21. For more on this, see Chapter 4 on 'Socrates and the Forms' in this volume.

22. Then again, we must bear in mind that Socrates appears to *retreat* from the identity conclusion in order to reinforce the part-whole doctrine in the *Laches* (Devereux 2006). This feature of the text will certainly require an explanation from proponents of the reconciliation interpretation.

23. An explanation is available to the bi-conditional interpretation however. Brickhouse and Smith (1997a: 322) observe 'this objection results from a failure to distinguish virtuous agents from virtuous acts'. In *Euthyphro*, Socrates requested the quality (*eidos*) distinctive of both pious acts and pious persons (7a). The definition is therefore supposed to serve as a model by which to identify pious acts and persons. When it comes to persons, the virtue-names might have the same extension. When it comes to actions, the virtue-terms might not. See also McPherran (2000).

SOCRATIC VIRTUE INTELLECTUALISM

24. It might appear that the result (*ergon*) is the most important feature here, since there are other arts (*technai*) that happen to concern the body. In the *Gorgias* (463a–465e), for instance, Socrates describes *both* medicine and gymnastics as arts that tend to the body. However, as Dodds (1959: 226) points out, there is still room for a distinction between 'corrective' and 'regulative' arts that concern the body (and similarly for the soul). Corrective arts seek to remove a bad condition, whereas regulative arts tend to strengthen a good condition. The medical art is corrective, while gymnastics is regulative.

25. This observation in response to Rudebusch (2017) was brought to my attention by Nicholas Smith in a helpful comment during the preparation of this chapter.

26. It is worth considering that, in the *Apology* (24a–26c, 29d–31c), Socrates depicts his own service to the gods as benefiting human beings.

27. This can also be explained by making a distinction between thinking of piety as producing a benefit *to the gods*, and thinking of piety as producing benefit *for the gods*. The gods cannot themselves be benefitted (13a), as we have seen, but they can perhaps appreciate those who produce benefit on their behalf or in their honour.

28. This is a subtle distinction. But there may be good reason for making it. For commentators who aim to reconcile an identity reading of the unity thesis with the part-whole doctrine by positing distinct applications of a single knowledge, there is one passage from the *Republic* that threatens the idea that they produce distinct results (*erga*). In Book 5, Plato offers a candid account of how different powers (*dunameis*) should be distinguished.

> Here's what I think about them. A power (*dunamis*) has neither colour nor shape nor any other feature of the sort that many other things have and that I use in my own case to distinguish those things from one another. In the case of a power (*dunamis*), I use only what it is set over and what it does: What is set over the same things and does the same I call the same power; what is set over something different and does something different I call a different power.
>
> – *Republic* 447c–d

This passage is from the middle of the *Republic*, not itself an early dialogue. But if this passage describes how Socrates understands powers in the early dialogues, then we have discovered something rather important. The individual virtues are 'set over' different relational categories – this is what makes them distinct applications. But now suppose that, in addition to being 'set over' something different, they also 'do something different' by producing different results. In this case, according to the passage above, we are in real danger of describing what (for Socrates) amounts to different powers. This would undermine the entire reconciliation project, fracturing the single power (*dunamis*) that unifies the virtues (Clark 2015: 13–14). For those who favour a reconciliation interpretation, therefore, care must be taken not to do too much to distinguish the virtues, lest we obliterate the thing that unifies them.

29. *Charmides* 174b–c; *Euthydemus* 280a–281e.

30. Temperance is never explicitly identified with knowledge of good and bad in the *Charmides*, though many support the inference (Santas 1969; Tsouna 2004). For a reconciliation interpretation of the *Charmides*, see Clark (2018a, 2022).

31. The account of wisdom as 'craft of measurement' makes Brickhouse and Smith's (1997a: 321) example of triangulation even more apt, since both involve measurement.

32. *Gorgias* 481b–527e, *Phaedo* 69a–b, et cetera.

33. These translations of *Apology* and *Crito* are borrowed from Vlastos (1985b), who gives justification for translating the verb *hypologizesthai* 'to give countervailing weight'. The verb is commonly rendered 'to give an account', but following Riddell (1867: 66, 167), Vlastos argues from the context that what is conveyed by the verb is not subtraction of one account from another, as it so often is, but instead a 'meeting from an opposite direction', just as in the case of *hypantan* or *hypōmosia*, to mean 'affidavit to stop proceedings'. It is used, in other words, to convey competing values weighed against one another. Santas (1979: 32–33) provides a similar reading, emphasising that there is a principle of choice operating here within the context of the verb. (See Vlastos 1991: 214, n. 59.)

34. Vlastos and Irwin are said to have had an exchange about this in a collection of letters. (See Roochnik 1986: 297, fn. 9.)

35. Brickhouse and Smith (2010) assert the relation between virtue and happiness is *nomological*. Socrates is not talking about necessary or sufficient conditions for happiness, he is merely claiming that, given the way the world works, the acquisition of wisdom constitutes the most reliable strategy for attaining *eudaimonia*.

36. Wolfsdorf (2005) also cites Socratic examples of the *ergon* as a distinct product and the *ergon* as characteristic activity. A craft will either produce something distinct from itself, or it will engage in a distinctive activity.

37. See *Gorgias* 521d and *Euthydemus* 289d–292b.

38. A question also arises whether wisdom and success are identical as well. Jones (2013a: 6) argues they are not: 'the relation between wisdom and good fortune is explicitly causal, and the causal passages (280a6, 281b2–4, 282a4–5, 282c8–9) militate strongly against the identity reading. A causal analysis implies that there are two different things involved: the cause (wisdom) and the effect (good fortune).'

39. See *Meno* 87b. For discussion, see Ferejohn 1984 and Annas 1994.

40. Some (Vlastos 1991: 305–306; Jones 2013a: 16) have denied that '*kath' auta*' means 'in themselves', preferring 'by themselves'. For discussion of the phrase in other Platonic works as it bears on the interpretation of the *Euthydemus*, see Jones 2019a: 239–240 and Jones 2019b. For the phrase in Greek literature more broadly, see Broackes (2009).

41. McPherran (2005: 58) also suggests the *Euthydemus* is 'a forerunner of Stoic theology', since the primary sense of *eutuchia* is divine providence rather than chance good luck.

42. In this context, perhaps such things will count as good only in conjunction with the virtue that produced them.

43. This role is already occupied by other areas of expertise (money-making, medicine, physical training, et cetera).

44. See, for instance, *Phaedrus* 279c.

45. The passage in question at 30b2–4: *Ouk ek chrēmatōn aretē gignetai, all' ex aretēs chrēmata kai ta alla agatha tois anthrōpois apanta kai idiai kai dēmosiai.*

CHAPTER EIGHT

Socratic Eudaimonism

PAUL WOODRUFF

His friends believed that Socrates was happy – *eudaimōn* – all through his life and, most remarkably, at the end of it (*Cr.* 43b, *Phd.* 58e, 117b–e). He would not have claimed *eudaimonia* for himself, as that would have been a dangerous boast, tantamount to claiming virtue. But he did speak on his last day of the wisdom-lover's joy in going down to be with his beloved (*Phd.* 68b), and of the swan's delight in singing during its last day (*Phd.* 85b).[1]

Gregory Vlastos, writing not long before his own death, concluded his book on Socrates with these words: 'If you believe what Socrates does, you hold the secret of happiness in your own hands. Nothing the world can do to you can make you unhappy. In the quest for happiness, the noblest spirits in the Greek imagination are losers: Achilles, Hector, Alcestis, Antigone. Socrates is a winner. He has to be. Desiring the kind of happiness he does, he cannot lose.'[2]

Socrates' friends believed also that he was the most virtuous person they had known, as we see from the last lines of the *Phaedo* (118a), which probably express Plato's own tribute to Socrates: 'the man who was by far the best and wisest and most just', echoing praise from the official whose job it was to see to his execution: 'I came to know you in this time as by far the most noble and most mild and best man of all who have come here' (*Phd.* 116c).[3]

Happiness and virtue appear to be conjoined in Socrates' life, and not by coincidence. Plato represents Socrates as holding that virtue leads to, and perhaps even constitutes, *eudaimonia*. 'Eudaimonism' is the name modern scholars have given to a family of ancient views that associate virtue with happiness. In this chapter I examine the various interpretations that scholars have proposed for Socratic eudaimonism and consider which of them are best supported by the texts.

In this chapter, I will take Socrates to be the figure we meet primarily in the *Apology* and *Crito* of Plato, and in other texts only in so far as they are consistent with these,[4] including the *Gorgias* and Book 1 of the *Republic*. In these works, Socrates treats character or soul as a single entity not divided into parts, so I will not cite the later books of the *Republic*. These later books employ the doctrine of the divided soul to present a vivid image of a soul that has been injured – made miserable – by acting unjustly; the injury consists in being divided against itself in such a way that the worse parts suppress the better, so that appetite or emotion takes charge of reason and makes it miserable. But this image for moral injury we do not have in the earlier dialogues, which do not dwell in the same way on a soul divided by powers of appetite or emotion.

What, then, is the nature of the injury to soul or character, caused by acting unjustly, that Socrates urges us to avoid (*Ap.* 30c–e, *Cr.* 47c–d)? We will need to try to understand this in order to understand Socratic eudaimonism, because, according to Socrates, such injuries are a major source of unhappiness. We will also need to try to understand what Socrates thinks happiness is, and how he believes it is related virtue. The answer to that may depend on how Socrates understands the knowledge or wisdom that (he thinks) constitutes virtue. Eudaimonism raises interesting ethical questions about what sort of aims are ethical: Does Socrates hold that it is ethical to aim primarily at one's own happiness in making ethical decisions? All these matters are controversial among scholars, including this: Did Socrates really combine virtue and happiness in his life?

IS SOCRATES HAPPY THROUGH VIRTUE?

If Socrates is really happy through being virtuous, then his life itself is evidence for eudaimonism. His friends thought that Socrates was both virtuous and happy, but he may not have agreed with them. Although we know he thinks he is free from culpable or punishable wrongdoing (*Ap.* 25e–26a),[5] he may not be able consistently to believe that he is both happy and virtuous as Vlastos contended he did. Scholars have objected to Vlastos' view for two reasons. First, Socrates seems to hold that virtue is necessary for happiness and that knowledge is necessary for virtue (*Euthd.* 81a–b). Socrates disclaims knowledge (*Ap.* 21b, 23a),[6] and, in doing so, disclaims happiness by implication.

Second, Socrates seems to have a bleak view of embodied human life. This leads him to declare that those who fear death are displaying culpable ignorance, not knowing that death is an evil (*Ap.* 29a); in fact, he will argue at the end of the *Apology* that death is either the blessing of an afterlife with gods and heroes, or total annihilation, and that either of these is better than embodied life (40c–41a); we are told, he says, that people in the afterlife are happier than people here (41c). Other texts seem to support the same conclusion.[7] I will address the objections in order:

How can Socrates be virtuous if he truly lacks wisdom? Socrates thinks of his human wisdom as consistent with his ignorance. To examine what he means by this is beyond the scope of this chapter.[8] I will take it here that Socrates does claim a human level of knowledge that falls short of the ideal; he knows some valuable things, but he cannot give elenchus-proof definitions of the virtues. If that sort of knowledge is necessary for virtue, then, however good Socrates may be, he would not be virtuous. Socrates is confident that he is good in being blameless, but not that he is virtuous.[9] He lays claim to goodness again and again, but never to any of the virtues. How can we explain that?

If knowledge of virtue is sufficient for virtue, and virtue for happiness, then a god-like being who could define virtue adequately would be virtuous and happy to the highest possible degree. Socrates would not meet that standard. But, at the same time, Socrates' human wisdom might be sufficient for lower levels of virtue and happiness, available to embodied human beings. Socrates' friends and his jailer, then, would be correctly testifying to his high *human* level of virtue. They are not attributing perfection to him, but merely saying that they have not encountered anyone better – in contexts that clearly limit the comparison range to human beings.[10] If Socrates held a scalar view of these concepts, then he could agree with his friends to this extent: He is virtuous at levels that are open to embodied human beings and allow for improvement. If Socrates did not hold a scalar view of knowledge and virtue, he could not have supposed that his mission to Athens was beneficial to the Athenians, as he insists it is. The benefit could only be an improvement on a scale.[11]

By learning of his own ignorance through self-questioning, he has saved himself from the vicious condition of thinking he knows what he does not. So Reeve:

SOCRATIC EUDAIMONISM

By means of the elenchus, by living the examined life, we can avoid *blameworthy* vice by avoiding culpable ignorance and thereby coming as close to being virtuous as is humanly possible. We can achieve *human* wisdom and with it what we might call *human* virtue.[12]

And from this, presumably, *human* happiness would spring. But the virtue of knowing one's own ignorance falls short of the goodness that Socrates' friends attribute to him, and does not explain, for example, the courage Socrates showed at the battle of Delium (*La.* 181b). Neither Socrates nor any other speaker in the dialogues explicitly treats knowledge of ignorance as leading by itself to any level of virtue. Socrates' human wisdom must go beyond a proof of his ignorance.[13]

One scholar has argued recently that Socrates' practice of philosophy could do harm, as it is not guided by the wisdom that must guide anything other than wisdom if it is to be good (*Euthd.* 281d). If so, then we cannot maintain the hope that Socrates could attain goodness through living his philosophical, elenctic life (Austin 2020). On this view, Socrates' practice would be a conditional good, but that is inconsistent with the *Apology*, which declares the goodness of Socratic inquiry with no reservations (e.g., *Ap.* 37e–38a).

Socrates at one point promises happiness to Callicles 'both while alive and after death' if he follows the call of virtue along with Socrates (*Grg.* 527c). The passage clearly implies that the living can be happy, and (somewhat less clearly) it implies that Socrates is happy or is on the way to happiness.[14] If so, and if Socrates lacks perfect knowledge, then, according to Socrates, perfect knowledge is not necessary for whatever level of virtue is necessary for happiness. In the same dialogue in which he disclaims knowledge, the *Apology*, he claims to be good in strong terms,[15] so he must believe that goodness is consistent with his degree of ignorance.[16] Socratic ignorance allows for a certain human level of knowledge, and this level may suffice to satisfy the knowledge condition for a high, but human, level of happiness. Knowledge, happiness and virtue may all be scalar or gradable; that is, they may come in degrees; if so, we can resolve a number of problems about Socratic theory.[17] We shall see, however, that the scalar thesis is controversial.

Is happiness possible in this life? The second challenge to Vlastos' position is the argument that Socrates finds the human condition so bleak that he could not have thought himself happy. Here the argument turns largely on interpretations of the case Socrates makes at the end of the *Apology* that his death may be an improvement over his current state (*Ap.* 40b–41d). Again, it helps to think of happiness as scalar.[18] Socrates' famous claim, at the end of this argument, that no evil can come to a good man living or dead (*Ap.* 41d), would not be consistent with treating his embodied life as misery. Indeed, he has escaped the worst misery by escaping from wrongdoing. I conclude that Plato's Socrates is humanly virtuous and humanly happy during his life in Athens; his example serves to support a practical form of eudaimonism.[19]

WHY DOES WRONGDOING LEAD TO MISERY?

Socrates insists that wrongdoing (*adikia*) inevitably leads to misery, as a result of injuries that wrongdoing inflicts on one's character or soul, a kind of injury he compares to a bodily injury. I shall call this 'moral injury'. On the inevitability of moral injury from wrongdoing he is clear, and he is clear that such moral injury is more to be feared than bodily injury (*Cr.* 47d, *Grg.* 471a). But he is not clear about the nature of moral injury.

Only recently have modern ethical thinkers and psychologists taken moral injury seriously, as a result of research on the experiences of combat veterans, who often report something like the disordered soul described by Socrates, a soul at war with itself.[20] Avoiding moral injury has come back now as a theme in practical ethics. This may lead to a revival of eudaimonism and the problems associated with it.

In the *Crito*, as we shall see in detail below, Socrates answers what we would call the 'why be moral' question by arguing that acting unjustly is damaging to one's character.[21] Socrates says little explicitly here about what this injury is or why we should avoid it. He does not even specify what it is that is injured beyond saying it is 'that in us which unjust [behaviour] harms and just [behaviour] benefits' (47e). The word for soul does not occur in this dialogue. As for the injury that unjust behaviour causes, he says that it is analogous to the damage done to the body by disease (47d). This damage, Socrates insists, is more serious than damage to the body, and it should, for this reason, be strictly avoided.

We are left to speculate as to the meaning of Socrates' analogy of the self-injury caused by unjust action to physical disease. I shall take it that what is injured by unjust behaviour is one's moral character, and that the injury consists in one's becoming less disposed to behave justly and more disposed to commit injustice – that is, by violating virtue one becomes less virtuous. What this means for Socrates depends on what he takes virtue to be. Socrates goes further in the *Gorgias*, where he makes clear that the injury is to the soul and illustrates it with the plight of the tyrant Archelaus and those who imitate him (e.g., 511a). Their injustice brings upon them the greatest evil and makes them miserable (471a), even though they are unaware of their misery (471b–d) and do not realise that their misery can be alleviated by punishment (472e). Caving in to one's undisciplined desires leads to the misery of injustice (507d–e), and this can be prevented by maintaining order (*kosmos*) in the soul through *sophrōsunē* (506e–507a). The injury then appears to be a kind of disordering of the soul in which appetites have too much influence.[22] What kind of influence could this be?

The *Gorgias* gives us a hint: The influence could be on one's beliefs, and the disorder could be internal disagreement. When Socrates sets out to show Callicles that it is worse to do injustice than to suffer it, he says 'if you leave me unrefuted, then . . . Callicles will not agree with Callicles, but be at dissonance all his life' (*Gorgias* 482b, cf. 473e–74b and 475e–476a). Socrates thinks Callicles has false beliefs that are due to his desires, and which he, Socrates, plans to correct through elenchus. And, at the same time, Socrates thinks Callicles has true beliefs conflicting with the ones that need to be corrected.[23]

An account of Socrates' concept of moral injury must explain how such disorder and/ or dissonance is possible in Callicles' soul, as well as how further wrongdoing could worsen that condition. We must keep in mind that Socrates believes at least some moral injuries can be healed only by punishments (rather than by instruction alone) and these punishments, like some physical cures, are painful.[24] We can understand moral injury best if we understand Socrates' rationale for punishment, on which much has been written.[25] Above all, we need to explain why Socrates thinks that moral injuries inevitably make the injured party miserable – even though many wrongdoers say they feel just fine.

Scholars have defended three main accounts of moral injury in Socrates' thought. A purely intellectualist account is widely accepted, a moderately intellectualist one has been well defended, and a third highly plausible account departs from intellectualism altogether.

On the purely intellectualist account, harm to the soul is purely cognitive: Damaging the soul is causing it to have more false beliefs, or stronger ones, than it had before.[26] This account makes no use of the disorder Socrates finds in the injured soul, nor does it

SOCRATIC EUDAIMONISM

explain the value Socrates attributes to painful punishments that go beyond instruction.[27] Defenders of this view will have to declare that the *Gorgias* passages on painful punishments are not truly Socratic unless they can show that Socrates means such punishments to be purely educational.[28]

The moderately intellectualist view is designed to correct these and other defects.[29] On this view, the injury is cognitive – strong false beliefs about what is best – but the cause is non-cognitive or non-rational. Unjust actions strengthen appetites and passions, these stronger appetites and passions in turn corrupt one's beliefs, and corrupted beliefs then lead to further unjust action. The ruined soul has lost the ability to 'manage, rule, and deliberate' (Brickhouse and Smith 2010: 128, citing *Rep.* 1.353d). Punishment is directed at the first step in this causal chain, in which appetites become unruly. Punishment puts appetites back in order, with beneficial consequences for the beliefs that guide action.[30]

The moderately intellectualist account is strong so far as it goes.[31] But it does not explain the disorder and dissonance that concern Socrates. On this account, the injured reason simply changes its mind under the influence of appetite; after that there is no dissonance, and the soul remains united. Reason is still making the decisions, and so the soul is not disordered on this view. But disorder is the main source of misery for the unjust.[32] And it is hard to explain how a unitary soul without parts could be disordered or orders; order seems to entail a plurality of items that are to be kept in order.

The third view is that moral injury is a blow to one's integrity or wholeness as a person. Moral injury on this view leads to a self that is divided against itself.[33] That would explain the disorder and dissonance of which Socrates speaks in the *Gorgias* (482b, 506e–507a, cf. 475e–476a). It also promises to explain the misery that Socrates believes accompanies moral injury. The experience of veterans with moral injuries is consonant with this; their misery leads all too often to self-destructive acts including suicide. Although promising in many ways, this line of interpretation faces a serious obstacle: It seems to be inconsistent with Socrates' intellectualism as well as with his commitment to an undivided soul. Defenders of this view may appeal to the psychology of the later books of Plato's *Republic*, but that is not an acceptable move for most Socratic scholars (Brickhouse and Smith 2010: 97–102). Scholars who deny that Socrates is any kind of intellectualist, however, may support versions of the third view.[34]

None of the scholarly interpretations of moral injury that I have seen is entirely successful in explaining Socrates' thought on the matter from the texts at hand. We must go beyond a purely intellectualist account, and therefore beyond the literal meaning of the texts, by supplying a theory of the soul that allows for moral injury. Brickhouse and Smith supply the theory that appetite can warp belief; Gerson imports Platonic psychology from later works. I think we can do without full-scale Platonic psychology and simply recognise that Socrates employs the assumption that everyone somehow feels the attractive pull of the good, and, if tempted into wrongdoing, will be wrenched apart by these opposing pulls.[35] Socrates will have no psychological mechanism to explain this wrenching apart, until Plato develops his tri-partite model of the soul.

EXTERNAL INJURIES AND BENEFITS: DEPENDENT GOODS

Moral injury is the greatest source of misery according to Socrates. If virtue and happiness are identical for Socrates, as the ancient Stoics and some modern scholars hold, then moral injury is the only source for real misery.[36] But a number of texts suggest that moral injury is not the only type of injury that Socrates would wish to avoid. The argument of the *Crito* depends on an analogy between physical and moral injury that will fail if physical injury is not to be avoided (*Cr.* 47d–e; cf. *Grg.* 512a). Also, Socrates says that he would prefer not to be the victim of injustice, although he thinks it far worse to be a perpetrator (*Grg.* 469c).[37]

How can Socrates' preference to avoid victimisation be explained unless injustice truly harms its victims? Supporters of the identity thesis hold that only true injustice is harmful, and it is harmful only because it makes its victims less just – in other words, vicious behaviour inflicts moral injury, which is the only true kind of injury, and so the only source of injury we should avoid. But in context, Socrates says he is averse to suffering the kind of injustice that is on Polus' mind – including unjust execution, confiscation of property and banishment (*Grg.* 466b-c). So this explanation is weak,[38] and Socrates' position here counts against the identity thesis, both Stoic and modern.

We must distinguish the identity thesis from the sufficiency thesis that it entails. A number of scholars, following Vlastos, defend the thesis that virtue is sufficient for happiness while denying the identity thesis.[39] If physical injuries can make you more miserable without making you less virtuous, then virtue and happiness cannot be identical.[40] But if virtue is the dominant constituent of happiness, then virtue can guarantee a measure of happiness even though other sources of misery abound – though it cannot guarantee perfect happiness.[41]

Socrates seems to hold a theory of dependent goods and evils: Physical health is good if used virtuously, bad if used viciously.[42] Surviving a voyage is good for the virtuous and healthy, bad for the vicious or the sick (*Grg.* 511d–512a). To live virtuously, one must practice virtue actively, as with anything like a craft. To practice virtue actively, you must meet certain enabling conditions, which may include physical health and membership in a community. If Socrates permanently lost his voice, he would be unable to carry out the gadfly mission he describes in the *Apology*. Exile from Athens would have the same effect; no philosopher from out of town could get away with the activity of a gadfly. So exile would reduce Socrates' virtue, and therefore his happiness, by reducing his opportunities to practice virtues.[43] This is an objective matter: Exile would lower Socrates' level of happiness whether or not he preferred to avoid it.

Suppose the practice of virtue did not require external goods such as membership in a community. Even then, the injustice of exile or loss of property could still lower your happiness by placing you in circumstances in which strong emotions such as fear and anger could reduce your ability to manage your life in a reasonable and therefore virtuous way.[44] Again, this loss occurs whether it pains you subjectively or not.

Subjective feelings must count for something, however. Many scholars follow Vlastos in supposing that no matter how virtuous he may be, even Socrates would prefer not to have to sleep in a vomit-soaked bed.[45] This leads Vlastos' followers to identify a category of subjectively preferred goods. We should ask, then, whether subjective preference has anything to do with happiness as Socrates conceives it.

HAPPINESS: WELL-BEING OR GOOD FEELINGS?

Philosophers and social scientists who study happiness today often rely on studies based on reports of life satisfaction, which appears to be a subjective psychological condition. Their approach contrasts with that of what some philosophers call 'objective listers', who number objective factors, such as knowledge and friendship, as the basis of true happiness. It is tempting to reserve 'happiness' for the subjective state of life satisfaction,

SOCRATIC EUDAIMONISM 185

and 'well-being' for the condition satisfying objective conditions. But to understand Socrates (or Aristotle, I think) we need a concept that bridges the two.

A number of English expressions may be used to translate '*eudaimonia*', leading to confusions I will try to clear up here. So far I have been using 'happiness', which I consider the best choice, but we must also consider 'living well', 'well-being' and 'flourishing'.[46] 'Living well' translates a Greek expression that Socrates seems to treat as equivalent to *eudaimonia* (e.g. at *Cr.* 48b). In English as in Greek 'living well' could mean living virtuously, but it could also mean living prosperously. 'Well-being' in English often covers objective features of a human life, such as health. 'Flourishing' has been introduced by translators of Aristotle.[47] This concept is based on the *nature* of a living thing: Being *eudaimōn* (on this view) is fulfilling a human being's natural potential. Aristotle's ethics is therefore generally considered to be naturalistic.[48] Socrates does not appear to have a naturalistic theory, and ancient Greek usage counts against a purely naturalistic reading of *eudaimonia*. Natural beings such as plants and animals may flourish, but in Greek they are not said to be *eudaimones*. Only human beings (and perhaps also gods) may be said to be *eudaimones*. A likely explanation of this is that to be truly *eudaimōn* one should be conscious of one's happiness. Surely a Socrates who feels happy in his virtue is better off than an equally virtuous character who feels miserable. Being conscious of your *eudaimonia* enhances it. That is, people who are objectively happy, because they are living well, are also subjectively happy: They feel good about their lives, as does Socrates. By contrast, many people who think they are *eudaimones* and feel good about their lives are not really *eudaimones* at all.[49] Good feelings come and go and may or may not be coincident with actual *eudaimonia*.[50]

Ancient Greek does not clearly mark distinctions between objective and subjective approaches to happiness, but the culture tended toward objectivity. A famous proverb told the ancient Greeks to call no one happy until after death; to claim *eudaimonia* before one's death is to ask for trouble from the gods, as Croesus learned to his cost.[51] This is standard ancient Greek wisdom, which probably explains why Socrates does not claim *eudaimonia* on his own behalf. The famous proverb implies that living subjects are not authorities on their own happiness – whether it is conceived as objective, subjective or both. Aristotle and Plato take a largely objective view of *eudaimonia*. In Socratic dialogues, it does not matter how good the unjust tyrant feels or says he feels; he is in fact at the peak of misery, unless he has the good fortune to be punished (*Grg.* 479e).

For the objective thesis that Socrates is living justly and happily we do not have to ask him how he feels; we have seen the testimony of his friends; his feelings are not at issue. Socrates has objective reasons, recognised by his friends, for believing that he is living well – if not with full virtue. Socrates takes a cheerful tone in the *Apology*, confident enough of his goodness to have no fear of evil in this life or after it (*Ap.* 41c–d). Plainly he thinks he has good reasons to feel good about his life. By contrast, if an unjust tyrant feels happy, it is because he is wrong about the nature of happiness. Such vicious people, on Socrates' view, do not have any idea what happiness truly is. If they did know how their unjust lives are destroying what is most important to them, they would feel miserable.[52]

Both our word 'happiness' and ancient Greek *eudaimonia* seem to bridge objective and subjective uses. For simplicity I will continue to translate *eudaimonia* as 'happiness', hoping that the reader will keep in mind this point: We moderns generally understand happiness as personal and subjective, so that we think of pursuing happiness as intrinsically egoistic. But Socrates and other ancient Greeks do not think of happiness in this way.

Socrates' claim that everyone wants to be happy (*Euthd.* 282a) does not in itself imply that everyone is driven by self-interest.[53] Below, we will consider the concept of altruistic eudaimonism.

EUDAIMONIST THEORIES ATTRIBUTED TO SOCRATES: A TAXONOMY

Socrates' ethical view is eudaimonist in that he believes that only those who live well ethically are *eudaimōn*: 'In my terms, Polus, I call the fine and good man or woman *eudaimōn*, and anyone who is unjust and bad I call miserable' (*Gorgias* 470e, cf. 507c). 'To live well (*to eu zēn*) and to live finely (*kalōs*) and to live justly (*dikaiōs*) are the same thing', where 'to live well' may be synonymous with *eudaimonia* (*Crito* 48b). 'Since we passionately wish to be happy, and since it turns out that we become so by using things and using them rightly, and since what furnishes rightness and success is knowledge, then it is necessary, as you might expect, that everyone should take steps to be superlatively wise' (*Euthd.* 282a).[54] Such statements have given rise to a number of different interpretations.

E1. A psychological eudaimonist holds that, as a matter of fact about human nature, all people pursue *eudaimonia*.[55] What this would mean for Socrates depends on what he means by *eudaimonia*, and also on how he understands the pursuit of such a good. Most scholars who attribute E1 to Socrates conjoin it with egoism, on the questionable assumption that pursuing happiness is self-interested.

Scholars who attribute E1 to Socrates often appeal to Socrates' claims that everyone wants to be happy (*Euthd.* 282a; cf. *Prt.* 358c-d) and also that everyone wants what is truly good and pursues it; those who are mistaken about what is truly good therefore do not get what they want (*Gorgias* 468a-b, *Meno* 77b-c; cf. *Republic* 6, 505d-505e). If Socrates' claim is meant to state a fact of human nature, and if he believes that what is truly good is identical with *eudaimonia*,[56] then Socrates would be a psychological eudaimonist. This would still leave open questions about the nature of *eudaimonia* as the good, and therefore about the relation between *eudaimonia* and virtue or self-interest. These questions are addressed in the normative formulations of eudaimonism, below (E2 through E6).

E1 is not necessarily egoistic, in view of the range of meanings that *eudaimonia* or the good life may have.[57] Charles Kahn puts the case against egoism clearly: 'It would be appropriate to speak of egoism here only if we thought (like Terry Irwin's Socrates) that it was possible to characterize the good life in morally neutral terms' – that is, conceptually independent of the virtues, which Socrates never represents as essentially self-regarding. The only passage that seems to present the good life in morally neutral terms is late in the *Protagoras*, the passage on *akrasia*.[58] We shall see that scholars' views on Socratic egoism depend heavily on whether they take this passage to express Socrates' considered view or a position he takes dialectically in response to Protagoras' claim that virtue can be taught and therefore is a kind of knowledge.[59]

Socrates' example, moreover, tells strongly against E1 on an egoist reading. In the *Apology* he explains to the jury his reasons for living as he has and most of these are not self-interested.[60] Indeed he says he has neglected his own interests in service to the god (*Ap.* 23b). If Socrates' account of his motivation in the *Apology* is correct, and not a falsehood calculated to win over the jury, then egoistic psychological eudaimonism is, as

SOCRATIC EUDAIMONISM

a matter of fact, false: Not everyone is moved solely or primarily by the egoistic pursuit of happiness. On any view, however, psychological eudaimonism grounds an approach to ethical education that clarifies *eudaimonia*. If everyone is motivated to do what *eudaimonia* requires, changing people's beliefs about *eudaimonia* would change their behaviour.

E2. An egoist eudaimonist holds that, in order to be virtuous, one ought to perform an action if and only if, and because, performing that action promotes (or can reasonably be expected to promote) one's *eudaimonia* better than the alternatives.[61] This is a form of ethical egoism.[62] It can be understood in at least two ways: (a) a hard egoist holds that a virtuous person ought to do good to others only as a by-product of that person's quest for personal *eudaimonia*; (b) a soft or benign egoist conjoins egoism with the principle that one person's interests cannot conflict with those of others.[63] Benign egoism is still a form of egoism because 'it tells us to maximize our own good, and it takes self-interest to be the best kind of reason for action' (Kraut 1989: 81). Most of those who attribute egoism to Socrates have in mind a form of egoism that is benign in effect, holding that benefits to others are bound up with the welfare of the agent.

A number of modern scholars have held that Socrates was an egoistic eudaimonist, and that in this he was going along with what was then common sense on ancient Greece. This is controversial. We have evidence in both literary and philosophical texts that Greeks in the classical period associated virtue with acting for the interests of others.[64] This need not imply selflessness or self-sacrifice. Both the concept of self-sacrifice and the concept of egoism depend on a distinction between one's self-interest and the interest of others, and such a distinction may be anachronistic. Some scholars have argued that ancient Greek ethical thinkers saw the good of the individual and that of the community as essentially fused.[65] Greek poets from Tyrtaeus on identify the interests of individuals with those of their *polis*, as does Pericles in the time of Socrates.[66] Socrates cannot conceive of living a good life outside his *polis*.[67] Radical thinkers such as Thrasymachus and Callicles try to separate their individual interests from those of others, but Socrates argues that they cannot succeed in this. Self-interest and other-interest are for him, as for many of his contemporaries, closely bound together, not merely by the contingencies of life in ancient city-states, but by the very nature of human beings.[68] Socrates is committed to the concept of a common good (*Grg.* 505e, *Chrm.* 166d), which is not consistent with thoroughgoing egoism (Ahbel-Rappe 2010: 42–43).[69] Benign egoism is attractive, but Socrates' position is unlikely to have entailed any form of egoism, as we shall see below.

Most scholars who discuss egoist eudaimonism in the Socratic context are focused on the reasons Socrates thinks we should use to guide our actions. This has led them to the rational version of egoistic eudaimonism (E3).[70]

E3. An egoistic rational eudaimonist holds either (a) that a person's greatest *eudaimonia* serves as a *decisive* rational consideration for all of that person's actions and choices, or (b) that a person's greatest *eudaimonia* serves as the *only* rational consideration for that person's practical reasoning.[71] Rational eudaimonism on this model entails some form of egoism. Socrates might hold rational eudaimonism as an ideal, but, if he were unable to find reasons he would count as rational in a given case, he would nevertheless have to fall back on non-rational considerations.[72] What this means depends on what reasons Socrates would count as good enough to be accepted as rational.[73] The word 'rational', however, does not translate a Socratic concept directly; we will find it helpful to distinguish between the ideal reasoning of a moral expert and the reasoning for which Socrates is capable in his human wisdom – reasoning good enough to serve as the basis for a decision he knew would lead to his death.

Defenders of E3 will have to explain why the practical reasoning Socrates exhibits in guiding his own life is based on other-regarding considerations which, in some cases, exclude self-regarding ones as these were usually understood.[74] Fortunately, rational eudaimonism need not be egoistic. As we have seen, *eudaimonia* may be altruistic and not self-interested. Socrates appears to have reasons he considers good for everything he says and does.[75] If so, then any position Socrates holds is rational on his view, and therefore, if he is a eudaimonist, he must be a rational one – but not necessarily egoistic.

E4. A teleological eudaimonist holds either (a) that the value of virtue lies only in its being instrumental for *eudaimonia*, or (b) that virtue is the only means to happiness (while virtue may also have value in itself). Irwin has called this sort of position 'moral solipsism' on the belief that Socrates identifies the good with pleasure.[76] Assigning either of these to Socrates has been highly controversial.[77]

For E4, the issue is this: Which is the primary goal; virtue or happiness? The question presupposes that virtue and happiness are not identical. Defenders of E4 could argue that, in the *Apology*, Socrates urges his fellow citizens to cultivate virtue as a means to happiness and only as a means. We do not need to be told to pursue our happiness; no gadfly seems necessary for that. But a gadfly is necessary for the difficult pursuit of virtue, if that is the only way to achieve happiness. But then the defenders will have to explain why Socrates does not make this explicit in the *Apology*.

Defenders of E4 will also have to explain why Socrates investigates the natures of the virtues in the dialogues of search rather than the nature of happiness. It is virtue, as the good condition of the soul,[78] not happiness, that Socrates urges his fellow citizen to cultivate in the *Apology*. And, in the *Euthyphro*, Socrates asks his companion to defend his decision by defining the virtue of reverence, not by defining happiness (5cd).

E5. An identity eudaimonist holds that virtue and *eudaimonia* are identical. The identity of *eudaimonia* with virtue was held by Socrates' student Antisthenes, and also by later Platonists in antiquity, as well as by Stoics, who believed that this was Socrates' position.[79] We might assign the identity thesis to Socrates on the basis of his identification of living well with living justly (*Cr.* 48b). Note that virtue can be identical with happiness and, at the same time, productive of happiness. Socrates does not draw a line between what is good in itself and what is productive of good.[80]

The strongest objection to E5 is that Socrates does not consistently identify living well or *eudaimonia* simply with living virtuously. If Socrates thought virtue and happiness were identical, he would see no threat to happiness in the loss of physical health. But he uses the following premise in his discussion with Crito:

> Would our lives be worth living once [the health of the body] has been destroyed? Surely not.

> – 47d–e

In itself, this text alone does not entail that a loss of health is a loss of happiness – merely that there is no point in continuing to confine your soul to a body that has been wrecked. After all, one might be quite happy in an afterlife without a body. But, as we have seen, a wider study of the texts shows that Socrates has reason to avoid bodily and other external injuries in addition to direct injuries to the soul. If, as seems likely, Socrates thinks that

SOCRATIC EUDAIMONISM

losing health diminishes one's happiness in this life, then he is at most what Vlastos calls a *constitutive* eudaimonist:

E6. A constitutive eudaimonist holds either (a) that virtue is the dominant part of *eudaimonia*, outweighing all other parts and therefore sufficient for *eudaimonia*, or (b) that virtue is a necessary part of *eudaimonia* (while other parts, such as physical health, may also be necessary for *eudaimonia*). On E6a, virtue is the dominant constituent in happiness; other constituents would include health and friends. Because virtue is dominant, it will be strong enough to make you happy even if all the other constituents go bad. On E6b, virtue is not dominant, and so cannot overcome other sources of misery. This is attractive as being the more common-sense view.[81] On E6a, in making a practical decision, Socrates would have no reason to consider anything but what it is that virtue requires, because loss of money, exile and even execution cannot outweigh virtue, while on E6b, since those troubles conceivably could outweigh virtue, they would have to be considered. On this point, the text supports E6a (*Cr.* 48c–d).

E6a, like E5, entails the sufficiency thesis, which is controversial. Rudebusch has given a detailed argument to show that the thesis can be proved on Socratic premises (1999); Irwin has argued that Socrates can promote the sufficiency thesis by holding an improbable approach to happiness – adaptive happiness, which adjusts to deprivations; Plato, seeing the weakness of this, abandons sufficiency on Irwin's view (1986). On the other side, Brickhouse and Smith deny that Socrates held the sufficiency thesis because, they contend, it would require us to be omnipotent in our ability to avoid troubles.[82] Virtue ethicist Christine Swanton rejects eudaimonism as an ethical theory because, in effect, she sees it as entailing a consequence of the sufficiency thesis – that a trait is not a virtue unless it contributes to human flourishing (2003). That, she thinks, would be too restrictive of what counts as a virtue. We need to consider whether that objection applies to Socrates. With some trepidation, however, I think that the Socrates of the *Apology* and *Crito* is committed to sufficiency, in spite of the problems to which the thesis leads.

A further distinction cuts across these interpretations: The relationship between virtue and happiness may be thought to be *a priori*, or it may be considered nomological. If it is *a priori*, then it holds in virtue of the essential natures of virtue and happiness, whether or not the two are identical.[83] The alternative to understanding the relationship as *a priori* is understanding it as contingent or nomological, meaning it turns out that pursuing virtue is an effective way, and the only effective way that we have found, of pursuing happiness, but virtue in itself, as a matter of logic, is neither necessary nor sufficient for happiness. Conditions are conceivable on this view under which virtue would not lead to happiness.[84] On the nomological view, then, eudaimonism represents a lawlike relationship between virtue and happiness that allows for exceptions; it does not follow from the essential natures of virtue and happiness. Socrates, however, does not explicitly treat the relationship as contingent. He treats eudaimonism as guaranteed by knowledge of virtue and happiness, rather than as a truth we learn from human experience.[85]

A shadow of egoism falls over any interpretation of eudaimonism, since an individual's happiness seems to be the personal concern of that individual. Much depends on what Socrates understands by *eudaimonia*, as we have seen. Much also depends on how he understands the pursuit of virtues such as justice. What kinds of reasons bear on the pursuit of virtue – on practical decisions as to what virtues require of us? Are we to start by determining where *eudaimonia* lies and infer from that where virtue lies? Or the other

190 THE BLOOMSBURY HANDBOOK OF SOCRATES

way around? Or both at once? If both at once, how do we manage that? Keep in mind also that 'egoism' can mean more than one thing; it can be hard or benign.

On eudaimonism, Socrates scholars can learn useful concepts from recent philosophers who have been developing virtue ethical theory. Although they are working in the tradition of Aristotle, these thinkers employ distinctions that may be applied in the debate about Socratic eudaimonism. For example, we now have the concept of *altruistic* eudaimonism, on which 'the virtuous agent may be understood as being motivated by human goodness, caring about herself and others based on human goodness, and where all of her reasons, values and justifications are cashed out in terms of human goodness 'all the way down'.[86]

Which of these views does Plato represent Socrates as holding? To understand Socratic eudaimonism we will need to attend to what Socrates says about justice, as that is the principal virtue (aside from wisdom) that he connects with *eudaimonia*. Can justice be a self-regarding virtue, or is it intrinsically other-regarding? Or is it, in some way, both? We will ask the same question about other Socratic virtues, with an emphasis on *sophrōsunē*. In all cases we will be looking at the reasoning process that Socrates practices or recommends, since that is one of the main points on which the scholarly debate hangs: Does Socrates' ethical reasoning treat personal happiness as its explicit goal, as E1, E2, E3 and E4 seem to require? Or is its goal a virtue such as justice or wisdom? I begin by examining the arguments in the *Crito*.

SOCRATIC REASONING: WHY AVOID MORAL INJURY

The reasons Socrates offers for living justly and avoiding moral injury – that is, for performing just actions and maintaining a just character – appear to be egoistic. Socrates would be a rational eudaimonist if he held that we ought to make moral decisions by taking our own *eudaimonia* explicitly as the target. And he would be an egoist if he held that we should be moved only by reasons that are related to our own good. But we shall see that the matter is not so simple.

The argument for avoiding moral injury is given in the *Crito*. As Vasiliou has shown, the argument there falls into two distinct stages.[87] Stage one gives Socrates' answer to what we would call the 'why be moral' question; stage two answers the question of what action morality requires in this case. These are different kinds of question; answering them calls for different kinds of reasons. Socrates' decision to act as he does is based on both arguments, but it does not follow that his reasons are the same in both cases.

Stage one begins around 46e and ends at 48c, explaining his reasons for *trying* to work out what action in a given case is just. These reasons appear to be *self*-regarding: Acting unjustly (he says) would wreck his character, and he would find life with a wrecked character unliveable. Stage two runs from 48c to the end of the dialogue.

Socrates' general plan for reasoning on such matters is to follow only the *logos* that, as he reasons about it, is revealed as the best (46b). In the course of the argument that follows, Socrates suggests a scenario in which he has found an expert. An expert on virtue knows virtue the way a physical trainer knows fitness, and on that basis the expert prescribes actions that maintain or improve the subject's virtue (47c–d). If he had an expert to consult, Socrates could explain his decision to Crito by saying: 'my expert said to remain in custody'. But Socrates has not found such an expert, and he nowhere claims

SOCRATIC EUDAIMONISM

to have such expert knowledge on his own.[88] In fact he claims not to have expert knowledge at all (*Ap.* 21b, 23b) and professes ignorance about the matters on which he questions others.[89] Stage one, then, identifies the question that he and Crito must answer:

> For us, now that the argument has chosen thus, there is nothing else we should ask than what we were just now talking about: whether we'd be doing justice by paying money and doing favours for those who'd get us out of here – we and those who'd get us out – or whether in truth we'd be doing all these things unjustly.
>
> – *Crito* 48c–d

Socrates' reason for drawing this conclusion is clear: Doing injustice wrecks one's character,[90] which has greater value than one's body (48a). Therefore, avoiding injustice has a higher value than avoiding physical injury. It follows that Socrates should pursue the family and social values to which Crito has appealed only insofar as they are just, or at least not unjust. In ranking the values one must live by, living justly must come first. If justice is the fundamental virtue for Socrates, then this is essentially the same doctrine as the one he preaches in the *Apology*, that one should take more care over the goodness of one's soul than of money or reputation or high office (29d–30a, cf. 32d).[91]

Note that, in coming to this conclusion, Socrates is considering not only his own character, but the characters of those who would accept the bribes his friends have offered, and indeed of anyone who would help him undermine the law of Athens. By escaping through these means he would implicate others in his act of injustice and so damage them as well. He is not considering his own interest to the exclusion of others at stage one.

Clearly Socrates holds that living justly confers a benefit on the agent. The benefit is to the character or the agent – that which 'becomes better' through justice. By performing just actions, you become more just in character, and by performing unjust actions, more unjust.[92] The health analogy suggests that you maintain a just character by living justly, in the same way that you maintain a healthy body by living healthily. And becoming healthier in body or character leads to an increase in *eudaimonia*, while losing ground in either way leads to lesser happiness or greater misery.

Underlying this belief about justice and character, I propose, is a principle of causation I will call the principle of synonymy. Just as heat cannot by its own nature have any effect on any object other than to increase that object's heat, so justice can have no other effect on anyone by its own nature than to make the person affected more just.[93] That, I suggest, would explain why (on Socrates' view) doing just actions renders the agent more just (if it has any effect on the agent) and also why just punishment is beneficial by making wrongdoers more just in character.[94] If, in the process of being punished, wrongdoers suffer some physical or material loss, that would not destroy their happiness, according to E5 or E6a. The improvement in justice resulting from undergoing punishment would make irrelevant any physical or material loss caused by, or involved in, the punishment.

The only effect of doing justice qua justice, on this view, is more justice, whether in the character of the agent or in the characters of other people affected by the agent's actions, or in the community of the agent. In effect, Socrates has been answering the question of why we should do what is right, and his answer has been that we should do what is right because doing so is always beneficial. Socrates characteristically uses 'beneficial' in an unqualified sense; apparently, what is truly beneficial is so for everyone who is touched by it.[95] Justice comes across as rather like a viral infection – highly contagious (barring an immune reaction). This contagiousness is an important feature of any virtue, although it is neutral with respect to what sort of life virtue actually calls for, and what actions virtue requires.[96]

So far, we have not gone beyond Socrates' reasons for trying to live justly. The question *what it is to live justly* is clearly still open at the end of stage one, and this openness is explicit at 48c: What is to be looked into is whether it would be just for Socrates to escape as proposed. At this point we might ask whether Socratic justice is an other-regarding virtue or a self-regarding one. But that would be misleading. We have seen that the causal influence of justice makes no distinction between self and other; it is indiscriminately beneficial.

SOCRATIC REASONING: JUSTICE[97]

Stage one aimed to lead Crito to see why justice is the only thing to consider; stage two will aim to show why justice forbids Socrates to escape from custody in these circumstances. Socrates will show in stage two that acting unjustly in this case could wreck the laws as well as his character, and so do damage to his friends (i.e., to his fellow citizens) and to his country (54c). So, in stage two, his reasons for *finding* that this particular action is unjust appear to be *other*-regarding – or at least they disregard the self-regarding reasons he gave in stage one for putting justice first. In this second phase of the *Crito* argument we learn that leaving prison through bribery would injure Socrates' character because it would be unjust for him to leave prison in this way. It would be unjust to do so for a number of contributing reasons relating to his obligations to the polis and its laws. But he does not argue that it is unjust for him to leave because it would damage his character. To say that would be to run the argument backward. In fact, the reasons Socrates cites here are all other-regarding.

We have three main lines of evidence in earlier dialogues for Socrates' conceptions of justice and injustice. For justice, we have the reasoning Socrates offers in stage two of the *Crito* for not agreeing to bribe the jailors. For injustice, we have the model of unjust behaviour set by such tyrants as Archelaus discussed in the *Gorgias*. In addition, we have what Socrates says about the unifying role of justice in any community in *Republic* 1, which explains how he thinks injustice wrecks a community (351c–352a).

The argument in stage two of the *Crito* appeals to a complex set of contributing reasons, all set against the background assumption that Socrates' action, if he chose to escape, would be destructive of Athenian law[98] and, as a result, damaging to Athens and to its citizens (50b).

Socrates uses two main principles to support his argument.[99] The first is explicit: (1) Justice requires us to keep our agreements, provided they are just (49e5–7). The second is implicit in the speech of the Laws:[100] (2) Justice requires reciprocation: We owe the benefits of respect and obedience to those, such as our parents, from whom we have received the benefits of life and education. These are plainly other-regarding principles, and they represent a conventional view of justice. Socrates need not believe that these hold without exception,[101] but he evidently believes that they apply in his case, and neither he nor Crito is able to come up with reasons for making exceptions here. The actions these two principles require remain, roughly, the sorts of actions that Socrates is defending here and elsewhere as contrary to the injustices of tyrants that are so attractive to Polus. Socrates' conception of justice under these two principles is conventional: The majority of his fellow-citizens would have agreed with them, although probably not with his conclusion.

In Socrates' case, his agreements are with the laws of Athens, and the benefit he has received is from the polis of Athens, his fatherland (*patris*), which, he has the laws say, has done more for him than even his parents. Individuals depend on community, and the community depends on the justice of its citizens. By bribing the guards and escaping the force of the law, Socrates would be inflicting harm on the very institutions that have made his life possible as well as on the people whose job it is to uphold the law.[102] Plato must have had in mind the history of Alcibiades, who went over to the Spartans and did irreparable harm to Athens.[103] He was one of the young men Socrates is supposed to have corrupted, and Plato, in giving Socrates this argument in the *Crito*, is showing how different are the values of the two men.

The opposite of justice is injustice. Socrates presents the tyrant as the paradigm of injustice, both in the *Gorgias* and in the whole of the *Republic*. Of tyrants, the paradigm is Archelaus, who murdered, lied and cheated his way to power in Macedon, where he laid the foundations for the rise of Macedon under Philip II. He was a useful ally to the Athenians, who therefore tended to overlook his crimes. Archelaus' success showed that a tyrant could kill those he thinks fit to kill,[104] banish others as he sees fit, and confiscate property – all of this with impunity. Polus, who deems the tyrant happy, admits that Archelaus has committed the greatest injustices in his rise to power (471a–b), and Socrates agrees. Archelaus has taken what was not his, deceived people, and killed his rivals, including young children. These are plainly violations of justice as Socrates and his fellow citizens understand it. In these passages, Socrates is appealing to received opinion about what counts as injustice: Archelaus' murdering, lying and taking what is not his.[105] The only novelty here is Socrates' view of how happiness relates to conventional justice.

Socrates implied, at the end of the *Crito*, that the proposed injustice would be damaging to the country and to its citizens. He evidently subscribes to the common views that people flourish best as citizens of a *polis*, that the *polis* cannot survive without the order that laws bring to it (53a) and that injustice destroys that order. This idea has a substantial history.

Protagoras, according to the dialogue bearing his name, holds that justice, along with *aidōs*, respect, is what human beings need in order to live together in communities sustained through order and friendship (322b–c). Socrates holds a similar view in *Republic* 1: Even a band of thieves cannot work together if they do each other injustice (351c). On this view, justice is the primary human virtue because human beings need community and cannot sustain community without justice. On this, Socrates seems to agree with the view of justice he attributes to Protagoras. As a virtue of community, justice is primarily an other-regarding virtue.

That is why Socrates has to face the challenge of Glaucon and others to show that it's in the interests of the agent to serve the community by practising justice. For this, in the later books of the *Republic*, he will develop a theory of the soul that shows how the agent is better off for being just. That theory lies outside the scope of this chapter, but I will point out here that the Platonic account of justice, based on the tripartite theory of the soul, does not pre-empt the basic other-regarding requirements of justice[106] such as we found in the earlier dialogues: for example, that one not be a tyrant,[107] and that one repay one's obligations to the community, as the philosopher rulers will do by returning to the Cave as a matter of justice (*Republic* 7.519e–520e). Socrates has no need to convince his audience that justice serves the interest of the community; everyone recognises that. His challenge is to show that it also serves the interest of the agent. In rising to this challenge, he appears to make himself vulnerable to the charge of egoism.

We may well ask whether what goes for justice goes for the other virtues. The virtue of *sophrōsunē*, temperance or sound-mindedness, appears to be personal and self-directed, but Plato and other thinkers of the period understood it to be a social virtue. Plato has Protagoras pair *sophrōsunē* with justice as the two civic virtues that every citizen must have if they are to maintain a polis (*Protagoras* 323a). In the Kallipolis of Plato's *Republic*, *sophrōsunē* is required of all citizens, along with justice, and is essential to the survival of the city in its noble form. In the *Gorgias* Socrates represents *sophrōsunē* as leading to appropriate action, and this makes it a cause of justice, piety and courage (507a–c). As such it appears to be necessary and sufficient for happiness (507c).

Justice is the principal virtue in Socrates' scheme of human virtue.[108] In Socrates' usage, 'just' and 'unjust' are almost equivalent to our 'right' and 'wrong'.[109] That is why we had to elucidate what Socrates means by living justly in order to understand what he means by living well. We have seen that Socrates' reasoning about what justice requires is largely other-regarding. Now we are tempted to ask whether Socrates understands justice as a self- or other-regarding virtue. We have seen evidence on both sides: We should aim at justice because it is beneficial to us individually to do so, but acting with justice requires us to consider the interests of others. But we have also seen that justice is by its nature directed at the welfare of all who are affected by it, including those who live justly and do justice.

THE CHARGE OF EGOISM

A frequent modern criticism of ancient ethics is that its eudaimonism is egoistic in a sense that is not benign but amoral.[110] Writing about the argument of the *Republic*, H. A. Prichard says that, in accepting Glaucon's challenge, Socrates agrees that 'for an action to be right, it must be advantageous', from which Prichard thinks it follows that 'advantageousness is what renders an action right' (1928: 15). He further attributes to the Platonic Socrates the doctrine that, even if we know an action is right, we will not do it unless 'we think we shall be better off for doing it', where 'better off' means 'happier'. This is a claim about the facts of human nature – psychological egoism. It is plainly false: We know of many cases of self-sacrificing action, and it is a mistake to attribute all such cases to the agent's thinking she will be happier sacrificing her own interests. Take the case of a parent giving up an activity she loves in order to take care of an ailing child. Indeed, she may well be happier in the long run for doing this, but she has not time to think of that, and that is not why she does it. She makes the sacrifice for the sake of the child's welfare; if that is possible, then it is false that no one ever acts for self-sacrificing reasons. We need strong textual evidence to attribute to Socrates a view that is so plainly false. A more plausible view would be that self-sacrificing choices are possible but irrational, but we have seen that this does not appear to be Socratic.

In a limited defence of Prichard's view, Brown argues that Socrates is an egoistic rational eudaimonist: 'The practically rational person always acts or chooses with a view, ultimately, to their own happiness' (2007: 47). On that account, a non-self-interested oddball (as she calls her) is not impossible but merely irrational. However, Brown agrees with Prichard that 'Socrates fails to recognize that a just person has reasons for a just action of a quite different sort from an appeal to one's own good' (2007: 59).[111]

Bobonich, in a chapter on this subject, also employs the notion of rational eudaimonism; he argues that Socrates holds an even stronger view, according to which Socrates believes that, ideally, we ought to make *eudaimonia*, and *only eudaimonia*, our conscious goal in making ethical decisions:

SOCRATIC EUDAIMONISM

> The principle of Rational Eudaimonism claims that there is a single, decisive rational consideration for all of a person's actions and choices – that is, the person's (greatest) happiness. We have found good evidence from the early dialogues that Socrates holds a stronger form of rational eudaimonism such that one's own happiness is the only rational consideration. . . . He seems to think that attaining happiness is best achieved by taking it as an explicit target [for practical deliberations].[112]

If Socrates is a eudaimonist of this sort, then it appears he must also be an egoist, because the *eudaimonia* it is rational to pursue appears to be one's own. Some modern critics have charged that Socrates' egoism has penetrated all of ancient ethics. Thomas Hurka complains that Aristotle 'grounds all my oughts and reasons in considerations about *my* good'. 'What makes something like benevolence a virtue isn't its benefitting me but its caring properly about goods in other people's lives.'[113] This is a plausible point: Aristotle builds the virtues into his concept of an agent's *eudaimonia*, and Socrates, who started us off on this journey into virtue, held that the goal of virtuous action is the moral health of the agent. In short, and put crudely, the charge against Socrates and the tradition that follows him is this: We moderns think ethics is essentially other-regarding, while Socrates and his successors thought it was mainly about self-interest. So runs a modern objection to the Socratic tradition.[114]

RATIONALITY

'Rational' does not have an exact equivalent in Socrates' usage. We will say that a rational argument is one that employs good reasons. What counts as a good reason for Socrates? I will consider three ways of answering this question. First, in the *Euthyphro*, Socrates assumes that if Euthyphro has a good reason for prosecuting his father, he must be able to ground his decision to do so in a definition of the relevant virtue, in this case piety – a definition that can withstand elenctic examination.[115] This is a high standard, which Socrates himself does not claim to meet – an ideal that perhaps the philosopher-kings of the *Republic* are educated to satisfy. A fully rational procedure, by this standard, would fit the model he attributes to physical trainers or doctors: Knowing precisely what fitness or health is, an expert for the body knows what to do to maintain health or restore it when it is lost.[116] In the same way, a moral expert – a doctor for the soul – would know how to keep one's character in good shape. Such an expert would take moral health as the goal, and ethical behaviour merely as the means. But we have seen that Socrates does not reason this way in his own case.

The second model of rationality we can take from what Socrates actually does. He stakes his own life on a weaker kind of reason – the reasons we have outlined in his argument against escaping in the *Crito*. He must consider these reasons good enough, if he is to die for them, but he may also consider them less than ideal. A moral expert who satisfied the ideal standard might have been preferable.

There is a third model I will mention only briefly here as it takes us out of the realm of Socratic studies. We might look at the argument Socrates thinks is good enough to persuade the philosopher kings to return to the Cave; it is similar to the *Crito* argument, except that it must meet the highest standard, since it is aimed at fully educated philosophers. Although this falls outside of Plato's most Socratic work, it gives us clues as to how Plato thought about rationality.[117]

I prefer the second model, as Socrates surely thinks the reasons he uses to guide his life and accept his death are good enough. In the *Crito*, we see that Socrates has to decide whether to escape or not because of the situation thrust upon him. We have seen that his reasoning at this stage is other-regarding. In the *Apology*, Socrates explains why he lives as he does, and there self-interest plays only a part of his explanation: He stresses the importance of looking after the goodness of one's soul, *epimeleisthai tes psyches* (30a–b), an activity that apparently involves the discussions of virtue that arise from questioning oneself and others. Notably, he is not trying to persuade his fellow citizens to look after each other, but to look after themselves as individuals. In this he makes it clear that he is trying to do good for them; he does not say that he has undertaken this mission in the interest of his own happiness. Quite the contrary: He thinks he deserves a reward for this service to the city.

Having discussions of virtue every day, he says, is the greatest good for a human being (38a). In the context, he is not saying that he performs this service in order to realise this good for himself; instead, he says it by way of explaining why he thinks that he has been bringing the greatest good to all in Athens as he carries out his mission. This mission he sees as given him by the god, and so the god's command may be his principal reason for living as he does. But reasons may overlap: Socrates may have arrived at his understanding of what the god commands from whatever reasoning led him to see the value of these discussions in the first place.

Defenders of assigning E3 (rational eudaimonism) to Socrates could argue, against opponents such as Ahbel-Rappe (2012), that Socrates could consider other-regarding reasons in making his own ethical decisions while still being a rational eudaimonist in theory. That would be so if Socrates limited rational decision-making to the ideal standard beyond the reach of those, like him, who cannot give a full account of the good. Then using other-regarding considerations would be second-best. We know that Socrates holds that much human success is irrational – that is, not logos-based – and that such success may be due to gifts from the gods.[118] The god's command to Socrates would be such a gift if Socrates did not have adequate reasoning to back up his mission.

This defence of E3 fails. Eudaimonism on the first model of rationality is impossible for Socrates and so not likely to be possible for any human beings. In the *Apology*, Socrates is not asking his fellow citizens to seek gifts from the gods, but to look after the care of their souls through discussion and self-examination. Nor is he seriously asking them to find human moral experts and obey them.

Suppose, however, that such an expert were to materialise in Socrates' prison. We do not know what a doctor for the soul would tell Socrates and Crito at their moment of decision. For all we know, the expert's reasoning might look just like Socrates'. Instead of starting with a definition of happiness or of the health of the soul, the expert might start with same principles as Socrates does. If so, the other-regarding reasons Socrates actually gives here would be rational by expert standards, and rational eudaimonism could not be egoistic. The expert on *eudaimonia* would be advising us that it is rational to take into account the *eudaimonia* of others, thus merging rational with altruistic *eudaimonia*. We cannot dismiss this possibility.

CONCLUSIONS

I cannot claim to have proved all the points that follow, but I think they are the most likely answers to the questions raised by Socratic eudaimonism. Most of these answers depend in turn on answers to large questions that are addressed elsewhere in this volume, such as the extent of Socrates' intellectualism, and I have not had space here to support

SOCRATIC EUDAIMONISM

my views on those matters. But here is where matters stand for me after reading widely on Socratic eudaimonism and reviewing the relevant texts: The most likely interpretation for Socrates' view on virtue and happiness is rational, altruistic, constitutive eudaimonism.

Further work on Socratic eudaimonism should allow for the collapse of a distinction that scholars and philosophers commonly make. Socrates does not distinguish sharply between self- and other-regarding reasons for pursuing virtue. Merely asking whether or not Socrates is or is not an egoist betrays a misunderstanding of Socrates' concept of virtue. Socrates would not ask whether we should aim at benefits only for ourselves or only for others, because he would not accept the 'only'. He believed that virtue is such by its very nature that it benefits everyone who is touched by it in any way. It follows that anyone who used exclusively self- or other-regarding reasons in ethical deliberation would be labouring under a serious misunderstanding of the nature of virtue. In any case, different sorts of reasons may properly bear on the same decision. Emphasising one sort of reason does not necessarily exclude others. You may do the right thing because it is the right thing and also because it gives you pleasure to do the right thing. One reason does not cancel the other.

Virtue is necessary for happiness; that's why moral injury diminishes one's happiness as it diminishes one's virtue. Virtue is not purely intellectual; moral injury is a blow to one's character, not merely to one's beliefs. Indeed, moral injury is painful partly because it often involves a clash between what one believes and what one does in difficult situations such as combat, or between two competing sets of belief.

As the dominant constituent of *eudaimonia*, virtue is sufficient for happiness, although not for ideal happiness. Virtuous persons such as Socrates will be humanly happy, so long as they are virtuous. But virtue does not stand as a bulwark against every kind of misery. And so virtuous people will prefer to avoid being treated unjustly because of the miseries that would entail.

NOTES

1. I presented an earlier and much shorter version of this chapter (quite different) at University College, London, on November 11, 2019. I am grateful to the audience there for helpful comments, especially Fiona Leigh and A. W. Price, whose 2011 book has helped me understand how reasons work. I presented a later version at the University of Pittsburgh, virtually, on October 9, 2020. Thanks to participants there for good comments and questions, especially to Jennifer Whiting and Christian Wildberg. Thanks also to Ward Farnsworth for comments on the written version. In this chapter I am much influenced by Julia Annas (1993), who is, in turn, influenced by the middle Platonist understanding of Plato's ethics. I have also been helped by Iakovos Vasiliou's work (2008). Comments from the editors of this volume have been extremely helpful.

2. Vlastos 1991: 235. In other words, virtue is sufficient for happiness; a controversial claim, as we shall see.

3. Translations are my own unless otherwise indicated.

4. If conflicts occur within the Socratic corpus, I take these two dialogues as definitive.

5. Reeve argues that Socrates' claim of innocence rests on his confidence that life examined by elenchus cannot go culpably wrong (1989: 152); cf. Kraut 1984: 268, n. 39. That confidence may also arise from his belief that he is carrying out a mission issued to him by a god.

6. On Socratic ignorance and knowledge, see Chapter 5 in this book.

7. This argument against Vlastos' view is made by Jones 2013b and disputed by Smith 2016.

8. See Chapter 5 in this book.

9. The distinction between 'good' and virtuous' is crucial. See Brickhouse and Smith 1990.

10. I take the superlatives at *Phd.* 116c and 118a as indicating not the highest possible level, but the highest level encountered in human beings by the speakers.

11. Smith 2016: 11–12; Martinez and Smith 2018: 65–66. Bobonich argues against a scalar view, 2002: 210–213, on the grounds that we have no textual evidence to support it anywhere in Plato. Jones argues for a 'minimal standard' view and, although he does not say what the standard is, he contends that Socrates does not think he meets the standard, 2016: 100–101.

12. Reeve 1989: 150. Author's emphasis.

13. Indeed, to arrive at the recognition of his own ignorance, Socrates must employ quite a lot of knowledge – logic and a basic concept of knowledge; in urging his fellow citizen to take care of their souls he depends on an understanding of the soul and its ethical needs (Burnet 1924: 88, note on *Ap.* 20d). See Smith (2016) on the gradable approach to knowledge, and, on the extent of Socrates' knowledge, Chapter 5 of this book.

14. My interpretation of this passage follows Jones (2013b) rather than Smith (2016: 11), although I agree more with Smith's general conclusion.

15. *Ap.* 20d, 30c–d, 41c–d, cf. *Grg.* 521b.

16. Kraut 1984: 268, ff., Brickhouse and Smith 1994: 129–131.

17. So Smith 2016.

18. See Jones 2013a and 2016 with Smith 2016.

19. By 'practical' here I mean not dependent on ideal agents or ideal conditions; some eudaimonists hold that virtue and therefore happiness are unobtainable for non-ideal agents or under less than ideal conditions. But this is not Socrates' view. He says that even Callicles can become happier by seeking virtue (*Grg.* 527c). On eudaimonism and idealisation, see Tessman 2009.

20. Sherman (2015) is essential reading on this topic. Some thinkers have gone so far as to argue that warfare cannot be justified by any theory, because it inevitably causes moral injury. People in many walks of life have experienced similar symptoms. For a study of moral injury by psychologists, see Litz et al. 2009.

21. In this chapter I will not distinguish, as some scholars do, between ethics and morality, the latter of which is associated with Kant. Devereux (1995) makes a reasonable case that Socratic and Kantian doctrines of virtue are not widely separated; Reshotko (2006) argues for a sharp distinction between Kant's moral theory and Socrates' prudential approach.

22. It is tempting to understand this disordering in terms of the tripartite soul of *Republic* 4, but the text does not take us so far, and we have reason to think that Socrates did not allow for irrational parts of the soul to be relevant to virtue. Aristotle says that he did not so allow, drawing an inference from Socrates' identification of virtue with knowledge (*Magna Moralia* 1.1, 1182a18–23).

23. See Vlastos 1994a: 25; Brickhouse and Smith 2010: 126–127.

24. *Grg.* 479b. On Socrates' views of punishment, see Chapter 9 in this volume.

SOCRATIC EUDAIMONISM

25. On the necessity of punishment, see *Grg.* 480b–c with Brickhouse and Smith 2010: 119–123. Injustice becomes ingrained if not punished.

26. Penner and Rowe 1994, Reshotko 2013: 182.

27. Brickhouse and Smith 2010: 113. Note that a penalty that is beneficial to one person may be harmful to another; banishment would harm a virtuous person who needs a community in order to exercise virtue, while benefitting one who lacks virtue by saving him from vicious acts (Ibid. 115).

28. On the philosophical issue here, see Hampton 1984.

29. For a recent defense of the moderately intellectualist interpretation, which they call the revisionary view, see Martinez and Smith 2018: 70–71, and, most recently, Smith 2021.

30. Brickhouse and Smith 2010: 89–106.

31. An additional argument in support: Insofar as Socratic virtue is like a *technē*, or craft, it may require more than intellectual knowledge; it requires skills that depend on actively practising the *technē* correctly. I can say quite precisely how to make fine turnings on a lathe, but I have fallen out of practice and can no longer produce good work. Practicing a *technē* badly – for example, botching navigation or playing music out of tune – leads to bad habits that are bad for the practitioner and could be corrected by punishments that lead to better habits. This is controversial. Some scholars would counter that intellectual knowledge is by itself motivating in a way that would prevent the development of bad habits.

32. See Jones and Sharma 2017: 130.

33. Gerson 1997: arguing that because soul is self, unity of self requires that reason not cede control in favour of the body.

34. Weiss, rejecting intellectualism, argues that injury to the soul is real, so that punishment 'aims not at changing a person's beliefs, but at changing his character' (2006: 99, 103). On the debate over Socrates' intellectualism, see Chapters 7 and 9 in this volume.

35. So Socrates in *Rep.* 1.352a speaks of civil war in the mind of the unjust person, without introducing the psychology of Book 4.

36. On the identity thesis, see below under E5.

37. But note *Grg.* 512de with 511a, where Socrates makes it clear that one must not act on this aversion, as it would deform the soul.

38. Martinez and Smith 2018: 66.

39. On the debate over the sufficiency thesis, see below under External Injuries and Benefits: Dependent Goods.

40. The argument of *Crito* 47d-e shows Socrates holding that physical injury can make one so miserable that dying would be preferable to living (Morrison 2003: 8).

41. Happiness, like virtue, may be a scalar or gradable concept. See Smith 2021.

42. 'Justice is the condition of any aspect of one's life being good for one' (Jones and Sharma 2017: 130n44). See Brickhouse and Smith 2010: 185, 238.

43. Martinez and Smith 2018: 66.

44. Martinez and Smith 2018: 73–74.

45. Vlastos 1991: 215.

46. For a taxonomy of these concepts, see Haybron 2010: 29–42. He argues that these are not different conceptions of the same thing, but different concepts. See also Kraut 1979 and 2018.

47. Some scholars translate Socratic *eudaimonia* as *human* flourishing, e.g. Cooper (1975: 89) and Reshotko (2006: 6).

48. For a discussion of Aristotelian naturalism, see Hursthouse 1999: 192, ff.

49. Archelaus, for example, *Grg.* 470e, ff.

50. See Brickhouse and Smith 2010: 49n2.

51. The proverb is supported famously in the anecdote Herodotus tells about Solon and Croesus: Croesus, believing that his great wealth made him the happiest of men, asked the wise Solon who was the happiest of those he had seen. Solon answered that he could render no judgment on a person's happiness until his life had closed happily. After his life turned bitter, Croesus remembered this and attributed his troubles to a nemesis he brought on himself by claiming happiness prematurely (Herodotus *History*, 1.30–34).

52. To know whether even the Great King is *eudaimōn*, Socrates says he would need to know how he is with respect to education and justice, and he assents to Polus' incredulous question: 'Is all of *eudaimonia* in that?' To that Socrates replies, 'So I say, Polus; the fine and good man and woman I say are happy, while the unjust and bad are miserable' (*Gorgias* 470e).

53. Vlastos discounts the differences between the ancient Greek and modern concepts (1991: 202–203) and this leads him to assume, wrongly, that desire for happiness is self-referential (1991: 203n14). See Jones and Sharma 2017: 132.

54. Note that wisdom is the paramount virtue in this context, placed over even justice and courage (*Euthd.* 279d ff.). My translation, following Brickhouse and Smith (2010: 170; Smith 2021: 113n15), takes *eutuchia* as 'success' instead of the usual 'good fortune'. Knowledge does not need, and does not produce, good fortune or good luck; it produces success (280b). *Pace* McPherran 2005, who takes *eutuchia* as divine providence. Sprague's translation in Cooper (1997) weakens the conclusion of the argument at 282a with 'appear to be' and 'seems'; the Greek is more definite.

55. Reshotko holds that Socrates believes we have no choice but to be eudaimonists: Whether or not we are aware of this, we are always aiming at *eudaimonia*. '*Eudaimonia* is the ultimate and inevitable goal. Every purposeful behavior is an effort to achieve *eudaimonia*' (Reshotko, 2013: 183; cf. her 2006). The following scholars also attribute E1 to Socrates: Kraut 1984: 211n40; Vlastos 1991: 177; Irwin 1977: 255; 1995: 62; Bobonich 2011: 329. These scholars oppose the attribution: Jones and Sharma 2017: 132, Morrison 2003, Weiss 2006 and Ahbel-Rappe 2010, 2012.

56. A similar idea in different terms: 'in wanting to be happy, people want what is truly good, and since what is truly good is justice . . .' (Weiss 2006: 20).

57. Pursuing *eudaimonia* is not necessarily self-interested. See Morrison 2003: 20.

58. *Protagoras* 351b, ff.; Kahn 1989: 41.

59. On Socrates' argument against *akrasia*, see Chapters 7 and 9 in this volume. Morrison 2003: 32 argues that the passage does not support egoism.

60. Weiss 2006: 6–7: 'It strains credibility' to attribute Socrates' life choices to self-interest; so also Ahbel-Rappe 2010: 37–38; 2012 *passim*.

SOCRATIC EUDAIMONISM

61. Shaver 2023: 'Ethical egoism claims that I morally ought to perform some action if and only if, and because, performing that action maximizes my self-interest'.

62. Ethical egoism is attributed to Socrates by Irwin 1977: 255 and Kraut 1984: 211n40, 313–314, as well as Brown 2007 and Bobonich 2002. E2 does not in itself entail the stronger instrumentalist view of E4. Kahn's 1989 argument against E1 also serves against E2. Other scholars arguing against assigning E2 to Socrates include Morrison 2003, Weiss 2006, Ahbel-Rappe 2010 and 2012, and Jones and Sharma 2017.

63. Egoism takes a benign form if it is conjoined with the no-conflict principle that self-interest and other-interest cannot conflict. A useful taxonomy of forms of ethical egoism is provided by Kraut, who, in his discussion of Aristotle, contrasts benign egoism with combative egoism (1989: 80–83); discussed by Ahbel-Rappe 2010: 29.

64. On the issue, and the scholars on both sides, see the thorough treatment in Schuh 2019.

65. For a recent expression of the fusion view, see Smith 2021: 42; for criticism of the view, see D'Souza 2021: 488–489, citing White 2002.

66. 'There is nothing more wretched than leaving one's city', wrote Tyrtaeus, who goes on to imply that it is far better to die (fr. 10), tr. Gagarin and Woodruff 1995: 24. Pericles, about two centuries later, utters the same sentiment in his last speech: 'It does not matter whether a man prospers as an individual: if his country is destroyed, he is lost along with it' (Thucydides 2.60), tr. Woodruff 2021: 75.

67. This is the implication of *Cr.* 53b–54a; consider also that Socrates' mission, given him he believes by the god, is to Athens (*Ap.* 37c–e).

68. Aristotle is summing up a traditional view when he says, 'a human being is a polis-dweller by nature' (*NE* 1.5 1097b11).

69. 'One's own flourishing requires active respect for the flourishing of others', wrote Gomez-Lobo of Socratic eudaimonism (1994: 113).

70. As a defining feature of egoism, Ahbel-Rappe writes that on this view, which she opposes, 'self-regarding reasons are either the best or the only kind of reason there is' (2012: 321).

71. Scholars who attribute E3 to Socrates include Brown 2007 and Bobonich 2011; those opposed include Morrison 2003, Weiss 2006 and Ahbel-Rappe 2010, 2012.

72. So Bobonich 2011, 327.

73. On this see Morrison 2003: 17.

74. For example, *Ap.* 32d, 36bc, *Cr.* 48c. In the *Crito*, Socrates gives an answer to the 'why be just' question in terms of a kind of self-interest, culminating in the conclusion that only justice matters (48c). But, as Ahbel-Rappe shows, this does not reveal Socrates to have been an egoist eudaimonist (2010: 43–44).

75. One may object that it is not rational by his standards for Socrates to heed his daimonion. On the issue, see Smith and Woodruff 2000 and Destrée and Smith 2005.

76. On the debate over hedonism and Socrates, see Zeyl 1980; Kraut 1984: 266n36, n37; Vlastos 1991: 300–302; Rudebusch 1999; Reshotko 2006: 179–188.

77. Irwin has made the case for assigning the instrumental view (E4a) to Socrates, while Vlastos has argued strenuously against attributing any form of teleological eudaimonism to Socrates (Irwin 1977: 255; 1995: 67–68, 73; Vlastos 1991: 6–10, 302–303; 1995). As this debate has been thoroughly aired in the past, I will not add to it here, except to say that I think

Vlastos makes the stronger case from the texts of Socratic dialogues. Socrates does not hold that virtue cannot be good in itself if it is good in virtue of what it brings about, which is, generally, more virtue. Again and again, as we shall see, Socrates says in the *Apology*, *Crito* and *Gorgias* that justice trumps every other consideration. In the *Crito*, he argues that the only question for him to answer is what it is that justice requires. Only the mindless majority take money, family and reputation as relevant considerations (48b–c). Justice does not outweigh these considerations (*pace* Jones and Sharma 2017: 130); it simply nullifies them.

78. 'It is the greatest good for one to discuss virtue every day', *Ap*. 37e–38a, cf. 29d–30b and 32d. But note that Socrates says he is causing his fellow citizens not to believe that they are happy, but to be happy.

79. Vlastos 1991: 208. I will discuss modern views below. Vlastos' argument that Socrates is not an identity eudaimonist has convinced many scholars (1991: 214–232). Scholars who attribute E5 to Socrates include Rudebusch 1999; those opposed, besides Vlastos, include Brickhouse and Smith 2010: 238, cf. 170.

80. As I have argued (Woodruff 1982: Chapter 8).

81. Vlastos, after much deliberation, attributes E6a to Socrates (1991: 203–209, 214–232). Brickhouse and Smith prefer a nomological version of E6b (2010: 170; Smith 2021: Chapter 5 and 162–163).

82. Brickhouse and Smith 2010: 170, 185n24; Smith 2021: 107–128.

83. Some scholars call this relationship *analytic* (e.g. Reshotko, 2006: 152), which would suggest that it is said to hold in virtue of the meanings of words. More likely Socrates thinks it holds in virtue of the true natures of happiness and virtue.

84. The nomological view, with a denial of the sufficiency thesis, is taken by Brickhouse and Smith (2010: 185n24, 187; cf. Smith 2021: 111) and Reshotko, who also argues that virtue is not necessary for happiness 2006: 135–155.

85. As far as I know, scholars have yet to develop arguments against the nomological interpretation, but it is vulnerable to this line of attack.

86. D'Souza introduced the concept of altruistic eudaimonism (2021: 475–476). In a seminal essay, Foot insists that in order to show that justice is truly a virtue we must show that it is in the interests of the person who is just to be just (1958). Most proponents of virtue ethics, however, have tried to distance their theories from egoism. Swanton rejects egoistic eudaimonism explicitly (2003: 77–90; 2016: 117); so does Sreenivasan, who takes *eudaimonia* to be a non-moral concept (2020: 15–20). Hursthouse develops a carefully nuanced position that excludes an amoral egoism (1999: chapter 8, concluding at 190–191). As we have seen, *eudaimonia* can be understood as a moral or semi-moral concept.

87. Vasiliou analyses the argument in these two stages in his 2008: 63–89.

88. So Vasiliou 2008: 63, 65, with n. 32.

89. For example, at *Grg*. 509a, implications of *Eu*. 5a, *La*. 200e–201a, *Chrm*. 175d, *Hi. Ma.* 304de. On Socrates' declaration of ignorance, see Chapter 5 in this volume.

90. 'Character': 'that which comes to be better by justice and is wrecked by injustice' (47d4–5). Socrates does not use the word for soul in the *Crito*.

91. This does not mean that money and reputation have no value for Socrates, although he does not weigh such matters against the loss of virtue; he would prefer not to suffer unjust losses (*Grg*. 469c).

SOCRATIC EUDAIMONISM 203

92. Vasiliou writes that this presupposes what he calls the principle of habituation (2008: 66), but that is not explicit in the texts.

93. It's not in the *nature* of justice to cause the pain of certain kinds of punishment, just as it is not in the nature of medicine to cause pain. And yet a cure for physical or moral injury may require pain.

94. *Republic* 1, 335c–d, *Gorgias* 472d–e, et cetera. The scholarly literature on Socrates' view of punishment is substantial; for more on this see the chapters by Austin and Möbus in this volume. See also the arguments in Brickhouse and Smith on how Socrates' views on punishment must shape our interpretation of his take on moral injury (2010: 108–131).

95. For Socrates' preference for using 'beneficial' and related terms in an unqualified sense, see *Prt.* 334a–d, where Socrates reacts negatively to Protagoras' use of qualifiers, and *Rep.* 1 336c, which suggests that Socrates has been using the term that way.

96. Cf. Woodruff 1982: 187–189. This is a special case of the general Socratic principle that what is good is productive of good. This principle does not serve to define the good or the fine, or to guide our actions, but it tells us something important about our principal good, virtue. Virtue brings about more virtue, in both others (by example) and self (by practice). Unlike a virus, virtues are self-strengthening, as is a *technē*. The more you practice a *technē* the better you are at doing it.

97. For more detailed discussions of the argument in the *Crito*, see Kraut 1984, Kahn 1989, Weiss 1998 and Chapter 12 in this volume.

98. Socrates does not explicitly defend this background assumption here, but it is congruent with common ideas of the period about the value of law for maintaining a successful *polis*. Where the rule of law breaks down, the horrors of civil war loom. On this see Thucydides, *History of the Peloponnesian War* 3.82 and Woodruff 2005: chapter 5.

99. In this brief summary I will not distinguish between what Socrates says in his own persona and what he supposes the Laws might say (50a, ff.).

100. Harte argues that the reasoning presented by the personified laws conflicts with that of Socrates on what is wrong with retaliation (1999; 130). Her case is well argued; I think the conflict results from Socrates' attempt to put his reasoning into a shape that Crito can understand. For more on whether the laws speak for Socrates, see Chapter 12 in this volume.

101. These rules – keeping one's agreements and returning benefits to one's benefactors – are not eclipsed by Socrates' refutation of Cephalus' account of justice in Book 1 of the *Republic* as telling the truth and returning what one has borrowed from another (331c ff.). Following these rules is not just without exception, that is, the prescribed behavior is not *haplōs dikaiōs* (just without qualification) because it may sometimes be done *adikōs* (unjustly) – as in the case of returning a borrowed weapon to a man who is running amok.

102. The rule of law entails that no one be allowed to be above the law; the institution of bribery puts the wealthy above the law (Woodruff 2005; chapter 5). Note that Socrates is concerned about the harm bribery would do to those who receive the bribes, presumably by tempting them to violate their just agreements (48cd).

103. Alcibiades' case is different in that he was denied a trial when the political situation was favourable to him, and he absconded before a trial at a time when his supporters were absent from Athens. But he showed no loyalty to the city, serving the interests of both Sparta and the Persian Empire. For his attitude toward Athens, see Thucydides 6.89 and 6.92.

104. 'He thinks fit': as opposed to 'he wishes'. Socrates thinks tyrants and orators are mistaken about what they want to do (466d).

105. Note that Socrates does not subscribe to these views without possibility of exception (470c). These are common examples of injustices, but in agreeing that this is so Socrates is not agreeing to a definition of injustice, and he is not agreeing that such actions are inherently unjust.

106. Socrates' aim in the *Republic* has been all along to defend such requirements against the charge that they violate the interests of the agent; it follows that his theory cannot undermine them.

107. E.g., *Republic* 9.579d–580a: The tyrant makes himself *and others* miserable.

108. This is presupposed in the *Crito* argument and made explicit at *Republic* 335c. But Socrates is believed to have held that the virtues are unified by their special relationship with wisdom; on the unity of virtue, see Clark in this volume.

109. Prichard 1928: 5–6.

110. See above E2 for the definition of egoism, and citations of scholars who attribute it to Socrates.

111. Cf. Verity Harte: 'There is no suggestion that others – and their relation to the agent in question – have a role to play in determining the justice of an action' (1999: 133; see Vasiliou's response, 2008: 69).

112. Bobonich 2011: 326–327.

113. Hurka 2013: 15–16. He cites Prichard 1928: 21–49 and (for the case of Plato's Socrates) Brown 2007: 42–60. For a generic response to Hurka on behalf of virtue ethics, see Annas 2007.

114. In adapting virtue ethics to modern ethical tastes, a number of philosophers have tried to steer virtue ethics away from egoistic eudaimonism, e.g. D'Souza 2021, Swanton 2003 and 2016, Hursthouse 1999.

115. *Eu.* 5c-d with 4e–5a.

116. Notably at *Gorgias* 464d, ff., he contrasts medical *technē* against the knack of pleasing people. See also *Laches* 190a–c.

117. The passage has been much discussed by scholars. Here is a simple summary: After the Kallipolis has seen to their education, Socrates says the philosophers should be compelled to return to the Cave. Glaucon complains that this would be unjust, since philosophers could live better outside the cave (519d8–9). Glaucon does not say, nor does Socrates admit, they would be more *eudaimones* outside the cave – simply that they would live better or do well (519e2). In reply, Socrates supplies an argument to show that justice requires them to return, and Glaucon accepts the argument: It would be impossible for just people to refuse to obey just orders (520e); this explicitly gives the sense of *anankē* that is conveyed by 'compel'. The philosopher-rulers, even in the Cave, are *eudaimones* in living a life that is good and rational (*emphrōn* – 521a2–4). And this reasoning is similar to the reasoning Socrates gives in the *Crito*: You have a special debt to those who have provided you with an education (implication of 520b3–4). This shows that Plato at this stage still thought it highly rational, in reasoning about justice, to appeal to such other-regarding considerations as the duty to repay debts.

118. For example, *Meno* 99c–d.

CHAPTER NINE

Socratic Motivational Intellectualism[1]

FREYA MÖBUS

WHAT IS MOTIVATIONAL INTELLECTUALISM?

Socrates' view about human actions in Plato's early dialogues has often been called 'intellectualist' because, in his account, we always do what we *believe* is the best (most beneficial) thing we can do for ourselves, given all available options.[2]

The main textual evidence for Socrates' intellectualism about human actions comes from the *Protagoras*:

> No one who knows (*eidōs*) or believes (*oiomenos*) there is something else better than what he is doing, something possible, will go on doing what he had been doing when he could be doing what is better. . . . No one goes willingly toward the bad or what he believes (*oietai*) to be bad; neither is it in human nature, so it seems, to want (*ethelein*) to go toward what one believes (*oietai*) to be bad instead of to the good. And when one is forced to choose between one of two bad things, no one will choose the greater if he is able to choose the lesser.[3]
>
> – *Prt.* 358b–d

In the *Protagoras*, Socrates seems to claim that our actions always follow a belief about the best thing to do; that is, a belief about what is in one's own best interest at the time of action.[4] This idea, we could say, makes Socrates an intellectualist regarding *actions*. But one might wonder why Socrates is considered to be an intellectualist regarding *motivations* as the title of this chapter suggests. What exactly are 'motivations'? Unfortunately, interpreters of Socrates generally do not define this term. Without a more specific definition, 'motivations' can refer to anything that moves us to act – desires, goals, emotions, facts, beliefs, reasons and so on. Our discussion here will not hinge on one particular understanding of 'motivation'. Instead, we will understand Socratic motivational intellectualism as the view that for any given intentional action our motivations – whatever moves us to act – are tied to the intellect, specifically to a belief about the best (most beneficial) thing we can do for ourselves.[5] Without such a belief, no action follows. How exactly motivations are 'tied to' beliefs about what is best is, as we will see, one of the major points of disagreement among interpreters.

Motivational intellectualism is often considered to be at the centre of Socrates' intellectualist account of actions, according to which:[6]

(1) We never act against our present judgment about what is best to do. Since we *always* do what we believe is the best thing for us to do, Socrates' motivational intellectualism implies the denial of *synchronic belief akrasia* (*Prt.* 358b–d).

(2) All wrongdoing is due to ignorance. Since we always do what we believe is best for us, any action that is in fact not best for us results from a false belief. Moral wrongdoing or injustice is never in our own best interest (*Ap.* 30c–d, *Cr.* 49a–b, *Grg.* 469b). Thus, all moral wrongdoing is due to ignorance.

In addition to these two claims, some interpreters have added a further, more controversial claim:

(3) Our beliefs about what is best generate action-causing desires. Desires that are not generated by such a belief, that is, 'non-rational desires', cannot motivate actions.[7]

Since motivational intellectualism – the idea that we always act according to our beliefs about what is best – can explain these Socratic claims, many interpreters place it at the core of Socratic philosophy.[8] Some have even argued that it is this theory of human motivation – and not, for example, Plato's theory of forms – that distinguishes Socrates' philosophy from Plato's, and that suggests a division of Plato's dialogues into different groups: 'intellectualist' (or pre-*Republic*) and 'non-intellectualist' or 'anti-intellectualist' (post-*Republic*) dialogues (Rowe 2007: 21–25).

In addition to the idea that 'we always do what we believe is best for us to do', Socrates' account of motivation includes another major idea, the desire thesis:

(4) We all desire the good (*Prt.* 358d, *Meno* 77d–e, *Euthd.* 278e, *Grg.* 466a–468e).

The desire thesis, in turn, is often considered to be the foundation for the claim that[9]

(5) No one does wrong willingly (*Prt.* 345e, 358d–e; *Grg.* 509e). When we do what is wrong (i.e., not in our own best interest), we act against what we want.

Despite their centrality for Socratic philosophy, interpreters disagree on the exact interpretation of these five claims and of Socrates' account of motivation. This chapter surveys the interpretative landscape so that the reader may more easily navigate the primary and secondary literature and decide for themselves whether Socrates is a motivational intellectualist and, if so, in what sense.

The answer to this question matters not only for those who are academically invested in Socratic philosophy, but also for all who have joined Socrates on his mission of living a good life. For Socrates, we live well if we act well; wrongdoing leads to a life lived poorly and miserably. Understanding why we act as we do, promoting right-doing, and preventing wrong-doing, are thus of utmost importance for anyone who wants to live well.

Further, one's stance on Socrates' motivational intellectualism has broader implications for understanding his philosophy of human nature. Do we always do what we believe is in our own best interest? Is it entirely up to us to figure out what is in our own best interest, or do we come equipped with some motivational orientation toward what is truly good for us? In other words, do we all come equipped with an inherent desire for our real good? We will start our discussion with this question.

WE ALL DESIRE THE GOOD

When discussing Socrates' theory of motivation and action, interpreters often refer to the 'desire thesis' (Barney 2010): We all desire the good. In this section, we will disentangle the different ways of understanding this thesis.

The claim that we all desire the good is initially puzzling. Many would rightly wonder: 'What do you mean by *the good*?' Katja Vogt (2017: 16–20) helpfully explains that we can take 'the good' to refer to at least three different kinds of things:

(a) Long-term goods: Some might think that 'the good' refers to the good life (e.g., 'the good is the examined life') or happiness. Long-term goods are those that we try to achieve over the course of our life.

(b) Mid-range goods: Others might think of 'the good' in terms of good things to have. Socrates might say that 'wisdom is the good', while Callicles might object that 'pleasure is the good'. Mid-range goods are those intermediate goods that we want in our lives (e.g., health, wealth, friends, wisdom).

(c) Small-scale goods: Still others might think that 'the good' refers to the good we aim for in individual actions. For example, 'eating these vegetables is the good (thing for me to do)'. Small-scale goods are those that we consider the best thing for us to do in any given situation (e.g., to eat these vegetables).

These different goods can be in a means-end relation to one another. For example, I want to eat these vegetables (small-scale good) in order to stay healthy (mid-range good), and I want to stay healthy (mid-range good) in order to live a good life (long-term good). Alternatively, one might think that, for example, being healthy, having friends and being financially well-off are specifications of what a good life looks like.

In Socrates' desire thesis, then, does 'the good' refer to small-scale, mid-range, or long-term goods? Interpreters of Socrates commonly do not make these distinctions and clarify what kind of good they have in mind. To better understand Socrates' desire thesis, I propose that we apply Vogt's concepts to the following passages: 'no one wants to go toward what one believes to be bad' (*Prt.* 358d); 'we desire the good' (*Grg.* 468b); and 'we all wish to do well' (*Euthd.* 278e).

We opened this chapter with a passage from the *Protagoras* in which Socrates says that in any given situation, we always want to do what we believe is the best (or the 'good') thing for us to do (*Prt.* 358d). If we put this into Vogt's terms, motivational intellectualism – as formulated in the *Protagoras* – refers to our desire for small-scale goods. In this reading, the desire thesis is a reformulation of Socrates' motivational intellectualism.

In the *Gorgias*, Socrates discusses small-scale goods in relation to mid-range goods: We sit or walk or embark on sea voyages for the sake of some further good that we hope to accomplish:[10]

> It's because we pursue the good (*to agathon*) that we walk whenever we walk; we suppose that it's better to walk. And conversely, whenever we stand still, we stand still for the sake of the same thing, the good (*tou agathou*). . . . Hence, it is for the sake of the good (*tou agathou*) that those who do all these things do them.
>
> – *Grg.* 468b

Here, 'the good' refers to mid-range goods: We do everything we do for the sake of some further good such as wisdom, health or wealth (*Grg.* 467e).

208   THE BLOOMSBURY HANDBOOK OF SOCRATES

Turning to the *Euthydemus*, we see Socrates holds that we all desire the same long-term good, namely happiness or 'doing well':

> Do all men wish (*boulometha*) to do well (*eu prattein*)? Or is this question one of the ridiculous ones I was afraid of just now? I suppose it is stupid even to raise such a question, since there could hardly be a man who would not wish to do well.
>
>   *– Euthd.* 278e

Later in the text, Socrates states that 'we all want to be happy (*eudaimones*)' (*Euthd.* 282a). We 'do well' and become happy, Socrates explains, by acquiring 'many good things' and using them well (*Euthd.* 278e–281b).

Given the textual evidence presented above, Socrates' desire thesis – we all desire the good – can be understood in three different ways: We all desire happiness or 'doing well' (long-term good); we all desire intermediate goods like health and friends that we want in our lives (mid-range goods); we all desire the good thing we aim for in individual actions (small-scale goods). For Socrates, that we desire 'the good' is a fact about 'human nature' (*Prt.* 358d) that we do not need to argue for or justify (*Euthd.* 278e). No one wants to be miserable, and no one wants what is bad for oneself.

Of course, I may incorrectly conclude that certain things are good when in fact they are not good or are perhaps even bad for me. But as Socrates explains in *Meno* 77c–e, we must be careful not to conclude that in such instances I desire something bad. I still desire what I believe is good for me:

> Those who do not know things to be bad do not desire what is bad, but they desire those things that they believe (*ōonto*) to be good but that are in fact bad. It follows that those who have no knowledge of these things and believe (*oiomenoi*) them to be good clearly desire good things.
>
>   *– M.* 77d–e

The *Meno* echoes Socrates' claim in *Protagoras* 358d that no one wants what they believe is bad for themselves. In the *Meno*, Socrates explains further that no one wants bad things because they make us miserable and unhappy. And no one wants to be miserable and unhappy (*M.* 77e–78a). The *Meno* is often considered to be the locus classicus for the so-called *apparentist* interpretation of Socrates' claim that we all desire 'the good': We all desire *apparently* good things, that is, things that we *think* are good even when they are in fact bad for us.[11]

In *Gorgias* 466a–468e, Socrates considers agents who go terribly wrong in determining what is best for them to do: tyrants. When explaining tyrants' actions – unjustly confiscating someone's property, exiling them, and putting them in prison or even executing them – Socrates eventually convinces his interlocutor, Polus, that while these agents do what they believe is best, they do not do what they *want*:

> Socrates: If a person who is a tyrant or an orator puts somebody to death or exiles him or confiscates his property because he believes (*oiomai*) that doing so is better for himself when actually it's worse, this person, I take it, is doing what seems (*dokei*) good to him, isn't he?
> Polus: Yes.
> Socrates: And is he also doing what he wants, if these things are actually bad? Why don't you answer?
> Polus: All right, I don't think he's doing what he wants. (*Grg.* 468d)

SOCRATIC MOTIVATIONAL INTELLECTUALISM

Socrates even goes on to claim that 'no one does what is unjust (*adikein*) because he wants to, but that all who do so do it unwillingly (*akontas*)' (*Grg.* 509e). Those who act unjustly do not do what they want, because in doing what is unjust, they harm themselves. For Socrates, 'doing what is unjust is the worst thing there is' for a person (*Grg.* 469b) because injustice harms one's soul and makes one miserable (*Grg.* 470e).

Notice that in the *Gorgias* Socrates seems to make a claim about desire that is quite different from the *Meno*. In the *Meno*, it seems that we always want what we (subjectively) take to be good. In the *Gorgias*, Socrates seems to say that we all always want what is in fact (objectively) good for us. The *Meno* suggests the '**apparent good**' interpretation of desire: We want what we think is good. In this interpretation, tyrants do what they want. The *Gorgias*, in contrast, seems to suggest the '**real good**' interpretation: We only want what is *really* or *truly* good for us. And in this interpretation, the tyrants do not do what they want. How can we resolve this seeming inconsistency?

Before we dive into the secondary literature on this question, let me outline why our answer matters in the context of Socratic motivational intellectualism. If all our desires are for apparent goods – if indeed we desire only what we think is good – then what we desire depends entirely on our beliefs. Motivationally, we would be born as blank slates. But if some of our desires are for the real good, regardless of what we believe is good, this would indicate that we come equipped with an inherent orientation toward the real good. Human nature would, to some extent, push us in the right direction. The apparent and real good interpretations lead to two different accounts of Socratic motivational intellectualism, and the former is more intellectualist than the latter, or so I will argue. According to the apparent good interpretation, *all* of our desires derive from beliefs. But according to the real good interpretation, our desire for the real good is inborn and precedes any of our beliefs. The central question thus becomes: *Are we born with an inherent desire for the real good?*

Let us first look at interpretations that maintain Socratic psychology includes an inherent desire for the real good:

> We, humans, are hardwired to seek our own good. What we want is, ultimately, to do well for ourselves. The striving for this condition of doing well, which Socrates calls 'the good', is something that every human soul comes equipped with.
>
> – Segvic 2006: 180

According to this line of interpretation, we humans are born with an inherent desire for our real long-term good: true happiness, or truly doing well and living a good life. Terry Penner developed this line of thought in detail, sometimes in collaboration with Christopher Rowe. According to Penner and Rowe, in each situation, we must figure out which action would most promote our happiness, that is, which action would be the best thing for us to do. If all goes well, we conclude correctly that a particular action is best for us to do. This true belief then transforms our overarching, general desire for true happiness into a particular desire to execute a specific action – 'the generalized desire . . . *becomes* the executive desire' (Penner 1991: 153). The combination of our inherent desire for the real good and our belief that action x is the best thing to do brings about an action-causing desire to do x – and so we do x.

But agents often deliberate incorrectly and are thus mistaken about their long-term, mid-range or small-scale goods. The tyrant, for instance, might incorrectly believe that living well consists in accumulating money and power and that executing political opponents is the best means toward this end. In such cases, the agent's belief about what is best for him to do brings about a 'defective' or 'false desire' (Penner and Rowe 2005: 221), which then leads to an action (e.g., executing political opponents). But since this action is not in fact the best means to the agent's overall real good, strictly speaking he does not do what he wants. In fact, according to Penner and Rowe, any action that does not *maximise* the agent's happiness is not truly a wanted action: one does what one wants to do only if one's action leads to 'the greatest amount of happiness attainable starting from where one is at right now' (Penner 1991: 182). Rowe sums up his interpretation as follows:

> Briefly, and at bottom, it [i.e., Socrates' intellectualist theory of motivation] consists in the claims (a) that all human agents always and only desire the good; (b) that what they desire is the real good, not the *apparent* good; and (c) that what we do on any occasion is determined by this desire together with whatever beliefs we have about what will in fact contribute to our real good. Hence the label 'intellectualist': we only ever do what we *think* will be good for us.
>
> – Rowe 2007: 23

We *do* what we think is good, but we *desire* what is truly good. For Penner and Rowe, we want only our real long-term good – true happiness – and that which would most promote our true happiness; that is, truly good small-scale and mid-range goods. The desire for the real long-term good, in this interpretation, is our first and only desire: We are born 'hardwired' to pursue the real good, and all subsequent desires for mid-range and small-scale goods that arise out of deliberation are simply particularisations of our general desire for the real good. According to Penner and Rowe (1994), Socrates in *Meno* 77d–78b does not in fact claim that we desire apparent goods. Instead, they argue that the *Meno* supports the same idea as the *Gorgias*: In everything we do, we desire what is really good.

Rachana Kamtekar (2006) agrees with Penner and Rowe that we have an inherent desire for our own real long-term good; that is, for true happiness. She also agrees that the *Gorgias* suggests that, strictly speaking, we only 'want' actions if they truly promote our long-term good. But Kamtekar differs from Penner and Rowe in maintaining that we also desire our apparent good; that is, what we think is good, as the *Meno* seems to suggest. In other words, our desire for the real good is not our only desire. To harmonise the 'apparent good' with the 'real good' interpretation, Kamtekar distinguishes between two kinds of conative attitudes: *boulēsis*, or the desire for the real good, which Kamtekar translates as 'wanting', and *epithumia*, or the desire for our apparent good, which she translates as 'desire'.[12] We *want* (*boulesthai*) the real good 'rather than what we think good (*Grg.* 468b–d)', but we *desire* (*epithumein*) the apparent good, that is, 'things that we think are good, which are sometimes in fact bad (*M.* 77d–e)' (Kamtekar 2006: 127). The tyrant, for example, 'desires' to murder his enemies; but he does not 'want' it.

Our 'wanting' what is truly good for us is an inherent motivational orientation. Thus, Kamtekar explains, no agent is entirely conatively cut off from the truth (Kamtekar 2006: 150–151). This conative connection to our real good explains why getting what we desire does not always lead to lasting fulfilment. Our 'striving comes to rest' only once we achieve our real good, but when we acquire things that are not really good, but only apparently so, 'we will not be stably fulfilled by them' (Kamtekar 2006: 156). When we do something that does not in fact promote our real good, our 'wanting' what is truly good for us remains unfulfilled, and thus we may experience a lingering feeling of dissatisfaction.

SOCRATIC MOTIVATIONAL INTELLECTUALISM

In contrast to Penner, Rowe and Kamtekar, Rachel Barney (2010) proposes that the *Gorgias* does not introduce an inherent desire for our real good; instead, the *Gorgias* offers an addition to or clarification of Socrates' claim in the *Meno* that we desire the apparent good. In Barney's interpretation, 'I pursue what seems good *as an attempt* to obtain what really is so' (2010: 53). In other words, agents desire the apparent good, believing that it is the real good (even if it is not):

> As the Appearance thesis says, I always desire what seems good to me. But, as the Reality thesis clarifies, that does *not* mean that I desire objects *under the description* 'what seems good to me', taking my subjective responses to be constitutive of value. Rather, in desiring I do my best to track what is antecedently valuable, insofar as I can detect it. Properly understood, the Desire thesis is really a claim about the priority of cognition to motivation.
>
> – Barney 2010: 38

Barney here explicates the apparentist interpretation that we always desire what we think is good, which goes back to Gerasimos Santas (1964). In this interpretation, we do not have an inherent desire for the real good. Certain things are truly good for us, Barney explains, but we are not hardwired to desire them; we do not have a 'latent teleological orientation' toward them (2010: 37). Instead, *all* desires are causally dependent on evaluative beliefs; for Socrates, 'we cannot desire something without first finding it good' (2010: 43).

Thomas Blackson (2015) also argues that, for Socrates, all desires follow beliefs and that we thus do not have an inherent desire for the good. But whereas Barney proposes that all desires are *caused* by beliefs (2010: 43), Blackson *identifies* desires with beliefs:

> All desires are identical to beliefs. In forming a belief that something is a suitable goal, a human being forms a desire, but there is no psychological state other than a belief that something is a suitable goal that functions as a motivational state.
>
> – Blackson 2015: 31

In Blackson's interpretation, our beliefs about what is good do not bring about the separate psychological state of desire; instead, these beliefs are in themselves motivating once they are combined with the belief that their objects are indeed best to pursue. For example, my belief that 'eating chocolate is good' becomes a desire to eat chocolate once I have concluded that eating chocolate is the best thing for me to do right now. In making all desires identical to beliefs, this interpretation attributes the perhaps most radical form of motivational intellectualism to Socrates.

At this point, let us return to Socrates' claim in *Gorgias* 509e that 'no one does what is unjust (*adikein*) because he wants to, but that all who do so do it unwillingly (*akontas*)'. Socrates repeats this idea with slight variation in the *Protagoras*, saying that 'no one errs (*examartanein*) willingly (*hekonta*) or willingly does anything shameful (*aischra*) or bad (*kaka*)' (345e). These claims are often summarised as **'no one does wrong willingly'**.[13]

Socrates himself does not explain this claim any further, and interpreters are left wondering why and in what sense exactly wrongdoing is 'unwilling'. Especially apparentists are in need of an explanation. Apparentists argue that the tyrant believes executing his enemies is best and he thus *wants* to do so, since all desires are 'causally dependent on' (Barney) or 'identical to' (Blackson) beliefs. Thus, in the apparentist interpretation, the tyrant does what he wants, which seems to contradict Socrates' claim. Below, we will review two arguments for 'no one does wrong willingly': one that premises motivational intellectualism and another that premises the desire thesis. I will propose that the latter is more convincing and open to both 'apparent good' and 'real good' interpreters.

Some argue that the tyrant acts 'unwillingly' because he acts from ignorance (see, e.g., Santas 1964: 160, n.25). We can reconstruct this argument as follows:

(i) We always do what we believe is the best (most beneficial) thing we can do for ourselves. [Motivational intellectualism]
(ii) Thus, if we do what is in fact bad (i.e., harmful) for us, we must falsely believe that what we are doing is good for us.
(iii) Actions done due to false beliefs (i.e., ignorance) are unwilling; if I act as I do because I made a mistake, then I do not really want to do what I am doing.[14]
(iv) So, no one does what is bad for oneself willingly.
(v) Doing injustice is bad for oneself.
(vi) So, no one does what is unjust willingly. (*Grg.* 509e)[15]

While *Protagoras* 358d lends some support to this argument by presenting 'no one does wrong willingly' and motivational intellectualism as being closely connected, Kamtekar (2017b: 71–72) argues that *Apology* 25c–26a raises doubts about understanding 'unwillingly' as 'acting from ignorance'. In *Apology* 25c–26a, Socrates says that if one does wrong willingly, it must be because one does not know that if one corrupts one's associates, they will harm one in turn. In other words, a certain kind of ignorance – not knowing that corrupting one's associates leads to harm to oneself – makes *willing* wrongdoing possible. The *Apology* thus suggests that not every action done due to ignorance is unwilling, contrary to premise (iii).

Others argue that the tyrant acts 'unwillingly' not because he acts from ignorance but because he does not do what he *really* wants (see e.g., Kamtekar 2017b: 69–128; Brickhouse and Smith 2018: 38 n. 2; 47). We can reconstruct this alternative argument as follows:

(i) We want to do what is truly good (truly happiness promoting) for ourselves. ['Real good' interpretation of the desire thesis]
(ii) 'Willingly' means 'acting in accordance with what one truly wants'; 'unwillingly' means 'acting against what one truly wants'.
(iii) So, no one does what is bad for oneself willingly.
(iv) Doing injustice is bad for oneself.
(v) So, no one does what is unjust willingly. (*Grg.* 509e)

'Real good' interpreters argue that we want to do what is truly good for ourselves because we have an inherent desire for our real good. When we pursue what is in fact bad for us, we act against this desire and – since this desire is part of our natural set-up – we act against 'human nature' (Kamtekar 2017a: 76). Apparentists, on the other hand, could argue that we want to do what is truly good (happiness promoting) for us not because of an inherent desire for the real good but because we believe that happiness is good. Since we believe that happiness is good, we desire happiness, and in desiring happiness, we are aiming at our true happiness or 'real good'; we are trying to get it right (Barney 2010: 53). When we do what is in fact bad for us, we act against what we truly want and thus unwillingly.

SOCRATIC MOTIVATIONAL INTELLECTUALISM

EMOTIONS, APPETITES AND NON-RATIONAL DESIRES

When identifying the motivations for our actions, we might think of emotions and appetites. Someone might explain, for example, 'I got a glass of water because I was thirsty' (appetite) or 'I walked away because I was angry' (emotion). But in Socrates' explanation of our actions, emotions and appetites do not seem to play an important role. According to Socratic motivational intellectualism, we act as we do because we *believe* it is best. The only conative element that seems to play a role in motivating our actions is our desire for the good. Thus, interpreters have traditionally paid little attention to emotions and appetites, sometimes even depicting 'Socrates as denying that people feel the urge to do things other than what they believe to be good for them'.[16] It seems to some that Socrates 'does away with' (Aristotle *MM* 1182a15–23) or at least totally 'disregard[s]' (Kahn 1996: 227) emotional or affective factors of human motivation. He seems to propose 'una erradicación total de factores irracionales que pueden interferir en el logro de una condición racional' (Fierro 2012: 60).

One might think that interpretations like these are supported by Socrates' apparent denial of *akratic* actions. According to Socratic motivational intellectualism, we *always* do what we believe is the best thing we can do. This entails that we never act against our belief that a certain action is best for us to do. But agents seem to act *akratically* all the time; that is, they seem to act against their better judgment because they are overcome by strong appetites or emotions. Imagine, for example, a pie eater who believes that eating pie is bad for him but eats the pie anyway. How could Socrates explain this action?

Socrates could describe this example differently: In the moment of action, when the agent reaches for a slice of pie, he believes that doing so is the best thing for him to do. Before reaching for the slice, he might have believed that eating pie would be bad for him; he may even return to this belief right after he takes a bite. But in the moment of action, Socrates could maintain, the agent believes that eating pie is the best thing for him to do. In other words, Socrates could deny that at the moment of eating, the agent believes that eating pie is bad for him.

We might still call this an instance of *akrasia* – acting against one's better judgement – but here it is understood diachronically instead of synchronically. With Penner (1990: 45–48), we can call the pie eater someone who exhibits 'diachronic belief *akrasia*':

✓ *Diachronic belief akrasia*: believing that x is best at t_1; believing that y is best at t_2; doing y at t_2; and then, at t_3, returning to one's belief that x is best.

What Socrates denies is what Penner calls 'synchronic belief *akrasia*', as well as 'knowledge *akrasia*':

X *Synchronic belief akrasia*: believing that x is best at t_1, but doing y at t_1; in other words, doing y while continuing to believe that x is best (rejected at *Protagoras* 358c–d).

X *Knowledge akrasia*: knowing that x is best and nevertheless doing y (rejected at *Protagoras* 352c, 356d–357a, 358b–c).[17]

Socrates' motivational intellectualism – we always do what we believe is the best thing we can do – implies that we never act against what we believe is best in the moment of action. But it leaves open the possibility of changing one's belief over time. Socrates could thus describe what happens to the pie eater as an instance of diachronic belief *akrasia* (see Brickhouse and Smith 2010: 199–210 for a very helpful discussion).

Notice that the Socratic explanation of *akratic* actions leaves room for the experience of mental conflict that we usually associate with acting against our better judgment. The agent might feel torn between eating and not eating pie. This experience could result from a conflict between appetites and desires: The agent's appetite for pie conflicts with his reasoned desire to abstain from eating (Singpurwalla 2006: 250–254). In this interpretation, the agent experiences two conative forces pulling him in different directions at the same time (i.e., synchronically). Alternatively, the agent might feel conflicted because he goes back and forth between two different beliefs about the best thing for him to do – eating or not eating pie; in this case, he alternates over time (i.e., diachronically) between two desires pulling him in different directions (Reshotko 2006: 87).

Agnes Callard (2014) has proposed a different explanation of the *akratic* experience. Callard argues that the *akratic* agent experiences a 'distinctive phenomenology of conflict and psychological strife' (2014: 36) because of his specific kind of ignorance. While all wrongdoers are ignorant – they all act on false beliefs about what is best for them to do – only the *akratic* wrongdoer has an experience (*pathos*) (*Prt.* 352e, 353a, 357c) of his ignorance; *akratic* ignorance is painful. The *akratic* agent's pain, Callard argues, is a symptom of this particular kind of ignorance:

> In akrasia, ignorance is felt as pain. Just as physical pain is the sensing of a bodily injury of which we are at times unaware, so too psychological pain can be the sensing of epistemic injury the person does not fully fathom. When he says that the akratic has an experience (*pathos / pathēma*) of his ignorance, Socrates is pointing to the fact that the akratic is the one whose ignorance does not *completely* escape his own notice.
>
> – Callard 2014: 36–37

The *akratic* agent himself might deny that he suffers from ignorance and experiences an 'epistemic injury'. After all, he claims to believe (or even to know) that eating more pie is in fact bad for him. He might explain that he only ate more pie because he was overcome by the pleasant appearance of the pie. But in Callard's interpretation, Socrates would diagnose this *akratic* person as suffering from belief–appearance confusion: In the moment of action, he did not actually *believe* that eating pie is bad for him (if so, he would not have eaten more pie); instead, it only *appeared* to him that eating pie is bad.[18] In fact, the *akratic* agent's appearance of the pie is correct (eating more pie is bad), but he acts on a false belief (eating more pie is good) while mistaking this false belief for a false appearance. *This* is the experience (*pathos*) of *akratic* ignorance.

When describing *akratic* actions as instances of ignorance (i.e., acting on a false belief about what is best to do), Socrates seems to pay no attention to the agent's emotions and appetites. This might seem to confirm some readers' suspicion that Socrates disregards our emotions and appetites. However, emotions like anger, shame and fear; appetites like erotic attraction; and states like pleasure and pain are clearly present in Plato's early dialogues and influence some characters' actions. The events of the *Euthyphro* start when a day-labourer kills a slave in drunkenness and anger (*Eu.* 4c). Anger also plays a central role in Socrates' trial in the *Apology*: The Athenians are angry with Socrates because he embarrassed them (*Ap.* 23c–d), and he appeals to them not to let their anger influence their vote (*Ap.* 34c–d). Then, after his conviction, Socrates explains that he lost his case because he lacked shamelessness and did not want to appeal to the judges' emotions by lamenting in tears and presenting his weeping wife and children (*Ap.* 38d). Shame and fear also dominate the discussion between Crito and Socrates about whether it is right for

SOCRATIC MOTIVATIONAL INTELLECTUALISM

Socrates to flee or to stay in prison: Crito suspects that Socrates refuses to flee because he fears that Crito and any others who help him will be punished (*Cr.* 44e–45b). He then tries to shame Socrates into fleeing (*Cr.* 45e–46a). In the *Laches*, Socrates discusses what it means to be courageous in the face of pain, pleasure, appetites and fear (*La.* 191d–e). As he explains in the *Gorgias*, some people do not withstand pain or fear: children, for instance, avoid medical treatment, and criminals try to avoid painful punishment (*Grg.* 479a–c). Socrates himself admits that he is afraid at times, specifically of thinking he knows something when he does not (*Chrm.* 166d) and of conducting investigations incorrectly (*Chrm.* 172e). Socrates also experiences erotic desire when facing the handsome young Charmides for the first time (*Chrm.* 155c–d).

In light of these passages, any interpretation of the Socratic psychology of action must include emotions and appetites and acknowledge that they play some role in generating our actions. But which role exactly is debated. Presently, there are three main actively defended interpretations: Penner's interpretation, which he sometimes defended in collaboration with Rowe, and which was further developed and defended by Naomi Reshotko; Rachel Singpurwalla's; and Thomas Brickhouse and Nicholas Smith's, which was originally inspired by Daniel Devereux. I will focus on the debate between Penner, Rowe and Reshotko on the one hand and Brickhouse and Smith on the other, which has dominated the secondary literature on Socrates' motivational intellectualism in recent years.[19]

The debate between these two accounts of Socratic motivational intellectualism is often presented as a debate over whether or not Socratic psychology includes a type of desire that is sometimes called '**non-rational**' or '**good-independent**'. But as we will see, framing the debate in these terms can be problematic because interpreters use the terms 'non-rational', 'good-independent' and 'desire' in different ways.[20]

The term '**non-rational**' is often used to refer to mental states that lack some kind of relation to beliefs or deliberation and reasoning: 'Non-rational' states are described by interpreters alternatively as not arising from, involving or responding to beliefs or deliberation.[21] Some interpreters take this further, arguing that non-rational states are not responsive to beliefs or reasoning *because* they are not or do not involve beliefs (i.e., if they were beliefs, they could be altered by belief changes).[22]

The term '**good-independent**' captures an alternative aspect of these types of mental states. 'Good-independent' mental states lack some kind of relation to goodness: They are understood as independent of our desire for the good or as independent of our beliefs or deliberations about goodness (either about goodness generally or about our overall, long-term good specifically).[23] But these alternative ways of defining 'good-independent' are not at all synonymous.

Finally, the term '**desire**' is itself used in different ways. Penner and Reshotko use 'desire' very narrowly, referring only to action-causing motivations – desires 'to do something', that is, desires that arise out of our inherent desire for the real good combined with beliefs about what is best to do (Penner 1992a: 128). They distinguish 'desires' from what they call 'itches' and 'hankerings' (Penner 1991: 201, n.45) or 'longings', 'drives', 'urges' and 'raw desires' (Reshotko 2006: 55, 76–77, 84–88). According to both Penner and Reshotko, emotions and appetites are not full-fledged desires; they are mere 'itches' or 'hankerings'. In the Socratic account of motivation, they argue, all 'desires' are particularisations of our inherent desire for the good. These particular (or 'executive') desires are brought about by the belief that a certain action is best. In this sense, all 'desires' are thus 'rational'; there are no non-rational executive desires within Socratic psychology (Penner 1990: 39, 1992a: 128).

Brickhouse and Smith, in contrast, use 'desire' very broadly to refer to feelings of attraction and aversion (Brickhouse and Smith 2010: 72, 2015: 14–15; see also Martinez and Smith 2018: 70). They argue that Socrates identifies three kinds of natural attractions and aversions in the *Charmides* (167e): 'appetite (*epithumia*), which aims at pleasure, wish (*boulēsis*), which aims at what is good, and love (*erōs*), which aims at what is beautiful. Each of these seems to have an aversive alternative, as well: we avoid pain, what is bad, and what is ugly' (2015: 14). In other words, we are naturally attracted to pleasure, goodness and beauty, and we feel aversive toward pain, badness and ugliness. These attractions and aversions are 'non-rational' in the sense that they 'seek their objects in a way that is independent of [i.e., not caused by][24] our reasoning or deliberation about what is really good for us' (2013b: 191). We desire pleasure, beauty and goodness because of inherent natural attractions to each.[25]

If we understand 'desire' broadly as 'attraction' and 'non-rational' as 'not caused by reasoning or deliberation', then Brickhouse and Smith's view is that we have three fundamentally 'non-rational desires' (our inherent desires for pleasure, goodness and beauty), whereas Penner and Reshotko's view is that we have only one such 'non-rational desire' (our inherent desire for the good). But if we understand 'desire' narrowly as 'desire to do something', then Brickhouse and Smith's view is that some of our 'desires' are rational while others are non-rational, and Penner and Reshotko's view is that all of our 'desires' are rational.

Against Brickhouse and Smith's very broad understanding of 'desires' as feelings of attraction and aversion, Singpurwalla has argued that feeling an attraction or aversion is different than 'actually desiring to act on that feeling' (2006: 252). For example, I might 'find a lifestyle of jet-setting and party-hopping attractive, but not really desire it, since I realize it is incompatible with fulfilling desires or goals that I believe make an essential contribution to living the good life' (2006: 252). Thus, Singpurwalla proposes that we distinguish full-fledged desires from attractions and aversions: Attractions and aversions are not themselves desires, but they can lead to desires if they are 'endorsed as true, and so give rise to a belief' (2006: 252). In Singpurwalla's interpretation, 'non-rational desires are evaluative beliefs' based on attractions and aversions (2006: 252).

Since the terms 'non-rational', 'good-independent' and 'desire' are used in very different ways, they invite misunderstanding. I will therefore centre this discussion around the phenomena that these terms were supposed to capture in the first place: emotions and appetites. What roles do emotions and appetites play in the Socratic account of action?

While Penner, Rowe and Reshotko consider emotions and appetites as belonging to the same class of mental states – namely 'itches' or 'hankerings' – and as influencing our actions in the same way, Brickhouse and Smith (2015) argue that we should distinguish between emotions and appetites. In the *Protagoras* (358d5–6), they argue, Socrates seems to endorse a cognitive account of emotions, claiming that emotions are beliefs. If Brickhouse and Smith are right that, for Socrates, emotions are beliefs but appetites are not, then these two states play different roles in generating actions and must be discussed separately. In this chapter, I will mainly focus on appetites. For a detailed discussion of emotions, see Chapter 12 of this volume ('Socrates on Emotion').

Interpreters on both sides of the debate – Brickhouse and Smith on the one side and Penner, Rowe and Reshotko on the other – agree that appetites can influence our actions by influencing our beliefs and deliberations.[26] For example, my craving for chocolate might affect my calculation of what is best; without this craving, I might not conclude that

SOCRATIC MOTIVATIONAL INTELLECTUALISM

buying a Snickers bar is the best thing for me to do right now (Reshotko 2006: 84–87). Both sides also agree that appetites are aversive or attractive; they drive or urge us.[27] Disgust, for instance, is aversive. However, they disagree about the extent to which appetites can drive or urge us.

The interpretive disagreement over the role of appetites in Socrates' account of motivation boils down to the following questions:

- Can appetites represent their objects as good or bad and thereby drive us toward or away from specific things?
- Can appetites incline us toward new beliefs about what is best to do?
- Can appetites distort already-formed beliefs about what is best to do?

Brickhouse and Smith answer these questions in the affirmative, while Penner, Rowe and Reshotko answer negatively.

Penner, Rowe and Reshotko have argued that appetites can influence our actions by *informing* our beliefs and deliberations:

> My thirst informs me that drinking something in the near future would be in my best interest, but my beliefs about what kinds of drinks are available, how they taste, how much they cost and how much effort it takes to obtain one of them will all be integrated into my executive desire to grab four quarters and to walk to the vending machine . . . to buy a bottle of grapefruit juice. . . . My non-rational urges do effect my behaviour, but they do not cause any behaviour all by themselves.
>
> – Reshotko 2013: 171

My thirst informs me that I should drink, but it does not tell me what I should drink (e.g., grapefruit juice or water) or how to get that drink (e.g., buying juice at the vending machine or getting tap water from the kitchen). Appetites like thirst do not tell us which things are good and worth pursuing or bad and worth avoiding. They cannot move us toward or away from specific things.[28] They thus cannot make us believe that any particular thing would be best to pursue. In other words, they cannot cause beliefs about what is best to do.[29]

According to Penner and Reshotko, my thirst is only one piece of information that I consider when I deliberate about what would be best for me to do. I may have any number of different appetites at any given moment – I might be thirsty, hungry and sleepy – and there may be many different ways of satisfying those appetites, but I 'always do just *one* particular action. How is it determined which one?' (Penner 1991: 202, n.45). Socratic motivational intellectualism provides a clear answer: We either drink, eat or sleep, depending on our belief about the best thing to do at the moment of action.

Once an agent has determined that doing x is best, he forms an (executive) desire to do x. While the agent might also feel an appetite, the satisfaction of which would require him to do y, this appetite ('non-rational desire') cannot trump his desire to do x ('rational desire').[30] However, the agent's appetite might change his calculation about what is best to do. For example, if he suddenly feels very hungry, he might determine that it is overall best to eat something first and then run errands. In other words, Penner, Rowe and Reshotko argue that appetites can inform us, but they cannot distort already-formed beliefs about what is best to do, nor can they compete with 'rational' desires (i.e., desires that arise from combining such beliefs with our inherent desire for the real good).

According to Brickhouse and Smith, on the other hand, appetites can distort already-formed beliefs about what is best. They argue that it is primarily this claim that distinguishes their interpretation from others:

> There is 'a fairly strong scholarly consensus that, according to the Socrates in Plato's Socratic dialogues, appetites, such as hunger and lust, and passions, such as anger and hatred, are not capable of altering an agent's judgment about what it is best for her to do. . . . The primary impetus behind *SMP* [Brickhouse and Smith's *Socratic Moral Psychology*] is to challenge *this particular consensus* and to provide an alternative account according to which Socrates recognizes the possibility that appetites and passions can, under certain conditions, not only affect, but even severely impair, judgment about what is best'.

> – Brickhouse and Smith 2012b: 325–326

According to Brickhouse and Smith, appetites can 'severely impair' beliefs about what is best because they present their objects as good and worth pursuing, or as bad and worth avoiding; this drives the agent toward or away from specific things and inclines him to believe that pursuing or avoiding those things is the best thing to do.[31] For example, my craving for chocolate might present a specific object (that chocolate bar in front of me) and a specific action (buying that chocolate bar in front of me) as good, which, by default, leads me to believe that buying the chocolate bar is the best thing for me to do, unless some other belief-forming process interferes (e.g., unless I consider some contrary evidence that convinces me that I should not satisfy this appetite).

In Brickhouse and Smith's interpretation, appetites can motivate actions under the condition that the agent believes satisfying his appetite is the best thing for him to do:

> Only if the soul ended up judging that what appeared to be good (because presented as such by an appetite, for example) was actually the best choice one could make in a given situation, would one become fully motivated to act. The stronger the appetite or passion, the more compelling the appearance of good would be. . . . But in this way, as we have shown, appetites and passions could never motivate us independently of what we believe is good for us, for although our beliefs about what is good for us might be unstable (particularly in those persons susceptible to strong appetites or passions), we will always act in the ways we presently believe are best for us.

> – Brickhouse and Smith 2010: 200; see also 2010: 62,
> 79, 107, 108; 2012b: 337; 2015: 16

In Brickhouse and Smith's account, therefore, Socrates is still a motivational intellectualist because our motivation for action is tied to a belief about what is best. Our *actions* always follow from such a belief: We *act* as we do because we believe it is best. However, Brickhouse and Smith argue that Socrates is not an intellectualist about *desires*: We do not *desire* what we desire because we believe it is best.[32] Instead, we desire what we desire (pleasure, beauty and goodness) because of an inherent natural attraction. In Penner, Rowe and Reshotko's interpretation, by contrast, Socrates is an intellectualist about both actions *and* desires; our actions and executive desires (i.e., our desires to do something) follow from our beliefs about what is best. Brickhouse and Smith might say that Penner, Rowe and Reshotko's interpretation got things backwards: According to Brickhouse and Smith, executive desires usually do not follow from beliefs, but beliefs can follow from desires. In other words, beliefs usually do not generate desires, but desires can generate beliefs.

SOCRATIC MOTIVATIONAL INTELLECTUALISM

Despite their disagreements, Brickhouse and Smith agree with Penner, Rowe and Reshotko that *appetites* 'do not cause any behaviour all by themselves' (Reshotko 2013: 171), that is, without a belief that this is the best thing to do. But when it comes to *emotions*, Brickhouse and Smith propose a fundamentally different account.

Brickhouse and Smith (2015) argue that emotions are evaluative beliefs brought about by natural attractions or aversions. Fear, for instance, is a belief that results from our aversion to pain (2015: 15). Our natural aversion to pain presents certain actions as best for us to do, thereby inclining us to believe that these actions are indeed best (2015: 19). According to Brickhouse and Smith, this resulting belief is fear. In this interpretation, emotions thus differ from appetites in a crucial way: Since emotions *are* beliefs about what is best to do, emotions can generate actions on their own.[33] An appetite, however, must generate or call to mind a belief – the belief that pursuing the object of the appetite is best – in order to bring about an action. Appetites can prompt us to believe that their objects are good and worth pursuing; emotions are beliefs that their objects are good and worth pursuing. This is in contrast to Penner, Rowe and Reshotko, who claim that neither emotions nor appetites can orient one toward an external object in the absence of other beliefs and the desire for the good.

We saw that Socrates does not disregard emotions and appetites. Emotions and appetites can play some role in generating our actions, even though all actions are ultimately explained in terms of beliefs (we act as we do because we *believe* it is best). Above, I reviewed the two dominant interpretations of Socratic motivational intellectualism and the roles they assign to these mental states. We will see in the next section that these two different interpretations of Socratic motivational intellectualism align with different interpretations of the Socratic response to wrongdoing and specifically of Socrates' stance on punishment. Penner, Rowe and Reshotko have argued that philosophical conversation is the only reliable means for correcting wrongdoers: Since emotions and appetites cannot cause actions (or beliefs about what is best, which then generate actions), they do not need correction through non-argumentative means such as punishment. Brickhouse and Smith, by contrast, have argued that Socrates believes some wrongdoers require punishment to correct their misguided appetites.

WRONGDOING AND PUNISHMENT

According to Socratic motivational intellectualism, we always do what we believe is in our own best interest at the moment of action. Moral wrongdoing ('acting unjustly') is never in our own best interest (*Cr.* 49a–b, *Grg.* 469b). Socrates believes that wrongdoing is the worst thing there is for the wrongdoer (*Grg.* 509b) because it harms the soul (*Cr.* 47d–48a, *Ap.* 30d), and those with harmed souls lead miserable lives (*Grg.* 511c–512b). So, wrongdoers do wrong because they have concluded falsely that their actions are in their own best interest (*Prt.* 357c–358d, *Grg.* 466d–468e). For Socrates, wrongdoing always reflects an intellectual failure.

Since agents do wrong because they are ignorant – they falsely believe that they benefit from wrongdoing – correction efforts must focus on making them less ignorant. One plausible way to make agents less ignorant is via philosophical conversations. Through conversations with Socrates, wrongdoers will become better deliberators; they will get rid of their false beliefs and acquire new true beliefs, and they are thereby more likely to abstain from future wrongdoing. The question at the centre of this discussion is whether philosophical conversations are appropriate for correcting *all* wrongdoers. Are philosophical conversations the *only* means of correction that Socrates endorses, or does Socrates' intellectualist account of motivation and action leave room for other means of correction?

To answer these questions, one must turn to Socrates' apparent approval of legal punishment in the *Gorgias*:

> Wrongdoing should not be kept hidden but brought into the open, so that [the wrongdoer] gets punished and gets healthy; he should force himself . . . and present himself courageously as to a doctor for cauterization and surgery, pursuing the good and admirable thing without taking into account the pain. And if he is so unjust that he deserves flogging, he should present himself to be beaten; if he deserves imprisonment, to be imprisoned; if a fine, to pay it; if exile, to be exiled; and if death, to die.

> *– Grg.* 480c–d

In this passage, Socrates seems to suggest that wrongdoers ought to be punished – fined, imprisoned, exiled and even flogged or put to death.[34] Elsewhere in the *Gorgias*, he explains that these punishments benefit the wrongdoer by improving his soul (*Grg.* 477a–b): The punished wrongdoer gets rid of the 'most serious bad thing', namely 'injustice, ignorance, cowardice, and the like', which lead to misery and a life lived poorly. It is thus in the wrongdoer's own best interest to disclose his wrongdoing and be punished.

The challenge interpreters face is: 'if it [i.e., wrongdoing] is all supposed to be a matter of intellectual error, what use is it to *punish* anyone? . . . How can making people suffer – fining, imprisoning, flogging, exiling, executing them – how can any of *that* make them *think* better?' (Rowe 2007: 28). Interpreters have answered this question in three different ways. Below, we will look at their answers in more detail.

Answer #1: Punishment cannot make us think better. Socrates does not approve of legal punishment.

Some interpreters have argued that, for Socrates, all wrongdoers can be improved *only* through philosophical conversations and thus Socrates does not in fact approve of legal punishment. We can reconstruct their argument as follows:

(i) In Socrates' intellectualist account of motivation and action, 'the only factor that is ever relevant to changing someone's conduct . . . is changing his beliefs' (Penner 2011: 289). If we want to correct wrongdoers, we must improve their beliefs.

(ii) Punishment cannot improve beliefs. For Socrates in Plato's early dialogues, '*only philosophical dialogue* can improve one's fellow citizens' (Penner 2000: 164; see also Penner 2018 and Rowe 2007).

(iii) Thus, Socrates cannot approve of punishment.

In this interpretation, our only hope to improve wrongdoers is changing their beliefs via extended philosophical conversations:

> 'If only we could *discuss* things for long enough, if only we could *understand* what is best,' Socrates seems to say, 'all would be well, and all conduct would be virtuous!' For Socrates, when people act badly or viciously or even just out of moral weakness, that will be merely a result of intellectual mistake.

> *– Penner 2000: 165*

Philosophical conversations are the only reliable means of correction, because the only thing that can make us do wrong is a false belief about what is best, and such intellectual

SOCRATIC MOTIVATIONAL INTELLECTUALISM

errors, these interpreters maintain, can only be corrected in an intellectual way: 'nothing apart from talking and reasoning with us will be necessary, because there is nothing apart from what we think and believe that is even in principle capable of causing us to go wrong' (Rowe 2006: 166).

Rowe contrasts this Socratic account of correction with Plato's. For Plato, our emotions and appetites can cause us to do wrong and act against our better judgment (in other words, Plato allows for synchronic belief *akrasia*; for a helpful discussion of this contrast between Socrates and Plato, see Brickhouse and Smith 2010: 199–210). Correction efforts may therefore need to target either a wrongdoer's ignorance *or* his misguided emotions and appetites, depending on the cause of wrongdoing. For Plato, 'our *desires as well as our reason needs persuasion, education, direction. That* is where punishment comes in, as a suitably irrational way of dealing with irrational drives' (Rowe 2007: 29). But for Socrates, by contrast, 'one can only go wrong through ignorance' (Rowe 2007: 24). Thus, in this interpretation, wrongdoers only need philosophical conversations to improve, and Socrates 'does not endorse flogging, imprisonment, or any other vulgar kind of punishment' (Rowe 2007: 36).

To explain *Gorgias* 480c–d, where Socrates seems to approve of legal punishment – imprisonment, paying a fine, exile and even bodily punishment – Rowe proposes that Socrates uses an ordinary notion of punishment simply to make it easier for his interlocutor, Polus, to understand his argument (Rowe 2007: 34). Nevertheless, so the argument goes, Socrates does not approve of any kind of 'punishment' beyond teaching and philosophical conversations, the only 'punishments' he believes can improve wrongdoers (Rowe 2007: 32, 34–35; see also Penner 2000, 2011, 2018; Edwards 2016[35]).[36]

> *Answer #2: Punishment cannot make us think better, but certain forms of punishment can deprive us of the means that facilitate wrongdoing. Socrates approves of these kinds of legal punishment.*

Shaw (2015) has argued that Socrates endorses only certain forms of punishment – the death penalty, exile and confiscation of property – because these punishments deprive the wrongdoer of the means that facilitate his wrongdoing. Paying a fine, for example, deprives one of money; exile deprives one of friends; and the death penalty deprives one of life. Money, friends and being alive are means that enable an agent to do wrong. In other words, Socrates approves of punishment only for the sake of incapacitation or the deprivation of the means to do wrong. But since certain bodily punishments like flogging cannot be justified in this way, according to Shaw, Socrates does not approve of them.

Shaw argues that Socrates' apparent endorsement of flogging in *Gorgias* 480c–d does not provide sufficient grounds for concluding that Socrates approves of this type of bodily punishment, because his approval of flogging is conditional: A wrongdoer should be flogged *if* he is so unjust that he deserves to be flogged. But this condition, Shaw argues, might never be met (2015: 79; see also Moss 2007: 232 n.8).

> *Answer #3: Punishment can make us think better by improving our misguided appetites. Socrates approves of legal punishment.*

Brickhouse and Smith (2010: 102–110; 2018: 45–47) have argued that we must distinguish between two different kinds of wrongdoers. Some wrongdoers commit crimes due to mere ignorance; they might miscalculate costs and benefits or lack certain information. Teaching and instruction are appropriate for correcting these wrongdoers. In the *Apology*, Socrates argues that he himself belongs to this group of wrongdoers, if indeed he harmed anyone (*Apology* 26a). But other wrongdoers, Brickhouse and Smith argue, commit crimes due to strong appetites. These wrongdoers are ignorant 'in a different sense' (2010: 123): Their appetites cause false beliefs and make them disinclined to follow reason. For such wrongdoers, 'calm conversation . . . would not be effective' (2015: 26). These wrongdoers cannot hope to improve 'unless they undergo punishment' (2010: 123).

When we act to satisfy our appetites, Brickhouse and Smith argue (2010: 117–124; 2018: 47), our appetites become stronger. In some wrongdoers, appetites have become so strong that they severely impair the ability to listen to reason. For these wrongdoers, appetites habitually cause them to believe that the objects of their appetites are good and worth pursuing; acting on those appetites then further strengthens them. According to Brickhouse and Smith, punishment can break this vicious cycle by changing wrongdoers' calculations about what is beneficial to them: The punished wrongdoer comes to believe that the pleasure from satisfying appetites is not worth the pain from punishment (2010: 124). Since punishment is unpleasant or even painful, it gives appetitive wrongdoers a convincing reason to avoid future wrongdoing; and when they abstain from wrongdoing and do not act on their appetites, their appetites are not 'filled up' and become 'weaker' (2010: 123–124; 2018: 51). Weakened appetites are less likely to cause the agent to believe that the objects of those appetites are good and worth pursuing. Once appetites are weakened, a wrongdoer can see the objects of those appetites for what they really are – merely apparent goods (2010: 124).

In this interpretation, painful punishment brings about a *conative* improvement by weakening the wrongdoer's excessively strong appetites. This conative improvement in turn may bring about an *epistemic* improvement: The weakened appetites are less likely to cause false beliefs about what is the best thing to do. Brickhouse and Smith thus conclude that Socrates is serious when he approves of legal punishment.

The advantage of Brickhouse and Smith's interpretation is that it takes the textual evidence in the *Gorgias* at face value. However, critics have argued that, even setting aside the question of whether painful punishment is consistent with Socrates' psychology of action, we still have reason to reject Socrates' apparent approval of painful punishment.

Critics have worried that painful punishment will not improve wrongdoers by making them less ignorant; instead, it could make them worse and more ignorant, either by enforcing what Socrates holds to be a false belief, namely that 'pain is bad' (Kamtekar 2016: 6, n. 13), or by creating a new false belief, namely that 'getting caught is bad' (as one might infer from Shaw 2015: 76). The agent would then become a sophisticated wrongdoer: someone who merely tries to avoid getting caught. For responses to these objections, see Möbus (2023).

Further, a critic could argue that Socrates' alleged approval of punishment is incompatible with his belief that no one does wrong willingly. In the *Apology*, Socrates argues that only wrongdoing done willingly should be legally punished. Unwilling wrongdoers should be taken aside and instructed privately. But if indeed all wrongdoing is unwilling, then it seems that no wrongdoer should be legally punished:

(i)   Only willing wrongdoing should be legally punished (*Ap.* 26a).
(ii) No one does wrong willingly (*Prt.* 345e, 358d–e; *Grg.* 509e).
(iii) So, no one should be legally punished.

SOCRATIC MOTIVATIONAL INTELLECTUALISM

But several interpreters (Kamtekar 2017b: 72; Brickhouse and Smith 2018) have argued that in the *Apology*, Socrates claims that some people actually do wrong willingly, namely, those who exhibit a certain kind of ignorance – those who do not know that if they harm their associates, they will be harmed in turn (*Ap.* 25c–d). How can Socrates claim both that all wrongdoing is unwilling and that some wrongdoers do wrong willingly and should be legally punished?

Brickhouse and Smith (2018) have proposed that all wrongdoing is involuntary (they translate *akōn* as 'involuntary' instead of 'unwillingly') because all wrongdoing is self-harm – it harms one's soul – and no one wants to harm oneself.[37] But they argue that this is perfectly compatible with the idea that the same agent could voluntarily harm others. An action 'can be voluntary in one sense and yet involuntary in another' (2018: 52): A wrongdoer can voluntarily harm his victim while at the same time involuntarily harming himself (Brickhouse and Smith 2018: 50–51). This is why Socrates can claim both that no one does wrong voluntarily *and* that some wrongdoers do wrong voluntarily and thus should be legally punished.

Against all three interpretations presented above, Freya Möbus (2023) has argued that Socrates in the *Gorgias* approves of painful bodily punishment like flogging (*pace* Penner and Rowe; *pace* Shaw) and that we can explain the efficacy of bodily punishment without introducing non-rational desires (*pace* Brickhouse and Smith). Möbus proposes that experiencing bodily punishment can benefit the wrongdoer in two ways: It can epistemically improve the wrongdoer by prompting him to form the new true belief that wrongdoing is bad for him, and it can prevent a further epistemic worsening of the wrongdoer by deterring him from future wrongdoing, at least sometimes. Bodily punishment can improve certain wrongdoers under certain circumstances, Möbus explains, because experiencing bodily pain and feeling that wrongdoing is bad is more persuasive than mere philosophical arguments. In Möbus' account, flogging can be educationally effective precisely because it is painful (*pace* Shaw).

IS SOCRATES AN INTELLECTUALIST ABOUT HUMAN MOTIVATION?

In this chapter, we discussed Socratic motivational intellectualism – the claim that we always do what we believe is the best thing for us to do, and we saw that many place motivational intellectualism at the centre of Socrates' account of human action. Some, however, have pushed back on this interpretation.

Kamtekar (2017a: 72–73, 2017b: 1–4, 69–128) has argued that we should not put so much weight on Socrates' alleged motivational intellectualism because we have only *one* piece of textual evidence for it, *Protagoras* 358c–d. Further, this one piece of evidence, Kamtekar argues, stands on shaky ground: Socrates says that '*if* the pleasant is the good', no one would do something if he believed there was something better that he could do. Since Socrates presents motivational intellectualism as premised on hedonism (i.e., 'the pleasant is the good'), our interpretation of his account of motivation hinges on the question of whether Socrates is a hedonist. While Kamtekar has argued that Socrates rejects hedonism (pointing us, for example, to *Grg.* 493a–495a), others have proposed that he only rejects a certain kind of hedonism (Rudebusch 1999, Moss 2014).

The foundation of Socrates' account of motivation is not intellectualism, Kamtekar proposes, but rather the desire thesis – we all desire our own real good. The desire for our real good, Kamtekar argues further, 'may be manifested in different ways: certainly by our pursuit of what we believe to be best, but also by our pursuit of pleasant things and fine things' (2017b: 3). In other words, we do not *always* and *only* do what we *believe* is best for us to do; sometimes we do what merely seems pleasant, for example. If Kamtekar is right, Socrates is not an intellectualist about human motivation after all.

The conversation about Socrates' account of motivation remains ongoing, and the implications for his philosophy of human nature have yet to be determined: Are we indeed beings who *always* do what we believe is in our own best interest? Do we come equipped with an inherent desire for what is truly good for us? For Socrates, our answers to these questions matter because if we act well, we live well; so, to live a good life, we must understand why we act as we do.

NOTES

1. I am very grateful to editors Rusty Jones, Nicholas Smith and Ravi Sharma for the invitation to write this chapter and for their extraordinarily helpful comments on earlier versions of it. I would also like to thank Naomi Reshotko and Antonio Chu, whose detailed feedback helped me present several arguments more clearly.

2. By 'Plato's early dialogues', I here mean the *Euthyphro, Apology, Crito, Charmides, Laches, Lysis, Euthydemus, Meno, Protagoras, Ion, Hippias Minor* and *Major, Gorgias* and *Republic I.*

3. All translations used in this chapter are from Cooper (ed.), *Plato: Complete Works* (1997). I have occasionally made small changes to the translation for certain passages, in which case I provide the Greek in brackets.

4. The view that I always do what I believe is best *for me* is often referred to as psychological egoism. Many understand Socrates' motivational intellectualism in this way (see e.g., Brickhouse and Smith 2013b: 185; Penner 1992a: 128), specifically his remarks in the *Protagoras* (see e.g., Reshotko 2013: 179; Taylor 2019: 60–62). Others, however, have pushed back against the claim that Socrates is a psychological egoist (see e.g., Jones and Sharma 2017: 132–133) and have offered alternative interpretations of the *Protagoras* passage (see e.g., Ahbel-Rappe 2012: 332–335). One might worry that if Socratic agents are psychological egoists, then they further their own good at all costs, even at the expense of the well-being of others. But some interpreters have argued that, for Socrates, the ethical good and our prudential good never come apart (Brickhouse and Smith 2010: 44–46): What I ethically ought to do is always also what is in my own best interest; likewise, wrongdoing is never good for me.

5. I hope to offer an understanding of 'motivational intellectualism' that is shared by many interpreters. Parts of the definition are thus intentionally left vague to avoid biases for or against certain views (I therefore propose, e.g., that motivations 'are tied to' beliefs instead of 'are', 'follow', 'are caused by' or 'derive from').

6. For a very helpful outline of Socrates' motivational intellectualism and its centrality for his ethics, see Taylor (2019: 60–62). Kamtekar (2017b: 1–3) has questioned what she calls the 'mainstream account', according to which motivational intellectualism is the 'theoretical basis' or 'foundation' for the 'Socratic intellectualist package'. I will return to her view at the end of this chapter.

7. Among those who have argued that, in the Socratic account, non-rational desires do not motivate actions are Irwin (1977: 78–82), Penner (in various articles; see e.g., 1992a) and Rowe (see especially his 2012a).

SOCRATIC MOTIVATIONAL INTELLECTUALISM

8. See e.g., Penner (2000), Rowe (2007), Brickhouse and Smith (2010: 199–210) and Taylor (2019: 60–62).

9. Kamtekar (2017b: 69–128).

10. While in this passage Socrates refers to wisdom, health and wealth as 'goods', he describes what I call 'small-scale goods' – for example, sitting, walking and embarking on sea voyages – as 'neither good nor bad'; they 'sometimes partake of what's good, sometimes of what's bad, and sometimes of neither' (*Grg.* 467e).

11. Penner and Rowe (1994) and Reshotko (2006: Chapter 2) argue against this widely accepted interpretation of the *Meno* passage.

12. Segvic (2009), Devereux (1995: 398ff.), Santas (1964: 152 n.15) and others also distinguish between *boulēsis* and *epithumia*.

13. Santas (1964) argues that we should not 'lump together' these passages. We must distinguish, Santas argues, between prudential and moral wrongdoing and thus between Socrates' prudential paradox that 'no one does what is bad for oneself (i.e., prudentially wrong or bad) willingly' and his moral paradox that 'no one does what is unjust (i.e., morally wrong or bad) willingly'. According to Santas, Socrates takes the prudential paradox to be a fact about human nature that serves as a premise in his argument for the moral paradox.

14. I thank Rachel Barney for a helpful discussion of this argument and this premise in particular.

15. For a similar reconstruction, see Kamtekar (2017b: 70–71).

16. Reshotko (2013: 170) attributes this view to Irwin (1977, 1995), among others.

17. Socrates believes that knowledge *akrasia* of any kind – diachronic or synchronic – is impossible (Penner 1990: 47). Diachronic knowledge *akrasia* is impossible because knowledge is stable; it does not vacillate. Synchronic knowledge *akrasia* is impossible because we never act against what we 'know or believe' is best for us in the moment of action (*Prt.* 358b–d).

18. Callard proposes 'simulacrum' instead of 'appearance' as a translation of 'phantasma' in *Prt.* 356d. 'A simulacrum is a representation not believed to be veridical by the one who has it' (2014: 52).

19. Rowe's 2012a discussion of Brickhouse and Smith's *Socratic Moral Psychology* and their 'Reply to Rowe' (2012b), as well as Reshotko's discussion of the different interpretations (2013: 170–172), are particularly helpful for understanding the debate. For a helpful discussion of similarities and differences between Devereux's (1995) interpretation and Brickhouse and Smith's, see Brickhouse and Smith (2013b: 193–194). For a critical discussion of Brickhouse and Smith's *Socratic Moral Psychology* by Jones (2012), Butler (2012) and Devereux (2012), as well as Brickhouse and Smith's response to these critics (2012a), see *Analytic Philosophy* (53.2).

20. As Kamtekar notes as well: 'the terms we use – desire, belief, appetite, nonrational – are so familiar that we do not usually stop to ask what we are saying' (2012: 259). She identifies two ways of understanding 'non-rational': 'good-independent motivations (that is, motivations that do not represent their objects as good), and uncritical (but quite possibly good-directed) motivations' (2012: 257).

21. See, for instance, Singpurwalla (2006: 243, n.1): 'a non-rational desire is a desire that arises independently of reasoning and so has the potential to come into conflict with our

reasoned conception of the good'. For the idea that non-rational desires are not responsive to belief and deliberation, see Penner (1992a: 128–129). See also footnote 22 below.

22. Singpurwalla (2006) argues that non-rational desires are beliefs and that they can thus be changed by reasoning: 'The fact that Socrates conceives of irrational desires as evaluative *beliefs*, as opposed to desires that are independent of any evaluation of the object of desire or appearances, opens up an interesting possibility, namely, for Socrates irrational desires are resistant to reason but not invariably or essentially so. Irrational desires are still beliefs, and the aim of beliefs is to represent the world; thus any evaluative belief is sensitive to evidence' (2006: 253). If non-rational desires did not involve beliefs, it would be a 'mystery' how they could affect or be affected by our beliefs (2006: 251).

23. For the idea that our non-rational desires are independent of our desire for the good, see, for instance, Reshotko (2006: 54–55, 74). For the idea that our non-rational desires are independent of our beliefs or deliberations about goodness, see, for instance, Rowe: 'Desire, taken by itself, i.e., until beliefs are "plugged into" it, will *always* be non-rational; . . . desires only become desires "to do something" when they are combined with beliefs, i.e., about what is best for the agent; and that is also the moment at which they become "rational" desires' (2012a: 309); Singpurwalla: non-rational desires arise independently of 'reasoned beliefs about value' (2006: 249); Irwin: rational or good-dependent desires (Irwin seems to use these terms interchangeably, 1977: 78) 'rest on deliberation about what would be best, all things considered, for myself as a whole' (1995: 215) – they are 'formed by deliberation about instrumental means to the final good' (1977: 170). Non-rational desires, by contrast, do not arise out of deliberation about the final, overall good. Brickhouse and Smith (2013b: 191) distinguish 'non-rational' from 'good-independent' desires as follows: Non-rational desires are 'desires that seek their objects in a way that is independent of our reasoning or deliberation about what is good for us'. Good-independent desires are 'desires that seek their objects in a way that is independent of our universal desire for what is really good for us'; for a discussion of different usages of the term 'irrational', see Carone (2005: 377, n.37).

24. The term 'independent' should here be understood as 'not caused by' or 'not dependent upon' reasoning or deliberation; it should not be understood as 'totally unresponsive to' reasoning or deliberation (Brickhouse and Smith 2013b: 196).

25. Note that Brickhouse and Smith think of our basic attractions and aversions as 'non-rational' but 'good-dependent' (Brickhouse and Smith 2013b: 191). Attractions and aversions are good-dependent because they present their objects as good.

26. Brickhouse and Smith (2010, 2015, 2018) and Martinez and Smith (2018: 70–73) have argued most prominently and extensively for the idea that emotions and appetites can influence our actions in the Socratic account of motivation. But Penner, Rowe and Reshotko have also acknowledged this idea. See e.g., Penner: '"Does desire for drink never generate an action? How can that be? Is it being denied that we have these desires?" No, the desire for drink does occur, but the way it gets us to act is to present itself to our desire for happiness, which turns to the belief-system to produce an estimate of the possible gains from various choices for fulfilling this desire' (2011: 263). See also Reshotko: 'I hold that urges and drives *do influence* our rational assessment of different courses of action. . . . My craving for chocolate makes my calculation of the good, and my consequent actions based on my desire for the good, come out differently than they would, had I not been craving

SOCRATIC MOTIVATIONAL INTELLECTUALISM

chocolate' (2006: 87); 'Intellectualism need only claim that these non-intellectualized factors never cause behavior in an unmediated fashion: They cause it by affecting our beliefs. These changed beliefs influence our deliberation concerning which action is the best means to the best end available to us in our situation, so we come to different conclusions about which action is most beneficial' (2006: 84); 'No purposeful action can be the result of a non-rational element (like emotion) except insofar as the non-rational element has influenced the agent's beliefs' (2006: 16). See also Penner and Rowe: 'For most such "feelings" *are* intimately connected with beliefs and actions. Indeed, it is hard to imagine a feeling that does not somehow influence some belief the subject has' (2005: 230).

27. Reshotko attributes the idea that, in the Socratic account, emotions and appetites drive or urge us to Penner: 'For many years, the dominant interpretation of the Socratic denial of *akrasia* . . . depicted Socrates as denying that people feel the urge to do things other than what they believe to be good for them. Penner challenges that tradition . . ., finding that Socrates acknowledges the experience of urges and desires that are not yet integrated with the desire for the good and, so, can be said to conflict with it' (2013: 170).

28. See Reshotko: 'Neither Penner nor I deny that an agent continues to feel an urge even while acting against it in an effort to do what is best. What we deny is that this urge can be a *pull towards a specific instance of a thing*' (2013: 171). See also Brickhouse and Smith's criticism of Penner's and Reshotko's account: 'Missing from this account, we contend, is what is peculiar to the appetites and passions, namely, that they are "drives" and "urges," that is, that they are psychic events that actually do *drive* or *urge* us towards and away from things' (2010: 52, n.6).

29. See Reshotko: 'Devereux believes that my appetite for chocolate can actively work to distort my beliefs concerning a candy, *causing* me to *see the candy as a means to my happiness*. . . . This is not how I have presented the role of unintellectualized drives and urges. In my view, an appetite never plays a role that is more instrumental than any other piece of information that the intellect has used in order to determine what it is best to do as motivated by the desire for the good. I hold that appetites are like sense impressions: they are phenomena that help us form our judgments, but they do not interact with judgments that have already been formed' (2006: 85–86). See also Rowe (2012a: 314) and Penner (2011: 263–264).

30. See, for example, Reshotko: 'While other drives and urges might exist, Socratic intellectualism dictates that they cannot trump or triumph over the desire for the good' (2006: 85, 76–77).

31. Brickhouse and Smith: 'non-rational desires influence [. . .] what we believe by representing their targets as goods or benefits to the agent, so that the agent would come to believe that pursuing or obtaining those targets would serve the universally shared desire for benefit, unless some other process interfered with this' (2015: 11); 'Our very natural attractions and aversions [. . .] present to the soul representations of what is best for us, inclining the agent to come to believe that doing whatever the attraction or aversion indicates actually is the best thing for the agent to do' (2015: 19). Brickhouse and Smith sometimes also describe this process in terms of causation (appetites can cause beliefs about what is best, see Brickhouse and Smith 2010: 53–62, 104; 2015: 11). Both 'causation' and 'inclination' are supposed to capture the same idea: Appetites lead to beliefs about what is best to do by default, unless some other belief-forming process intervenes (Brickhouse and Smith 2015: 19).

32. Jones (2012).

33. In order to be able to generate actions, these beliefs will have to present very specific actions as the best actions to do. Brickhouse and Smith do not give examples of such beliefs. However, in the case of a hoplite's fear, for example, they might suggest a belief such as 'throwing away my shield and running north up the mountain path is the best thing for me to do'.

34. Ravi Sharma has noted that the quoted passage (*Grg.* 480c–d) is dependent upon an antecedent of the form 'if oratory is to be used to expose wrongdoing'. He points out that the 'should' in 'wrongdoing should not be kept hidden' is thus a function of the way one must use oratory to accomplish that goal. Socrates is, then, not making a moral demand, and it is not clear that he is expressing his own view.

35. Fay Edwards (2016) has argued in support of Penner and Rowe's view that Socrates understands teaching as a form of punishment. Her argument focuses mainly on a puzzle in the *Euthyphro*: Socrates claims that if he were to gain knowledge of piety, Meletus should drop the charges of impiety because he will have been punished. But why would learning about piety secure Socrates' acquittal? Edwards argues that the answer lies in understanding instruction as punishment. If Socrates learns about piety, he will have been appropriately punished and there is no need to bring him to court. Edwards suggests that this result 'might encourage us to approach Socrates's statements about punishment in other dialogues, such as the *Gorgias* and *Protagoras*, with caution, as Penner and Rowe themselves suggest, as what Socrates means when he talks about punishment may not be what it, at first, seems' (2016: 18). Brickhouse and Smith have responded to Edwards, arguing that Socrates distinguishes between instruction and punishment: 'Socrates seeks education from Euthyphro that would make further pursuit of the prosecution against him otiose, but not because that education counts as a form of punishment, but because any errors Socrates may have made in the past are the sorts *that do not merit punishment*' (2017: 61).

36. Another possible explanation of Socrates' endorsement of punishment in the *Gorgias* is that this dialogue (either partially or completely) is not in fact 'Socratic' but instead is 'transitional', serving as a point of transition between Plato's early and middle dialogues (Irwin 1977: 291 n.33; 1995: 114). In his transitional dialogues, Plato uses Socrates more and more to express his own views. Thus, one could argue that it may be Plato, not Socrates, who endorses painful punishment.

37. How exactly does wrongdoing harm the soul? Brickhouse and Smith (2007a, 2013b: 204–207) discuss two possible explanations: Wrongdoing harms the soul because it leads the wrongdoer to acquire new false beliefs, or wrongdoing harms the soul because it leads the wrongdoer's appetites and passions to become less disciplined. They argue for the second explanation.

CHAPTER TEN

Socrates On Love

SUZANNE OBDRZALEK

INTRODUCTION: SOCRATES AS LOVER

In the famous Catalogue Aria of *Don Giovanni*, Leporello recounts how his master seduced 2,065 ladies in France, Germany, Italy, Turkey and Spain; reading Plato's Socratic dialogues, one gets the sense that, while he may have had few actual conquests, at least in terms of overall susceptibility to beauty, Socrates was not far behind.[1] In the *Charmides*, Socrates describes himself as a poor judge of youthful beauty because, like a broken yardstick, he finds almost all young men appealing (154b). In the *Symposium*, Alcibiades accuses Socrates of being 'crazy about beautiful boys; he constantly follows them around in a perpetual daze' (216d).[2] Though Socrates is famous for professing ignorance, there is one area where he trumpets his expertise: In the *Symposium*, he declares that the only thing he understands is *ta erōtika* (matters of love, 177d); in the *Lysis*, he describes himself as mean and useless in all else, but possessed of the god-given skill to recognise lovers and beloveds (204b–c).

Perhaps the most noteworthy of Socrates' infatuations was with Alcibiades: In the *Gorgias*, Socrates calls himself the dual lover of philosophy and of Alcibiades (481d). In the *Protagoras*, teased for hunting after the ripe Alcibiades, Socrates defends himself, alluding to Homer's observation that young men are at their most seductive when their beards are in first bloom (309a–b). However, Alcibiades was not the only youth to catch Socrates' eye: In the opening of the *Charmides*, Socrates famously describes himself as aflame with passion when he catches a glimpse beneath the boy's cloak.[3] This description is paralleled in Xenophon's *Symposium*, where Socrates describes the effect of rubbing his naked shoulder against Critobulos' as the bite of a wild beast, which leaves a sting in his heart (4.27–8). This depiction of Socrates is not confined to Plato and Xenophon; Dover cites a remark by Aristoxenos, that Socrates had strong heterosexual appetites, which he indulged, though without injustice (f. 55; Dover 1978: 153). Kahn alludes to a fragment from Phaedo's *Zopyrus*, in which the physiognomist concludes on the basis of Socrates' bulging eyes that he is a womaniser; Socrates acknowledges this as his native weakness, which he has mastered through rational training (1996: 11–12).

If we look more closely at these passages, something strange emerges. As the fragments from Phaedo and Aristoxenos already suggest, though Socrates may have had unusually strong sensual appetites, he seems to have had them firmly under control. In the *Symposium*, after mockingly comparing Socrates to the debauched Silenus, Alcibiades reveals that the boy-crazy exterior is just a veneer (216d–e). Alcibiades goes on to recount the humiliating story of his failed seduction of Socrates. In a striking inversion of pederastic convention,[4] Alcibiades becomes so infatuated with Socrates' wisdom and

230 THE BLOOMSBURY HANDBOOK OF SOCRATES

virtue that he is transformed into the lover, seeking to seduce Socrates, in order to trade physical for spiritual benefits. To this, Socrates replies:

> If I really have in me the power to make you a better man, then you can see in me a beauty that is really beyond description and makes your own remarkable good looks pale in comparison ... You seem to me to want more than your proper share: you offer me the merest appearance of beauty, and in return you want the thing itself, 'gold in exchange for bronze'.

> – 218d–e

This is echoed in Aeschines' *Alcibiades*, where Socrates rebukes Alcibiades for his vanity, and Alcibiades, reduced to tears, begs Socrates for help in becoming virtuous (cited in Kahn 1996: 19–23). Socrates declares that he had hoped that through keeping company with Alcibiades, *dia to eran* (through loving him), he might improve him. Kahn speculates:

> Perhaps [Aeschines] is saying in his simpler way ... what Plato indicates more explicitly in the Alcibiades speech: that what looked to the world like Socrates' flirtatious interest in handsome young men was in fact his way of focusing upon them the magnetic power of his own personality and thus drawing them to him 'through the power of love', instilling in them a desire to imitate in their own lives the philosophical pursuit of *aretē* which they saw in his.

> – 22–23

Supposing that Kahn is correct, that Socrates' flirtatious exterior is actually a means of seducing promising youths to philosophy, then we are left with a puzzle regarding Socrates' motivation. In classical Athens, pederastic relations typically had a transactional nature: Older male citizens offered their beloveds moral and physical training in exchange for sexual favours. Yet in taking on the cast of lover in order to draw boys to philosophy, Socrates' philosophical seduction appears unmotivated. The evidence does not suggest that Socrates was hoping to exchange philosophical for sexual favours.[5] And, while Socrates typically flatters his interlocutors, claiming that he hopes to gain wisdom from them, in the case of the very young and inexperienced – Lysis, Menexenus and Charmides come to mind – it seems unlikely that he could have believed they had much to teach him. Perhaps in engaging philosophically with these boys, Socrates is acting out of disinterested beneficence. But what prompts this? Why, as Socrates puts it, trade gold for bronze?

This worry becomes acute if we consider the theory of love and motivation that Vlastos and others locate in the *Lysis*. In his seminal paper, 'The Individual as Object of Love in Plato', Vlastos 1981a argues that Socrates' theory of love in the *Lysis* is a failure, since it is incapable of accommodating disinterested concern for the beloved. According to Vlastos, Socrates argues that 'if A loves B, he does so because of some benefit *he* needs from B and for the sake of just that benefit' (8). We are to love others only for the sake of our own possession of happiness and never for their own sakes. This leads us to be attracted to others who are beautiful and useful solely insofar as they are such, and to potentially abandon them should someone more beautiful or useful come along. As a consequence, 'Plato is scarcely aware of kindness, tenderness, compassion, concern for the freedom, respect for the integrity of the beloved, as essential ingredients in the highest type of interpersonal love' (30).

We can see why the *Lysis* lends itself to precisely this worry. In his opening elenchus with Lysis, Socrates concludes that we are not going to be loved by anyone insofar as we are useless (210c). In his subsequent discussion, Socrates rules out the possibility that

SOCRATES ON LOVE 231

good could love good on the grounds that the good are self-sufficient; he who is self-sufficient needs nothing and therefore loves nothing (215a–b). However, at the same time as the *Lysis* advances an egoistic analysis of love, its dramatic frame problematises this very theory. The dialogue begins with Socrates demonstrating to Hippothales how to seduce a haughty boy, and he succeeds in eliciting Lysis' and Menexenus' friendship: The boy is described as turning to Socrates *paidikōs kai philikōs* (in a playful and friendly manner, 211a); Socrates addresses Menexenus as *ō phile hetaire* (dear friend, 213b); and the dialogue concludes with Socrates describing himself, Lysis and Menexenus as friends (223b).[6] Socrates' method of seduction is to demonstrate to Lysis that he is ignorant and therefore needy; by humbling the boy, Socrates makes him vulnerable to his advances. But this leads us to question Socrates' motives. On the one hand, if Lysis is knowledgeable, then, in convincing him that he is ignorant, Socrates advances his own interests, but also emerges as a disturbingly manipulative character. On the other hand, if, as is more plausible, Lysis is ignorant, then Socrates does him a service in revealing to him his need for knowledge. But if Lysis is ignorant then, according to Socrates' own theory, he has nothing to offer Socrates, and we are left to wonder what Socrates' motives are in seeking friendship with the boy and in benefitting him via the elenchus.[7]

In this chapter, I focus on what has come to be called the Vlastos problem, the question of whether the theory of love that Socrates advances in the *Lysis* can allow for love of other persons, and whether it can allow for a form of such love that is not problematically egoistic. In the first part of this chapter, I concentrate on the dialogue itself. I begin by offering a close examination of Socrates' initial elenchus with Lysis, leading to the question of whether Lysis' parents love him. I then turn to Socrates' positive account of the *philos* (lover, friend),[8] agreeing with those interpreters who take Socrates to endorse the proposal that the neither-good-nor-bad (henceforth NGNB) is *philos* to the good.[9] In the second part of this chapter, I address critical responses to Socrates' theory of love in the *Lysis*. I divide these into four groups:

1. those that deny the *Lysis* seeks to offer an account of the conscious motivations of the lover;
2. those that maintain it allows for non-egoistic love between persons;
3. those that concede it treats all love as egoistic, but attempt to reconcile this with contemporary intuitions regarding love as an other-regarding state;
4. those that, like Vlastos, reject Socrates' theory as implausibly and repellently egoistic.

I argue against the first group that the *Lysis* clearly seeks to offer an account of the lover's motives. I contend against the second group that the *Lysis* does contain an egoistic theory of love, and against the third, that this theory cannot be reconciled easily with contemporary intuitions. I conclude by suggesting, against the last group, that while Socrates' theory may strike us as repellent, it is not without explanatory power.

DO LYSIS' PARENTS LOVE HIM?

The *Lysis* opens with Socrates questioning Lysis in order to demonstrate to Hippothales how to humble a boy, making him receptive to one's advances. Socrates begins by asking Lysis whether his parents love him, eliciting the admission that they do love him and therefore want him to be as happy as possible. Socrates then proposes that happiness is being free to do whatever one pleases. However, Lysis' parents do not let him do as he pleases in most areas: They trust their charioteer, not Lysis, with their horses, their muleteer with their mules and will not let him anywhere near his mother's loom. On the other hand, in areas where Lysis does have knowledge, such as reading, writing and playing the lyre, his parents give him free rein. Socrates extrapolates that if Lysis possesses the relevant knowledge, his neighbours will allow him to manage their estates and the Athenians their affairs. Even the Great King will trust Lysis rather than his own son to treat his son's eyes if Lysis has medical expertise. If Lysis becomes wise, everyone will be *philos* to him because he will be useful and good; if he remains ignorant, then Lysis will be no one's *philos*, and no one will love him, not even his parents. Socrates concludes by observing that Lysis is in need of mental training; the implication is painfully obvious: Lysis lacks knowledge, and so is not loved, even by his parents.

This conclusion has, nonetheless, been resisted by most interpreters, who find it so morally repellent and psychologically implausible that they conclude Socrates cannot be serious. Price, for example, argues that, just as we are not to believe that the Great King would entrust Lysis with his possessions, so we should not take seriously the proposal that Lysis' parents do not love him (2004: 3); Robinson, similarly, suggests that the passage is an exaggerated homily, which needs to be taken with a grain of salt (1986: 69 n. 15).[10] Vlastos is the notable exception to this trend. Vlastos observes that Socrates' conclusion at 210c–d, that no one will love Lysis insofar as Lysis is useless, does not necessarily imply that Lysis must benefit his parents in order to be loved by them; it is possible that Socrates means they wish him to be wise in order that he may benefit himself (1981a: 7–8). However, Vlastos argues that at 213e and 215b–c Socrates advances a purely egoistic model of love, which makes no room for wishing Lysis well for his own sake. In that case, the conclusion stands, that Lysis' parents only love him insofar as he is useful to them; since he is not yet wise, they cannot love him very much.[11]

Before turning to arguments suggesting that Lysis' parents do love him after all, it is worth emphasising that interpretative charity does not demand we interpret the *Lysis* such that Socrates does not advance a utilitarian model of parental love. Plato is a great philosopher, but as the *Republic* demonstrates, he has highly unconventional views regarding interpersonal and familial relations.[12] While these views might be unattractive to us, they do not mire him in the sort of conceptual or logical confusion that, as sympathetic interpreters, we should avoid attributing to him.

Nonetheless, it seems most likely to me that Socrates does hold that Lysis' parents love him. The reasons for this emerge if we look more closely at his elenchus with Lysis. First, consider the unfavourable comparison of Lysis to his parents' muleteer. If Socrates is in fact endorsing a biconditional claim at 210d that one is loved if and only if one has knowledge, then it would emerge that Lysis' parents love their slaves more than Lysis, given that the slaves have greater expertise. Given Athenian attitudes toward slaves, it seems unlikely that Socrates actually thinks that Lysis' parents love their slaves more than Lysis; he thus cannot be serious when he concludes: 'It seems, then, that [Lysis'] parents think more even of a slave than their own son' (208b). Turn next to Socrates' observation that Lysis' parents do not let him rule his own self (208c). What could their motive be? They do not let him do as he wishes with his mother's loom for fear that he may damage it; by analogy, they do not let him govern himself for fear that he may harm himself. This makes sense only if they value him highly. This, in turn, should cause us to recognise that in the case of the horses and mules, the most plausible reason why they prevent Lysis from having his way with the animals is not that they fear he will damage the animals, but,

SOCRATES ON LOVE 233

rather, that they fear the animals will damage him. Finally, when Socrates observes that Lysis' parents let him do as he wishes when it comes to reading and playing the lyre, we have reason to question whether his expertise in these areas can really be the basis of their love for him; if this were so, they would have even more reason to love a scribe or musician.

Later in the dialogue, Socrates refers twice to cases of parental love that are in apparent tension with his initial exchange with Lysis. At 212e–3a, Socrates observes that newborn infants are dearest of all things to their parents. If Lysis is useless, how much more so a crying infant. And at 219d–20a, Socrates describes a father who values his son more highly than all his possessions; this father's supreme regard for his son causes him to value other things derivatively – for example, he would value a cup if it contained an antidote to some hemlock his son had drunk. This passage calls to mind the example of the Great King and suggests that if Lysis' medical knowledge makes the Great King value him, this is only because he values his son even more, despite his son's medical ignorance.[13]

Where does this leave us? Do Lysis' parents love him or not? In assessing Socrates' initial elenchus with Lysis, we are left with the following interpretative options:

1. Lysis' parents do not love him;
2. Lysis' parents do love him, but their love is not grounded in utility;
3. Lysis' parents love him with a love grounded in utility; Lysis is useful to his parents in some way as yet to be determined;
4. Socrates is in a state of *aporia* regarding the nature of Lysis' parents' love for him.

I have raised considerations that cast doubt on the first option. In order to decide between the remaining three, we must first determine what, if any, positive account of love Socrates offers.

SOCRATES' POSITIVE PROPOSAL

As Santas observes, the *Lysis* is, formally at least, an aporetic dialogue: Socrates entertains, then attacks a number of hypotheses concerning who is the *philos*, and the best we can do as interpreters is to speak, speculatively, of the favoured hypothesis (1988: 81). Before considering what this may turn out to be, it will be helpful to offer an overview of the remainder of the dialogue. After revealing to Lysis that his ignorance renders him unworthy of love, Socrates turns his attention to Menexenus, asking him the question that remains the focus for the remainder of the dialogue – who is the *philos*? Is it the one loving, the one loved or both? Menexenus initially opts for both, so long as one of them loves the other. Socrates replies that if this is sufficient for both to be *philoi* (friends), then, absurdly, it will turn out that one can be *philos* to someone who hates him. Menexenus therefore proposes that both are *philoi*, but only if they love one another. Socrates retorts that this precludes the possibility of there being horse-lovers, quail-lovers and even philosophers, people who love objects that cannot possibly reciprocate their affection. Menexenus' third proposal is that what is loved is *philos* to that which loves; however, since the beloved can hate the one loving, this returns us to the absurdities of his first proposal. Finally, Menexenus suggests that a lover is a friend to the beloved; again, this leads to the possibility that one might be a *philos* to an enemy.

Having reached *aporia* with Menexenus, Socrates returns to questioning Lysis. Appealing to the poets, Socrates suggests that like is friend to like. But if this is correct, then bad will be friend to bad; this is impossible, since the bad do one another injustice. Perhaps, then, only the good are friend to the good. Socrates rejects this for two, related reasons. First, insofar as the good are alike, they cannot benefit one another, and so cannot be friends. Second, the good are, by definition, self-sufficient; he who is self-sufficient lacks nothing and therefore loves nothing. Socrates next considers the opposite possibility, that unlikes are friends. This, however, fails for the familiar reason that a friend will then be friend to an enemy.

There is one possibility they have overlooked: that that which is neither good nor bad is a friend to the good. Just as a sick man is friend of a doctor on account of sickness and for the sake of health, so, more generally, the NGNB is a friend of the good on account of the presence of the bad and for the sake of the good. Socrates takes issue with this account for two reasons. First, according to this proposal, all friendships arise from some cause and exist for the sake of some end. If this end, in turn, is the friend of something else, then this would lead to an infinite regress; Socrates therefore posits a terminus for this telic chain, a *prōton philon* (first friend, henceforth FF) for the sake of which all other friends are friends, but that is not, itself, the friend of anything further. In that case, all the dependent friends turn out to be false friends; only the FF is truly a friend. Second, this account assumes that all friendship occurs on account of the presence of some bad. However, Socrates maintains that there would be friendship even if there were no bad. In that case, there must be some other cause of friendship. Socrates ends the dialogue by proposing that desire is this cause. Since we all desire what we lack, that is, what has been taken from us, the object of friendship is revealed to be the *oikeion* (what is one's own).[14] Socrates concludes by observing that they may have something useful to say about friendship if there is a difference between being *oikeion* and being alike. However, the two boys miss this warning: When asked whether the good is *oikeion* to everyone, or whether good is *oikeion* to good, bad to bad and NGNB to NGNB, they opt for the latter; this mires them, again, in the incoherence of good being friend to good et cetera. Since they have eliminated all possible candidates for the *philos*, the dialogue ends in *aporia*.

Most interpreters assume that Socrates endorses some version of the thesis that the NGNB is friend to the good. Before turning to such interpretations, I will first consider a few alternate proposals. There are very few interpreters who locate any other positive analysis of friendship in the *Lysis*. One exception is Hoerber. In 'Plato's *Lysis*' (1959), Hoerber argues that according to the *Lysis*, the highest form of friendship is mutual friendship between the good.[15] The difficulty with Hoerber's argument is that he can only adduce the most tenuous textual support. According to Hoerber, Plato's ostensible reason for rejecting the reciprocal analysis of friendship is that it cannot account for usages such as *quail-lover* and *philosopher*, where the friendship is non-mutual.[16] However, Hoerber maintains that Plato rejects Menexenus' proposal that the lover is the *philos* because this would allow for contexts where friendship is non-mutual; Plato is thus indicating that friendship is necessarily mutual, and we can therefore disregard his argument against the reciprocal hypothesis (21–22). Against Hoerber, Plato's issue with the proposal that the lover is the *philos* is not that this might lead to non-mutual friendship, but, more problematically, that it might lead to friendship with an enemy. Furthermore, Hoerber's argument that we should disregard Socrates' argument opposing reciprocal friendship cuts both ways; perhaps we can deploy the argument opposing reciprocal friendship as evidence for disregarding Socrates' objections to one-way friendship. Hoerber adds that, in listing the views that have been refuted at the end of the dialogue, Socrates ignores

SOCRATES ON LOVE   235

reciprocal friendship. Against Hoerber, the very last substantive philosophical point Socrates makes in the dialogue is that good cannot be friend to good (222d).

A more plausible alternative to Hoerber is the proposal that, far from advancing any positive account of friendship, the *Lysis* is genuinely aporetic. Two prominent proponents of this view are Robinson and Mackenzie.[17] According to Robinson (1986), the aporetic conclusion of the dialogue stems from Plato's ignoring an ambiguity in the sense of *philos*: One sense of the term applies to those engaged in a reciprocal relationship between humans, while another refers to what makes some object valuable.[18] Plato's error is to analyse human friendship in terms of this second sense of *philos*, to assume that people are valuable in the same way as objects; as a result, he is unable to explain the reciprocal aspect of friendship. While we can see why the NGNB should be friend to the good, it is left unclear why the good should reciprocate this affection. Robinson's argument assumes that human friendship is necessarily a mutual relation and that Plato took it to be such, but neither claim is obvious.[19] Robinson appeals to passages from Xenophon and Aristotle to establish that the Greeks took friendship to be necessarily reciprocal (67–68); however, Aristotle's emphasis on reciprocity (at, for example, *NE* 1155b–6a) can be seen as a rebuttal of Plato's allowing for non-reciprocal cases of friendship (at 212d–e). In fact, in the *Laws*, Plato distinguishes two kinds of *philia*, between equals and unequals, and specifies that the latter is rarely reciprocal (837a–b): Reciprocity does not appear to be a requirement on *philia* for Plato. To turn to the *Lysis*, Plato deliberately sets the dialogue in an erotic context, and depicts Hippothales' *erōs* for Lysis as one-sided. Why, then, is it out of the question that Plato should allow for cases of *philia* that are one-sided as well, particularly since he emphasises non-reciprocal cases of *erōs* at 212b–c, and at 221b claims that *erōs* entails *philia*?

In her ingenious paper, 'Impasse and Explanation: from the *Lysis* to the *Phaedo*' (1988), Mackenzie proposes that the dialogue contains 'a complex structure of thesis and counter-thesis, which end without resolution and with no hint of a saving clause' (31). In particular, the proposal that the NGNB is friend of the good is undermined by the argument that there would be friendship even if there were no bad; the thesis that all friendship is for the sake of some FF is attacked by the arguments that the good is loved for the sake of the bad and that desire is the ultimate cause of friendship; the claim that desire is what explains friendship is countered by the suggestion that friendship is explained by some feature in the beloved, which renders it *oikeion* (one's own); and, finally, the thesis that all friendship is directed at the *oikeion* is rejected because this amounts to the previously rejected proposal that friendship is felt by like for like. Against Mackenzie, not all of her counter-theses need be construed as such, and it is not clear that the dialogue ends with 'no hint of a saving clause'. Socrates' argument that friendship would persist in the absence of the bad does nothing to undermine his proposal that the NGNB is *philos* to the good, only the additional clause, that it is *philos* on account of the bad. The claim that all friendship originates in desire does not contradict the thesis that it is all directed toward the FF. Similarly, the proposals that friendship is due to desire and that it is directed towards the *oikeion* are not clearly incompatible. Finally, the collapse of the proposal that *philia* is felt for the *oikeion* into the previously rejected hypothesis that like is friend to like is due to an argumentative error on the part of Lysis and Menexenus, an error of which Socrates clearly warns them at 222b. While the dialogue may formally end in *aporia*, if anything, Plato implies at 222b that Socrates is far from stumped.

Most interpreters take Socrates to endorse some version of what I shall call the NGNB thesis, the thesis that the NGNB is *philos* to the good.[20] There is, I believe, substantial

236   THE BLOOMSBURY HANDBOOK OF SOCRATES

evidence that Socrates subscribes to the NGNB thesis. First, consider the manner in which it is introduced (see Penner and Rowe 2005: 243–244). The first phase of the investigation into what is the *philos* centres on Menexenus' replies to the alternatives Socrates poses to him, and the second examines answers given by the poets. But the third and final phase of the dialogue, in which the NGNB thesis is introduced, begins in a striking manner. It is *Socrates* who notes that they have overlooked the possibility that the NGNB is friend to the good. He then announces his intention to wax prophetic (*apomanteuomenos*) and asks Lysis to listen to his mantic sayings (*ha de legōn manteuomai*). That Plato should place the NGNB thesis in the mouth of Socrates and draw attention to it by comparing it to an oracular utterance demands explanation; the most plausible is that Plato is signalling that this is the hypothesis Socrates treats most seriously.

According to the NGNB thesis, friendship aims at the good; the example of the sick body suggests that it is directed toward one's own good. This conception of friendship as grounded in utility is repeatedly endorsed earlier in the dialogue. In his elenchus with Lysis, Socrates concludes that we are loved if and only if we are wise and hence useful to others (210c–d). In rejecting the proposal that good is friend to good, Socrates produces two arguments, both of which rely on the assumption that friendship aims at benefitting oneself: The argument that likes cannot be friends because, being alike, they cannot benefit one another; and the argument that the good cannot be friends because, being self-sufficient, they can be of no use to one another.

Finally, at the conclusion of the dialogue, Socrates tells his friend, 'Wanting to review the argument, I said, "It seems to me, Lysis and Menexenus, that if there is some difference between belonging and being like, then we might have something to say about what a friend is"' (222b). This suggests that, so long as we do not commit Lysis' and Menexenus' error of identifying the *oikeion* (one's own) with the *homoion* (like), on Socrates' own telling, we will have a plausible account of friendship. Socrates goes on to list all the accounts of friendship that have been rejected; as Tessitore (1990: 128) and Gonzalez (2000: 394 and 2003: 31) note, the suggestion that the NGNB is friend to the good is conspicuously absent from this list.

Apart from evidence internal to the *Lysis*, there are suggestive parallels of the NGNB thesis to claims that Plato appears to endorse in other dialogues. Kahn (1996: 266–267), Rowe (2000: 205–211) and Versenyi (1975: 194) all emphasise parallels to the *Symposium*. In the *Symposium*, Plato makes the following claims, all of which echo statements made in the *Lysis*:

1. Love is directed at some object (*Symp.* 199d; cf. *Ly.* 221c);
2. This object is something the lover lacks (*Symp.* 200a–b; cf. *Ly.* 221d–e);
3. This object is the beautiful or the good (*Symp.* 201a–c; cf. *Ly.* 216d);
4. Something can be neither good nor bad (*Symp.* 201e–2b; cf. *Ly.* 217e);
5. That which loves is neither good nor bad (*Symp.* 204a–b; cf. *Ly.* 216d);
6. There must be a terminus to desire, which is not desired for the sake of anything else; this terminus is the good (*Symp.* 204d–5a; cf. *Ly.* 219c–20b).

Conjoined, these claims give us the view that that which is neither good nor bad loves the good that it lacks, a good that is not desired for the sake of anything further. Though less striking, there are also parallels to the *Gorgias*, where Plato draws a distinction between the good, the bad and the NGNB (467e–8a), and maintains that people pursue the NGNB for the sake of the good (468a–b; see Robinson 1986: 75). As Rowe notes, on their own,

SOCRATES ON LOVE

these parallels perhaps do not offer decisive evidence for what, if any, positive proposals Socrates advances in the *Lysis*, but when conjoined with evidence internal to the dialogue, they strongly suggest that the NGNB thesis is Socrates' own (2000: 210–211).

INTERPRETATIVE PROBLEMS FOR THE POSITIVE PROPOSAL

Suppose we follow the majority of interpreters in taking the NGNB thesis to be Socrates' favoured proposal. This still leaves us with a number of interpretative questions. Does Socrates hold that the NGNB loves the good on account of the bad? What is the FF? Can there be more than one FF? And, finally, in what sense, if any, is the dialogue aporetic?

The Role of the Bad

When Socrates first introduces the NGNB thesis, his proposal is that the NGNB is friend of the good *on account of the presence of the bad*. Socrates goes on to reject this last clause for two reasons. First, Socrates argues that if we identify the bad with the enemy, then we arrive at the paradoxical result that, whereas all other friends are loved for the sake of a friend, the good is loved for the sake of an enemy. As many scholars note, this argument is baffling: In it, Socrates slides from saying, unproblematically, that the good is loved on account of (*dia*) the bad, to advancing the questionable claim that the good is loved for the sake of (*heneka*) the bad.

There have been several attempts to salvage Socrates' argument. Mackenzie proposes that Socrates is driven to this position because, as the end of a chain of consequential goods, the good cannot be loved for the sake of some further good; in that case, the only possibility is that it is loved for the sake of the bad. In advancing this paradoxical result, Socrates is implying that if we posit the FF as what is lovable in itself, we fail to explain its value (1988: 43–44). Though this proposal is intriguing, it is somewhat far-fetched. To object that the good is loved for the sake of the bad would be a highly indirect way of indicating the explanatory vacuity of positing the FF; furthermore, this opens the question of why Socrates has no qualms about assigning the good the role of first principle in the *Republic*. Penner and Rowe have suggested that when Socrates claims that the good is loved for the sake of the bad, what he really means is that it is loved for the sake of *getting rid of* the bad (2005: 134). The difficulty with this proposal is that it does not lend itself to the opposition between the FF and all the other friends that Socrates alludes to at 220d–e, since all of the dependent friends are also loved for the sake of getting rid of the bad. While it is dissatisfying to attribute such an elementary error to Socrates, in the absence of a better explanation, it is perhaps best to side with interpreters such as Santas, who accuse Socrates of confusing the *dia* and *heneka* relations (1988: 86).

Socrates' second reason for rejecting the role of the bad is his insistence that we would love the good even if there were no bad. Socrates imagines a world in which the bad did not exist; in such a world, we would still experience desires such as hunger. Hunger is sometimes beneficial, sometimes harmful; if the bad were abolished, bad hunger would disappear with it, but beneficial hunger would remain. Desire entails love; thus, if desire can occur in the absence of the bad, the same follows for *philia*. This argument is taken more seriously by interpreters; Santas concludes, on its basis, that *philia* is not reliant on the presence of the bad (1988: 86).[21] However, it is just as unsound as its predecessor. Just because hunger is beneficial, it does not follow that we can feel it in the absence of the

238 THE BLOOMSBURY HANDBOOK OF SOCRATES

bad. Even if hunger is, typically, the beneficial awareness of the body's lack of food, it is still the awareness of a bad state – lacking food. More generally, given Socrates' analysis of love and desire as grounded in lack, if we grant that lack is a bad state, then it is hard to see how these could ever occur in the absence of the bad (see Bolotin 1989: 225). Socrates appears quite sincere in rejecting the role of the bad in his account: The objection is of his own devising; is unrefuted; and is introduced in a striking manner when, at 218c–d, he shouts out that his arguments are imposters. It thus seems best to follow Versenyi in concluding that Socrates' rejection of the role of the bad is an argumentative error, which he would have done well to avoid (1975: 196).

The First Friends

What is the first friend? Plato clearly gives us a preliminary answer – the good; however, it is unclear whether he has any more substantive account to offer. Some scholars propose that the FF is the form of the good.[22] They appeal to parallels between the status of the FF as the only thing that is truly a friend and the role of the form of the good in the *Republic* as the first principle. They take Plato's discussion of *parousia* (participation) at 217c–18b to offer further confirmation that the theory of forms is operative in the dialogue. However, as Mackenzie notes, the *parousia* relation Socrates introduces in the *Lysis* is quite different from that which is part of the theory of forms (1988: 32–33).[23]

More persuasively, interpreters have suggested that the FF is happiness, virtue and/or wisdom. All of these proposals are plausible in light of evidence external to the *Lysis*; however, they are completely lacking in direct textual support internal to the dialogue. The suggestion that it is happiness, for example, advanced by Irwin (1977: 52), Vlastos (1981a: 10–11), Wolfsdorf (2007: 253–256) and others (see Versenyi 1975: 195), while attractive, has no support from within the *Lysis* – at most, we might take Socrates' claim that Lysis and Menexenus are happy since they have friends (212a) to imply that friendship is desired for the sake of happiness. Roth (1995: 17–18) has argued that the FF is virtue (see also Bolotin 1989: 193 and Guthrie 1975: 145). According to Roth, at 218a–b, Socrates states that wisdom is to ignorance and the soul as medicine is to disease and the body. The FF stands in relation to the soul as health stands in relation to the body; we can conclude, therefore, that the FF is virtue. *Contra* Roth, Plato does not state at 218a–b that wisdom is to the soul as health is to the body; in this passage, Socrates only claims that the non-terminally ignorant desire wisdom. Furthermore, at 219c, Socrates suggests that we value health for the sake of something else; if virtue is indeed analogous to health, then it, too, is valued for the sake of some further good and is not the FF.

Penner and Rowe argue at length for identifying the FF with wisdom, offering two passages as evidence for their position (2005: 143–153, 273–275; see also Tessitore 1990: 128). First, at 218a–b, Plato gives philosophers as an example of those who love the good on account of the presence of the bad. It is true that this passage implies that wisdom is *a good*, but it does not establish that wisdom is *the good*, that is, the FF. The passage occurs before Plato introduces the FF; as Penner and Rowe concede (274–275), Plato also refers to the desire for health, but we are not to conclude on this basis that health is the FF. Second, at the conclusion of the dialogue, Plato implicitly identifies the FF with the *oikeion* (what is one's own); Penner and Rowe treat this as a deliberate allusion to the opening of the dialogue, where Socrates concludes that wisdom makes all things *hēmetera* (our own). Against Penner and Rowe, in the conclusion of the dialogue, the *philon* is not identified with that which *makes* things *oikeia*, but with the *oikeion*,

SOCRATES ON LOVE

239

simpliciter. By contrast, in the opening discussion, wisdom is what *makes* things useful and *hēmetera*. If wisdom is what makes things useful, then it appears that it is a means to the FF rather than the FF itself. Penner and Rowe concede this objection, but insist that wisdom can still be identified with the FF, since it is always a means to the FF (275–276). However, nowhere in the dialogue does Plato draw a distinction between means that sometimes lead to the FF and means that always lead to the FF. In sum, then, Socrates does not appear to offer any positive account of the FF in the *Lysis*, beyond identifying it with the good.[24]

Multiple First Friends?

The question of what the FF is lends itself to a related concern, whether there can be multiple FFs. This will be important later in this chapter, when we turn to the question of whether people can function as FFs, and so be loved for their own sakes. Again, the text gives us no clear answer. Many interpreters, such as Annas (1977: 538)[25] and Irwin (1977: 51–52), accuse Socrates of committing the error of concluding, on the basis of the fact that there cannot be an infinite chain of dependent friends, that there can be only one FF. However, Plato nowhere states that there can be only one FF; the best evidence for their criticism is the fact that Plato always refers to the FF in the singular. Those who hold that there can be multiple FFs can accommodate this fact. Even if Plato refers to the FF in the singular and identifies it with the good, the good may have many constituents, each of which is an FF.[26]

Mackenzie has argued that when Plato describes a father as valuing a cup full of healing wine for the sake of his son, whom he values above all else, Plato is not merely providing an analogy, but is actually giving an example of the relation of a dependent *philon* to the FF (1988: 35). If the father can have two sons, presumably he can have two FFs; anything that one legitimately values for its own sake will turn out to be a FF (see Versenyi 1975: 192–193). Against this proposal, Penner and Rowe argue that the son is an analogue to, and not an example of, the FF (2005: 141–142). They emphasise that Plato only refers to the father as valuing his son, and not to the son being a *philos* to the father. However, as Mackenzie observes, Plato seems to hold that there is a close relation between valuing something and viewing that thing as a *philos* (see, for example, 215a, 215b–c, 215d). More persuasively, Penner and Rowe note that at 220a, Socrates asks, 'Isn't the same account true of the friend?' If the son were truly a FF to his father, then this phrasing would be odd; it would be more natural to say, 'Isn't the same account true of all friends?' In defence of Mackenzie, it is implausible that the father should value his son above all else, but that his son should fail to be an FF for the father; if the son is a dependent friend, loved for the sake of the father's happiness, then the father would not, in fact, value his son above all else.

Aporia

As my discussion of the FF has suggested, even if the *Lysis* contains a core positive view, Socrates leaves much unresolved. This enables us to offer a tentative answer to our fourth question: In what sense, if any, is the dialogue aporetic? I argued earlier that the dialogue contains a positive proposal, the NGNB thesis. Nonetheless, there are still strong indications that it is, in some way, aporetic (see Mackenzie 1988: 15). Socrates begins by claiming that he is so far from possessing a friend that he does not know how people become friends (212a), and concludes by noting that, while he takes himself, Lysis and

Menexenus to be friends, he still does not know what a friend is (223b). It would therefore be preferable to come up with some deeper explanation of the aporetic conclusion of the dialogue than the boys' error. Plato has them err for a reason, and to attribute this to an attachment to the formal structure of the aporetic dialogue is unsatisfying. The most persuasive explanation is that the dialogue is aporetic because Socrates has not yet discovered what the FF is (see Bordt 2000: 171; Gonzalez 1995: 81; Mackenzie 1988: 36–37; Penner and Rowe 2005: 187–188; Rowe 2000: 215 and Tessitore 1990: 124–125). Even if it is the good, Socrates does not tell us what the good is. Socrates maintains that dependent goods are imposters because they pretend to be valuable for their own sakes, while they are actually valuable only for the sake of the FF (219d–220b). If we do not know what the FF is, then we do not know what the dependent goods are valuable for; in that case, we will not know why they are valuable, and they will remain phantom goods. However, if this is the true source of Socrates' *aporia*, then we are left to wonder why Plato does not have the dialogue founder on these grounds, rather than on the conflation of the *oikeion* (what is one's own) with the *homoion* (the same).

THE VLASTOS OBJECTION

As I mentioned in the opening of this chapter, Socrates' theory of love has been subject to an influential line of attack by Vlastos (1981a); subsequent critical work on the dialogue is, in large part, a response to Vlastos.[27] Vlastos' overall critique of the Socratic theory is that it is problematically egoistic: We are to love others only insofar as they contribute to our own good, and not for their own sakes. Further difficulties emerge when Vlastos turns to Plato's theory of love in the *Symposium*. On this theory, we love others only insofar as they instantiate admirable qualities, such as beauty and goodness, qualities that are perfectly exemplified only by forms. While I follow Vlastos in not finding the theory of forms in the *Lysis*, if we assume that in the *Lysis* people are to be loved for their possession of useful qualities, then many of the objections Vlastos raises against the Platonic theory in the *Symposium* apply to the Socratic theory of the *Lysis* as well. According to Vlastos, if love is solely responsive to valuable qualities in the beloved, then we fail to love him for his true self, for 'the uniqueness and integrity of his or her individuality' (31). Furthermore, we fail to do justice to his subjectivity; we treat him as we might an object – to love persons as 'objectifications of excellence is to fail to make the thought of them as *subjects* central to what is felt for them in love' (32). Finally, should a person with more valuable qualities come along, we would be rationally obliged to trade up.

Before I turn, in the next section, to discussing various responses to Vlastos' objection, I will spend the remainder of this section attempting to throw light on what, exactly, the objection amounts to. There is a tendency to run together a number of distinct objections to utility-based love: that it is egoistical, that it is not directed at the beloved's true self, that it is potentially transient, that it does not involve a desire to benefit the beloved for his own sake, et cetera. Carefully exploring and distinguishing these will help us to get a better sense of what, exactly, the charges are against Socrates, whether these charges are legitimate and whether he can meet them.[28]

The broadest charge critics raise against Socrates is that of *egoism* (see Irwin 1977: 99–100). Consider two lovers – call them Romeo and Juliet. According to this objection, on the Socratic theory, Romeo loves Juliet only insofar as Juliet contributes to Romeo's own good. Penner and Rowe offer a helpful refinement: The charge of egoism can be

SOCRATES ON LOVE 241

distinguished from that of *selfishness* (2005: 289–290).[29] Socrates' theory is selfish if, in addition to being egoistic, it claims that the good at which love aims is necessarily a state of the lover, such as pleasure; in that case, the good of Juliet can only ever play an instrumental, but not a constitutive, role in Romeo's good. Thus, a theory could be egoistic but not selfish, if it allowed that the well-being of Juliet is a constituent of Romeo's good, independently of the contribution her well-being makes to his psychological state. What, exactly, is the problem with egoism? The worry might be that Romeo would not love Juliet if she did not contribute to his own good. Call this the charge of egoism proper. Alternately, the problem might be that Romeo does not love Juliet for her own sake; call this worry *instrumentalism*.[30] Though this might appear identical to the first concern, in fact they are distinct. For example, it is possible that Romeo might not love Juliet if she did not contribute to his good, but that the love generated by her contribution to his good causes him to love her for her own sake as well as his own, with the proviso that, should she cease to contribute to his good, his other-directed concern would vanish. Conversely, it is possible that Romeo might love Juliet whether or not she contributes to his good, but that his love does not involve valuing her for her own sake; self-destructive love often takes precisely this form.

The instrumentalism objection contains a core ambiguity: It is not obvious what, exactly, it means to love the beloved for his own sake. Vlastos is inconsistent on this issue. In the opening of his paper, he suggests that to love the beloved for his own sake is to wish for his good independently of its contribution to one's own good (4–6). However, Vlastos goes on to speak of the philosopher as loving the forms for their own sakes (34), and it is unclear how he could possibly hope to benefit them. Relatedly, Vlastos objects that in loving the beloved as an instantiation of good qualities, we fail to value him for his own sake (31–34). This might suggest that to love the beloved for his own sake is to value him for those qualities that constitute his true essence. These two issues are frequently linked: Often the reason we fail to wish for another's good for his own sake is because we fail to love him for those qualities that really matter, as opposed to the qualities that merely make him useful or pleasant to us. Nonetheless, the two worries are distinct. Let us call the concern that Socratic love does not involve wishing the beloved well for his own sake *instrumentalism*; I will refer to the second concern, that Socratic love fails to respond to the beloved's true self, *objectification*.

For Vlastos, part of what makes egoism worrisome is two potential consequences. The first is *interchangeability*: Insofar as Romeo loves Juliet for certain qualities she exemplifies, he has no more reason to love her than someone else who exemplifies these qualities equally, and he ought, rationally, to abandon her should a more attractive woman come along. As Kolodny observes, this is distinct from a second, related concern: *transience* (2003: 140–141). On transience, Romeo ought to cease loving Juliet should she cease to possess the qualities that made her initially lovable. Two additional concerns are *impersonalism* and *non-reciprocity*. According to Vlastos, in the *Lysis*, Socrates claims that whatever we love for the sake of the FF is not truly lovable. On the assumption that the FF is happiness or some other impersonal object, then Socrates' theory cannot accommodate other persons as objects of love. Relatedly, Robinson, among others, raises the concern that if we love something impersonal, or another person who is perfectly good, then Socrates' theory of love cannot do justice to the fact that love is typically a reciprocal relation (1986: 79). In the first case, reciprocity is a conceptual impossibility – happiness, wisdom and virtue cannot love you back; in the second case, it would be unmotivated – a perfectly good person needs nothing and, given egoism, can love nothing.

242 THE BLOOMSBURY HANDBOOK OF SOCRATES

Methodology

Before turning to critical responses to Vlastos' challenge, it will be helpful to emphasise certain methodological principles. Vlastos' attack on Socrates assumes that a correct theory of love will reveal it to be a reciprocal, other-regarding relation between two persons, in which each desires the other's good for his own sake; call this the *other-regarding theory of love*. It is unclear what, exactly, the status of this theory is. As a descriptive claim, it appears false: Most interpersonal love falls short of the other-regarding ideal, and some cases of love are completely selfish. As a normative claim, the other-regarding theory needs defence; however, this is typically not provided, and the theory is taken to be obviously true. Thus, our first interpretative constraint in assessing Socrates' theory of love is to avoid baldly assuming that either the normative or descriptive versions of the other-regarding theory is correct. Our second constraint is not to force Socrates to conform to the other-regarding theory on the grounds that it is normatively or descriptively correct. Even if the other-regarding theory is correct, this approach risks being grossly anachronistic and doing violence to Socrates' actual claims. The Greeks had quite different approaches to love – sexual and familial – than we do, and even if they did not, Socrates appears to have had views radically at odds with his community's. We should not allow according with contemporary intuitions – let alone a contemporary philosopher's construal of contemporary intuitions – to constrain our interpretation of Plato, and we should be open to the possibility that he has a position that may strike us as odd or even repellent.

Critical Assessment of Vlastos' Position

As I mentioned earlier, Vlastos' critique has served as the foundation for virtually all subsequent discussion of Socrates' theory of love. Some interpreters reject his critique on interpretative grounds. Of these, one group argues that Vlastos' attack mistakes the purpose of Socrates' theory: Socrates is not attempting to analyse the lover's motivations, and therefore cannot be accused of offering an egoistic theory of love. The second group argues that Socrates' theory is not necessarily egoistic; if persons can serve as the FF, then they can be loved for their own sakes. In contrast to these two approaches, other interpreters accept Vlastos' reading of Socrates' theory as egoistic. However, of these, one group maintains that, though the theory is egoistic, it is not at odds with contemporary intuitions about love. The second follows Vlastos in rejecting Socrates' theory as unacceptably egoistic.

Socrates offers a theory of value, not love The most prominent proponent of this approach is Glidden (1981).[31] According to Glidden, the charge of egoism Vlastos raises against Socrates is misdirected. In the *Lysis*, Socrates is not offering an account of the lover's subjective motivation; instead, he is advancing a general theory of value. As evidence for his position, Glidden notes that at 214b and 215e, Socrates emphasises the universal scope of his theory: He is not merely offering an account of interpersonal relations, but of what feature in anything, sentient or non-sentient, renders it *philos*. Glidden also argues that Socrates' claim, that anyone will turn himself over to Lysis if Lysis has knowledge (210a–b), would be absurd if it concerned conscious intentions; Socrates is discussing what is in people's interests, not what actually interests them. Insofar as Socrates offers a theory of desire, and not just of value, he does not examine desire as a conscious state of the agent, but as a subconscious psychological force; on Glidden's reading, Socrates is a forerunner of psychoanalytic theory.

SOCRATES ON LOVE 243

Against Glidden, even if Socrates is offering a theory that applies to impersonal objects, he is also proposing one that applies to persons. There is no reason to suppose that, as this theory applies to persons, it does not concern their conscious motivations: One key difference between persons and other animals is that persons are capable of deliberating about the good. The framing of the dialogue draws attention to the conscious motives that drive lovers and beloveds: Socrates is attempting to convince Lysis that he needs knowledge, so that he will become *philos* to Hippothales; on Glidden's theory, Lysis would need no convincing. In Socrates' initial elenchus with Lysis, he proposes that Lysis' parents *think more of* (*hēgountai peri pleionos*) a slave than their own son because they entrust their slave, and not Lysis, with their livestock (208b): He is reading Lysis' parents' conscious attitude toward Lysis off their behaviour. At 209c–d, Socrates states that Lysis' neighbours will entrust themselves and their goods to Lysis if they believe (*hēgēsētai*) that he has knowledge. Belief is a conscious state, and Glidden's proposal, that Socrates' claim is so preposterous that it must be ironic, is dismissive of the textual evidence. In rejecting the possibility of love between the good, Socrates states that it is a requirement on love that the lover think highly of (*peri pollou poioumenoi*) his beloved (215b–c); this claim clearly concerns the lover's assessment of the beloved's value, an assessment that serves as the motivation for love. Finally, in distinguishing the NGNB from the bad, Socrates says that the ignorant do not love wisdom because they do not believe they are lacking (218a–b). If Socrates is not concerned with the conscious intentions of lovers, then there should be no difference between the NGNB and the bad, since both are equally lacking; the gap between them lies in the fact that the NGNB *believes* that he is lacking. At any rate, even if Glidden is correct, and Socrates is not concerned with lovers' conscious motives, the theory would still be egoistic, since it claims that love aims solely at the good of the lover. Often the most egoistic are those who are unaware that they use others, but who are solely motivated by a (subconscious) desire for their own gain.

Socrates' theory of love is non-egoistic Numerous interpreters find the egoistic analysis of love so counter-intuitive that they offer alternative interpretations of the *Lysis*, on which Socrates' theory is non-egoistic.[32] One approach is to maintain that Socrates does in fact allow that love, or at least the best form of love, is felt by the good for the good. I have already discussed Hoerber's attempt to defend such a view. One of its earliest proponents is von Arnim, who distinguishes *philia* from *erōs*, and argues that *philia* is not occasioned by lack. *Philia* in its highest form is felt by the good for the good for their own sakes.[33] More recently, Kahn argues that Socrates is not serious in advancing a utility-based model of love and that he does, in fact, allow that love can occur between the good (1996: 282–284). Why should the good feel love? Rudebusch proposes that the good love others because this enables them to act beneficently on their prudential wisdom and thereby achieve happiness (2009: 193–194). Bordt suggests that the good love the form of the good and therefore desire to realise it in themselves and others, an aim that is furthered through friendship (2000: 170). Against these proposals, Socrates states quite clearly, on numerous occasions, that the good cannot love the good (215a–b, 222d). Furthermore, there is absolutely no evidence that Socrates gives up on the view that love is occasioned by lack: It is present from his initial elenchus with Lysis, when he proposes that Lysis will be loved only insofar as he is useful (210d), through to the conclusion of the dialogue, when he argues that the cause of love is desire occasioned by need (221d–e).

Another approach is to propose that love of the FF is, by its very nature, non-egoistic. Annas argues that Socrates' account of love in the *Lysis* appears egoistic only insofar as it seemingly maintains that all non-I-desires – desires whose propositional content does not make reference to 'I' – depend on I-desires (1977: 537–538). However, Socrates rejects this, since it would land him in an infinite regress of *teloi* (ends). He therefore introduces the FF, which is not loved for the sake of anything further. Where all other desires make reference to the lover, love of the FF does not derive from an I-desire (see also Curzer 2014: 362–364 and Gadamer 1980: 17–18). Against Annas, it is unclear why an infinite regress of *teloi* can be avoided only if the terminal object of desire makes no reference to the lover; why can't the FF be, say, the lover's happiness? Socrates' position will be non-egoistic only if the FF is not the lover's own good, but there is nothing to suggest that this is the case. Annas maintains that love of the FF is not grounded in lack; however, after introducing the FF, Socrates proposes that love is caused by desire for what the agent lacks (221d–e).

A final approach is to maintain that a beloved person can serve as the FF. If a beloved person is the FF, then we can avoid the objection that I raised against Annas, that the FF is the lover's own good. On this proposal, love might involve appreciating the worth of another person independently of his contribution to one's own well-being and desiring his good for its own sake.[34] There is little to suggest such a model of love in the dialogue, with the exception of Socrates' reference to the father who values his son above all else (219d–220a). If, as Mackenzie maintains, the son is an example of, and not merely an analogue to, the FF, then this would be a case of a person being valued for his own sake (1988: 35). However, it is difficult to reconcile this proposal with Socrates' need-based model of love, especially if we parse love of persons along the lines of Kantian respect for their rational natures. On the need-based model, we love others only insofar as we are lacking and they are useful to us; it is not obvious why this should give rise to respect for the rational nature of the beloved.

Even if we concede that Socrates allows for other-regarding love in the *Lysis*, it also appears that he allows for egoistic love, and this is sufficient to generate Vlastos' objection (see, for example, Adams 1992: 3, 6–7). There is much in the text to suggest that the egoistic model is at work. The analogy of love to sickness (217a–b) suggests a need-based model, on which love aims at fulfilling a lack in the agent; this is confirmed at the conclusion of the dialogue, when love is said to aim at what we lack (221d–e). Socrates argues that good cannot love good because the good need nothing and thus love nothing (215a–b). But if love is, in fact, respect for the inherent value of another person, then it is hard to see why the good cannot feel love. Finally, if we turn outside Plato, Xenophon provides further support that Socrates was thought to have advocated an egoistic theory of love. According to Xenophon, Socrates gave a lecture in which he maintained that friends are the most useful of all possessions, more useful than even a horse or an ox (*Mem.* 2.4–5). A good friend must therefore be cultivated like fruit on a tree; conversely, you should make yourself worth as much as possible to your friends, so that they will not betray you.

Socrates' theory of love is egoistic but not selfish   Given that the text strongly suggests an egoistic theory of love is at work, some interpreters seek to demonstrate that this is at least partially compatible with the other-regarding model. Thus, Penner and Rowe propose that a theory of love can be egoistic without being selfish if it holds that all love is motivated by concern for one's own happiness, but retains an expansive conception of

SOCRATES ON LOVE   245

happiness, on which the good of the beloved is closely linked to that of the lover (2005: 280–291).

There are two ways in which one could defend an egoistic but unselfish theory of love. The first would be to maintain that, while the lover's happiness is the FF, the beloved is somehow part of the lover's happiness. Lesses (1996: 38–40) has argued, against Irwin (1977: 85), that Socrates' model of valuation does not rule out constituent means. Building off of Lesses' argument, if a beloved person can serve as such a constituent means, then Socrates' theory can allow for valuing persons for their own sakes, while still advancing an egoistic analysis of love.[35] Against this, it is unclear what it would mean for a *person* to be a constituent of one's happiness: Logically, only states of affairs can play this role. Perhaps, then, it is the beloved's well-being, and not the beloved himself, that is a constituent of the lover's happiness. However, it is difficult to reconcile this with the need-based analysis of love. These difficulties can be bypassed if we posit, instead, that it is being in a loving relationship that serves as a constituent of the lover's good. This proposal is easy to align with the need-based analysis. Humans are characteristically lonely creatures, who need loving relationships with others in order to feel complete; forming such a relationship would thus satisfy a genuine need in the lover. Such a relationship could, in turn, give rise to genuine, other-regarding concern for the well-being of the beloved.[36]

This proposal faces several difficulties. First, it possesses many of the features that give rise to the kinds of objection Vlastos made: It is guilty of selfishness, instrumentalism, objectification and replaceability. If what the lover loves is being in a relationship, then it seems that his love is directed at his own good, and that he is treating the beloved as a mere means to that good. If asked why he loves the beloved, the lover would have to reply because he is lonely, or because he wishes to be in a relationship. But surely the beloved would be troubled to learn that he is merely a means to keeping loneliness at bay; he might feel that his lover does not really love *him*, that any suitable companion would do the trick. Second, it is doubtful that Socrates would allow that loving relationships ought to function as constituents of the FF. Though Socrates does not specify in the *Lysis* what the FF is, if we look to other dialogues, he typically maintains that we ought to aim at happiness, where this is equivalent to or strongly dependent on virtue. Relationships with others are valuable insofar as they are conducive to virtue – particularly via joint philosophical enquiry – but are never presented as constituents of happiness in themselves; I suspect Socrates would insist that to pursue such relationships for their own sakes and independently of their contribution to virtue is irrational and even morally irresponsible.

Penner and Rowe have therefore offered an alternate account of how love might be egoistic yet unselfish (2005: 280–291). On their model, the FF is happiness, where this is closely linked to wisdom. However, they maintain that such a model of love can avoid selfishness if the beloved person is treated as a high-level means to the lover's happiness. The beloved is a high-level means if he is 'rather a major premise in all calculations of [one's] good' (270). Even if the beloved is merely a means, this is not problematic, since Penner and Rowe contend that there are no conceivable circumstances in which the lover could secure his own good in conflict with that of his beloved (288).

Against Penner and Rowe, so long as the good of the beloved is valued as a means to some state of the lover, the model of love is selfish. Suppose that some parent thought that his happiness consisted in securing the admiration of his peers, and concluded that the only way to accomplish this was to promote the flourishing of his children. This parent's concern for the well-being of his children would be objectionably selfish, since he would value it only for the sake of his own good. Penner and Rowe might object that what makes this example unattractive is not that the good of the children is a mere means, but that the end in question is base. Perhaps if the end were something more admirable – say, wisdom – the love would no longer be objectionable. However, it seems that whatever the end, so long as it is a state of the lover, the beloved has grounds for complaint. Surely my beloved might be hurt if he learned that my primary reason for caring for him was that he is a mathematical genius with the ability to further my understanding of advanced algebra.

Second, once the beloved is a means to some other end, distinct from and independent of the good of the beloved, then the good of the lover and that of his beloved can always conflict. Suppose that, as Penner and Rowe maintain, the FF is wisdom. There are surely many possible circumstances in which the beloved might fail to be an optimal means to wisdom; in fact, according to Plato, the beloved will succeed in being an efficient means to wisdom only if he is a philosophical discussion-partner, and a very good one at that! This would render parental love, and many cases of friendship and romantic love, inexplicable and even dispensable. Penner and Rowe might reply that my understanding of wisdom is too narrow: There are important life-lessons to be gained from, say, raising a child. But even if there is something to be learned, it is not clear that one's pursuit of wisdom would not be better served by abandoning the child for the library, or at least a philosophical discussion-group. Perhaps one who would abandon his child so callously would reveal himself to be dangerously lacking in moral wisdom. Granting that, if wisdom is indeed the FF, then he is rationally obliged to pursue whatever means will most reliably and efficiently secure him wisdom, and it is at least conceivable that this may not be child-rearing. One difficulty raised by these sorts of possibilities is transience and replaceability: Should the beloved cease to serve the pursuit of wisdom, or should a more efficient means be discovered, the lover ought, rationally, to abandon his beloved. Another concern lies not in the expendability of the beloved, but in the motivation of the lover. So long as the lover's motivation is centred on his own psychological state – be it wisdom, virtue or mere pleasure – then his motivation is revealed to be not merely egoistic, but also selfish. And this is precisely what reveals the Socratic theory of love to be deeply at odds with the other-regarding model.[37]

Socrates' model of love is objectionably egoistic   This is not to say that Penner and Rowe's treatment of Socratic love is incorrect on interpretative grounds. What Penner and Rowe miss is that the theory that emerges is selfish, and therefore sharply at odds with the other-regarding ideal.[38] I am therefore in agreement with interpreters such as Guthrie (1975: 143–144) and Irwin (1977: 99–100), who follow Vlastos in maintaining that Socratic love is utilitarian and egoistic. Nonetheless, interpreters who side with Vlastos in criticising the Socratic theory typically do not do justice to its explanatory strengths, nor do they recognise the weaknesses of the other-regarding model.

These strengths can be clarified by contrasting Socrates' theory with two of the most influential recent philosophical treatments of love. The first is advanced by Frankfurt in 'On Caring' (1999). According to Frankfurt, love is disinterested concern for the well-being of the beloved. Being in such a disinterested relationship is one way in which we make our lives meaningful. Love is not a response to value, but, rather, a creator of value; it is not directed at any valuable qualities of the beloved, but, rather, at his concreteness. One considerable strength of Frankfurt's analysis is that it is not subject to transience and replaceability: If love is not a response to value, then there is no worry that the beloved may cease to be valuable to the lover, nor that he will be abandoned for someone with

SOCRATES ON LOVE

more valuable qualities. This, however, reveals a worry with Frankfurt's model. If love is not a response to value, then it seems irrational. Furthermore, if what is loved is the beloved's concreteness, rather than any of his qualities, then it seems that the beloved is not loved at all; Frankfurt secures the permanence of love at the expense of bypassing the person as object of love. Finally, if the beloved has value to the lover in virtue of serving as the means for the lover to participate in an other-regarding relationship then, as I suggested earlier, the beloved has grounds to complain that he is being used in order to satisfy the lover's desire to be in such a relationship, even if the relationship in question is other-regarding.

The second theory is advanced by Velleman in 'Love as a Moral Emotion' (1999). According to Velleman, love is a response to value; the value in question is not the beloved's beauty or intellect, but his Kantian rational nature. While all persons merit respect, love involves a heightened vulnerability in response to the arresting awareness of the value of the beloved's rational nature. One attractive feature of Velleman's model is that, like Frankfurt's, it avoids the problems of transience and replaceability. The lover has no cause to abandon the beloved or trade up, since his love is a response to a value that all persons have simply in virtue of being persons, a value that, according to Velleman, prohibits comparison. However, just as Frankfurt avoids transience by bypassing the person, so Velleman focuses on a feature of persons that gives us no more reason to love one person than another.[39]

This examination of Frankfurt and Velleman has brought to light a difficulty that confronts any attempt to explain love: The demands that we place on an account of love are in conflict. In assessing theories of love, we expect them to render love motivated, discriminating and non-transient. However, if love is responsive to qualities that are particular to the beloved, then it is transient; if not, then it is either unmotivated or undiscriminating. Socrates' theory thus fails in the first regard, Frankfurt's in the second and Velleman's in the third. We can now also see that Socrates' theory has a significant strength: It offers a powerful account of motivation. It is intuitively plausible that, other things being equal, everyone desires his own happiness, and desires it as a final good; the desire for happiness, as Plato notes in the *Symposium*, does not give rise to the further question, 'What's the point of wanting happiness?' (204e–205a). If love is a species of the desire for happiness, then we can see why it has such a hold on us.[40] And if the beloved is a means to happiness, then it is clear why he should be lovable.[41]

This, in turn, suggests that some of the supposed strengths of the other-regarding model of love may be merely apparent. While Socrates' theory may be guilty of most of the charges Vlastos directs against it, we have reason to question the cogency of some of these charges. Consider transience. Transience is necessarily a problem for any quality-based theory of love, so long as the qualities in question are not, as on Velleman's theory, possessed by everyone.[42] If one is loved for his qualities, then there is always a risk that these qualities will change or that a better exemplar will come along. In order to avoid transience, then, we must abandon the quality-based approach.[43] But in giving up the quality-based approach, we give up a great deal: Love becomes either indiscriminate or irrational. Furthermore, to be loved independently of one's qualities seems dehumanising. Nor is it obvious that transience is necessarily problematic. If the beloved ceases to promote one's happiness, then perhaps one should not continue to love him. We may think we want to be loved no matter what but, in the end, this is absurd. Perhaps it is commitment, rather than love, that demands permanence.

Next, turn to objectification. This charge, as raised by Vlastos, is incoherent. As Kosman has persuasively argued, to love someone for his valuable qualities is not to objectify him, to bypass his true self (1976: 57). What else could his true self consist in? To love him warts and all, for his bad breath and occasional cruelty, as well as his admirable qualities, seems both fetishistic and irrational. The alternative Frankfurt poses, on which we love the concreteness of the beloved, is even more guilty of objectification than the Socratic approach: After all, persons, like objects, can be bearers of qualities, but it is the sorts of qualities persons bear – intelligence, wit, kindness – that make them potentially special.

Finally, let us examine egoism. The charge of egoism claims that it is problematic to love the beloved for the sake of one's own good; instead, the beloved ought to be loved for his own sake. However, it is unclear what it even means to love someone for his own sake. Perhaps the thought is that his good should be valued independently of its relation to one's own. But this raises a further question: What could motivate such love? Price observes that if one requires that love aim solely at the good of the beloved, and not that of the lover, then 'the thought expresses a moral obscurantism' and invents 'values in a vacuum created by the expulsion of motivation' (2004: 13; see also Penner and Rowe 2005: 280–282). Philosopher's fantasies aside, it seems that many people do think of their beloveds primarily in relation to their own happiness, and that there is nothing so bad about this. I suspect that what people worry about when they worry about egoism and transience is not that their lover loves them only for the sake of his own happiness and will abandon them should they cease to contribute to it, but that they will cease to make such a contribution. This would spell the end of love, or at least any form of love that falls short of self-destructive obsession or cold dutifulness.[44]

CONCLUSION

In this chapter, I have argued that interpreters are correct to attribute the NGNB thesis to Socrates. This model of love is of a piece with Socrates' egoism: Love is a species of the desire for one's own good, the desire that motivates all intentional action. This apparent egoism has sparked considerable debate among interpreters, since it conflicts with the other-regarding model of love, on which love is a reciprocal relation between two individuals, each of whom desires the good of the other for his own sake. In the second part of this chapter, I turned to critical responses to Socrates' egoistic model of love, dividing interpreters into four groups: those who absolve Socrates' model of love of egoism, claiming that it does not seek to account for the lover's conscious motivations; those who maintain that it is innocent of the charge of egoism because it allows for disinterested concern for the beloved; those who concede that it is egoistic but maintain it is not problematically selfish; and those who, like Vlastos, reject it as unacceptably egoistic. I then argued that Socrates' model of love is indeed egoistic and therefore sharply at odds with the other-regarding ideal. However, I also proposed that Socrates' theory possesses a core strength that the other-regarding model lacks: It renders love rational and motivated.

This leaves us with two questions, questions with which I opened this chapter. First, why does Socrates befriend ignorant youths such as Lysis and Menexenus, who do not appear to be useful to Socrates in any way? Second, if Lysis' parents do love him, what can motivate their love, given his uselessness?

SOCRATES ON LOVE

To begin with the second of these questions, earlier, I argued it is unlikely that Socrates sincerely believes Lysis' parents do not love him, but I left open three other interpretative options: their love is not grounded in utility; he is useful to them in some way as yet to be determined; and Socrates is genuinely puzzled by their love. The first option, that their love is not grounded in utility, fits best with the proposal I discussed earlier, that they love him as an FF; this is supported by the example of the father who values his son above all else. However, it is unclear what it would even mean for a person to be the FF; the FF seems to be the *lover's* good, and a person cannot be a constituent of that. Perhaps, then, it is best to opt for the second proposal, that Lysis is, after all, useful to his parents in some way.[45] One possibility is that what Lysis' parents value is their relationship with Lysis; Lysis is a means for them to participate in a loving parent–child relationship. Alternately, if we turn to the *Symposium*, Socrates, in fact, explains the use children have to their parents: They enable them to achieve a mortal form of immortality (207a–8b). Neither proposal paints a particularly attractive picture of parental love, since according to both, Lysis is merely a means. However, both are at least descriptively plausible: Many people do have children because they want the experience of being a parent or because they feel that they will somehow live on through their children; the second proposal has the further advantage of actually being advanced by Socrates (albeit in a later dialogue). Even if Socrates allows that Lysis' parents do love him because he is useful to them, he might still maintain that their love is grounded in a mistaken conception of their own good. What they should value is wisdom and virtue, and they should only value Lysis insofar as he contributes to these ends; perhaps when Socrates concludes that Lysis' parents do not love him very much, what he means is that they ought not to.

Let us now turn to the question of Socrates. Why does he befriend beautiful boys and lovingly introduce them to philosophy? Again, we can attribute utilitarian and non-utilitarian motives to him. On the one hand, he may act out of disinterested beneficence; however, this would be completely at odds with his professed egoism. The text suggests that the NGNB thesis is Socrates' preferred analysis of love, and it rules out selfless love. Furthermore, in advancing the NGNB thesis, Socrates treats the love of wisdom as a paradigmatic desire of the NGNB for the good (218a–b); this suggests that Socrates should be viewed as the NGNB *par excellence*. This, however, makes the motivational problem acute: If Socrates subscribes to the NGNB-thesis and is, himself, NGNB, then he has no reason to befriend Lysis and Menexenus, who, at best, are on their way to becoming NGNB under Socrates' tutelage.[46] My answer to this quandary is aporetic: I believe that Plato was genuinely puzzled by the tension between Socrates' professed egoism and his selfless engagement with others, and sought to highlight this tension in framing the *Lysis* in terms of Socrates' philosophical seduction of Lysis and Menexenus.[47]

This tension is one which Plato attempts to resolve in the *Symposium* and *Phaedrus*. In these dialogues, Plato offers a fully developed theory of the way in which a loving relationship with a beautiful boy can serve as a conduit to philosophy: The beautiful boy powerfully awakens the lover's desire for beauty and causes him to recollect the forms. This fits neatly with the general analysis of love Socrates offers in the *Lysis*: The lover loves the boy because the boy enables the lover to achieve happiness, that is, philosophical understanding. It is worth emphasising that the theory of love at work in these later dialogues remains self-centred; in the *Symposium*, for example, Plato refers to beautiful boys as steps to be trodden on the path to enlightenment (211c; see my 2010 and 2012). Some interpreters argue that the theory of love in the *Lysis* is deficient, corrected by the *Symposium* and *Phaedrus*.[48] This is not at all my proposal. What Plato explains in these later dialogues is why loving a beautiful boy should serve as a means to philosophy, but the general analysis of love remains the same. The *Lysis* merits our philosophical attention because it offers Plato's closest analysis of love as a species of the egoistic desire for one's own good. This is a theory that is jarring and perhaps even repellent. Nonetheless, it may be at least partially descriptively correct; furthermore, it offers the prospect that love should be subject to rational assessment and eventually directed to whatever is genuinely good. In studying Socrates' theory of love, we come to see the limitations of its rival, the other-regarding model; we also come to recognise that perhaps no theory of love can do justice to all of our intuitions, and that love, like beauty, remains slippery (216c–d).

NOTES

1. In this chapter, I discuss the views on love advanced by the character, Socrates, who appears in Plato's dialogues, particularly those assigned to Plato's early period. Though I occasionally appeal to non-Platonic sources, such as Xenophon, to corroborate my interpretation, I do not make any claims as to whether the views of the character, Socrates, were shared by the historical Socrates. I focus on Plato's *Ly.*, since this dialogue offers the most sustained discussion of love among the early dialogues. I thus subscribe to the commonly held assumption that the *Ly.* precedes the *Symp.* and *Phdr.* and belongs to Plato's early period. For defence of this assumption, see Brandwood 1992: 112; though at 115, Brandwood offers some considerations which suggest that the *Ly.* and *Symp.* belong to the same group, Guthrie 1975: 134–135, Kraut 1992: 4–5 (Guthrie and Kraut identify the dialogue as early-middle, but take it to precede the *Symp.*), Levin 1971: 236–237, Robin 1964: 44–46 and Robinson 1986: 63; for a summary of contrary views, see Robin 1964: 44–46 and Guthrie 134–135. No recent interpreters contest the authenticity of the *Ly.*; for a summary of the nineteenth-century debate concerning its authenticity, see Robin 1964: 44 n. 1.

2. See Xen. *Sym.* 8.2.

3. See also Plat. *M.* 76a–c and *Phdr.* 227c–d for further depictions of Socrates' flirtatiousness.

4. Plato's dialogues suggest that pederastic relationships were prevalent in Socrates' circle. Such relationships were characteristically asymmetrical: The man was in love with the boy, while the boy, at most, felt affection for the man; the man ideally served as a mentor to the boy, imparting philosophical, political or athletic skills, while the boy offered the man sexual favours in return. For further discussion of this important topic, see Dover's classic 1978, as well as Halperin's more recent 1990.

5. Though Lucian takes a sceptical view of Alcibiades' depiction of Socrates' chastity (*Philosophies for Sale* 15, cited in Dover 1978: 156).

6. For helpful discussion of Socrates' methodology in seducing Lysis, see Walker 2020.

7. Vlastos notes this tension, but explains it by positing that 'a man can be better than his theory' (1981a: 9 n. 21).

8. The translation of *philos* and its cognates, *philein*, *philoumenos* and *philia*, is notoriously difficult. The term, *philein*, has a wider sense than either *to love* or *to be the friend of*; at its broadest, it means *to value*, and it can be directed at both personal and impersonal objects. (It should be noted that in Attic Greek, *philein* is often used in opposition to *eran*, to denote non-sexual or familial love. In the *Ly.*, however, Plato is concerned to treat *philein* as a catch-all for all forms of valuation, including sexual ones; he therefore claims at 221b

SOCRATES ON LOVE 251

that *eran* entails *philein*.) Thus, interpersonal relationships count as one species of *philia*, and both lovers and friends turn out to *philein* their objects, since both are attracted to or value their objects. I attempt to capture this ambiguity by alternating between translating *philia* as *love* and as *friendship* as the context demands; similarly, I translate *philos* as both *lover* and *friend*. Since there are no suitable English expressions related to *friend*, I solely translate *philoumenos* as *beloved*, and *philein* as *to love*. For a very helpful discussion of the senses of these terms, see Robinson 1986: 65–68, though I do not agree with Robinson's claim that *philia* between humans is necessarily a reciprocal relationship (see my comments below).

One frequent response to the *Ly.* is to suppose that Socrates erroneously applies his general analysis of valuing relationships to interpersonal relationships. This may be correct. However, as I argue below, Socrates' reasons for doing so are deeply rooted in his moral psychology. For Socrates, all valuing relationships are grounded in the agent's desire for his own good; whether one loves wine or another human, this love is aimed at the good of the agent.

9. Strictly speaking, the *Ly.* is concerned with the question of who is the *philos*, and not what is *philia*. However, in his attempt to identify the *philos*, Socrates commits himself to a broader theory of *philia*, of the nature of the relation that makes one count as a *philos*. Sedley 1989 notably argues that the *Ly.* is not concerned with defining *philia*; for a contrary view, see, e.g., Adams 1992: 16 n. 7 and Bordt 2000: 157. Belfiore makes a related point, that while the dialogue problematises the meaning of philos, it takes the sense of philein for granted (2012: 71–73).

10. See also Bordt 2000: 160–161, though Bordt's rejection of the utilitarian analysis of friendship is at odds with his concession that utility is a necessary condition for friendship (162); Lockwood 2017; and Penner and Rowe 2005: 233–234. Penner and Rowe suggest, plausibly, that the absurd conclusion, that Lysis' parents do not love him, is a *reductio* of the childish conception of happiness as doing whatever one thinks one wants.

11. Rider 2011 argues that Socrates' aim in reaching this counter-intuitive conclusion is protreptic, to spur Lysis (and the audience) to engage in further philosophical investigation. This suggestion is plausible; however, it does not resolve the issue of whether Socrates himself endorses the conclusion (as Rider notes at note 36).

12. See Gonzalez 2000, who provides compelling evidence that the historical Socrates was perceived to advance a radically unconventional conception of the *philos* and the *oikeios*; Gonzalez, like Vlastos, takes at face value Socrates' claim that Lysis' parents do not love him insofar as he lacks wisdom.

13. The significance of these passages is noted by Jenks 2005: 71–72, Lockwood 2017: 325–326, Penner and Rowe 2005: 33 and Price 2004: 3.

14. In what follows, I leave *oikeion* untranslated, since no English word captures its sense; its core meaning is what pertains to one's household, but it can mean what is proper to or akin to oneself.

15. Bordt 2000 advances a similar interpretation, on which *philia* is only felt between the good on account of their love of the Good. Like Hoerber, Bordt's proposal lacks direct textual support; Bordt is forced to appeal to significantly later dialogues, and to ignore Plato's claim in the *Ly.* that the good are self-sufficient (164–166).

16. Adams 1992: 9 proposes that this passage is, in fact, compatible with Socrates' taking reciprocity to be a requirement on friendship: Quails and horses can be friends to us

because we can benefit them. Adams adds, 'This theory also makes sense of the fact that Socrates never mentions the possibility of being a friend to an inanimate object' (9). This is puzzling since, in the passage under consideration, Socrates goes on to refer to those who are friends of wine, exercise and wisdom.

17. See also Belfiore 2012: 69–70 and Trivigno 2011: 81–82, who emphasise the protreptic role of *aporia*.

18. Cf. Lockwood 2017: 329–331, who argues that Socrates' equivocal use of *oikeios* is tied to the dialogue's aporetic status.

19. Note that if Robinson were to claim, instead, that Plato mistakenly thought that *philia* between humans need not be reciprocal, then the dialogue would yield a false conclusion, but would not be aporetic.

20. See Curzer 2014, Gonzalez 1995: 82–83, Gonzalez 2003: 30–31, Rudebusch 2009: 191, Santas 1988: 84–85, Versenyi 1975: 188 and Wolfsdorf 2007: 248–250. Robin 1964: 39–40 concurs that according to the *Ly.*, the NGNB is the *philos*, but is agnostic as to the object of *philia*. Rowe argues that Plato endorses the NGNB proposal, though he raises doubts concerning whether the *philon* is necessarily *oikeion* (2000: 211–213); these doubts are not shared by Penner and Rowe 2005: 174–175.

21. See also Bolotin 1989: 178–179, Gadamer 1980: 17–18, Guthrie 1975: 148 and Robin 1964: 39.

22. Glaser, cited in Glidden 1981: 39 n. 4, and, more recently, Bordt 2000 and Levin 1971: 247–248.

23. See also Glidden 1981: 43 n. 37 and Vlastos 1981a: 35–37 for further arguments that the *Ly.* does not make reference to the theory of forms.

24. See Rowe 2000: 210, 214–215. While it is important to emphasise that Socrates does not offer a positive account of the good in the *Ly.*, the evidence in other dialogues that he takes happiness to constitute one's good is very strong; in what follows, I therefore occasionally appeal to the proposal that the FF is happiness.

25. Annas 1977 qualifies this claim at 538.

26. Irwin concedes this 1977: 53; see also Lesses 1996: n. 6 and Versenyi 1975: 194.

27. See also Irwin 1977: 85, 99–100, who argues persuasively that Socrates' egoistic theory of love in the *Ly.* stems from his commitment to LG, the principle that if x and y are goods and x contributes to y, then x is not good in itself. According to Irwin, in the *Ly.*, Socrates suggests that we only love others for the sake of our own happiness; LG therefore entails that we can never love them for their own sakes.

28. See also Kosman's 1976: 54–56 and Kolodny's 2003: 139–142 for helpful discussions.

29. See also Irwin 1977: 54, though Irwin refers to selfishness as egoism.

30. An alternate version of instrumentalism might claim that it is not sufficient for Romeo to love Juliet for her own sake; he must also never treat her as a means. In its raw form, this is implausible: Surely it is acceptable that he should, say, value Juliet as a dance partner, so long as he primarily loves her for her own sake. Perhaps this version of instrumentalism should be modified such that Romeo must never treat Juliet merely as a means, or that his love must never be conditional on her serving as a means to some other end.

31. For a similar line of argument in relation to the *Symp.*, see Sheffield 2012.

SOCRATES ON LOVE

32. Curzer 2014 takes the instrumental model of friendship that appears in the *Ly.* to be so counter-intuitive that he maintains that the dialogue should be understood as a *reductio* of that model. Curzer argues that the instrumental model yields 'wildly counterintuitive' consequences, such as the claims that the good are friends with no one, and that wise people do not love wisdom, consequences that serve to reveal the absurdity of the instrumental model (368). Against Curzer, given that Plato advances virtually identical claims in the *Symp.* (200e–1c, 204a), it is not at all clear that Curzer is entitled to treat these as implying a *reductio* of the instrumental model in the *Ly.* Curzer also appeals to features of the dramatic context, for example, he takes the friendship between Lysis and Menexenus to undercut the instrumental model; it is not obvious, however, that Plato's intention is not, instead, to suggest that the boys' friendship is instrumentally-based or, alternatively, that it is problematic.

33. See Bolotin's 1989: 201–225 summary of von Arnim.

34. Gonzalez makes a related proposal, that nonreciprocal love for the FF can give rise to reciprocal interpersonal love: Two individuals who are NGNB might recognise that each is *oikeios* to the good, and hence that they are *oikeioi* to one another; their shared kinship to the good can cause them to love one another for who they really are (2003: 30–35). It is unclear whether Gonzalez means that they love one another due to an appreciation of their kinship to the good; in that case, it would be rational for them to prefer the good to that which is merely akin (but presumably inferior) to it. Alternatively, he may mean that they love one another in virtue of the contribution their joint, competitive pursuit of the good makes to securing it for each of them (34); in that case, Vlastos' instrumentalism and selfishness charges apply, a consequence to which Gonzalez is, perhaps, not averse (35–36).

35. Note that Lesses does not propose that persons can serve as constituent means.

36. This model of love bears some resemblance to what Frankfurt 1999 proposes, which I discuss in the following section. Nichols 2009: 190 perhaps has in mind something along these lines when she suggests that friendship is felt between the NGNB for the sake of experiencing one's own as another or another as one's own.

37. Roth claims that it is not egoistic to prioritise one's own virtue over friendship where these conflict (1995: 18–19); against him; while this may be righteous, it still seems egoistic.

38. Penner and Rowe acknowledge that the egoistic theory of love they attribute to Socrates is somewhat at odds with the other-regarding ideal: For example, it does not demand that the beloved's good be valued independently of its contribution to that of the lover. Nonetheless, they minimise the degree to which the theory is selfish, to which it may prescribe that the lover pursue his own good even when it runs contrary to the good of the beloved or the commitments implicit in the love relationship.

39. Velleman attempts to circumvent this by proposing that love is prompted by the beloved's empirical persona as this reveals his rational nature (1999: 370–372). This is unsatisfactory: If what we really love is the rational nature *as revealed by* the empirical persona, then we do have to worry about replaceability, since it is conceivable that someone else's empirical persona could reveal his rational nature in a more loveable form; on the other hand, if what is loved is simply the rational nature, then it is hard to see why the empirical persona should be what prompts love.

40. As I note above, Socrates does not explicitly identify the FF with happiness in the *Ly.*; however, the evidence from other dialogues for this identification is quite strong. At any

rate, even if we can only identify the FF with one's own good, my claim that Socrates has a powerful account of motivation will still hold.

41. Note that the beloved will only be loved as a means; strictly speaking, then, he will not be truly lovable (219d). However, at the conclusion of the dialogue, Plato deploys a looser vocabulary, on which persons can still be called lovable (221e–222a, 222a, 223b), even though they are not the FF.

42. One might avoid replaceability if the list of qualities which one values in the beloved were so extensive and unusual that no other person could possibly replicate these. However, as Velleman 1999: 368–370 notes, such love would cease to be rational; furthermore, such love could not accommodate changes in the beloved and would therefore be particularly susceptible to transience.

43. Kolodny 2003 has suggested a third alternative: We can love others for their relational qualities – e.g., for their being one's child or wife. Kolodny's theory strikes me as the most persuasive among recent proposals; it offers a particularly powerful account of familial love. I take it that Socrates would reject Kolodny's theory on the grounds that unless relational qualities are conducive to one's own good, the love is irrational. Cf. *Symp.* 205e–206a. See also Penner and Rowe (2005: 280–282).

44. Our intuitions about love appear strikingly inconsistent in this area. On the one hand, were I to learn that I no longer make any contribution to my lover's happiness, I would conclude that he no longer loves me; in this case, I would be assuming that love is egoistic. On the other hand, were my lover to tell me that he loves me only insofar as I contribute to his happiness, I might object that he is using me and does not really love me; in this case, I would be supposing that love is necessarily non-egoistic. Some of these inconsistencies depend on the conception of happiness at work: Is it being in a giving relationship with the beloved or, say, using him for sexual or even intellectual purposes? Others derive from the perspective assumed in the thought-experiment: Do I imagine myself to be the lover or the beloved; the beloved being wooed or the beloved being scorned?

45. One concern about this strategy is that, as Rider notes, Socrates appears to argue at 210d for the claim that Lysis is ignorant and hence useless (2011: 55 n. 30). Perhaps this can be resolved along the lines I sketch out below, that, while Lysis' parents ought only to love him insofar as he is wise, in fact they love him because they take him to be useful in other dimensions.

46. A further tension is that if Socrates is really NGNB, then it seems that he should be lacking in wisdom and so be ignorant of the NGNB thesis; perhaps this can be resolved by insisting that Socrates' ignorance lies solely in his lacking a full account of the good.

47. A possibility I do not pursue is that Socrates' sole motive for engaging philosophically with others is that he was ordered to do so by the gods. See Rudebusch 2009: 197.

48. See, e.g., Guthrie 1975: 143, Levin 1971: 246, Robin 1964: 40, Santas 1988: 88. For a contrary view, see Gonzalez 1995: 88–89, Penner and Rowe 2005: 298–299 and Versenyi 1975: 185–186.

CHAPTER ELEVEN

Socrates on Emotions

IRINA DERETIĆ

I. INTRODUCTION

The scholarly study of the role of emotions in Socratic[1] moral psychology has not received the attention it deserves. This can probably be explained by Socrates' intellectualism about virtue and motivation.[2] It has seemed to many scholars, accordingly, that there is nothing of philosophical significance to say about the mentions of emotions in Socratic conversations, since all that appears to matter in human affairs has been taken to be explicable wholly in terms of cognition.

The dominant scholarship in the past, for example in Santas (1979: 185–189), Vlastos (1969, 1991) and Walsh (1963), interpreted Socrates as denying that the non-rational aspects played any role at all in the explanation of human actions. According to this view, Socrates believes that everyone always rationally desires what they think is good. Penner (1990, 1991, 1996, 1997), Reshotko (2006, 2013) and Rowe (2002, 2006, 2007) challenge the traditional view by acknowledging a role for non-rational desires and urges. They are integrated, according to Penner, with beliefs forming 'executive desires which will lead directly to, or cause, a particular action' (1991: 152). Reshotko supplements Penner's view by arguing that this integration provides an agent 'with information about what might be best for him in the present circumstances and how to get it' (2013: 170). These scholars[3] consider that Socrates at least recognises the non-rational aspects of our personality, but they deny that these elements can cause action independent of or contrary to a rationally endorsed belief.

By contrast, there are the Socratic scholars who not only regard the existence of appetites and emotions as important in Socratic philosophy, but also consider that they can contribute to a better understanding of human action. These include (in alphabetical order): Brickhouse and Smith 2010, 2015; Candiotto 2015; Carone 2004; Devereux 1995; Moss 2007; Sanderman 2004; Segvic 2000; Singpurwalla 2006; Smith 2019; and Woodruff 2000. According to this group of scholars, Socrates finds that, apart from reason, there are non-rational aspects of a person that might function in a way independent of and even possibly contrary to what reason might support. They contend that the relation between beliefs and emotions is more complex than the way it is represented in Penner's view that emotions must 'always automatically adjust to the agent's beliefs about what is the best means to their ultimate end' (Penner 1992a: 128). This other basic approach to Socrates' views about emotions provides the framework for the account I will offer.

In this chapter, I endeavour to explain the Socratic account of emotions in general, and fear, shame, anger, envy and grief, in particular,[4] to show how they influence the way we act – especially in cases where our actions do not seem to be rational. I will advance my discussion of the Socratic understanding of emotions in stages. First, I will consider illustrative passages from Plato's early dialogues in order to show that there are clear cases in our texts where emotions are recognised by Socrates as playing a critical role in Socrates' explanation of human behaviour. Second, I will elucidate the nature, origin and structure of emotions in his philosophy. Then, I will discuss how my general account of emotions applies to the particular emotions of fear, shame, anger, envy and grief as they appear particularly in Plato's Socratic dialogues. In the end, I hope to have shown how Socrates understood emotions and the role they play in human ethical behaviour.

II. THE MOTIVATIONAL EFFICACY OF THE NON-RATIONAL ASPECTS OF THE HUMAN SOUL

In Plato's early dialogues, there are a number of places where Socrates not only describes a variety of appetites and emotions, but also seems to ascribe to them a certain role in explaining human conduct. Among Plato's early dialogues, the *Gorgias* seems to be the one where the non-rational elements of the soul have the most prominent place. Particularly interesting is the following passage:

> Once I even heard one of the wise men say that we are now dead and that our bodies are our tombs, and that the part of our souls in which our appetites reside is actually the sort of thing to be open to persuasion and to shift back and forth. And hence some clever man, a teller of stories, a Sicilian, perhaps, or an Italian, named this part a jar (*pithos*), on account of its being a persuadable (*pithanon*) and suggestible thing, thus slightly changing the name. And fools (*anoētoi*) he named uninitiated (*amuētoi*), suggesting that that part of the souls of fouls where their appetites are located is their undisciplined part, one not tightly closed, a leaking jar, as it were. He based the image on its insatiability.
>
> *– Gorgias* 493a–b[5]

Socrates argues that the life of unrestrained appetites is like a leaky jar that can never be filled up. What appetites seem to have in common is that they are chaotic, unstructured and insatiable. When we indulge our appetites, they increase and become more difficult to master. Given this explicit reference to the appetitive 'part', Socrates seems to suggest that the soul is composed of parts, one of which is an appetitive one.[6] However we are to conceive of the nature of the soul in the *Gorgias*, it is clear at least that it is something that can be disordered in such a way as to be detrimental to one's well-being. It is this condition that Socrates finds in his interlocutor, Callicles, whose soul is so distracted by conflicting urges that he is 'out of harmony' with himself (*Gorgias* 481d–482c). Socrates argues that the life of unrestrained appetites – proposed by Callicles – will prevent one from having a well-structured, i.e., good soul. Callicles' intense and unrestrained appetites are what explain his views and actions, but this explanation remains consistent with Socratic motivational intellectualism, in that Callicles acts in accordance with his belief that it is best for him to indulge his most intense appetites. By arguing in this fashion, Plato's Socrates seems to hold that non-rational desires can play a significant role in the explanation of human behaviour.

In 1995, D. T. Devereux published an important paper that called for more focused attention to the way that non-rational factors appear in Socratic explanations of human personality and action. Devereux argues that Socrates does not treat the appetites as a distinct source of motivation, independently of cognition. Explicitly following Devereux, Brickhouse and Smith (2010, 2013b, 2015) have argued that the way the appetites motivate is by representing things to the soul as beneficial, which can cause an agent to believe that they are beneficial and then act to achieve those perceived benefits. All sorts of unruly appetites, they argue, explain why some people behave in an unrestrained fashion, but the way they explain it is compatible with – and a part of – Socratic motivational intellectualism. In their view, people may come to believe that doing X is best for them (among the options available to them that they are aware of at the time of action) because it has been represented as the best choice by certain appetites. Appetites can influence what we believe, and our actions always follow what we believe. Therefore, the manner in which appetites contribute to an explanation of behaviour is by virtue of the role they play in belief-formation, but not independently of cognition (Brickhouse and Smith 2010).

Carone 2004, Segvic 2000 and Singpurwalla 2006[7] seem to hold the view that both appetites and emotions are just evaluative beliefs about their objects. Their view is also obviously compatible with motivational intellectualism, because one who is motivated to do something by an appetite would still be doing what one thinks is best at the time of action. Brickhouse and Smith rightly criticise this view on the ground 'that it rules out any possibility of having to struggle against an appetite or passion, because the agent believed that it would be best to refrain from what the appetite or passion inclined him or her to do. Or if there could be such conflict, it could only be a case of cognitive dissonance' (Brickhouse and Smith 2013b: 195).

Does Socrates take appetites to be different from emotions? In their 2010 book, Brickhouse and Smith supposed appetites and emotions were all to be understood simply as non-rational urges in the soul that could explain beliefs, but which were not themselves beliefs. In their 2015 article, they change their account and claim that Socrates treats appetites and emotions differently. If appetites are different from emotions in Socrates' philosophy, then one must ask what emotions are and how they relate to appetites and reason, and thus, how they function within human motivation. It is to these questions that I now turn.

III. EMOTIONS AS COGNITIONS

Socrates does not offer an explicit analysis of emotion as such. But from the way he talks about fear and the fear of death, it is obvious that he was committed to a cognitivist view of fear. Fearing is identified as the expectation of something bad (*Laches* 198b, *Protagoras* 358d).[8] In what follows, I will accordingly make two assumptions, but admit that they are somewhat speculative: (i) I will assume that Socrates categorises emotions – as opposed to other psychological conditions – in the same way that we do, by which I mean that he would count anger, love, shame, envy and grief (to name a few examples) as belonging to the same general kind of psychological condition (i.e. emotion) as fear; and (ii) I will also assume that Socrates is also a cognitivist about these other emotions. I will attempt to support these assumptions by the way in which Socrates and his interlocutors discuss particular emotions, such as shame, anger, envy and grief. In doing this, I will endeavour to provide a plausible understanding of all that Socrates has to say about the emotions, and how these play important roles in our lives.

In my view, it is not just that 'emotions depend on judgements' (Austin 2010: 3), for that makes them distinct from the judgments they depend on. Instead, the textual evidence indicates that we should suppose Socrates understood emotions actually to be evaluative cognitions or beliefs (Brickhouse and Smith 2015, Deretić and Smith 2021). If so, it follows that internal struggle involving the emotions will be at least partly explicable as either cognitive dissonance, or at least as internal conflict about what the agent is inclined to believe. If our emotions are beliefs, the question is then whether they are generated in a similar or different fashion compared to other beliefs. Plainly, there are a number of different processes that can generate beliefs, including memory, deduction, induction, sense perception and testimony. Not all belief-forming processes are veridically reliable, however; one that is notoriously unreliable is the process of belief-formation based upon wishful thinking.

In their 2015 paper, Brickhouse and Smith argue that Socrates recognises different etiologies for belief-formation and belief-supporting processes. Some of them have a non-rational origin, involving our most basic natural urges and aversions. They cite Plato's *Charmides* (167e), where Socrates seems to distinguish several types of desire, which have different targets:

> These [desires] include appetite (*epithumia*), which aims at pleasure, wish (*boulēsis*), which aims at what is good, and love (*erōs*),[9] which aims at what is beautiful. Each of these seems to have an aversive alternative, as well: we avoid pains, what is bad, and what is ugly. Our natural attractions and aversions, we contend, are the grounds for a variety of non-rational beliefs: Insofar as something seems or promises to be pleasurable, beneficial, or beautiful, the agent will be naturally inclined to believe it to be something good; and insofar as something seems to be painful, detrimental, or ugly, the agent will be naturally inclined to believe it to be something bad. Unless the natural inclination to believe in such cases is mitigated or defeated by some other (for example, rational) belief-forming process, one will form beliefs about goods and evils accordingly. The beliefs created by these natural attractions and aversions, because they derive from non-rational processes, are veridically unreliable, but are also to some degree (by their nature as non-rational) resistant to rational persuasion and other belief-forming processes.
>
> – Brickhouse and Smith 2015: 14–15

Brickhouse and Smith take this evidence to show that our basic attractions and aversions are the etiological sources of particular kinds of beliefs that are emotions. They are based upon an attraction to pleasure, good and the beautiful, while avoiding pain and what is bad and ugly.[10]

Given that emotions are cognitions, in the Socratic view, our experience of them allows us to consider and evaluate whether they are true or false. But because emotions have origins in non-rational desiderative processes,[11] they (1) are less veridically reliable compared to the beliefs generated by several other sources of belief- formation, and (2) may also be resistant to correction by other belief-forming processes. In addition, (3) because they are veridically unreliable, emotions can provide the cognitive basis for inappropriate attitudes and immoral actions. How can one correct these cognitive and moral errors? One might think of what Socrates in *Protagoras* (356d–e) calls the art of measurement. He describes it as follows:

> SOCRATES: Since it has turned out that our salvation in life depends on the right choice of pleasures and pains, be they more or fewer, greater or lesser, farther or nearer, doesn't our salvation seem, first of all, to be measurement, which is the study of relative excess and deficiency and equality?
>
> – *Protagoras* 357b

SOCRATES ON EMOTIONS

Our salvation depends on acquiring the craft of measurement, which will enable a person to judge correctly and make right choices regarding appetites, pleasures, pains and emotions in real-life situations. In other words, the art of measurement involves knowledge of the true balance of long-term and short-term pleasures and pains, knowledge that can thus guide a person's actions. Those 'who wrongly choose to indulge in immediate pleasure do not know that they are selecting the worse course of action' (Wilburn 2015: 3). In a properly functioning soul, such knowledge allows one to exercise full self-control over pleasures, appetites and emotions. The errorless knowledge required for the full mastery of the craft of measurement does not seem to be available, however, at least to human beings. According to the oracle given to Chaerephon (*Apology* 20e–21a), no one is wiser than Socrates; we may infer that no one is better at the craft of measurement than Socrates is. But it is plain that Socrates does not regard himself as having mastery of this craft. Instead, when he insists that 'the unexamined life is not worth living for a human being' (*Apology* 38a) Socrates indicates a way we can achieve some cognitive control over the unreliability of non-rational belief-forming processes: We shouldn't simply accept the ways in which we instinctively evaluate things in our world; instead, we should consider what is valuable to us in more thoughtful and deliberate ways. Even this way of life, however, provides no complete or absolute assurance that we will not continue to be vulnerable to the cognitive effects of the strong desires within us. Socrates himself, as his response to the young Charmides at the beginning of the dialogue named after him shows, remains vulnerable to the natural urges to which human beings are susceptible.

The examined life, for Socrates the only kind of life that is worth living, includes refuting the beliefs of his fellow citizens who value less important things more than more significant things. Leading a philosophical life includes subjecting our beliefs and dispositions to critical evaluation. This is, however, not only an epistemic, but also an ethical process, because those who know what piety, courage and justice are, are pious, courageous and just. Knowledge of virtue combines with our general desire for what is good/beneficial to motivate virtuous action. Socrates promises his jurors that he will not give up practising philosophy, i.e. questioning, examining and testing his fellow citizens about virtue. While having a philosophical conversation with his interlocutors, Socrates endeavours to refute their false beliefs about the most valuable issues. Having this in mind, as it seems, Penner says that 'only philosophical dialogue can improve one's fellow citizens' (Penner 2000: 164–165). This, however, seems to idealise humans as perfectly rational beings who can be persuaded only by good reasons, and is not what we find in Plato's dialogues. Socrates' interlocutors often do not accept his refutations when Socrates has shown them that their beliefs are inconsistent, as we see with Callicles and Thrasymachus, who continue to resist even when their confusions and errors have become evident. Philosophical dialogue seems not to be sufficient for correcting all cognitive and moral errors. Even the philosophical way of life, which includes dialogue with fellow citizens, 'is no complete or absolute assurance that we will not continue to be vulnerable to the cognitive effects of strong desires within us' (Deretić and Smith 2021: 117). We will not always or inevitably stop feeling something, even if the argumentation shows how ineffective and inappropriate what we feel is.

Precisely because emotional responses seem to derive from more basic desiderative processes and responses, Plato does not have Socrates engage only in purely rational argumentation. At times we find him employing tactics that appear to focus more on disrupting or interfering with non-rational processes, rather than just offering cool appraisals of evidence. So it is that we find Socrates sometimes:

1. using myths with a deeper moral as an additional support to an argument;
2. encouraging others to keep their appetitive urges in what he calls a 'disciplined' condition;
3. shaming his interlocutors, humiliating them because their beliefs are inconsistent;
4. appealing to concerns like honour and dignity.

As for myths, Emily Austin highlights that Socrates, when having a dialogue with his interlocutors, sometimes employs myths to supplement his rational arguments. She claims that credible myths sometimes can 'alter a person's psychology independent of rational assent' (Austin 2013: 2). Such myths can support the right ethical norms by appealing to the same kinds of non-rational belief-forming processes as those that can lead us astray – by appealing to attractions and aversions that help to support the right evaluations, instead of the wrong ones.

As for natural urges, Socrates advises how we should diminish our vulnerability to the unreliable cognitive processes that are based on appetites (*Gorgias* 505b, 507c–e). What Socrates tells Callicles – who is characterised as someone who has very severe problems with self-control – is that appetites should be in 'disciplined' condition. 'The more we keep our appetites . . . in a *disciplined* condition, the more able we will be to engage in and appreciate the epistemic value of reasoning. But the more one indulges those natural attractions and aversions, the stronger their role in belief production becomes, with the effect that one becomes increasingly less responsive to reason in one's cognitive processes' (Brickhouse and Smith 2015: 22). The power of this veridically unreliable process might be reduced to some extent by attention to rational argumentation, 'but never entirely eliminated' (Deretić and Smith 2021: 117).

Because of their non-rational origins, only when emotions are in accordance with our reason are they both worthy of acceptance and of guiding our actions, and only then will the way in which they add motivational urgency to our decision-making function in ways that can benefit us. Socrates regards emotional processes as significantly epistemic ones, because they involve a process of belief-formation. But we must regard this process with a certain mindful and sceptical detachment – one that will not be possible for us unless we keep our appetites under significant control. It is not, therefore, that Socrates seeks for us not to experience attractions and aversions, nor is it the case that he would think we can or should cease to experience emotions. The evaluation beliefs that are expressed in emotions, when appropriate, can be even more powerfully motivating than purely rational beliefs. As I will now go on to show, Socrates thinks that there are things that we may rightly fear, that make us feel appropriately angry, and that rightly may sadden us, and the like. But we should feel these things when and only when the beliefs in which they consist are supported by other, more veridically reliable, cognitive processes.

IV. FEAR

Very frequently, persons are deemed fearless, although they might be confronting serious danger. In the *Laches*, Plato has Nicias reject this idea in such a way as to call to mind Socrates' own virtue intellectualism:

> By no means, Laches, I do not call courageous beasts or anything else that, for lack of understanding, does not fear what should be feared. Rather I would call them fearless (*aphobon*) and dull (*moron*). Or do you suppose I call all children courageous, who

SOCRATES ON EMOTIONS

fear nothing which should be feared, because they have no sense? I rather hold that the fearless and the courageous are not the same things.

– Laches 197a–b[12]

Herein, fearlessness is associated with rashness, thoughtlessness and lack of reason. Such behaviour can be attributed to wild beasts and children that often cannot identify even the features of the danger. Socrates' intention is to distinguish a courageous person from only an apparently brave, but in fact a reckless and dull person, by pointing to their different relation to fear or dread.

> SOCRATES: Dread is an expectation (*prosdokian*) of a future evil (*Laches* 198b).
> SOCRATES: I say that whether you call it fear or dread, it is a kind of expectation (*prosdokian tina*) of something bad [. . .]. If what I have said up to now is true, would anyone be willing to go toward what he dreads, when he can go toward what he does not? Or is this impossible from what we have agreed? For it was agreed that what one dreads one holds (*hegesthai*) to be bad (*Protagoras* 358d–e).[13]

The kind of cognition that Socrates has in mind is an assessment of what should be feared and not feared, i.e., what is a real and what is only an apparent evil. It is also a judgment of the level of risk (*Laches* 194e–195a) one should undertake when confronting a future evil.

In both dialogues, Socrates seems to be correct when he argues that past and present evils do not cause fear, but future evils do, since fear is the anticipation of bad things that will happen to us. We are not afraid of the bad things that we have already experienced and overcome. Although we are afraid of a prospective evil, our experiences with past dangers can contribute to our assessment of what is to be feared in the future.

That fear is an evaluative belief – as Socrates suggests – can be supported by the fact that when choosing between two future evils, one assesses which one is lesser. Even when one determines what is to be feared and not feared, one judges what can be harmful to oneself or one's associates. A person might have a misconception of what is really bad and harmful or his anticipations of bad things might be inaccurate.

If we accept that all emotions are based on natural non-rational attractions and aversions, then fear, too, is grounded in an aversion to what is considered harmful. All humans instinctively avoid what they think might harm them. Both the courageous person and the coward avoid what they fear; what distinguishes them, as Socrates argues (*Protagoras* 359d–e), is that the courageous person rightly judges what is truly likely to be harmful, and this is deserving of fear, while the coward is much more likely to judge wrongly.[14] In many of Plato's early dialogues, Socrates claims that the experience of fear in the face of what an agent knows to be bad is appropriate (*Apology* 29b–c, 37b; *Crito* 47b, 47d; *Gorgias* 522e).

Unlike the brave individual, the coward seems to be the one who is afraid of many things, assessing wrongly that most of what is feared is bad and harmful. 'The fearful person, as we all know, is *much more likely* to form false beliefs about threats in his or her environment; the courageous person is much less likely to make such mistakes' (Brickhouse and Smith 2015: 19). Socrates seems to think that the fear of death is a false or at least unfounded belief that death is bad.

Deretić and Smith (2021: 113–114) hypothesised that the ubiquity of the fear of death is explicable in terms of 'familiarity bias', 'which is the form of cognitive bias that shows undue preference for whatever is more familiar'. They argue that Socrates seems 'to

262 THE BLOOMSBURY HANDBOOK OF SOCRATES

regard the concern for losing the things that one values in life as insufficient to support the rationality of the fear of death' (Deretić and Smith 2021: 114). In their view, the fear of death is intractable and eliminating it would be possible only if someone failed to have the natural aversion, common to all living beings, to having one's own life end, and who, thus, would be entirely immune to the disposition to form the belief that death is bad. Due to its non-rational origin, the fear of death often has an impact on creating false judgments about what really matters in our lives and, thus, frequently keeps us from acting justly and consistently with our own ethical assessments.

Reeve (1989: 112–114), Austin (2010) and Deretić (2020) argue that Socrates' argument in Plato's *Apology* against the fear of death can serve the purpose for which Socrates employs it – namely, to show that his will is to continue to lead a philosophical life, which is for him the only life worth living, even though it might lead to his death. Socrates not only contrasts his own disavowal of any knowledge of death with his knowledge of what is really bad and contrary to morality (*Apology* 29a–b), but also connects the fear of death with the fear of shame.

Socrates contends that fear and shame are interrelated not only in content, but also logically. While discussing this with Euthyphro, Socrates points out (*Euthyphro* 12c) that 'where there is shame there is also fear, for fear covers a larger area than shame'. I now turn to what Socrates has to say about shame.

V. SHAME AND ITS ROLE IN PERSUASION

Since Homer, shame (*aidos*)[15] has become one of the key concepts of Greek culture and its understanding of what is virtuous and valuable. Shame is associated with a recognition of a threat to one's self-esteem that is deeply connected with a social value system of appropriate behaviour.

Several scholars[16] have rightly emphasised Socrates' employment of shame (*aidos*) in philosophical discussion. Paul Woodruff defines shame as follows: 'Shame is a painful emotion one feels at the thought of being exposed in weakness, foolishness, nakedness, or perhaps even wickedness, to the view of a community whose laughter would scald. Shame is closely related to fear of exclusion from one's group, since derision generally marks the exposed person as an outsider' (Woodruff 2000: 133).

Recently, Nicholas D. Smith proposes a cognitively-based definition of shame:

> Shame might be the belief that one has been exposed or perceived by ones whose opinions of one matter to one, as deserving rejection or exclusion, where such rejection or exclusion from the group would qualify as the 'bad' the fear of shame would expect.
>
> – Smith 2019: 166

This belief that one has been exposed and viewed as deserving exclusion is based upon a non-rational, natural aversion to being excluded from or a desire for acceptance by and affirmation in a social group. As a motivational intellectualist, Socrates can acknowledge that the emotion of shame can generate action, because being ashamed can guide the action in such a way as to respond to the fact that one has done something that merits rejection or exclusion from one's preferred social group. In Plato's dialogues, shame is highlighted as one of the chief motives for human action. And his use of shame has significant philosophical implications. In the *Charmides*, for example, Socrates describes what an interlocutor can feel when he confronts Socrates' argumentation.

SOCRATES ON EMOTIONS

SOCRATES: But since his consistently high reputation made him feel ashamed in the eyes of the company and he did not wish to admit to me that he was incapable of dealing with the question I had asked him, he said nothing clear, but concealed his predicament.

– Charmides 169c–d

Critias wishes to be recognised for aristocratic excellence. As a man of high reputation, he is expected by his company to be up to the task of responding to Socrates' questions in an effective and admirable way. This is also what Critias expects from himself, because he internalises the social norms and pursues the values that his fellows admire and respect. In this case, Critias is ashamed, since he is certain that his intellectual shortcomings are exposed as failing to live up to the high opinion that Critias' associates have of him, and that Critias has of himself. The mutual dependence of self-esteem on the regard of others is significant for experiencing shame. Critias' shame hinders acknowledging his confusion, as it triggers a defence mechanism that causes Critias not to admit his shortcomings. Unlike Critias, his young cousin, Charmides, does not hide his ignorance: He does not know whether he is wise or not. He blushes when talking of his ignorance, showing that modesty is linked with shame.

The *Gorgias* is the dialogue in which Socratic 'shame tactics' are the most obviously displayed. Socrates appeals to shame to refute each of his three interlocutors: Gorgias, Polus and Callicles.[17] He describes an example where the experience of shame would be appropriate:

SOCRATES: Now if someone were to refute me and prove that I am unable to provide *this* protection for myself or for anyone else, I would be ashamed at being refuted, whether this happened in the presence of many or of a few, or just between the two of us.

– Gorgias 522d

Socrates reveals how his own method and its consequences can be applied to himself. He would have been ashamed if his own beliefs had been proven to be inconsistent. The shame he would feel does not depend on how many persons would be present at his being refuted. Gorgias and Polus are 'ashamed', as Callicles highlights, to say frankly what they think because they are afraid to be caught in contradiction or in speaking against public opinion (*Gorgias* 482d, 487b–c). Callicles, on the other hand, is not ashamed to say what he thinks. Although he is a bold hedonist, Socrates makes him concede that some unseemly pleasures like itching or being the passive partner in homosexual relations[18] are shameful and disgusting, forcing Callicles to reconsider his conception of what brings value to a life.

By shaming his opponents, Jessica Moss contends, Socrates shows a possible perspective of how non-virtuous persons can be guided toward virtue (Moss 2005: 138). She also compellingly points out that the discussion in the *Gorgias* reveals significant aspects of shame that are associated both with (1) 'how an agent sees himself' (Moss 2005: 152) and (2) what are his 'deepest moral intuitions' (Moss 2005: 149).

Recently, Laura Candiotto (2015) characterises the Socratic elenchus as not only a rational process of testing out the inconsistency of the interlocutor's beliefs but also an 'emotional process acting inside reasoning and where shame . . . has a leading role' (Candiotto 2015: 234). By causing shame in his soul, Socrates' intention is not only to call attention to his cognitive, but also to his moral error, which the interlocutor finds difficult and shameful to admit, particularly when surrounded by an audience, who will witness his failure. Even though interlocutors often attempt to conceal their shame, such a strategy usually backfires, contends Candiotto (2015: 234), because the audience can readily perceive both the cognitive error and the resultant shame.

Nonetheless, as Paul Woodruff notices, not all sorts of shame should be accepted and applied. Public shame is frequently dependent on what the public regards as valuable or disgraceful. This is rarely 'vulnerable to rational criticism' (Woodruff 2000: 144). One could be ashamed of violating a publicly accepted value, even when that value is not in accordance with one's own beliefs as to what is good and just (*Protagoras* 333c). By contrast to public shame, 'more intimate and disturbing' shame can invoke painful self-awareness that one has betrayed one's own most cherished values. This can bring one to 'two discoveries about oneself – that one is truly committed to these values, and that one is not living up to them' (Woodruff 2000: 144). These two discoveries of our self-examination could evoke our reflection of how we can find the best way of implementing our values in a life worth living.

Given that shame is a response to being confronted with one's cognitive or moral error, it begins the process of becoming aware of one's own failings. Moreover, one can, by experiencing shame, become aware that one's errors are in conflict with one's deepest moral convictions. The appropriate response to such an experience, in Socrates' view, is to undertake more careful self-examination, in order to correct oneself and pursue moral improvement.

A typical reaction to being shamed, however, is, as Candiotto has shown, not to admit one's errors, and worse, to actually become angry at those who have exposed them. Let us, then, turn to this emotion and see how it appears in the dialogues.

VI. ANGER

In Plato's early dialogues, Socrates never defines anger, although anger seems to be what many Athenians feel toward him. In Plato's *Apology*, Socrates describes his philosophical activity as cross-examining his interlocutors in front of other people and showing that his interlocutors' beliefs reveal their lack of wisdom. The effect of his questioning is often that his interlocutors are left feeling as if their pride has been hurt; having been publicly humiliated, they become angry at Socrates. This anger was the powerful force that inspired the nasty slander against Socrates which leads to his formal accusation by Meletus, supported by Anytus and Lycon, that he did not believe in the state's gods and corrupted the youth. Their hidden intentions were different, though. Some citizens of Athens wanted to punish Socrates for revealing to them the truth they did not want to admit – that they were humiliated and angry because of their own ignorance. In Socrates' account, the anger was evoked not because his prosecutors really believed that Socrates was an atheist who seduced the youth into wrongdoing, but because of the damage done to their excessive pride and vanity.

From what is said in the *Apology* about the anger at Socrates, one can draw some conclusions about anger itself. It is a response to what an individual perceives as some unwarranted insult or injury. This perceived insult or injury causes those who are questioned to be exposed to shame, as I have already discussed, and their response (or the response of their supporters) is to be angry with the one responsible for it. This response, accordingly, would be represented, in Socratic cognitivist terms, as a belief that something or someone one values has been or is being mistreated in some way. Typically, this response

SOCRATES ON EMOTIONS

comes in the form of retaliation, a return of a harm for a harm or a wrong for a wrong. Socrates holds that 'blameworthy ignorance' dooms those who think that they are wiser than others, whereby they are, in fact, ignorant of their own capacities and accomplishments. If Socrates publicly exposes their follies, then they believe he has belittled them, so much that they become wrathful, resulting in their desire to avenge themselves against Socrates. In the case of his interlocutors, this belief is shown to be false: It is no injustice, and neither insult nor injury to have one's ignorance recognised as such. A better reaction than anger would be to regard what Socrates reveals as a ground for self-improvement. In some accounts of Socrates' motivational intellectualism, such as the one given by Penner, emotions must 'always automatically adjust to the agent's beliefs about what is the best means to their ultimate end' (1992a: 128). Brickhouse and Smith (2010: 57) claim that Penner gets 'exactly backward the way Socrates thinks the relationship between anger and belief works. Rather than anger "automatically adjusting" to what the person believes, the anger seems to have effects on *what the angry person believes*, namely, that he should try to do something damaging to Socrates. Such anger, then, plays a conative role and resists and even impairs good reasoning.'

My claim in this chapter is that it is wrong to think that Socrates treats anger and belief as distinct phenomena and must then determine which one influences the other. In the view I am proposing, anger is an evaluative belief which motivates the prosecutors' response. The prosecutors' anger is a belief that Socrates did them wrong by mocking and criticising them, and by exposing their ignorance. This motivates their response in the form of charges against him that are more aimed at retaliation than truth. My interpretation is also consistent with Socrates' motivational intellectualism, since the prosecutors did what they thought was best – their anger is an evaluative belief that motivates their actions against Socrates.

In my discussions of other emotions, I have shown how Socrates recognises that even the negative emotions of fear and shame can be appropriate and even helpful. Although there are fewer examples of appropriate anger in Plato's early dialogues, there is at least one in which Socrates deals with his own anger. In this instance, Socrates is not angry at others, but at himself:

> SOCRATES: He[19] questioned me this way, really insultingly: 'Socrates, how do *you* know what sorts of things are fine and foul? Look, would you be able to say what the fine is?' And I, I'm so worthless, I was stuck and I wasn't able to answer him properly. As I left the gathering, I was angry and blamed myself, and I made a threatening resolve, that whomever of you wise men I met *first*, I would listen and learn and study, then return to the questioner and fight the argument back. So, as I say, it's a fine thing you came now.
>
> – *Hippias Major* 286c–d

When he is confronted with the question in a Socratic fashion, Socrates says to Hippias that he, Socrates, was worthless, not being capable of defining what fine things are. Because of his own ignorance, Socrates was angry at and blamed himself. Unlike most of his interlocutors, rather than trying to hide it or lash out at anyone who might expose it – or for that matter, seek to injure himself in some retaliatory way – Socrates' own assessment of himself as being ignorant motivates him to make a philosophical effort to listen, learn and study from someone wiser than he. He seeks not revenge, but self-improvement. Here, it is not his belief that adjusts to his anger, but the anger that motivates Socrates so positively that he enhances his philosophical study to such a degree that he responds effectively and appropriately to the one who had questioned him.

One other example of how one should treat anger deserves a mention. Socrates interprets Simonides' verses in a free fashion while telling us what good men should do, even if they are angry at their parents and country:

> SOCRATES: Good men conceal the trouble and force themselves to give praise, and if they are angry because their parents or country wronged them, they calm themselves down and reconcile themselves to it, and they force themselves to love and praise their own people.

> *– Protagoras* 346b

Socrates holds that good men are aware that what their parents and country have given them is so considerable that it is incomparable with any wrongs they might receive from either of them.[20] Additionally, if one is angry at parents or other loved ones, Socrates advises that it is always prudent and reasonable to calm down and to consider whether it is more worthwhile to be angry at or to reconcile oneself with the situation and with those who have angered one. One of the features of the emotions I have observed is that their non-rational etiologies can make them especially resistant to rational persuasion. In *Republic* I, Plato provides us at least a glimpse of how Socrates tried to manage the project of persuading an interlocutor who reacts in irrationally emotional ways. Thrasymachus' response to Socrates is heated.[21] Socrates seems not only to refute Thrasymachus' arguments but – by understanding the dynamic of his psychic life – also to educate him in a way the angry sophist would never expect.

> He coiled himself up like a wild beast about to spring, and he hurled himself at us as if to tear us to pieces.

> *– Republic* I.336b

Socrates' most ferocious interlocutor, Thrasymachus cares inordinately about honour, power and reputation. His rashness and impatience are characteristics of an angry person. His behaviour seems not to be consonant with his political and philosophical views, because his ideal political leader should be intelligent, brutal and unscrupulous, and therefore not distracted or vulnerable to excessive emotional responses that might cloud his ruthless judgments. Socrates employs his irony and apparent fear (*Republic* I.336b) to expose both 'Thrasymachus' overactive passion, and his intellectual instability and lack of self-control to everyone, but most importantly to Thrasymachus himself' (Hoesly and Smith 2013: 192). Having delivered his panegyric speech on the ideal of an unjust ruler, he is compelled to answer Socrates' philosophical questions, which aim at establishing what justice is. At the end of Socrates' refutation, Thrasymachus becomes emotionally and physically exhausted. Plato's description of his psychosomatic reactions after he was refuted by Socrates is striking: Thrasymachus sweats, 'a quantity of sweat that was a wonder to behold', and blushes, which Socrates did not expect to see (350c–d). At that moment, he does not want to participate in the dispute anymore, saying that he will just 'nod yes and no, as one does to old wives' tales' (350e).

At the end of Book I of the *Republic*, we find that Thrasymachus has calmed down, and later on in the *Republic* he has become tamer and even collaborates in the discussion. When Adeimantus and Glaucon ask to clarify the concept of the community of women and children that Socrates seems not to have fully explained, Thrasymachus says, 'In fact, Socrates, you can take this as the resolution of all of us' (450a). Further on, Socrates

SOCRATES ON EMOTIONS

defends him by saying: 'Don't slander Thrasymachus and me just as we've become friends – not that we were enemies before' (498c–d).

'By performing this psychic therapy in Book I', as Hoesly and Smith (2013) show, Socrates seems to transform Thrasymachus from a hostile interlocutor into a partner in the quest for justice. By exposing Thrasymachus' vulnerability to anger, 'Socrates is able to shame him into becoming *more* psychically and intellectually stable, more receptive to reasoning, and hence, more just' (Hoesly and Smith 2013). Just as in the case of Thrasymachus, Socrates 'does not merely refute others; he also says he *exhorts* and *shames* them, *irritates*, *angers*, and *annoys* them' to restore and enhance their reasoning and attitude. In the case of Thrasymachus, his anger affects his reasoning so that he was too rash and too impatient to elaborate and advance his conception of (in)justice. By depicting the anger of an interlocutor such as Thrasymachus, Plato shows that one's emotions are often faulty assessments of things, and thus motivate inappropriate reactions. When Socrates exposes Thrasymachus' inconsistent thoughts, Thrasymachus' anger and shame are engaged in such a way as to have an impact on the further discussion and on Thrasymachus himself, who seems to become a more reasonable partner in the discussion. His purpose from then on was not only to express his view, but to collaborate with Socrates and the other interlocutors on their common enterprise of seeking justice. Plato's portrayal of Thrasymachus is not just a literary ornament. Instead, Plato issues it to explain how hostility and anger affect philosophical dialogue.

VII. ENVY

How to account for envy has remained a puzzling issue that has persisted to this day, with a variety of approaches on offer. Many contemporary scholars[22] posit a distinction between two kinds of envy: a malicious or invidious form, and a benign, emulative or admiring variety of envy. In this section, I will attempt to show how Socrates contributed to the understanding of envy, because he seems to conceive of a version of this emotion that is both the negative form of envy and the one positive, in contrast to many ancient accounts which highlight the negative aspect of envy.[23]

Socrates himself is the object of an invidious form of envy. In the *Apology* (28a), we are told that citizens of Athens envy Socrates due to his intellectual and moral superiority. According to a later tradition, Socrates said that 'envy is the ulcer of the soul' (Stobaeus, *Greek Anthology* III 38.48). However, a benign, emulative or admiring variety of envy plays a role in Plato's Socratic dialogues, although Socrates does not frequently concur with his interlocutors about who is the one that should be envied in such a way. This sort of envy is at stake when Polus in the *Gorgias* (468e–469a) endorses his object of admiration:

> POLUS: Really, Socrates! As if *you* wouldn't welcome being in a position to do what you see fit in the city, rather than not! As if *you* wouldn't be envious whenever you'd see anyone putting to death some person he saw fit, or confiscating his property or tying him up!
> SOCRATES: Justly, you mean, or unjustly?
> POLUS: Whichever way he does it, isn't he to be envied either way?
> SOCRATES: Hush, Polus.
> POLUS: What for?
> SOCRATES: Because you're not supposed to envy the unenviable or the miserable. You're supposed to pity them.

Polus' envy seems to be an admiring one, though aimed at an unjust person. It is approval of someone for some desired quality, possession or position they have. I propose that this belief has a non-rational source in our natural attraction to the beneficial, however misapplied in this instance. In having such a non-rational belief Polus seems to follow, as Irwin argues (Irwin 1979: 146), the traditional Greek belief that one should 'envy' powerful, fortunate and successful people. Socrates does not simply reject that we should ever envy others; instead, he regards Polus as simply wrong about who merits such (positive) envy. Those who manage their affairs in such a way as to violate both laws and justice will fully corrupt their own souls. Therefore, such a 'powerful' person is the proper object not of envy, but of pity. Socrates seems to understand pity as the feeling we have toward those who do or suffer things that will make them wretched or miserable, and therefore rightly applies to anyone who is corrupted, ill-controlled, and in whom reason does not play an adequate role. This kind of pity might influence our negative moral judgments of the pitiable, especially when those rightly pitied are admired for the wrong reasons. Those we should properly envy, according to Plato's Socrates, are those who can manage to keep themselves free of the corrupting effects of wrongdoing and injustice – and our envy for such persons would deserve to be even greater for those who can help others to achieve that same psychic order in themselves.

VIII. GRIEF

Grief[24] plays a particularly prominent role in all cultures, although there are cultural differences in what qualifies as socially acceptable ways for its expression. It might be tentatively defined in cognitive terms as a belief that one has suffered some significant loss, usually the death of a beloved person. It is obviously based on our natural aversion to pain, in this case the anguish caused by the experience of the deprivation of persons we love, or of something that we highly value. Grief can be intolerable when the persons whom we love are irrevocably cut off from us. Moreover, grief can be the result of a more or less accurate judgment that the loss of some especially beloved other amounts to a permanent loss to one's own well-being. For some losses, there can never be fully adequate remedies. Grief is one of several other-related emotions, which shows how we relate to one another as humans. If we experience grief for another, it obviously implies that we highly value and love that person.

In Plato's *Phaedo* and Xenophon's *Apology*, the last moments before Socrates dies are described very subtly. In Xenophon's *Apology*, Socrates sees his friends in tears and he knows that they feel grief for him, because they soon will be deprived of him forever, from the teacher they love and esteem highly. Given all that they had gained from association with Socrates – whose wisdom and ethical attitude were paradigms for them – his friends will experience bereavement, which can cause considerable mental anguish in them. When one who has participated so essentially in our life dies, we might feel that we are losing something we regard as required for our own well-being. In Xenophon's *Apology*, Socrates' intention is to convince his friends and disciples not to grieve for him but to 'feel cheered', because he will be happy. If he will flourish, they should not experience grief. Phaedo, in the dialogue bearing his name, before Socrates' death describes his feeling as mixed: as sorrow or joy, because Phaedo's teacher will not be in his own life anymore, and as a kind of joy, because Socrates 'appeared happy in both manner and words' (*Phaedo* 58d–59b).

SOCRATES ON EMOTIONS 269

In the famous Funeral Oration, which Socrates attributed to Aspasia in Plato's *Menexenus*, deceased soldiers speak to their fathers and mothers. In this Oration, we find this advice about how to cope with grief:

> For they will stand in no need of a stimulus for grief; the misfortune that has befallen them will be enough to provide that. A better course is to try to heal and soothe them, by reminding them that the gods have answered their most earnest prayers. For they prayed for their sons to live not forever, but bravely and gloriously.
>
> *– Menexenus 247d–e*

In these poignant words one finds the love and care that the brave warriors have for their parents. Given that they know their parents will experience bereavement when they hear their children have passed away, the deceased, being thoughtful and caring, through their words show that they do not want their parents to grieve excessively, and want them to overcome their pain. The father and mothers 'ought ceaselessly' to be encouraged not to indulge in grief, since deep, long and intense grief can be self-destructive. Too much calamity had befallen them, so – as it is advised – their souls should be healed, by finding the proper words to remedy their pain. Moreover, if their mothers and fathers reveal too much anguish, it may seem as though the fathers did not properly respect what their sons so courageously and gloriously did for their country. Even so, others – and particularly one's own children – might figure so significantly in one's own sense of well-being, that such deaths can result in permanent reductions in one's capacity for happiness in life. Nevertheless, parents must not succumb to their grief, because this is the wish of their dead sons. Rather, the bereaved parents should cope with grief: (i) by being moderate in mourning, (ii) 'by turning their minds to the concerns of the living,' (248c) instead of mourning for those who died, and (iii) by limiting lamentation of the dead (249c).

This understanding of grief seems to show that Socrates was aware of how difficult it is to modify negative emotions by rational persuasion. However, the grief must be controlled and limited, if not eliminated. In his own case, Socrates reassesses the value of death which causes grief. Given that death for him is a blessing, Socrates is felicitous. If our grief is caused by our unhappiness for the one who will die, then his friends and students should not grieve, because what is to happen to him is a good, and not a bad thing. In the case of parents' mourning for their dead sons, they should overcome their grief by devoting themselves not to the dead sons, but to their living grandchildren. Socrates seems to recognise the power of grief, which can be a genuine threat to human beings. However, he offers ways of assuaging grief, by philosophically re-assessing the cause of grief and telling proper words to remedy grief, and by giving ethical advice to be moderate in grief, appealing to honour and dignity. If grief cannot be entirely avoided or eliminated, all citizens must respect the official limits on the period of mourning.[25]

IX. CONCLUDING REMARKS

Some scholars have held the view that emotions were not important for the explanation of the Socratic account of human motivation. Since Devereux's important paper (1995) appeared, a new way of understanding Socratic moral psychology has been proposed and may be gaining broader support among scholars. This view highlights the irrational aspects of the human soul as an important factor in the explanation of Socrates' theory of motivation. Although the result of non-rational psychological processes, emotions are motivationally potent within Socratic moral psychology in virtue of being themselves evaluative beliefs.

In this chapter, I have accepted the view, posited by Brickhouse and Smith (2015), that Socrates was a cognitivist about emotions: They are beliefs derived from natural attractions and aversions. Socrates seems to think that emotions are very significant in our cognitive life. They have an impact on our other beliefs, to the degree that they can even alter or replace our rational or apparently rational beliefs. Emotions are evaluative beliefs that indicate to us how to act. As such, they can contradict and override or themselves be contradicted and overridden by other, contrary beliefs that derive from other belief-forming processes. This is one of many reasons why Socrates cautions Callicles about the perils of being 'out of tune' with himself, in cognitive conflict and thus inconsistent in the ways in which he might pursue the best life that is possible for him. Similarly, Socrates did not want to beg his jurors for mercy (*Apology* 32c) – as many do when facing the death-penalty – because he thought it was an inappropriate way to behave in court. But he also knew that in refusing to make such an appeal, he might elicit anger in his jurors. Aware that, in the same situation, they would have reacted differently from Socrates, this anger motivated some of them to condemn him. Such jurors followed the path of anger instead of the path of rational persuasion, and a terrible injustice was done as a result. The view of emotion as being motivationally efficacious is consonant with Socratic motivational intellectualism because those who are motivated by emotion do what they think is best when they act. The emotions, in this account, just are the beliefs that motivate their actions – beliefs that are engendered by a non-rational process and are thus unreliably associated with truth.

Second, Socrates employs and elicits emotions to support his own arguments or to discourage his interlocutors from holding faulty views so firmly and to accept the fact that it is a fault in them which has caused them to be refuted. When he appeals to emotions, however, his own moral psychology can count it as an appropriate way to manage the improper cognitive processing that he finds operating within an interlocutor. Without some intervention to reduce the hold that veridically unreliable processes can have on an interlocutor, Socrates will be unable to persuade them. Eliciting emotional reactions can serve to make his interlocutors sceptical about their firmly held beliefs and to encourage them to begin questioning these beliefs. For example, by mocking and shaming Callicles, who says that he is aware of Socrates' shaming tactics, Socrates makes him admit that some pleasures, such as those of scratching itches or being a catamite, are shameful and disgusting, whereby Socrates intends that Callicles brings into question his firmest belief that the experience of pleasure is the ultimate purpose of our lives.

Moreover, by exploring the use of emotions in Socratic dialogues, my goal was also to find out what for Socrates fear, shame, anger, envy and grief are, and how they are interrelated and to interpret them in a more systematic fashion. On the basis of what Socrates says about fear, I have proposed that he understood all emotions in cognitive terms. The fact that emotions are cognitions explains how it is that they can both motivate action and also influence other beliefs. Although they have non-rational etiologies, they compete with other belief-forming processes and are thus at least to some degree responsive to reason. The capacity of emotion to be rational is for Socrates the reason for accepting some instances of it. Because they are veridically unreliable, emotions must be regarded with scepticism in the ways they would lead us. But when they lead us in the right way, they can add potency to the motivations that help us to follow the right path.

In the context of Plato's early dialogues, Socrates reveals the workings of specific emotions, and also the ways in which they are interconnected. Fear and shame seem to be connected in a way that we are afraid to do something that could lead to our being ashamed afterward. Likewise, those who were shamed by what they did are afraid to do it again. Fear of death might be associated with grief. Both emotions are caused by death. Nevertheless, the fear of death is most frequently fear of one's own death, whereas grief is triggered by the death of another, whom we love, and from whom we will be deprived. Anger at oneself increases susceptibility to shame, as the example with Thrasymachus shows. Being refuted by Socrates, Thrasymachus is angry at himself and ashamed at the same time. Anger seems to trigger shame, and shame can, when constructive, lead to the self-awareness that one has done something wrong. A malicious form of envy, when we become aware of it, might evoke shame. To put it otherwise, we can become ashamed when we realise that we suffer pain at our friend's successes, instead of the joy we should feel. Envy and pity are associated as a pair of opposites. Having in mind one of the meanings of both emotions, one may say that those we envy are also those we admire. In deciding who is worthy of envy and admiration – and thus of emulation, we may err, as Socrates' dispute with Polus shows. Socrates seems to connect shame with most emotions because it is deeply involved with our basic moral intuitions, particularly when we are ashamed in our own eyes.

Socrates holds that all emotions are somewhat resistant to reason, which makes them especially dangerous as guides to behaviour. He associates feeling excessive fear with vice and ignorance, and persons who are always fearful are cowards. Excessive anger blocks one's reasoning and can motivate doing injustice to other people, which can fully corrupt our souls. Socrates strongly disapproves of malicious envy, as also the later tradition recognised. He seems to disagree with indulging oneself in immoderate ways in other-regarding emotions such as grief and pity, the former because it is self-destructive, and the latter for making our character weak. But it is the human condition that we feel these emotions, for they all have their bases in our most basic attractions and aversions. We can experience emotions at the wrong times, and to the wrong degrees; but we cannot exist as human beings without experiencing them at all.

The Socratic dialogues point out how human beings should control their emotions in order to lead a philosophical life. In these dialogues, Socrates often gives advice about how to be righteous and successful in leading lives that are worth living. Some belief-forming processes are fully rational ones; for example, the craft of measurement or attending to evidence. Due to their non-rational aetiology, however, Socrates was aware that emotions play a different role in how we act and respond – even within a philosophical discussion. He makes arguments, obviously, and attempts to persuade people through reason; but he also sometimes employs emotions to mock and shame his interlocutors. Both sorts of practices are aimed at improving the souls of his interlocutors by promoting the right, and by problematising the wrong, sorts of cognitive processing. The purpose of his philosophical dialogues was not only to teach his interlocutors how to examine things and to become critical of only apparent truths, but also to appeal to interlocutors to make the effort it takes to manage their non-rational propensities and to subject any of the impulses they might experience to rational scrutiny and reflection. Only when our non-rational processes are brought into alignment with reason can we hope to lead virtuous and flourishing lives. In this way, for Socrates, mindfulness is the best path to wisdom, virtue and happiness, at least to the degree that such things are possible for human beings at all.

NOTES

1. By 'Socrates' and 'Socratic' in this chapter, I intend to refer to the character of that name in Plato's early dialogues. I will also sometimes mention other works by Plato, and also works by other authors (in particular, Xenophon) when I find contrasts or comparisons revealing.

2. For discussions of which, see the chapters on each in this book.

3. Alongside the views already discussed, C. C. W. Taylor considers that there is no 'possibility of interference by conflicting desires' in Socrates' account of motivation. See Taylor 1998: 63.

4. Not, however, love, since there is another whole chapter devoted to that emotion in this collection. (See Chapter 10.)

5. Unless I indicate otherwise, all translations of Plato are those that appear in Cooper 1997. When I have revised these, I will say so.

6. This reading seems to be supported by the later characterisation in the *Gorgias* of keeping the soul in an orderly condition (see 504b–505b, 506d–507a, 507e–508a). It is not clear that this should be taken as an anticipation of the partitioning of the soul provided in *Republic* Bk. IV, since the actual account of motivation assumed in the *Gorgias* appears to be different from the one provided in the *Republic*. For discussion, see Brickhouse and Smith 2010: 199–210.

7. Singpurwalla argues 'that Socrates accepts the existence of distinct sources of motivation, and in particular, irrational desires, and uses them to explain mental conflict and weakness of the will in the *Protagoras*'. See Singpurwalla 2006: 2.

8. I will discuss both passages in more detail in the section on fear.

9. Socrates here treats *erōs* as a kind of desire, and so does not seem here to intend to refer to an emotion. Greek has a number of terms that might be translated as 'love' and so what he says here should not be taken as decisive with respect to how Socrates might think about the experience that we regard as the emotion of love. Again, since Chapter 10 in this volume addresses Socrates' conception of love, I will not address this specific topic further here.

10. Brickhouse and Smith leave it somewhat unclear as to whether they take all appetitively generated beliefs to be emotions. This is not the view that I am proposing here. Appetites such as thirst or hunger, for example, may influence us to form evaluative beliefs about their targets, but the relevant evaluative beliefs would not count as one of the generally recognised emotions, but simply interests that we are motivated to pursue. For Socrates, the beliefs that constitute emotions would be a subset of those with their etiological origins in appetitive urges.

11. A psychological process is non-rational when it arises independently from operations of reason. This is not to say that such processes are *irrational*, which would be a psychological process that is not only generated from non-rational sources but which is also consciously recognised as conflicting with our reasoned conceptions. As I will show, Socrates does not believe that all emotional responses are *irrational*, though all have non-rational etiologies.

12. This is R. K. Sprague's translation, which I slightly modified. See Cooper 1997: 682. Xenophon's Socrates also rejects this identification: 'Over-boldness instills carelessness, negligence, and heedlessness, whereas fear makes people more attentive, more obedient, and more orderly' (Xenophon *Memorabilia* 3.5.5; trans. Konstan 2006: 135).

SOCRATES ON EMOTIONS 273

13. It is the translation of Stanley Lombardo and Karen Bell. See Plato 1992: 56.

14. Josh Wilburn interprets Socrates' argument as follows: 'Fear, Socrates and his interlocutors agree, is an expectation of something bad. Since no one chooses what he expects to be bad (or worse, when the choice is between two bad things), it follows that neither the coward nor the courageous individual chooses what he (most) fears (358e). Rather, they both avoid what they fear, and what distinguishes them is that the courageous person rightly judges what is deserving of fear, while the coward judges wrongly. Courage, therefore, is knowledge or wisdom about the fearful, and cowardice is a form of ignorance.' See Wilburn 2015: 4.

15. The most comprehensive book on *aidos* is by Cairns 1993.

16. See Candiotto 2015, Kahn 1983, Moss 2005, Smith 2020, Woodruff 2000, for discussions.

17. Charles Kahn is one of the first scholars who highlights a role for shame in Socratic philosophising, which is particularly at work in Socrates' discussion with Callicles. See Kahn 1983: 106–107.

18. In Jeffrey Henderson's *The Maculate Muse* (1991: 213–215), there is a list of forty-two who are identified by comic poets as passive homosexuals, which makes it one of the most common insults (indeed, perhaps the most common) in comedy.

19. Socrates seems to be referring to himself in the third person.

20. Emily Austin points out Socrates' 'unwillingness to use his friends and family for advantage, even in order to save his life'. See Austin 2009: 52.

21. My account here follows the analysis given in Hoesly and Smith 2013.

22. See, for examples, Farrell 1989, Neu 1980, Young 1987.

23. For examples of the purely negative ancient accounts of envy, see Xenophon, *Memorabilia* 3.9.8; Plato, *Philebus* 49a–50a; and Aristotle, *Nicomachean Ethics* 1107a9–1107a27.

24. The reasons why Aristotle did not include grief in his discussion of emotion in the *Rhetoric* are excellently discussed in Konstan. He also elaborates on the social aspect of grief. See Konstan 2006: 244 ff.

25. An interesting interpretation of grief in the *Republic* is given by Emily Austin. See Austin 2016: 1–20.

CHAPTER TWELVE

Socrates' Political Philosophy

CURTIS N. JOHNSON

I. INTRODUCTION

Is it possible to attribute a 'political philosophy' to Socrates? Whatever it might be, it will have to be assembled from several dialogues that purport to capture, more or less, various conversations between Socrates and assorted people in and around Athens, as recorded mainly by Plato.[1] Complicating matters is that these conversations have little to do with 'politics' as it is generally understood today. They have rather to do typically with 'virtue' (*aretē*) under its many aspects, and virtue is today generally considered to belong to the discipline of ethics rather than political philosophy. There is also the problem of Socrates' self-claimed 'ignorance' about 'the most important things', particularly how 'virtue' is to be understood (*Ap.* 30a). How can someone who claims 'not to know' about virtue (in the broad sense used here to encompass 'politics') be said to have a political philosophy? Having a political philosophy would seem to assume at least some knowledge about the political questions constitutive of it and some ability to say what this knowledge is. Socrates usually says he cannot give an account of virtue because he does not know what it is.

Nevertheless an endeavour to discover a Socratic political philosophy is entirely worthwhile, both for showing how Socrates would and did answer questions that people today would call 'political' – his 'ignorance' was not 'total ignorance' – and more importantly, for bringing into clearer relief how and why Socratic notions of 'virtue' were very much what he and his auditors would understand as 'political' ideas, however much we have today drifted away from that perspective.

The discussion that follows is presented in three parts. The first part attempts to orient the reader in a general way to what might plausibly be taken to be Socrates' political philosophy. The second part reviews the various controversies that have appeared in the recent scholarly literature about what this philosophy might be in its details. Many lines of interpretation have been developed, as one might expect. The hope is that most of the key arguments have been captured and that references in the text will lead interested readers onto more detailed discussions. The final section undertakes a deeper examination of a cluster of arguments about the extent of Socrates' obligations to obey the commands of civic authority, especially when those commands, if obeyed, would result (in Socrates' opinion) in Socrates being implicated in an injustice.

II. SOCRATES AS POLITICAL PRACTITIONER

Any account of Socrates' political philosophy must begin with an understanding of what Socrates took 'politics' to mean. His understanding was decidedly unconventional, even for the Athens of his day, and more so for a modern audience. A useful guide is what he says to Callicles in *Gorgias*. 'I think I am', Socrates claims, 'one of the few, not to say the only one in Athens who attempts the true art of politics and the only man of the present time who engages in politics' (*Grg.* 521d).[2] This statement, like many other Socratic utterances, appears absurd on its face. Obviously, many Athenians engaged in what they understood as political activity, the activity appropriate to and defining of the *polis* – particularly, voting in the Assembly, serving on the Council, filling political 'offices', and participating in judicial proceedings (Aristotle, *Politics* V.13–15). Indeed, quite paradoxically, Socrates in *Apology* notoriously claimed to *avoid* these activities as much as possible.[3] How could 'the only one in Athens' who engages in genuine political activity also be one of the few people in Athens actively to avoid politics, while everyone else who did 'engage in politics' was found by Socrates not really to do so at all?

The answer hinges on the qualification 'the *true art* of politics' as presented in *Gorgias*. Here, Socrates is engaged in a discussion with Callicles, known by virtue of this dialogue as a champion of the speech-craft of rhetoric. Rhetoricians as a group held significant power in the ancient Greek city-states, including Athens. They sometimes appeared before assemblies and other political bodies in order to effect persuasion to favour or oppose proposed legislation or other matters up for political decision-making; or more commonly, they taught others with political ambitions how to do so. Socrates regarded this entire line of work with grave misgivings. As we know from his great speech against rhetoric earlier in the dialogue (*Grg.* 463a–466a), Socrates shows rhetoricians, along with so-called politicians generally, to be engaged in counterfeit speech, that is, speech designed merely to sway audiences by emotional appeals rather than aimed at educating or enlightening them by appeals to reason. Audiences under the sway of such people were no better, wanting only to be pleased or entertained, not educated. Socrates, by contrast, aims only at 'what is just' or 'what is best' (*Grg.* 464c).

What, though, is 'justice' for Socrates? First is his statement in *Gorgias* that justice is a part of the 'craft' (*technē*) of politics. While it is hard to say what 'justice' is, much *can* be said about what the craft of politics is:

> I'm saying that of this pair of subjects there are two crafts. The one for the soul I call politics; the one for the body, though it is one, I can't give you a name for offhand, but while the care of the body is a single craft, I'm saying it has two parts: gymnastics and medicine. And in politics, the counterpart of gymnastics is legislation, and the part that corresponds to medicine is justice. [. . .] These, then, are the four parts, and they always provide care, in the one case for the body, in the other for the soul, with a view to what's best. Now flattery takes notice of them, and – I won't say by *knowing*, but only by *guessing* – divides itself into four, masks itself with each of the parts, and then pretends to be the characters of the masks. It takes no thought at all of what is best; with the lure of what's most pleasant at the moment, it sniffs out folly and hoodwinks it, so that it gives the impression of being most deserving. Pastry baking has put on the mask of medicine. [. . .] Cosmetics is the one that wears [the mask of] gymnastics in the same way. [. . .] What cosmetics is to gymnastics, sophistry is to legislation, and what pasty baking is to medicine, oratory is to justice.
>
> – *Grg.* 464b–465c, trans. Zeyl in Cooper 1997

SOCRATES' POLITICAL PHILOSOPHY

Socrates nowhere claims that he is a *practitioner* or a *craftsman* of justice, only that he *is* just and that he knows 'how [rightly] to live', if we take 'living rightly' to mean (for Socrates) practising the 'true art' of politics (Johnson 2005: 17–35).[4] Socrates does claim this art for himself in *Gorgias*, claiming to be the only one in his time to practise it (*Grg.* 521d). Because he is contrasting his 'craft' with that of the counterfeit practitioners of rhetoric and sophistry, Socrates suggests that he practises non-counterfeit speech. Proper speech is the one craft he practises in greater measure than any other Athenian, or more strongly still, that he is the only Athenian to practise or at least to attempt to practise this craft (*Grg.* 521d).[5] The 'true' business of politics, Socrates is saying, is not to aim at what pleases but rather at what 'improves' the city and its citizens. As true doctors aim only at the health of bodies, no matter how painful medical treatments may be, so too true statesmen aim only at what is best for the citizens' minds, even if what is best causes temporary psychic pain – and it often will (*Grg.* 464b–465c).[6]

It is natural, then, to suppose that Socrates associated his own wisdom, 'human wisdom', with his proficiency in 'proper speech', which he associated with the elenchus. It was, after all, through his practice of questioning others that he came to understand the nature of his own 'wisdom' and how it differed from the false wisdom of others (*Ap.* 20d–23b). What Socrates learned about a 'political philosophy' from his cross-examinations (beyond this 'self-wisdom') is hard to determine: Most of his dialogic encounters with others ended without firm resolution. At the least, it is safe to say that Socrates did learn some important things about virtue from his cross-examinations, e.g., that it is better to suffer wrong than to do wrong (*Grg.* 469b), even if they did not yield complete knowledge about what virtue is.

Still, as we shall see, a positive Socratic moral philosophy does emerge from an examination of how he lived, and of the account he gave of how he lived. Many lines of evidence converge on the view that, to live justly, Socrates believed he was obliged to live according to the commands of 'the god' (to pursue philosophy) and to the legal commands of the city to obey what they command (*Ap.* 29b). He claims also to be obliged always to 'follow the reason (*logos*) that seems best to me' wherever it may lead (*Cr.* 46b–c). How he came to believe that living justly entails 'obeying legal and moral authorities' is not spelled out in any Socratic texts, leading to difficulties for a proper interpretation. But that he associated living justly with obeying his commanders (with some qualification, discussed below), is as safe a conclusion about his political philosophy as any other that is available to us.

II.I Socrates' Political 'Mission'

Socrates is the only one who attempts 'the true art of politics' because he *does* attempt to improve the city and its citizens, and is, as far as he knows, the only one to do so in his own generation. Many others, including some of the greatest names in Athenian political history, may have gained a reputation for improving the city, but Socrates finds all of them – democrats and oligarchs alike – to have fallen far short of the mark of effecting genuine improvement. Many, in fact, have actually corrupted those they tend to, as a medical practitioner lacking proper medical training may inflict harm on human bodies – i.e., make them worse rather than better (*Ap.* 25b). As Socrates explains to his jury, people often regarded as 'benefactors', such as those who have won 'victories with a team of horses at the Olympic games' have only made the Athenians *think* they are well-off and happy, whereas Socrates has brought to the Athenians 'real' happiness (*Ap.* 36d–e; cf. *Grg.* 516e–517a), even if (again in seeming paradox) the Athenians themselves do not know that they have been made happy by Socrates.

How Socrates improves the city and makes its citizens genuinely happy is a complicated story, but essentially centres on his 'divine mission'. He explained to his jury that he had been ordered by 'the god' (i.e., Apollo) to 'pursue philosophy'. The oracle in fact had affirmed only that 'no one is wiser than Socrates', but for whatever reason Socrates took this as a divine command to himself to pursue philosophy, and believed the command was reaffirmed in dreams and by other manifest signs (*Ap.* 33c).[7] But how does one 'pursue philosophy'? Socrates decided, apparently on his own authority, that one pursues philosophy by engaging other people in conversations about their beliefs, especially their beliefs about virtue. Such conversations often led to Socrates questioning people and then subjecting their answers to merciless scrutiny and usually refutation – the notorious Socratic elenchus.[8]

These conversations, even if they did not yield positive beliefs about virtue, did perform a valuable (or harmful, depending on one's perspective) function for those who were involved in them, either as participants or auditors. They showed that, often unwittingly, people hold beliefs that are in conflict with one another. Socrates believed it to be a great misfortune for the human soul to hold contradictory beliefs (*Grg.* 482a–c). The *elenchus* was useful for bringing these inner conflicts into light, for which attentive interlocutors should be grateful, even if often they were not.

For Socrates, then, 'the true art of politics' is not what most people then or now think it is. It is not practiced in 'public' spaces such as assemblies or law-courts. It is not aimed at producing results, such as laws or verdicts, that are merely pleasing or that satisfy temporary appetites. Its true practitioners are not those who win a sufficient number of votes or who have been chosen by the lottery or who are sufficiently wealthy or prestigious to attain political office. Most people, in fact, would not recognise Socrates' politics as politics at all. It really resembles much more what we today would call 'philosophy', or perhaps better, the craft of 'teaching' philosophy, particularly ethics. But this statement also needs to be qualified. Socrates insisted that he was *not* a teacher, perhaps even that complete virtue is something that *cannot* be taught (*Prt.* 319a–328d; *M.* 92d–94e). Nevertheless, when we examine how Socrates actually lived and what he did with his life, it is hard to escape the conclusion that 'politics' for him was nothing other than engaging himself and others through conversation in attempting the pursuit of knowledge about virtue and about 'how one should live'. Politics for Socrates *was* philosophy, and philosophy *was* politics. To speak of Socrates' political philosophy is thus at one and the same time to speak about his politics and his philosophy; they are indistinguishable.

III. INTERPRETATIONS AND CONTROVERSIES

III.1 Was Socrates a Democratic or an Oligarchic Theorist?

From what has been said, a Socratic political philosophy is difficult to assimilate to modern conceptions, even when those conceptions trace an ancestry back to ancient Greek thought or practice. In brief, the Socratic conception of political philosophy, as characterised above, rules out several candidates that have been brought forward in recent scholarship as describing what Socrates *really* believed as a political philosophy.

SOCRATES' POLITICAL PHILOSOPHY

Some scholars have found Socrates to be a champion of democratic political thought (e.g., Popper v. 1 1945: 128, 191, 194, 305 n. 53; Santas 1979: 38; Gulley 1968: 168–179; Burnet 1924: 173; a dissenting view is Kraut 1984: 22 and chapter 7); or of 'democratic republicanism' (Arendt 1958: 22–78; Villa 2001: chapter 1). This belief centres mainly on Socrates' loyalty to the Athenian laws and constitution when they were constituted as a democracy, that is, for most of his life (two short-lived oligarchic regimes in 411 and 404–403 BCE being the only exceptions). He showed his loyalty in many ways, many of which are recounted in *Apology* (cf. especially 28d–e; 36a–c), but no greater demonstration could be given than his willing submission to accept the unjust penalty of the Athenian jury that he be executed for his 'wrongs'. By contrast, when the Thirty Tyrants were in power Socrates showed his *lack* of respect for that government by openly disobeying one particular order they issued directly and specifically to Socrates, an order that he participate in the arrest of Leon (*Ap.* 32c–d; Xenophon *Mem.* 1.2.31–38 and 4.4.1). Moreover, when Plato has the personified 'Laws' in *Crito* question Socrates about whether he may rightfully escape, they remind him in the clearest possible terms that he has shown throughout his life his 'satisfaction' with the city and its laws. So great, in fact, has been his satisfaction that his decision to live in Athens rather than to go into exile in another city may be construed as a sort of 'agreement' on Socrates' part to abide by the city's laws and other commands (*Cr.* 51e–52d). Socrates appears to agree with this entire line of reasoning; certainly, he does not protest any of it. Because Athens was a democracy for nearly the entire time Socrates lived there, a conclusion might be drawn that Socrates was sympathetic to democratic thought through and through.

Against this view is the belief that Socrates was really an oligarch, or at least more sympathetic to oligarchic rule and ideology than to democratic practices and beliefs (e.g., E. Barker 1959: 97; A. E. Taylor 1933: 103; Stone 1988: 117–139; Grote 1888 vol. 7: 144–146; Guthrie 1971: 61–64; Vlastos 1983b: 495–516; Winspear and Silverberg 1939/1960: 84; Wood and Wood 1978: 97; Ober 2011: 142–143 is a critical examination of this view; cf. also the discussion of this issue in the context of relevant ancient texts in Brickhouse and Smith, 1994: 155–175, reprinted in Brickhouse and Smith 2002b: 190–223). A stronger version of this thesis is that Socrates was in fact anti-democratic (this opinion is critically surveyed, with references to additional literature, in Ober 2011: 142, 163 and n. 48; Ober 1998: 159 and n. 9; and Brickhouse and Smith, 2002b: 191–192).

In favour of the opinion that Socrates was sympathetic to an oligarchic political philosophy is that his most famous friends and companions, including Plato himself, were oligarchs, and some, like Critias and Charmides, were closely associated with the oligarchic faction in Athens, both having even been members of the Thirty. There is, secondly, Socrates' apparent scorn for the views of 'the many', people who, Socrates is quite convinced, have never given much careful thought to anything of real importance and whose views should be set aside by anyone who wishes to make correct decisions about how to live a virtuous life (e.g., *Cr.* 47a–48c; *Ap.* 24e–25c; *Grg.* 474a–b). This is not, we are told, an attitude that any democrat would hold. In addition, Socrates appears explicitly to cast doubt on some core elements of what is usually taken to be a 'democratic ideology', especially the beliefs, conveyed by Protagoras in the dialogue that bears his name, that virtue can be taught and that all people have a share in the possession and teaching of virtue (*Prt.* 319a–328d; cf. *M.* 92d–94e).[9] The assumption here is that anyone who is as contemptuous of democratic ideals and democratic men as Socrates plainly is must therefore be friendly to the obvious alternative, oligarchic ideals and men.

Closer inspection reveals, however, that Socrates' thought cannot be considered to be simply 'democratic' or simply 'oligarchic'.[10] We have no strongly positive evidence in any of Plato's Socratic dialogues for a Socratic preference for any sort of existing regime (Brickhouse and Smith 1989b: 170–173; Kraut 1984: chapter 7). He did, it is true, have great (though not unbounded) respect for political authority. But this respect did not derive from the character or the particular form of government under which he lived. He demonstrates no principled approval or disapproval of any particular form of government, whether democracy or oligarchy (he lived under regimes of both types in Athens during his lifetime), or any other. As Kraut (1984: chapter 7) points out, his allegiance to democratic Athens in *Crito* could just as well have been given to an oligarchy or even a monarchy; it is not based on Athens being a democracy.

Indeed, in *Crito*, the 'Laws' remind Socrates that, while he has been satisfied with democratic Athens and 'how we conduct our trials and manage the city' (*Cr.* 51e), he has also often praised Crete and Sparta (both oligarchies) as 'well-governed' (*Cr.* 52e–53a). Kraut plausibly suggests that his approval of all three governments had less to do with the form of the constitution than with the fact that all three cities took seriously the important business of inculcating moral principles into the young. Socrates' conception of politics, if we take it to mean or to include practicing the elenchus, brought him around to the belief that conventional politicians of every stripe are among the *least* virtuous and wise of all persons (*Ap.* 21c–e). Neither wealth nor free birth (the defining marks of oligarchies and democracies, respectively) bore any relation to one's ability to withstand a Socratic cross-examination, let alone to bring forward positive beliefs about virtue that Socrates could deem to be well-founded. A standard Socratic assumption is that someone lacking knowledge of virtue, or at least a commitment to discover what it is, is in no position to 'do well' or to improve his city, and is in fact much more likely to do it real harm (*Ap.* 24d–25c; *Cr.* 47c–d). Neither democrats nor oligarchs scored very well on the standard of 'improving' the city or its citizens, and on these grounds, Socrates had little sympathy for either side.

As for Socrates' friends and associates, just because Socrates may have conversed or been on friendly terms with some oligarchs does not mean that he embraced an oligarchic political philosophy. For one thing, people of oligarchic sympathy were more likely than the working classes to have had the leisure time necessary to engage in philosophic conversations. But also, Socrates may have deliberately targeted oligarchs more often than democrats because he believed they needed more help in the hard business of virtue than democrats (Brickhouse and Smith 2002b: 205). In any case, Socrates counted not only oligarchs among his companions – Chaerephon, for example, who brought the Delphic wisdom back to Athens, was a prominent democrat, as were some others who apparently were quite comfortable living in democratic Athens, like Crito, Laches, Nicias and others. And Socrates makes perfectly clear in *Apology* that he wants to talk with all citizens, rich or poor or whatever their station (*Ap.* 33a–b). The elenchus, and by extension Socrates himself, does not discriminate.

Finally, we should consider briefly the argument that Socrates was a proponent of 'democratic republicanism' (Arendt 1958: 22–78; Villa 2001: chapter 1). This is a complex argument, much of which falls away for the same reasons that the argument for 'Socrates the democrat' fails. But the notion of 'republicanism' brings in a dimension that is not fully present in the democratic view, namely, the suggestion that Socrates was a champion of public virtue and civic engagement, and would therefore support a political philosophy that gave a prominent place to the values of concern for the city over concern

SOCRATES' POLITICAL PHILOSOPHY   281

for oneself and of active civic discourse, preferably in an 'ideal speech setting', among all citizens. The republican position, moreover, generally favours a 'mixed' or 'blended' constitution to ensure a role for 'the many' as a counterpoint to the typical dominance within government by 'the few'.[11]

The first and most apparent difficulty with this view is that Socrates eschewed 'politics' (in the conventional sense) as much as possible. 'Civic engagement' was quite a different thing for Socrates than what it is to the republican tradition. Socrates' position does make allowance for, even requires, the 'discursive community' and the 'ideal speech condition' posited by theorists like Arendt and Habermas. But Socrates' notion of a discursive community is much more private and intimate than the free-wheeling public arena of debate and discourse contemplated by republicans. Beyond that, Socrates' ideal constitution can no more be said to be a 'mixed' or 'blended' regime than it can be said to be a 'democracy' or an 'oligarchy'. In time, *Plato* appears to have come to embrace the mixed regime as a 'second best' form of government, as spelled out, for example, in the *Statesman*. But a defence of that particular form of constitution is not found in the Socratic dialogues. If neither the many nor the few could be said reliably to care for the 'most important things' and to know how to enact the best policies, then no more could a mix between the two be hoped to do so.

III.II Was Socrates a 'Liberal/ Social Contract' Theorist?

Some scholars have found a 'liberal, social contract' political philosophy in Socrates' thought, particularly as they believe it is spelled out by the 'Laws' in *Crito*. While liberal political philosophy has taken many forms, it generally reduces to the notions that: i) the relation between the citizen and the city is a 'social contract', in which cities and citizens agree voluntarily to exchange rights and obligations for the sake of mutual self-benefit (the 'just agreement' condition[12]); ii) citizens are understood to be morally autonomous and 'unencumbered' individuals who decide for themselves through acts of individual and independent conscience that they wish to enter into the contract (the so-called 'consent' condition, including 'tacit' consent); iii) the contract, to be sufficiently attractive for such morally autonomous citizens to consent to their obligations (including, above all, the obligation to obey the government) must include benefits granted by the state to its citizens (normally conceived as protection of 'natural rights', but not always); and finally, iv) that if the state should fail in its side of the contract (to provide benefits to the citizens), the citizens may, as autonomous individuals, justifiably disobey the government on the grounds that the state has broken the contract (cf. Kraut's illuminating discussion 1984: chapter 6; also Brickhouse and Smith 2004: 217–225; Ober 1998: 181, 184; and Ober 2011: 156–157).

The belief that Socrates was a proponent of this view stems in part from the speech of the Laws in *Crito* and in part from Socrates' practices as described mainly in *Apology* (cf. Gr. 483a–c). Many scholars have found the Laws to be proposing a social contract theory in *Crito*, based on their invocation of Socrates' 'just agreements' to obey the city (most recently Ober 2011: 156); or his agreements to perform only just *acts* the city commands him to perform (Harte 1999). The idea the Laws want to present is that anyone who 'agrees justly' to a city's government, seeing how it is run and having the opportunity to leave the city if he is not satisfied, thereby incurs an obligation to obey its laws, even if the citizen is required by those laws unjustly to go to his death. The city has conferred benefits on the citizen, the citizen has accepted those benefits, and so, on this reading, the contract is consummated and the citizen is obliged to obey.[13]

One benefit that seems especially important in the case of Athens is 'freedom of speech' (*parrhēsia*). Athens, unlike many other ancient cities, allowed great latitude to citizens to speak on all manner of subjects, almost without restraint. Citizens were allowed to propose laws, to express opinions about proposed and actual laws, to vote in assemblies and on juries, even to bring fellow citizens forward on criminal charges and to prosecute them before a jury of their peers. It is sometimes argued that this enshrining of 'free speech' as among Athens' most cherished values shows the signs of a nascent form of liberalism (Villa 2001: 49–50; Brickhouse and Smith 2004: 231; Weiss 1998: 23, 123 n. 88), in the sense that the citizen has the right to exercise a fundamental liberty, and the state has an obligation to protect him in that exercise, or at least not to interfere.[14]

Athens, however, based solely on what the Laws say in *Crito*, cannot be considered a 'liberal' state (but see Ober 2011: 150, 156–157; and Kim 2011: 107–111). It did pride itself on its generosity to its citizens: providing a stable framework of laws for marriage, nurture and education of children, and a share of 'all the good things we can [give]' to its citizens (*Cr.* 50c–52a). What we do not find in the speech of the Laws or in Socrates' acquiescence to it is any idea that Socrates (or the Laws) *ties* Socrates' obligations to these benefits, or that Socrates believes he is absolved of his obligation to obey if he thinks the city has failed to comply with its side of the contract. Conspicuously absent from the speech of the Laws is any notion that the *city* has agreed to anything. We are not told that the Laws think they are obliged to confer these benefits; the city and its Laws are simply generous, for which Socrates (and other citizens) should be grateful.[15] Much less are we told that Socrates has 'rights' to these benefits. Reading a liberal social contract philosophy into *Crito* requires supplying one half of the contract idea that is simply not in the text – the half that imposes *obligations* on the city and gives 'rights' and 'goods' to the citizens that the city is obliged to supply.[16]

The Laws, in fact, make the opposite case: Because of the city's generosity to its citizens it may rightfully assume that anyone who decides to remain in the city shows *by his act of remaining* that he accepts state authority without condition (*Cr.* 51d–e). They explicitly point out the mistake in thinking that just because a city might decide to 'undertake to destroy you [the citizen], thinking it is just', the citizen gains a parallel freedom to act in the same way in return, i.e., to try to destroy the city by disobeying its commands (*Cr.* 51a). There is, the Laws say, no 'equality' between the city and the citizen (cf. Ober 1998: 181–182). Rather, the relation between city and citizen is better likened to that between a master and slave or a parent and child. Slaves, children and even more so citizen-subjects owe obedience to their superiors. This is a claim any city could make to its subjects, and is apparently a claim actual cities, no matter how liberal (or tyrannical), do often make. The fact that Socrates has been unjustly convicted by the jury and unjustly sentenced to death does not free Socrates of his obligation to obey. If liberalism is to be detected in the speech of the Laws, it is much closer to the authoritarian liberalism of Thomas Hobbes than to the liberal liberalism of John Locke or John Rawls. But even that assimilation is quite misleading (Kim 2011: 67 n. 2).

Socrates shows by his reaction to the speech of the Laws and his subsequent decision to remain in prison and accept execution that he essentially agrees with what the Laws have said. If the Laws are not liberal, neither is Socrates. He nowhere ties his loyalty to the Athenian state to its institutions allowing free speech and 'universal' (i.e., adult Greek male) citizenship, and providing the other 'good things' it provides. These institutions may have helped satisfy Socrates that he should remain in Athens rather than go into voluntary exile to another city. But we do not find Socrates specifically praising these

SOCRATES' POLITICAL PHILOSOPHY

institutions or, more importantly, hinting that he would somehow feel free of his obligation to obey the civic authorities were these institutions lacking.

III.III Was Socrates a 'Proceduralist'?

Some scholars have found Socrates to be an early proponent of the 'procedural state' (cf. Kraut 1984: 166–171; Ober 2011: 174–175; Harte 1999: 117–125). According to this conception, just decisions are contingent upon just procedures, sometimes referred to as 'due process' considerations (e.g., Brickhouse and Smith, 2002b: 240). Since Socrates was allowed a 'fair trial' and because other relevant norms and laws were adhered to in his arrest, trial and execution, a temptation may exist to find him to have obeyed the state in the matter of his execution *because* the proper procedures were followed and *because* those procedures were fair. He was given 'due process of law', and accordingly believed himself bound to obey the state in the matter of his execution.[17]

The evidence supporting this view is again to be found in *Crito* (assuming here that the Laws speak authentically for Socrates). The Laws point out to Socrates that he had entered into 'just agreements' with the city, and that the justice of these agreements is apparently contingent upon the agreements having been neither 'forced, nor tricked, nor rushed' (*Cr.* 52d–e). In addition, the city allowed citizens to 'leave the city' if they were not satisfied with how the city was governed. The Laws also say on several occasions that Socrates must 'persuade us where justice really lies', or obey its commands. One might infer from these statements that one's 'agreements' to obey one's city and its laws are qualified by these procedural requirements (Brickhouse and Smith 2004: 239; Harte 1999; Kraut 1984: 166 ff.). Since Socrates could not claim any procedural violation, he found himself obliged to obey. But, some scholars argue, had he discovered a procedural violation, he may have justifiably escaped.

Generally, it is a mistake to find a doctrine of 'rights' or a foreshadowing of the 'procedural republic' in the thought of either Socrates or Plato. (Discussions include Johnson 1990: 730, 733 and n. 23; Woozley 1979: 32 ff.; Kraut 1984: 90, 100–101; Walzer 1970: chapter 4; Strauss 1983: 62–63; Brickhouse and Smith 2002b: 240; I postpone a fuller discussion of the so-called 'persuade-or-obey' doctrine to a later section of this chapter.) The weakness in this line of reasoning lies in the assumption that, had the procedures been absent or different or had Socrates found them to be 'unjust', he would no longer have believed himself obliged to obey. One is hard-pressed to find clear evidence in the dialogues that would support that assumption. The Laws say only that the city provided citizens with good reasons to be satisfied with it. Socrates, by remaining in Athens, has shown he was satisfied with the city and how it was governed. The Laws do not say what the procedural interpretation requires, that Socrates' obligation to obey the state *depends upon* or is *conditional upon* the presence of these (or some other) procedures, and that the obligation to obey would be suspended if these procedures were lacking.

In fact, the Laws make the opposite point. If a citizen believes he has been harmed or wronged by the city, his *only* options are to 'persuade or obey' (*Cr.* 52a).

But when it comes to deciding whether the citizen has been harmed or wronged, the Laws are explicit that the city, not the citizen, decides. The citizen gains no reciprocal right to retaliate (*antipoiein*) against the city if persuasion has been attempted and has failed; the citizen is not on an equal footing with the Laws (*Cr.* 50e–51a). The city is simply generous in allowing persuasion and other benefits. No suggestion is made that the procedural benefits create the obligation to obey. As the Laws see it, the obligation is

284 THE BLOOMSBURY HANDBOOK OF SOCRATES

created by the fact of the citizen choosing to remain in the city, thereby signifying his satisfaction with it and removing any pretext for disobeying.

III.IV Socrates and Civil Disobedience

A related claim in recent years about Socrates' political philosophy is that he was an early proponent – perhaps the first – of a civil disobedience theory of political philosophy (Martin 1970; Kraut 1984: 90, 100–101; Walzer 1970: Ch. 4; Strauss 1983: 62–63; Allen 1980: 86, 109–113; E. Barker 1918: 123; Murphy 1974: 17; Santas 1979: 26; Vlastos 1974: 530–534; Wade 1971: 324; Woozley 1971: 307–308; Woozley 1979: 8–40; Kim 2011: 67–110). On this theory, a just citizen may or must disobey the commands of his city when: i) those commands are 'unjust' (or the city itself is unjust); and ii) the citizen, not the city, decides whether civic commands are just. Do we find a foreshadowing of this theory in the Socratic dialogues?

One notes, importantly, that a command may be unjust in two ways: A command may order a citizen to *commit* injustice; or a command may be 'unjust' though without ordering a citizen to commit injustice, even if it orders him to *suffer* an injustice (*Grg.* 474b). (An example of the second would be the jury's command that Socrates be executed.[18]) As usually presented, the civil disobedience stance would allow or require disobedience in both cases. But it is possible that Socrates accepted only the first idea but not the second. Some scholars believe he would refuse to carry out only commands that he believed would require him to *commit* an injustice. Commands of this sort – if any happened to come his way – he would simply disobey. But, on this reading, he would (and did) carry out 'unjust commands' of the other sort, those that he regarded as 'unjust commands', such as the command that he die, but that did not require him to commit injustice.

The civil disobedience reading of *Crito* generally proceeds along lines similar to the proceduralist argument, with an important difference. The proceduralist assesses the justice of commands from the standpoint of the procedures that gave rise to those commands. The civil disobedient, by contrast, looks mainly to what has been commanded; that is, to the results of those procedures. Just procedures might result in unjust commands (e.g., the command that Socrates be executed), and unjust procedures may, by fortuity, result in just commands. For the civil disobedient, procedures are secondary; what matters is whether the state, through whatever procedures, imposes unjust commands upon the citizen. Do we find such a doctrine spelled out, or even hinted at, in *Crito*?

The Laws in *Crito* do explain to Socrates that he has been treated fairly and generously by the city. Socrates seems to agree – he does not disobey, or even challenge the Laws' reasons. The question for a civil disobedience theory in *Crito* is whether the Laws (or Socrates) suggest that *if* Socrates had been commanded to participate in injustice, he either might or must disobey. Do his obligations *depend upon* the city issuing only 'just' commands, or being a 'just' city?

The answer, based on the text, must be 'no.' The problem with the 'civil disobedience' view outlined above when applied to Socrates is that the theory of the Laws in *Crito* is not really a civil disobedience theory. In its traditional form, civil disobedience explicitly allows or even requires dissent and disobedience if the state is unjust or commands its citizens to participate in injustice. Good government – meaning government that is not unjust – is a condition of the civic duty to obey. The Laws of *Crito* make no such claim. They only claim that people who remain in the city show *by remaining* their 'satisfaction'

SOCRATES' POLITICAL PHILOSOPHY

with the city and how it is run. And, unlike modern disobedience theory, the Laws do not allow private citizens to decide what laws to obey or disobey. Leaving it to private judgments about what justice requires opens up a great deal of leeway for disobedience on spurious grounds. Indeed, one ventures to say that almost anyone else besides Socrates, when faced with his situation in prison, would jump at the opportunity to escape without giving the matter much if any rational consideration at all.

In truth, *Crito* is more naturally read as a defence of almost unlimited obedience to state authority than as a manifesto of disobedience.[19] In this dialogue Socrates not only agrees that he must submit willingly to his unjustly ordered execution, but also stands as a staunch defender of *Staatsrecht*: Whatever the state orders must be obeyed by the just citizen. *Crito* offers a powerful and almost unqualified version of unlimited state power, and Socrates appears to endorse this theory (Brickhouse and Smith 2004: 234; but cf. Weiss 1998, and Harte 1999, who believe the Laws do not speak for Socrates). Modern political philosophy may look back to *Crito* for guidance on a citizen's duty to the state, but it takes a strained form of reasoning to get the *Crito* to add up to a civil disobedience doctrine.

III.V 'Persuade or Obey'

Of possible 'proceduralist' considerations that may have influenced Socrates' thinking, one seems especially important: The Laws' statement to Socrates that he has been 'allowed' (*ephiêmi*) to 'persuade' the city why it is wrong before he is obliged to obey its commands:

> Is your wisdom such as not to realize that your country is to be honoured more than your mother, your father, and your ancestors, that it is more to be revered and more sacred, and that it counts for more among the gods and sensible men, that you must worship it, yield to it, and placate its anger more than your father's? You must either persuade it, or obey its orders. [. . .] One must obey the commands of one's city and country, or persuade it as to the nature of justice.
>
> – *Cr.* 51a–c; Grube/Cooper trans. in Cooper 1997

The passage has an important bearing on the question of the extent of Socrates' obligation to obey state authority. The clear import is that Socrates' obligation is not absolute: He has the opportunity (literally, 'is allowed') to attempt to persuade the state that its commands are unjust, and thus to cause the state to rescind such commands, if the state is persuaded the commands are unjust, before he incurs any obligation to obey them.

It may be questioned, however, whether the city is suggesting anything like the proceduralist idea that Socrates has a 'right' to persuade before he is obliged to obey, or that, if denied this right, his obligation to obey would cease. While the Laws do seem implicitly to be making a case that 'persuade or obey' is foundational in a citizen's obligations to obey – they mention the point three times in *Crito* – it goes beyond the text to see the Laws offering anything more than a gift, not a promise or guarantee (Brickhouse and Smith 2002b; S. Yonezawa, 1991: 11–12 notes that 'persuade or obey' 'was not in the Athenian law system'). Athens just happens to give its citizens this opportunity without being required to and, they seem to be saying, Socrates should be grateful. And Socrates is: He has shown his satisfaction with the city and Laws by remaining in Athens. Had he been dissatisfied he was free to leave (cast as another opportunity, not a 'right').

However that may be, the passages in which 'persuade or obey' appears still leave a number of questions open for further interpretation. First, we should ask, when does the citizen attempt to 'persuade', before or after an unjust command has been given? Some scholars believe the persuasion should come before the command, at least before the command directly impinges upon a citizen's activity (Brickhouse and Smith 2004: 222; Kim 2011: 84–92). On this view, citizens may rightly appeal to the Assembly (the main legislative body of Athens) to pass only laws that are just, or to rescind laws that they deem to be unjust. If a citizen fails to persuade the Assembly in either of these ways, he is obliged to obey even 'unjust' laws (i.e., laws that appear unjust to him) when they impinge upon his actions. Socrates, as we know, eschewed all conventional political activity as much as possible, and therefore did not succeed in persuading – did not even try to persuade – the Assembly to rescind its unjust laws or to refrain from passing other laws he may have believed to be unjust. In effect, he forfeited the opportunity to free himself of the obligation to obey unjust laws because he: i) did not exercise his opportunity to persuade, perhaps thinking the Athenian laws were just (*Cr.* 51c–52c); and ii) would have presumably failed to persuade the city of the injustice of its laws even if he had exercised his opportunity. Either way, having failed at persuasion, he was bound to obey (Brickhouse and Smith 2002b: 235–242).

Other scholars believe, not necessarily in conflict with the previous interpretation, that the attempted persuasion is to come *after* one has been accused and/or convicted of a crime, and that its purpose is to persuade the jury that one is innocent (e.g., Kraut 1984: chapter 3; Johnson 1990: 733 and n. 23; Reeve 1989). An accused citizen is to have his day in court. Here the question is not so much about the justice of the laws that one is commanded to obey – although that option may have been available to defendants at trial – as about the guilt or innocence of a citizen who has been accused of violating such laws.[20] On this reading all sides can agree about the justice (or legality) of the state's commands. What is at issue, rather, is the factual question of whether violations to those admittedly just laws have occurred. The Laws are thus to be read as making the uncomplicated point that Socrates was allowed to address the jury with his defence against the accusations, and failed to persuade it that he was innocent (i.e., 'what we have ordered is not right' [*Cr.* 51e–52a]). His failure has the consequence that he is obliged to abide by the verdict to remain in prison and die.

Two other questions raised by the 'persuade or obey' passages are: i) to whom is the persuasion to be directed? and ii) is it enough to *try* to persuade or must one *succeed* in persuading, if persuasion is to have any impact on one's obligation to obey? Since the Laws do not make their meaning clear on either point, we are free to speculate.

Different scholars have offered different answers to the first question: the Assembly, the Laws or the jury – or all three. An answer to the first helps to answer the second. If the Assembly is the intended audience for persuasion, the usual argument is that since Socrates did not ever try to persuade it that its laws were unjust, he forfeited any warrant for disobedience that may have accrued from his attempt at persuasion (whether his attempted persuasion had been successful or not). If the Laws are the intended target of persuasion, Socrates may be seen in *Crito* to attempt to persuade them about their injustice to him. Since he failed to change their mind, and since he remained to accept his execution, this interpretation suggests that 'persuade or obey' influences one's obligation to obey only if one has attempted to persuade. If the jury is the proper object of persuasion, then Socrates is again seen as having attempted to persuade (in this case, to persuade the jury that he was innocent of the charges), and that, having failed (and accepting his punishment),

SOCRATES' POLITICAL PHILOSOPHY 287

he shows again that he thinks persuasion must be successful if it is to absolve one of one's obligations to the city.

Finally, we may ask, how much disobedience is justified under the 'persuade or obey' doctrine? Some scholars find the doctrine to open up 'wide scope' for disobedience (Kraut 1984: 111). Others argue that Socrates' commitments to the state, on a strict reading of 'persuade or obey', remove any room for disobedience. The citizen has only two options: to persuade, or obey. If the citizen tries to persuade and fails, he is obliged to obey. If the citizen does not try to persuade, he forfeits that opportunity, and so again, is obliged. If the citizen succeeds in persuading, he is then no longer confronted with an unjust command and thus with a dilemma about obeying. However you look at it, on this reading, Socrates *must* obey whether he succeeds or fails at persuasion; no third option exists (Brickhouse and Smith 2004: 220–235).

The worry with that reading for some scholars is that it would make Socrates too 'authoritarian'. It seems to remove any place for what some call 'moral autonomy' (Harte 1999; Weiss 1998) or 'critical rationality' (Nussbaum 1985; Kim 2011; Vlastos 1991) argues that at least divine commands required 'rational interpretation' by Socrates, raising the possibility that state commands did too). Despite a seemingly unambiguous text, many scholars find the portrait of Socrates as *always* obliged to obey the state no matter what it commands to be incompatible with his steadfast devotion to 'the just life,' and to his equally strong commitment to 'always be persuaded by the best reasons'. The concern, again, is: What if the state orders Socrates to commit injustice, or to accept reasons for obeying that he finds to be flawed, or weak? But that concern may be prompted more by what thoughtful people today think than by what is in the text. Defenders of 'strict compliance' argue that when the Laws say the citizen must 'persuade or obey', that appears to be precisely what they mean and precisely what Socrates agreeably takes them to mean (Brickhouse and Smith 2002b: 236–239; Brickhouse and Smith 2004: 220–221; Allen 1980: 105; Woozley 1979: 62–75; Santas 1979: 21–26; Young 1974: 16–17, 21–22).

No matter how one resolves the questions posed above, one can scarcely doubt the importance of 'persuade or obey' either for the Laws, who make and repeat the point several times in *Crito*, or for Socrates, who appears to agree with the Laws that 'persuade or obey' is an important consideration in assessing one's obligations to obey the city. Despite ambiguities and uncertainties, one may, I think, safely infer from the evidence of *Crito* that the Laws believe giving citizens an opportunity to 'persuade' was an important factor in their believing that citizens who, having been given this opportunity but nevertheless failed, should be *all the more* willing to recognise that their obligation is to obey, without much further question. And, Socrates appears to accept the Laws' verdict on that matter.

IV. WAS SOCRATES AN 'AUTHORITARIAN' OR A 'LIBERTARIAN' POLITICAL PHILOSOPHER?

At the heart of the controversies discussed above lies a deeper layer of interpretive disagreement: Was Socrates an 'authoritarian' philosopher, or a more 'libertarian' thinker? Disagreement centres on whether Socrates held a *consistent* political philosophy, both between *Apology* and *Crito*, and within *Crito*. One nagging concern for many scholars is that Socrates seems to affirm different, even conflicting views about his relation to the state in different places. In particular, beliefs Socrates expresses in the *Apology* seem not entirely to align with beliefs he expresses in *Crito* (the '*Apology/Crito*' problem); and also claims he makes in *Crito* seem to conflict with other claims he makes in the same dialogue (the '*Crito*' problem). These apparent discrepancies have led scholars to divergent opinions about a Socratic political philosophy. Some, relying on *Apology* and a particular interpretation of *Crito*, find Socrates to be 'morally autonomous', or even 'libertarian'; others, relying primarily on a straightforward reading of *Crito*, discover in Socrates an obedient servant of the state, or more strongly, an 'authoritarian' political philosopher.

IV.I The 'Apology/Crito' Problem

The *Apology/Crito* problem is generated by the fact that, in *Apology*, Socrates seems willing, not only in principle but in actual self-described conduct, to countenance disobedience to state authority in certain situations (the 'libertarian' or 'morally autonomous' Socrates), whereas in *Crito* he articulates (through the speech of the 'Laws') a commitment to nearly unqualified obligation to obey whatever the state commands (the 'authoritarian' Socrates). Can the two views be reconciled or be made consistent?

Broadly, two kinds of resolution to the '*Apology/Crito*' problem have been proposed. One is to acknowledge inconsistency and then to give an explanation for it. Some scholars declare either that Socrates is simply inconsistent, a common human failing, as Socrates discovered was true of many of his interlocutors (e.g., Villa 2001: chapter 1; Beverslius 2000: *passim*); or that he changed his mind (or, more precisely, that Plato did: Grote, 1865); or that Socrates offered the arguments of the Laws only to pacify Crito while not believing in those arguments himself (sometimes called the 'separation' view, to be discussed in a later section).

The other strategy for removing the '*Apology/Crito*' difficulty is to deny inconsistency and then to explain how a proper interpretation allows this to be done: either by showing the Socrates of *Apology* to be 'more authoritarian' than he may seem to be (the Brickhouse/Smith solution, and the 'hierarchy of authority' solution, both discussed below); or by showing the Socrates of *Crito* to be 'more libertarian' (i.e., open to disobedience to the state) than he may at first appear (the 'civil disobedience' reading discussed above; or the 'separation' reading of *Crito*: Harte 1999; Weiss 1998, discussed below).

Scholars who find a disobedient Socrates in *Apology* generally base their interpretations on three cases that Socrates himself brings forward to the jury: i) his refusal to comply with the order of the Thirty that he participate in the arrest of Leon – a direct breach of loyalty to the state (*Ap.* 32c–e); ii) his refusal to go along with (i.e., his decision to 'oppose') the Assembly's decision to try the ten Arginousae generals as a group (*Ap.* 32a–c); and iii) his refusal of the hypothetical 'offer' made by the jury that he would be allowed to go free if only he would agree to give up his cross-examinations, in other words, give up 'philosophy' as Socrates understood it (*Ap.* 29c–30b; Socrates calls this a 'conditional acquittal' offered by the jury, one he claims he would decline if it were offered).

To show that Socrates was more obedient to state commands than the foregoing examples from *Apology* might suggest, some scholars deny that any of these alleged acts of disobedience really count as disobedience to 'authentic' state authority (e.g., Brickhouse and Smith 2004: 230–235). Socrates refused to obey the Thirty, it is pointed out, because the Thirty was not a legally constituted state authority and, for that reason, could claim no valid expectation of obedience from Socrates. Socrates' response to the Assembly on the matter of the ten generals was not an act of disobedience as much as an act of

SOCRATES' POLITICAL PHILOSOPHY

'opposition' to the Assembly's proposal (i.e., a 'nay' vote), and in any case the Assembly was in violation of Athenian law – thus, again, rendering their 'authority' over Socrates to be invalid. The jury's offer of 'conditional acquittal' could not be accepted because the jury had no legal standing to make such an offer in the first place. But even if such an offer were legally issued in an attempt to get Socrates to stop philosophising, Socrates would not necessarily decline the offer. If he believed that the offer would make his continuation of practising philosophy *unjust*, he would accept it because, as we know from *Crito*, his agreements with the city to obey its legal commands placed him under a moral obligation to do whatever the city thought was right. The city and not Socrates, on this reading, is the 'final arbiter between it and the citizen regarding what justice requires' (Brickhouse and Smith 2004: 234).

IV.Ia The 'Crito' Problem

The *Apology/Crito* problem arises because of an apparent conflict between Socrates' seeming willingness to disobey state authority (in some circumstances) in the former, and his seeming unwillingness to disobey state authority (under any circumstances) in the latter. The concern with the *Crito* is that Socrates appears to be affirming two conflicting opinions within the same dialogue: that he will never disobey the city (strict compliance, or SC), *and* that he will never knowingly commit injustice (absolute prohibition of injustice, or APOI). What, then, if he is ordered by the city to commit injustice – that is, something that *Socrates* believes to be unjust?

Some believe the concern is more imaginary than real because the sort of situation imagined here – a direct legal command from the state to Socrates to participate in doing an injustice (in contrast to suffering an injustice) just does not come up. The concern is hypothetical. Others, however, have brought forward actual cases from Socrates' life in which he might be seen as doing this very thing: obeying legally issued commands that led Socrates to commit acts that are regarded by some modern authorities as morally reprehensible. One such instance, it is alleged, is his participation in possible war-crimes in the war against Potidaea; another is his accepting the hemlock (cf. Woodruff 2007; Balot 2008; Anderson 2005: 82–86). There is no question here about the legality or authenticity of the commands. The question, rather, is whether in obeying these commands, Socrates was guilty of doing what APOI prohibits absolutely: participating knowingly in the commission of injustice.

One rescue is simply to deny that Socrates in these cases was 'doing wrong knowingly'. Marching into battle at the order of the military officials could well have been regarded by Socrates as exactly what the 'just' citizen must do. He says as much to his jury: 'I would have done a dreadful thing', he says, if I had abandoned my post for fear of death or anything else [rather than to maintain my station]' (*Ap.* 28d–e). The idea of 'war crimes' seems not to have entered Socrates' thinking: The soldier's duty is to obey. As to the hemlock, Socrates may well have thought that, by taking it, he was participating in an injustice, even to the point of suffering an injustice, but not that he was involved in committing an injustice. Again, he can be seen as a loyal servant of the state, even as he willingly died for it.

A different approach is to suggest that Socrates did in fact knowingly carry out unjust orders (as in participating in the Potidaea campaign or taking the hemlock) but that, in doing so, he was not 'culpable' of wrongdoing (Brickhouse and Smith 2004: 236–237). People sometimes do terrible things, even in direct response to state commands, but

290 THE BLOOMSBURY HANDBOOK OF SOCRATES

nevertheless should *not* be held 'responsible' because the citizen is an 'instrument of the state'. 'Responsibility' or 'blame' for any wrongdoing pursuant to obeying legal authority belongs to the state issuing the commands. Authentic state commands are to be obeyed by the just citizen. But if the citizen obeys an unjust command only because he has legally been ordered to, and if he has no realistic alternative than to obey, his obedience is not 'culpable'; culpability belongs to the state. The same is true of Socrates' accepting the hemlock, and also the jailor's administration of it: He could obey without violating APOI because in none of these instances is he (or the jailor) to 'blame' for the injustice. On the contrary, because Socrates held a strict compliance view, obeying the state even in these unfortunate circumstances is exactly what the just citizen must do.

How, though, could someone completely devoted to an 'absolute prohibition of injustice' (i.e., a 'moral saint', as he has been called) submit to unlimited state authority? Having chosen to remain in Athens, should he not be aware that the state has sometimes commanded him to commit morally repugnant deeds? Is it not at least conceivable that some of these commands might lead to 'culpable wrongdoing'? Some scholars prefer a Socrates who, placing his own moral judgment above the state's, would choose to disobey the state when *he* believed the state's commands went too far. He would be compliant, but only within moral boundaries that were agreeable to him, not necessarily ones that were agreeable to the state. But, if that were true, would he not be in violation of SC?

The problem here is that the 'Laws' in *Crito* appear to leave almost nothing up to the citizen's independent judgment when it comes to the question of obedience and loyalty to the state (Brickhouse and Smith, 2004: 234). The Laws' arguments strongly affirm the citizen's duty to obey, and Socrates does not object, or even question, their reasons. In fact, he is the one who manufactures them! And obviously, he remains in prison and accepts execution. What, then, of his commitment to APOI? Would Socrates obey even a legal command to commit injustice? In short, do his twin commitments to SC and APOI lead Socrates into more or less straightforward self-contradiction?

IV.II The 'Hierarchy of Authority' Argument

To avoid that conclusion, some scholars have had recourse to what is often called the 'hierarchy of authority' view (Santas 1979: 37, 208; Vlastos 1974: 517–534; Johnson 1990: 719–740; Vlastos 1991: 286; Kraut 1984: 26 and n. 2 and 133–134; Woozley 1971: 315; Martin 1970: 25–26; Dybikowski 1974: 524). In general, 'hierarchy' supports an 'authoritarian' version of Socrates, but with an important qualification: Some authorities, i.e., 'higher' authorities, have a greater claim on Socrates' loyalties than other, 'lower' authorities. When authorities make conflicting commands, Socrates will obey the 'higher' ones, with the consequence that he will be disobeying the lower.

On the hierarchy view, Socrates genuinely believed that he is obliged to obey all legal commands of the state (the command of the Thirty does not qualify as 'legal'). But he also believed that he must obey 'the god'. Socrates is thus sometimes forced to choose to obey one authority at the expense of disobeying another. For example, when Socrates in *Apology* tells the jury that he would 'disobey' (or, more precisely, not be persuaded by) an injunction to stop philosophising, even if he were given his freedom in exchange, and even if the result of persisting in philosophical activity were that he die, he really means that he would disobey (not be persuaded).[21] One might suppose that Socrates would disobey such a command even if it were legally valid (the jury's offer was not valid). Yet, on the hierarchy view, he would disobey the state only as an immediate and accidental

SOCRATES' POLITICAL PHILOSOPHY

consequence of obeying the god. His highest allegiance is to the god (*Ap.* 29c–d; 30b; 37e–38a), and that means to him that he must practice philosophy because that is what he understood the god to require of him:

> Men of Athens, I am grateful [for your conditional offer of acquittal] and I am your friend, but I will obey the god rather than you. As long as I draw breath and am able I shall not cease to practice philosophy ... Be sure that this is what the god orders me to do, and I think there is no greater blessing to the city than my service to the god.
>
> – *Ap.* 29d–30a: Grube/Cooper trans

Hierarchists tend to find in this passage Socrates' opinion about the relative importance to him of obeying the god and obeying the state: In a case of conflict, he will obey the god. His continued practice of philosophy might be 'unjust' from the standpoint of the state, but not 'unjust' in Socrates' eyes because he would still be obeying the god, and obeying the god is what the just man must do in this situation. The god's command 'trumps' the state's command, in Vlastos' expression.

The same line of reasoning would help to explain how Socrates would decide if confronted with two conflicting commands of state authority: He would yield to what he took to be the 'higher' authority. The hierarchy view establishes a pecking order of state commanders. It must do so because the state does not necessarily speak with one voice. The Laws, the Assembly, the military commanders, the jury – all of these have a legal voice. If conflicting commands were ordered, Socrates would (according to the hierarchy view) have recourse to his understanding of the hierarchy: Let us suppose the god comes first, then the Laws, then the Assembly (the source of the Laws but also of 'decrees' [*psephismata*]), then other state and military officials (Johnson 1990). Thus, if one legal authority countermanded a different legal authority, Socrates might well be confronted with conflicting commands in such a way as to be unable to obey one without disobeying the other.

The most likely source of such a confusion of legal voices in Socrates' Athens, if it occurred, would be the Assembly. Unlike the laws, especially permanent or constitutional laws, the Assembly was apparently often subject to the vagaries of the fleeting passions of the multitude. Aristotle notes this point with disapproval in his discussion of the habit of democratic assemblies, in particular to exercise their authority of legislating by passing 'decrees' (*psephismata*) instead of laws (*Politics* 1292a4–8 and n. 494, Reeve trans.). One specific action of this sort mentioned by Socrates seems to be the decision by 'the many' to try the ten Arginousae generals as a group. Socrates did not call this action a 'decree', but he did explicitly note that he could not go along with the Assembly because the action was in violation of Athenian Law (*para nomous: Ap.* 32b–c). Yet, for hierarchists, it is hard to deny that the proposal was issued by a legal state authority, making it impossible for Socrates to go along non-culpably with the trial without 'committing injustice'. The instance could be said to constitute an actual example of Socrates *disobeying* a legal state authority because he felt bound to obey the more permanent, and 'higher', authority of Athenian Law. He could not go along with the Assembly without violating the Law. The Law had a stronger claim on his allegiance than spur-of-the-moment decisions made by the accidental make-up of an Athenian democratic faction (which, incidentally, changed its mind shortly after the trial). The example, if valid, shows how Socrates could refuse to go along with a legal state authority and yet remain 'just', i.e., obedient to a higher authority.

The hierarchy view is not without its critics. This argument for hierarchism (i) assumes that the hypothetical command given to Socrates by the jury would be an example of a

292   THE BLOOMSBURY HANDBOOK OF SOCRATES

legal command (as required by 'persuade or obey' in the *Crito*), when, as scholars have shown, this is actually not possible under Athenian law (Brickhouse and Smith 2004); (ii) Hierarchists, in fact, fail to find any clear and uncontroversial cases where Socrates would both recognise a command as genuinely legal and also find he must disobey it, so the very idea that there could be such a conflict is purely speculative. Finally, (iii) the example of the Athenian assembly issuing commands (*psephismata*) that are unconstitutional (*para nomous*) commits Socrates to disobedience of a genuinely legal command only by assuming that unconstitutional *psephismata* would be regarded as nonetheless legal (by Socrates, Plato or Plato's intended audience), and if so, has Socrates disobeying a legal command only in circumstances where it would be logically impossible to obey all of the (putatively legal) commands put upon him. From the fact that a citizen, as a matter of logical necessity, can't fail to disobey some (putatively legal) authority, it doesn't follow that Socrates found any exceptions to 'persuade or obey'. So this example does not solve the problem the hierarchy view takes upon itself to solve.

IV.III *The 'Separation' View*

A different resolution to the *Crito* problem in particular is to have recourse to what is usually called the 'separation' view, mentioned earlier (separation is defended by Weiss 1998: 3–24; Strauss 1983: 38–66; Harte 1999: 117–147; Coliaco 2001: 199 ff.; G. Young 1974: 1–29). This view, in its extreme form, dispenses with any attempt to support an 'authoritarian' or 'strict compliance' reading of *Crito*. In brief, it holds that the words and arguments Socrates puts into the speech of the Laws do not represent his own actual beliefs, but were invented by him only to assuage Crito. Privately, it is argued, Socrates was much more morally agreeable to disobeying the state, or at least more morally independent, than he allows the Laws themselves to affirm. The speech of the Laws thus allows Crito to be persuaded (by 'the Laws') that Socrates must be executed (unjustly), while allowing Socrates privately to hold views at odds with this stated position – sometimes called the 'individual moral autonomy' view (e.g., Weiss 1998: 7–15).

To bolster their position, separationists point out Socrates' steadfast commitment to 'reason' (*logos*), that is, to 'listen to nothing within me but the reason that, on reflection, seems best to me', wherever it might lead (*Cr.* 46b–c). Accordingly, when he is confronted with commands that are possibly unjust, he appeals to what might be called a 'justice test': to subject the arguments for obedience to rational assessment (the idea that rational beliefs should be 'tested' for their truth is introduced at *Grg.* 487e).[22] If Socrates finds upon rational scrutiny that he has been commanded to commit injustice, or believes the reasons he has been given to obey were poor or weak reasons, it is argued that he would 'be persuaded by the strong or best reasons' and would disobey.[23] On the other hand, commands that can be defended by rational argument, by the fact that they have been successfully defended, are to be obeyed. 'The reason' (i.e., *logos*) – whether for obedience or disobedience – will, on this reading, prevail in Socrates' deliberations in how to act.

This test, we surmise, would not at all satisfy the Laws or strict compliance theorists, even though the Laws do not make their opposition explicit. (Crito, by contrast, does explicitly accept this test: *Cr.* 46b–47a.) The Laws would naturally point to the imperfection of humans' reasoning ability, including their own, as they so much as say in *Crito* (50c; 51e–52a). Given this imperfection, who is one to believe in cases of disagreements? The Laws insist, as they believe they must, that the final arbiter in such cases is the city and the Laws, not the private citizen. Without that 'hard line' authoritarian

SOCRATES' POLITICAL PHILOSOPHY

293

stance, too much leeway is opened up for civic disobedience on spurious grounds. Yes, disagreements are bound to occur, but to avoid the shipwreck of widespread civic disruption, the Laws must insist on their having the final say.

The separation view does extricate Socrates from the charge of holding conflicting beliefs, and from being 'too authoritarian', but at a cost. For one thing, it begs the question of whether 'authoritarian' is the proper way to characterise the Socrates of the anti-separationists; some of them, at least, reject that portrait. Moreover, it requires us to imagine Socrates fabricating views that departed from his own strong moral convictions, even if for the noble endeavour of making Crito more comfortable with Socrates' imminent execution (Brickhouse and Smith 2013a). Indeed, Crito had just earlier (*Cr.* 46b–47a) affirmed his own commitment to 'follow the strongest arguments', and not to be swayed by 'rhetorical manipulations' and 'emotional appeals'. So why would Socrates suddenly shift gears by using specious arguments to calm Crito down? Even more difficult for the separation view is to explain why Socrates would have invented arguments for the Laws he did not believe himself, and then immediately proceed to *follow them*, particularly when these inferior arguments resulted in him going unjustly to his death. Why would Socrates have taken the trouble to do that? If his aim was to appease Crito by the manufactured arguments of the Laws, that aim is undermined by Socrates' decision just moments later to abide by the Laws' judgment and accept execution.

The separation view runs into yet another difficulty: It stands in stark opposition to the doctrine of 'persuade or obey'. This doctrine holds that a citizen confronted with a choice of obeying or disobeying authentic legal authority has but two choices: either to persuade the state where it is wrong, or, failing that, to obey. The Laws give no third option. Socrates either did not attempt to persuade, or his attempts failed. Either way, by the logic of persuade or obey, Socrates *must* obey. Separationists may, of course, sweep this objection away by denying Socrates agreed with the Laws even about 'persuade or obey'. The problem here is that, of all the arguments of the Laws, 'persuade or obey' seems the one most completely affirmed by Socrates. Moreover, this doctrine is not the one separationists usually have in mind when claiming Socrates did not share the views of the Laws. Rather, they generally want to attack 'strict compliance'. In any case, if persuade or obey is an acceptable doctrine to Socrates, separation cannot be true.

The positions and objections I have reviewed in this section represent the best efforts of scholars to resolve the puzzles about Socrates' doctrine of obedience to law, which seems to fit only uneasily with his categorical prohibition against injustice. The difficulties with each of the positions reviewed explain why no general scholarly consensus has yet been reached on this question.

V. CONCLUSION

In what sense, then, does Socrates have a 'political philosophy'? Whatever it is, it is unusual. It has little to do with conventional politics. But it does offer answers to those who ask themselves how they ought to live, even and perhaps especially those who come into direct contact with 'political authority' in the conventional sense and are commanded by the authorities about what they must or must not do. This includes more or less all citizens in all cities. It encourages obedience to the state as a rule, but also asks citizens to examine reasons for obeying, finding good and strong reasons (whatever they may be) and following them.

It is easier to say what Socrates does not counsel than what he does. He does not counsel that we should prefer democracy to oligarchy or the other way around. His best constitution, if one were to guess, would be similar to the *kallipolis* of Plato's *Republic*, but to make that guess goes beyond the evidence.[24] Nor did Socrates espouse what would today be called 'liberalism' or 'proceduralism'. In that regard he was a person of his time, supportive of the authority of the state and its powers over the prerogatives of its citizens and their putative rights. Equally doubtful is the proposition that he was a forerunner of a civil disobedience tradition of political philosophy. He was a staunch and unapologetic upholder of state authority and the unlimited obligation of citizens to obey that authority.

What stands out about Socrates for virtually all interpreters is that he is almost defined by his cross-examinations. Socrates was above all one who asked questions, and in the dialogues we have examined here, the central question is about the obligations of a citizen to his state. States sometimes ask citizens to do things that seem unreasonable, even unconscionable. An easy way around mental anguish in such cases is simply to assume either: i) the state is right, and so one's duty is to obey; or ii) the individual citizen is right (or some group to which he or she belongs or thinks he or she belongs is right), and so the citizen may justifiably disobey.

Socrates took neither of these easy ways out. Both are essentially unreflective responses, and that is the problem. What one desires in citizenship, he insists, is precisely reflection and careful deliberation. The Laws are compliant; they provide reasons for their opinions about civic obligation. Socrates appears to find them to be good reasons, ones he accepts. Ultimately that is what justice requires: neither blind subjection nor knee-jerk dissidence. Socratic justice is nothing other than Socratic philosophy: leading the examined life wherever it may lead.

NOTES

1. I assume without argument that the 'Socrates' under inspection here is best thought of as 'Plato's Socrates'. My sources for the views of this person are chiefly: *Apology, Crito, Gorgias, and Republic* Book I. I thus acknowledge putting to one side (for the most part) evidence from Xenophon's *Memorabilia*.

2. Irwin 1979: 240 takes Socrates to mean that he only attempts (*epicheirein* at *Grg.* 521d) the political craft, not that he has reached it, so that 'this remark need not conflict with his previous disavowal of knowledge' (similar is Kraut 1984: 227; and Griswold 2011: 340). But in the same sentence Socrates says he does practice politics, indeed that he is 'the only one of the present time' who does so. This is strong evidence that he believes he actually does practice the craft of politics, not that he only attempts it. Cf. also Brickhouse and Smith 1994: 8.

3. Socrates says to the judges at his trial in *Apology* that he never engages in politics (*Ap.* 31c–d); and to Polus in *Gorgias* that 'I am not one of the political men' (*Grg.* 473e). How, then, can he claim in *Gorgias* to be the only practitioner of politics? The answer is that he intends two different senses of politics in these two passages. The context at *Grg.* 473e makes clear that his disclaimers apply to conventional politics; cf. Dodds 1959: 247, 276; but at 369, Dodds doubts whether the historical Socrates would have made any such claim, and credits Plato with the discovery of this new political ideal. I argue that the claim is 'Socratic' and displays a continuity (along with other positive moral convictions expressed by him in *Gorgias*) with *Crito* and *Apology*.

SOCRATES' POLITICAL PHILOSOPHY

4. Socrates often refers to the several virtues in terms appropriate to other 'crafts' like shoemaking and medicine, e.g., *Chrm.* 165c–166b; *Euthd.* 288d–292e; the particular virtue of justice seems to be (though is not called) a craft at *Grg.* 464b3– 465c5. At *Rep.* 332d an imaginary questioner asks 'Simonides' about the 'craft' of justice. Socrates does not claim the craft of justice as his own in either of these passages, but seems to allow that justice might be considered a craft insofar as it exhibits itself in certain kinds of practices. When justice is a state of soul (*Grg.* 504d), the craftsman is the one who brings such a soul into existence (*Grg.* 503e), but justice itself (as the proper order of the soul) is not itself a craft. 'Philosophy' (under that term) is a craft only at *Rep.* VI.495d, but the appellation 'craft' is given to what Socrates does when he practices philosophy at *Grg.* 465a and 521d, where it is differently called the *technē logōn* and *the politikē technē*. Discussions of the craft-analogy of virtue and other ways of thinking about Socrates as a craftsman include: Reeve 1989: 124–144; Irwin 1977: 71–73, 93–95, 127–129; Klosko 1981: 95 ff.; Brickhouse and Smith 1994: 6–10; Parry 1996: 47–60; Tiles 1984: 49–66; Lesses 1982: 93 ff.; Roochnik 1986; Johnson 2005: 21, 38, 99, 211–213.

5. It is by no means universally accepted that Socrates possessed a craft or even believed he did (e.g., Brickhouse and Smith 1994: 6–10; Irwin 1979: 240; Kraut 1984: 233). His explicit statements at *Grg.* 465a and especially 521d, however, are strong testimony that he did believe he possessed at least the craft of true speech.

6. Recent scholarship has homed in on the question of Socrates' motives for 'avoiding' conventional politics, or even whether he is sincere in claiming that he did. Ober 1998 thinks Socrates knew more about the courts, the assembly, the agora and the speech-conventions of those places than he let on in *Apology* (citing evidence from *Gorgias*). Both Woodruff 2007 and Balot 2008 think he did avoid conventional politics (establishing a model for Plato's Socratic 'philosopher' at *Tht.* 172c–176b), but they have different reasons for supposing so. Woodruff argues that Socrates could not have engaged in conventional politics without ceasing to be a philosopher; whereas Balot believes Socrates could not have entered the 'public' arena of Athenian politics without being destroyed by the demos. Such accounts bear on another question (also treated by Anderson 2005): If Socrates was a 'moral saint' (as Balot puts it), why did he not speak out against moral atrocities committed by Athenians during the war, and why did he not speak out against Athenian imperialism more generally? More on this to follow.

7. Griswold 2011: 342–343 argues that Socrates' argument to the jury that he was 'commanded' by Apollo to pursue philosophy is 'unconvincing'. Ober 1998: 172–173 and nn. 32–35 calls Socrates' interpretation of the oracle's statement a 'tenuous thread' for justifying his philosophical activity because statements by oracles were notoriously open to competing and conflicting interpretations. Socrates does, however, attempt to justify his own peculiar interpretation (*Ap.* 21b–c). Ober acknowledges Socrates' additional testimony at *Ap.* 33c.

8. See Chapter 3 of this book.

9. Socrates may be thought to be defending democratic ideology in *Gorgias* when he argues, against Callicles' übermensch philosophy, that natural justice really means everyone should get an equal share, on Callicles' own premises. But, like Kraut, I take this argument to be inserted only to give Callicles trouble by showing that Callicles' beliefs lead him to conclusions he cannot accept. The argument reveals nothing about Socrates' beliefs.

10. Ober 2011: 164 n. 49 notes that 'Socrates was a critic', hence neither for nor against democracy or oligarchy. A different view is Stone 1988, for whom Socrates was

296 THE BLOOMSBURY HANDBOOK OF SOCRATES

'fundamentally anti-oligarchic' as shown in his response to the Thirty that he arrest Leon by 'going away'. Griswold 2011: 349 and n. 30 leans toward a 'democratic' Socrates, and provides citations to other scholars who share this opinion.

11. See Ober's 1998: 6–7 paean to republican 'freedom', defined as 'the condition of not being under, directly subject to the will of, other human beings' (from Dunn 1996: 105). In democratic Athens this 'freedom' did not rule out a political role for the elite few in governing the city, but did ensure an even greater political role for the 'masses'. Kim 2011: 101–110 emphasises the freedom of the autonomous will of interlocutors who are engaged in Socratic conversations, even if the outcome of a conversation is uncertainty, as it often is.

12. The term employed in *Crito* that is often taken as rendering the idea of a contract is 'agreement' (*homologekenai*: e.g., 51e). The Laws tell Socrates he has 'agreed to obey' by various manifest signs, and so, having agreed, he now finds he must do so. Weiss 1998: 74–76 argues that Socrates' 'agreement' to do things he has agreed to do (in this case, to obey the city's command) derives from his pledge to his jury to 'abide by my penalty' (*Ap.* 39b); but see following notes.

13. As one might expect, different liberal theorists endorse or differentially weigh different parts of the liberal formula. Kraut, for example, defends what he calls a 'liberal' reading of *Crito*, but he does not endorse the view that this dialogue includes a defense of all the elements of liberalism I have identified here. In particular, while he places great weight on the 'argument from just agreements' as underwriting Socrates' obligations to obey, he rightly does not construe that argument as a Lockean social contract argument; and he rightly finds no defense of a doctrine of 'natural rights' in the dialogue, which is, he thinks, its greatest defect. Villa 2001: chapter 1 and Kim 2011: 95ff. find an attractive exemplar of the moral autonomy of the individual in Socrates, but neither place any weight on the idea of the 'procedural republic' in Socrates. Kim 2011: 67–68 and n. 2 gives a useful account of some vital differences between modern 'social contract' theory and the theory of obligation set out by the personified Laws in *Crito*.

14. Cf. Stone 1988, who finds *Apology* to be intensely anti-liberal in this sense; Weiss 1998: 123 n. 88 acknowledges Athens' toleration of free speech but believes that this tolerance did not extend to Socrates' method of doing philosophy.

15. Ober 2011: 158–163 believes the 'goods received' by Socrates that lead to his obligation to obey the city are 'birth, upbringing, and education', but he does not claim these are 'natural rights', only that they are 'goods' that create an obligation.

16. Ober 2011: 156 acknowledges in his 'social contract' reading of *Crito* that the contract is 'unequal'. Socrates is obliged to give more (complete obedience to the Laws) than the Laws are obliged to give him (birth, nurture and education; Ober does not mention the additional unspecified 'goods' that the Laws claim to provide). But for Ober it is still a contract. I depart from this view insofar as I see no evidence at all that the Laws believed they were obliged to give Socrates, or citizens more generally, anything at all – except perhaps a city to live in. The notion of a city's obligations to citizens is not in the text. The point of the Laws, rather, is that Socrates should be even more happy to obey the Laws of the city because, compared to other places, Athens' Laws are fairly generous. The city gives Socrates a 'gift', not a quid pro quo.

17. Ober 1998: 183–187 and n. 56 believes that Socrates' acceptance of the jury's verdict that he suffer the death penalty owed much to his conviction that Athens had fair procedures, that these were followed in the case of his trial, and that a just person must obey judgments

SOCRATES' POLITICAL PHILOSOPHY

thus rendered. Ober's case is bolstered by his sensitivity to Athenian political culture at the time of Socrates' trial, wherein he shows a general concern on the part of Athenian citizens with procedural requirements, especially regarding the role of juries in defining what acts constituted crimes and what punishments to mete out to those convicted. I depart from Ober's view only insofar as I find no 'proceduralist' arguments being offered in *Crito* by either Socrates or the Laws, except perhaps inferentially.

18. Does Socrates violate his own proscription against committing injustice by agreeing to take the hemlock? Most scholars find this to be an instance of the acceptable act of suffering injustice (e.g., Kraut 1984: 37–38), perhaps less desirable than neither doing nor suffering, but more desirable than doing it. Cf. Reeve 1989: 120–121 and n. 18 (and citations). Colson's 1989: 34–35 argument that Socrates is doing injustice to himself by taking the hemlock has found few adherents.

19. Weiss 1998: 7–15, and Harte 1999, argue that Socrates does not agree with the Laws in *Crito*, at least with their arguments about his obligations to obey the city. Socrates fabricates a speech for the Laws that is designed to satisfy Crito, not to reflect his own private views. A more complete discussion is found below.

20. Modern jurisprudence recognises two different ways in which states may err in condemning persons accused of wrongdoing: 1) in wrongly thinking the laws that have supposedly been broken are 'good' or 'right' laws (in modern parlance, 'constitutional' laws); and 2) in wrongly believing defendants have broken such laws. Neither the Laws of *Crito* nor Socrates himself quarrels with the rightness of the law prohibiting impiety. Both are focused on whether Socrates disobeyed that law. The distinction would help remove some of the difficulty in understanding just what the Laws were telling Socrates he should do when they presented 'persuade or obey'. Ober 2011: 140 is one of the few modern scholars to discuss the 'fact/law' distinction in Athenian legal practice.

21. Socrates also reminded the jury in *Apology* that he refused to go along with the decision of the Council when he was a member to try the ten admirals of Arginusae as a group, on the grounds that he believed Athenian law prohibited capital trials of several individuals at once. Whether his refusal can be construed as disobedience has been disputed, but at the very least it shows that he did not regard himself as bound to agree with every decision of state authority (Weiss 1998: 13–14 assumes that Socrates' behaviour in the case of the ten admirals was an example of disobedience).

22. Bostock 1990: 1–21, who reads *Crito* as strictly authoritarian (i.e., the just man must always obey every law), overlooks entirely the significant role of *logos* here. Vlastos 1991: 170–171, while acknowledging the crucial role of *logos*, seems to brush aside even the theoretical possibility of a conflict between it and at least one other authority in Socrates' life, viz., commands of divine origin, on the grounds that the latter always required Socrates' rational interpretation of them in order to be understood; but Vlastos does not provide the evidence that would assure us that in every case the divine monitions required interpretation (cf. McPherran 1996: 178–208 for a useful critique, although he too does seem to allow [201 n. 57] some room for Socrates' interpretation of the *daimonion*; cf. Reeve 1989: 69, and n. 17 above; Nussbaum 1985: 234–235 argues that the *daimonion* is Socrates' own critical rationality).

23. *Ap.* 29b–d. The hypothetical offer which Socrates imagines the jury making to him may not quite resemble an 'argument', but it is comparable to the 'arguments' brought forward by Crito to induce him to escape. Both have the form, 'doing "x" would be advantageous to

sustaining your physical existence; therefore you should do (or might want to consider doing) "x"'. Cf. Colson 1989: 27 ff. The authority of the *daimonion* is not presented as overruling or interdicting the *logos*, it is true. But Socrates does say it 'often prevented me from doing something I was about to do', and since he always led the examined life as much as possible, one must assume that 'what I was about to do' was itself at least sometimes the determination of a process of rational reflection. On the other hand, Socrates would no doubt have wished to investigate the reason for daimonic intervention after the fact of its occurrence (cf. McPherran 1996: 157 ff.).

24. Nevertheless, the opinion is not uncommon: Schofield 2006: 315–316; Kraut 1984: 10; Ober 1998: 10. It may be the case that Socrates would find the *kallipolis* too 'oligarchic', given his evident concern for the health of the souls of all citizens in his native Athens. Colson 1989: 27 ff. rightly emphasises the centrality of the examined life to Socrates' conduct in both *Apology* and *Crito*, suggesting (on the basis of *Ap.* 21c) that 'even the god must pass the test [and] measure up to Socrates' investigative standard' (Colson 1989: 48–49; for a similar view cf. Vlastos 1991; Lamb's introduction to the *Charmides* in his Loeb Classical Library edition). This last statement seems to me to go beyond the evidence, for Socrates nowhere indicates that he would disobey the god under any circumstances. If we can imagine the god failing the test (whatever that might mean), we must suppose that Socrates would conclude that he, not the god, was in error.

CHAPTER THIRTEEN

Socratic Theology and Piety

MARK L. MCPHERRAN

Socrates is acknowledged to have been a moral philosopher of the first order: the founder of virtue ethics and the chief exponent of the Socratic Method (the elenctic method of question-and-answer cross-examination).[1] It has also been, however, common to underplay the idea that he was very much a man of his own time in respect of the supernatural, assuming in his speech and thought the existence of gods vastly superior to ourselves in power and wisdom, and other such conventional Greek religious commitments. Of course, Socrates' trial and execution on a charge of impiety further indicates that he did not insulate his religious beliefs from those many other novel ones he had arrived at philosophically. Rather, our texts indicate that Socrates understood his religious commitments to be integral to his philosophical mission of moral examination and rectification; conversely, he used the rationally-derived convictions underlying that mission to reshape the religious conventions of his time in the service of establishing the new enterprise of philosophy. The direct legacy of that project is the rational theology of Plato, the Stoics and others. That, in any case, is the overarching thesis of this chapter. My goal in what follows is to delineate and justify it by offering a sketch of the religious dimension of Socratic philosophy; one that illustrates the way Socrates both challenged and renewed the religious conceptions of his time.

I. HISTORY OF THE PROBLEM

Although for most of our intellectual history the general postulate of a religious Socrates has been something of a commonplace, it has had its critics; first ancient, now modern. A rough historical sketch of its career goes as follows. The ancient critics of Socrates' own era seemed to discern in his philosophical interests and his methodical interrogations of others the marks of an atheistic nature philosopher and the amoral argumentative twistings of a professional teacher of rhetoric: or a religious Socrates, but an impious critic of the gods and religious institutions of Athens (cf. *Ap.* 18a–19d). In the *Apology*, Socrates eloquently and vehemently denies the truth of these charges, and those denials — I shall be arguing — are reinforced by the portraits of the other early dialogues. These fictional recreations of Socrates are, among other things, so engaging and life-like, that, when taken in tandem with the corroborating testimony of other Socratic apologists (primarily Xenophon), they quite naturally won the posthumous case of Socrates against his various accusers' allegations of atheism.[2] Indeed, on a straightforward reading of those accounts, Socrates appears to be in many ways the most pious Greek of his day. Having won that debate, however, these ancient defenders also inadvertently prepared a fertile ground for the subsequent heroisation of Socrates by many of the early Christian apologists and Church Fathers.[3]

Plato's and Xenophon's emphatic portraits of Socratic piety made it inevitable that Christians would compare Socrates' 'human wisdom' with the divine wisdom of Christ, his unjust prosecution as an atheist with theirs,[4] Socrates' proposed penalty at his trial of thirty minae with Judas' thirty pieces of silver, Socrates in his cell with Christ in the Garden of Gethsemane, and the former's martyrdom by hemlock with the latter's sacrifice on the cross. For many, that comparison revealed Socrates to be a proto-Christian and prophet of Christ, a valuable link between the virtues of intellectual paganism and the revealed truths of Christianity.[5] Hence, the tradition of an unjustly persecuted, religious Socrates became an inspirational fixture and a subject of idealising literature for thinkers up to and including Petrarch, Ficino and Erasmus.[6]

The image of Saint Socrates, however, also began to unravel with the onset of the Italian Renaissance. First, the very real interpretive problems involved in the use of the diverse accounts left by authors as different as Aristophanes and Plato began to be fully appreciated. This weakened previous confidence in the received conception of Socrates and thus gave to those battling for intellectual liberty and religious tolerance new license to follow their interpretive imaginations in a manner favourable to their own political and religious sympathies. Thus, some rejected or modified the 'myth' of Socrates as a pious and unjustly condemned servant of God, developing in its stead the picture of a free-thinking Socrates, a subverter of traditional and civic religion.[7] In tandem with this development, the increasingly philosophical — as opposed to theological — interests of succeeding generations of scholars led to a greater focus on Socrates' contributions to the triumph of rational, scientific culture, to the neglect of those traditional, religious elements he retained within his own thinking.[8] Thus began a process of secular canonization that – even now in some quarters – portrays Socrates as a figure straight out of the Enlightenment. This is the Socrates I and many others in philosophy were introduced to in graduate school: A consummate intellectualist, wholly taken up in agonistic argument, whose 'paradoxical' view that 'virtue is *knowledge*' (e.g., *Prt.* 349e–350d, 360d; *Mem.* 3.9.5) grounds a moral theory that takes discursive rationality as our only trustworthy guide in life.

Thus, rather than arriving at a reasonably accurate – or at least, a reasonably balanced – assessment of Socrates and his views, one biased reading of the materials, one mythical personage, has sometimes been joined by another mythical extreme. Where before Socrates had been a fifth century John the Baptist, today we can find others emphasising the antithesis: a philosophical figure inextricably tied to our own contemporary self-conceptions, cultural values and educational practices.[9] This has given to popular and scholarly culture a Socrates who is not so much a man of his own time as a paradigm of the modern 'rationally-examined life', an 'early apostle of the liberal ideals of sincerity and self-realization'.[10]

This version of Socrates – as opposed to what I shall contend is the more accurate (and more puzzling, more interesting) one – has Socrates pursuing the fundamental questions of human conduct and moral value by essentially one method alone: the 'elenctic' examination of belief-consistency by the interrogation of an interlocutor.[11] On the standard 'secular' portrait, this dialogical belief-testing procedure rigorously obeys the canons of logic and constitutes Socrates' primary method of philosophical investigation, moral decision-making and pedagogy. When Socrates claims that 'the unexamined life is not worth living' (*Ap.* 38a), he is thus to be understood as advising all human beings to

SOCRATIC THEOLOGY AND PIETY

spend part of each day elenctically examining themselves and others in accordance with the rational principles of proper philosophical investigation.[12] For this Socrates, extrarational religious experiences do not themselves contribute to philosophy's proper methodology, but rather, are the very sorts of things demanding our philosophical scrutiny. Hence, it is not surprising that advocates of this portrait have sometimes understood Socrates to have been a kind of atheist or agnostic, where his positive references to divine beings and 'signs' are thus construed as instances of his infamous alleged irony.[13] He may talk as though he is the recipient of a 'divine voice' (*Ap.* 31d), but *really* – goes this line of thinking – this is but a *façon de parler*: or by such phrases he is simply referring surreptitiously in the language of 'the many' to the 'divine' inner promptings of his utterly secular, human powers of ratiocination.[14] Once again, on this reading the Socrates of the *Apology* stands guilty as charged.[15]

In my judgment, this portrait of Socrates is the result of slighting and misinterpreting the evidence of our texts (not to mention the cultural forces at work on Socrates from birth). Proponents of this sort of view have at least to come to terms with the compelling evidence for a Socrates who was genuinely religious in the primary sense, a sense recognised both then and now; namely, possessing intellectual, heartfelt commitment to the view that there exist divine, otherworldly beings possessing intelligence and power; that is, gods.

II. GREEK RELIGION

The distinct phenomena we designate by using terms such as 'religion' and 'the sacred' were, for Socrates and his contemporaries, seamlessly integrated into everyday life.[16] Moreover, no ancient text such as Homer's *Iliad* had the status of a Bible or Koran, and there was no organised church, trained clergy or systematic set of doctrines enforced by them. What marked out a fifth century BCE Greek city or individual as pious (*hosios; eusebēs*) – that is, as being in accord with the norms governing the relations of humans and gods – was therefore not primarily a matter of belief, but rather, correct observance of ancestral tradition.[17] The most central of these activities consisted in the timely performance of prayers and sacrifices.[18] Such sacrifices ranged from an individual's libation of wine at the start of a meal to the great civic sacrifices of cattle held on the occasion of a religious festival, culminating in a communal banquet that renewed the ties of city-protecting deities with the citizenry through the mechanism of the shared meal (a portion of meat being set aside as a burned offering for the gods; see, e.g., Homer *Odyssey* 3.418–72). Besides such activities designed to ensure the favour of a divinity, however, we must also set those other rituals which aim to harm, not help, others; in particular, curses (see e.g. Pindar *Olympian* 1.75–115; Homer *Iliad* 3.299–301, *Odyssey* 2.134–145; Sophocles, *The Women of Trachis* 1238–1240).[19] Whatever the ritual, the actions composing it were typically aimed at a specific deity and were tied to the community, ranging from households to more complex groupings such as the *deme*.[20] The most obvious organising principle, however, was the city and its religious officials, who exercised final authority over all religious functions and which oversaw the most prominent displays of public piety provided by the city's numerous festivals.[21]

It should be clear that ancient Greek religion presupposed a notion of divinity rather different from those central to monotheistic traditions. Socrates and his peers were brought up on the portrait of the gods drawn in the works of Homer and Hesiod, and these gods did not create the cosmos or humankind, but rather, were themselves created.

Their power was often gained through duplicity and violence, they were neither omniscient nor omnipotent nor eternal, and it was assumed that they regularly intervene in human affairs for good or ill, inflicting, for example, famine, war and plague.[22] Here on earth, then, there is no clear separation of the religious from the secular, and thus every human action, every facet of nature, had what we would call a religious dimension. But although the ancient Greek world is permeated by the divine, its most potent expression is in beings distinctly different from perishable, mortal creatures: gods, *daimones* and heroes.[23]

Even though these ancient conceptions of divinity were not elaborated or enforced by an official theological body, religious education was not left entirely to chance. Both Homer and Hesiod were recognised as having established for the Greeks 'a kind of canonical repertory of stories about the Powers of the Beyond'.[24] It was on the basis of this repertory that 'the elegiac, lyric, and tragic poets drew unstintingly while simultaneously endowing the traditional myths with a new function and meaning.'[25] Thus, for example, the dramas of Aeschylus and Sophocles (e.g. *Antigone*) juxtapose some present situation against the events represented in Homer's texts, extending that mythology while also calling into critical question some facet of the human condition and contemporary society's response to it. By the time of Socrates, some of this probing of the traditional stories was influenced by the speculations and scepticism of those thinkers working within the new intellectualist traditions of nature philosophy (e.g. Heraclitus) and sophistry (e.g. Protagoras). As a result, in the work of authors like Euripides and Thucydides even the fundamental tenets of popular religion concerning the efficacy of sacrifice and prayer became targets of criticism.[26] Although it is beyond the scope of this chapter to trace the influences of such thinkers on Socrates, I will make brief allusions to some of them as we proceed.

III. THE PUZZLES OF 'SOCRATIC RELIGION'

Socrates' philosophical reputation rests on his adherence to the highest standards of rationality, one given its clearest expression in the *Crito*:

> T1 **Rationality Principle:** Not now for the first time, but always, I am the sort of man who is persuaded by nothing except the argument (*tō logō*) that seems best to me when I reason (*logizomenō*) about the matter.
>
> – *Cr.* 46b

Socratic reasoning commonly employs the Socratic Method, and we are encouraged to believe that for many years Socrates subjected a wide variety of self-professed experts on the topic of virtue to this form of examination (*Ap.* 20d–23c). The result of this long effort, however, appears to be not a body of knowledge, but the meagre payoff of moral scepticism:

> T2 **Ignorance Principle:** I am aware of being wise in nothing, great or small . . . (*Ap.* 21b). . . . [except that] . . . I am wiser in that what I do not know, I do not even suppose that I know . . . (21d).

This would not be so surprising an outcome were it not that Socrates represents this awareness as resulting from a quest performed at the behest of Greece's pre-eminent religious authority, the Delphic Oracle. For as Socrates sees it, the god Apollo, speaking through the Oracle, has stationed him in Athens as though he is a warrior, ordering him

SOCRATIC THEOLOGY AND PIETY

to philosophise by elenctically examining himself and others (28d–29a, 30e–31a). As he summarises the matter:

> T3 **Divine Mission:** I . . . go around seeking and investigating in accordance with the god. . . . I come to the god's aid. . . . because of my devotion to the god (*Ap.* 21e–23c). . . . the god stationed me . . . ordering me to live philosophizing and examining myself and others. . . .
>
> – *Ap.* 28e–29a

Socrates also emphasises that his interpretation of Delphic Apollo's pronouncement that 'no one is wiser' than he as an order to philosophise has been confirmed through other extrarational sources:

> T4 **Extra-rational Information:** To do this [philosophizing] has been commanded of me . . . by the god through oracles and through dreams and by every other means in which a divinity has ever commanded anyone to do anything.
>
> – *Ap.* 33c; cf. *Ap.* 30a; *Cr.* 43d–44b; *Phd.* 60c–61c

In addition, Socrates tells the jurors at his trial that he has been assisted in his philosophical mission through the frequent warnings of his divine sign, the *daimonion*:

> T5 **Daimonion:** . . . a sort of voice (*phonē*) comes, which, whenever it does come, always holds me back from what I'm about to do but never urges me forward.
>
> – *Ap.* 31d

Our texts that depict the Divine Mission (T3), Extrarational Information (T4) and *Daimonion* (T5) should now prompt us to ask how it is that Socrates can also subscribe to his Ignorance Principle (T2): For, lacking wisdom, how can Socrates be confident that gods such as Apollo even exist, let alone be assured that Apollo always speaks the truth (21b) and that his divine dreams and signs are not mere delusions? Moreover, since he also endorses the Rationality Principle (T1), we can expect him to justify the claims implied by these texts; but it is hard to see how the Socratic Method could provide that sort of warrant (since it appears to reveal only the inconsistency of interlocutors' beliefs; hence, their lack of expert knowledge). Texts such as Extrarational Information (T4) and *Daimonion* (T5) also make Socrates appear to be far more superstitious than the average Athenian: not the sort of behaviour we expect from the paradigm of the rationally self-examined life. After all, if enlightened contemporaries such as Thucydides could stand aloof from comparable elements of popular religion, and if even traditionally minded playwrights such as Aristophanes could poke cruel fun at seers and oracle-mongers (e.g., *Birds* 521, 959–991), how could Socrates not do so as well? Worse yet, it is hard to see how the Socrates who accepts the Rationality Principle (T1), Divine Mission (T3) and Extrarational Information (T4) as he investigates the religious claims of his interlocutors can be self-consistent when he goes on to criticise such interlocutors for acting on ungrounded religious judgments:

> T6 **Euthyphro Principle:** . . . if you [Euthyphro] did not know clearly the pious and the impious, there is no way you would ever have attempted to prosecute an elderly man, your father, for murder on behalf of a hired man. Rather, as to the gods, you would have dreaded the risk that you would not do it correctly, and as to human beings, you would have been ashamed.
>
> – *Eu.* 15d

304 THE BLOOMSBURY HANDBOOK OF SOCRATES

Here a rational principle of morality is implied: actions that are morally ambiguous ought not to be performed in the absence of a full understanding of the relevant concepts involved. So we are then left to wonder how the epistemically modest Socrates of the Ignorance Principle (T2) would respond if pressed to defend his risky conduct of challenging the moral and religious views of his fellow Athenians. The mere citation of divine authority instanced by the Divine Mission (T3), Extrarational Information (T4) and *Daimonion* (T5) texts would appear inadequate in view of the demands of the Rationality Principle (T1); such a citation would also open up to interlocutors such as Euthyphro (a self-professed diviner) the possibility of replying in kind that they too, like Socrates, have been commanded in divinations and in dreams to contest conventional norms.

The preceding texts exemplify the way that Plato presents us with a puzzling, street-preaching philosopher who is both rational and religious, and whose relationship to everyday Athenian piety is anything but clear. To begin to make sense of that relationship, and thereby resolve the tensions between these and related texts, it is useful to examine Socrates' own examination of a self-professed expert in Greek religion: Euthyphro.

IV. SOCRATIC PIETY AND PHILOSOPHY

The *Euthyphro*'s discussion of the virtue of piety makes it a key text for determining the religious dimension of Socratic philosophy.[27] It also provides vivid examples of the Socratic Method though its portrayal of Socrates' relentless interrogation of Euthyphro's five attempted definitions of piety.[28] Definition (1) – piety is proceeding against whomever does injustice (5d–6e) – is quickly dispensed with because it is too narrow: Euthyphro holds there to be cases of pious action that do not involve proceeding against wrongdoers (5d–e). Socrates also reminds Euthyphro that he is seeking a complete account of the *one* characteristic (*eidos*) of piety: that unique, self-same, universal quality the possession of which makes any pious action pious and which Euthyphro had earlier agreed was the object of their search (6d–e; cf. 5c–d; M. 72c). Definition (2) – piety is what is loved by the gods (6e–7a) – is next rejected on the grounds that since Euthyphro's gods quarrel about the rightness of actions, a god-loved, hence pious action could also be a god-hated, hence impious action; thus, definition (2) fails to specify the real nature of pious actions (7a–9d). Note, however, that by presupposing without restriction in his definitional search that the definition of piety must apply to *every* pious action – and given his apparent rejection of divine enmity and violence (6a–d, 7b–9c) – Socrates is committed to the claims (i) that there is but one universal moral canon for all beings, gods and humans alike, and thus must reject the tradition of a divine double-standard of morality (cf., e.g., *Rep.* 378b). Socrates' examination also suggests that his gods (ii) are perfectly just and good, and so (iii) experience no moral disagreements among themselves.

Socrates' rebuttal of Euthyphro's third attempt at definition (3) – piety is what is loved by all the gods (9e) – constitutes the most logically complex section of the *Euthyphro* (9e–11b).[29] Socrates' apparent rejection of this definition comes at the end of a long and complex passage (10e–11b) where he first drives home his conclusion that Euthyphro's various concessions undercut this third definition of piety and then explains the apparent source of Euthyphro's confusion; namely, given Euthyphro's claim that something is god-loved because it is pious, his purported definition 'god-loved' appears to designate only a non-essential property of piety (a *pathos*) rather than specifying piety's essential nature (its *ousia*). With this Socrates makes it evident that he is no Divine Command Theorist:

SOCRATIC THEOLOGY AND PIETY

That is, unlike gods modelled after Homeric royalty, his gods do not issue morality-*establishing* commands such that a pious action is pious simply because it is god-loved; rather, it seems, his gods love things that are independently pious because they themselves are by nature wise, virtue-loving beings. By tacitly allowing that the gods are *of one mind* on the topic of virtue, Socrates here lays the groundwork for the view that there is ultimately only one divinity (see 'Socratic Theology', below).

Socrates assists Euthyphro in producing a fourth definition of piety by confronting him with the question of piety's relation to generic justice: Is all the just pious, or is justice broader than piety such that piety is then a part of justice (11e–12e)? Subsequent to his adoption of the part-of-justice view, Euthyphro attempts to differentiate pious justice from the remainder ('human justice') by stipulating that piety involves the *therapeutic tendance* of gods (*therapeia theōn*) (12e6–9). This differentia, however, is rejected by reference to a craft analogy comparing those who would tend the gods in this fashion to those who tend horses, dogs and cattle (13a–d). Such therapists possess the sort of expert knowledge that includes the capacity to benefit their particular kind of subjects substantially by restoring or maintaining their health, or by otherwise meeting their essential needs and improving the way in which they function. Obviously, then, since mere mortals cannot benefit gods in these ways, the virtue of piety cannot be a form of therapy (13c–e). By contrast, *skilful service (hupēretikē)* along the lines of assistants to craftspeople contributes to an acceptable differentia of generic justice; assistants to a shipwright, for example, serve the shipwright by satisfying his or her desire to receive assistance in building ships but do not restore or improve upon the shipwright's own nature or functioning. Socrates has thus brought Euthyphro to the point of agreeing that:

> Piety is that part of justice that is a service of humans to gods, assisting the gods in their primary task to produce their most beautiful product (*pagkalon ergon*).
>
> – 12e–14a

Within the constraints of this account, Euthyphro is then asked to specify precisely the nature of that most beautiful product of the gods' chief work in whose production the gods might employ our assistance (13e–14a). Euthyphro, however, tenaciously avoids answering this question (13d–14a), citing instead a fifth definitional attempt: (5) piety is knowledge of sacrificing and praying (14b–15c). To this Socrates emphatically responds that Euthyphro is abdicating their search just at the point where a *brief* answer – one analogous to 'food', the product of the craft of farming (14a) – might have finally given Socrates all the information that he really needed to have about piety (14b–c). Many scholars have found this good evidence for ascribing something like P to Socrates.[30] The question then becomes how Socrates would have answered the question of the identity of the gods' beautiful, chief product?

First, we can expect Socrates to maintain that although we humans cannot have a complete account of the gods' work, since the gods are wholly good, their chief project and product must be superlatively good. But what reasons, *per* the Rationality Principle (T1), does Socrates have for holding that the gods are entirely good? His thinking would seem to run roughly as follows. Since gods are perfectly knowledgeable, they must be entirely wise (*Ap.* 23a–b; *Hi.Ma.* 289b3–6); but because wisdom and virtue are mutually entailing (and since there is but one moral realm), it would follow that a god must be at least as good as a good person; but then since the latter can only do good, never evil (*Cr.* 49c; *Rep.* 335a–d), the same goes for the former (cf. *Rep.* 379a–391e).[31]

Socrates' moral reformation of the gods indicates that his gods cannot be fully identified with those of tradition. For Greek popular thought assumed as a fundamental principle from Homer on that justice consists in reciprocation, in repayment in kind: a gift for a gift, an evil for an evil (the *lex talionis*).[32] Even among the gods the principle of *lex talionis* is assumed as basic (e.g., Zeus suggests that Hera might allow him to destroy one of her favourite cities in return for abandoning Troy [*Iliad* 4.31–69]; cf. Sophocles *Ajax* 79).[33] In respect of this venerable principle, Socrates must be ranked a self-conscious moral revolutionary (*Cr.* 49b–d): As he sees it, since we should never do injustice, we should never do evil, and from that it follows that we should never do an evil in return for even an evil done to us (*Cr.* 48b–49d, 54c; cf. *Grg.* 468e–474b; *Rep.* 335a–d). For Socrates, then, not even Zeus (rather, least of all Zeus) can return one injury for another.[34]

Next, the Socratic view that the only or most important good is virtue/wisdom (e.g., *Ap.* 30a–b; *Cr.* 47e–48b; *Grg.* 512a–b; *Euthd.* 281d–e) makes it likely that the only or most important component of the gods' chief product is virtue/wisdom. But, then, since piety as a virtue must be a craft-knowledge of how to produce goodness (e.g., *La.* 194e–196d, 199c–e; *Euthd.* 280b–281e), *our* primary service to the gods – the one we are best suited to perform – would appear to be to help the gods produce goodness in the universe *via* the protection and improvement of the human mind/soul. Because philosophical examination of oneself and others is for Socrates the key activity that helps to achieve this goal *via* the improvement of moral-belief-consistency and the deflation of human presumptions to divine wisdom (e.g., *Ap.* 22d–23b), philosophising is a pre-eminently pious activity.[35]

Finally, Socrates' treatment of Euthyphro's fifth definition – (5) piety is knowledge of sacrificing and praying – makes evident that he rejects the idea that piety consists in traditional prayer and sacrifice motivated by hopes of a material payoff (14c–15c).[36] In addition, Socrates' view that the only real good is virtue means that one ought not to pray for any particular material payoff, since any such payoff could in fact diminish one's happiness. Nevertheless, from his perspective the sacrificial gifts of time, pride and conventional goods offered up in the pursuit of philosophical activity do gratify the gods to a greater extent than any burnt offering might (e.g., *Ap.* 23b–c, 31b–c, 37e–38a; *Mem.* 4.3.17–18).[37]

This appropriation and reconception of piety as demanding of us philosophical self-examination would, however, seem to be a direct threat to everyday piety. For now it would appear that for Socrates, time spent on prayer and sacrifice is simply time stolen from the more demanding, truly pious task of rational self-examination *per* the Rationality Principle (T1). More threatening still, Socrates' theology of entirely just, 'relentlessly beneficent' gods in conjunction with his moral theory seems to make sacrifice and prayer (and especially curses) entirely useless.[38] For such practices appear to rest on the traditional and fundamental assumption that justice consists in reciprocation, in repayment in kind (i.e. the *lex talionis*): a principle of returning evil for evil that Socrates rejects (*Cr.* 49b–d). To what extent, then, is Socrates at odds with the ritual bedrock of Greek religion?[39]

I think it is clear that Socrates does not reject conventional religious practices *in general*, but only the narrowly self-interested motives underlying their common observance. Xenophon, for example, portrays him as 'the most visible of men' in cult service to the gods (*Mem.* 1.2.64) and has him testify that he often sacrificed at the public altars (*Apol.* 10–12; cf. *Mem.* 1.1.1–2, 4.8.11). It seems unlikely that Xenophon would offer as a defence a portrait of Socrates that simply no Athenian could take seriously.[40] There is, in addition, some corroborating Platonic evidence on this point.[41] Although it

SOCRATIC THEOLOGY AND PIETY

would not seem that Socrates could consider prayers or sacrifices alone to be *essentially* connected to the virtue of piety (since, independent of the right intention, such actions in themselves do not necessarily serve the purpose of the gods *per* P), their performance is nonetheless compatible with the demands of piety reconceived as philosophising. After all, since Socrates embraces the positive side of the *talio* – the return of one good for another – we should reciprocate as best we can the gods' many good gifts (see, e.g., *Eu.* 14e–15a) by honouring the gods in fitting ways through performing acts with the inner-intention to thank and honour them (*Mem.* 1.4.10, 18; 4.3.17). While, again, serving the gods *via* philosophical self-examination has pride of place in providing such honours, there is no reason why such actions cannot include prayers and sacrifices (cf. *Mem.* 4.3.13, 16). Socrates may well hold that prayers and sacrifices that aim to honour or thank the gods, or that request moral assistance from them, serve both ourselves and the gods: They help to induce our souls to follow the path of justice (thus producing god-desired good in the universe) by habituating us to return good for good. These actions also help to foster and maintain a general belief in the existence of good and helpful gods and an awareness of our inferior status in respect of wisdom and power; something that Socrates is clearly interested in promoting (see, e.g., Xen. *Mem.* 1.4.1–19, 4.3.1–17; Plat. *Ap.* 21d–23c). Of course, no such action can be expected to establish a claim on any deity that would give us a right to expect any specific or immediate return.

Nevertheless, Socrates appears to think that the gods aid those who do what is virtuous. Xenophon, for example, represents Socrates as accepting the view that he receives goods from the god(s) (e.g., his *daimonion*) *because*, apparently, of the piety of his mission to the Athenians (*Mem.* 1.1.9, 1.1.19, 1.3.3, 1.4.15–19, 4.3.16–17, 4.8.11; *Symp.* 47–49). Hence, since petitionary prayers and sacrifices that offer honour to the gods *are* virtuous by attempting to offer good for good, Socrates will expect that good things will be returned to us for such efforts in some fashion (*Mem.* 1.3.2; 2.1.28): Just as a master-craftsman offers guidance, nourishment and tools to his assistants when they ask, Socrates would have thought, so the gods may be expected to aid us in a similar way. Again, however, although for Socrates the gods are always pleased in some sense by the honour such sincerely motivated practices display toward them, they – unlike the gods entertained by some Athenians – are not responsive to the material basis of the sacrifice or the specificities of the request (since any particular item requested might not be conducive to our real good; *Mem.* 1.3.2) (especially Socratically unjust petitions; e.g. unjust curse-imprecations).

It appears, then, that with the perfectly wise and just deities of Socrates we have few specific, materially rewarding imprecations to make: Beyond the sincere, general prayer that one be aided in pursuing virtue, there are few requests or sacrifices to which all-wise deities can be counted on to respond (since in our ignorance, we can never know if any specific request would be virtue-aiding, and since the gods have no need of our sacrifices) (see, e.g., Socrates' prayer at *Phdr.* 279b–c). This implication of Socrates' moral theory cuts straight at the root of everyday self-interested motivations underlying many cult-practices. But if Socrates rejected the efficacy of improperly motivated requests, then he was a threat to popular piety – whether he was recognised as such by any of his jurors. After all, to many Athenians the assistance of a Heracles would have meant, above all, help against the unseen, non-human forces bearing down on one (e.g. plague), and for most of them this meant material help against oppressive *other deities*. By taking away the enmity of the gods and conceiving of them as fully beneficent, then, the need for and the efficacy of *this* Heracles is also removed.

It seems clear that those jurors able to recognise the implications of Socrates' views for sacrificial cult would have seen him as threatening the stability of the state: For if you take away the conflicts of the deities and the expectations of particular material rewards and physical protections in cult, you disconnect the religion of everyday life and the state from its practical roots. To those not already centred on the development of their inner lives, the substitute of the difficult, pain-producing activity of philosophical self-examination would seem to offer little solace in the face of life's immediate, everyday difficulties. Socrates, therefore, raised the stakes for living a life of piety considerably by making its final measure the state of one's philosophically purified soul.

V. SOCRATIC REASON AND REVELATION

As our Divine Mission (T3), Extrarational Information (T4) and *Daimonion* (T5) texts demonstrate, Socrates is portrayed as a man who gives clear credence to the alleged god-given messages and forecasts found in dreams, divinations, oracles and other such traditionally-accepted incursions by divinity.[42] But the degree of trust Socrates places in such sources appears to put him at odds with the Rationality and Ignorance Principles (T1 and T2): What is the rational justification for heeding them, and in doing so, are they not regarded as sources of wisdom? The natural response is, I think, to hold that while Socrates accepts the everyday notion that the gods provide us with extrarational signs and so does not pursue a form of the intellectualist rejection of divination's efficacy,[43] he also does not take the operations of traditional divinatory practices at face value. Rather, he insists in accord with the Rationality Principle (T1) that conventional methods of oracular interpretation must give way to a rational method for evaluating such phenomena. These extrarational sources, however, do not supply Socrates with general, theoretical claims constitutive of the expert moral knowledge he seeks and disavows having obtained *per* the Ignorance Principle (T2). Rather, they yield items of what we might call non-expert moral knowledge (e.g. that his death is good; *Ap.* 40a–c).[44] Let us consider a few examples.[45]

Early in his defence speech, Socrates explains that his reputation for wisdom can be best understood by attending to the testimony provided by the god who speaks through the Delphic Oracle: Apollo (*Ap.* 20d–23b).[46] As Socrates relates the tale, his friend Chaerephon travelled to Delphi to ask the Oracle if anyone was wiser than Socrates, and the response was 'No one is wiser' (21a). This report, however, was at odds with Socrates' own conviction that he possessed no real wisdom (namely, full comprehension of virtues such as piety), and so – given that 'it is not lawful (*themis*) for the god to speak falsely' (21b) – he was provoked to discover an interpretation that would preserve Apollo's veracity. He does this by going from one self-professed expert to another in hopes of finding someone wiser than himself so as to refute the apparent meaning of the oracular pronouncement (and so uncover its real meaning). After continually failing to find such a person, Socrates concludes that what the god actually meant is that Socrates is wisest by best grasping his own lack of real wisdom (this is 'human wisdom'). This, in turn, is taken to mean that Apollo has stationed Socrates in Athens ordering him to philosophise and *examine* himself and others (28d–29a). Thus, since one ought always to obey the command of a god at all costs, Socrates is obliged to philosophise regardless of any dangers (29d; cf. *Rep.* 368b–c). His jurors, therefore, should understand that the Oracle's pronouncement marked a turning point in his life so profound that he now philosophises under a unique and divine mandate (Divine Mission [T4] and 29c–30b). Socrates also

SOCRATIC THEOLOGY AND PIETY

continually interrogates others because he has come to believe that the god is using him as a *paradigm* to deliver the virtue-inducing message that that person is wisest, who – like Socrates – becomes most cognizant of how little real wisdom he/she possesses (23b).[47]

This account, despite its complexity, suggests that Socrates takes it to be obligatory to subject extrarational signs to rational interpretation and confirmation whenever possible, and especially if they urge him to act in ways that appear to run counter to tradition or prudential considerations.[48] That postulate dissolves two of our initial puzzles. First, the conflict between reason *per* the Rationality Principle (T1) and revelation *per* the Divine Mission (T3), Extrarational Information (T4) and *Daimonion* (T5) texts is mitigated by noting how Socrates allows *rationally* interpreted and tested revelations to count *as reasons* in the sense of the Rationality Principle (T1) (see below).[49] The second tension between revelation and the Euthyphro Principle (T6) is dissolved as well: This principle can be understood to claim that actions traditionally held to be unjust ought to be refrained from in the absence of compelling rational or *rationally* interpreted and tested divinatory evidence to the contrary. Euthyphro himself threatens with his suit traditional filial piety but cannot, under examination, defend his conduct; and his purported mantic abilities manifestly fail to give him any revelations whose meaning he could decipher or rationally justify. Socrates, on the other hand, has engaged in few activities that actually violate the traditional code, and has never violated the essential dictates of traditional piety (especially once these are rightly understood). And although he has run some moral risk in pursuing his life of philosophical examination, his belief in its overriding moral worth has survived a lifetime of such testing. He has, in particular, laboured at great length to derive his understanding of the Delphic Oracle's pronouncement and has received varied and consistent extrarational indications that back up his interpretation (that are, in turn, subject to philosophical testing). Finally, Socrates has secular justification and confirmation of this *via* his conception of the virtues for believing that his mission to the Athenians is a great good (*Ap.* 30a, 30d–31a).[50] To confirm this account of Socrates' treatment of extrarational indicators, let us consider his reliance of his divine sign, the *daimonion*.[51]

Socrates' *daimonion*, we are told, is an internal, private admonitory 'sign' (*sēmeion*; *Ap.* 40b, c; *Euthd.* 272e; *Phdr.* 242b; *Rep.* 496c; *Mem.* 1.1.3–5) and 'voice' (*phonē*; *Ap.* 31d; *Phdr.* 242c; Xen. *Apol.* 12.) caused to appear within the horizon of consciousness by a god (probably Apollo).[52] It has occurred to few or none before Socrates (*Rep.* 496c) and it has been his companion since childhood (*Ap.* 31d). The *daimonion*'s intervention in his affairs is frequent and pertains to matters both momentous and trivial (*Ap.* 40a). That Socrates receives and obeys these monitions is well-known in Athens (*Ap.* 31c–d; *Eu.* 3b), and they are understood to be apotreptic signs that warn him *not* to pursue a course of action that he is in the process of initiating (*Ap.* 31d; *Phdr.* 242b; *Thg.* 128–131a).[53] These interventions are regarded as unfailingly correct in whatever they indicate (*Mem.* 1.1.4–5), just as we would expect the gift of an unfailingly good divinity to be. The *daimonion*'s generosity even extends to warning Socrates of the inadvisability of the actions intended by others (*Tht.* 150c–151b; cf. *Thg.* 128d–131a; *Mem.* 1.1.4; *Apol.* 13), but in no case does it provide him with general, theoretical claims constitutive of the expert moral knowledge he seeks and disavows having obtained *per* the Ignorance Principle (T2). Neither does it provide him with ready-made explanations of its opposition. Rather, its occurrences yield instances of non-expert moral knowledge of the inadvisability of pursuing particular actions because those actions are disadvantageous to Socrates and others; e.g., the knowledge that it would not be beneficial to let a certain student resume study with him (see, e.g., Xen., *Sym.* 8.5; *Tht.* 150c–151b; *Alc. I* 103a–106a). Finally, these divine 'signs' always target *future* unbeneficial outcomes, and especially those whose reasonable prediction lies beyond the power of human reason (*Ap.* 31d; *Euthd.* 272e–273a; *Mem.* 1.1.6–9, 4.3.12). It is, in short, a species of the faculty of divination, true to Socrates' description of it as his 'customary divination' (*Ap.* 40a4) and himself as a seer (*mantis*) (*Phd.* 85b; cf. *Phdr.* 242c).

One important example that displays Socrates' reliance upon and rational confirmation of a daemonic warning is found at *Apology* 31c–32a, where Socrates notes his obedience to the *daimonion*'s resistance to his entering public partisan politics (cf. *Rep.* 496b–c) and then offers an explanation for its warnings; namely, that such political activity would have brought him a premature death, thus curtailing his vastly beneficial mission to the Athenians (cf. *Phdr.* 242b–243a; *Alc. I* 103a–106a). This account is introduced in the manner of one wholly convinced of not only that explanation, but of the extrarationally indicated truth that prompted that explanation; namely, that the *daimonion* opposes now, as it has in the past, his every attempt at going into politics.

Another instance of daemonic activity is found at *Euthydemus* 272e–273a. There we find that Socrates had formed the intention to leave his seat, but just as he was getting up the *daimonion* opposed him, and so he remained. In this case, Socrates exhibits no doubt that its warning is utterly reliable; rather, Socrates implicitly trusts the *daimonion*, although *how* or *why* it is that the result of his obedience will be good-producing is opaque to reasoned calculation (*Tht.* 150c–151b; *Mem.* 4.3.12; 1.1.8–9). But this trust is in no way *ir*rational – and so does not contradict the Rationality Principle (T1) – for it may be rationally confirmed in its wisdom and so given credence on an inductive basis; since (i) in Socrates' long experience of the *daimonion*, it has never been shown not to be a reliable warning system (Xen. *Apol.* 13; *Ap.* 40a–c), and (ii) the reliability of its alarms has been confirmed by the good results that flow from heeding it (i.e., we should suppose that from an early age Socrates observed subsequent to its warning that he would most likely have experienced a harm had he not heeded its advice). Some sense of its level of activity can also be ascertained by attending to the end of the *Apology* (40a–b).

Subsequent to his conviction and condemnation in the *Apology*, Socrates closes his defence speech with a friendly chat (39e–40a) designed to console the jurors who voted for his acquittal by persuading them that his death will be a good thing. Socrates offers them two reasons for the truth of this claim, the second of which is his famous argument for the goodness of death (40c–41d).[54] This argument, however, is intended to buttress his initial reason for taking this stance, namely, the fact that his *daimonion* has never once interfered with his trial proceedings (*Ap.* 40a–c; 41d). Socrates represents this failure as a 'great indication' (*mega tekmērion*: 40c) of the goodness of both his death and death in general. For this to be so, he must assume that the *daimonion* has generally opposed him when he was about to do something unbeneficial and that it is the gift of a being who gives us nothing but good (cf. *Eu.* 14e–15a), who would never deceive us (*Ap.* 21b, *Rep.* 381e–382a), and who is superlatively wise (*Ap.* 23a; *Hi.Ma.* 289b): in short, a divinity. But since Socrates' trust in the accuracy of the *daimonion* has been achieved inductively, the resulting beliefs that various intended plans of action are unbeneficial are not so secure that they amount to certain knowledge (thus, they do not threaten the Ignorance Principle [T2]). That would seem to be why he goes on to confirm his argument from daemonic silence with the argument of 40c–41d; even then, he takes himself to have established only a rational expectation that death is good (40c).

SOCRATIC THEOLOGY AND PIETY   311

Given the preceding, the *daimonion* appears to be compatible with Socrates' profession of his Rationality and Ignorance Principles (T1 and T2): If during or after a process of deliberation the *daimonion* should oppose his action, then given the prior rationally established reliability of the *daimonion*, it would seem that an occurrence of the *daimonion* would count in a perfectly straightforward way *as a reason* for not performing that act. For if one had very frequently in the past always obeyed the promptings of an internal warning that one has reason to believe come from all-wise gods, and this had always been judged to have resulted in the best outcome, then one has good reason for letting this internal warning trump one's merely human judgment (although this does not provide the sort of complete account of the virtues that would contradict the Ignorance Principle [T2]).

VI. SOCRATIC THEOLOGY

Socrates' claims to receive guidance from the gods brings us to our last puzzle: How can Socrates satisfy the rational demands of the Rationality Principle (T1), the sceptical restraint marked by the Ignorance Principle (T2), and yet affirm that gods exist and that they have characteristics such as wisdom (*Ap.* 41c–d; *Eu.* 14e–15a; *Grg.* 508a; *Hi.Ma.* 289b; *Mem.* 4.4.25)? Unfortunately, Plato's texts show Socrates simply assuming and never proving the existence of gods (although Plato's Socrates might perhaps take the *daimonion* as evidence that its god exists). However, in Xenophon we are given an innovative teleological cosmology and theodicy grounded on an argument for the existence of an omniscient, omnipresent God: The Maker of an orderly and beautiful universe, a deity who also now governs it in a fashion analogous to the way in which *our* minds govern *our* bodies (1.4.1–19; 4.3.1–18; cf. Sextus Empiricus, *Adversus Mathematicos* 9.92–94).

The primary teleological argument contained in the *Memorabilia* holds that since individual beings in the universe are either the products of intelligent design (*gnome*) or mere dumb luck (*tuche*), and since human beings are clearly products of intelligent design, we then ought to be persuaded that there exists a vastly knowledgeable and powerful God, a God who is moreover a 'loving and wise Maker (*demiourgos*)' (1.4.2–7; cf. 4.3.1–18). The argument – with a bit of interpretive polishing – can be given this formal structure:

(1) Everything that is clearly purposeful (*ophelia*; a beneficial adaptation of means to ends) is the product of intelligent design (*gnome*; i.e., art [*techne*]) (and not mere dumb luck [*tuche*]).
(2) Human beings (and other features of the universe, living and non-living; 1.4.8) exhibit 'signs of forethought' (1.4.6); for example, eyes have protective eyelids and lashes, teeth are adapted to cutting and the anus is far removed from the nostrils.
(3) Things that exhibit signs of forethought are clearly purposeful.
(4) Thus, human beings are the product of intelligent design.
(5) The existence of products of intelligent design implies the existence of an intelligent designer-creator (one possessing the intelligence and power necessary for producing its products; cf. 1.4.2–4).
(6) Thus, an intelligent designer-creator of the cosmos exists.

This is a fairly impressive piece of philosophy to find in any section of fourth century text, since the argument is no mere prototype but close to being a full-fledged version of the classic Argument from Design.[55] Socrates, then, conforms to his Rationality Principle (T1) when he affirms the existence of god. It also appears that because of the analogical relationship Socrates postulates between this Maker-god and the human soul (e.g. both are invisible), his conception of this god is an extrapolation from his own understanding of the human soul. This explains why he is confident that the Maker-god has many human mental characteristics raised to the level of perfection. We are told, for example, that this being has – unlike the divinities of popular imagination – complete knowledge of the present, possessing an awareness of all things at once by being present everywhere (*Mem.* 1.4.17–19). The Deity also has knowledge of the past thanks to Its possession of an all-encompassing divine memory, and It has sufficient knowledge of the future to allow It to send us reliable portents of the things to come (cf. *Sym.* 4.47–49). Vast power, as well, must be ascribed to this Being: power sufficient to allow It to implement Its cosmic plans (*Sym.* 4.48). Finally, as we saw earlier in section III, the wisdom of this god ensures its complete goodness.

Given its extrapolated characterisation, it is not surprising to find that Socrates' Maker has desires and affective states. Indeed, here Socrates shows himself to be a bolder theologian than many modern teleological philosophers: The actual argument goes beyond conclusion (6)'s mere assertion of existence by characterising the Demiurge as 'loving' (1.4.7).[56] This appellation, naturally, does not strictly follow from the argument, but Socrates offers support for it later on when he responds to Aristodemus' postulation of an indifferent Demiurge (*Mem.* 1.4.10.19; cf. 4.3.2–14): We appear, says Socrates, to have been not only designed, but designed to the *greatest advantage* in respect of other living creatures. First, we exhibit a superior adaptation of means to ends in our physical being; e.g., our versatile hands, our capacity for speech and the fitness of our bodies for housing the kind of soul we have been given (1.4.11–12, 13–14; cf. 4.3.11). In addition, the rest of the material Universe also exhibits a solicitous design insofar as it appears especially constructed with the requirements of human happiness in mind, for it offers light, seasons and food crops adapted to those seasons. Furthermore, when our reason is unable to discern the future adequately, the gods send portents to our aid (1.4.15, 18; cf. 4.3.12). So generous does Socrates' theodicy become in the *Memorabilia*'s book four account – and so seemingly neglectful of earthquakes, tyrants and plagues – that he even claims that *everything* in the Universe is 'fair and good' (4.3.13; cf. 1.4.13).[57] This God is also capable of pleasure, since Socrates recommends that we honour and venerate It and other gods on the grounds of prudence given that these Deities confer benefits on those who *please* them with obedience and honour (4.3.17).

The relation between this omniscient, omnipresent Deity and the other gods is left entirely obscure. Socrates speaks at one moment of that singular Deity as responsible for our creation and aid, and in the next breath depicts the plural gods as doing the same (e.g., 1.4.10–11, 13–14, 18). Next, he distinguishes this one Deity *from* the other gods by characterising It as that particular god who 'coordinates and holds together the entire cosmos' (4.3.13) but also treats that Deity as fulfilling *all* the functions of the gods. To reconcile such oddities with what evidence there is that Socrates would affirm a belief in Delphic Apollo and plural Greek gods, we might credit him with being a henotheist; that is, he may understand the Maker-god to be a supreme Deity overseeing a community of lesser deities in the manner of Xenophanes' 'greatest one god' (DK 21 B23). Alternatively, it is also possible that Socrates shared the not-uncommon view which understood the gods to be manifestations of a singular supreme Spirit.[58] In any event, we may expect that Socrates holds that his reasons for affirming the existence and nature of his Maker-god do

SOCRATIC THEOLOGY AND PIETY

not constitute the sort of complete and certain account that would give him the kind of theological wisdom he disclaims with his Ignorance Principle (T2).

VII. SOCRATES ON TRIAL

According to the report of Diogenes Laertius (DL 2.40) and Xenophon (*Mem.* 1.1.1), and as Socrates himself recounts at *Ap.* 24b–c (cf. *Eu.* 3b–d), Socrates was prosecuted on a charge of impiety that consisted of three distinct specifications: (I) Socrates does not recognise (*nomizein*) the gods recognised by the state; (II) Socrates introduces new divinities (*kaina daimonia*); and (III) Socrates corrupts the youth by *teaching* youths the notions specified by the other two allegations.[59] Socrates takes up these claims in reverse order, beginning with III, but he first addresses the informal concerns that he takes to motivate them: These are the old rumours that Socrates investigates natural phenomena in the style of Anaxagoras and is a crafty practitioner of sophistical argument like Protagoras, and teaches others his results and methods in these areas (18b–c, 19b–c, 23c–d). These allegations are especially dangerous because popular opinion holds that such intellectuals 'do not recognize the gods [to exist]' (18c). Later, when Socrates addresses the formal accusations by interrogating Meletus as to the precise nature of charge I, atheism again becomes the chief allegation (26a–e). But as our Divine Mission (T3), Extrarational Information (T4) and *Daimonion* (T5) texts – and now the teleological argument of the *Memorabilia* (section V) – indicate, Socrates is no atheist; moreover, Socrates has no trouble showing that Meletus' allegation II of introducing new divinities is inconsistent with a charge of atheism (26a–28a).

However, as discussed earlier in the section on 'Puzzles of Socratic Thought', it would not seem possible to fully identify the gods of Socrates with either the civic deities of Athens or those of the poets. For example, in response to Euthyphro's mention of the story that Zeus bound his father Kronos for committing an injustice, Socrates exclaims:

> Is this, Euthyphro, why I am a defendant against the indictment: that whenever someone says such things about the gods [e.g., that Zeus bound his own father, that gods quarrel], I receive them with annoyance? Because of this, as is likely, someone will assert that I am a wrongdoer.
>
> – *Eu.* 6a; and see his similar reaction to the myths of conflict at 6b–d; cf. 7a–9b

This piece of pre-trial speculation, however, is not decisive, and later on Socrates affirms his belief in the civic gods:

> ... plainly, if I should persuade and force you by begging, after you have sworn an oath, I would be teaching you not to hold that *there are gods*, and in making my defence speech I would simply be accusing myself of *not believing in gods*. But that is *far* from being so. For *I do* recognize [*nomizō*] them [the civic gods] . . . as none of my accusers do (*Ap.* 35c–d).
>
> – my emphasis

Nevertheless, the evidence we saw regarding Socratic theology in preceding sections argues that while Socrates is committed to the existence of gods, and is willing to 'recognize' them both intellectually and through traditional sacrificial practice under their civic names, they cannot be fully identified with the civic or poetic gods insofar as those gods are conceived of as being at variance with other gods, or given to retributive justice, or as lacking in wisdom or power.[60] Again, Socrates' conception of the gods as thoroughly good does appear to undermine the everyday motivations underlying conventional conceptions of prayer and sacrifice. But if so, then Socrates would have been associated with the sorts of criticisms of popular religion found in Xenophanes, natural scientists and those of the sophists who followed a similar revisionary line.[61] To what extent then is Socrates actually guilty of non-recognition of the civic gods (allegation I)?

Although his revisionary theology puts Socrates at variance with some of his fellow Athenians, it does not seem by itself sufficiently problematic to warrant a conviction on charge I. After all, Socrates' practical, legal guilt before the court on this allegation would be very much a matter of the meaning each juror placed on the phrase 'gods of the state': but for most Athenians of the end of the fifth century, it would have been no great shock to hear expressions of doubt or outright denial concerning the poets' tales of divine capriciousness, enmity, immorality and lack of response to sacrifice. They had been exposed to such criticisms for years by thinkers such as Solon, Xenophanes, Heraclitus and Euripides, none of whom appear to have suffered from religiously based persecution.[62] Moreover, others such as Pindar could speak plainly of 'Homer's lies' (*Nemean* 7.23) without incurring legal sanctions, and we have no evidence of anyone being prosecuted for disbelieving the stories of Homer or Hesiod.[63] Hence, although there may be problematic implications for traditional religion in Socrates' conception of divinity, charge I does not seem able to bear the entire explanatory weight of Socrates' conviction. Let us consider allegation II then.

So far as we know, Socrates was the first person in the history of Athens to be formally accused of the crime specified by II,[64] but despite the lack of precedent, there is every reason to think that the allegation is legally permissible. The Athenian *polis* took an active role in overseeing all religious activity; in particular, it had the power to exclude or allow forms of worship, and those wishing to introduce new cults into Athens had to seek official sanction.[65] Since such representations to the *polis* implied privileged access to the divine, were in the last analysis unverifiable, presented competition to the established cults and could easily be based on self-interested or political motives, a significant burden of proof would have been borne by the petitioner. Even then, however, 'new gods and their sponsors were by no means assured of a warm welcome when they petitioned for entry into a Greek community'.[66]

What sorts of *daimonia*, then, did Socrates and his jurors take the '*kaina daimonia*' of allegation II to refer to? Although it is possible that the term targets the morally-purified gods of Socrates, there are a number of reasons for taking the view that the *daimonion* was central to the allegation. Primary among these is Euthyphro's suggestion (to which Socrates does not object) that Socrates has been indicted because of his *daimonion*.[67] It seems, then, that all Socrates' prosecution needed to do was suggest to the jurors that the source of Socrates' *daimonion* has not been formally 'licensed' by the state and thereby incite the natural suspicions Athenians had toward foreign religious imports.[68] There are, then, at least three areas of potential danger the prosecution might point to: (1) the source of the *daimonion* may be an unlicensed deity to whom Socrates pays unlicensed cult; (2) his characterisation of this sign puts him on special, private terms with a deity; and (3) this sign and the deity behind it may be illusory or the deity may have hostile intentions towards Athens.[69] Although the first concern, (1), is the explicitly actionable one, items (2) and (3) can also be understood to generate the sort of ill will that Socrates cites as the true causes of his conviction (28a). Socrates must have only deepened such fears in some of his jurors when he claimed that it was the *daimonion* that kept him from

SOCRATIC THEOLOGY AND PIETY

entering public politics (*Ap.* 31d–32a), and then threatened to disobey any order they might concoct to discontinue his *daimonion*-assisted mission on behalf of Apollo (29b–d).

As Socrates surely realised, he was not in an ideal position to soothe these sorts of reactions to the *daimonion* (e.g., the time allotted for his defence speech is inadequate to the formidable task of removing by reason what are very much emotional responses; cf. *Ap.* 18e–19a). Socrates cannot deny that the *daimonion* gives him a unique advantage in life, and other sorts of denials unaccompanied by adequate proof are all he has time to offer in response to suspicions that his voice offers evil counsel (e.g., by noting that its content is always dissuasive, never proscriptive; 31d). Moreover, once Meletus opted for his allegation of complete atheism (26b–c), Socrates was obliged to focus most of his defence against that claim, not all the other suspicions that the jury might still be weighing against him. Thus, here in the second specification I think we find one potent source that Meletus might have called upon in pressing an allegation of non-conformity and one source for the jury's actual vote for conviction: Meletus' invocation of the *daimonion* may well have inflamed the prejudices of the jury, leading a good number of them to vote for his conviction on the specification of introducing *kaina daimonia*.[70]

While certain jurors might have been discerning enough to see or intuit the danger to traditionally-motivated cult in Socrates' philosophical revisioning of the gods and the virtue of piety, the attention of the jurors who voted for conviction was most likely to have been drawn to his apparent introduction of a new dispensation without seeking the sanction of the *polis: that* will have seemed his most obvious and glaring violation of accepted norms.[71] Naturally, given the over-determining constellation of factors working against Socrates, jurors who believed him guilty of illegally introducing a new divinity may well have made further damning inferences concerning his teachings.

We should not be surprised, then, that Socrates' defence ultimately failed. In the end, the prejudices and allegations ranged against Socrates proved so numerous and broad-ranging that he was in effect put on trial for the conduct of his entire life. His strange, provocative, street-preaching conduct, purportedly commanded by a divinity and exemplifying the new intellectualist conception of piety that Socrates had forged, proved all too prone to misrepresentation before an undiscerning crowd. From outside the circle of Socratic philosophy, that revised piety looked all too similar to the newfangled impiety Aristophanes had lampooned in his *Clouds* long before (423 BCE), an impiety that Socrates himself would have condemned (*Ap.* 19c–d). It is, then, part of the drama and irony of Socrates' martyrdom that the sign of his god is also the sign of his demise. But, on my account, it is also natural that even with his last words Socrates gave thanks to a god for the extrarational assistance that gave him a life of extraordinary rationality.[72]

NOTES

1. Aristotle *Metaphysics* 1078b7–32, *Eudemian Ethics* 1216b3–1216b26; Cicero, *Tusculan Disputations* 5.4.10–11. See Eric Brown in this volume on the Socratic Method. This essay does not attempt to identify the views of the historical Socrates, but rather, those of the cross-dialogue, literary figure that emerges from the Socratic dialogues of Plato in concert with the recollections of Xenophon and others (e.g., Aristotle). These portraits constitute a mosaic of the characteristics, methods, views and activities of a Socrates who manifests distinctly different philosophical attitudes from those expressed by the Socrates of Plato's *Republic* and other such constructive and, arguably, later dialogues. This qualification permits me to avoid the difficult issue of how we might accurately arrive at the views of the

actual teacher of Plato, yet still allows us to confront many of the most interesting questions Plato's works provoke. There is not sufficient space here to address the complex issue of whether and how we might legitimately use the testimony of Aristotle in conjunction with that of Plato's dialogues and Xenophon's work to triangulate to the views of the historical Socrates in the manner of Gregory Vlastos 1991, chaps. 2 and 3; but see, e.g., M. L. McPherran 1996, sec. 1.2.

2. E.g., the theistic Stoics claimed to be following in Socrates' footsteps, and assigned the origins of their main proof of God's existence to him; cf. Sextus Empiricus *Math.* 9.88–104, esp. 9.101; J. DeFilippo and P. Mitsis 1994; A. A. Long 1988; and my 1996, sec. 5.2. Sextus also finds it natural to lump Socrates in with Pythagoras and Plato as one of the leading ancient theists (*Math.* 9.64).

3. And many Muslim thinkers as well; see I. Alon, who notes 'Next to Aristotle and Plato, . . . Socrates . . . was the most mentioned philosopher in Arabic literature' (1991: 12).

4. In the first centuries of Christianity, Christians were liable for prosecution as 'atheists' in the same way a theistic Socrates could be thought atheistic: by 'not recognizing the gods of the state' but 'new (unlicensed) divinities' instead; Athenagoras *Presb. Chris.* 4.

5. Justin Martyr appears to have been the first to make the parallel (cf. Justin Martyr I *Apol.* V, 3–4, II *Apol.* X, 4–8), and was followed in his admiration by Clement, Origen, Lactantius and Augustine; Clem., *Strom.* I, XIV 63, 3; V, XIV 99, 3; I, XIX 92, 3; *Prot.* VI, 71, 1 ff.; Orig. *Adv. Cels.* III 66, 67; IV 89; VII 56; August. *De vera relig.* c. 39, n. 72; II, 1; *Confess.* I, II; *De consensu evangelist.* I, 12, 18. Not all the Fathers were so impressed, however. Tertullian, for one, accused Socrates of being an immoralist (*Apology* 39, 12) whose attention to a 'familiar voice' (Socrates' 'little divine voice' [the *daimonion*]) shows him to be acting in the service of a disreputable daemonic power (*Apology* 46; *On the Soul* 1, 2–6). There was a similar reaction in the Islamic world: While many thinkers saw important parallels between Socrates and Muhammad, a minority saw otherwise, e.g., al-Ghazâlî attacks Socrates as a non-believer: Alon 1991: 11, 34–35, 41–100.

6. Cf. Petrarch, *Familiar. rer.* I, 9; *rer.* VIII, 4; *Seniles* XI, 14; D. Erasmus, *Colloquia*, Ulmae 1712, *Convivium Religiosum*, 175; and his letter to John Colet. See Montuori 1981a: 6–12. For Ficino, see P. J. FitzPatrick 1992: 165. The temptation to compare and contrast the secular philosopher with the sacred saviour, often to the detriment of both, still proves irresistible; see, e.g. Davar 1972, Deman 1944, Kaufmann 1951, Toynbee 1954 and Wenley 1889.

7. E.g., Marechal and Voltaire; see also Montuori 1981a: 12–25.

8. The popular 1749 biography of Socrates by J. G. Cooper is in this line, where Socrates' fate is taken to show how false religion can undermine true morality and rational understanding.

9. As Burnet 1916: 236, observes:

The most diverse philosophies have sought to father themselves upon him, and each new account of him tends to reflect the fashions and prejudices of the hour. At one time he is an enlightened deist, at another a radical atheist.

For further and more detailed discussion of Socratic historiography, see Montuori 1981a and FitzPatrick 1992. As the next section of this chapter makes clear, however, my account of Socrates differs substantially from Montuori's own attempt to get beyond the many conflicting images of Socrates presented by the literary tradition.

10. Nussbaum 1980: 44; and see also her n. 5.

SOCRATIC THEOLOGY AND PIETY 317

11. Thorough reviews of the vast literature on 'the Socratic method' may be found in Wolfsdorf 2013 and Chapter 3 by Eric Brown in this volume.

12. Cf. Brickhouse and Smith 1994: ch. 1 and 1991; and Vlastos 1994a on Socrates' use of the *elenchos*. Why think, however, that Socrates would allow *all* human beings to engage in philosophy? First, notice that although we never see Socrates engaged in the elenctic examination of women, he does foresee the possibility of interrogating both men and women in the afterlife (*Ap.* 41c). We also see testimony that he holds virtue and the means to it – the practice of philosophy – to be free of class and gender distinctions, open even to slaves, foreigners and young and old alike; *Ap.* 30a; *M.* 85c, 73b-c; Xen. *Sym.* 2.10; and McPherran 1996, sec. 4.2.

13. For discussions of Socratic irony, see Vasiliou 2013.

14. Nussbaum 1985: 234.

15. For the most recent example of this line of interpretation, see L. Versenyi 1982. Also note, in particular, the attempts of Nussbaum 1985: 234–235, and Nehamas 1987: 305–306, to explain away Socrates' trust in various forms of divination. Vlastos 1991: ch. 6, and 1989, also finds Socrates guilty of disbelieving in the gods of the Athenian state, but allows that he was nonetheless religious in some sense.

16. Note, for example, that there is no Greek term for 'religion' (the root '*religio*' is Latin).

17. See Mikalson 2010: 6–9 and chapters 4–5 on the subtle differences between *eusebēs* 'proper respect' and *hosios* 'religious correctness'.

18. For examples of prayer, see *Iliad* 1.446–58; Hesiod *Works and Days* 724–726, 465–468; and Aeschylus, *The Seven Against Thebes* 252–260.

19. See e.g. Watson 1991, chapter 1.

20. See Parker 1996 on the nature of the reciprocity of sacrificial gift-giving. On his account, prayer and sacrifice occur in the context of a *charis*-relationship, where *charis* is delight, favour, gratitude and kindness; the mutual exchange of pleasing favors in reciprocal relations between gods and humans; see also Mikalson 2010: 14, 39.

21. For discussion, see Burkert 1985: chapters 2 and 5; Cartledge 1985; and Zaidman and Pantel 1992, part 2.

22. See e.g. Zaidman and Pantel 1992, chapter 13.

23. *Daimones* were sometimes thought of as 'intermediary powers'. However, 'every god can act as *daimon*', and so the term is better understood as referring to the 'veiled countenance of divine activity' (Burkert 1985: 180). A hero was a long-dead individual, about whom epic adventures might be told, usually tied to a specific locale (e.g. such as Theseus at Athens; although some, like Heracles, were widely worshipped). As much as any god, a hero had attained the status of divinity, and thus could respond to prayers and sacrifices by providing protection, retribution and so forth. On *daimones*, see Burkert 1985, sec. 3.3.5; on heroes, see Burkert 1985, chapter 4; and Zaidman and Pantel 1992, chapter 13.

24. Vernant 1980: 193.

25. Zaidman and Pantel 1992: 144.

26. For Euripides, see, e.g., *Bacchae* 216–220, *Trojan Women* 1060–1080, *Andromache* 1161–1165. For Thucydides, see e.g. *The Peloponnesian War* 2.8.2.

27. Not everyone agrees with this assessment: Whether the *Euthyphro* is a source of positive Socratic doctrine or merely an aporetic inquiry is a much-debated issue; see below.

28. For a more complete account of Socrates' examination, see Geach 1966, Heidel 1900 and McPherran 1996, chapter 2.

29. For analysis of this argument, see Cohen 1971 and Benson 2000: 59–62. McPherran 1996: 43 n. 43, provides a bare bones version: 'Euthyphro agrees that (1a) the pious is loved by the gods because it is pious and that (1b) it's not that the pious is pious because it is loved by the gods (b). He also agrees that – as with the examples of seer and seen thing, carrier and carried thing, lover and loved thing – (2) a god-loved thing is god-loved because the gods love it, and (3) it's not that the gods love a god-loved thing because it is god-loved. But if D3 [his third definition: piety is what is loved by all the gods] were true (viz., that the pious = the god-loved), then by substitution from D3 into (1a), it would be true that (4) the god-loved is loved by the gods because it is god-loved, and by substitution from D3 into (2) it would be true that (5) a pious thing is pious because the gods love it. However, (4) contradicts (3), and (5) contradicts (1b). Thus, (1a), (1b), (2), and (3) cannot be jointly affirmed while also affirming D3 (resulting in D3's rejection).' To conclude, 'the god-loved is not the pious . . . nor is the pious the god-loved, as you say, but the one is different from the other' (10d; cf. 10e–11a).

It should be noted that although Socrates takes himself to have established that D3 is inconsistent with Euthyphro's other commitments (to, e.g., [1a]), he need not be taken to also conclude that D3 is false; see Benson 2000: 59–61.

30. Among those 'constructivists' willing to do so are Brickhouse and Smith 1994: chapter 6.1; Burnet 1924: 136–137; Rabinowitz 1958; Reeve 1989: sec. 1.10; Taylor 1982; and Vlastos 1991: chapter 6. Those who do not think a Socratic account of piety is implied by the text ('anticonstructivists') include Allen 1970: 6–9, 67; and Grote 1865: 437–457. Beckman 1979: sec. 2.1; Calef 1995; and Versenyi 1982 are qualified anticonstructivists, since they argue that no definition of piety *involving reference to the gods* may be culled from the dialogue's explicit statements, and that in fact, the notion of piety *toward* which Socrates directs Euthyphro is a secular one that identifies it with the whole of virtue (Reeve 1989: 64–66, seems to head in this direction as well). For additional references, see McPherran 1985: nn. 2 and 3, and 1996: 30 nn. 4 and 5.

31. For further discussion, see McPherran 1996: secs. 2.2.2–6, 3.2; and Vlastos 1991: 162–165.

32. Cf., e.g., Aeschylus *The Libation Bearers* 306–314, *Agamemnon* 1560–1566; Aristotle *Nicomachean Ethics* 1132b21–1133a6; Hesiod fr. 174 Rzach; Pindar *Pythian* 2.83–85; and Plato *M*. 71e.

33. Yunis 1988: chapters 1 and 3.

34. Cf. Xenophanes, who testifies that 'Homer and Hesiod have attributed to the gods everything that is a shame and reproach among humans, stealing and committing adultery and deceiving each other' (Sextus Empiricus *Math.* 11.193).

35. For further discussion, see McPherran 1996: secs. 2.2 and 4.2.

36. For a detailed treatment of Socrates' examination of this definition, see McPherran 2003b.

37. See, e.g., McPherran 1996: secs. 2.2 and 4.2.

38. Vlastos 1989: 235.

39. See McPherran 2000 for full discussion of this issue.

40. Some modern critics dismiss Xenophon's categorical affirmations of Socratic piety as instances of telltale overkill. For example, Vlastos 1971b: 3 argues that Xenophon's

SOCRATIC THEOLOGY AND PIETY   319

account of Socratic piety 'refutes itself', since 'had the facts been as he tells them, the indictment would not have been made in the first place'.

41. For example, Plato is willing to put twelve prayers into the mouth of his Socrates (see B. D. Jackson 1971; *Euthd.* 275d; *Phd.* 117c; *Symp.* 220d; *Phdr.* 237a–b, 257a–b, 278b, 279b–c; *Rep.* 327a–b, 432c, 545d–e; *Phlb.* 25b, 61b–c). *Euthydemus* 302c–303a, *Menexenus* 243e–244b and *Phaedrus* 229e testify to Socrates' orthopraxy, and note the stage-setting of the start of the *Republic* (327a), where Socrates has travelled down to the Piraeus in order to pray to the goddess Bendis and observe her festival.

42. During Socrates' lifetime, divination was widely employed by both states and individuals, and appeared in roughly three forms (in order of prestige): (1) divination by lots; (2) interpretation of signs such as thunder, the direction of flights of birds, dreams and the reading of sacrificial entrails; and (3) the production and interpretation of oral oracles by a seer (*mantis*) (with these being recorded, collected and interpreted by 'oracle-mongers'). See, e.g., Zaidman and Pantel 1992: 121–128.

43. E.g., in the manner of the characters of Euripides, who challenge both the abilities and honesty of traditional seers (e.g., *Philoctetes* fr. 795) and the existence of the gods who allegedly provide foreknowledge (*Bellerophon* fr. 286; *The Trojan Women* 884–887; Fr. 480; Sextus Empiricus *Math.* 9.54). See M. Ostwald 1986: 279–290, for discussion.

44. For discussion of how Socrates can endorse the Ignorance Principle (T2) but also know (or justifiably believe) things, see Brickhouse and Smith 1994: chapter 2; Vlastos 1994a. See also the chapter by McPartland in this book.

45. For a comprehensive discussion of Socrates' relation to the extrarational, see McPherran 1991 and 1996: chapter 4.

46. On the Oracle and its functions, see Fontenrose 1978; Parke and Wormell 1956.

47. For discussion of the problem of how Socrates is able to derive a prescriptive claim that he *ought to* philosophise from the merely descriptive claim of the Pythia that he *is* the wisest, see Brickhouse and Smith 1983; McPherran 2002; Stokes 1992: 29–33; Vlastos 1989: 229–230 and 1991: 166–173.

48. See McPherran 1996: sec. 4.2

49. See Vlastos 1989 and 1991: chapter 6, opposes this view, and is replied to by Brickhouse and Smith 1994: chapter 6, and McPherran 1991 and 1996: chapter 4.

50. See McPherran 1996: sec. 4.2.

51. For discussion of the *daimonion* – and opposition to Vlastos 1989, and Nussbaum 1985, who downplay the epistemic significance of the *daimonion* – see Brickhouse and Smith 1994: sec. 6.3; and McPherran 1991 and 1996: sec. 4.1.

52. See *Ap.* 40b together with 26b–28a. See also *Ap.* 31c–d, 40a, 40c, 41d; *Eu.* 3b; *Tht.* 151a; *Thg.* 128d–131a; Xen. *Mem.* 1.1.2–4, 4.8.1; *Apol.* 4–5, 8, 12–13; *Sym.* 8.5. What evidence there is (see esp. *Ap.* 27c–28a) suggests that Socrates is uncertain as to the nature and identity of the divinity behind his 'sign', but Apollo is surely a prime candidate since it is Apollo who has charged him with his philosophical mission to the Athenians, one that exposes him to the sort of danger that would warrant a god's help.

53. Although in Xenophon (e.g., *Mem.* 1.1.4; 4.3.12; 4.8.1; *Apol.* 12) the *daimonion* offers positive advice.

54. I argue in McPherran 1996: sec. 5.1 that we have reason to believe Socrates holds the alternatives of his first premise – that death is either nothingness or migration to another place where he can philosophise – to be equally probable; hence, that he is an agnostic on the topic of the soul's immortality. For a critical response, see Brickhouse and Smith 1994: sec. 6.5.

55. This inference was adopted by the Stoics as their main theological proof and made a crucial contribution to their thinking about natural law; see, e.g., DeFilippo and Mitsis 1994; Long 1996; and Sedley 2002. For further discussion and the argument that Xenophon's testimony ought to be accepted, see McPherran 1996: sec. 5.2.

56. The attribute of 'loving' marks a new and startling development, for the traditional attitude held that being a human-lover is beneath the dignity of Zeus; Burkert 1985: 274.

57. Although we never see Socrates grapple directly with the problem of reconciling the existence of good and wise god(s) with the existence of natural disasters and moral evil, his view that piety involves serving the gods by improving our souls *via* philosophical examination, and his seeming view that we are – *qua* human beings – constrained from fully possessing the knowledge of virtue constitutive of divine wisdom (*Ap.* 20d–e, 23a), suggest that he might have held something akin to a traditional 'soul-building' response to the problem. On this sort of account, there really are no natural evils: Ocean storms, diseases and death itself are not in themselves evil, but assume value only in relation to the moral development of a person's soul (see, e.g., *Euthd.* 277d–282e; *Grg.* 511c–512e). Moral evils, on the other hand, are a consequence of our having imperfect human souls, an imperfection that is a necessary condition of non-divine human beings having been created in the first place, a creation that is – all things considered – a good thing.

58. Guthrie 1971: 156; Zaidman and Pantel 1992: 176: 'As the Greeks saw it, the divine simply manifested itself in multiply diverse aspects.'

59. *Ap.* 26b; a reduction paralleled at *Eu.* 3b–4e; Reeve 1989: 75–76. For the argument that the specifications are historically accurate and authentic, see Brickhouse and Smith 1989b: 30; Versnel 1981: 124 n. 122.

60. Plato makes the same point, in a clear reference to the *Euthyphro* (*Rep.* 377e–378e; cf. *Laws* 886c–d). Note too that even a critic of the new intellectualism like Aristophanes sees this same problem, but foists it onto the intellectuals, not the traditionalists (correctly so, since it is these who are responsible for advocating a unitary conception of justice); e.g., in the *Clouds* he has Wrong Argument advocate using the example of Zeus to excuse one's own adulteries (1079–84; cf. 904).

61. E.g., Democritus, a probable contemporary of Socrates, declared that the gods are the source of all good and that man is responsible for the evils that he suffers (DK B 175); while the speaker of the Sisyphus fragment (probably by Euripides) held the gods and their justice to be the false invention of certain 'shrewd and clever-minded man' (DK 88B.25).

62. See, e.g., Euripides, *Heracles* 1340–1346.

63. Lloyd-Jones 1971: 134; Burnet 1924: 114; Dodds 1951: 141–143; Yunis 1988: 39.

64. Garland 1992: 136, 146; Versnel 1981: 127.

65. For detailed discussion of this procedure, see, e.g., Parker 1996: chapters 9 and 10; Garland 1992: esp. 14–22, 137, 149. Cf. *Laws* 738b–739a. As the influx of foreign deities such as Bendis into Athens increased during and after the life of Socrates, there even seem

SOCRATIC THEOLOGY AND PIETY

to have been a number of prosecutions for failure to meet the requirements for proper religious innovation; see Garland 1992, chapter 7, and Parker 1996, chapters 9 and 10.

66. Garland 1992: 146. Versnel 1981: 121, writes: '. . . the very nature of the notion 'foreign' [e.g. god] evoked various unpleasant associations. . . .'

67. *Eu.* 3b; cf. 5a. Xenophon also claims that the second count derives from Socrates' talk of the *daimonion* (*Mem.* 1.1.2–3; *Apol.* 12), and the Socrates of Plato's *Apology* reports that 'Meletus wrote about it [the *daimonion*] in the indictment' (31d). Add to this the fact that Xenophon feels the need to defend Socrates against this sort of understanding of the second allegation (*Mem.* 1.1.3–4; *Apol.* 12–14; cf. *Mem.* 4.3.12–13) and we have solid grounds for supposing that Socrates' *daimonion* was indeed its primary target. Cf. Burkert 1985: 317; Garland 1992: 149.

68. Versnel 1981: 121–122 notes that foreign cults tended to be associated with private rituals, which in turn fostered all sorts of suspicions. He also persuasively shows through a survey of cult-introduction in Athens (102–131) that 'in addition to the negative connotations of *foreign* cults . . . there is also a marked resistance to the *novelty* of non-traditional gods and cults' (130): a resistance to religious change that extends back to Hesiod (fr. 322) and which shows up in Xenophon's advice from Delphi to 'follow established custom' (*Mem.* 4.3.16). Thus, the *daimonion* could represent to some Athenians the worst possible religious threat: not only a foreign import, but a new one as well.

69. McPherran 1996: 135; cf. Kraut 2000: 17.

70. Cf. Garland 1992: chapter 7; Kraut 2000.

71. Although Socrates himself never names the *daimonion* as a source of the 'first accusations' that led to the formal specifications, it may be alluded to when he speaks at *Apology* 23a of unspecified slanders connected with the allegations that he possesses wisdom and when he notes at 23d–e the allegation that he teaches about 'the things aloft'. In fact, since it is clear that the *daimonion was* the source for the formulation of one of the formal specifications, it seems likely that Meletus would try to use a formulation that *does* pick up a pre-existing prejudice and that the *daimonion* – as the source for the second specification's formulation – was, then, a source of pre-trial prejudice.

72. Namely: 'Crito, we owe a cock to Asclepius: please pay the debt and do not forget' (*Phd.* 118a). In McPherran 2003a I argue that we should understand Socrates here as instructing Crito to repay their mutual debt for (1) the philosophy-encouraging dreams Socrates has received from Asclepius (e.g., *Apology* 33c, 43d–44b; *Phd.* 60c–61c); and (2) for Asclepius having saved both Crito and himself from death during the plague of 430–420, and thus, having saved them for a life of philosophising.

CHAPTER FOURTEEN

Socrates on Death and the Afterlife

EMILY A. AUSTIN

Death did not sneak up on Socrates like a thief in the night. In fact, some people think Socrates actively pursued his death, relishing the prospect of an afterlife or of annihilation's release from a human existence he found increasingly tiresome. Regardless of whether he wanted to die, though, one thing is certain – he spent time preparing. He talks regularly of his own death, what it might be like and whether it will benefit or harm him. He repeatedly acknowledges that he might eventually be killed by Athens and recounts tales of having almost been killed by Athens before. Others regularly praise him, and he occasionally praises himself, for his prowess and courage in battle at the risk of death.

This chapter explores how Plato and Xenophon characterise Socrates' views on death, though I focus primarily on Plato, whose Socrates has long merited the lion's share of scholarly attention. While much of the chapter will focus on Socrates' claims specifically about death and whether he or anyone else should fear it, I also tease out how his views on death intersect with both long-standing and recent debates in the scholarly literature on Socratic ethics and moral psychology. Socrates' dogged belief that committing injustice is worse than death is woven into almost every part of his developed philosophy, including his emblematic disavowal of knowledge, his view that emotions like fear are (in some fashion or other) within our control, his belief in divine providence and the goodness of the gods, and his speculation about post-mortem reward and punishment.

The first four sections concern Plato's Socrates. Section One addresses Socrates' arguments against the fear of death in Plato's *Apology*, which present philosophical problems independently and when taken together. Section Two addresses Socrates' intellectualist conception of the emotions and explores how intellectualism affects our ability to control or eliminate the fear of death. Section Three addresses the role of Socrates' myths of the afterlife and their relationship to his intellectualism, his justification for various forms of punishment and his view that virtuous living is its own reward. Section Four briefly explores the relationship between the fear of death and Socratic courage. The final section turns to Xenophon's characterisation of Socrates' views on death in *Socrates' Defence to the Jury*.

DEATH IN PLATO'S *APOLOGY*

In Plato's *Apology*, Socrates offers three key arguments against fearing death. In his first, pre-verdict argument, Socrates extends his characteristic epistemic modesty to the question of whether death is good or bad for the one who dies. He claims that people fear death because they suffer from the 'blameworthy ignorance' of thinking they know that death is bad, when in fact they have no such knowledge. Socrates, on the other hand, does not fear death because he does not know whether death is good or bad (*Ap.* 29a–c). After the verdict, though, Socrates offers two arguments to the effect that death is a benefit. First, he claims to have 'convincing proof' from his *daimonion* that his death will benefit him (*Ap.* 40a–c). The *daimonion* has offered no resistance to his defence, his defence has ended in a death sentence, so the *daimonion* must consider the verdict the better result. He then offers an additional argument, often called the 'Two Things Argument', that others should likewise have 'good hope' that both annihilation and an afterlife offer an improvement on life (*Ap.* 40c–41c).

Scholars have noted that none of these arguments are exceptionally strong on their own merits. Worse, they appear contradictory when taken together, since the post-verdict arguments seem to violate the epistemic modesty upon which the pre-verdict argument depends. Most scholars resolve the tension between the arguments by diminishing Socrates' commitment to the final 'Two Things Argument', in part because they consider it a weak and uncharacteristically immodest argument (Armleder 1966; Roochnik 1985, Brickhouse and Smith 1989a, 1989b; Reeve 1989, 182; de Strycker and Slings 1994). A few scholars have sought to defend parts or all of the final argument and resolve the inconsistency (McPherran 1996, Rudebusch 1999; Austin 2010, Jones 2013b, Smith 2016). In this section, I will walk through the three arguments, pointing out common objections and candidate responses on behalf of Socrates.

The Sceptical Argument

After his examination of Meletus, Socrates imagines an objector who asks him why he has persisted in practising philosophy even though it has led to mortal peril. Most of us, given the choice between refraining from philosophy and being killed, would likely express a sudden interest in learning to code or economics. Socrates, less fickle than the average philosopher, thinks the objector's reasoning depends on an unwarranted assumption that death is bad. In fact, Socrates thinks many people consider death the *worst* thing. Socrates, however, contends that people labouring under this assumption suffer from intellectual immodesty:

> To fear death, gentleman, is no other than to think oneself wise when one is not, to think one knows what one does not know. No one knows whether death may not be the greatest of all blessings for a man, yet men fear it as if they knew it was the greatest of evils. And surely it is the most blameworthy ignorance to believe that one knows what one does not know. It is perhaps on this point and in this respect, gentleman, that I differ from the majority of men, and if I were to claim that I am wiser than anyone in anything, it would be in this, that as I have no adequate knowledge of things in the underworld, so I do not think I have.
>
> – *Ap.* 29a–b

Socrates here puts his characteristic epistemic modesty to good use. If having a rational fear requires knowing that the thing one fears is bad or harmful, then Socrates rightly points out that he, knowing not whether death is bad, lacks reason to fear it.

Yet it is not clear how far Socrates' argument can take him. It cannot establish that death will be good, since advancing a positive claim on the basis of ignorance is a textbook

SOCRATES ON DEATH AND THE AFTERLIFE

fallacy. All he can establish is that death's badness is uncertain. Yet this uncertainty might itself be sufficient reason to fear death. One might consider it rational to fear something simply because one does not know whether it will be bad. If you tell me that something will benefit me or result in a lifetime of excruciating pain, it would be odd for you to chastise me for my fear that it could result in excruciating pain (Austin 2010; Long 2019, 92–93). Even given a negligible chance of harm, it would remain rational to fear it. Socrates' sceptical argument, then, can only do so much to show that death is not bad or to diminish a person's fear of death.

Reeve (1989, 112–114) and Austin (2010) argue that in its intended context, the sceptical argument can serve the purpose for which Socrates uses it – namely, to show that he has reason to continue to practise philosophy, even though it might lead to his death. Socrates believes the gods ordered him to philosophise, and he thinks everyone should agree that ignoring the commands of the gods would be impious. Given a choice between something he knows would be bad (disobeying the gods by giving up philosophy) and something that could be good (death), he thinks death is the better choice. Perhaps death will be bad, and perhaps a person can rationally fear it. But Socrates thinks a person should not fear something that might be good more than something that is certainly bad.

Socrates' agnostic attitude toward death gives way at the end of the dialogue, though, to newfound confidence stemming from 'convincing proof' that death is a good thing, perhaps even a 'blessing'. For reasons discussed below, most scholars have chosen to resolve this apparent contradiction in favour of the pre-verdict argument, which fits more squarely with Socrates' characteristic modesty. The pre-verdict sceptical argument is also, by most accounts, the philosophically more respectable of the two. The closing passage contains two sustained arguments against fearing death – 'The Argument from Daimonic Silence' (40a–c) and 'The Two Things Argument' (40c–41c).

The Argument from Daimonic Silence

Once the jury hands down its verdict, Socrates moves from castigating those who voted to execute him to a more intimate conversation with those who voted for his acquittal, whom he now addresses as 'friends' (40a). He begins by noting his own surprise that his distinctive divine sign, the *daimonion*, remained silent throughout his defence, never interrupting him to signal that his words or actions were incorrect. The *daimonion*'s silence means that it endorsed not only his actions, but also their result – his death (interestingly, he does not seem to consider that it might have endorsed the guilty verdict). This leads Socrates to conclude that 'what has happened to me may well be a good thing, and those of us who believe death to be an evil are certainly mistaken' (40b). Unfortunately, the first clause about Socrates, even if true, does not necessarily license the second clause about everyone else.

Scholars have noted that the argument from daimonic silence can only show so much, perhaps less than Socrates assumes. Brickhouse and Smith (1989b, 250–267) argue that Socrates is justified in concluding that his defence has been successful, in part because the defence was so elaborate that the *daimonion*'s failure to register concern at any point does reasonably constitute endorsement. Nevertheless, the *daimonion* only keeps Socrates from doing things. It does not tell Socrates *why* he should not do them. Socrates must speculate about the *daimonion*'s intentions, as he does when he offers a reason for the *daimonion*'s prohibition against his taking part in politics (*Ap.* 31d–32a). Socrates might

326 THE BLOOMSBURY HANDBOOK OF SOCRATES

safely conclude that his death has divine endorsement, but he must give his own account of the *daimonion*'s reasoning.

More importantly, while the *daimonion*'s silence might be sufficient to warrant Socrates' confidence, it does not license any such conclusion for others about their own death. After all, the *daimonion* is private (Roochnik 1985, 212; McPherran 1996, 255), and most people do not die after having lived Socrates' life and offered his defence (Reeve, 1989, 182). Socrates' friends lack a private *daimonion* and will face death under different circumstances. Any effort to convince his audience that they should not fear their own death, then, requires a separate argument. Granted, some jurors might take the testimony of Socrates' *daimonion* seriously out of piety, and Socrates might himself believe the argument should generalise (Austin 2010, 7–8). Whether that confidence is merited is a legitimate matter of dispute.

The 'Two Things Argument'

Socrates takes up this more general task in what is often called the 'Two Things Argument'. The argument begins with a disjunctive premise about the nature of death:

> Let us reflect in this way, too, that there is good hope that death is a blessing, for it is one of two things: either the dead are nothing and have no perception of anything, or it is, as we are told, a change and a relocating for the soul from here to another place.
>
> *– Ap.* 40c

One might worry that this starting disjunction might itself be false, since surely there are other options. For example, why not think the soul can persist, but remain here rather than going 'to another place', a possibility entertained in both the *Phaedo* (81c–d) and the *Theaetetus* (177a)? On a charitable reading, we can at least grant Socrates an exhaustive premise – we are annihilated or we are not annihilated.

However, Socrates' argument that annihilation is good is more difficult to assess charitably. He develops the first disjunct as follows:

> If it is a complete lack of perception, like a dreamless sleep, then death would be a great advantage. For I think if one had to pick out that night during which a man slept soundly and did not dream, put beside it the other nights and days of his life, and then see how many days and nights had been better and more pleasant than that night, not only a private person but the great king would find them easy to count compared with the other days and nights. If death is like this, I say it is an advantage, for all eternity would then seem to be no more than a single night.
>
> *– Ap.* 40d–e

The objections to this argument largely stem from Socrates' comparison of annihilation to a 'dreamless sleep' that is 'more pleasant' than most of the days of one's life. Roochnik (1985, 214) claims that what makes a night of dreamless sleep pleasant is that one wakes up from it 'refreshed and vitalized', and one clearly does not wake up from annihilation. Smith (2016), on the other hand, thinks that we often look forward to the release of sleep independent of whether we will wake up. This is a relatively small disagreement, however, since Smith concedes Roochnik's larger point that the argument does not license Socrates' apparent claims that an endless dreamless sleep is itself pleasant or better than most of the days and nights of our life. The state of annihilation is not the sort of thing that can even be pleasant, since annihilation is the absence of the capacities of sense-experience upon

SOCRATES ON DEATH AND THE AFTERLIFE

which pleasure depends (Roochnik 1985, 213). If Socrates thinks annihilation benefits because it is more pleasant than most of the days of one's life, then he is hopelessly confused about the nature of annihilation.

Scholars who are inclined to help Socrates escape this apparent confusion have generally taken one of two approaches, either affirming or denying that Socrates considers annihilation pleasant. Rudebusch (1999, 68) argues that while annihilation makes 'sensory' pleasure impossible, perhaps annihilation permits another kind of pleasure that does not require capacities for sensory awareness. Drawing on Aristotle and Ryle, Rudebusch distinguishes between 'sensate' pleasures, of which we must be aware, and 'modal' pleasures, of which we need not be aware (e.g., getting lost in a book or a game). Austin (2010, 10–11) worries that even pleasure of which one is not *currently* aware is pleasure of which one *could* become aware, as when one finishes the book or the game. Annihilation makes such awareness impossible.

The second way of defending Socrates is to deny that he thinks annihilation is pleasant. Instead, Socrates argues that annihilation is a 'benefit' compared to the many days of one's life, the vast majority of which are quite unpleasant. An eternal dreamless sleep, on this line of argument, offers an improvement on life, since life is overall bad and unpleasant (McPherran 1996, 257–258; Austin 2010, 11–12; Jones 2013b, 84–85 and 2016). Brickhouse and Smith (1989b, 259) write: 'No doubt, not everyone would share Socrates' very negative assessment of the typical enjoyments of daily life, but surely his point here cannot be dismissed', singling out Roochnik in particular for this too easy dismissal.

McPherran (1996, 257–258) and Austin (2010, 12) support this interpretation by suggesting that Socrates' argument might allude to the story of Cleobis and Biton in the first book of Herodotus. Croesus asks Solon, visiting while on vacation, to name the happiest human being, hoping of course that Solon will name Croesus himself. Croesus, to his chagrin, does not register in the competition. Second place goes to the twin brothers Cleobis and Biton. According to Solon, when their mother's oxen proved unable to transport her to the festival, the brothers took on the role of oxen and pulled her there themselves. Bursting with pride, their mother asked the gods to reward them with 'whatever is best for a man to win'. The gods complied, allowing them to spend their evening feasting, then putting them both to sleep eternally. According to Solon, the take-home message of their eternal sleep is that 'the god showed thoroughly how much better it is for a man to be dead than alive' (i 31, Greene 1987 trans.). The connection between eternal sleep as superior to human life maps neatly onto Socrates' claim that an eternity of 'dreamless sleep' might be superior to almost all of the days of our lives.

While the idea that humans are 'better off dead' helps Socrates escape the confusion about the pleasure of annihilation, some scholars think it comes at too great a cost. In particular, it is difficult to call anyone meaningfully happy if annihilation is better than living. Jones (2013b, 84–85) uses this very point in support of his argument that even Socrates cannot be happy. Jones argues that the first disjunct of the 'Two Things Argument' squares with Socrates' claims in the *Euthydemus* that happiness requires wisdom. Since Socrates lacks wisdom, Jones argues that Socrates cannot be happy. He is only less miserable than others, which is not the same as being happy.

Those preferring a happy Socrates have recourse to some supporting textual evidence (see esp. Smith 2016). Socrates, when entertaining free meals as a possible counter penalty, tells the jury that the Olympic victor makes 'you think yourself happy; I make you be happy' (*Ap.* 36d–e). He notes that people in the afterlife are 'happier', the comparative suggesting that the living are at least to some extent happy (*Ap.* 41c). In a text receiving significant attention in this debate, Socrates entreats Callicles in the *Gorgias*: 'listen to me and follow me to where I am, and when you come here, you'll be happy both during life and at its end' (*Grg.* 527c, trans. Zeyl). Jones (2016, 102–103), however, argues that the perspicuous rendering shows that Socrates merely encourages Callicles to join him in *pursuing* happiness, not in being happy.

In the end, readers who reject the possibility of pleasant annihilation and judge Socrates happy must either dismiss the first disjunct as incoherent or, with Smith (2016), tease out a set of reasonably defensible claims needlessly adorned with 'kindly overstatement' and 'innocent hyperbole'.

The Second Disjunct

Socrates then turns to the second arm of the disjunct and considers the benefits of an afterlife:

> If, on the other hand, death is a change from here to another place, and what we are told is true and all who have died are there, what greater blessing could there be, gentleman of the jury? If anyone arriving in Hades will have escaped those who call themselves jurymen here, and will find those true jurymen who are said to sit in judgment there, Minos and Rhadamanthus and Aeacus and Triptolemus and the other demi-gods who have been upright in their own life, would that be a poor kind of change?

> – 40e–41a

Socrates notes that residents of the afterlife are 'happier' (41c), which might have some bearing on the previous concern about Socrates' happiness. The comparative suggests that humans are to some extent happy here, unless 'happier' means that they are happier by being happy at all. Socrates imagines himself continuing his examinations in the company of famous men and heroes, noting that they will not put him to death for philosophising in the afterlife, or perhaps that they cannot because metaphysics precludes killing the immortal.

Scholars have worried that Socrates again makes unwarranted assumptions. On what grounds can he claim that the afterlife will be pleasant rather than torturous? As Roochnik (1985, 213) points out, absent good evidence to the contrary, the afterlife might involve 'being chained to a cliff and having one's liver daily eaten'. It might involve unmerited suffering meted out by capricious gods. The idea that the underworld would be good is complicated by the fact that many familiar stories of the afterlife did not offer a compelling advertisement. On what grounds can Socrates or his audience rule out an afterlife that inspired Achilles to tell Odysseus that he would rather till the ground than be king of the dead?

Deretić and Smith (2021, 111–113) rightly point out that Homer was not the only, or even the most authoritative, source for tales of the afterlife. When Socrates refers to 'what we are told', he might appeal to a more widely known and cherished conception of the afterlife than that offered from the Homeric era. While more harrowing tales might have some residual hold on them, we have no good reason to think that his audience takes that conception more seriously than the positive stories to which Socrates clearly appeals.

McPherran (1996) and Austin (2010) argue that Socrates and his sympathetic audience likely discard those stories of capricious gods because they operate on a foundational principle that the gods are good. Any afterlife ruled by the gods, then, must also be good

SOCRATES ON DEATH AND THE AFTERLIFE

in some fashion. While such assumptions about piety and the nature of the gods might themselves be open to philosophical challenge, questioning them in the context of a trial for impiety would not only be uncharacteristic of Socrates, but also subvert the sort of defence he has offered. If there is an afterlife, the gods would not make it bad.

Rudebusch (1999) argues that Socrates need not commit himself to the idea that the afterlife is good at all. Socrates believes that 'a good man cannot be harmed either in life or in death' (41c–d), so Socrates must also believe that he could readily endure a bad afterlife. While he hopes for a good result, his commitment to virtue will shield him from harm.

One last point about the benefit and harm of death remains – the final sentence of the *Apology*. In his parting words, Socrates tells the jurors, 'Now the hour to part has come. I go to die, you go to live. Which of us goes to the better lot is known to no one, except the god' (42a). Socrates' apparent uncertainty fits more naturally with his sceptical, pre-verdict argument in that it acknowledges that human life might be superior to annihilation or even an afterlife. Both of those possibilities were ruled out in the 'Two Things Argument', where death promises a better result on either condition.

Long (2019, 97) argues that this final line gives further credence to the view that we should take Socrates' pre-verdict, sceptical argument more seriously than the closing 'Two Things Argument'. Those scholars who find the 'Two Things Argument' weak or even hopelessly confused likewise welcome this return to epistemic modesty.

Setting aside the merits of the arguments themselves, it is worth noting that Socrates offers them all in the service of his dogged claim that doing injustice is worse than suffering it. If suffering injustice sometimes means death, and death were the worst thing, then it would be prudent to choose injustice (especially a minor injustice) rather than suffer death. Even at his most sceptical about the nature of death, Socrates thinks we have reason to choose justice instead because we can know that disobeying the gods is bad, whereas we cannot know that death is bad. One might still have reason to fear death because of its uncertain nature, but one has less reason to fear death than injustice. It would admittedly make it easier to choose justice if one did not fear death at all, which is a result marketed by the post-verdict arguments. Either way, justice wins.

Socratic Intellectualism and the Fear of Death

Socrates, in both Plato's *Apology* and elsewhere, tries to convince his audience to fear death less or not at all, so it makes sense to determine how he thinks a person might effectively manage or eliminate fear. Scholars generally agree that Socrates advocates some variety of an intellectualist account of emotions, according to which emotions are either exhausted by or importantly depend on judgments. The fear of death, on such a model, depends on or is exhausted by a judgment that death is a bad thing. The fear of an early death, a violent death, a childless death or a painful death would likewise track corresponding judgments that death under such circumstances is bad. Lessening or eliminating the fear of death would require revising or replacing those judgments.

Perhaps the key point of scholarly disagreement concerns not whether emotions crucially involve judgments, but how those judgments are replaced or revised. On one interpretation, sometimes called 'cognitivism', Socrates thinks we change our beliefs, and thereby our emotions, by engaging in rational argumentation. If I encounter and accept a convincing argument, that should lead me to revise my false judgment that something should be feared. For example, if I tell you I am afraid of being eaten alive in the sharp jaws of dust mites, then you can quite readily convince me that my understanding of dust mites is confused and that, while gross, they will not eat me. If I persist in my fear, it indicates that I have not actually accepted the argument.

According to Penner (1992a, 128), Socrates thinks this sort of rational revision in light of argument is not merely *a* way to alter emotions. Instead, Penner claims that for Socrates, 'the *only* way to influence my conduct is to change my opinion as to what is best' (his emphasis). In fact, 'desires *always automatically* adjust to one's beliefs' (145, my emphasis). Scholars who adopt this view of rational revision think sound rational examination alone suffices to alter the beliefs, desires and emotions of Socrates' interlocutors (see also Rowe 2007, chapter 4). A long and successful encounter with the elenchus, then, should make your irrational fears go away. Whenever Socrates fails to convince his interlocutors, the cause is either a failure of argumentative execution or of the interlocutor's rational understanding (Woolf 2000, Carone 2004, 87–94). Socrates fails because he uses the wrong arguments, not because he uses arguments.

Against this parsimonious Socratic intellectualism (rational beliefs altered by arguments alone), some scholars have sought to preserve intellectualism while recognising that some beliefs cannot be readily reasoned away, or even reasoned away at all. These new, more baroque intellectualisms seek to recognise a role for non-rational resistance that does not undermine traditional Socratic resistance to soul division and weakness of will. Brickhouse and Smith (2010) offer the most sustained articulation of such a view, motivated in part by their agreement with Devereux (1995). On their account, some emotions (which still depend on beliefs) must be cultivated or revised through means other than, or in addition to, straight-line argumentation. Such beliefs and attitudes are 'reasons-resistant' and cannot be 'talked' away. A person could, for example, fully recognise a very good argument, yet report that the argument proves insufficient to alter the fear. To revisit the fabulist example, a person might find herself nevertheless fearing the wrath of dust mites because of a long history of looking at scary blown-up pictures and watching horror films.

Brickhouse and Smith (2010) collect textual evidence from across the Socratic dialogues to support their view that Socrates recognises that some reasons-resistant beliefs require practical, non-argumentative interventions. For the purposes of this chapter, though, their account intersects with Socrates' views about death on two key fronts, both prominent in the *Gorgias*. First, they think some forms of punishment succeed in improving a person by means other than argumentation. In their words (2010, 134–135), 'Socrates quite explicitly endorses the uses of various penalties and punishments that simply cannot be adequately understood in standard intellectualist terms.' These penalties range from minor embarrassment to exile, flogging and death. Since some of these punishments also extend in the myth of the afterlife in the *Gorgias*, they will be taken up in more detail in the next section on the afterlife.

The question of Socratic intellectualism also influences how scholars address the fear of death in the pre-mortem part of the *Gorgias*. Austin (2013) and Deretić and Smith (2021) argue that Socrates thinks the fear of death in particular can prove intractable and that controlling or eliminating it requires a set of strategies, some of them non-argumentative. Austin (2013) argues that Callicles suffers from an intransigent fear of death that gives rise to and reinforces his other desires, including for fame and pleasure. This fear is manifest most clearly in his persistent cautionary threat that Socrates' philosophical activity will get him killed, while Callicles' own political career will keep him alive (*Grg.* 486a–b, 508c–d, 521b–d).

SOCRATES ON DEATH AND THE AFTERLIFE

In a well-studied passage at 513c, though, Callicles confesses that he finds himself agreeing with Socrates that a person should not let his fear of death control his life choices. Despite this nagging sense that Socrates is right, Callicles tells Socrates that 'the thing that has happened to most people has happened to me. I'm not really persuaded by you' (*Grg.* 513c–d). Austin argues that this agreement, coupled with his resistance, indicates that Callicles possesses an intransigent fear of death. Callicles recognises that his willingness to conform to political authority to stay alive indicates a servile cowardice, but he is unable to automatically adjust his feelings accordingly and change his life. As a result, he will continue to pander to the people because that is the best way to avoid the fate that awaits Socrates.

Deretić and Smith (2021) also argue that the fear of death might prove 'ubiquitous and intractable' in a way that traditional Socratic intellectualism cannot account for. They argue that the source of this ubiquitous fear of death is not frightening myths, but a 'familiarity bias' that causes our belief-forming mechanism to fear what is uncertain. They write that, 'given the natural processes by which fears are generated, even if one were to acquire some kind of plausible evidence of there being a favourable afterlife ... the recognition of such evidence as evidence would not automatically and effectively preclude the fear of death' (10 of pre-print). They nevertheless suggest that Socrates himself has managed to fight this bias, which explains his own apparent confidence about death, though they leave unspecified how and to what extent he has successfully managed or eliminated his fear.

The extent to which Socrates fears death, if he fears it at all, bears on the discussion of courage in Section Four. In the next section, though, I turn to the stories of the afterlife, which offer a well-spring of available evidence for Socrates' views on death and the role of non-rational persuasion in Socratic intellectualism.

THE AFTERLIFE

Socrates discusses the afterlife in three Socratic dialogues – the *Apology*, *Crito* and *Gorgias*. All three accounts describe some sort of post-mortem judgment, explicitly or implicitly recognising both punishment and reward. In each case, Socrates intends the accounts to play some role in persuading his audience to pursue virtue and to have the appropriate attitudes toward death. In the *Apology*, he seeks to console the jurors who voted for his acquittal. In the *Crito*, Socrates uses the prospect of the afterlife to both console Crito about Socrates' impending execution and to convince him that Socrates should not escape prison in violation of the laws. In the *Gorgias*, Socrates uses his two tales of the afterlife in hopes that they will persuade Callicles to adopt the life of virtue and self-control, though Socrates himself admits they will likely prove ineffective with Callicles. In this section, I will address scholarly treatments of these accounts of the afterlife, focusing on the nature of post-mortem judgment and their role as a persuasive technique. Since the *Gorgias* receives the lion's share of scholarly attention, the same will be true in this section.

First, though, a general point about how philosophers have approached the myths. Many have either set the myths aside as literary confections irrelevant to Socrates' philosophical arguments or as embarrassments best ignored. Penner (1992a, 125), for example, argues that Socrates expresses 'little interest' in the afterlife, despite its role in the *Apology*, *Crito* and *Gorgias*. Yet, the myths cannot be excised from the text, and recent scholars have drawn on their content to inform or complicate standard interpretations of

Socratic intellectualism, rehabilitationism and the advantages of virtue. There is an understandable temptation to see in Socrates those views we ourselves might have, but Socrates discusses both annihilation and the afterlife, and we need good reason to think he only takes one or the other seriously as an option.

Apology

The *Apology*, as discussed in Section One, features an account of the afterlife in which Socrates imagines himself continuing his examinations among 'happier' and less litigious people than his fellow Athenians. The myth appears in the second disjunct of the 'Two Things Argument', which aims to convince those who voted to acquit him not to fear death. He speculates that, upon arrival in Hades, souls will be assessed by the 'true jurymen who are said to sit in judgment there, Minos and Rhadamanthus and Aeacus and Triptolemus, and the other demi-gods who have been upright in their own life' (*Ap.* 41a). These true jurors are presumably to be contrasted with the Athenian jurors, who have moments ago unjustly sentenced him to death.

Socrates leaves unclear whether this afterlife involves punishment and what its nature would be, other than more conversation with Socrates himself. The existence of judges, though, indicates that some people fare better than others in some way or fashion. While Sisyphus suffers great torment in the *Gorgias* (525d–e), Socrates happily anticipates conversing with him in the *Apology* (41c). There is no mention of physical punishment, and obviously no one can be put to death in a place where everyone is immortal.

Scholars disagree about how seriously Socrates takes the possibility of the afterlife in the *Apology*. Remember that Socrates considers two possible results of death – annihilation or an afterlife. The *Apology* is the only place in the Socratic dialogues where Socrates explicitly entertains the possibility of annihilation, and it is perhaps the only place in the Platonic corpus where he argues that annihilation benefits the virtuous (though Austin 2019 has argued that the Socrates of the *Phaedo* believes the same). The logical form of the 'Two Things Argument' only requires that he consider the ramifications of both options, not that he think each option is equally likely. The surface of the text, though, is silent on the matter of likelihood.

McPherran (1996, 266–267) argues that Socrates considers both options equally likely, since Socrates would have reason to make it clear if he thought the afterlife were more likely. His audience would draw greater consolation from the afterlife, so the fact that Socrates withholds that additional consolation means he could not offer it in good conscience. He would be misleading the jurors by offering a result his argument cannot license. Combined with Socrates' pre-verdict scepticism about death, Socrates manifests agnosticism about the result of death and indifference to either result. For that reason, McPherran thinks Socrates' epistemically confident excitement about the eschatological myth of the *Gorgias* signals a departure from Socratic views to a Platonic conception of immortality. More on that point below.

Brickhouse and Smith (2010, 250–256) argue that the text of the 'Two Things Argument' can sustain a reading according to which the afterlife is certainly preferable and perhaps more likely. Socrates' lengthy and colourful depiction of the afterlife suggests that the jurors would prefer an afterlife, which McPherran concedes. It also suggests that Socrates himself prefers the afterlife. Brickhouse and Smith, though, argue that he might think that is the more likely option as well. Their point, roughly, is that the argument could just as well take the following form: 'Friends, even in the unlikely result that death

SOCRATES ON DEATH AND THE AFTERLIFE 333

is annihilation, it would still be good. The afterlife is, we all agree, a more likely and certainly a preferable option. But even if the gods withhold the afterlife for their own good reasons, we will still benefit from that result.' I myself suspect that Brickhouse and Smith have the correct reading, but I also agree with them that the text itself leaves the matter underdetermined.

Crito

Talk of the afterlife bookends the *Crito*, and here, too, it features post-mortem judgment and plays a persuasive role. At the opening of the dialogue, Crito marvels at Socrates' ability to sleep soundly despite the 'misfortune' of his impending death (*Cr.* 43b). Socrates explains his easy slumber by recounting a pleasant dream in which a goddess promises him that he will 'arrive at fertile Phthia on the third day' (*Cr.* 44a–b). At the close of the dialogue, Socrates imagines the Laws cautioning him that if he escapes prison against their will, then their 'brothers, the laws of the underworld, will not receive [him] kindly' (*Cr.* 54c). His escape would not help him when he arrives 'yonder' (*Cr.* 54b). This final point – that Socrates will fare poorly in the afterlife – likely plays some role in Crito's subsequent acquiescence to Socrates' decision to remain in prison.

With respect to *Crito*, Penner (1992a, 125) notes that the final passage about the afterlife is 'in the mouth of the Laws'. McPherran concurs that the *Crito* offers 'dubious evidence' of Socrates' belief in an afterlife because 'the personified laws of Athens, not Socrates in his own voice, assume the soul's migration' (1996, 265). This is not an entirely ad hoc exclusion on the part of Penner and McPherran, since other scholars have argued that we should also view the Laws' endorsement of authoritarianism as un-Socratic (Harte 1999, Bostock 1990; for an opposing view, see Brickhouse and Smith 2013a). The Laws do deliver the bulk of the dialogue, so attempts to excise them admittedly come at some textual cost.

Gorgias

The most detailed and contentious myth of the afterlife in the Socratic dialogues closes out the *Gorgias*, which Penner (1992a, 125) refers to, with little elaboration, as 'the horrific myth at the end of the *Gorgias*.' McPherran (1996) agrees with Penner and seeks to isolate the myth from other Socratic discussions about death because it threatens the view that Socrates himself does not care about the afterlife and also, for reasons discussed below, because it threatens intellectualist moral psychology. Annas (1982, 125), on the other hand, claims that the myth is, at root, 'morally optimistic' because it promises rewards for justice, even if that optimism depends on 'a hypothesis we have no reason to believe'.

Before turning to the *Gorgias'* closing myth, though, it is worth noting an earlier myth of the afterlife that gets less scholarly attention. In his effort to convince Callicles to moderate his pleasures, Socrates borrows a depiction of the afterlife from 'a Sicilian', in which the 'uninitiated' are forced to carry water with a sieve and put it into another leaky vessel (*Grg.* 493a–d). McPherran (1996, 268) claims this has overtones of the Pythagorean or Orphic accounts of the afterlife more common to the *Phaedo* (see also Penner 1992, 125). Socrates hopes this myth, in addition to the subsequent Myth of the Jars, will persuade Callicles to pursue moderation. Callicles, however, affirms Socrates' suspicion that such stories will have little or no persuasive effect on Callicles (*Grg.* 493c–d).

Nevertheless, Socrates tries again with another, much more elaborate account of the afterlife at the end of the dialogue. As in the *Apology* and *Crito*, it features post-mortem judgment. Here, though, the nature of the judgment and its after-effects, especially in terms of punishment, are much more fully developed. Socrates admits in advance that he doubts that his story will be effective for Callicles. Callicles will probably consider it an 'old wives' tale,' but Socrates confesses that he considers it 'true' (523). Though his entreaties are directed at Callicles, perhaps Socrates thinks others in the assembled audience will prove less intractable than Callicles.

Scholars all agree that Socrates does not consider his account literally true in its entirety. Even in the decidedly non-Socratic myth in the *Phaedo*, Socrates claims that 'no sensible man would insist that these things are as I have described them'. Nevertheless, Socrates thinks good people should 'risk' believing that 'this, or something like this, is true' (*Phd.* 114d). The 'part true' nature of such myths, though, leaves the reader with the difficult task of determining exactly what parts merit the term 'true' – the afterlife itself, the divine judgment, the specific punishments and rewards?

The Incurables and Just Punishment

Socrates opens with a mytho-historical account of divine judgment. In the early days, back when Cronus oversaw matters, even the divine judges found themselves ruling in error. They saw only the outward trappings of the dead, their beauty and riches beguiling the judges into the false belief that the people must have been good and upright because of their prosperity (*Grg.* 523a–c). When Zeus took charge, he was frustrated that the judgments were incorrect, so he solved the problem by stripping the dead of their bodies to reveal the souls underneath.

As a result, the soul market underwent a correction. Rich and beautiful bodies often hid scarred and twisted souls, while the poor and ugly often appeared with unmarred souls. Scholars have generally noted that this admittedly overwrought narrative illustrates a contrast between Athenian courts, which judge by externals, and the gods, who see the soul itself (Rowe 2012b, 2007; Sedley 2009, Annas 1982). Betegh (2009, 82–89) calls attention to this interesting theme of divine problem-solving in other myths, including the *Protagoras* and the *Symposium*. Betegh argues that the *Gorgias*, as in other myths, features gods who are 'fundamentally benevolent agents' (86). Only on such an assumption can Socrates rule out the possibility of an afterlife ruled by capricious, jealous or vengeful gods.

The verdicts of these new, Zeus-era post-mortem judgments, though, threaten the traditional Socratic conception of punishment in two ways. First, some defendants are judged 'incurable', yet these 'incurables' are nevertheless punished. Second, those who are 'curable' appear to be punished not with mere argumentation, but by physical force and horror at the punishment of the 'incurables'. The first point suggests that Socrates does not, despite his own suggestions to the contrary, strictly adhere to a rehabilitationist model of punishment. Punishment does not always improve the punished. The second point suggests that Socrates thinks the elenchus often proves insufficient for even the curable, which threatens the traditional 'cognitivist account' of Socratic intellectualism.

The 'curables' are souls who engaged in garden-variety injustice and escaped detection and punishment while alive. These souls, in Socrates' words, 'become better and profit' from punishment (*Grg.* 525b). The 'incurables', on the other hand, 'no longer derive any profit from their punishment' (*Grg.* 525c). They are punished not for their own benefit,

SOCRATES ON DEATH AND THE AFTERLIFE

but as an example to others. The incurable is 'made an example for others, so that when they see him suffering what it is he suffers, they may be afraid and become better' (*Grg.* 525b). The curables 'profit' from watching the incurables 'undergoing for all time the most grievous, intensely painful and frightening sufferings for their errors, simply strung up there in the prison in Hades as examples, visible warnings to unjust men who are ever arriving' (525c–d). The incurables, however, get nothing from the deal.

Some scholars see Socrates' apparent endorsement of retributivism and deterrence without hope of benefit as a break from his regular adherence to rehabilitationism. Socrates consistently tells Polus that punishment benefits the transgressor by making them less miserable (473b), and he famously contends one should not return harm with harm (*Cr.* 49b–d). He suggests to Polus that everyone can come to recognise that doing injustice is better than suffering it, so it seems that no one could be incurable. Yet the incurables do not benefit at all and seem beyond the reach of what Socrates suggests everyone can grasp. Mackenzie (1981, 225–239) and Saunders (1991) identify this feature of the myth as consistent with Plato's later account of punishment. Rowe (2007, 35) likewise considers it evidence that the *Gorgias* myth is not properly Socratic.

Inwood (2009, 28–31) worries that the myth punishes as 'incurable' those who had the bad luck to confront opportunities for grave injustice, despite having souls no worse than those who lacked such opportunities. Socrates considers two people with equivalent desires to commit injustice, one who by chance encounters the opportunity to act on those desires (e.g., Archelaus), the other who does not (e.g., Thersites). The latter can be reformed, while the former's opportunities for injustice render him incurable. Inwood thinks that if the two men have the same desires, but one suffers the bad luck of having the chance to fulfil them, it is unfair that the incurable suffers without benefit while the other can be cured. Those who fall into extreme vice seem to be victims of bad moral luck.

This worry is not isolated to the *Gorgias*, since Socrates elsewhere suggests that it is better for the unwise to lack opportunities. In the *Euthydemus*, Socrates argues that the unwise are better off poor, ugly and talentless because at least then they do less damage to themselves and others for lack of opportunity (*Euthd.* 280e–281e).

The 'Curables' and Just Punishment

The treatment of the 'curables' presents two chief problems that stem from Socrates' apparent endorsement of physical punishment both before and in the myth. The first puzzle concerns whether physical punishment is an effective means of rehabilitation. The second is whether, even if physical punishment proves effective, it is consistent with Socratic intellectualism. These points are a continuation of the debate about Socratic psychology from the previous section.

Those who adhere to the traditional account that dialectic exhausts Socratic punishment point to Socrates' frustration when Callicles tries to escape the argument. Socrates announces to the audience, 'This fellow won't put up with being benefitted and with his undergoing *the very thing* the discussion's about, with being disciplined' (505c, my emphasis). Similarly, Socrates encourages Polus to answer: 'You won't get hurt in any way. Submit yourself nobly to the argument, as you would to a doctor' (475d). Edwards (2016) argues, quite creatively, that Socrates is not always the doctor in this transaction, since he submits himself to Euthyphro for education in piety, hoping to show Meletus that his education was sufficient punishment for his crimes of impiety. For an opposing view, see Brickhouse and Smith (2017).

Brickhouse and Smith (2010, esp. 108–131), however, point out that Socrates tells Polus that candidate punishments include being 'lectured', but also being 'lashed' (478e). Socrates claims the just person should 'present himself to be whipped' if he merits that punishment (480c–d). Other less violent, but also non-conversational punishments include exile, the confiscation of wealth, even death. Socrates makes clear that these latter punishments can be done 'justly', though the one carrying out the just punishment does not have an enviable task (468e–469b). Barring an afterlife, though, one cannot rehabilitate a dead person, certainly not by conversing with him. Granted, the afterlife of the *Apology* does feature a conversant Socrates who continues his work examining others in the afterlife. He happily converses with Sisyphus in the *Apology*, presumably the same Sisyphus who suffers so greatly in the *Gorgias*. In the *Gorgias*, though, the myth includes the same panoply of physical and non-rational punishments Socrates discusses with Polus.

Rowe (2012b, 193; 2007) argues that physical punishment does not improve people, so we should resist taking Socrates' discussion of such punishments literally on grounds of charitable interpretation, if nothing else (see also Penner (2018)). Physical pain would not transform us; it could merely serve as 'encouragement to be cleverer in future about covering our tracks' (2012b, 192). As Rowe puts it, 'If by 'punishment' here Socrates really intends flogging, imprisonment, fines, exile or execution, what kind of sense could that possibly make ... insofar as neither Socrates nor anyone else has any reason to believe – even on standard assumptions – that such form of treatment will reliably improve anybody' (193). Standard retributivism is admittedly indifferent to whether punishment reforms – that would just be a happy accident.

Reasserting his own commitment to traditional intellectualism, Rowe asserts that '[t]he only sure-fire way of changing people's beliefs is to *reason* with them' (192, his emphasis). On Rowe's account, Socratic punishment is dialectic (195). Socrates adheres to the common account of intellectualism according to which belief alteration in light of rational argumentation is the way to a better life, and the *Gorgias* myth threatens a break with that intellectualism. This serves as another reason to excise the myth from the Socratic tradition.

Shaw (2015, 75) agrees with Penner that Socrates does not endorse flogging 'because such procedures do not remove injustice from the soul'. Shaw also agrees with Rowe that physical pain only serves to incentivise more successful injustice rather than justice itself (84). As Shaw notes, Brickhouse and Smith (2010, 118–119, 122), who argue that Socrates does endorse corporal punishment, concede that its intended reformative effect might only motivate more sophisticated injustice. For my part, I am not sure that dialectical punishment does much more than give the transgressor incentive to avoid Socrates or kill him. That dialectic reliably improves the transgressor does not seem self-evident to me either.

Shaw also agrees with Rowe that Socrates' discussion of whipping and lashing is a way of engaging with his interlocutor on their terms rather than an expression of his own view. When Polus and Callicles think of punishment, they think of physical abuse, and Socrates simply repurposes that language to suit his own surprising and counterintuitive views. Shaw writes that Socrates 'foregrounds *Polus*' view of punishment by using hitting, cutting, and burning in his *epagōgē* and analogy; he thus provokes Polus, even as he carefully avoids saying that expert judges use these procedures' (82, my emphasis). As Rowe puts it, '[Socrates] is responding to Callicles in terms that Callicles can understand, even if he would utterly reject the ideas Plato has Socrates use those words to express'

SOCRATES ON DEATH AND THE AFTERLIFE

337

(194). If only Socrates had said something like, 'Hey, everyone, when I say "whipping", I don't mean it literally!'

Shaw departs from Rowe in one key respect. Socrates, Shaw points out, is explicit in supporting other painful non-argumentative strategies, including exile, wealth confiscation and even death. Shaw argues that Socrates thinks these can be carried out justly because they take away opportunities for successful injustice. Other forms of punishment that Socrates endorses in physical life (for Shaw, exile, confiscation, death) are ruled out in the afterlife, leaving dialectic standing on its own (92–95). One might think, though, that these punishments are endemic to the afterlife, since punished souls have been exiled from the world, and their beautiful bodies and external goods have been removed so that they can no longer hide their injustice. Perhaps these other punishments also make injustice more difficult to hide in the afterlife.

Again, Brickhouse and Smith (2010) take the physical punishments of the *Gorgias* myth seriously, just as they consider Socrates in earnest when he mentions 'whipping' and 'exile' in the discussion with Polus. As such, there is no break between the discussions with Polus and the myth. Though it lies beyond the scope of this chapter, they argue that such non-rational punishments are consistent with Socratic intellectualism more generally. On such a reading, Socrates always thinks that improving the soul of the transgressor can sometimes require practical, non-argumentative intervention, even occasionally physical force. Pouring someone's alcohol down the drain might occasionally be more effective than a series of isolated discussions.

The dispute is not merely about what sorts of punishment improve the unjust. It is also a methodological dispute about whether the *Gorgias* is a 'Socratic' dialogue at all, at least in its entirety. The greatest challenge of mythic interpretation, in the end, might be that we can be a bit too prone to use our own interpretive preferences to differentiate between those mythic elements we should take seriously and those we should not. We should be careful lest 'he doesn't really mean that' or 'that is inconsistent with my methodology' is more an expression of our own views than those reflected in the text. I cannot, of course, settle this question of whether the *Gorgias* myth constitutes a break with Socratic intellectualism, the effect of such intellectualism on his penology, or Socrates' level of commitment to the afterlife. What is clear is that these points intersect in the *Gorgias* myth in a way that sets the terms for what counts as 'Socratic'.

Virtue's Intrinsic Reward

What, though, of the people in the afterlife who reap the rewards of their justice, the ones who go off to the 'Isles of the Blessed' (526c–527a)? Sedley (2009) acknowledges that the myth risks undermining the general message of Socrates' arguments in a more fundamental way. Socrates argues throughout the dialogue that the just are happy and the unjust are unhappy *in this life*. Recourse to post-mortem reward and punishment seems to undermine this key point or unnecessarily adorn it. If the just life is already better, why gild the lily with something extra? The Myth of Er that closes Plato's *Republic* has generated a similar concern that the prospect of post-mortem rewards undercuts or at least weakens the central thesis that virtue is its own reward. It also risks steering people away from injustice through fear rather than from a conviction that the life of justice is superior.

Sedley (2009), like Rowe, argues that the *Gorgias* myth can be read as merely providing commentary on the current state of the world rather than an account of the afterlife itself.

338   THE BLOOMSBURY HANDBOOK OF SOCRATES

The initial bad judgments indicate that the Athenian political system is broken, and the 'incurables' illustrate what it means to be beyond the reach of philosophical persuasion, as perhaps Callicles himself is. The rewards of people like Socrates are likewise a mirror image of the benefits of justice in this life. On Sedley's account, Socrates tells a story that is essentially the same as the arguments he advances. One need not take the myth literally to see how it captures lessons from the dialogue in narrative form. Sedley, though, does not rule out that Socrates might instead intend us to take the myth literally, which would undermine the central argument preceding the myth. He himself thinks the choice is 'underdetermined by the text' (68). His reading, then, is not dogmatic, and recognises that the myth could, in fact, threaten the main line of argument.

Russell (2001, 560–561) argues that we would benefit from a literal interpretation that does not undermine the central message of the dialogue. It is fine to 'demythologise' the account to say that it reflects Socrates' larger point that virtue is its own reward, but one should demythologise something that, *if* taken as literally true, actually supports the argument of the dialogue. The problem, Russell argues, is that scholars have read the afterlife as offering 'extra bonuses' that do not often or always accrue to the possession and exercise of virtue in life. Russell argues that the text actually sustains a reading according to which the Isle of the Blessed is essentially more of the same. The reward for living virtuously is greater time living virtuously, doing what one loves (563–564). On the flip side, the 'punishment' is more time spent in vice, albeit without any hope of avoiding detection. This allows readers to read both the literal and the 'demythologised' version as consistent. It also brings the myth into closer connection with the afterlife of the *Apology*, where Socrates imagines the life of the just as more of the same.

Still, one might have the nagging worry that Socrates should not be motivating people to choose justice from fear or sustaining them in their justice through hope. One's thoughts on the matter again turn importantly on one's model of intellectualism. If one thinks the fear of death is sometimes reasons-resistant, then we should not be surprised that Socrates offers an additional mechanism for motivating those who need additional assistance altering their beliefs. Sometimes persuasion involves stories, even for people who accept an argument, but might need some help overhauling their motivations accordingly.

COURAGE AND THE FEAR OF DEATH

Courage is the virtue most commonly associated with one's attitudes toward death, since paradigmatic cases of courage generally occur in contexts where one risks death for some perceived good (e.g., military service, running into a burning building to save others, resisting unjust oppressors). We have evidence from the dialogues that many of Socrates' contemporaries considered him courageous in the context of his military service. In the *Laches*, the seasoned general Laches praises Socrates' behaviour in the Athenian retreat from the Battle of Delium (*La.* 181a–b). In his wine-soaked praise of Socrates, Alcibiades tells of watching that same retreat from the safety of horseback, claiming that Socrates was more composed than Laches and that everyone could see from a great distance that Socrates was 'a very brave man' (*Symp.* 221a–c). Alcibiades claims that this visible bravery provided protection for others by scaring off the enemy. He also recounts how Socrates rescued him during the campaign at Potidaea (*Symp.* 220d–4). Socrates himself appeals to his own military service in the *Apology*, noting that he fought at Delium, Amphipolis and Potidaea (*Ap.* 28d–e).

SOCRATES ON DEATH AND THE AFTERLIFE

Socrates also flirts with the idea that his insistence on risking death for the sake of philosophy is courageous. He compares himself to Achilles for persisting in his philosophical actions despite almost certain death (*Ap.* 28b–d). In the *Gorgias*, Socrates tells Callicles that he does not mind death, since 'no one who isn't totally bereft of reason and courage is afraid to die; doing what's unjust is what he's afraid of' (*Grg.* 522e). In this case he appears to attribute some form of courage to himself for his persistent belief that doing injustice is worse than suffering it, even if suffering injustice involves death.

It is unclear, though, whether Socrates can be judged courageous by his own lights. Scholarship on the Socratic conception of courage and its bearing on whether Socrates was himself courageous has generally addressed three questions: 1) does courage require wisdom; 2) is courage consistent with not fearing death; and 3) can a person be courageous in the service of unjust military ends? Since Socrates denies possessing wisdom, seems at points to deny fearing death and quite likely served in unjust military campaigns, these questions also bear on our assessment of Socrates himself.

Does Courage Require Wisdom?

The view that courage requires wisdom serves as the foundation for arguments that Socrates is not courageous. Given that Socrates generally cashes out virtue in terms of wisdom and that he repeatedly denies possessing wisdom, it seems by logical implication that Socrates could not consider himself to possess any virtue, including courage. There is some evidence in the text that Socrates doubts his own courage as he doubts almost everything else. In the closing part of his pre-verdict defence in the *Apology*, Socrates says, almost as an aside, 'whether I am brave in the face of death is another matter' (*Ap.* 34e). The fact that he refuses to pander for the sake of justice is insufficient to establish bravery. In the *Laches*, he denies knowledge of courage, and both Laches and Nicias acknowledge that they know 'nothing about courage' at the end of the dialogue (*La.* 200a–c). If courage requires knowledge plus an account, and we respect Socrates' disavowals of knowledge, Socrates is not courageous.

One might argue, though, that wisdom and the other virtues are not all or nothing, but rather come in degrees. Smith (2016) argues that Socrates commonly employs the craft analogy for virtue. Crafts such as carpentry are 'gradable', in the sense that even the novice is in some sense practising carpentry. Smith argues that Socrates thinks that the knowledge of virtue, like carpentry and house building, is gradable. He need not be a 'master craftsman' in order to possess competency. Alternately, one might think that while full virtue requires true belief plus an account, one can possess meaningful virtue if one's beliefs about virtue are never refuted. A consistent set of psychological attitudes about the role of virtue in the good life might be enough to ground confidence in one's virtue (see Brown and Shaw forthcoming). Socrates has some beliefs that are made of 'iron and adamant', perhaps because he has never met anyone who can deny them without falling into inconsistency (*Grg.* 508e). Finally, one might also think that the 'human wisdom' Socrates does attribute to himself would involve some sort of 'human courage' as well. There are, then, ways to afford Socrates some sort of wisdom and courage.

Those who seek to lower the bar for virtue, though, must account for Socrates' occasional flirtation with the idea that virtue seems to require something like an omniscience of moral value. In his final discussion with Nicias in the *Laches*, he and Nicias conclude that if courage were knowledge about what is to be feared or hoped, then that would require knowledge of all good and bad, past, present and future (*La.* 199b–e).

In the *Charmides*, temperance appears to require not only knowledge of good and evil, but also knowledge of the objects of all of the other crafts. Reshotko (2016, 156–176) has argued that this commitment to 'universal knowledge' is Socrates' genuine view, which prices virtue out of the market for us all. One might also find a similar all or nothing account in Socrates' account of wisdom in the first protreptic of the *Euthydemus*, where wisdom on some readings seems to require exceptionless success. Some, though, have argued in support of degreed wisdom in the *Euthydemus* (Smith 2016; Austin 2020). If Socrates thinks courage requires full wisdom, though, the answer to the question of whether Socrates is courageous is a straightforward 'no'.

Does Courage Require Fearing Death?

Socrates' attitudes toward death raise a second puzzle about courage, again concerning both knowledge and the emotions. Recall that the *Apology* leaves us with two, possibly contrary, accounts of what Socrates believes about the relative harm or benefit of death. On the sceptical account, Socrates is unsure whether death is good or bad. On the second, post-verdict account, Socrates maintains that death is a benefit, at least until the final sentence of the dialogue. Whether one considers death a harm or benefit has some bearing on whether one dies courageously, and both options affect interpretations of Socratic virtue and moral psychology.

Consider first the idea that death benefits, providing perhaps even the 'greatest' benefit. Some scholars find it odd to think one can courageously welcome a benefit. As Murphy (1976, 195) puts it,

> Socrates (at least according to Plato) seemed to have this kind of other-worldly outlook . . . This seems to me to be a way of not facing death and certainly does not deserve to be characterized, as many people have characterized it, as facing death with courage. For what is courageous about accepting the fact that one will move to a place where one will be better off than ever before?

On Murphy's account, courage requires recognising a loss of some sort and coming to terms with it. Similarly, Baxley (2007) argues that Aristotle's conception of courage must also countenance the view that one loses something of value by dying and that one has reason to fear it, even if one nevertheless chooses the courageous action.

The conception of courage as having a price can be sustained, though, on the sceptical reading. On this account, Socrates recognises that death could harm him, though not as much as committing injustice. When he chooses to risk death, he recognises that he risks suffering a harm that he might have reason to fear; he just lacks reason to fear it as much as he fears injustice. While a lesser fear of death allows Socrates to escape Murphy's complaint, it runs up against some accounts of Socratic moral psychology. Most philosophers working in the Socratic studies tradition think Socrates denies the kind of synchronic soul division that Plato endorses. It is unclear whether Socrates thinks a person can consider something bad and worthy of fear (death), yet choose that very same thing at the same time as good. It might be difficult on some models of intellectualism to choose an action while simultaneously fearing it. Such an account also suggests that Socrates employs a quasi-hedonistic model of virtuous action that includes weighing benefits and harms, and some scholars think Socrates rejects hedonism outright. Whichever way one goes, one makes decisions about the role of fear in courage and about whether Socrates thinks one can fear what one chooses as best.

SOCRATES ON DEATH AND THE AFTERLIFE

Finally, some scholars have also challenged the legitimacy of considering the historical Socrates courageous on the grounds that his military service was unjust. While Vlastos (1987) and Brickhouse and Smith (1994) offer defences of Socrates' military involvement, Anderson (2005) argues that Socrates' likely service under the leadership of Cleon, possibly in the campaign against Scione, amounts to his willing participation in war crimes. The military aim of the battle at Scione was to indiscriminately kill male citizens and enslave the women and children for their refusal to pay taxes to the empire. Anderson argues, on far more speculative grounds, that Socrates served eagerly in such efforts rather than by legal compulsion, perhaps motivated by a desire for the social status afforded to hoplites.

Xenophon's Socrates as 'Better Off Dead'

Plato is a tough act to follow. For that reason, we should extend some grace to Xenophon. His Socrates is the guy berating you for the hangover you earned from drinking and talking with Plato's Socrates until dawn. Xenophon's Socrates does, though, say some strident and interesting things about death that seem, at least on the surface, to depart from Plato's account in the *Apology*. In fact, Xenophon advertises his account of Socrates' defence as distinctive because others failed to make clear that Socrates 'already believed he would be better off dead' before the trial began (1). This point could not have been terribly new to many of Xenophon's local readers, since Xenophon supplies Hermogenes as his source on this score, and Hermogenes had apparently been reporting these anecdotes widely. One might wonder, though, to what extent Xenophon and Plato's accounts of Socrates' attitudes about death substantively differ.

Some of the differences are overstated. Xenophon's Socrates goes into the trial knowing he is better off dead, whereas Plato's Socrates reaches that conclusion after the verdict. Their justification, however, is the same. Specifically, Xenophon and Plato agree that Socrates' private voice licensed his conclusion that that he was better dead than placating the jury to allow him to stay alive. Xenophon's Socrates reaches that conclusion *before* the trial begins. He tries to prepare the sort of speech that might motivate the jurors to let him off easy, but the *daimonion* stops him, thereby sealing his fate. He concludes that the *daimonion* thinks he's better off dead (*Apol.* 4–7). Plato's Socrates gives the speech he thinks appropriate, not the one that will placate the jury, and the *daimonion* signals its approval by sitting back and enjoying the show. He, too, concludes the *daimonion* thinks he is better off dead. Perhaps there is something unseemly about Xenophon's Socrates needing to be stopped from pandering, but they both conclude that the *daimonion* would rather them die than pander (see Dorion 2005 for further exploration).

There are, however, two meaningful differences, which I will note, but not here defend.

First, Xenophon's Socrates never discusses the afterlife. This might be a divergence in Xenophon and Plato's historical record of the trial, of their accounts of Socrates' beliefs on the matter, or of both. Maybe Socrates did mention the afterlife at the trial or perhaps he did not. Perhaps Socrates did believe in the afterlife, or perhaps Plato preferred him that way. The important point is that Plato's Socrates is willing to entertain the possibility that death is 'one of two things', whereas Xenophon's seems to think there is one thing – annihilation.

Second, Socrates' Xenophon has much more conventional views about the disadvantages of old age and the desirability of a good post-mortem reputation. In his *Apology*,

Xenophon's Socrates speculates that the *daimonion* wants to save him from the embarrassments of old age – diminishing sight and hearing, slow learning, quick forgetting and the other indignities of an ailing body. While Plato's Socrates does mention multiple times that he is old and could die any minute, he takes old age on the chin and does not seem to see it as an impediment to philosophising.

Xenophon's Socrates also wants to leave a good impression so that his friends will grieve his death. He claims that people are remembered more fondly and grieved more intensely if they die before losing control of their mind and body. Plato's Socrates, on the other hand, seems to have little interest in the grief of others. Again, though, this difference might be overstated, since Socrates recognises in both accounts that being killed by Athens will make him famous. Plato's Socrates warns those who sentenced him to death that they will bring upon themselves a horrible reputation for killing him, a supposed wise man, when they could have just let him die of old age without fanfare.

In sum, Xenophon and Plato agreed that Socrates was prepared to die for having practiced philosophy, that he refused to pander at his trial even though he recognised it would likely get him killed, and that the *daimonion*'s silence licensed his conclusion that death was a benefit, at least for him. Xenophon's Socrates chiefly distinguishes himself by not generalising his claim about the benefits of death to others or coveting the possibility of an afterlife.

CONCLUSION

In this chapter, I have explored the way that Socrates' views about death and the afterlife intersect with important interpretive puzzles within Socratic virtue ethics and moral psychology. Whether Socrates fears or does not fear death is tied up with how much he thinks he knows about death, and how much Socrates knows about anything lies at the core of Socratic studies. In addition, if Socrates thinks we have reason to regulate our fear of death (he does), then he requires some account of what fear is and what psychological mechanisms cause and regulate it. Socrates' moral psychology is likewise at the core of Socratic studies. If Socrates thinks one of the ways to regulate our fear is to imagine an afterlife, then we have reason to determine what role those myths actually play in his ethics and psychology. Lastly, since courage often involves risking death, then whether death is bad lies at the heart of Socrates' conception of courage. In other words, one cannot explore Socrates' views on death and the afterlife without exploring almost everything he thinks about how to live.

CHAPTER FIFTEEN

The Trial of Socrates

NICHOLAS D. SMITH

I. INTRODUCTION

In 399 BCE, Socrates was tried in the Heliastic court at Athens on the charge of impiety, found guilty by a majority of the jurors and condemned to death. His execution was achieved in a way that was commonly employed for executions in Athens: He was given a cup of hemlock, a powerful poison, and died of its effects.[1] These facts are about as much as can be said about the trial of Socrates without encountering scholarly controversy. In this chapter, I will investigate and review the main controversy concerning the trial, conviction and condemnation of Socrates, which is why it happened at all. In order to try to answer this question, I will focus primarily on what was said about the trial in the ancient sources, and explain how these sources have influenced later scholarly explanations. Because the sources say very different things about the trial, it is not surprising that scholars have drawn very different conclusions themselves. My own conclusions will be motivated mainly by close attention to the testimony to be found in Xenophon and Plato – sources that some scholars have dismissed as too biased to have been reliable.[2] Such views of Xenophon and Plato are themselves based on what other ancient sources have to say. In order to assess which of our sources are the most credible, we will need to work our way through them and try to see how and why they came to be a part of the very complicated ancient fascination with Socrates.

II. LEGAL PRELIMINARIES

Most prosecutions in ancient Athens were pursued entirely by private citizens. With a very few exceptions (none of which are pertinent to the trial of Socrates), the state's role was limited, in the first place, to a decision by an officer known as the 'king archon' as to whether the prosecution should be brought to court. Presumably, those cases that seemed to the king archon to have no legal basis would simply be dismissed. A king archon's decision to empanel a jury to try a case was in no way regarded an indicator of probable guilt.[3] Instead, the Athenian legal system had a mechanism to prevent and punish abusing the legal system for personal reasons: Those who prosecuted cases that eventuated in fewer than 20 per cent of a jury's members voting in favour of guilt would be made to pay a significant fine for frivolous prosecution.[4]

Once the determination was made to send the case to trial, a jury would need to be empanelled (randomly selected from a large group of volunteers), at a cost to the state of three obols per juror – subsistence in terms of wages, to be sure, but not an entirely negligible cost for the state, since juries were typically quite large at that time,[5] presumably as a way to discourage litigants from bribing jurors. In the case of Socrates, the number of jurors empanelled to the case was 500.[6] In Plato's *Apology*, Socrates remarks that had he managed to win an extra thirty votes, he would have won the case (*Apology* 36a). If we accept this as accurate, it follows that the vote to convict Socrates was 280–220.

Socrates was accused of having violated the constitutional law prohibiting impiety, an offense that might be achieved in indefinitely many ways within Athenian religion and law. There were some offenses that had punishments already mandated by law, but that was not the case for a crime like impiety, which might be committed in wildly diverse ways. As such, the indictment would need to provide specifications of precisely how the prosecutor alleged the crime to have been committed; and the prosecutor would need to propose a specific punishment for the specific violation. In the case of Socrates, the ancient sources all agree that the alleged crime was specified in three ways: (i) Socrates was guilty of not acknowledging the gods acknowledged by the state; (ii) Socrates introduced (bogus) new divine things; and (iii) Socrates corrupted the youth.[7]

The first two of these specifications seem to contemporary readers plausibly to qualify as impious. Different translators have struggled a bit to render what I have above rendered as 'acknowledge'. The Greek for this allegation was '*ou nomizein*', which could indicate a failure of belief in the relevant gods, or could indicate any of a number of failures of appropriate behaviour, such as a refusal to perform customary sacrifices. So even in this specification, there remains significant vagueness. The same may be said for the second specification, charging Socrates with recognising '*kaina daimonia*'. The description here could hardly be vaguer. '*Kaina daimonia*' could be a description of either entities – other divine beings – or activities – other divine doings.[8]

The vagueness of these specifications of the charge against Socrates have lent themselves to significant speculations among scholars as to what the prosecutors may have meant by them – or for that matter, whether there was any specific meaning intended at all. For prosecutors at risk of being fined for abusing the legal system, such vagueness might be strategic: It would allow jurors to imagine for themselves different ways in which a defendant might be guilty and thus produce more votes to convict.[9] Accordingly, defendants would do well to force the prosecution to make clearer precisely what such offenses were actually supposed to include, and thus to make it more difficult for jurors to understand the indictment in their own ways. But to be clear, there was no legal requirement for jurors to base their decisions entirely on the evidence as it was presented in court. There was no legal constraint on what grounds they were permitted to use in making their own decisions.

The other specification of the charge against Socrates was that he did wrong by corrupting the youth. It may be difficult from a contemporary perspective to see how this could count as a religious crime, but that is because contemporary notions of impiety mainly have to do with violations of orthodoxy, of which there was almost none in ancient Greece. The ideal of filial piety, involving centrally respect for one's parents, was deeply ingrained in ancient Greek culture, and so turning youths against their parents and making them rebellious against parental authority (as Socrates is portrayed as having done to Pheidippides in Aristophanes' *Clouds*) could certainly be construed as a type of impious malefaction. On the other hand, this other specification of the charge of impiety could be seen as directly linked to the other two – it would be impious for Socrates to teach youths not to recognise the gods recognised by the state and also to recognise bogus new divine things, instead. It is not impossible that the prosecution was also strategically vague on this issue, but here, too, ancient evidence may provide more details. Regardless of

THE TRIAL OF SOCRATES 345

what the prosecutors intended, however, the jurors, again, were permitted to convict a defendant entirely on the basis of their own understanding of the alleged crime.

III. THE POLITICAL INTERPRETATION

Speculation about what the prosecutors actually may have said at Socrates' trial – which could have clarified considerably precisely how Socrates was supposed to be guilty of the charge and its specifications – has been a fixation among scholars, because ancient evidence on the question is sparse and not obviously reliable (when, that is, it is not obviously *unreliable*). Similarly, we are confronted with even less evidence about what might have led jurors actually at the trial to have found Socrates guilty. Not long ago, the historian Robert Parker argued that it would be folly even to try to discern what precise motives may have come into play.

> Different arguments will have had different weight with different jurors; and the motives of most individual jurors were surely also mixed. It is pointless to attempt to clarify that complex mess of human resentment, and declare religious or social or political factors decisive.
>
> – Parker 1996: 207[10]

Parker is no doubt right to say that there may have been a variety of motives for why the jurors at Socrates' trial voted the ways that they did, and the same may also be true for the individual motives of the prosecutors. But to declare 'pointless' any effort to try to understand the motives that may have played the greatest role in the prosecution and conviction ignores that there actually is a significant amount of ancient evidence and scholarship that takes such evidence into account. Rather than follow Parker's implicit advice, then, let us consider what the different interpretations of prosecutors' and jurors' motives might have been, and how well these interpretations are supported by evidence.

In fact, there is an abundance of evidence from antiquity for thinking that the most important reason for the trial and condemnation of Socrates had to do with his associations with (and putative influence on) some of Athens' most notorious traitors.[11] Several fragments of ancient texts make or at least seem to support this claim.

An important Greek orator from the second century CE has this to say:

> I wonder how one ought to deal with the fact that Alcibiades and Critias were the associates of Socrates, against whom the many and the upper classes made such strong accusations. It is hard to imagine a more pernicious person than Critias, who stood out among the Thirty, the most wicked of the Greeks. People say these men ought not to be used as evidence that Socrates corrupted the youth, nor should their sins be used in any way whatsoever with respect to Socrates, who does not deny carrying on conversations with the young.
>
> – From Publius Aelius Aristides, *In Defence of Oratory* 110D335[12]

The concern about Socrates' reputation as a bad influence on some of Athens' worst criminals is clear enough here. What is not clear enough, however, is how – or even if – this tells us anything about the actual trial of Socrates. Aelius Aristides' concern is what 'the many' and 'the upper classes' have said about Critias and Alcibiades, on the one hand, and then, on the other, what 'people say' about how this reflects on Socrates. Nothing in what is said here tells us anything directly about what might have been said at the trial. So we are left to wonder – is Aelius Aristides talking about the trial, or about

346 THE BLOOMSBURY HANDBOOK OF SOCRATES

some other controversy about this very controversial figure in Athenian history? As Parker said, of course, both may be true, and even if the associations of Socrates with Critias and Alcibiades were not a specific focus of the prosecution, they could well have played a role in how the jury reached its verdict. But there is more ancient evidence to consider.

In 345 BCE, some fifty-four years after the trial, Aeschines (Rhetor), a former ambassador for the state of Athens, brought a pre-emptive charge against a certain Timarchus, who had been planning to team up with another former ambassador to charge Aeschines himself with treason. As he presses his attack against Timarchus, Aeschines asks the jurors,

> Did you, O men of Athens, put Socrates, the sophist, to death because he was revealed to be the teacher of Critias, one of the thirty who abolished the democracy?
>
> – Aeschines, *Against Timarchus* 173

The jurors to whom Aeschines made his address could hardly themselves have been responsible for the decision against Socrates, and so the question he asks in this passage is obviously asked for purely rhetorical effect. Moreover, Aeschines (389–314 BCE) had not yet been born in 399, so we might wonder where he got this information. The question is worth pursuing a bit further.

Aeschines could have gotten this idea from reading Plato. It is true, of course, that Critias is mentioned several times by Plato as someone with whom Socrates actually did associate, but is never portrayed as someone who could be regarded as having Socrates as his teacher. The relationship between the two is sometimes depicted as amiable, but in other instances, less so. In the *Protagoras*, Critias is one of many at the gathering, and only speaks up when it seems the conversation is about to end prematurely (*Protagoras* 336d–e). In the *Timaeus*, Critias gives a short speech about a story Solon brought back from Egypt, and Critias relates the tale of the conflict between Athens and Atlantis in the (unfinished) *Critias*. But in none of these places is he characterised as anything but among Socrates' associates, and never as one receiving instruction.

A greater intellectual engagement occurs in the *Charmides*. As sometimes happens with Socrates' interlocutors, however, things get a bit spiky when Critias begins to wilt under Socratic examination (at 166b–c) and Socrates seems to imply that Critias should be more courageous in the discussion (at 166d). The dialogue ends in a way that seems only superficially light-hearted: Critias's cousin, Charmides, vows to devote himself to learning from Socrates (when the dialogue clearly indicates that Charmides is no more deficient than Critias is, and thus in no greater need of instruction). Charmides ends the dialogue by joking that he is ready to use force to get what he wants from Socrates. At any rate, if there is any indication here that anyone was to become Socrates' student, it is Charmides, not Critias.

But whatever amicability may be depicted elsewhere in Plato is not at all confirmed by the way Plato has Socrates describe Critias' later, infamous role as a ringleader among the Thirty. Although not mentioning Critias by name, Socrates recalls when the Thirty were in power and commanded him to bring in Leon of Salamis for summary execution. Socrates says he did not obey, and simply went home instead, but characterises the Thirty in a sharply negative way: 'They often ordered many others to do such things, since they wanted to implicate as many as possible in their guilt' (*Apology* 32c[13]).

The association with Alcibiades reported by Aelius Aristides is much more prominent in Plato's dialogues, where Alcibiades is often represented as not just a young associate of Socrates, but as one eager for (but sometimes averse to) instruction and also as something

THE TRIAL OF SOCRATES

of a lover to Socrates.[14] Whatever popular prejudice at the time might have thought about this association, however, the closest Plato comes in representing Socrates' associations with Critias or Alcibiades as a focus at the trial is when (without naming names) he has Socrates disclaim teaching anything to anyone (at *Apology* 33a).

There is also no indication in Aristophanes that Socrates was the teacher of Critias or Alcibiades – at least as far as the Aristophanic evidence that has survived. Socrates' main appearance in Aristophanes is, of course, in the *Clouds*, of which we only have a second version that was (as far as we know) never actually produced in antiquity. In that dialogue, Socrates is depicted as a quack natural scientist and a teacher of rhetorical cheap tricks, but is not in any obvious way associated with political conspiracies or sedition. In *Birds* (produced in 414), those associated with Socrates are said to be 'laconized', but the context makes it seem more about personal style and lack of concern for one's appearance than about any specific political agenda.

But the lack of evidence in these two sources is not the whole story. Aeschines certainly could have gotten all the evidence he needed for making Socrates the teacher of Critias from Xenophon's *Memorabilia*. Xenophon begins the *Memorabilia* in a somewhat revealing way:

> I have often wondered what the arguments could have been by which the writers of the indictment (*hoi grapsamenoi*) persuaded the Athenians that Socrates deserved death from the city. Now, the indictment against him was something like this: 'Socrates does wrong by not recognizing the gods that the city recognizes, but (instead) introducing other, new divine things, and he also does wrong by corrupting the youth.'
>
> – Xenophon, *Memorabilia* 1.1.1

Xenophon's expression of wonderment is itself puzzling. As his writings show, the trial of Socrates was an extremely important event for Xenophon. Although he was not in Athens when Socrates was tried (off on a military mission in Asia Minor, as reported in his *Anabasis*), in the first lines of his *Apology*, Xenophon makes clear that he is aware that others had written about the trial, and in both the *Apology* and the *Memorabilia*, he repeats for his readers some things that he had heard from one who was present at the trial – Hermogenes, son of Hipponicus. So one might suppose it very unlikely that Xenophon actually didn't know what arguments the prosecutors had used against Socrates at the trial. On the other hand, none of what Xenophon reports from Hermogenes actually gives any detail about how the prosecutors had argued the case, and the only other writing about the case from among Socrates' contemporaries that survives today (that is, Plato's *Apology*) is also frustratingly undetailed about the actual arguments given by Socrates' prosecutors.[15] At any rate, scholars are divided about what to make of Xenophon's expression of wonder here. David M. Johnson (2021) has recently argued extensively for the first of the two options mentioned above: Xenophon knew perfectly well what arguments were given by Socrates' prosecutors, and goes on (somewhat later in his discussion of the trial) to enumerate and reply to them. In what follows, on the contrary, I will argue for the latter option: Xenophon either actually did not know what specific arguments were given by the prosecutors, or feigns ignorance of those arguments when discussing Socrates' trial.

At any rate, as the passage quoted above shows, Xenophon's own argumentative strategy first expresses wonderment about the actual arguments used by the prosecutors, but immediately switches from that focus to what was stipulated in the indictment itself. Xenophon then undertakes a fairly detailed defence of Socrates in response to 'the writers

348 THE BLOOMSBURY HANDBOOK OF SOCRATES

of the indictment'. We learn that the Socrates he had known was a model of piety. Xenophon opines that the source of the 'new divinities' claim was probably Socrates' well-known reports to have a divine sign (*daimonion*; *Memorabilia* 1.1.2; see also 4.8.1), but cannot see why this would provoke anyone into the conviction and execution (1.1.2–5). Xenophon goes on to express repeatedly his failure to understand how the jurors could have convicted Socrates of 'not recognizing the gods' (1.1.5, 1.1.20), and how or why they had supposed that Socrates was guilty of 'corrupting the youth' (1.2.1).

The rhetorical pattern of the opening section of the *Memorabilia* is thus clear: Xenophon considers the points covered by the indictment and then expresses his own astonishment that the jury could have convicted Socrates and condemned him to death on the basis of such claims, recalling his friend and mentor in quite the opposite ways: as a very pious and religious man who was also a model of virtue for the youths who associated with him. If Xenophon actually did know what the prosecutors had said against Socrates, again, he has elected to efface their arguments altogether from his narrative and simply focus, instead, on the specifications of the legal charge and how poorly those specifications fit the man he knew and remembered. But having created this as the platform for his very positive recollections of Socrates, Xenophon now seems to interrupt his own narrative with another voice:

> But by god, the accuser (*ho katēgoros*) said, he made his companions despise the established laws, telling them how foolish it was to select public officials by lot, when no one would ever select the captain of a ship, or a builder, or a flutist in such a way, nor any other for work in which errors are less harmful than errors in the works of the city. By saying such things, he turned the youth against the established constitution and made them violent.
>
> – 1.2.9[16]

Again, Xenophon's argument had been focused entirely on how entirely inapt, mistaken and, indeed, unjust the allegations made in the indictment were. Xenophon has, however, not reported anything specific about the actual case the prosecutors had made against Socrates in order to show that Socrates was actually guilty of what the indictment had alleged. But suddenly now, Xenophon knows quite well what 'the accuser' (*ho katêgoros*) had said against Socrates, and as one reads this report of what 'the accuser' has said, it is not difficult to see that the accusation fits the allegation, reported by Aeschines, with which I began. Critias certainly seems to be a clear example of one who opposed 'the established laws' and 'the established constitution', and also had readily resorted to violence to secure his political goals.

Xenophon goes on to defend Socrates again, only now against 'the accuser' (1.2.10–11). But Xenophon's engagement with 'the accuser' has only just begun. It turns out that Xenophon knows a good deal more about what 'the accuser' has said. Now 'the accuser' makes it explicit who he has in mind as among those who were corrupted by Socrates:

> 'But', the accuser added, 'Critias and Alcibiades became intimates of Socrates, and the two of them did the city the most grievous wrongs. Critias became the biggest thief and the most violent and murderous of all those in the Oligarchy, while Alcibiades became, for his part, the most irresponsible and high-handed and violent of those in the democracy.'
>
> – *Memorabilia* 1.2.12

Here, we not only get precisely the association of Socrates to Critias, but also one to Alcibiades: It seems that Socrates' influence was a completely non-partisan evil; he could

THE TRIAL OF SOCRATES

manage to corrupt not only those who favoured overthrowing the democracy, but also Alcibiades, who had been the darling of the democracy but whose eventual crimes involved wrongdoings that aligned him with both factions at different times.

Here, too, Xenophon has a response to make, the gist of which is that, while not at all defending the two men 'the accuser' claimed were Socrates' students, instead makes the case that both of the bad men had sought out association with Socrates because the latter had such a well-established reputation for prudence, which they supposed they could find useful. And while they were associates of Socrates, they actually behaved very well (*Memorabilia* 1.2.18, 1.2. 24). Once they began to enjoy political success, they abandoned their associations with Socrates, who would never have approved of their excesses (1.2.14–28). Xenophon then continues to tell a few anecdotes intended to explain how and why Critias had ended up in conflict with Socrates (1.2.29–39). He follows these with a story intended similarly to distance Socrates from Alcibiades (1.2.40–46). The upshot, says Xenophon, is that both of these bad men had sought Socrates out for the sake of their political ambitions, and this same reason led to them being estranged from him (1.2.47). Xenophon then goes on to give a list of Socrates' actual associates, all of whom Xenophon finds blameless throughout their lives (1.2.48).[17]

Xenophon goes on to report and respond to several other complaints made by 'the accuser':

- Socrates taught the young to abuse their fathers (1.2.49)

- And not just their fathers, but also other relatives (1.2.51)

- He taught that friends and family members who did not give actual help were useless, even if they acted from good wishes, and convinced them that Socrates himself was the only person worthy of their esteem (1.2.52)

- Socrates also chose excerpts from the famous poets that he could interpret in ways that would help persuade the young to become wrongdoers and tyrants (1.2.56)

- He also especially liked to do this with quotations from Homer, citing some lines from the *Iliad* and explaining how he interpreted them to teach his students to treat common and poor people badly (1.2.58).

At *Memorabilia* 1.2.64, Xenophon returns to the actual indictment against Socrates and once again expresses disbelief that Socrates could have been charged with not recognising the gods of the city or corrupting the youth, as the indictment claimed. These accusations are attributed not to 'the accuser', but again to 'the writer of the indictment'.

I have gone into so much detail about the claims of 'the accuser' because I believe these are the original source of what I am calling 'the political interpretation' of the trial of Socrates. Most importantly, I have tried to show that Xenophon's reports of what 'the accuser' had said are strikingly unlike what he has to say about 'the writer(s) of the indictment'. With respect to the arguments of the latter individual(s), Xenophon claims only to wonder at what arguments he (or they) may have used to convince the jurors of Socrates' guilt. With respect to the former, it is almost as if Xenophon has an actual text in front of him, and is able to quote directly what arguments 'the accuser' used against Socrates. Moreover, when going into such detail about the arguments given by 'the accuser' the jurors and their responses are never mentioned. In order to explain these discrepancies, some scholars have concluded that, as a matter of fact, 'the accuser' is not someone whose accusations were spoken at the trial, but was a sophist named Polycrates whose 'Accusation of Socrates' was published a few years after the trial.[18]

It was common in this era for teachers of rhetoric to write speeches intended as rhetorical displays (*epideixeis*). Many of these speeches by various authors have survived, and none make any claim to historical veracity. Instead, the aim of such speeches is to give examples of how the author could give interesting and even persuasive arguments to defend what might otherwise be regarded as doubtful or even indefensible positions. For example, there still exist such speeches written by the great sophist, Gorgias, in which he defends the innocence of Helen of Troy, and the putatively philosophical thesis that nothing exists. Polycrates' other works, too, follow a similar pattern.[19]

In his own rhetorical response to Polycrates' defence of Busiris, Isocrates (426–338 BCE) includes a reference to Polycrates' 'Accusation of Socrates': 'When you were accusing Socrates, as though you were trying to praise him, you gave him Alcibiades as a pupil' (*Busiris* 5). Many centuries later, Diogenes Laertius gives a confused report about the role of Polycrates, initially claiming that Polycrates had written the speech given by the prosecutor (whom Diogenes reports as having been Polyeuctus, who is not mentioned in any of our other sources), but then citing Favorinus (c. 80–c. 160 CE), who claimed that the speech of Polycrates mentioned events in Athens that hadn't yet taken place when Socrates was tried (Diogenes Laertius 1.5.38–39).

All of these reports seem to indicate that Xenophon's 'accuser' was actually Polycrates, and thus what Xenophon has to say about 'the accuser', and also what Aelius Aristides and Aeschines said about Critias and/or Alcibiades, may have had nothing to do with what was said and done at the actual trial of Socrates. Instead, all of these reports and reactions may have had their origins in an *epideixis* speech by Polycrates, written a few years after the actual trial of Socrates. But if so, then all of the ancient evidence that the real motives for Socrates' trial and condemnation were political is effaced.[20]

Such considerations, however, have not at all prevented scholars from taking the evidence I have now reviewed as nonetheless strongly favouring the political interpretation. Most noteworthy among such scholars is, of course, I. F. Stone, who entirely mistrusts Plato and Xenophon, but takes the claims made by Polycrates as if they followed a journalistic ethic for truth: 'the few tantalizing bits that Xenophon gives us from this vanished work provide our only glimpse of the case as seen by the prosecution' (Stone 1988: 28[21]). Much more recently, in the first edition of this collection (2013), Robin Waterfield advises that if we want to know the *real* Socrates, we will do best to ignore the portraits in Aristophanes (because comedy does not require accuracy; 2013: 7–8), and in Xenophon and Plato, and indeed, in all of the so-called 'Socratic writings' generally (because all simply used fictions involving 'Socrates' to advance their own philosophical views; 2013: 9–13). Waterfield also dismisses any of the evidence to be found in Aristotle because, Waterfield claims, Aristotle relied almost entirely on what he found in Plato and is anyway 'a notoriously unreliable historian of others' ideas' (2013: 8). Instead, Waterfield endorses the reliability of what Stone had called 'this vanished work' by Polycrates,[22] on the ground that too many later sources cite Socrates' alleged political influence on Critias (Waterfield 2013: 17–18 and note 91) for the charge to have originated with Polycrates. Waterfield thus concludes that 'It is still plausible, then, to suggest that Polycrates was not entirely misrepresenting the trial, and that there was a political element to the prosecution speeches' (Waterfield 2013: 18).

Problems with this resuscitation of Polycrates abound. First, to take up this last quotation from Waterfield, the only evidence that Polycrates was *representing* the trial itself is that Libanius (4th c. CE) makes Anytus the speaker of the accusations that Libanius wishes to refute (Libanius *Apology* 136–141). This could be because Polycrates' 'Accusation' had put

THE TRIAL OF SOCRATES   351

his 'accusations' into the mouth of Anytus. This bit of ventriloquism, however, seems to have been ignored by Isocrates, at least, who attributes the accusation not to anyone at the trial, but to Polycrates himself: again, Isocrates says, 'when *you* were accusing Socrates . . .' (my emphasis). At any rate, the fact remains that the work itself seems to have been a rhetorical display piece, which, as I said earlier, never made any claims of historical or any other sort of accuracy. The whole point of such speeches was to display the rhetorical teacher's ability to argue persuasively for absurdities and lost causes!

Waterfield's dismissal of all of our other main sources, too, leaves much to be desired. While it is true, for example, that ancient comedy did not make sure that its depictions of historical persons were accurate, such depictions could hardly serve their comedic purpose if the characters portrayed bore no resemblance to those being satirised.[23] As for Plato and Xenophon, though I will say more about both below, it is simply not enough to note that some of their anecdotes contradict those given by the other one, so as to discard the entire testimony given by both of them. Were this to be a reasonable way to proceed, most contemporary uses of eye witnesses would be dismissed as useless. We should be rather more suspicious of witnesses who report historical events in exactly the same ways, than when we get accounts that seem to reflect predictable differences of emphasis or perspective, and even when we detect the altogether human propensity for bias. As this edition of *The Bloomsbury Companion* has hopefully made clear, there is a great deal of value to be derived from careful and cautious attention to the testimonies of very different witnesses. And as for Waterfield's dismissive treatment of Aristotle, it will simply have to suffice here to say that recent study of the Aristotelian testimony about Socrates[24] shows that as much as Plato surely had an influence on Aristotle, a good deal of Aristotle's testimony almost certainly has other origins. So while it is true that none of what Aristotle has to say about Socrates was from his own direct experience (Aristotle wasn't yet born when Socrates died), nonetheless Aristotle seemed to have access to plenty of testimonial material (as well as live reports of some who had actually known Socrates) in order to form his own opinions. From Aristotle, too, we should of course expect bias and his own personal perspective. Nonetheless, a great deal of what we take ourselves to know about other ancient philosophers (including especially the presocratics) comes directly from Aristotle's testimony. Refusing to credit Aristotle as at least somewhat reliable forecloses any access to whole areas of ancient Greek philosophy.

So what does this review of the best sources that would support the political interpretation show us? Plainly, the answer to this question depends entirely on how much evidential weight one assigns to Xenophon's report of what 'the accuser' said. Obviously, if we assume that Xenophon's 'accuser' is not Polycrates, but was actually Meletus[25] or one of the other prosecutors at the actual trial, then this would provide significant support to the political interpretation of the trial. If, however, we take 'the accuser' to refer to Polycrates, as I have suggested, then we need to make some decisions about what genre Polycrates' 'Accusation of Socrates' belonged to, and what degree of historical reliability we should assign to works within that genre. My own view is that we may expect no reliability of any kind; Stone and Waterfield, among others, disagree. Finally, looking through the several mentions of the same sort of charge that we find given by Xenophon's 'accuser', we may regard all of these as having their origins entirely in Polycrates' 'Accusation', or we may imagine that the putative influence of Socrates on Alcibiades and Critias is too often repeated not to represent some genuine historical truth about Socrates. But there are other aspects and ramifications of the political interpretation that deserve further scrutiny.

352   THE BLOOMSBURY HANDBOOK OF SOCRATES

The first such aspect we should consider is to try to get just a bit clearer about what the 'political' part of 'the political interpretation' amounts to.[26] Stone summarises his own version succinctly: 'I believe the case against Socrates was political and that the charge of corrupting the youth was based on a belief – and considerable evidence – that he was undermining their faith in Athenian democracy' (Stone 1979). This way of understanding the real motives for the case against Socrates derives from a complicated mix of the ancient source materials discussed above, together with various anti-democratic statements that can be culled from the very sources that Stone (and Waterfield) regard with such scepticism – Plato and Xenophon, neither of whom would be mistaken by anyone as having political views favourable to democracy. There is no shortage of such evidence, to be sure, but a problem for this part of the construction of the argument for the political interpretation is that, unless one cherry picks evidence that scholars generally acknowledge to express the view of these authors themselves, and not Socrates', critiques of democratic ideology in Plato and Xenophon are never accompanied by any kind of advocacy of sedition or 'regime change'. Instead, a theme strongly present in both Plato's and Xenophon's portraits of Socrates is that citizens must always obey the law – including laws that might change, where obedience is required both before and after the change (see Plato's *Crito* and Xenophon's *Memorabilia* 4.4.12–25).[27] It is also extremely easy to find examples in which Plato's Socrates in particular is critical of famous democratic political leaders (for example, in Plato's *Gorgias* 515c–517a and *Meno* 92d–94e), but one can see this as clear evidence of an anti-democratic bias only if one ignores that famous anti-democratic leaders of Athens are also disparaged with the same degrees of criticism.[28] As I said above, the association of Socrates with Critias and Alcibiades made by Xenophon's 'accuser' actually seem designed to show that Socrates was a bad influence on those associated with any of the existing political divisions during this bitter period in Athenian history (see esp. *Memorabilia* 1.2.12).

Here, too, however, the lack of decisive evidence for regarding Socrates as an anti-democratic ideologue or a supporter of oligarch revolutionary activities does not at all mean that it would have been impossible for jurors to perceive him in such terms. So here, too, we should be reminded of Parker's caution that we should not hope to be able to explain all of the considerations that may have led to Socrates' trial and condemnation by the Athenians. My point is simply that we also need to avoid depicting what evidence there is as clear support for the political interpretation.

An even more obvious issue the political interpretation must confront is, perhaps, the most obvious one: If the *real* antipathy toward Socrates that led to his trial and condemnation was political, then why did Meletus and his supporting prosecutors, Anytus and Lycon, resort to a charge that, on the face of it, seems to be grounded in a religious concern, and not a political one? Defenders of the political interpretation of Socrates' trial offer different answers to this question. The one that has perhaps been the most often repeated is that the prosecutors actually couldn't prosecute Socrates for his allegedly seditious political views because of a general amnesty that was passed when the democracy was restored after the ousting of the Thirty from power.[29] Under the terms of the amnesty, no one could be prosecuted for crimes allegedly committed during or before the time the Thirty were in power. So it is true that the amnesty would have ruled out the possibility of prosecuting Socrates for his alleged influences on Critias or Alcibiades. But an appeal to the Amnesty cannot explain why the prosecution did not charge Socrates as having violated the law against sedition – a law that was in effect at that time (see Andocides, *On the Mysteries* 96–97, a speech given the same year that Socrates was tried) – on the

THE TRIAL OF SOCRATES

353

ground that Socrates' allegedly seditious 'teachings' had continued even after the passage of the amnesty. Anyone willing to testify that he had heard Socrates continuing to spread his supposed hatred for the democracy more recently could provide the ground for such a charge. And then, once in court, nothing in the amnesty ruled out recalling the effects Socrates is supposed to have had on the likes of Critias and Alcibiades.

So to return to the original question, why, then, did the prosecution charge Socrates with impiety, if the real reason for the trial and condemnation were Socrates' allegedly unsavoury effects on criminals such as Critias and Alcibiades? A particularly ingenious answer to this question has been offered by Paul Cartledge,[30] who argues that religious interests were generally recognised as overlapping with political interests, since offenses to the gods would put the entire community at risk. According to this line of interpretation, then, 'it is anachronistic and misleading to distinguish a "political" from a "religious" charge' (Cartledge 2009: 77). Following this thought, Waterfield regards the question of why the charge was impiety, rather than sedition, as essentially irrelevant: 'The question is too black and white. There is no reason why the Athenians should not have had several instruments with which they could eliminate political undesirables' (Waterfield 2013: 15).

This response to the question, however, strikes me as simply an evasion of the question itself. Plainly, we can grant that the law against impiety (or any other religious crime) was regarded as a way to protect the welfare of the city and those within it. In that sense, religious crimes were regarded as crimes against the *polis*. Of course, the same can be said for sedition, which would also very obviously be a crime against the *polis*. So in attempting to discern what the motives may have been for the prosecution and condemnation of Socrates, it isn't helpful to say that the motives were 'political' in the broad sense Cartledge has suggested. We can readily acknowledge, without an answer to the question I am pursuing here, that *whatever* led to Socrates' trial and execution, it no doubt was framed and conceived in terms of some threat to the *polis*. The question is: *In what way* did the prosecutors hope to convince the jurors, and *in what way(s)* did a majority of the jurors think that Socrates endangered the *polis*? Was it because of his affiliations with and influence on those who sought to destroy the democracy at Athens (as Stone and others have said, and as 'the accuser' in Xenophon argued), or is it because he was perceived as committing certain acts or spreading certain ideas that were seen as religiously unacceptable, and thus likely to undermine the support Athens might otherwise have received from some god or gods?

I now turn to the evidence for the second of these options, which seems to me to be better and more credible evidence than what convinced Stone and others that Socrates was a threat to Athens for seditious behaviours and teachings. But to be clear, I fully accept that the evidence for the so-called 'religious interpretation' of the motives for the trial and condemnation was presented and accepted by those who believed it as evidence that Socrates was a threat to the Athenian *polis*.

IV. THE RELIGIOUS INTERPRETATION

Even when Xenophon is not reporting the claims made by 'the accuser', he has a great deal to say about the motives for the trial and execution of Socrates. Indeed, except for the sections in which Xenophon reports and disputes what was claimed by 'the accuser', the first two chapters of the first book of the *Memorabilia* are entirely devoted to a review of the indictment against Socrates with Xenophon's explanation of why he found each of the specifications of the indictment entirely inapplicable to Socrates.

Xenophon begins by considering the first specification that Socrates failed to recognise the gods recognised by the state. Xenophon reports that he finds it difficult to imagine what arguments the prosecutors might have made for such a claim (*Memorabilia* 1.1.1–2). As evidence that Socrates certainly did recognise the gods recognised by the state, Xenophon reports that Socrates often (*pollakis*) engaged in religious behaviours that were plainly visible (*phaneros*) both in his home and also at the altars of state temples, and also frequently used divination without hiding it in the least (1.1.2; see also *Apology* 11–12). Xenophon immediately then goes on to express his own belief that it was Socrates' claim to be guided by 'the divinity' (*to daimonion*) that led to the specification of the indictment that Socrates invented new divine things (1.1.2; see also *Apology* 12). Xenophon goes on to shrug off the idea that this was anything novel or blameworthy. Instead, he characterises it as of a piece with any other kinds of divination widely accepted in Athenian society: oracles, voices, signs, offerings, birds or chance meetings (1.1.3; see also *Apology* 13). Xenophon argues for how useful Socrates' sign had been not just for Socrates, but for his friends as well (1.1.4; see also *Apology* 13). Xenophon makes an argument from probability that his friends would have taken him for a fool on this issue, if his sign had not proven to be extremely reliable and Socrates' confidence in the sign could only have come from a god (1.1.5). Xenophon counts it as an indication of Socrates' piety that he often told his friends to seek divinatory evidence in matters that human inquiry could not penetrate (1.1.5–9).

From this very specific defence of Socrates' piety with respect to divination, Xenophon broadens his defence: Socrates lived very much out in the open and his words and deeds were readily available to anyone who cared to look. But no one ever knew him to be impious, whether in word or in deed (1.1.11). Unlike so many nature-philosophers (of the sort Socrates is assimilated to in Aristophanes' *Clouds*, for example), who were generally regarded with religious suspicion for their teachings, Xenophon insists that Socrates never talked about those subjects and regarded them as foolish nonsense (1.1.11). Instead of attending to things human beings could never hope to understand, Socrates was only interested in talking about 'human things' (1.1.16), such as what is and is not pious, beautiful, just, prudent and courageous, and what makes someone a statesman or a ruler (1.1.16).

Xenophon then goes on to recall the time that Socrates defied the mob who wanted to try the generals who had been in charge during the Arginousae affair in a single trial, on the ground that doing so was against the law (1.1.18; for which see also Plato, *Apology* 32b–c). Xenophon explicitly ties Socrates' obedience to the law in this case to his having taken an oath to act in accordance to the law (1.1.18), and says that the way Socrates responded to the threats of the mob proved that it mattered more to him to keep the oath he had sworn than to placate the crowd, despite the dangers they posed to him (1.1.18). Here, too, Xenophon emphasises Socrates' pious respect for the gods of the state. Xenophon concludes this section by repeating his incredulity that the jurors could have supposed that Socrates was guilty of failing to recognise the gods recognised by the Athenians (1.1.20).

To complete his review of the specifications of the indictment, Xenophon now turns to the question of how Socrates might have corrupted the youth. Had Xenophon supposed that the actual animus against Socrates has been focused on seditious political teachings, here is where we would expect his defence to respond to Socrates' alleged political influences. Instead, Xenophon emphasises how well Socrates controlled his own sexual and gustatory appetites, how well he endured extremes of hot, cold and labour (1.2.1)

THE TRIAL OF SOCRATES
355

and helped to improve others in these same ways (1.2.2). He kept himself physically fit, and encouraged others to do the same, to the extent, at least, that it also served to help one to care for one's soul (1.2.4). He disapproved of inappropriate delicacy or dandyism in clothing, footwear or behaviour, and also discouraged the love of money in his companions (1.2.5). Unlike those who might be thought actually to corrupt the youth, Socrates refused to take money from his companions for his company (1.2.6–7). Xenophon now concludes that these well-known facts about Socrates make it abundantly clear that he did not corrupt the youth (1.2.8). As much as Xenophon's portrait of Socrates here seems well designed to prove that he was actually a good influence on youths, it is anything but evident how Xenophon's report could be intended to address some specific partisan political taint on Socrates.

But now, and then for almost the rest of book 1 chapter 2, Xenophon turns to the complaints made by 'the accuser'. In response to these, Xenophon has many narratives and anecdotes that prove the opposite of what 'the accuser' claimed about Socrates, but even in these, Xenophon's focus is always on Socrates' own self-control, justice and unwillingness to do wrong, rather than on making some attempt to sugar-coat political views that would be anathema to democracy. For example, to the complaints that Socrates criticised Athens' use of the lot to appoint public officials and led the young to hate 'the established constitution' (1.2.9), Xenophon actually makes no specific reply. Instead, he takes up 'the accuser's' claim that Socrates made his associates violent, and emphatically denies it (1.2.10–11). Had Xenophon's readers known full well that Socrates advocated the overthrow of Athenian democracy, Xenophon's simply shrugging off what 'the accuser' had to say about that would be remarkably inept. Instead, Xenophon focuses on the issue of advocacy of violence and on Socrates' very visible relationships with two notorious traitors. In the conclusion of this long response to 'the accuser', Xenophon states clearly what he thinks the truth is about Socrates in terms of what might have been at stake if the motives for the trial and execution were political: 'to the state he was never the cause of disaster in war, or strife or treason or any evil whatever' (1.2.63). Xenophon then returns to the actual indictment against Socrates, and repeats his earlier responses to its specifications: Socrates was a devoted servant of the gods, and a man who dedicated his life to reforming those who had given way to excessive desires and to exhorting them to virtue. Xenophon might have served his own anti-democratic political views through his depiction of Socrates by defending some of Socrates' allegedly anti-democratic political doctrines. Instead, Xenophon focuses on Socrates' strength of character and how this strength was what had been so attractive to Alcibiades and Critias. The same silence about specifically seditious political activities or teachings may be noted in Xenophon's two accounts of Hermogenes' report on what Socrates did and said before and at the trial (*Memorabilia* 4.8.4–11 and *Apology*). Not a whisper of political taint may be found in these, either. Instead, the emphasis is entirely on how little Socrates was concerned about his death, and how enacting virtue was all that mattered to him.

In Plato's account of the trial, too, the allegedly political motives of the prosecution are never taken up. In Plato's version, Socrates actually takes up the very question that has been the focus of this discussion. The relevant passage is too long to quote in full, but it begins with Socrates explaining that, in fact, there are two sets of accusers who are responsible for his being there in court. The 'older' ones, including Aristophanes (18a, 18d, 19c), had depicted him as one who teaches sophistry and absurd speculations about nature. It is on these 'first accusations', Socrates insists, that the 'later' accusers, including especially Meletus, relied in writing up the legal indictment (19a–b).

As a way to characterise why he had landed in the Athenian court, this first part of Socrates' explanation is noteworthy for the fact that it is not at all any political taint that he associates with his 'first' accusers, such as Aristophanes. Whereas the Socrates of the *Clouds* may clearly be seen failing to recognise Athens' gods and inventing new divinities, and also corrupting the youth in obvious ways, despite Aristophanes' own very adroit and frequent political satire and critique, nothing in Aristophanes' caricature of Socrates makes the philosopher out to be an advocate for anti-democratic overthrow of the Athenian government. Instead, as I say, the Socrates of *Clouds* fits very nicely into the specifications of the later indictment against him, which on its face is about religious offenses. And Socrates is quite explicit in saying that the 'later' accusations – namely, his actual prosecutors – had relied on this earlier association of him to the notorieties of the free-thinkers of the fifth century in bringing their case to court. Had it been true that, in fact, the actual prosecution of Socrates was focused more on political actions or doctrines, there would be no such continuity between the 'first' and the 'later' accusers and their accusations.

Plato's Socrates emphatically denies having had anything to do with nature-philosophy or sophistry and challenges members of the jury to claim that they have heard him talking about such things, if they had (19c–d; again, compare this to Xenophon, *Memorabilia*. 1.1.11). If that is true, then it plainly follows that the slanders on which the prosecution relied in making its charges against Socrates are entirely inapt. But now Socrates imagines one of his jurors interrupting and asking him why, if not for teaching sophistry and absurd speculations about nature, has he come to have such a bad reputation in Athens – surely he has been saying or doing *something* different from what most people do or say (*Apology* 20c). Now Socrates embarks on his story about the oracle to Chaerephon, and Socrates' subsequent attempts to figure out what the oracle might have meant.[31]

The story of the oracle to Chaerephon is given a very different form in Xenophon (for which, see his *Apology* 14). In Plato, however, the gist of the story is that Socrates is at first profoundly puzzled by the oracle's pronouncement that no one is wiser than Socrates, but then, in questioning first people highly regarded for their wisdom (politician and then poets) and then various artisans, he comes to realise that those reputed for wisdom lack it while also thinking they have it, whereas the artisans at least have some wisdom in their crafts, but then make the mistake of thinking that they are also wise in more important matters. Socrates thus learned that he was indeed the wisest, because at least he recognised how deficient in real wisdom he was (*Apology* 21b–23b). He concludes by acknowledging that young people with the leisure to witness Socrates' questionings of others ('the sons of the very rich' – *Apology* 21c) were entertained by the spectacle, and often imitated him. This, then, is enough to explain how and why he has come to have such a bad reputation in Athens, and also why Meletus and the other prosecutors were moved to bring Socrates to trial. When people found themselves questioned by some of Socrates' young imitators, he explained to the jurors,

> Those who are examined by them get angry with me and not with them, and say that a certain Socrates completely pollutes the land and corrupts the youth. And when someone asks them what I do and what I teach, they have nothing to say and draw a blank, but so they don't appear to be confused, they say what's commonly said against all philosophers – 'what's in the heavens and below the earth', 'doesn't believe in gods', and 'makes the weaker argument the stronger'. But I think they wouldn't want to say what's true, that they're plainly pretending to know, and they don't know

THE TRIAL OF SOCRATES   357

anything. In so far, then, as they are, I think, concerned about their honour, and are
zealous, and numerous, and speak earnestly and persuasively about me, they've filled
your ears for a long time by vehemently slandering me. It was on this account that
Meletus, Anytus, and Lycon came after me: Meletus angry on behalf of the poets;
Anytus on behalf of the craftsmen and politicians; and Lycon on behalf of the orators.
The result is that, as I was saying when I began, I'd be amazed if I were able to refute
in such a little time this slander you accept and that has gotten out of hand. There you
have the truth, men of Athens, and in what I'm saying, I'm neither hiding nor even
shading anything large or small. And yet I know pretty well that in saying these things,
I'm making myself hated, which is evidence that I'm telling the truth and that such is
the slander against me and that these are its causes. And whether or not you investigate
these things now or later, you'll discover that they're so.

– Apology 23d–24b[32]

I have chosen to quote this conclusion of Socrates' explanation of the prejudices against
him for several reasons. The first of these is obvious, but deserves emphasis: (i) Socrates
offers this explanation of why he has been brought to trial by the prosecutors as part of a
long history of slanders against him. But not just that; (ii) Socrates also makes it very plain
that the account he has offered is *comprehensive*: 'I'm neither hiding nor even shading
anything large or small.' Moreover, (iii) he challenges his jurors to 'investigate these
things now or later' and claims that his explanation of the animus against him will prove
to be both accurate and complete.

If the real motives for the trial were those provided by the political interpretation, then
Stone is right to say that Plato's account is 'a masterpiece of evasion' (Stone 1979),
because there is not even a whisper of such political concerns represented here. It is, of
course, entirely possible for us to dismiss Plato as a witness in precisely the way that Stone
does. As we have seen, except for what Xenophon has to say about 'the accuser', nothing
else in his work lends support to the political interpretation, and so we can also dismiss
all that evidence in the same way. Scholars have proven to be very inventive about
dismissing the most proximate (and prolific) ancient sources on Socrates, by 'clearing the
ground' of all of these,[33] and then selecting some other evidence as more credible. In
historical matters of this kind, it is plain that the evidence we have has allowed very
different interpretations by scholars.

The long passage just quoted above, however – while of course, it could be a clever
cover-up by an author who is certainly clever enough to tell convincing lies – actually
manages to give a completely credible story of why Socrates could have been brought to
trial, and also could explain why a majority of jurors found him guilty. Socrates engaged
in practices that would almost certainly manage to offend those who presented themselves
as leaders in the community. It is certainly obvious enough to anyone with any experience
of the world that politicians and demagogues in particular do not respond well to having
their ignorance and folly made publicly evident. That the same angry and vindictive sort
of response could be provoked from leading literary figures or prominent artisans seems
also to be entirely credible – even familiar.

Athens was still reeling from a shattering loss in a war her leaders had continued to
promise would be won. One does not need to be devoutly religious to suspect, in such
circumstances, that Athens' woes – which were considerable at the time – indicated an
abandonment by the gods that had formerly protected her. And there was, at that time,
also a well-known and highly controversial intellectual movement – the very sorts of

people that Plato has Socrates complain he has been assimilated to – whose teachings and fancies cast doubt on traditional religious views. Finally, we also know from Aristophanes' play (*Clouds*), produced in 423 BCE, that for at least a quarter-century, Socrates had been assimilated to that group of intellectuals. So, the basis for the explanation that Plato has Socrates give to the jurors seems to me to be entirely credible. Such prejudice *could* happen. Bias can most certainly lead to acts of vengeance and retribution against people who never committed the imagined 'crimes'. We know this painfully well from our own time. I see no reason for thinking that the ancient Athenians could not also be guilty of bias and prejudice, and also find no reason to think that these could not boil over into judicial homicide during very troubled times. Rather than 'clear away' entirely credible evidence that directly addresses the scholarly question I seek to answer herein, I am accordingly inclined to accept it completely. Socrates, according to Plato's credible account, was a troublesome fellow who antagonised too many of his fellow Athenians – especially the proud and powerful ones – and they spread false, but all-too-plausible rumours about him. These rumours eventually led to his being charged with the kinds of religious 'crimes' that the people of Athens were quite familiar with and were themselves quite sure were being committed by certain intellectuals. I also find entirely credible the claim that Plato's Socrates makes about the circumstance he found himself in at the trial itself. Given a single day to disabuse the jurors of the rumours and scandals they had heard about, Socrates' chances of actually winning the case were poor. As he also says once he has been found guilty, it is actually more surprising that the vote against him was as close as it ended up being: Had only thirty additional jurors voted in his favour, Socrates would have been found innocent (*Apology* 36a).

The evidence from both Plato and Xenophon, then, strikes me as decisively favouring what has been called 'the religious interpretation'. But even those who agree that the motives for the trial and condemnation were aptly described in the actual indictment have disagreed on what we might find to be the more important question: Was Socrates actually guilty of the impieties described in the indictment, at least from the standpoint of what would qualify as fairly typical Athenian religious concerns?[34] Famously, some scholars have found evidence in Plato for contending that the jurors' verdict was actually reasonable and apt. The evidence cited for this disturbing conclusion is said to be found in the *Euthyphro*. Euthyphro reminds Socrates of several myths in which the gods, at least by human standards, behave in violent and shocking ways. In the Grube translation,[35] Socrates replies,

> Indeed, Euthyphro, this is the reason why I am a defendant in the case, because I find it hard to accept things like that being said about the gods, and it is likely to be the reason why I shall be told that I do wrong.
>
> – *Euthyphro* 6a

The problem that Socrates seems to identify as the reason for the indictment is that he doesn't think the gods do vicious and evil things to one another, or even to human beings. This 'moralising' of the Greek gods struck Gregory Vlastos, for example, as a shocking and dangerous departure from orthodoxy:

> To heirs of the Hebraic and Christian traditions this will hardly seem a bold conclusion. For those bred on Greek beliefs about the gods it would be shattering. [. . .] Required to meet [Socrates' moralizing] standards, the city's gods would have become unrecognizable. Their ethical transformation would be tantamount to the destruction

THE TRIAL OF SOCRATES   359

of the old gods, the creation of new ones – which is precisely what Socrates takes to be
the sum and substance of the accusation at his trial.

– Vlastos 1991: 165–166[36]

There are, however, several problems here. The first of these – though not a mistake
repeated by Vlastos himself[37] – may be seen in Grube's translation of the relevant text
from the *Euthyphro*. As a matter of fact, the translation makes into one sentence what is
in the Greek two sentences, the first of which is a question. Brickhouse and I offered this
translation in our 2002b book:

> Is *this*, Euthyphro, why I'm being indicted – because whenever someone says such
> things about the gods, I have trouble accepting it for some reason? Surely it's for this
> reason that some, it seems, will say that I've committed a crime.

– Brickhouse and Smith 2002b: 30

Why doesn't Socrates already *know* why he has been indicted – as the Grube translation
suggests he does, but which the text plainly does not support? The answer to this question
requires a closer look at the way in which legal charges were made in ancient Athens.[38]
Because, as I said at the very beginning of this chapter, legal cases were nearly always
initiated by private individuals, one who wished to prosecute a case first had to decide
which legal official would be responsible for administering the case. For the trial of
Socrates, this official was called the 'king archon' or just 'king' (*basileus*). The translation,
though technically accurate, was already an anachronism – the 'king' was not a king in
any familiar sense, but only one of many public officials, and like most of them, he would
be appointed by lot for a single year of service. At any rate, the prosecutor would then
have to find out when the king's office would be open, so the charge could be registered.
The very fact that it is this archon who administered the case against Socrates all by itself
counts as evidence that the charge was intended and taken to be about a matter of religion:
Different archons in the Athenian system administered the legal procedures for different
domains. The special domain of the king was for cases involving religion, homicide and
deliberate wounding.[39] Euthyphro came to the king because his case involved the charge
of murder. Socrates is there because he faces a charge of impiety.

Once a prosecutor identified which was the appropriate archon for a case of the kind he
sought to prosecute, and also found out when that archon would receive new cases, the
prosecutor must then issue a summons, which was achieved by finding two witnesses who
could testify that the summons had actually been issued, and then confronting the accused
party with those witnesses in attendance. The summons itself would be an oral (not written)
statement of the charge together with the actual summons to appear before the king on the
appropriate date. At this initial meeting before the king, the prosecutor would provide a
written version of the accusation (the *graphê*). At that meeting, the king would then schedule
a preliminary inquiry (*anakrisis*). The text of the charge would then be publicly displayed in
the Agora, and the litigants could make whatever preparations they wished for the inquiry.

At the inquiry, the charge would be stated, and the litigants would be asked several
questions by the king and could also at that time ask questions of one another. In that
process, the actual nature and presumably (official) basis of the charge would be disclosed
and explicated.

> This would give each of them a clearer idea of what the other was alleging and what
> were the exact points in dispute, and it would help them to decide how it would be

best to present their arguments in the trial and what supporting evidence would be needed.

– MacDowell 1978: 241

In the passage from the *Euthyphro* quoted above that seems to support the version of the religious interpretation of the trial in which Socrates turns out to be guilty of the charge, it seemed that Socrates wasn't really sure exactly why he had been indicted. Socrates' lack of familiarity with the case and his prosecutor is evident right from the start of that dialogue, where Socrates confesses not really knowing much about Meletus, his prosecutor. He knew what Meletus looked like (since Meletus would have had to initiate the legal process by confronting Socrates in person), and might also at that time have been informed of Meletus' deme. But Socrates' uncertainties and speculations seem to indicate that he has not yet attended the preliminary inquiry, where all that he is vague about in the *Euthyphro* would likely have been revealed, discussed and clarified (even if the prosecutors' underlying motives might still have remained hidden). Instead, the way Plato represents Socrates' responses to his own prosecution to Euthyphro makes clear that this is his first visit – the one he was summoned to – with the king, where he could expect to learn when the preliminary inquiry would then be scheduled.

I have gone on at some length about just where in the pre-trial procedures Socrates was when he is depicted as having his conversation with Euthyphro, because in that depiction, he is very plainly shown not (yet) to know why he has been charged or what arguments the prosecution plans to make. Socrates' speculation that it is his 'moralising' of the gods that has led to his being charged is plainly not confirmed by the time the trial actually takes place, or else we would expect to hear more about that understanding of the charges in other ancient sources. Euthyphro's own speculation that it is Socrates' claim to have a divine sign that motivated the specification involving 'new divine things' (*Euthyphro* 3b) provides a different interpretation of that part of the indictment: Socrates is allegedly guilty of 'inventing new divine things' not because the gods he recognises are so different from the ones recognised by the state, but because he claims to have contact with a 'divine thing' that is not recognised by the state as a divinity.[40] In Plato's representation of the trial itself, this explanation for the 'new divinities' specification is repeated by Socrates himself (*Apology* 31d). I conclude that the religious interpretation of the motives for the trial and condemnation of Socrates offered by Vlastos and others is without basis.

But perhaps one still inclined to defend this view would claim that my focus on the 'new divine things' specification of the indictment is either misleading or simply mistaken. Instead, it might be argued, I should pay more attention to another point that Vlastos makes with respect to Socrates' 'unrecognisable' gods: 'that he believes in *gods* he makes clear enough; that he believes in the *gods of the state* he never says' (Vlastos 1991: 166 n. 141; emphasis in original).[41] The claim now seems to be that Socrates' moralised gods were so different from 'the gods of the state' that he really was guilty of 'not recognising the gods recognised by the state', as the indictment specified. Vlastos rightly goes on to note that Xenophon directly defends Socrates against the claim that he did not recognise the gods *of the state* (at *Memorabilia* 1.1.2 and *Apology* 11 and 24) (Ibid.).

As for Plato's Socrates, while Vlastos is strictly right that Socrates does not continue to specify that it is the gods *of the state* that are at issue, it seems to me that the implication of this omission that Vlastos perceives is mooted by the way in which this specification gets treated in Plato's *Apology*. First, recall that when Socrates explains to his jurors why he thinks he has been brought to trial (in the long quote given earlier), he says his public

THE TRIAL OF SOCRATES

361

humiliation of politicians, poets and artisans is what led to his being hated by so many Athenians, but that, rather than admit it was the exposure of their ignorance that had made them angry, 'so as not to appear at a loss, they mention those accusations that are available against all philosophers, about "things in the sky and things below the earth", about "not believing in the gods" and "making the worse the stronger argument"'. He claims that his actual prosecutors relied upon these long-standing prejudices in composing their indictment. In this way of accounting for the motives of his prosecutors, 'not recognizing the gods recognized by the state' was intended and taken to mean that Socrates didn't believe in the gods – the only gods anyone at the trial thought were relevant to the charge.

Plato manages to go on to establish this point even more securely. Although we may reasonably expect that Socrates already understood what Meletus had intended in his indictment as a result of the preliminary inquiry, the jurors might not have gotten the same information from the speeches already made by the prosecutors. So Plato has Socrates engage Meletus in a discussion that will allow his jurors to see very clearly what Meletus intended when he alleged that Socrates 'did not recognise the gods recognised by the state'. It seems to me that the way Plato has Meletus clarify his own allegation provides a completely adequate answer to Vlastos' doubts:

> In the name of these very gods that we're arguing about, Meletus, tell me and these men here still more clearly. I'm not able to understand whether you're saying that I teach people not to believe that some gods exist – and therefore that I myself believe gods exist and am not a complete atheist, nor am I a wrongdoer in that way – and yet I do not believe in the ones that the city believes in, but others, and this is what you're accusing me of, because I believe in the others? Or are you saying that I don't believe in gods at all and that I teach others such things.
>
> I'm saying that you don't believe in the gods at all.
>
> – *Apology* 26b–c[42]

It is, of course, true that because Meletus gives the answer that he does, Socrates is subsequently able to show that Meletus' indictment is actually contradictory: Socrates invents 'new divinities' according to one specification of the charge, but is now being said to be an atheist, according to one of the other specifications of the charge. But the only thing forcing Meletus to answer as he does here is what Socrates had alleged earlier – that in writing the indictment as he did, Meletus was relying on the old prejudice against all philosophers, a prejudice that included a stereotype that they were atheists. It is certainly convenient to Meletus' case, if what Socrates reports of the old prejudice is accurate, to have Socrates tarred by a long-standing prejudice and stereotype to which the jurors have already been exposed. If Vlastos' view of what was really going on were correct, however, Meletus should not have answered as he did. So here, too, in Plato's account 'not recognising the gods recognised by the state' amounted to the charge of atheism. Religious innovation is neither mentioned nor even implied in Plato's account to have played any role in the prosecution, conviction or condemnation of Socrates. Instead, Socrates was portrayed as an atheist because that was the prejudicial stereotype of philosophers at that time. He was alleged to 'invent new divine things' because he claimed to have a divine sign. And he corrupted the youth by teaching them the kinds of things that the stereotypical philosopher was supposed to teach. In depicting these as the grounds for why he was brought to trial, Plato has Socrates explain, 'I'm neither hiding nor even shading anything large or small' (*Apology* 24a).

In the first edition of *The Bloomsbury Companion to Socrates*, Mark Ralkowski argued for a version of what he terms 'the mixed motivations theory' of the trial, which has it that 'in Socrates' Athens religion and politics were so interrelated and inseparable' as to make an appeal to neither all by itself an accurate way to explain Socrates' trial: 'In Athens, impiety was always political, because it always ran the risk of endangering the city as a whole' (both quotes from Ralkowski 2013: 323). If we insist on this sense of what is and is not 'political', any threat to the welfare of the city will be seen as a 'political' threat. But such a 'refinement' of the sense in which the trial of Socrates is alleged to have been 'politically motivated' or motivated with 'mixed motives' strikes me as simply obfuscation. I see no mixture of motives in the way the prosecution, the litigants themselves or the jurors perceived the case. The trial of Socrates was undertaken as a way to rid the city of a difficult man. A majority of jurors showed they regarded Socrates as a threat to the welfare of the city. The precise ways in which Socrates was regarded as a threat to the city had clear and unambiguous roots in Athenian religion. We may grant, accordingly, that the trial was based on a view of Socrates that made him a threat to the common good. But the plainest and best way to understand the motives for the trial and condemnation do not require either the abandonment of or radical revision to our familiar concepts of politics and religion. Socrates was tried on a religious charge, and his jurors convicted and condemned him to death because they thought he was guilty of one or more of the quite obviously religious interpretations of how that charge was specified in the indictment.

In reaching this conclusion, to be clear, I do not take myself to be reporting what each and every juror might have had in mind when he cast his votes against Socrates (that is, the vote to convict, and then the vote to condemn). Different issues would surely have mattered in different degrees to different jurors. As for the prosecutors, each of their motives might, too, have been different, with different focuses and perhaps different aims. It seems to me entirely open to question whether any one of the prosecutors even believed the charge they prosecuted against Socrates, and if so what part(s) of it. In the account Plato has Socrates actually give of the prosecutors' strategy, their accusation is motivated entirely differently, by a distrust of intellectuals generally, and antagonism toward Socrates in particular for the ways in which he humiliated important people in public. I see no reason to suppose that their motives might not have included any number of considerations that were never made explicit. It is certainly common enough for people to allege wrongdoing of some kind as a way of responding to entirely other perceived grievances. What I do take myself to have explained, however, is how the motivation for the trial of Socrates was characterised by those who were in the best position to report it accurately. Whether our best sources actually did report what they knew accurately may (and likely will) continue to be a matter for speculation. But the meaning of what the sources actually say is clear enough, I think. Better yet, our best sources on the matter – Plato and Xenophon – are consistent in their representations on this issue, which is that Socrates was tried for religious reasons. Tragically, in both accounts, Socrates was innocent, but convicted and condemned to death anyway. In Socrates' time, as in ours, prejudice and bias are responsible for fatal injustices.

NOTES

1. As strange as it may seem, even Socrates' death has been a source of controversy. It used to be believed that the way Plato depicted the death of Socrates was obvious fiction – a medical impossibility. A decisive more recent study, however, has shown that

THE TRIAL OF SOCRATES

Plato's description was so accurate it might have come from a toxicology textbook. See Bloch 2002.

2. The most extreme examples of these sorts of responses to Xenophon and Plato may be found in Stone 1979 and 1988, and Waterfield 2013. I will cite other scholars who take similar approaches within.

3. *Contra* Nails 2006: 11.

4. The fine would be for 10 minas (1 mina = 100 drachmas = 600 obols) of silver. The average daily wage for free Athenian labourers at that time was one drachma per day, so the fine would be for 1,000 times that amount – around three years' worth of such wages. Socrates' jurors would be paid just half of a drachma (three obols), subsistence pay that Aristophanes often mocked as a security net for the aged and infirm. (See MacDowell 1978: 34–35 for discussion.)

5. Numbering anywhere from a few hundred to a few thousand (see MacDowell 1978: 36–38).

6. Most translations and scholarly sources report the number as 501, with the odd number intended to break ties. But the change to odd-numbered juries seems to have come later (see MacDowell 1978: 37–39; Burnet 1924: note on 36a5). In the older system, tie votes were counted in favour of the defendant.

7. I have listed the order of the specifications as they appear in Xenophon's *Memorabilia* 1.1.1 and Diogenes Laertius 2.40. The same specifications are also given in almost the same words in Plato's *Apology* at 24b–c, but the order in which the specifications are given there is (iii), (i), (ii), and it is in this order that Plato has Socrates discuss the charges with Meletus. I cannot see that any important interpretive or historical issue rests on which order was the actual one.

8. Robert Parker renders '*daimonia*' as 'powers' (Parker 1996: 201).

9. On the vagueness in the indictment against Socrates, see Ober 2011: 140.

10. Ober 2011: 140–141 seems to think that the closeness of the vote to convict Socrates indicated a lack of consensus regarding what would or would not count as grounds for thinking that Socrates was guilty of what was specified in the indictment.

11. See, for example, the most famous proponent of what I am calling 'the political interpretation' of Socrates' trial, Stone 1988: 178. Contrast the assertion by Nails (who explicitly works from just the Platonic evidence): 'there is no evidence that there was an underlying political motive in Socrates' case' (Nails 2006: 7).

12. Trans. Brickhouse and Smith 2002b.

13. Trans. Brickhouse and Smith 2002b, slightly amended.

14. The Platonic texts associating Socrates with Alcibiades in these ways are too abundant to review individually here. But for the association of the two as lovers, see especially *Gorgias* 481d and *Symposium* 213c–d.

15. 'Plato's *Apology* is a very poor guide to the arguments for the prosecution' (Johnson 2021: 60).

16. Both this and the next translation from the *Memorabilia* are those of J. Fogel in Brickhouse and Smith 2002b.

17. Plato's Socrates makes a similar move in his own defense at *Apology* 33c–34b, naming numerous of his younger associates and their fathers who Socrates says would gladly testify on his behalf.

18. For which, see Chroust 1957; Brickhouse and Smith 1989b: 69–87; Ober 2011: 143. Although Johnson 2021: 75 reports that this identification 'remains that of the scholarly consensus', he rejects it, and attributes the views Xenophon reports as having been made by 'the accuser' to Meletus, who was also the (nominal) writer of the indictment. Johnson, therefore, also rejects the distinction I am making here between Xenophon's references to 'the writer(s) of the indictment' and 'the accuser'. Johnson's own citations of the scholarship do not seem to me to indicate any broad consensus on this question (See Johnson 2021: 105, n. 14).

19. 'In addition to his piece in praise of the cannibal Busiris, Polycrates wrote in praise of Clytemnestra, in praise of mice, of pebbles, and, probably, in praise of a pot. He wrote a work in which Thersites (or a figure like him) was treated as a hero on a grand scale' (Johnson 2021: 80)

20. This conclusion would obviously include even later reports of how Socrates' associations with Critias and Alcibiades might have been sources of bias against Socrates; for which, see Maximus of Tyre (second century CE) in *Oration* III.8, and Libanius' (314–393 CE) *Apology of Socrates*, which Chroust 1957 used to reconstruct Polycrates' 'Accusation'. All of the major and minor sources on the trial of Socrates are included and translated in Brickhouse and Smith 2002b.

21. It is puzzling that Stone never cites Chroust 1957. He does cite a different work by Chroust elsewhere (Stone 1988: 244), but seems not to be aware of Chroust's efforts to reconstruct Polycrates' 'Accusation of Socrates'.

22. Waterfield, at any rate, seems to rely heavily on Chroust's reconstruction of the work that Stone had ignored (see Waterfield 2013 and n. 90, and my note 9, above).

23. For more detailed assessment of Aristophanes as a source on Socrates, see Chapter 1 of this book.

24. Smith 2018.

25. *Pace* Johnson 2021.

26. A long list of those who have advocated versions of 'the political interpretation' is given by Brickhouse and Smith in their 1989b: 70 n. 29. What I say here does not deviate from what we argued there.

27. See also Ober 2011: 148–158, who concludes that this shows 'Socratic philosophy and Athenian democracy were compatible' (158).

28. See the discussion of the political associations of leaders criticised by Socrates in Plato in Brickhouse and Smith 1994: 161–162.

29. Scholars who have made this claim include Allen 1975: 12; Burnet 1924: 101; Bury 1940: 393; Davies 1983: 187; Navia 1984: 14 and 32 n. 2; Reeve 1989: 99; and Ober 2011: 170.

30. And repeated in the first edition of this *Companion* by Waterfield 2013: 15, and Ralkowski 2013: 323.

31. Some scholars and translators have found Socrates' response to the oracle itself to be an indication of a religious offense. So, for example, Grube's translation in Cooper 1997 has Socrates seeking to 'refute the oracle' for 21c and Fowler's Loeb translation has it as 'prove the utterance wrong'. The Greek says that Socrates sought to '*elenchein* to *manteion*', which could be translated as 'refute the oracle' except for what Socrates had said only a few lines above, which was that it is not possible for the god to have spoken

THE TRIAL OF SOCRATES   365

falsely (*pseudetai*; 21b). This pair of claims, it seems to me, can only mean that Socrates realised the oracle certainly had to be true, but the sense in which it would turn out to be true would be something other than the superficial sense of what it said. Once Socrates later came to understand what the oracle had said, it did turn out to have been true all along. No disrespect or genuine doubt of the god is expressed or implied here.

32. Unless otherwise noted, all translations from Plato's *Apology* provided herein are those of Brickhouse and Smith in Brickhouse and Smith 2002b.

33. This is the expression Waterfield (2013) uses for dismissing entirely the evidence from Aristophanes, Xenophon, Plato and Aristotle, and then favouring the evidence provided by Polycrates, which (paradoxically) has survived almost exclusively in the work of Xenophon, which is otherwise treated as ground to be 'cleared'.

34. Ober 2011: 141 finds the question of whether Socrates was guilty a 'red herring' because of the lack of legal standards for determining guilt or innocence other than the specific votes of specific juries. But it seems to me that we can ask for ourselves whether or not a judgment of guilt or innocence would be warranted, given what we can discern of Socrates' actual views and behaviours, and certainly Socrates' ancient detractors and defenders supposed that the question of guilt was both meaningful and important.

35. It is this translation that is included in Cooper 1997.

36. For another expression of this view, see also Connor 1991: 56 and Burnyeat 1997. McPherran 1996: 141–160 finds Socrates' moralized beliefs about the gods a genuine threat to Athenian religious life, but ultimately argues that this threat probably did not play as great a role in the jury's condemnation of Socrates as did the connection jurors made between the 'new divinities' charge and Socrates' *daimonion* (McPherran 1996: 173).

37. See Vlastos 1991: 166 n. 42.

38. The source for all that follows is MacDowell 1978: 24–25 regarding the role of the king-archon and 237–242 for the description of procedure.

39. MacDowell 1978: 25.

40. See Ober 2011: 142.

41. Another instance of this distinction: 'The gods acknowledged by the polis were those of the poets, gods who often wished, and even caused, evil: but Socrates acknowledged no such gods' (Nails 2006: 8). I think McPherran's analysis, that the gods acknowledged by the state were simply the gods recognised in publicly sponsored festivals and rituals (see McPherran 1996: 121–122), is more apt. To acknowledge these gods, one needn't conceive of them in any terms other than those required for the performance of the relevant rituals, which Xenophon is careful to say that Socrates did often and very visibly.

42. Ober 2011: 145 claims that 'a reasonable judge' could take this exchange as actually proving that 'Socrates actually disbelieved in state-approved gods'. It seems to me that the text is intended to block such response.

BIBLIOGRAPHY

Adams, D. 1992. 'The *Lysis* Puzzles.' *History of Philosophy Quarterly* 9: 3–17.

— 1998. 'Elenchos and Evidence.' *Ancient Philosophy* 18: 287–307.

Adler, J. E. and Armour-Garb, B. 2007. 'Moore's Paradox and the Transparency of Belief'. In J. Green and M. Williams (eds), 146–164.

Ahbel-Rappe, S. 2010. 'Cross-examining Happiness: Reason and Community in Plato's Socratic Dialogues.' In A. W. Nightingale and D. Sedley, (eds), 27–44.

— 2012. 'Is Socratic Ethics Egoistic?' *Classical Philology* 107: 319–340.

Ahbel-Rappe, S. and Kamtekar, R. (eds). 2006. *A Companion to Socrates*. Malden, MA and Oxford: Blackwell Publishing Ltd.

Alesse, F. 2004. 'Euripides and the Socratics.' In V. Karasmanis (ed.), 371–381.

Allen, R. E. 1970. *Plato's 'Euthyphro' and the Earlier Theory of Forms*. London: Routledge & Kegan Paul, Ltd. and New York: Humanity Press.

— 1971. 'The Earlier Theory of Forms.' In Vlastos (ed.), 319–334.

— 1975. 'The Trial of Socrates: A Study in the Morality of the Criminal Process.' In M. L. Friedland (ed.), 3–21.

— 1980. *Socrates and Legal Obligation*. Minneapolis: University of Minnesota Press.

Alon, I. 1991. *Socrates in Mediaeval Literature*. Leiden: E. J. Brill.

Ambrosino, D. 1983. 'Nuages et sens. Autour des *Nuées* d'Aristophane.' *Quaderni di Storia* 9: 3–60.

Anagnostopoulos, G. and Santas, G. (eds). 2018. *Democracy, Equality, and Justice in Ancient Greece*. Cham: Springer.

Anderson, M. 2005. 'Socrates as Hoplite.' *Ancient Philosophy* 25: 73–89.

Annas, J. 1977. 'Plato and Aristotle on Friendship and Altruism.' *Mind* 86, 532–554.

— 1982. 'Plato's Myths of Judgement.' *Phronesis* 27: 119–143.

— 1993. *The Morality of Happiness*. New York: Oxford University Press.

— 1994. 'Virtue and the Use of Other Goods.' In T. H. Irwin and M. C. Nussbaum (eds), 53–66.

— 1999. *Platonist Ethics Old and New*. Ithaca: Cornell University Press.

— 2002. 'Platonist Ethics and Plato.' In M. Canto-Sperber and P. Pellegrin (eds), 1–24.

— 2007. 'Virtue Ethics and the Charge of Egoism.' In P. Bloomfield (ed.), 205–222.

Annas, J., Narvaez, D. and Snow, N. E. (eds). 2016. *Developing the Virtues: Integrating Perspectives*. Oxford: Oxford University Press.

Annas, J. and Rowe, C. (eds). 2002. *New Perspectives on Plato, Modern and Ancient*. Cambridge, MA: Harvard University Press.

Anton, J. 1980. 'Dialectic and Health in Plato's *Gorgias*.' *Ancient Philosophy* 1: 49–60.

Anton, J. P. and Kustas, G. L. (eds). 1971. *Essays in Ancient Greek Philosophy*. Albany: State University of New York Press.

Anton, J. P. and Preuss, A. (eds). 1989. *Essays in Ancient Greek Philosophy* (Vol. 2). Albany: State University of New York Press.

Arendt, H. 1958. *The Human Condition*. Chicago: University of Chicago Press.

Arieti, J. A. and Barrus, R. M. 2011. *Plato's* Protagoras: *Translation, Commentary, and Appendices.* Lanham: Littlefield.

Aristotle, 2002. *Nicomachean Ethics.* Trans. C. Rowe. Oxford: Oxford University Press.

Armleder, P. J. 1966. 'Death in Plato's Apologia.' *Classical Bulletin* 42: 46.

von Arnim, H. 1923. *Xenophons Memorabilien und Apologie des Sokrates.* Copenhagen: Høst & Søn.

Arrighetti, G. 1994. 'Socrate, Euripide e la tragedia (Aristoph., *Ranae* 1491–1499).' In F. Del Franco (ed.), 35–44.

Ausland, H. W. 2002. 'Forensic Characteristics of Socratic Argumentation.' In G. A. Scott, 36–60.

Austin, E. A. 2009. *Fear and Death in Plato.* Dissertation, Washington University in St Louis.

— 2010. 'Prudence and the Fear of Death in Plato's *Apology*', *Ancient Philosophy* 30: 39–55.

— 2013. 'Corpses, Self-Defense, and Immortality: Callicles' Fear of Death in the *Gorgias.*' *Ancient Philosophy* 33: 33–52.

— 2016. 'Plato on Grief as a Mental Disorder.' *Archiv für Geschichte der Philosophie* 98: 1–20.

— 2019. 'Piety and Annihilation in Plato's *Phaedo.*' *Apeiron* 52: 339–358.

— 2020. 'Socrates on Why we Should not Practice Philosophy.' *Ancient Philosophy* 30: 247–265.

Bagordo, A. 2014. *Alkimenes–Kantharos. Einleitung, Übersetzung, Kommentar.* Heidelberg: Verlag Antike.

— 2018. 'Κομψευριπικῶς. Tracce di Euripide socratico-sofistico nella commedia attica.' In S. Bigliazzi, F. Lupi and G. Ugolini (eds), 457–490.

Bakhtin, M. M. 1981. *The Dialogic Imagination: Four Essays.* Austin: University of Texas Press.

— 1984. *Problems of Dostoevsky's Poetics.* Edited and Translated by C. Emerson. Minneapolis: University of Minnesota Press.

— 1986. *Speech Genres and Other Late Essays.* Translated by V. W. McGee. Austin: University of Texas Press.

Balot, R. 2008. 'Socratic Courage in Athenian Democracy,' *Ancient Philosophy* 28: 4–26.

Bandini, M. and Dorion, L.-A. 2010. *Xénophon: Mémorables,* Tome I [Introduction générale, livre I] (Budé series). 3rd ed. [1st ed., 2000]. Paris: Les Belles Lettres.

— 2011a. *Xénophon: Mémorables,* Tome II, 1ᵣₑ partie [Livres II-III] (Budé series). Paris: Les Belles Lettres.

— 2011b. *Xénophon: Mémorables,* Tome II, 2ᵉ partie [Livre IV] (Budé series). Paris: Les Belles Lettres.

Barker, E. 1918. *Greek Political Theory: Plato and His Predecessors.* New York: Routledge.

— 1959. *The Political Thought of Plato and Aristotle.* New York: Dover.

Barnes, J. 1979. *The Presocratic Philosophers.* London and New York: Routledge.

— 1984. *The Complete Works of Aristotle: The Revised Oxford Translation.* Princeton, NJ: Princeton University Press.

— 1984. *The Complete Works of Aristotle: The Revised Oxford Translation* (ed.). Oxford: Oxford University Press.

— (ed.) 1984. *The Complete Works of Aristotle: The Revised Oxford Translation.* Princeton: Princeton University Press.

Barney, R. 2010. 'Plato on the Desire for the Good.' In S. Tenenbaum (ed.), 34–64.

Baxley, A. M. 2007. 'The Price of Virtue.' *Pacific Philosophical Quarterly* 88: 403–423.

Beckman, J. 1979. *The Religious Dimension of Socrates' Thought.* Waterloo: Wilfred Laurier University Press.

BIBLIOGRAPHY

Bekker, I. 1831. *Aristotelis Opera*. 4 vols. Leipzig: Reimer.

Belardinelli, A. M. 2013. 'Aristofane e la *Medea* di Euripide.' *Dionysus ex machina* 4: 63–84.

Belardinelli, A. M., Imperio, O., Mastromarco, G., Pellegrino, M. and Totaro, P. (eds). 1998. *Tessere. Frammenti della commedia greca. Studi e commenti*. Bari: Adriatica Editrice.

Belfiore, E. S. 2012. *Socrates' Daimonic Art: Love for Wisdom in Four Platonic Dialogues*. Cambridge: Cambridge University Press.

Benson, H. H. 1987. 'The Problem of the Elenchus Reconsidered.' *Ancient Philosophy* 7: 67–85.

— 1989. 'A Note on Eristic and the Socratic Elenchus.' *Journal of the History of Philosophy* 27: 591–599.

— 1990a. 'Misunderstanding the "What Is F-ness?" Question.' *Archiv für Geschichte der Philosophie* 72: 125–142.

— 1990b. 'The Priority of Definition and the Socratic Elenchos.' *Oxford Studies in Ancient Philosophy* 8: 19–65.

— (ed.) 1992. *Essays on the Philosophy of Socrates*. Oxford: Oxford University Press.

— 1995. 'The Dissolution of the Problem of the Elenchus.' *Oxford Studies in Ancient Philosophy* 13: 45–112.

— 2000. *Socratic Wisdom*. Oxford: Oxford University Press.

— 2002. 'Problems with Socratic Method.' In G. A. Scott (ed.), 101–113.

— 2003. ''The Method of Hypothesis in the *Meno*.' *Proceedings of the Boston Area Colloquium in Ancient Philosophy* 18: 95–126.

— (ed.) 2006. *A Companion to Plato*. Malden, MA and Oxford: Blackwell Publishing.

— 2011. 'Socratic Method.' In D. Morrison (ed.), 179–200.

— 2013. 'The Priority of Definition.' in J. Bussanich and N. D. Smith (eds), 136–155 and 342–347.

— 2015. *Clitophon's Challenge: Dialectic in Plato's Meno, Phaedo, and Republic*. Oxford: Oxford University Press.

Betegh, G. 2009. 'Tale, Theology, and Teleology in the *Phaedo*.' In C. Partenie (ed.), 77–100.

— 2013. 'Socrate et Archélaos dans les *Nuées*. Philosophie naturelle et éthique.' In A. Laks and R. Saetta Cottone (eds), 87–106.

Beversluis, J. 1987. 'Does Socrates Commit the Socratic Fallacy?' *American Philosophical Quarterly* 24: 211–223.

— 2000. *Cross-Examining Socrates: A Defense of the Interlocutors in Plato's Early Dialogues*. Cambridge: Cambridge University Press. Reprinted 2004.

Bevilacqua, F. 2010. *Memorabili di Senofonte*. Turin: Unione Tipografico-Editrice Torinese.

Bierl, A. and von Möllendorff, P. (eds). 1994. *Orchestra, Drama, Mythos, Bühne*. Stuttgart and Leipzig: B. G. Teubner.

Bigliazzi, S., Lupi, F. and Ugolini, G. (eds). 1994. Συναγωνίζεσθαι. *Studies in Honour of Guido Avezzù*. Verona: SKENÈ.

Bjelde, J. 2021. 'Xenophon's Socrates on Wisdom and Action.' *Classical Quarterly* 71: 560–574.

Blackson, T. 2015. 'Two Interpretations of Socratic Intellectualism.' *Ancient Philosophy* 35, 23–39.

Bloch, E. 2002. 'Hemlock Poisoning and the Death of Socrates: Did Plato Tell the Truth?' In T. C. Brickhouse and N. D. Smith, 255–278.

Bloomfield, P (ed.). 2007. *Morality and Self-Interest*. Oxford: Oxford University Press.

Bobonich, C. 2002. *Plato's Utopia Recast: His Later Ethics and Politics*. Oxford: Clarendon Press.

— 2011. 'Socrates and *Eudaimonia*.' In D. R. Morrison (ed.), 293–332.

— (ed.) 2017. *The Cambridge Companion to Ancient Ethics*. Cambridge: Cambridge University Press.

Bobonich, C. and Destrée, P. (eds). 2007. *Akrasia in Greek Philosophy: From Socrates to Plotinus*. Boston: Brill.

Boeri, M., Kanayama, Y. and Mittelmann, J. (eds). 2018. *Soul and Mind in Greek Thought: Psychological Issues in Plato and Aristotle*. Cham: Springer.

Bolonyai, G. 2007. 'Protagoras the Atheist.' *Rhizai* 2, 247–269.

Bolotin, D. 1989. *Plato's Dialogue on Friendship*. Ithaca, NY: Cornell University Press.

Bolton, R. 1993. 'Aristotle's Account of the Socratic Elenchus.' *Oxford Studies in Ancient Philosophy* 11: 121–152.

Bonanno, M. G. 1979. 'II. La commedia.' In R. Bianchi Bandinelli (ed.), 311–350.

Bordt, M. J. 2000. 'The Unity of Plato's *Lysis*.' In T. M. Robinson and L. Brisson, 157–171.

Bostock, D. 1990. 'The Interpretation of Plato's *Crito*.' *Phronesis* 35: 1–20.

Boys-Stones, G. and Rowe, C. (eds). 2013. *The Circle of Socrates: Readings in the First-Generation Socratics*. Indianapolis: Hackett.

Brandwood, L. 1992. 'Stylometry and Chronology.' In R. Kraut (ed.), 90–120.

Brickhouse, T. and Smith, N. 2018. 'Socrates on Punishment and the Law: *Apology* 25c5–26b2'. In M. Boeri, Y. Kanayama, and J. Mittelmann (eds), 37–53.

Brickhouse, T. C. and Smith, N. D. 1983. 'The Origin of Socrates' Mission.' *Journal of the History of Ideas* 44: 657–666.

— 1984a. 'Vlastos on the Elenchus.' *Oxford Studies in Ancient Philosophy* 2: 185–196.

— 1984b. 'The Paradox of Socratic Ignorance in Plato's *Apology*.' *History of Philosophy Quarterly* 1: 125–132.

— 1987. 'Socrates on Goods, Virtue, and Happiness.' *Oxford Studies in Ancient Philosophy* 5: 1–27.

— 1989a. 'A Matter of Life and Death in Socratic Philosophy.' *Ancient Philosophy* 9: 155–165.

— 1989b. *Socrates on Trial*. Oxford: Oxford University Press. Reprinted in 1990.

— 1990. 'What Makes Socrates a Good Man?' *Journal of the History of Philosophy* 28: 169–179.

— 1991. 'Socrates' Elenctic Mission.' *Oxford Studies in Ancient Philosophy* 13: 395–410.

— 1994. *Plato's Socrates*. Reprinted in 2004. Oxford: Oxford University Press.

— 1996. 'Socratic Ignorance and Skepticism.' *Skepsis* 7: 14–24.

— 1997a. 'Socrates and the Unity of Virtues.' *The Journal of Ethics* 4: 311–324.

— 1997b. 'The Problem of Punishment in Socratic Philosophy.' *Apeiron* 30: 95–107.

— 2000. *The Philosophy of Socrates*. Boulder, CO: Westview Press.

— 2002a. 'The Socratic *Elenchos*?' In G. A. Scott (ed.), 145–157.

— (eds) 2002b. *The Trial and Execution of Socrates: Sources and Controversies*. New York: Oxford University Press.

— 2004. *Routledge Philosophy Guidebook to Plato and the Trial of Socrates*. New York: Routledge.

— 2007a. 'Socrates on How Wrongdoing Damages the Soul.' *The Journal of Ethics* 11: 337–356.

— 2007b. 'Socrates on Akrasia, Knowledge, and the Power of Appearance.' In C. Bobonich and P. Destrée (eds), 1–17.

— 2010. *Socratic Moral Psychology*. Cambridge: Cambridge University Press.

— 2012a. 'Response to Critics.' *Analytic Philosophy* 53: 234–248.

— 2012b. 'Reply to Rowe.' *The Journal of Ethics* 16: 325–338.

— 2013a. 'Persuade or Obey.' *The Harvard Review of Philosophy* 19: 69–83.

BIBLIOGRAPHY

— 2013b. 'Socratic Moral Psychology.' In J. Bussanich and N. D. Smith (eds), 185–209.

— 2015. 'Socrates on the Emotions.' *Plato Journal: The Journal of the International Plato Society* 15: 9–28.

— 2017. 'Why Socrates Should Not Be Punished.' *History of Philosophy & Logical Analysis* 20: 53–64.

Brisson, L. 1989a. 'Alcibiade.' In R. Goulet (ed.), *Dictionnaire des philosophes antiques*. Vol. 1. Paris: Éditions CNRS, 100–101.

— 1989b. 'Aristodèmos d'Athènes.' In R. Goulet (ed.), *Dictionnaire des philosophes antiques*. Vol. 1. Paris: Éditions CNRS, 393–394.

— 1994. 'Chéréphon de Sphettos.' In R. Goulet (ed.). *Dictionnaire des philosophes antiques*. Vol. 2. Paris: Éditions CNRS, 304–305.

Broackes, J. 2009. '*ΑΥΤΟΣ ΚΑΘ᾽ΑΥΤΟΝ* in the *Clouds*: Was Socrates Himself a Defender of Separable Soul and Separate Forms?' *Classical Quarterly* 59: 46–59.

Broad, C. D. 1952. 'Egoism as a Theory of Human Motives.' In *Ethics and the History of Philosophy*, Volume 1. London: Routledge and Kegan Paul, 218–232.

Broadie, S. 2021. *Plato's Sun-Like Good: Dialectic in the Republic*. Cambridge: Cambridge University Press.

Bromberg, J. A. 2018. 'A Sage on the Stage: Socrates and Athenian Old Comedy.' In A. Stavru and C. Moore (eds), 31–62.

— 2019. 'Greek Tragedy and the Socratic Tradition.' In C. Moore (ed.), 41–74.

Brown, E. 2003. 'Knowing the Whole: Comments on Gill, 'Plato's *Phaedrus* and the Method of Hippocrates.' *The Modern Schoolman* 80: 315–323.

— 2022. 'Plato's Socrates and his Conception of Philosophy.' In Kraut and Ebrey (eds), 117–145.

Brown, E. and Shaw, J. C. forthcoming. 'Socrates and Coherent Desire.' In J. Shaw (ed.).

Brown, L. 2007. 'Glaucon: Challenge, Rational Egoism, and Ordinary Morality.' In D. Cairns and F.-G. Herrmann (eds), 42–60.

Bühler, W. (ed.) 1999. *Zenobii Athoi proverbia vulgari ceteraque memoria aucta*. Göttingen: Vandenhoeck & Ruprecht.

Burkert, W. 1985. *Greek Religion*. Cambridge: Harvard University Press.

Burnet, J. 1899–1907. *Platonis Opera*, 5. vols., Oxford: Clarendon Press.

— 1911. *Plato's* Phaedo. Oxford: Clarendon Press.

— 1916. 'The Socratic Doctrine of the Soul.' *Proceedings of the British Academy* 7 (1915–1916): 235–259.

— 1924. Plato's *Euthyphro, Apology of Socrates,* and *Crito*. Oxford: Oxford University Press.

— 1928. *Greek Philosophy: Thales to Plato*. London: Macmillan.

Burnyeat, M. F. 1977. 'Socratic Midwifery, Platonic Inspiration.' *Bulletin of the Institute of Classical Studies* 24: 7–16. Reprinted in H. H. Benson 1992, 53–65.

— 1997. 'The Impiety of Socrates.' *Ancient Philosophy* 17: 1–12.

— 2003 'Apology 30b 2–4: Socrates, Money, and the Grammar of "Gignesthai".' *Journal of Hellenic Studies* 123: 1–25.

Bury, J. B. 1940. 'The Life and Death of Socrates.' *Cambridge Ancient History*. Third Edition Vol. 5, ch. 13.4. Cambridge: Cambridge University Press, 386–397.

Bussanich, J. and Smith, N. D. (eds). 2013. *The Bloomsbury Companion to Socrates*. First Edition. London and New York: Bloomsbury Academic.

Butler, J. 1726/1841. *Fifteen Sermons Preached at the Rolls Chapel, to Which are Added Six Sermons Preached on Public Occasions*. New edition. London: Thomas Tegg.

Butler, T. 2012. 'Intellectualism in the *Phaedo*: Comments on Socratic Moral Psychology.' *Analytic Philosophy* 53 (2): 208–215.

Butrica, J. J. 2001. 'The Lost *Thesmophoriazusae* of Aristophanes.' *Phoenix* 55: 44–76.

Cairns, D. L. 1993. *Aidos: The Psychology and Ethics of Honour and Shame in Ancient Greek Literature*. Oxford, New York: Clarendon Press.

Cairns, D. L and Herrman, F.-G. (eds) 2007. *Pursuing the Good*. Edinburgh: Edinburgh University Press.

Cairns, F. 1972. *Generic Composition in Greek and Roman Poetry*. Edinburgh: Edinburgh University Press.

Calef, S. 1995. 'Piety and the Unity of Virtue in Euthyphro 11e–14c.' *Oxford Studies in Ancient Philosophy* 13: 1–26.

Callard, A. 2014. 'Ignorance and Akrasia-denial in the *Protagoras*.' *Oxford Studies in Ancient Philosophy* 47: 31–80.

Campbell, L. 1867. *The Sophistes and Politicus of Plato*. Oxford: Clarendon Press.

Candiotto, L. 2015. 'Aporetic State and Extended Emotions: The Shameful Recognition of Contradictions in the Socratic Elenchus.' *Etica & Politica/Ethics & Politics* 2: 233–248.

Canto-Sperber, M. and Pellegrin, P. (eds). 2002. *Le Style de la pensée: recueil de texts en homage à Jacques Brunschwig*. Paris: Les Belles Lettres.

Capra, A. 2001. *Ἀγὼν λόγων: il* Protagora *di Platone tra eristica e commedia*. Milano: Edizioni Universitarie di Lettere Economia e Diritto.

— 2016. 'Transcoding the Silenus: Aristophanes, Plato and the Invention of Socratic Iconography.' In M. Tulli and M. Erler (eds), 437–442.

— 2018. 'Aristophanes' Iconic Socrates.' In A. Stavru and C. Moore (eds), 64–82.

Carey, C. 2000. 'Old Comedy and the Sophists.' In D. Harvey and J. Wilkins (eds), 419–436.

Carone, G. R. 1998. 'Socrates' Human Wisdom and *Sophrōsunē* in Charmides 164c ff.' *Ancient Philosophy* 18: 267–286.

— 2004. 'Calculating Machines or Leaky Jars? The Moral Psychology of Plato's *Gorgias*.' *Oxford Studies in Ancient Philosophy* 26: 55–96.

— 2005. 'Plato's Stoic View of Motivation.' In R. Salles (ed.), 365–381.

Carpenter, M. and Polansky, R. M. 2002. 'Variety of Socratic Elenchi.' In G. A. Scott (ed.), 89–100.

Cartledge, P. 1985. 'The Greek Religious Festivals.' In P. E. Easterling and J. V. Muir (eds), 98–127.

— 2009. *Ancient Greek Political Thought in Practice*. Cambridge: Cambridge University Press.

Casanova, A. 2007. 'La difesa dell'educazione tradizionale nell'agone delle *Nuvole* di Aristofane.' In J. Fernández Delgado, F. Pordomingo and A. Stramaglia (eds), 84–95.

Cassio, A. C. (ed.) 1977. *Aristofane*. Banchettanti (Δαιταλῆς). *I frammenti*. Pisa: Giardini.

Catoni, M. L. and Giuliani, L. 2019. 'Socrates Represented: Why Does He Look Like a Satyr?' *Critical Inquiry* 45: 681–713.

Cerri, G. 2012. 'Le *Nuvole* di Aristofane e la realtà storica di Socrate.'. In F. Perusino and M. Colantonio (eds), 151–194.

Charalabopoulos, N. 2012. *Platonic Drama and its Ancient Reception*. Cambridge: Cambridge University Press.

Charles, D. 2006. 'Types of Definition in the *Meno*.' In L. Judson and V. Karasmanis (eds), 110–128.

Chroust, A.-H. 1957. *Socrates, Man and Myth: The Two Socratic Apologies of Xenophon*. Notre Dame, IN: University of Notre Dame Press.

Clark, J. C. 2022. *Plato's Dialogues of Definition: Causal and Conceptual Investigations*. Cham, Switzerland: Palgrave Macmillan.

BIBLIOGRAPHY

Clark, J. C. 2015. 'Socrates, the Primary Question, and the Unity of Virtue.' *Canadian Journal of Philosophy* 45: 445–470.

— 2018a. 'Knowledge and Temperance in Plato's *Charmides.' Pacific Philosophical Quarterly* 19, 763–789.

— 2018b. 'Socratic Inquiry and the "What is F?" Question.' *European Journal of Philosophy* 26: 1324–1342.

Cohen, D. 1983. *Theft in Athenian Law.* München: Beck.

Cohen, S. M. 1971. 'Socrates on the Definition of Piety: Euthyphro 10a–11b.' In G. Vlastos (ed.), 158–176.

Coliaco, J. 2001. *Socrates Against Athens.* London: Routledge.

Collins II, J. H. 2015. *Exhortations to Philosophy: The Protreptics of Plato, Isocrates, and Aristotle.* Oxford: Oxford University Press.

Collobert, C., Destrée, P. and Gonzalez, F. J. (eds). 2012. *Plato and Myth: Studies on the Use and Status of Platonic Myths* (*Mnemosyne* Supplements 337). First edition. Leiden: Brill.

Colson, D. 1989. 'Crito 51a–c: To What Does Socrates Owe Obedience?' *Phronesis* 34: 27–55.

— 1985. 'On Appealing to Athenian Law to Justify Socrates' Disobedience.' *Apeiron* 19, 133–151.

Compton-Engle, G. 2015. *Costume in the Comedies of Aristophanes.* Cambridge: Cambridge University Press.

Connor, W. R. 1991. 'The Other 399: Religion and the Trial of Socrates.' In M. A. Flower and M. Toher (eds), 49–56.

Cooper, J. G. 1749. *The Life of Socrates.* London: Dodsley.

Cooper, J. M. 1975. *Reason and the Human Good in Aristotle.* Cambridge, MA : Harvard University Press.

Cooper, J. M. 1982. 'The *Gorgias* and Plato's Socrates.' *Review of Metaphysics* 35: 577–587.

— (ed.). 1997. *Plato: Complete Works.* Indianapolis: Hackett.

— 1999. *Reason and Emotion: Essays on Ancient Moral Psychology and Ethical Theory.* Princeton: Princeton University Press.

Curd, P. 2007. *Anaxagoras of Clazomenae: Fragments and Testimonia.* Toronto, Buffalo and London: University of Toronto Press.

Curzer, H. J. 2014. 'Plato's Rejection of the Instrumental Account of Friendship in the *Lysis.' Polis* 31: 352–368.

Dancy, R. M. 2004. *Plato's Introduction of Forms.* Cambridge: Cambridge University Press.

— 2006. 'Platonic Definitions and Forms.' In H. H. Benson (ed.), 70–84.

Danzig, G. 2010. *Apologizing for Socrates: How Plato and Xenophon Created Our Socrates.* Lanham, MD: Lexington Books.

— 2017. 'Xenophon and the Socratic *Elenchos*: The Verbal Thrashing as a Tool for Instilling *Sophrōsunē.' Ancient Philosophy* 37: 293–318.

Danzig, G., Johnson, D. M. and Morrison, D. (eds). 2018. *Plato and Xenophon: Comparative Studies.* Leiden and Boston: Brill.

Davar, F. 1972. *Socrates and Christ.* Ahmedabad, India.

Davies, J. K. 1983. *Democracy and Classical Athens.* Stanford: Stanford University Press.

DeFilippo, J. G. and Mitsis, P. T. 1994b. 'Socrates and Stoic Natural Law.' In P. A. Vander Waerdt (ed.), 252–271.

Del Franco, F. (ed.) 1994. *Storia, poesia e pensiero nel mondo antico. Studi in onore di Marcello Gigante.* Napoli: Bibliopolis.

Deman, T. 1944. *Socrate et Jésus.* Paris: L'Artisan du livre.

Demont, P. 2012. 'Protagoras d'Abdère.' In R. Goulet (ed.), 1700–1708.

Denyer, N. 2001. *Plato: Alcibiades*. Cambridge Greek and Latin Classics. Cambridge: Cambridge University Press.

Derenne, E. 1930. *Les procès d'impiété intentés aux philosophes à Athènes au Vme et au IVme siècles avant J.-C.* Champion: Paris.

Deretić, I. 2020. 'Socrates Facing Death in the *Apology*.', *Theoria* 2, 5–16.

Deretić, I. & Smith, N. D. 2021. 'Socrates on Why the Belief that Death is a Bad Thing is io Ubiquitous and Intractable.' *The Journal of Ethics* 25: 107–122.

Desmond, W. 2008. *Cynics*. Stocksfield: Acumen.

Destrée, P. and Smith, N. (eds) 2005. 'Socrates' Divine Sign: Religion, Practice and Value in Socratic Philosophy.' *Apeiron* 38 (2).

Devereux, D. T. 1992. 'The Unity of the Virtues in Plato's *Protagoras* and *Laches*.' *Journal of the History of Philosophy* 101: 765–789.

— 1995. 'Socrates' Kantian Conception of Virtue.' *Journal of the History of Philosophy* 33 (3): 381–408.

— 2006. 'The Unity of the Virtues.' In H. H. Benson (ed.), 325–340.

— 2012. 'Comments on Socratic Moral Psychology.' *Analytic Philosophy* 53, 216–223.

Dimas, P. 2002. 'Happiness in the *Euthydemus*.' *Phronesis* 47: 1–27.

Dimas, P., Jones, R. E. and Lear, G. R. (eds). 2019. *Plato's* Philebus. Oxford: Oxford University Press.

Dodds, E. R. 1951. *The Greeks and the Irrational*. Berkeley: University of California Press.

— 1959. *Plato: Gorgias; A Revised Text with Introduction and Commentary*. Oxford: Clarendon Press.

Dorion, L.-A. 2003. '*Akrasia* et *enkrateia* dans les *Mémorables* de Xénophon.' *Dialogue* 42, 645–672.

— 2005. 'The *Daimonion* and the *Megalēgoria* of Socrates in Xenophon's *Apology*.' Translated by Matthew Brown, in N. Smith and P. Destrée (eds), 127–142.

— 2006. 'Xenophon's Socrates.' In S. Ahbel-Rappe and R. Kamtekar (eds), 93–109.

— 2010. 'The Straussian Exegesis of Xenophon: The Paradigmatic Case of *Memorabilia* IV 4.' In V. J. Gray (ed.), 283–323. Revised and expanded version of 'L'exégèse straussienne de Xénophon: le cas paradigmatique de Mémorables IV 4.' *Philosophie antique* 1, 2001, 87–118.

— 2011. 'The Rise and Fall of the Socratic Problem.' In D. Morrison (ed.), 1–23.

— 2013. *L'Autre Socrate. Études sur les écrits socratiques de Xénophon*. (L'Âne d'or 40.) Paris: Les Belles Lettres.

Dover, K. J. 1967. 'Portrait-Masks in Aristophanes.' In *Komoidotragemata: Studia Aristophanea Viri Aristophanei W. J. W. Koster in Honorem*. Amsterdam: Hakkert, 16–28.

— (ed.) 1968. *Aristophanes: Clouds*. Oxford: Clarendon.

— 1976. 'The Freedom of the Intellectual in Greek Society.' *Talanta* 7: 24–54.

— 1978. *Greek Homosexuality*. Cambridge, MA: Harvard University Press.

D'Souza, J. 2021. 'Altruistic Eudaimonism and the Self-Absorption Objection.' *Journal of Value Inquiry* 55, 475–490.

Dunn, J. 1996. *The History of Political Theory and Other Essays*. New York: Cambridge University Press.

Dupréel, E. 1922. 'La masque socratique.' In Id., *La légende socratique et les sources de Platon*. Bruxelles: Sand, 312–334.

Dybikowski, J. 1974. 'Socrates, Obedience and the Law: Plato's Crito.' *Dialogue* 13: 519–535.

Edmonds, J. M. (ed.). 1957. *The Fragments of Attic Comedy after Meineke, Bergk, and Kock*, vol. IIIa. Leiden: Brill.

BIBLIOGRAPHY 375

Edmonds, R. G. 2012. 'Whip Scars on the Naked Soul: Myth and Elenchos in Plato's Gorgias'. In C. Collobert, P. Destrée and F. J. Gonzalez (eds), 165–185.

Edmunds, L. 2004. 'The Practical Irony of the Historical Socrates.' *Phoenix* 58: 193–207.

— 2006. 'What Was Socrates Called?' *Classical Quarterly* 56: 414–425.

Edwards, F. G. 2016. 'How to Escape Indictment for Impiety: Teaching as Punishment in the *Euthyphro*.' *Journal of the History of Philosophy* 54: 1–19.

Egli, F. 2003. *Euripides im Kontext zeitgenössischer intellektueller Strömungen. Analyse der Funktion philosophischer Themen in den Tragödien und Fragmenten.* München and Leipzig: Saur.

Engstrom, S. 1996, 'Happiness and the Highest Good in Aristotle and Kant.' In S. Engstrom and J. Whiting (eds), 102–138.

Engstrom, S. and Whiting, J. (eds). 1996. *Aristotle, Kant, and the Stoics: Rethinking Happiness and Duty.* Cambridge: Cambridge University Press.

Erbse, H. 1954. 'Sokrates im Schatten der aristophanischen *Wolken*.' *Hermes* 82, 385–420.

Erler, M. and Tulli, M. (eds). 2016. *Plato in* Symposium. *Selected Papers from the Tenth Symposium Platonicum.* Sankt Augustin: Academia.

Everson, S. (ed.). 1990. *Companions to Ancient Thought: Epistemology.* Cambridge.

Fabrini, P. 1975. 'Sulla rappresentabilità delle *Nuvole* di Aristofane.' *Annali della Scuola Normale Superiore di Pisa. Classe di Lettere e Filosofia* 5, 1–16.

— 1989. 'Of Jealousy and Envy.' In G. Graham and H. LaFollette (eds), 245–268.

Ferejohn, M. 1982. 'The Unity of Virtue and the Objects of Socratic Inquiry.' *Journal of History of Philosophy* 20: 1–21.

— 1984. 'Socratic Virtue as the Parts of Itself.' *Philosophy and Phenomenological Research* 43: 377–388.

— 2013. *Formal Causes: Definition, Explanation, and Primacy in Socratic and Aristotelian Thought.* Oxford: Oxford University Press.

Fernández Delgado J., Pordomingo F., Stramaglia A. (eds). 2007. *Escuela y Literatura en Grecia Antigua. Actas del Simposio Internacional Universidad de Salamanca 17–19 Noviembre de 2004.* Cassino: Università degli Studi di Cassino.

Feugère, F. 1874. *De Socraticae doctrinae uestigiis apud Euripidem.* Dissertation, Paris.

Fierro, M. 2012. 'El residuo de lo irracional: reflexiones a propósito de algunos diálogos Platónicos.' In A. Lozano-Vásque (ed.), 51–80.

Fine, G. 1979. 'Knowledge and Logos in the Theaetetus.' *Philosophical Review* 88: 366–397.

— 1992. 'Inquiry in the *Meno*.' In R. Kraut (ed.), 200–226.

— 1993a. 'Vlastos on Socratic and Platonic Forms.' *Apeiron* 26, 67–83.

— 1993b. *On Ideas.* Oxford: Clarendon Press.

— 2003. *Plato on Knowledge and Forms.* Oxford: Clarendon Press.

— 2004. 'Knowledge and True Belief in Plato's *Meno*.' *Oxford Studies in Ancient Philosophy* 27, 41–82.

— (ed) 2008a. *The Oxford Handbook of Plato.* Oxford.

— 2008b. 'Does Socrates Claim to Know That He Knows Nothing?' *Oxford Studies in Ancient Philosophy* 35: 49–88.

— 2010. 'Signification, Essence, and Meno's Paradox: A Reply to David Charles's "Types of Definition in the *Meno*".' *Phronesis* 55: 125–152.

— 2014. *The Possibility of Inquiry.* Oxford: Oxford University Press.

FitzPatrick, P. J. 1992. 'The Legacy of Socrates.' In B. S. Gower and M. C. Stokes (eds), 153–208.

Flower, M. A. and Toher, M. (eds) 1991. *Georgica: Greek Studies in Honour of George Cawkwell*. London: University of London Press.

Fontenrose, J. 1978. *The Delphic Oracle*. Berkeley: University of California Press.

Foot, P. 1958. 'Moral Beliefs.' *Proceedings of the Aristotelian Society* New Series 59: 83–104.

Forster, M. 2006a. 'Socratic Refutation.' *Rhizai* 3, 7–57.

— 2006b. 'Socrates' Demand for Definitions.' *Oxford Studies in Ancient Philosophy* 31, 1–47.

— 2007. 'Socrates' Profession of Ignorance.' *Oxford Studies in Ancient Philosophy* 32, 1–35.

Frankfurt, H. G. 1998. 'On Caring.' In H. G. Frankfurt (ed.), *Necessity, Volition, and Love*. Cambridge: Cambridge University Press 1998. 155–180.

Friedland, M. L. (ed.). 1975. *Courts and Trials: A Multidiscplinary Approach*. Toronto: University of Toronto Press.

Friedländer, P. 1964. *Plato vol. 2 The Dialogues: First Period*. Princeton. Princeton University Press.

Fronterotta, F. 2007. 'The Development of Plato's Theory of Ideas and the "Socratic Question".' *Oxford Studies in Ancient Philosophy* 32: 37–62.

Gadamer, H.-G. 1980. *Dialogue and Dialectic: Eight Hermeneutical Studies on Plato*. Translated by P. C. Smith. New Haven, CT: Yale University Press.

Gagarin, M. and Woodruff, P. (eds). 1995. *Early Greek Political Thought from Homer to the Sophists*. Cambridge: Cambridge University Press.

Gaiser, K. 1959. *Protreptik und Paränese bei Platon: Untersuchungen zur Form des Platonischen Dialogs*. Stuttgart: W. Kohlhammer Verlag.

Gallo, I. 1983. 'Citazioni comiche nella *Vita Socratis* di Diogene Laerzio', *Vichiana* 12: 201–212.

Galy, J. 1979. 'Les Panoptes englottogastres ou les philosophes dans la comedie grecque des 5e et 4e siècles.' *Annales de la Faculté des lettres et sciences humaines de Nice* 35: 109–130.

Garland, R. 1992. *Introducing New Gods: The Politics of Athenian Religion*. Ithaca: Cornell University Press.

Geach, P. T. 1966. 'Plato's *Euthyphro*: An Analysis and Commentary.' *Monist* 50: 369–382.

Geissler, P. 1969. *Chronologie der altattischen Komödie*. Berlin: Weidmann.

Gelzer, T. 1956. 'Aristophanes und sein Sokrates.' *Museum Helveticum* 13: 65–93.

— 1960. *Der epirrhematische Agon bei Arsitophanes. Untersuchungen zur. Struktur der attischen alten Komödie*. München: Beck.

—1970. 'Aristophanes.' In W. Kroll (ed.) 1392–1569.

Gentzler, J. 1994. 'Recollection and "The Problem of the Socratic Elenchus".' *Proceedings of the Boston Area Colloquium in Ancient Philosophy* 10: 257–295.

Gerson, L. 1997. 'Socrates' Absolute Prohibition of Wrongdoing.' *Apeiron* 30: 1–11.

Gettier, E. L. 1963. 'Is Justified True Belief Knowledge?' *Analysis* 23: 121–123.

Gigon, O. 1946. 'Studien zu Platons *Protagoras*.' In Phyllobolia *für Peter von der Mühll zum 60. Geburtstag am 1. August 1945*. Basel: Schwabe, 91–152.

Glidden, D. K. 1981. 'The *Lysis* on Loving One's Own.' *Classical Quarterly* n.s. 31: 39–59.

Gomez-Lobo, A. 1994. *The Foundations of Socratic Ethics*. Indianapolis: Hackett Publishing Company.

Gonzalez, F. J. 1995. 'Plato's *Lysis*: An Enactment of Philosophical Kinship.' *Ancient Philosophy* 15: 69–90.

— 2000. 'Socrates on Loving One's Own: A Traditional Conception of *Philia* Radically Transformed.' *Classical Philology* 95: 379–398.

— 2002. 'The Socratic Elenchus as Constructive Protreptic.' In G. A. Scott (ed.), 161–183.

— 2003. 'How to Read a Platonic Prologue: *Lysis* 2013a–207d.' In A. N. Michelini (ed.), 15–44.

BIBLIOGRAPHY

Gosling, J. C. B. and Taylor, C. C. W. 1982. *The Greeks on Pleasure*. Oxford: Clarendon Press.

Goulet, R. (ed.). 2012. *Dictionnaire des philosophes antiques*. Vol. 5. Paris: Éditions CNRS.

Gower, B. S. and Stokes, M. C. (eds). 1992. *Socratic Questions*. London: Routledge.

Graham, D. 1991. 'Socrates, the Craft Analogy, and Science.' *Apeiron* 24: 1–24.

Graham, G. and La Follette, H. (eds). 1989. *Person to Person*. Philadelphia: Temple University Press.

Gray, V. J. 1998. *The Framing of Socrates: The Literary Interpretation of Xenophon's Memorabilia*. (Hermes-Einzelschriften 79.) Stuttgart: Franz Steiner Verlag.

— (ed.). 2010. *Oxford Readings in Classical Studies: Xenophon*. Oxford: Oxford University Press.

Green, M. and Williams, J. N. (eds). 2007. *Moore's Paradox: New Essays on Belief, Rationality, and the First Person*. Oxford: Oxford University Press.

Greenberg, N. A. 1964. 'Socrates' Choice in *Crito*.' *Harvard Studies in Classical Philology* 70: 45–82.

Grey, W. R. 1896. *The Treatment of Philosophy and Philosophers by the Greek Comic Poets*. Dissertation, Johns Hopkins.

Grilli, A. and Morosi, F. (eds). 2020-2-21. *Il mondo di Aristofane. Forme e problemi della commedia attica antica*, *Dioniso* (special double issue) 10–11.

Griswold, C. (ed.). 1988. *Platonic Readings, Platonic Writings*. New York: Routledge.

— 2011. 'Socrates' Political Philosophy.' In D. R. Morrison (ed.), 333–354.

Grote, G. 1849. *A History of Greece*. London: Lewis and Co.

— 1865. *Plato and the Other Companions of Socrates*. Vols. 1–3. London: John Murray.

— 1888. *Plato and Other Companions of Sokrates*, third edition. London: John Murray.

Grube, G. M. A., translation Plato, *Euthyphro*. In J. Cooper (ed.), 2–16.

Guidorizzi, G. and Del Corno, D. (eds). 1996. *Aristofane. Le Nuvole*. Milano: Mondadori.

Gulley, N. 1968. *The Philosophy of Socrates*. London: Macmillan.

Guthrie, W. K. C. 1969–1978. *History of Greek Philosophy* Vols. 3–5. Cambridge: Cambridge University Press.

— 1971. *Socrates*. Cambridge: Cambridge University Press.

— 1975. *History of Greek Philosophy*. Vol. 4: *Plato: The Man and his Dialogues: Earlier Period*. Cambridge: Cambridge University Press.

— 1977. *The Sophists*. Cambridge: Cambridge University Press.

Hackforth, R. 1933. *The Composition of Plato's Apology*. Cambridge: Cambridge University Press.

Halperin, D. M. 1990. *One Hundred Years of Homosexuality and Other Essays on Greek Love*. London and New York: Routledge.

Hampton, J. 1984. 'The Moral Education Theory of Punishment.' *Philosophy and Public Affairs* 13, 208–238.

Hardy, J. 2010. 'Seeking the Truth and Taking Care for Common Goods – Plato on Expertise and Recognizing Experts.' *Episteme* 7: 7–22.

Harte, V. 1999. 'Conflicting Values in Plato's *Crito*.' *Archiv für Geschichte der Philosophie* 81: 117–147.

Harvey, D. and Wilkins, J. (eds). 2000. *The Rivals of Aristophanes*. London: Duckworth and The Classical Press of Wales.

Havelock, E. A. 1972. 'The Socratic Self as It Is Parodied in Aristophanes' *Clouds*.' *Yale Classical Studies* 22: 1–18.

Haybron, D. 2010. *The Pursuit of Unhappiness: The Elusive Psychology of Well-Being*. Oxford: Oxford University Press.

Heidel, W. A. 1900. 'On Plato's Euthyphro.' *Transactions of the American Philological Society* 31: 164–181.

Heidhues, B. 1897. *Über die* Wolken *des Aristopjanes*. Köln: Beilage zum Progamm des Koniglichen Friedrich-Wilhelms-Gymansiums zu Köln 449.

Henderson, J. 1991. *The Maculate Muse: Obscene Language in Attic Comedy*. New York and Oxford: Oxford University Press.

Hobden, F. and Tuplin, C. (eds). 2012. *Xenophon: Ethical Principles and Historical Enquiry*. (Mnemosyne Supplements 348.) Leiden and Boston: Brill.

Hoerber, R. G. 1959. 'Plato's "Lysis".' *Phronesis* 4: 15–28.

Hoesly, D. and Smith, N. D. 2013. 'Thrasymachus: Diagnosis and Treatment.' In N. Notomi and L. Brisson (eds), 188–194.

Hubbard, T. K. 1986. 'Parabatic Self-Criticism and the Two Versions of Aristophanes' *Clouds*.' *Classical Antiquity* 5, 182–197.

Hurka, T. 2013. 'Aristotle on Virtue: Wrong, Wrong, and Wrong.' In J. Peters (ed.), 9–26.

Hursthouse, R. 1999. *On Virtue Ethics*. Oxford: Oxford University Press.

Hutchinson, D. S. and Johnson, M. R. 2005. 'Authenticating Aristotle's *Protrepticus*.' *Oxford Studies in Ancient Philosophy* 29: 193–294.

Imperio, O. 1998a. 'La figura dell'intellettuale nella commedia greca.' In Belardinelli, A. M., Imperio, O., Mastromarco, G., Pellegrino, M. and Totaro, P. (eds), 43–130.

— 1998b. 'Callia.' In Belardinelli, A. M., Imperio, O., Mastromarco, G., Pellegrino, M., and Totaro, P. (eds), 195–254.

Inwood, M. 2009. 'Plato's Eschatological Myths.' In C. Partenie (ed.), 1–27.

Irwin, T. H. 1974. 'Review of Leo Strauss, *Xenophon's Socrates*.' *The Philosophical Review* 83: 409–413.

— 1977. *Plato's Moral Theory: The Early and Middle Dialogues*. Oxford: Clarendon Press.

— 1979 (ed.). *Plato: Gorgias*. Oxford: Clarendon Press.

— 1983. 'Euripides and Socrates.' *Classical Philology* 78: 183–197.

— 1986. 'Socrates the Epicurean?' *Illinois Classical Studies* 11: 85–112.

— 1995. *Plato's Ethics*. Oxford: Oxford University Press.

Irwin, T. H. and Nussbaum, M. C. 1994. *Virtue, Love and Form: Essays in Memory of Gregory Vlastos*. Edmonton: Academic Printing and Publishing.

Jackson, B. D. 1971. 'The Prayers of Socrates.' *Phronesis* 16: 14–37.

Janko, R. 2006. 'Socrates the Freethinker.' In S. Ahbel-Rappe and R. Kamtekar (eds), 48–62.

Jenks, R. 2005. 'Varieties of *Philia* in Plato's *Lysis*.', *Ancient Philosophy* 25: 65–80.

Jirsa, J. 2009. 'Authenticity of the *Alcibiades I*: Some Reflections.' *Listy filologické* 132: 225–44.

Joël, K. 1893/1901. *Der echte und der xenophontische Sokrates*. 2 vols (in 3 parts). Berlin: Gaertners.

Johnson, C. N. 1989. 'Socrates' Encounter With Polus in Plato's *Gorgias*.' *Phoenix* 43: 196–216.

— 1990. 'Socrates on Obedience and Justice.' *Western Political Quarterly* 43: 719–740.

— 1992. 'The "Craft" of Plato's Philosopher-Rulers.' *Politikos* 2: 108–126.

— 2005. *Socrates and the Immoralists*. Lanham: Lexington Books.

— 2013. 'Socrates' Political Philosophy.' In J. Bussanich and N. D. Smith (eds), 233–256.

Johnson, D. M. 2005. 'Xenophon's Socrates at his Most Socratic (*Mem.* 4.2.).' *Oxford Studies in Ancient Philosophy* 29: 39–73.

— 2012. 'Strauss on Xenophon.' In F. Hobden and C. Tuplin (eds), 123–159.

— 2021. *Xenophon's Socratic Works*. London and New York: Routledge.

BIBLIOGRAPHY

Jones, R. E. 2012. 'Rational and Nonrational Desires in *Meno* and *Protagoras.*' *Analytic Philosophy* 53: 224–233.

— 2013a. 'Wisdom and Happiness in *Euthydemus* 278–282.' *Philosophers' Imprint* 13 (14).

— 2013b. 'Felix Socrates?' *Philosophia* 43: 77–98.

— 2016. 'Socrates' Bleak View of the Human Condition.' *Ancient Philosophy* 36: 97–105.

— 2019a. 'Cooking up the Good Life with Socrates.' In P. Dimas, R. E. Jones and G. R. Lear (eds), 235–252.

— 2019b. 'The Real Challenge of Plato's *Republic.*' *Ancient Philosophy Today* 1: 149–170.

Jones, R. E. and Sharma, R. 2017. 'The Wandering Hero of the *Hippias Minor*: Socrates on Virtue and Craft.' *Classical Philology* 112: 113–37.

— 2018. 'Virtue and Self-Interest in Xenophon's *Memorabilia* 3.9.4–5.' *The Classical Quarterly* 68: 79–90.

— 2019. 'Xenophon's Socrates on Harming Enemies.' *Ancient Philosophy* 39: 253–265.

— 2020. 'Xenophon's Socrates on Justice and Well-being: *Memorabilia* 4.2.' *Ancient Philosophy* 40: 19–40.

Joyal, M. 2003. 'Review of Denyer 2001.' *Bryn Mawr Classical Review*, 01.28.

Judet de La Combe, P. 2006. 'Strepsiade présocratique. Petites réflexions sur la grandeur de la bêtise dans les *Nuées.*' *Dioniso* 5: 54–69.

Judson, L. and Karasmanis, V. (eds). 2006. *Remembering Socrates: Philosophical Essays.* Oxford: Clarendon Press.

Kahn, C. H. 1983. 'Drama and Dialectic in Plato's *Gorgias.*' *Oxford Studies in Ancient Philosophy* 1: 75–121.

— 1985. 'The Beautiful and the Genuine: A Discussion of Paul Woodruff's Plato: *Hippias Major.*' *Oxford Studies in Ancient Philosophy* 3: 261–287.

— 1989. in T. Penner and R. Kraut (eds), 29–44.

— 1996. *Plato and the Socratic Dialogue: The Philosophical Use of a Literary Form.* Cambridge: Cambridge University Press.

— 2002. 'On Platonic Chronology.' In J. Annas and C. Rowe (eds), 93–127.

Kamtekar, R. 2006. 'Plato on the Attribution of Conative Attitudes.' *Archiv für Geschichte der Philosophie* 88: 127–162.

— 2012. 'Review: Socrates and the Psychology of Virtue (review of Brickhouse and Smith, *Socratic Moral Psychology* and Iakovos Vasiliou, *Aiming at Virtue in Plato*).' *Classical Philology* 107 (3): 256–270.

— 2016. 'The Soul's (After-) Life.' *Ancient Philosophy* 36: 115–132.

— 2017a. 'Plato's Ethical Psychology.' In C. Bobonich (ed.), 72–85.

— 2017b. *Plato's Moral Psychology: Intellectualism, the Divided Soul, and the Desire for Good.* Oxford: Oxford University Press.

Kanavou, N. 2011. *Aristophanes' Comedy of Names: A Study of Speaking Names in Aristophanes.* Berlin and New York: Walter de Gruyter.

Karasmanis, V. (ed.) 2004. *Socrates 2400 Years After His Death (399 B.C.–2001 A.D.).* Athens: European Cultural Centre of Delphi.

Kaufmann, W. 1951. 'Socrates and Christ.' *Harvard Studies in Classical Philology* 60: 205–233.

Kerferd, G. B. 1974. 'Plato's Treatment of Callicles in the *Gorgias.*' *Proceedings of the Cambridge Philological Society* 20: 48–52.

— 1981. *The Sophistic Movement.* Cambridge: Cambridge University Press.

Keuls, E. C. 1993. *The Reign of the Phallus: Sexual Politics in Ancient Athens.* Berkeley, Los Angeles and Oxford: University of California Press.

Kim, A. 2011. 'Crito and Critique.' *Oxford Studies in Ancient Philosophy* 41: 67–113.

Klosko, G. 1981. 'The Technical Conception of Virtue.' *Journal of the History of Philosophy* 19: 98–106.

Kolodny, N. 2003. 'Love as Valuing a Relationship.' *The Philosophical Review* 112: 135–189.

Konstan, D. 2006. *The Emotions of the Ancient Greeks: Studies in Aristotle and Classical Literature.* Toronto, Buffalo and London: University of Toronto Press.

— 2011. 'Socrates in Aristophanes' *Clouds.*' In D. Morrison (ed.), 75–90.

Kosman, L. A. 1976. 'Platonic Love.' In W. H. Werkmeister (ed.), 53–69.

Kraut, R. 1979. 'Two Conceptions of Happiness.' *The Philosophical Review* 88: 167–197.

— 1980/81. 'Plato's *Apology* and *Crito*: Two Recent Studies.' *Ethics* 91: 651–664.

— 1983. 'Comments on Gregory Vlastos, 'The Socratic Elenchus'.' *Oxford Studies in Ancient Philosophy* 1: 59–70.

— 1984. *Socrates and the State.* Princeton: Princeton University Press.

— 1989. *Aristotle on the Human Good.* Princeton: Princeton University Press.

— (ed.) 1992. *The Cambridge Companion to Plato.* Cambridge: Cambridge University Press.

— 2000. 'Socrates, Politics, and Religion.' In N. D. Smith and P. Woodruff (eds), 13–23.

— 2018. *The Quality of Life: Aristotle Revised.* Oxford: Oxford University Press.

Kraut, R and Ebrey, D. (eds). 2022. *The Cambridge Companion to Plato.* Cambridge: Cambridge University Press.

Kroll, W. (ed.). 1970. *Paulys Real-Encyclopädie.* Suppl. 12. Stuttgart: Metzler.

LaBarge, S. 1997. 'Socrates and the Recognition of Experts.' *Apeiron* 30, 51–62.

— 2005. 'Socrates and Moral Expertise.' In L. M. Rasmussen (ed.), 15–38.

Laks, A. and Saetta Cottone, R. (eds). 2013. *Comédie et philosophie. Socrate et les 'Présocratiques' dans les* Nuées *d'Aristophane.* Paris: Éditions Rue d'Ulm.

Lamari, A. A. 2017. *Reperforming Greek Tragedy: Theater, Politics, and Cultural Mobility in the Fifth and Fourth Centuries BC.* Berlin and Boston: de Gruyter.

Lapatin, K. 2006. 'Picturing Socrates.' In S. Ahbel-Rappe and R. Kamtekar (eds), 110–155.

Lefkowitz, M. 2016. 'Euripides, Socrates and Other Sophists.' in Id., *Euripides and the Gods.* New York: Oxford University Press, 24–48.

Lenfant, D. 2002. 'Protagoras et son procès d'impieté: peut-on soutenir une thèse et son contraire?' *Ktema* 27, 135–145.

Lesher, J. H. 1987. 'Socrates' Disavowal of Knowledge.' *Journal of the History of Philosophy* 25: 275–288.

— 2002. 'Parmenidean *Elenchos.*' In G. A. Scott (ed.), 19–35.

Lesses, G. 1982. 'Virtue as Technē in the Early Dialogues.' *Southwest Philosophical Studies* 13: 93–100.

— 1996. 'Plato's *Lysis* and Irwin's Socrates.' In W. J. Prior (ed.) 1996, 33–43.

Levin, D. N. 1971. 'Some Observations Concerning Plato's *Lysis.*' In J. P. Anton and G. L. Kustas (eds), 236–258.

Lewis, D. 1996. 'Elusive Knowledge.' *Australasian Journal of Philosophy* 74: 549–567.

Littman, R. J. 1970. 'The Loves of Alcibiades.' *Transactions and Proceedings of the American Philological Association* 101: 263–276.

Litz, B., Stein, N., Delaney, E., Lebowitz, L., Nash, W., Silva, C. and Maguen, S. 2009. 'Moral Injury and Moral Repair in War Veterans: A Preliminary Model and Intervention Strategy.' *Clinical Psychology Review* 29: 695–706.

Lloyd, G. E. R. 1966. *Polarity and Analogy, Two Types of Argumentation in Early Greek Thought.* Cambridge: Cambridge University Press.

Lloyd-Jones, H. 1971. *The Justice of Zeus.* Berkeley: University of California Press.

BIBLIOGRAPHY

Lockwood, T. C. 2017. 'Do Lysis' Parents Really Love Him? Non-Argumentative Arguments in Plato's *Lysis*.' *Ancient Philosophy* 37: 319–332.

Long, A. A. 1988. 'Socrates in Hellenistic Philosophy.' *Classical Quarterly* n.s. 38, 150–171. Reprinted with postscript in A. A. Long 1996, *Stoic Studies*, 1–34.

Long, A. G. 2019. *Death and Immortality in Ancient Philosophy*. Cambridge: Cambridge University Press.

López Eire, A. (ed.). 1997. *Sociedad, política y literatura: comedia griega antigua: actas del I Congreso Internacional*. Salamanca: Logo.

Lozano-Vásque, A. (ed.). 2012. *Platón y la irracionalidad*. Ediciones Uniandes: Universidad de los Andes.

MacDowell, D. M. 1978. *The Law in Classical Athens*. Ithaca, NY: Cornell University Press.

— 1995. *Aristophanes and Athens: An Introduction to the Plays*. Oxford: Oxford University Press.

Mackenzie, M. M. 1981. *Plato on Punishment*. Berkeley, Los Angeles and London: University of California Press.

— 1988. 'Impasse and Explanation: From the *Lysis* to the *Phaedo*.' *Archiv für Geschichte der Philosophie* 70: 15–45.

Maier, H. 1913. *Sokrates: sein Werk und seine geschichtliche Stellung*. Tübingen: J. C. B. Mohr.

Major, W. E. 2006. 'Aristophanes and *Alazoneia*: Laughing at the Parabasis of the *Clouds*.' *The Classical World* 99: 131–144.

Manuwald, B. 2005. 'The Unity of Virtue in Plato's *Protagoras*.' *Oxford Studies in Ancient Philosophy* 29: 115–135.

Marchant, E. C. 1921. *Xenophontis Opera Omnia*. Vol. 2 (Oxford Classical Texts). 2nd ed. [1st ed. 1901.] Oxford: Oxford University Press.

Marchant, E. C., Todd, O. J. and Henderson, J. 2013. *Xenophon. Memorabilia, Oeconomicus, Symposium, Apology*. (Loeb Classical Library 168.) Revision of 1st edition by Marchant and Todd, 1923.

Marshall, C. W. 1999. 'Some Fifth-Century Masking Conventions.' *Greece & Rome* 46: 188–202.

Marshall, C. W. and Kovacs, G. (eds). 2012. *No Laughing Matter: Studies in Athenian Comedy*. London: Bloomsbury.

Marshall, H. R. 2012. '*Clouds*, Eupolis and Reperformance.' In C. W. Marshall and G. Kovacs (eds), 63–76.

Martin, R. 1970. 'Socrates on Disobedience to Law.' *Review of Metaphysics* 24: 21–38.

Martinez, J. A. and Smith, N. D. 2018. 'Socrates' Aversion to Being a Victim of Injustice.' *Journal of Ethics* 22: 59–76.

Marzullo, B. 1953. 'Stepsiade.' *Maia* 6: 99–124.

Matthews, G. 1999. *Socratic Perplexity and the Nature of Philosophy*. Oxford: Oxford University Press.

— 2006. 'Socratic Ignorance.' In H. H. Benson (ed.), 103–118.

— 2008. 'The Epistemology and Metaphysics of Socrates.' In G. Fine (ed.), 114–138.

McLaughlin, Robert J. 1976. 'Socrates on Political Disobedience.' In *Phronesis* 21: 185–197.

— 2007. 'The Socratic Corpus: Socrates and Physiognomy.' In M. Trapp (ed.), 65–88.

McLean, D. R. 2002. *Refiguring Socrates: Comedy and Corporeality in the Socratic Tradition*. Dissertation, University of Pennsylvania.

McLean, D. R. 2007. 'The Socratic Corpus: Socrates and Physiognomy.' In M. Trapp (ed.), 65–88.

McPherran, M. L. 1985. 'Socratic Piety in the *Euthyphro.' Journal of the History of Philosophy* 23, 283–309. Reprinted in H. H. Benson 1992, 220–241; and in W. J. Prior (ed.) 1996, Vol. 2, 118–143.

— 1988. 'Commentary on Paul Woodruff's "Expert Knowledge in the *Apology* and *Laches*: What a General Needs to Know".' *Proceedings of the Boston Area Colloquium in Ancient Philosophy* 3: 116–130.

— 1991. 'Socratic Reason and Socratic Revelation.' *Journal of the History of Philosophy* 29, 345–374. Reprinted in W. J. Prior (ed.), 1996, v 2, 167–194.

— 1996. *The Religion of Socrates*. University Park, PA: The Pennsylvania State University Press.

— (ed.). 1997. *Wisdom, Ignorance, and Virtue: New Essays in Socratic Studies*. Edmonton: Academic Printing and Publishing.

— 2000. 'Piety, Justice, and the Unity of Virtue.' *The Journal of the History of Philosophy* 38: 299–328.

— 2002. 'Elenctic Interpretation and the Delphic Oracle.' In G. A. Scott (ed.), 114–144.

— 2003b. 'Socrates, Crito, and Their Debt to Asclepius.' *Ancient Philosophy* 23: 71–92.

— 2003b. 'The Aporetic Interlude and Fifth Elenchos of Plato's Euthyphro.' *Oxford Studies in Ancient Philosophy* 25: 1–37.

— 2005. '"What Even a Child Would Know": Socrates, Luck, and Providence at *Euthydemus* 277d–282e.' *Ancient Philosophy* 25: 1–15.

— 2007. 'Socratic *Epagōgē* and Socratic Induction.' *Journal of the History of Philosophy* 45: 347–364.

Meynersen, O. 1993. 'Der Manteldiebstahl des Sokrates (Ar. *Nub*. 175–9).' *Mnemosyne* 46: 18–32.

Michelini, A. N. (ed.) 2003. *Plato as Author: The Rhetoric of Philosophy*. Brill: Leiden.

Mikalson, J. D. 2010. *Greek Popular Religion in Greek Philosophy*. Oxford: Oxford University Press.

Miller, M. 1996. '"The Arguments I Seem to Hear": Argument and Irony in the *Crito*.' *Phronesis* 41: 121–137.

Möbus, F. 2023. 'Can Flogging Make Us Less Ignorant? Socrates on Bodily Punishment.' *Ancient Philosophy* 43: 51–68.

Moline, J. 1975. 'Euripides, Socrates and Virtue.' *Hermes* 103, 45–67.

Mondolfo, R. 1956. *Alle origini della filosofia della cultura*. Bologna: Il mulino.

Montgomery, J. D. (ed.). 1954. *The State Versus Socrates: A Case Study in Civic Freedom*. Boston: Beacon Press.

Montuori, M. 1966. 'Socrate tra *Nuvole prime* e *Nuvole seconde*', Atti dell'Accademia di Scienze Morali e Politiche della Società Nazionale di Scienze, Lettere ed Arti in Napoli 77: 3–56.

— 1981a. *Socrates: Physiology of a Myth*. Amsterdam: J. Gieben.

— 1981b. *De Socrate Juste Damnato: The Rise of the Socratic Problem in the Eighteenth Century*. Amsterdam: J. Gieben.

Moore, C. 2013. 'Chaerephon the Socratic.' *Phoenix* 67: 284–300.

— (ed.). 2019. *Brill's Companion to the Reception of Socrates*. Leiden: Brill.

Moore, G. E. 1962. *Commonplace Book 1919–1953*. London: Allen and Unwin.

Moravcsik, J. 1979. 'Understanding and Knowledge in Plato's Philosophy.' *Neue Hefte für Philosophie* 15/16: 53–69.

Morrison, D. 1987. 'On Professor Vlastos' Xenophon.' *Ancient Philosophy* 7: 9–22.

— 1994. 'Xenophon's Socrates as Teacher.' In Vander Waerdt (ed.), 181–208.

— 1995. 'Xenophon's Socrates on the Just and the Lawful.' *Ancient Philosophy* 15: 329–347.

BIBLIOGRAPHY

— 2003. 'Happiness, Rationality, and Egoism in Plato's Socrates.' In J. Yu and J. J. Garcia (eds), 17–34.

— 2010. 'Xenophon's Socrates on Sophia and the Virtues.' In L. Rossetti and A. Stavru (eds), 227–240.

— (ed.). 2011. *The Cambridge Companion to Socrates*. Cambridge: Cambridge University Press.

Moss, J. 2005. 'Shame, Pleasure, and the Divided Soul.' *Oxford Studies in Ancient Philosophy* 29: 137–170.

— 2007. 'The Doctor and the Pastry Chef: Pleasure and Persuasion in Plato's *Gorgias*.' *Ancient Philosophy* 27: 229–249.

— 2014. 'Hedonism and the Divided Soul in Plato's *Protagoras*.' *Archiv für Geschichte der Philosophie* 96 (3): 285–319.

Mourelatos. A. 2013. 'Xénophane et son "Astro-néphologie" dans les *Nuées*.' In A. Laks and R. Saetta Cottone (eds), 31–60.

Murphy, J. G. 1974. 'Violence and the Socratic Theory of Legal Fidelity.' In P. Wiener and J. Fisher (eds), 15–33.

— 1976. 'Rationality and the Fear of Death.' *The Monist* 59, 187–203.

Murray, G. 1993. *Aristophanes: A Study*. Oxford: Clarendon.

Nails, D. 2002. *The People of Plato: A Prosopography of Plato and Other Socratics*. Indianapolis and Cambridge: Hackett.

— 2006. 'The Trial and Death of Socrates.' In S. Ahbel-Rappe and R. Kamtekar 2006, 5–20.

Napolitano, M. 2012. *I Kolakes Di Eupoli: Introduzione, Traduzione, Commento*. Mainz: Verlag Antike.

Napolitano Valditara, L. M. (ed.). 2020 *Curare le emozioni, curare con le emozioni*. Milano and Udine: Mimesis.

Navia, L. E. 1984. *Socrates: The Man and His Philosophy*. Lanham, MD: University Press of America.

Nehamas, A. 1975. 'Confusing Universals and Particulars in Plato's Early Dialogues.' *Review of Metaphysics* 29: 287–306.

— 1987. 'Socratic Intellectualism.' *Proceedings of the Boston Area Colloquium in Ancient Philosophy* 2: 275–316.

— 1992. 'What Did Socrates Teach and to Whom Did He Teach It?' *Review of Metaphysics* 46: 279–306.

Nestle, W. 1940. *Vom Mythos zum Logos*. Stuttgart: Kröner.

Neu, J. 1980. 'Jealous Thoughts.' In Rorty (ed.), 425–463.

Neukam, P. (ed.). 1993. *Motiv und Motivation*. Munich: Bayerische Schulbuch-Verlag.

Newiger, H.-J. 1957. *Aristophanes und die alte Komödie*. München: Beck.

Nichols, M. P. 2009. *Socrates on Friendship and Community*. Cambridge: Cambridge University Press.

Nicolai, R. (ed.). 2003. *ΡΥΣΜΟΣ. Studi di poesia, metrica e musica greca offerti dagli allievi a Luigi Enrico Rossi per i suoi settant'anni*. Rome: Quasar.

Nightingale, A. W. 1995. *Genres in Dialogue: Plato and the Construct of Philosophy*. New York: Cambridge University Press.

Nightingale, A. W. and Sedley, D. (eds). 2010. *Ancient Models of the Mind*. Cambridge: Cambridge University Press.

North, H. 1966. *Sophrosyne: Self-Knowledge and Self-Restraint in Greek Literature*. Ithaca, NY: Cornell University Press.

Notomi, N. 2013. 'A Protagonist of the Sophistic Movement? Protagoras in Historiography.' In J. M. van Ophuijsen, M. van Raalte and P. Stork (eds), 11–36.

Notomi, N. and Brisson, L. (eds). 2013. *Dialogues on Plato's 'Politeia' ('Republic')*: Selected Papers from the Ninth Symposium Platonicum. Sankt August in: Academia Verlag.

Nussbaum, M. 1980. 'Aristophanes and Socrates on Learning Practical Wisdom.' *Yale Classical Studies* 26: 43–97.

— 1985. 'Commentary on Edmunds.' *Proceedings of the Boston Area Colloquium in Ancient Philosophy* 1: 231–240.

Obdrzalek, S. 2010. 'Moral Transformation and the Love of Beauty in Plato's *Symposium*.' *Journal of the History of Philosophy* 48: 415–444.

— 2012. 'Contemplation and Self-Mastery in Plato's *Phaedrus*.' *Oxford Studies in Ancient Philosophy* 42: 77–107.

Ober, J. 1998. *Political Dissent in Democratic Athens: Intellectual Critics of Popular Rule*. Princeton: Princeton University Press.

— 2011. 'Socrates and Democratic Athens.' In D. R. Morrison (ed.), 138–178.

O'Brien, D. 2003. 'Socrates and Protagoras on Virtue.' *Oxford Studies in Ancient Philosophy* 24: 59–131.

Olson, D. 2007. *Broken Laughter: Select Fragments of Greek Comedy*. Oxford: Oxford University Press.

— 2021. *Aristophanes' Clouds: A Commentary*. Ann Arbor: University of Michigan Press.

O'Regan, D. E. 1992. *Rhetoric, Comedy, and the Violence of Language in Aristophanes' Clouds*. New York and Oxford: Oxford University Press.

Orth, C. 2013. *Alkaios – Apollophanes. Einleitung, Übersetzung, Kommentar*. Heidelberg: Verlag Antike.

Ostwald, M. 1986. *From Popular Sovereignty to the Sovereignty of the Law: Law, Society, and Politics in Fifth Century Athens*. Berkeley: University of California Press.

Pangle, T. L. 2018. *The Socratic Way of Life: Xenophon's* Memorabilia. Chicago: The University of Chicago Press.

— 2020. *Socrates Founding Political Philosophy in Xenophon's* Economist, Symposium, *and* Apology. Chicago: The University of Chicago Press.

Papageorgiou, N. 2004. 'Prodicus and the Agon of the Logoi in Aristophanes' *Clouds*.' *Quaderni Urbinati Di Cultura Classica* 78: 61–69.

Parke, H. W. and Wormell, D. E. W. 1956. *The Delphic Oracle*. Oxford: Basil Blackwell.

Parker, R. 1996. *Athenian Religion: A History*. Oxford: Clarendon Press.

Parry, R. 1983. 'The Craft of Justice.' *Canadian Journal of Philosophy* 4: 19–38.

— 1996. *Plato's Craft of Justice*. Albany: State University of New York Press.

— 2003. 'The Craft of Ruling in Plato's *Euthydemus* and *Republic*.' *Phronēsis* 48: 1–28.

Partenie, C. (ed.), 2009. *Plato's Myths*. Cambridge: Cambridge University Press.

Paton, W. R. (ed.) 1916. *The Greek Anthology*. Book 1–6. Cambridge, MA: Harvard University Press.

Patzer, A. 1993. 'Die *Wolken* des Aristophanes als philosophiegeschichtliches Dokument'. In P. Neukam (ed.), 72–93.

— 1994. 'Sokrates in den Fragmenten der Attischen Komödie.' In A. Bierl and P. von Möllendorff (eds), 50–81.

— 1998. 'Sokrates in der Tragödie.' *Würzburger Jahrbücher für die Altertumswissenschaft* 22: 33–45.

— 2006. 'Sokrates und Archelaos: historische und fiktionale Texte über den jungen Sokrates.' In W. von der Weppen and B. Zimmermann (eds), 9–56.

— 2012. 'Sokrates in den *Vögeln* und in den *Fröschen* des Aristophanes.' In Id., *Studia Socratica: Zwölf Abhandlungen über den historischen Sokrates*. Tübingen: Narr, 54–63.

BIBLIOGRAPHY

Penner, T. 1973. 'The Unity of the Virtues.' *Philosophical Review* 82: 35–68.

— 1990. 'Plato and Davidson: Parts of the Soul and Weakness of Will.' *Canadian Journal of Philosophy* (Supplementary Volume 16): 35–74.

— 1991. 'Desire and Power in Socrates: The Argument of *Gorgias* 466a–468e that Orators and Tyrants have no Power in the City.' *Apeiron* 24 (3): 147–202.

— 1992a. 'Socrates and the Early Dialogues'. In R. Kraut (ed.), 121–169.

— 1992b. 'What Laches and Nicias Miss – and Whether Socrates Thinks Courage is Merely a Part of Virtue.' *Ancient Philosophy* 12: 1–27.

— 1996. 'Knowledge vs True Belief in the Socratic Psychology of Action.' *Apeiron* 29: 199–230.

— 1997. 'Socrates and the Strength of Knowledge: *Protagoras* 351B–357E.' *Archiv für Geschichte der Philosophie* 79: 117–149.

— 2000. 'Socrates.' In C. Rowe and M. Schofield (eds), 164–189.

— 2011. 'Socratic Ethics and the Socratic Psychology of Action: A Philosophical Framework.' In D. Morrison (ed.), 260–192.

— 2018. 'Inequality, Intention, and Ignorance: Socrates on Punishment and the Human Good.' In G. Anagnostopoulos and G. Santas (eds), 83–138.

Penner, T. and Kraut, R. (eds). 1989. *Nature, Knowledge, and Virtue*. Cambridge: Cambridge University Press.

Penner, T. and Rowe, C. 1994. 'The Desire for the Good: Is the Meno Inconsistent with the Gorgias?' *Phronesis* 39: 1–25.

— 2005. *Plato's Lysis*. Cambridge: Cambridge University Press.

Perusino, F. and Colantonio, M. (eds). 2012. *La commedia greca e la storia. Atti del Seminario di studio*. Pisa: ETS.

Peters, J. (ed.). 2013. *Aristotelian Ethics in Contemporary Perspective*. New York: Routledge.

Peterson, S. 2011. *Socrates and Philosophy in the Dialogues of Plato*. Cambridge: Cambridge University Press.

Picot, J.-C. 2013. 'L'image du ΠΝΙΓΕΥΣ dans les *Nuées*. Un Empédocle au charbon.' In A. Laks and R. Saetta Cottone (eds), 113–129.

Pieters, J. T. M. F. 1946. *Cratinus. Bijdrage tot de geschiedenis der vroeg-attische comedie*. Leiden: Brill.

Pirrotta, S. 2009. *Plato comicus. Die fragmentarischen Komödien. Ein Kommentar*. Berlin: Verlag Antike.

Plato, 1992. *Protagoras*. Translated by S. Lombardo & K. Bell. Indianapolis: Hackett Publishing Company, Inc.

Polansky, R. 1985. 'Professor Vlastos' Analysis of Socratic Elenchus.' *Oxford Studies in Ancient Philosophy* 3: 247–260.

Politis, V. 2015. *The Structure of Enquiry in Plato's Early Dialogues*. Cambridge: Cambridge University Press.

Popper, K. R. 1945. *The Open Society and Its Enemies, vol. 1: Plato*. London: Routledge.

Price, A. W. 2004. *Love and Friendship in Plato and Aristotle*. Oxford: Oxford University Press.

Prichard, H. A. 1928. 'Duty and Interest: An Inaugural Lecture Given at Oxford University.' Reprinted in Id., *Moral Writings*, J. MacAdam (ed.). Oxford: Oxford University Press, 21–49.

Prior, W. J. (ed.). 1996. *Socrates: Critical Assessments*. Routledge.

— 1998. 'Plato and the "Socratic Fallacy".' *Phronesis* 43: 97–113.

— 2004. 'Socrates Metaphysician.' *Oxford Studies in Ancient Philosophy* 27: 1–14.

— 2013. 'Socratic Metaphysics.' In J. Bussanich and N. D. Smith (eds), 68–93 and 337–338.

Pucci, P. 1960. 'Saggio sulle *Nuvole*.' *Maia* 12: 3–42.

Rabinowitz, W. G. 1958. 'Platonic Piety: An Essay Toward the Solution of an Enigma.' *Phronesis* 3: 108–120.

Raines, J. M. 1934. 'Critical Notes on Archippus, Phrynichus, Callias, and Aristophanes.' *Classical Philology* 29: 338–341.

Ralkowski, M. 2013. 'The Politics of Impiety.' In J. Bussanich and N. D. Smith (eds), 301–327.

Rappe, S. 'Cross Examining Happiness.' In Nightingale, A. and Sedley, D. (eds), 27–44.

Rasmussen, L. M. (ed.). 2005. *Ethics Expertise: History, Contemporary Perspectives, and Applications.* Dordrecht: Springer.

Rau, P. 1967. *Paratragodia: Untersuchung einer komischen Form des Aristophanes.* München: Beck.

Redfield, J. 2010. 'Philosophical *egkrateia*.' Accessed December 18, 2021. https://www.academia.edu/6017167/enkrateia.

Reeve, C.D.C. 1989. *Socrates in the* Apology: *An Essay on Plato's* Apology. Indianapolis: Hackett.

— (ed.). 2002. *The Trials of Socrates: Six Classic Texts.* Indianapolis and Cambridge: Hackett Publishing Company.

— 2006. 'Plato on Eros and Friendship.' In H. H. Benson (ed.), 294–307.

Reid, H. L., Ralkowski, M. and Zoller, C. P. 2020. *Athletics, Gymnastics, and Agon in Plato.* Sioux City: Parnassos Press.

Reshotko, N. 1992. 'The Socratic Theory of Motivation.' *Apeiron* 25: 145–70.

— 2006. *Socratic Virtue: Making the Best of the Neither-Good-Nor-Bad.* Cambridge: Cambridge University Press.

— 2013. 'Socratic Eudaimonism.' In J. Bussanich and N. D. Smith (eds), 156–184.

Revermann, M. 2006. *Comic Business: Theatricality, Dramatic Technique, and Performance Contexts of Aristophanic Comedy.* Oxford: Oxford University Press.

Riddell, J. 1867. *The* Apology *of Plato.* Oxford: Clarendon Press.

Rider, B. A. 2011. 'A Socratic Seduction: Philosophical Protreptic in Plato's *Lysis*.' *Apeiron* 44: 40–66.

Roberts, J. W. 1984. *City of Sokrates: An Introduction to Classical Athens.* London: Routledge.

Robin, L. 1910. 'Les *Mémorables* de Xénophon et notre conaissance de la philosophie de Socrate.' *Année philosophique* 21: 1–47.

— 1964. *La théorie platonicienne de l'amour.* Paris: Presses universitaires de France.

Robinson, D. B. 1986. 'Plato's *Lysis*: The Structural Problem.' *Illinois Classical Studies* 11: 63–83.

Robinson, R. 1953. *Plato's Earlier Dialectic.* 2nd ed. Oxford: Clarendon Press.

Robinson, T.M. and Brisson, L. (eds). 2000. *Plato: Euthydemus, Lysis, Charmides: Proceedings of the V Symposium Platonicum.* Sankt Augustin: Academia Verlag.

Röck, H. *Der unverfälschte Sokrates, der Atheist und 'Sophist', und das Wesen aller Philosophie und Religion.* Innsbruck: Wagner.

Romeyer Dherbey, G. and Gourinat, J.-B. (eds). 2001. *Socrate et les Socratiques.* Paris: Librarie Philosophique J. Vrin.

Roochnik, David. 1985. 'Apology 40c4–41e7: Is Death Really a Gain?' *The Classical Journal* 80: 212–220.

— 1986. 'Socrates's Use of the Techne-Analogy.' *Journal of History of Philosophy* 24: 295–310.

— 1996. *Of Art and Wisdom Plato's Understanding of Techne.* University Park, PA: The Pennsylvania State University Press.

Rorty, A. O. (ed.). 1980. *Explaining Emotions.* Berkeley: University of California Press.

BIBLIOGRAPHY

Rosen, R. M. 1988. *Old Comedy and the Lambographic Tradition.* Atlanta: Scholars Press.

— 1997. 'Performance and Textuality in Aristophanes' *Clouds.' The Yale Journal of Criticism* 10: 397–421.

Rosen, R.M. and Farrell, J. (eds). 1993. *Nomodeiktes: Greek Studies in Honor of Martin Ostwald.* Ann Arbor: University of Michigan Press.

Ross, W. D. 1924. *Aristotle's Metaphysics.* Vol. 1. London: Clarendon Press.

— 1951. *Plato's Theory of Ideas.* Oxford: Clarendon Press.

Rossetti, L. 1974. 'Le Nuvole di Aristofane: perché furono una commedia e non una farsa?' *Rivista di cultura classica e medievale* 16: 131–136.

— 2008. 'Socrate *enkrates.' Zbornik Matice srpske za klasicne studije* 10: 65–79.

Rossetti, L. and Stavru, A. (eds) 2010. *Socratica 2008: Studies in Ancient Socratic Literature.* Bari: Levante Editori.

Roth, M. D. 1995. 'Did Plato Nod? Some Conjectures on Egoism and Friendship in the *Lysis.'* *Archiv für Geschichte der Philosophie* 77: 1–20.

Rowe, C. J. 2000. 'The *Lysis* and the *Symposium: Aporia* and *Euporia?'* In T. M. Robinson and L. Brisson (eds), 204–216.

— 2002. 'Comments on Penner.' In Annas, J. and Rowe, C. J. (eds), 213–225.

— 2006. 'Socrates in Plato's Dialogues.' In S. Ahbel-Rappe and R. Kamtekar (eds), 159–170.

— 2007. 'A Problem in the *Gorgias:* How is Punishment Supposed to Help with Intellectual Error?' In C. Bobonich and P. Destrée (eds), 19–40.

— 2012a. 'Socrates on Reason, Appetite, and Passion: A Response to Thomas C. Brickhouse and Nicholas D. Smith, *Socratic Moral Psychology.' The Journal of Ethics* 16: 305–324.

— 2012b. 'The Status of the Myth of the Gorgias, or: Taking Plato Seriously.' In C. Collobert, P. Destrée and F. J. Gonzalez (eds), 187–198.

Rowe, C. and Schofield, M. (eds). 2000. *The Cambridge History of Greek and Roman Political Thought.* Cambridge: Cambridge University Press.

Rudebusch, G. 1999. *Socrates, Pleasure, and Value.* New York: Oxford University Press.

— 2009. *Socrates.* Malden, MA and Oxford: Wiley-Blackwell.

— 2017. 'The Unity of Virtue, Ambiguity, and Socrates' Higher Purpose.' *Ancient Philosophy* 37: 333–346.

Russell, D. C. 2001. 'Misunderstanding the Myth in the Gorgias.' *Southern Journal of Philosophy* 39: 557–573.

— 2005. *Plato on Pleasure and the Good Life.* Oxford: Clarendon Press.

Russo, C. F. 1962. *Aristofane autore di teatro.* Firenze: Sansoni.

Rusten, J. 2011. *The Birth of Comedy: Texts, Documents, and Art from Athenian Comic Competitions.* Baltimore: The Johns Hopkins University Press.

Saetta Cottone, R. 2013. 'Aristophane et le théâtre du soleil. Le dieu d'Empédocle dans le chœur des *Nuées.'* In A. Laks and R. Saetta Cottone (eds), 61–85.

Saetta Cottone, R. and Buarque de Holanda, L. 2020–2021: 'Le retournement du chœur et l'appropriation comique de la tragédie dans les *Nuées* d'Aristophane: un dialogue.' In A. Grilli and F. Morosi (eds), 227–254.

Salles, R. (ed.). 2005. *Metaphysics, Soul, and Ethics in Ancient Thought: Themes from the Work of Richard Sorabji.* Oxford: Clarendon Press.

Sanderman, D. 2004. 'Why Socrates Mocks His Interlocutors.' *Skepsis* 15: 431–441.

Santas, G.X. 1964. 'The Socratic Paradoxes.' *The Philosophical Review* 73: 147–164.

— 1969. 'Socrates at Work on Virtue and Knowledge in Plato's *Charmides.' Review of Metaphysics* 22: 433–460.

— 1972. 'The Socratic Fallacy.' *Journal of the History of Philosophy* 10: 127–141.

— 1979. *Socrates: Philosophy in Plato's Early Dialogues*. London: Routledge & Kegan Paul.

— 1988. *Plato and Freud*. Oxford: Basil Blackwell.

Sarri, F. 1975. *Socrate e la genesi storica del concetto occidentale di anima*. Roma: Abete.

Saunders T., J. 1994. *Plato's Penal Code: Tradition, Controversy, and Reform in Greek Penology*. Clarendon Press.

Scafuro, A. and Boegehold, A. (eds). 1994. *Athenian Identity and Civic Ideology*. Baltimore: Johns Hopkins University Press.

Schiappa, E. 1991. *Protagoras and Logos*. Columbia: University of South Carolina Press.

Schofield, M. 1984. 'Ariston of Chios and the Unity of Virtue.' *Ancient Philosophy* 1: 83–96.

— 2006. *Plato: Political Philosophy*. Oxford: Oxford University Press.

— 2019. 'Plato in his Time and Place.' In G. Fine (ed.), 2008a, 41–68.

Schorn, S. 2004. *Satyros aus Kallatis. Sammlung der Fragmente mit Kommentar*. Basel: Schwabe.

Schuh, G. 2019. 'Was Eudaimonism Ancient Greek Common Sense?' *Apeiron* 52: 359–393.

Scott, D. 2006. *Plato's Meno*. Cambridge: Cambridge University Press.

Scott, G. A. 2000. *Plato's Socrates as Educator*. Albany, NY: SUNY Press.

— (ed.). 2002. *Does Socrates Have a Method?* University Park, PA: The Penn State University Press.

Sedley, D. N. 1989. 'Is the *Lysis* a Dialogue of Definition?' *Phronesis* 34: 107–108.

— 2002. 'The Origins of Stoic God.' In D. Frede and A. Laks (eds), 41–83.

— 2004. *The Midwife of Platonism: Text and Subtext in Plato's* Theaetetus. Oxford: Oxford University Press.

— 2007. *Creationism and its Critics in Antiquity*. Berkeley, Los Angeles and London: University of California Press.

— 2008. 'Socrates' Place in the History of Teleology.' *Elenchos* 29: 317–334.

— 2009. 'Myth, Punishment, and Politics in the "Gorgias".' In C. Partenie (ed.), 51–76.

Segal, C. 1969. 'Aristophanes' Cloud-Chorus.' *Arethusa* 2: 143–161.

Segoloni, L. M. 1994. *Socrate a banchetto: il Simposio di Platone e i Banchetannti di Aristofane*. Roma: GEI.

— 2003. 'Socrate musico e poeta.' In R. Nicolai (ed.), 303–317.

Segvic, H. 2000. 'No One Errs Willingly.' *Oxford Studies in Ancient Philosophy* 19: 1–45. Reprinted in S. Ahbel-Rappe and R. Kamtekar (eds), 2006, 171–185.

Shaver, R. 2023. 'Egoism.' Accessed April 25, 2023, https://plato.stanford.edu/archives/spr2023/entries/egoism/.

Shaw, J. C. 2015. 'Punishment and Psychology in Plato's Gorgias.' *Polis* 32: 75–95.

— (ed.). forthcoming. *Plato's Gorgias: A Critical Guide*. Cambridge: Cambridge University Press.

Sheffield, F. 2012. 'The *Symposium* and Platonic Ethics: Plato, Vlastos, and a Misguided Debate.' *Phronesis* 57: 117–141.

Sherman, N. 2015. *Afterwar: Healing the Moral Wounds of Our Soldiers*. New York: Oxford University Press.

Shorey, Paul. 1903. *The Unity of Plato's Thought*. Chicago: The University of Chicago Press.

Silk, M. S. 1993. 'Aristophanic Paratragedy.' In A. H. Sommerstein (ed.), 477–504.

Singpurwalla, R. 2006. 'Reasoning with the Irrational: Moral Psychology in the *Protagoras*.' *Ancient Philosophy* 26: 243–258.

Slings, S. R. 1999. *Plato: Clitophon*. Cambridge: Cambridge University Press.

Smith, N. D. 1989. 'Diviners and Divination in Aristophanic Comedy.' *Classical Antiquity* 8: 140–158.

BIBLIOGRAPHY

— (ed.) 1998. *Plato: Critical Assessments*. 4 vols. London: Routledge.

— 2000. 'Plato on Knowledge as a Power.' *Journal of the History of Philosophy* 38: 145–168.

— 2004. 'Did Plato Write the *Alcibiades I?*' *Apeiron* 37: 93–108.

— 2009. 'Review of Scott 2006.' *Ancient Philosophy* 29: 414–418.

— 2014. 'Socratic Metaphysics?' *Apeiron* 47: 419–434.

— 2016. 'Socrates on the Human Condition.' *Ancient Philosophy* 36: 81–95.

— 2018. 'Aristotle on Socrates.' In A. Stavru and C. Moore (eds), 601–622.

— 2019. *Summoning Knowledge in Plato's Republic*. Oxford: Oxford University Press.

— 2020. 'Socrates' Agonistic Use of Shame.' In H. L. Reid, M. Ralkowski and C. P. Zoller (eds), 157–171.

— 2021. *Socrates on Self-Improvement: Knowledge, Virtue, and Happiness*. Cambridge: Cambridge University Press.

Smith, A. 1998. "Knowledge and Expertise in the Early Platonic Dialogues." *Archiv für Geschichte der Philosophie* 80: 129–161.

Smith, N. D. and Destrée, P. (eds). 2005. *Socrates' Divine Sign: Religion, Practice and Value in Socratic Philosophy* (*Apeiron* 38.2). Kelowna, BC: Academic Printing and Publishing.

Smith, N. D. and Woodruff, P. (eds). 2000. *Reason and Religion in Socratic Philosophy*. New York: Oxford University Press.

Snell, B. 1948. 'Das früheste Zeugnis über Sokrates.' *Philologus* 98: 125–134.

Sommerstein. A. H. (ed.). 1993. *Tragedy, Comedy, and the Polis: Papers from the Greek Drama Conference, Nottingham, 18–20 July 1990*. Bari: Levante.

Souto Delibes, F. 1997. 'La figura de Sócrates en la comedia ateniense.' In A. López Eire (ed.), 339–345.

Sreenivasan, G. 2020. *Emotion and Virtue*. Princeton: Princeton University Press.

Stanley, J. and Williamson, T. 2001. 'Knowing How.' *Journal of Philosophy* 98: 411–444.

Starkie, W. J. M. (ed.). 1911. *The* Clouds *of Aristophanes*. London: Macmillan and Co.

Stavru, A. 2011. 'Socrate: la *kalokagathia* del filosofo'. In Id., *Il potere dell'apparenza: percorso storico-critico nell'estetica antica*. Napoli: Loffredo, 99–130.

— 2016. 'Socrate *karterikos* (Platone, *Simposio* 216c–221b).' In M. Erler and M. Tulli (eds), 347–53.

— 2018. 'Socrates' Physiognomy: Plato and Xenophon in Comparison.' In G. Danzig, D. Johnson and D. Morrison (eds), 208–251.

— 2020. 'Piacere e dolore nella letteratura socratica.' in L. M. Napolitano Valditara (ed.), 41–70.

Stavru, A. and Moore, C. (eds). 2018. *Socrates and the Socratic Dialogue*. Leiden and Boston: Brill.

Stephens, J. 1985. 'Socrates on the Rule of Law.' *History of Philosophy Quarterly* 2: 3–10.

Stokes, M. C. 1992. 'Socrates' Mission.' In B. S. Gower and M. C. Stokes (eds), 26–81.

— 2012. 'Three Defences of Socrates: Relative Chronology, Politics and Religion.' In F. Hobden and C. Tuplin (eds), 243–267.

Stone, I. F. 1979. 'I. F. Stone Breaks the Socrates Story.' Interview in *The New York Times Magazine*, April 8, 1979, accessed April 25, 2023, https://www.nytimes.com/1979/04/08/archives/if-stone-breaks-the-socrates-story-an-old-muckraker-sheds-fresh.html.

— 1988. *The Trial of Socrates*. Boston: Little, Brown and Company.

Storey, I. C. 1988. 'Thrasymachos at Athens: Aristophanes fr. 205 (*Daitales*)', *Phoenix* 42: 212–218.

— 1993. 'The Dates of Aristophanes' *Clouds II* and Eupolis' *Baptai*: A Reply to E. C. Kopc.' *The American Journal of Philology* 114: 71–84.

— 2003. *Eupolis: Poet of Old Comedy*. Oxford: Oxford University Press.

— 2011. *Fragments of Old Comedy*. Cambridge: Loeb.

Strauss, L. 1966. *Socrates and Aristophanes*. New York and London: Basic Books.

— 1970. *Xenophon's Socratic Discourse: An Interpretation of the* Oeconomicus. Ithaca, NY: Cornell University Press.

— 1972. *Xenophon's Socrates*. Ithaca, NY: Cornell University Press.

— 1983. *Studies in Platonic Political Philosophy*. Chicago: University of Chicago Press.

de Strycker, E. and Slings, S. R. 1994. *Plato's Apology of Socrates: A Literary and Philosophical Study with a Running Commentary*. Leiden, New York and Köln: Brill.

Stump, J. 2020. 'On Socrates' Project of Philosophical Conversion.' *Philosophers' Imprint* 20 (32).

Swanton, C. 2003. *Virtue Ethics: A Pluralistic View*. Oxford: Oxford University Press.

— 2016. 'Developmental Virtue Ethics.' In J. Annas, D. Narvaez and N. E. Snow (eds), 116–34.

Taillardat, J. 1965. *Les images d'Aristophane, études de langue et de style*. Paris: Les Belles Lettres.

Tarrant, H. 1991. '*Clouds I*: Steps Towards Reconstruction.' *Arctos* 25: 157–181.

— 2002. '*Elenchos* and *Exetasis*: Capturing the Purpose of Socratic Interrogation.' In G. A. Scott (ed.), 61–77.

Taylor, A. E. 1911. 'The *Phrontisterion*.' In Id., *Varia Socratica, First Series*. Edinburgh: St Andrews University Publications, 129–177.

— 1933. *Socrates*. Edinburgh: Davies.

— 1937. *Plato: The Man and His Work*. London, Methuen.

Taylor, C. C. W. (ed.). 1976. *Protagoras*. Oxford: Clarendon Press.

— 1982. 'The End of the Euthyphro.' *Phronesis* 27, 109–118.

— 1998. *Socrates: A Very Short Introduction*. Oxford: Oxford University Press.

— 2019. *Socrates: A Very Short Introduction*, 2nd edn. Oxford: Oxford University Press.

Tell, H. 2011. *Plato's Counterfeit Sophists*. Cambridge: Harvard University Press.

Telò, M. 2016. *Aristophanes and the Cloak of Comedy: 'Affect, Aesthetics, and the Canon'*. Chicago: Chicago Scholarship Online.

Teloh, H. 1981. *The Development of Plato's Metaphysics*. Philadelphia: Pennsylvania State College.

— 1986. *Socratic Education in Plato's Early Dialogues*. Notre Dame: University of Notre Dame Press.

Tenenbaum, S. (ed.). 2010. *Desire, Practical Reason, and the Good*. Oxford: Oxford University Press.

Tessitore, A. 1990. 'Plato's *Lysis*: An Introduction to Philosophic Friendship.', *Southern Journal of Philosophy* 1990: 115–132.

Tessman, L. (ed.). 2009. *Feminist Ethics and Social and Political Philosophy: Theorizing the Non-Ideal*. Dordrecht: Springer.

Tessman, L. 2009. 'Feminist eudaimonism: eudaimonism as Non-ideal Theory.' in Id. (ed.), 41–70.

Thür, G. 2006. 'Antomosia.' In H. Cancik and H. Schneider (eds). *Brill's New Pauly*, accessed 7 December 2021, http://dx.doi.org/10.1163/1574-9347_bnp_e125890.

Tiles, J. E. 1984. 'Technē and Moral Expertise.' *Philosophy* 59, 49–66.

Toynbee, A. 1954. 'The Search for a Prophet: Socrates and Jesus.' In J. D. Montgomery (ed.).

Trapp, M. (ed.). 2007. *Socrates from Antiquity to Enlightenment*. London: Routledge.

Trivigno, F. V. 2011. 'Philosophy and the Ordinary: On the Setting of Plato's *Lysis*.' *Greek, Roman and Byzantine Studies* 51: 61–85.

BIBLIOGRAPHY

391

Tsamalikos, P. 2016. *Anaxagoras, Origen, and Neoplatonism: The Legacy of Anaxagoras to Classical and Late Antiquity.* Berlin and Boston: de Gruyter.

Tsouna, V. 2004. 'Interpretations of Socratic Self-Knowledge.' In V. Karasmanis (ed.), 319–330.

Tulli, M. and Erler, M. (eds). 2016. *Plato in Symposium: Selected Papers from the Tenth Symposium Platonicum.* Sankt Augustin: Academia Verlag.

Tuozzo, T. M. 2011. *Plato's* Charmides: *Positive Elenchus in a 'Socratic' Dialogue.* Cambridge: Cambridge University Press.

Tylawski, E. I. 2002. *Saturio's Inheritance: The Greek Ancestry of the Roman Comic Parasite.* New York and Oxford: Lang.

Untersteiner, M. 1967. *I Sofisti.* Firenze: La Nuova Italia.

van Leeuwen, J. 1898. *Aristophanis Nubes.* Lugduni Batavorum: Brill.

van Ophuijsen, J. M., van Raalte, M. and Stork, P. (eds). 2013. *Protagaras of Abdera: The Man, His Measure.* Leiden: Brill.

van Ophuijsen, J. M., van Raalte, M. and Stork, P. (eds). 2013. *Protagoras of Abdera: the Man, His Measure.* Leiden: Brill.

Vander Waerdt, P. A. 1993. 'Socratic Justice and Self-Sufficiency: The Story of the Delphic Oracle in Xenophon's *Apology of Socrates.' Oxford Studies in Ancient Philosophy* 11: 1–48.

— 1994a. 'Socrates in the *Clouds.'* In P. A. Vander Waerdt (ed.), 48–86.

— (ed.). 1994b. *The Socratic Movement.* Ithaca, NY: Cornell University Press.

Vasiliou, I. 2008. *Aiming at Virtue.* Cambridge: Cambridge University Press.

— 2013. 'Socratic Irony.' In J. Bussanich and N. D. Smith (eds), 20–33.

Velleman, J. D. 1999. 'Love as a Moral Emotion.' *Ethics* 109: 338–374.

Vernant, J.-P. 1980. *Myth and Society in Ancient Greece.* Atlantic Highlands: Harvester Press.

Versenyi, L. 1963. *Socratic Humanism.* New Haven: Yale University Press.

— 1975. 'Plato's *Lysis.' Phronesis* 20: 185–198.

— 1982. *Holiness and Justice: An Interpretation of Plato's Euthyphro.* Washington, DC: University Press of America.

Versnel, H. S. 1981. 'Religious Mentality in Ancient Prayer.' In H. S. Versnel (ed.), 1–64.

Viano, C. 2001. 'La cosmologie de Socrate dans les *Mémorables* de Xénophon.' In G. Romeyer Dherbey and J.-B. Gourinat (eds), 97–119.

Vickers, M. 1993. 'Alcibiades in Cloudedoverland.' In R. M. Rosen and J. Farrell (eds), 603–618.

Villa, D. 2001. *Socratic Citizenship.* Princeton: Princeton University Press.

Vlastos, G. 1965. 'Anamnesis in the *Meno.' Dialogue* 4: 143–167.

— 1969. 'Socrates on Akrasia.' *Phoenix* 23, 71–88.

— (ed.). 1971a. *The Philosophy of Socrates.* Garden City, NY: Anchor Books.

— 1971b. 'Introduction: The Paradox of Socrates.' In Vlastos, G. (ed.), 1971a, 1–21.

— 1972. 'The Unity of the Virtues in the *Protagoras.' Review of Metaphysics* 25: 415–458.

— 1974. 'Socrates on Political Obedience and Disobedience.' *Yale Review* 63: 517–534.

— 1976. 'What did Socrates Understand by his What is F? Question?' In *Platonic Studies,* edited by G. Vlastos. Princeton: Princeton University Press, 410–417.

— 1981a. *Platonic Studies,* 2nd edn. Princeton: Princeton University Press.

— 1981b. 'What Did Socrates Understand by His "What Is F?" Question.' In G. Vlastos (ed.), 410–417.

— 1983a. '"The Socratic Elenchus" and "Afterthoughts on the Socratic Elenchus".' *Oxford Studies in Ancient Philosophy* 1: 27–58 and 71–74.

— 1983b. 'The Historical Socrates and Athenian Democracy.' *Political Theory* 2: 495–516. Reprinted in R. W. Sharples 1993, 66–89; G. Vlastos 1994, 87–108. W. J. Prior (ed.) 1996, Vol. 2, 25–44; R. Brooks 2007, 123–144.

— 1984c. 'Happiness and Virtue in Socrates' Moral Theory.' *Proceedings of the Cambridge Philological Society* 30: 181–213.

— 1985a. 'Socrates' Disavowal of Knowledge.' *Philosophical Quarterly* 35, 1–31. Reprinted in 1994. G. Vlastos (ed.), 39–66.

— 1985b. 'Happiness and Virtue in Socrates' Moral Theory.' *Proceedings of the Cambridge Philological Society* 30: 181–213.

— 1987. 'Socrates and Vietnam.' In M. Burnyeat (ed.), 127–133.

— 1988. 'Socrates.' *Proceedings of the British Academy* 74: 89–111.

— 1989. 'Socratic Piety.' *Proceedings of the Boston Area Colloquium in Ancient Philosophy* 5: 213–238. Revised in ch. 6 of Vlastos 1991; revised version reprinted in W. J. Prior (ed.) 1996, vol. 2, 144–166; N. D. Smith and P. Woodruff (eds) 2000, 55–73; R. Kamtekar (ed.) 2005, 49–71.

— 1990. 'Is the "Socratic Fallacy" Socratic?' *Ancient Philosophy* 10: 1–16.

— 1991. *Socrates: Ironist and Moral Philosopher.* Cambridge: Cambridge University Press and Ithaca, NY: Cornell University Press.

— 1994a. 'The Socratic Elenchus: Method is All', with its Appendix and Postscript. In G. Vlastos 1994c, 1–37. This is a revised version of Vlastos 1983a.

— 1994b. 'Socrates' Disavowal of Knowledge.' In G. Vlastos 1994c, 39–66. [Reprint with alterations of G. Vlastos, 1985. "Socrates' Disavowal of Knowledge." *Philosophical Quarterly* 35: 1–31.]

— 1994c. In M. F. Burnyeat (ed.), 127–133.

— 1995. 'The Virtuous and the Happy: Irwin's *Plato's Moral Theory*'. In D. Graham (ed.). *Gregory Vlastos – Studies in Greek Philosophy, Volume II, Socrates, Plato, and Their Tradition.* Princeton: Princeton University Press, 126–132.

Vlastos, G. 1994c. *Socratic Studies.* Edited by M. F. Burnyeat. Cambridge: Cambridge University Press.

Vogt, K. 2017. *Desiring the Good: Ancient Proposals and Contemporary Theory.* Oxford: Oxford University Press.

Wade, F. C. 1971. 'In Defense of Socrates.' *Review of Metaphysics* 25: 311–325.

Walker, M. D. 2020. 'Socrates' Lesson to Hippothales in Plato's *Lysis.' Classical Philology* 115 (3): 551–565.

Wallace, R. W. 1994. 'Private Lives and Public Enemies: Freedom of Thought in Classical Athens.' In A. Scafuro and A. Boegehold (eds), 127–155.

Walsh, J. J. 1963. *Aristotle's Conception of Moral Weakness.* New York: Columbia University Press.

Walzer, M. 1970. *Obligations: Essays on Disobedience, War and Citizenship.* Cambridge, MA: Harvard University Press.

Warren, Edward. 1989. 'The Craft Argument: An Analogy.' In J. P. Anton and A. Preuss (eds), 101–116.

Waterfield, R. 2013. 'The Quest for the Historical Socrates.' In J. Bussanich and N. D. Smith (eds), 1–19.

Watson, L. 1991. *Arae.* Leeds: Cairns.

Weiher, A. 1913. *Philosophen und Philosophenspott in der attischen Komödie.* Nordlingen: Beck.

Weiss, R. 1994. 'Virtue Without Knowledge: Socrates' Conception of Holiness in Plato's *Euthyphro.' Ancient Philosophy* 14: 263–282.

BIBLIOGRAPHY

— 1998. *Socrates Dissatisfied: An Analysis of Plato's* Crito. New York: Oxford University Press.
— 2001. *Virtue in the Cave: Moral Inquiry in Plato's* Meno. Oxford: Oxford University Press.
— 2006. *The Socratic Paradox and its Enemies*. Chicago: University of Chicago Press.
Wenley, R. M. 1889. *Socrates and Christ: A Study in the Philosophy of Religion*. Edinburgh: Blackwood.
von der Weppen, W. and Zimmermann, B. (eds). 2006. *Sokrates im Gang der Zeiten*. Tübingen Attempto, University of Tübingen.
Werkmeister, W. W. (ed.) 1976. *Facets of Plato's Philosophy*. Assen: Van Gorcum.
White, N. 2002. *Individual and Conflict in Greek Ethics*. New York: Oxford University Press.
— 2008. 'Definition and Elenchus.' *Philosophical Inquiry* 30: 1–18.
Whitman, C. H. 1964. *Aristophanes and the Comic Hero*. Cambridge: Harvard University Press.
Wiener, P. and Fisher, J. (eds). 1974. *Violence and Aggression in the History of Ideas*. New Brunswick, NJ: Rutgers University Press.
Wilburn, J. 2015. 'Courage and the Spirited Part of the Soul in Plato's *Republic*.' *Philosophers' Imprint* 15 (26): 1–21.
Wildberg, C. 2006. 'Socrates and Euripides.' In S. Ahbel-Rappe and R. Kamtekar (eds), 21–35.
Willi, A. A. 2003. *The Languages of Aristophanes: Aspects of Linguistic Variation in Classical Attic Greek*. Oxford: Oxford University Press.
Williamson, T. 1996. 'Knowing and Asserting.' *Philosophical Review* 105: 489–523.
— 2000. *Knowledge and its Limits*. Oxford: Oxford University Press.
Winspear, A. D. and Silverberg, T. 1939. *Who Was Socrates?* Rahway: Quinn & Boden. Reprinted New York, 1960.
Wolfsdorf, D. C. 2003a. 'Socrates' Pursuit of Definitions.' *Phronesis* 48: 271–312.
— 2003b. 'Understanding the "What Is F?" Question.' *Apeiron* 36: 175–188.
— 2004a. 'Socrates' Avowals of Knowledge.' Phronesis 49: 75–142.
— 2004b. 'Interpreting Plato's Early Dialogues.' *Oxford Studies in Ancient Philosophy* 27: 15–40.
— 2004c. 'The Socratic Fallacy and the Epistemological Priority of Definitional Knowledge.' Apeiron 37: 35–67.
— 2005. 'ΔΥΝΑΜΙΣ in *Laches*.' *Phoenix* 59: 324–347.
— 2007. '*Philia* in Plato's *Lysis*.' *Harvard Studies in Classical Philology* 103: 235–259.
— 2008. *Trials of Reason: Plato and the Crafting of Philosophy*. Oxford: Oxford University Press.
— 2013. 'Socratic Philosophizing.' In J. Bussanich and N. D. Smith (eds), 34–67.
Wood, E. M. and Wood, N. 1978. *Class Ideology and Ancient Political Theory: Socrates, Plato, and Aristotle in Social Context*. New York: Oxford University Press.
Woodbury, L. 1965. 'The Date and Atheism of Diagoras of Melos.' *Phoenix* 19: 178–211.
— 1981. 'Anaxagoras and Athens.' *Phoenix* 35: 295–315.
Woodruff, P. 1976 'Socrates on the Parts of Virtue.' *Canadian Journal of Philosophy* Suppl. 2, 101–116.
— 1978. 'Socrates and Ontology: The Evidence of the Hippias Major.' *Phronesis* 23: 101–117.
— 1982. *Plato: Hippias Major*. Indianapolis and Cambridge: Hackett Publishing Company, Inc.
— 1988. 'Expert Knowledge in the *Apology* and *Laches*: What a General Needs to Know.' *Proceedings of the Boston Area Colloquium in Ancient Philosophy* 3: 79–115.
— 1990. 'Plato's Early Theory of Knowledge.' In S. Everson (ed.), 60–84.
— 2000. 'Socrates and the Irrational.' In N. D. Smith and P. Woodruff (eds), 130–150.

— 2005. *First Democracy: The Challenge of an Ancient Idea*. New York: Oxford University Press.

— 2007. 'Socrates and Political Courage.' *Ancient Philosophy* 27: 49–70.

— 2019. 'Wrong Turns in the *Euthyphro*.' *Apeiron* 52: 117–136.

— 2021. *The Essential Thucydides: On Justice, Power, and Human Nature*. Indianapolis: Hackett Publishing Company.

Woolf, R. 2000. 'Callicles and Socrates: Psychic (Dis)harmony in *Gorgias*.' *Oxford Studies in Ancient Philosophy* 18: 1–40.

Woozley, A. D. 1971. 'Socrates on Disobeying the Law.' In G. Vlastos (ed.), 299–318.

— 1979. *Law and Obedience: The Arguments of Plato's Crito*. London: Duckworth.

Xenophon. 1997. *Xenophon: Memorabilia. Oeconomicus. Symposium. Apology*. Translated by E. C. Marchant and O. J. Todd. Cambridge, MA: Harvard University Press.

— 2008. *Xenophon: Apology and Memorabilia* I. Edited with Introduction, Translation and Commentary by M. D. Macleod. Warminster: Liverpool University Press.

Yonezawa, S. 1991. 'Socrates's Two Concepts of the Polis.' *History of Political Thought* 12: 565–576.

Young, C. M. 2006. 'The Socratic Elenchus.' In H. H. Benson (ed.), 55–69.

Young, G. 1974. 'Socrates and Obedience.' *Phronesis* 19: 1–29.

Young, R. 1987. 'Egalitarianism and Envy.' *Philosophical Studies* 52: 261–276.

Yu, J. and Garcia, J. J. (eds). 2003. *Rationality and Happiness: From the Ancients to the Early Medievals*. Rochester: University of Rochester Press.

Yunis, H. 1988. *A New Creed: Fundamental Religious Belief in the Athenian Polis and Euripidean Drama*. Hypomnemata 91, Göttingen: Vandenhoeck & Ruprecht.

Zaidman, L. B. and Pantel, P. S. 1992. *Religion in the Ancient Greek City*. Translated by Paul Cartledge. Cambridge: Cambridge University Press.

Zeyl, D. 1980. 'Socrates and Hedonism: *Protagoras* 351b–358d.' *Phronēsis* 25: 250–269.

— 1982. 'Socratic Virtue and Happiness.' *Archiv für Geschichte der Philosophie* 14: 225–238.

— 2006. 'Review of Dancy, *Plato's Introduction of Forms*.' *Notre Dame Philosophical Reviews*, 9 June 2006.

Zimmermann, B. 1993. 'Aristophanes und die Intellektuellen.' In *Aristophane (= Entretiens sur l'Antiquité Classique 38*, edited by J. M. Bremer and E. W. Hendley, 255–286.

GENERAL INDEX

Adams, D. 244, 251, 252
Aelian 3, 7, 15, 17
Aelius Aristides 345, 346, 350
Aeschines (Rhetor) 346, 347, 348, 350
Aeschines (Socraticus) 16, 230
Aeschylus 13, 302, 317, 318
Aesop 4
afterlife 98, 103, 180, 181, 188, 317, 320, 323–342
  Hades 13, 70, 85, 328, 332, 335
Ahbel-Rappe, S. 187, 196, 200, 201, 224
akrasia 30, 153, 186, 200, 206, 213–214, 221, 225, 227
  see also intellectualism (motivational), moral psychology, voluntary and involuntary
Alcibiades 6, 8, 18, 27, 34–39, 44, 193, 203, 229, 250, 345–353, 355, 363, 364
  see also Alcibiades (Aeschines'), *Alcibiades* I (Plato's), *Symposium* (Plato's)
Alcibiades (Aeschines') 230
Alcibiades I (Plato's?) 21, 57, 62, 310
Alesse, F. 15
Alexis 16
Allen, R. 63, 64–69, 73, 75, 77, 78, 79, 82, 83, 163, 284, 287, 318, 364
Alon, I. 316
altruism, *see* egoism
Ambrosino, D. 21
Ameipsias 1, 2, 4, 5, 6, 7, 9, 14, 16
Ammianus Marcellinus 4, 16
Amphipolis (battle in 422 BCE) 17, 338
  see also Peloponnesian War
Anaxagoras 11, 21, 313
Anaximander 10, 20
Anaximenes 14
Anderson, M. 289, 295, 341
anger (*orgē, thumos*) 98, 130, 169, 184, 213, 214, 218, 255, 256, 257, 260, 264–267, 270, 271, 285, 356, 357, 361
  see also emotion(s)
Annas, J. 171, 173, 178, 204, 239, 244, 252, 333, 334

annihilation (death as), *see* death
Antiphon 26
Antisthenes 16, 61, 188
Anton, J. 168
Anytus 55, 96, 264, 350, 351, 352, 357
Apollo 4, 28, 278, 295, 302, 303, 308, 309, 312, 315, 319 (*see also* Delphic Oracle, religion)
Apology (Justin Martyr's) 316
Apology (Libanius's) 350, 364
Apology (Plato's) 17, 19, 21, 46, 47, 48, 49, 52, 53, 54, 55, 56, 59, 60, 69, 86, 87, 88, 89, 90, 91, 92, 93, 95, 98, 99, 101, 102, 103, 104, 106, 112, 115, 116, 135, 145, 146, 151, 153, 170, 173, 174, 177, 178, 179, 180, 181, 184, 185, 186, 188, 189, 191, 196, 198, 201, 202, 206, 212, 214, 219, 222, 223, 224, 259, 261, 262, 264, 267, 270, 275, 276, 277, 278, 279, 280, 281, 287, 288, 289, 290, 291, 294, 295, 296, 297, 298, 299, 300, 301, 302, 303, 305, 306, 307, 308, 309, 310, 311, 313, 315, 317, 319, 320, 321, 323–329, 331, 332–333, 334, 336, 338, 339, 340, 341, 344, 346, 347, 354, 356, 357, 358, 360, 361, 363, 365
Apology (Tertullian's) 316
Apology (Xenophon's) 16, 24, 25, 26, 28, 32, 33, 43, 44, 268, 306, 309, 310, 319, 321, 341–342, 347, 354, 355, 356, 360
appetite (*epithumia*), *see* desire
Archelaus 20, 182, 192, 193, 200, 335
Archippus 17
Arendt, H. 279, 280, 281
argument from design, 34, 311, 312
Arieti, J. 19
Aristippus 16, 61
Aristodemus 8, 18, 34, 312
Aristophanes viii, 1–21, 87, 300, 303, 315, 320, 344, 347, 350, 354, 355, 356, 358, 363, 364, 365

Aristophon 16
Aristotle 17, 50, 51, 59, 61, 66, 73, 83, 108,
113, 127, 128, 146, 154, 174, 185,
190, 195, 198, 201, 213, 235, 273,
276, 291, 315, 316, 318, 327, 340,
350, 351, 365
Armleder, P. 324
von Arnim, H. 41, 243, 253
Arrighetti, G. 15
art (*technē*), *see* craft
asceticism 2, 4, 5, 8, 10, 12, 13, 16
see also poverty
Aspasia 15, 269
associate(s), *see* friend/friendship
astronomy 7, 11, 171
see also geometry, nature
atheism 2, 11, 14, 21, 41, 49, 264, 299, 300,
301, 313, 315, 316, 361
see also religion
Athenaeus 4, 16
Athenagoras 316
Augustine 316
Austin, E. 181, 203, 257, 260, 262, 273,
324, 325, 326, 327, 328, 330, 331,
332, 340

Bagordo, A. 15
Bakhtin, M. 61
Balot, R. 289, 295
Bandini, 23, 40, 41, 42, 43, 44
Banqueters (Aristophanes' *Daitaleis*) 6, 7–8, 17
Barker, E. 279, 284
Barnes, J. 14, 66, 84, 174
Barney, R. 207, 211, 212, 225
Barrus, R. 19
Baxley, A. 340
beauty, *see* fine
Beckman, J. 318
Belardinelli, A. 20
Belfiore, E. 55, 59, 251, 252
benefit (*ōpheleia*) 25, 26, 33, 34, 38, 56, 62,
129, 139, 167, 169, 171, 172, 173,
174, 177, 180, 182, 183, 187, 191,
192, 193, 194, 195, 197, 199, 203,
205, 212, 219, 220, 221, 222, 223,
227, 230, 231, 232, 234, 236, 237,
238, 240, 241, 252, 257, 258, 259,
260, 268, 281, 282, 283, 305, 309,
310, 311, 312, 323, 324, 325, 327,
328, 329, 332, 333, 335, 338, 340,
342
see also good, happiness, virtue(s), wisdom

Benson, H. 44, 51, 52, 59, 60, 91, 94, 107,
114, 121, 123, 146, 147, 150, 151, 318
Betegh, G. 20, 334
Beversluis, J. 138, 139, 147, 148, 149
Bevilacqua, F. 23
Birds (Aristophanes') 1, 6, 7, 12, 14, 15, 17,
20, 303, 347
Bjelde, J. 40
Blackson, T. 211
blessed/blessings 25, 41, 90, 102, 180, 259,
291, 324, 325, 326, 328, 337, 338
see also benefit, good
Bloch, E. 363
Bobonich, C. 194, 198, 200, 201, 204
Bolonyai, G. 14
Bolotin, D. 238, 252
Bolton, R. 113, 114, 118
Bonanno, M. 13
Bordt, M. 240, 243, 251, 252
Bostock, D. 297, 333
Boys-Stones, G. 16
Brandwood, L. 63, 250
bravery (*andreia*) 6, 51, 162, 261, 269, 338,
339
see also courage, fear, virtue(s)
Brickhouse, T. 45, 46–48, 49, 50, 51, 52, 53,
55, 86, 91, 104, 117–121, 123, 125,
140–141, 144, 146, 147, 148, 149,
150, 151, 161, 164–166, 171,
173–174, 176, 177, 178, 183, 189,
198, 199, 200, 202, 203, 212, 213,
215, 216, 217, 218, 219, 221, 223,
224, 225, 226, 227, 228, 255, 257,
258, 260, 261, 265, 270, 272, 279,
280, 281, 282, 283, 285, 286, 287,
288, 289, 290, 292, 293, 294, 295,
317, 318, 319, 320, 324, 325, 327,
330, 332, 333, 335, 336, 337, 341,
359, 363, 364, 365
Brisson L. 18, 21
Broackes, J. 178
Bromberg, J. 13, 15, 19
Brown, E. 59, 60, 315, 317, 339
Brown, L. 194, 201, 204
Buarque de Holanda, L. 20
Bühler, W. 17
Burkert, W. 317, 320, 321
Burnet, J. 14, 21, 39, 174, 198, 279, 316,
318, 320, 363, 364
Burnyeat, M. 59, 150, 173, 174, 365
Bury, J. 364
Butrica, J. 19

GENERAL INDEX 397

Cairns, D. 273
Cairns, F. 61
Calef, S. 318
Callard, A. 214, 225
Callias 1, 2, 3, 4, 5, 9, 13, 15, 16
Campbell, L. 49
Candiotto, L. 255, 263, 264, 273
Capra, A. 17, 19
Carey, C. 13, 14, 15
Carone, G. 59, 226, 255, 257, 330
Carpenter M. 48, 49
Cartledge, P. 317, 353
Casanova, A. 18
Cassio, A. 14, 17
Catoni, M. 17
cause(s) (*aitia*)
    of cognitive or affective conditions of the
      soul 1, 8, 9, 13, 37, 48, 61, 88, 92, 93,
      116, 130, 160, 162, 167, 169, 171,
      172, 173, 179, 182, 183, 187, 188,
      196, 202, 211, 216, 224, 226, 233,
      241, 244, 249, 259, 263, 264, 265,
      268, 269, 271, 277, 305, 306, 308,
      311, 314, 331, 333, 334, 336, 337,
      346, 353, 357
    forms as 65, 67, 77, 79, 82, 84
    of things, actions, or events 9, 10, 46, 48,
      55, 93, 106, 118, 119, 165, 166, 167,
      169, 171, 172, 173, 174, 177, 178,
      182, 188, 191, 200, 203, 206, 209,
      215, 221, 227, 270, 278, 305, 309,
      310, 311, 314, 343, 357, 365
    virtue as 162, 163, 167, 171, 172, 173,
      174, 176, 177, 178, 188, 191, 192,
      203, 307
    see also intellectualism (motivational),
      moral psychology
Cerri, G. 19
Chaerephon 12, 13, 21, 28, 88, 90, 259, 280,
    308, 356
Charalabopoulos, N. 17, 19
Charles, D. 146, 148
Charmides 57, 143, 215, 229, 230, 259, 279
    see also Charmides (Plato's)
Charmides (Plato's) 47, 49, 51, 53, 59, 60, 80,
    92, 93, 127, 132, 134, 135, 140, 143,
    146, 147, 148, 149, 150, 153, 168,
    169, 171, 174, 175, 177, 187, 202,
    215, 216, 224, 229, 230, 258, 259,
    262, 263, 295, 298, 340, 346
Chroust, A.-H. 39, 364
Cicero 315

Clark, J. 40, 161, 177, 204
Clement 316
Clouds (Aristophanes') 1–21, 315, 320, 344,
    347, 354, 356, 358
cognitivism (with respect to emotions) 216,
    257–273, 323, 329, 334
Cohen, D. 21
Cohen, S. 318
cold (weather) 4, 5, 6, 8, 12, 17, 21, 354
Coliaco, J. 292
Collins, J. 58, 61, 62
Colson, D. 297, 298
comedy 1–21, 87, 273, 350, 351
companion(s), *see* friend/friendship
Compton-Engle, G. 21
Cooper J. G. 316
Cooper, J. M. 19, 29, 41, 58, 122, 147, 174,
    200, 224, 272, 276, 285, 291, 364, 365
Connor, W. 365
Cornford, F. 68
courage (*andreia*) 56, 92, 127, 134, 135, 141,
    143, 145, 153, 155, 156, 158, 159,
    160, 161, 162, 163, 164, 168, 175,
    176, 181, 194, 200, 215, 220, 259,
    260, 261, 269, 273, 323, 331,
    338–341, 342, 346, 354
    see also cowardice, virtue(s)
court (of law) 57, 99, 278, 280
    see also law/lawful, trial
cowardice (*anandreia*) 24, 127, 220, 271, 273,
    331
    see also courage, ignorance
craft (*technē*) 2, 3–4, 8, 10, 11–13, 27, 30, 31,
    32, 35–36, 39, 42, 43, 45–48, 51, 52,
    55, 58, 59, 60, 66, 86, 87, 88, 89, 90,
    91, 92, 108, 109, 115–121, 122, 124,
    125, 139, 140, 149, 153, 154,
    165–166, 168, 169–174, 177, 178,
    184, 188, 190–191, 195–196, 199,
    203, 204, 229, 232, 233, 250, 259,
    271, 276, 277, 278, 294, 295, 302,
    303, 304, 305, 306, 308, 309, 311,
    336, 339, 340, 356, 357
    see also cause(s), knowledge, wisdom
Critias 27, 34–39, 43, 44, 46, 57, 279,
    345–353, 355, 364
    see also Charmides (Plato's)
Critias (Plato's) 346
Cratinus 1, 2, 3, 4, 6, 14, 15, 18
Crito (Plato's) 21, 46, 49, 51, 54, 62, 102,
    112, 114, 146, 147, 170, 174, 178,
    179, 181, 182, 184, 185, 186, 188,

189, 190, 191, 192, 193, 195, 196,
  199, 201, 202, 203, 204, 206, 214,
  215, 219, 224, 261, 277, 279–293,
  294, 296, 297, 298, 302, 303, 305,
  306, 331, 333, 335, 352
Curd, P. 21
Curzer, H. 244, 252, 253
Cynics 5
Cyropaedia (Xenophon's) 21

daimonion 103, 111, 113, 201, 297, 298,
  303, 304, 307, 308–311, 313–315,
  316, 319, 321, 324–326, 341, 342,
  348, 354, 365
  see also divination
Dancy, R. 69, 71–72, 73, 75, 78, 137, 146,
  147, 148, 149, 150
Danzig, G. 23, 42, 43
Davar, F. 316
Davies, J. 364
death 1, 4, 5, 16, 44, 90, 98, 99, 101, 102,
  103–105, 170, 179, 180, 181, 185,
  195, 257, 261–262, 268–269, 270,
  271, 281, 282, 289, 293, 308, 310,
  320, 321, 323–342, 355, 362–363
  as a penalty 41, 44, 99, 135, 170, 188,
  208, 220, 221, 267, 268–269, 281,
  282, 296, 343, 346, 347, 362
  see also afterlife, punishment
DeFilippo, J. 44, 316, 320
definition(s) 3, 20, 29, 30, 32, 33, 41, 42, 44,
  46, 49, 50, 52, 55, 64, 66, 67, 70, 71,
  72, 73, 75, 76, 77, 78, 79, 81, 82, 83,
  92, 94, 115, 121, 127–151, 156, 159,
  160–163, 164, 175, 176, 180, 195,
  196, 203, 204, 205, 224, 262, 268,
  294, 304, 305, 306, 318
  see also essence
Del Corno, D. 14, 20
Delium (battle of, 424 BCE) 6, 16, 181, 308
Delphic oracle 28, 41, 53, 88, 89, 90, 92, 145,
  259, 278, 295, 302, 308, 309, 356,
  364–365
Deman, T. 374
Demont, P. 14
Denyer N. 62
Derenne, E. 21
Deretić, I. 258, 259, 260, 261, 262, 328, 330,
  331
desire (*boulēsis, epithumia, erōs*) 26, 27, 28,
  33, 36, 37, 47, 55, 59, 104, 105, 120,
  141, 154, 157, 172, 174, 179, 182,

200, 205–227, 228, 230, 234, 235,
  236, 237, 238, 240, 242, 243, 244,
  247, 248, 249, 250, 251, 255, 256,
  258, 259, 262, 265, 268, 272, 294,
  297, 305, 307, 312, 330, 335, 341,
  355
Desmond, W. 17
Destrée, P. 201
D'Souza, J. 201, 202, 204
developmentalism 63, 64, 69–79, 80, 81, 82,
  83, 84, 85, 86, 137, 145, 156, 159
Devereux, D. 156, 158–160, 161, 164, 175,
  176, 198, 215, 225, 227, 255,
  256–257, 269, 330
dialectic(al) 30, 31, 34, 35, 36, 39, 59, 67, 68,
  157, 186, 335, 336, 337
Dimas, P. 61, 171, 172
Diocles 19
Diogenes Laertius 4, 6, 14, 15, 16, 20, 21,
  313, 350, 363
Diogenes of Apollonia 11, 14, 20
Diogenes of Sinope 16
Dionysodorus, *see Euthydemus* (Plato's)
Diopeithes 21
discipline, *see* craft, moderation, punishment
disobedience, *see* obedience/disobedience
divination (*mantikē*) 34, 96, 141, 236, 304,
  308, 309, 310, 317, 319, 354
  see also daimonion, oracle(s), Delphic
  oracle
divine providence (*eutuchia*), *see* success
Dodds, E. 168, 177, 294, 320
Dorion, L.-A. 16, 23, 39, 40, 41, 42, 43, 44,
  341
Dover, K. 13, 14, 17, 18, 19, 21, 229, 250
drinking/drunkenness 6, 18, 67, 214
  non-alcoholic 217, 226
  see also wine, symposium
Dunn, J. 296
Dupréel, E. 17
Dybikowski, J. 290

Edmonds, J. 17
Edmunds, L. 13, 16
education (*paideia*) 2, 6, 7, 8, 13, 14, 38, 44,
  59, 60, 69, 171, 183, 187, 192, 200,
  204, 221, 223, 228, 282, 296, 300,
  302, 335
  see also teacher/teaching
Edwards, F. 221, 228, 335
effect(s) (of causes), *see* cause(s)
Egli, F. 15

GENERAL INDEX

egoism 185–158, 189, 190, 193, 194–195, 196, 200, 201, 202, 204, 221, 224, 226, 227, 231, 232, 240, 241, 242–246, 248, 249, 250, 252, 253, 254
   see also happiness

elenchus (*elenchos*) 31, 43, 49, 50, 52, 60, 76, 77, 89, 92, 93, 101, 106, 107, 109, 110, 111, 112, 114, 115, 116, 117, 124, 125, 128, 141, 143, 144, 145, 147, 151, 175, 180, 181, 182, 195, 197, 230, 231, 232, 233, 236, 243, 263, 277, 278, 280, 299, 300, 301, 303, 317, 330, 334, 364
   see also method

emotion(s) (*pathos*) 179, 184, 205, 213, 214, 215, 216, 219, 227, 255–273, 276, 293, 315, 323, 329, 330, 340
   see also cognitivism

Empedocles 11, 14, 20

envy (*pthonos*) 255, 256, 257, 267–268, 270, 271, 273, 336
   see also emotion(s)

epistemology, *see* craft, knowledge, ignorance, wisdom

Erasmus 316

Erbse, H. 18

essence (*ousia*) 29, 31, 32, 33, 37, 65, 66–68, 74, 77, 79, 80, 81, 84, 85, 111, 112, 114, 117, 139, 140, 149, 161, 163, 176, 189, 230, 241, 304, 307
   see also definition, form, paradigm

ethics, *see* moral psychology, virtue(s)

Eudemian Ethics (Aristotle's) 174, 315

Eupolis 1, 2, 3, 4, 5, 6, 9, 14, 19

Euripides 3, 4, 5, 6, 11, 13, 15, 302, 314, 317, 319, 320

Euthydemus 43 *see also Euthydemus* (Plato's)

Euthydemus (Plato's) 52, 55, 56, 57, 59, 62, 80, 97, 120, 138, 148, 168, 170, 172, 173, 174, 177, 178, 180, 181, 186, 200, 206, 207, 208, 224, 295, 306, 309, 310, 319, 320, 327, 335, 340

Euthyphro (Plato's) 46, 47, 51, 52, 59, 63–66, 68, 69, 70, 71, 73, 74, 75, 76, 79, 80, 81, 83, 84, 92, 94, 97, 98, 109, 120, 127, 131, 132, 134, 138, 147, 149, 167, 140, 141, 153, 156, 157, 158, 161, 163, 164, 165, 166, 167, 174, 175, 176, 188, 195, 202, 204, 214, 224, 228, 262, 303–306, 307, 309, 310, 311, 313, 314, 317, 318, 319, 320, 321, 335, 358, 359, 360

Evenus 88
   see also sophist(s)

excellence (*aretē*), *see* virtue(s)

exemplar, *see* paradigm

exhortation, *see* protreptic

experience (*pathos*), *see* suffering

expert/expertise, *see* craft

Farrell, D. 273

fear 10, 37, 90, 93, 94, 98, 99, 103, 104, 105, 131, 132, 135, 154, 158, 159, 163, 164, 169, 175, 180, 181, 184, 185, 214, 215, 219, 228, 232, 233, 255, 256, 257, 260–262, 265, 266, 270, 271, 272, 273, 289, 314, 323–325, 326, 329, 330, 331, 332, 337, 338–339, 340–341, 342
   see also emotion(s)

Ferejohn, M. 149, 161, 163, 164, 167, 175, 178

Feugère, F. 15

Ficino 316

Fierro, M. 213

fine (*kalon*) 73, 89, 90, 92, 94, 96, 122, 130, 131, 136, 139, 143, 148, 153, 186, 200, 203, 224, 265
   translated as "beauty" 8, 71, 72, 127, 142, 216, 218, 229, 230, 240, 247, 249, 250, 334

fine (as punishment) 37, 220, 221, 343, 363
   see also money, punishment

Fine, G. 75, 76, 84, 107, 114, 121, 122, 123, 124, 144, 146, 147, 151

FitzPatrick, P. 316

flattery (*kolakeia*) 2, 4, 5, 6, 9, 14, 15, 19, 61, 168, 230, 276

Fontenrose, J. 319

form(s) (*eidos, idea*) 63–84, 134, 136, 148, 163, 176, 206, 238, 240, 241, 243, 249, 252

Forster, M. 60, 141–143, 146, 147, 150, 151

fortune (*eutuchia*), *see* success

Frankfurt, H. 246, 247, 248, 253

Friedländer, P. 156

friend/friendship (*philos, philia*) 6, 26, 28, 30, 32, 33, 34, 61, 88, 92, 93, 95, 96, 127, 132, 140, 145, 173, 179, 180, 181, 184, 185, 189, 191, 192, 193, 207, 208, 221, 229–254, 267, 268, 269, 271, 273, 279, 280, 291, 308, 310, 325, 326, 332, 342, 348, 349, 354

400 GENERAL INDEX

Frogs (Aristophanes') 1, 3, 4, 6, 7, 13, 15, 16, 19
Fronterotta, F. 80, 81–83

Gadamer, H.-G. 244, 252
Gaiser, K. 61
Gallo, I. 13, 15
Galy, J. 13
Garland, R. 320, 321
Geach, P. 136, 144, 145, 148, 318
Geissler, P. 13, 14
Gelzer, T. 16, 18, 21
geometry 11, 14, 60, 171
  see also astronomy, mathematics
Gettier, E. 87
Gigon, O. 14
Giuliani, L. 17
Glidden, D. 242, 243, 252
god(s), *see* atheism, religion
Gomez-Lobo, A. 201
Gonzalez, F. 240, 251, 252, 253, 254
good(s) (*agathon*) 8, 25, 26, 28, 29, 30, 32,
    33, 34, 35, 37, 40, 41, 47, 53, 54, 55,
    56, 57, 62, 89, 93, 95, 96, 98, 99, 100,
    101, 102, 103, 104, 105, 115, 119,
    120, 121, 122, 133, 135, 136, 143,
    145, 148, 237–238, 240, 243, 252,
    256, 258, 259, 264, 266, 269, 282,
    296, 297, 302, 304, 305, 306, 307,
    308, 309, 310, 312, 314, 320, 362
  and bad(s) 25, 62, 98, 156–170, 173, 175,
    176, 177, 225, 231–243, 248–249,
    252, 253, 254, 339
  death as 323–342
  desire for 205–228
  knowledge of 153–178 relation to
    happiness (*eudaimonia*) 179–204
  and love 229–254
  see also intellectualism (motivational),
    virtue(s)
Gorgias 88, 350
  see also Gorgias (Plato's), *Meno* (Plato's),
    sophist(s)
Gorgias (Plato's) 21, 46, 47, 48, 49, 51, 53,
    56, 57, 59, 61, 62, 99, 102, 103, 116,
    117, 127, 146, 147, 167, 168, 174,
    177, 178, 179, 181, 182, 183, 184,
    185, 186, 187, 192, 193, 194, 198,
    199, 200, 202, 203, 204, 206, 207,
    208, 209, 210, 211, 212, 215, 219,
    220, 221, 222, 223, 224, 225, 228,
    229, 236, 256, 260, 261, 263, 267,

    272, 276, 277, 278, 279, 284, 292,
    294, 295, 306, 311, 320, 328,
    330–331, 332, 333–338, 339, 352, 363
Gosling, 41, 169
Graham, D. 171, 172
gratification, *see* pleasure
Gray, V. 23
Grey, W. 14
grief (*lupē*) 255, 256, 257, 268–269, 270,
    271, 273, 342
  see also emotion(s)
Griswold, C. 294, 295, 296
Grote, G. 21, 49, 156, 279, 288, 318
Grube, G. 64, 65, 84, 88, 89, 132, 135, 285,
    291, 359, 358, 359
Guidorizzi, G. 14, 20
Gulley, N. 108, 109, 279
Guthrie, W. 13, 14, 21, 175, 238, 246, 250,
    252, 254, 279, 320

Hackforth, R. 41
Hampton, J. 199
happiness (*eudaimonia*) 26, 30, 32, 39, 88, 93,
    94, 97, 104, 111, 116, 122, 132, 134,
    139, 168, 169, 171, 172, 173, 178,
    179–204, 207, 208, 209, 210, 212,
    226, 227, 230, 231, 238, 239, 241,
    243, 244, 245, 247, 248, 249, 251,
    252, 253, 254, 268, 269, 271, 278,
    306, 327, 312, 327, 328, 332, 337
  see also good, virtue(s)
Hardy, J. 58
harm (*blabē*) 25, 27, 33, 39, 42, 56, 85, 99,
    112, 179–180, 181–184, 188,
    190–192, 193, 197, 198, 199, 203,
    209, 212, 214, 219, 222, 223, 228,
    232, 237, 254, 261, 265, 277, 278,
    280, 283, 301, 306, 310, 323, 324,
    325, 329, 335, 340, 348
  see also benefit, good and bad, misery,
    suffering, vice
Harte, V. 62, 204, 281, 283, 285, 287, 288,
    292, 297, 333
Havelock, E. 21
Haybron, D. 200
hedonism 41, 56, 169, 170, 201, 223, 263,
    340
  see also pleasure
Heidel, W. 318
Heidhues, B. 18
Heliodorus 18
Henderson, J. 18, 41, 42, 273

GENERAL INDEX

Heraclitus 11, 20, 302, 314
Herodotus 200, 327
Hermogenes 25, 341, 347, 355
Hesiod 4, 15, 301, 302, 314, 317, 318, 321
Hippias 12, 21, 29, 88
   see also Hippias Major (Plato's), *Hippias Minor* (Plato's), sophists
Hippias Major (Plato's) 59, 72, 73, 75, 76, 78, 93, 94, 127, 130, 131, 134, 136, 138, 139, 140, 141, 146, 148, 174, 202, 224, 265, 305, 310, 311
Hippias Minor (Plato's) 46, 49, 51, 93, 146, 151, 174, 224
Hippon 2, 14
Hoerber, R. 234–235, 243, 251
Hoesly, D. 266, 267, 273
holy (*hosios*) 3, 43, 65, 132
   see also piety, religion
Homer 8, 12, 15, 229, 262, 301, 302, 305, 306, 314, 317, 318, 328, 349
Hubbard, T. 18, 19
hubris 9, 10, 19
hunger 4, 5, 6, 218, 237, 238, 272
   see also appetite(s), desire(s), moral psychology
Hurka, T. 195, 204
Hursthouse, R. 200, 202

identity (of virtue), *see* intellectualism (virtue)
   of virtue and happiness; *see* happiness, necessity thesis, sufficiency thesis
ignorance (*amathia, agnoia*) 20, 24, 25, 46, 74, 85–125, 127, 135, 136, 137, 140, 144, 145, 147, 148, 151, 153, 164, 173, 180, 181, 191, 198, 202, 206, 212, 214, 219, 220, 221, 222, 223, 228, 231, 232, 233, 238, 243, 248, 254, 263, 264, 265, 271, 273, 275, 302–304, 307–311, 313, 319, 324, 347, 357, 361
   see also knowledge, wisdom
Imperio, O. 13, 15
impiety (*asebeia*) 11, 21, 24, 27, 64, 65, 70, 74, 86, 92, 94, 120, 131, 228, 297, 299, 303, 304, 313, 315, 325, 329, 335, 343–365
   see also piety, new divinities, religion
injury, *see* harm
injustice (*adikia*) 20, 24, 35, 53, 59, 94, 98, 99, 102, 103, 111, 112, 116, 118, 122, 123, 127, 135, 157, 170, 179, 182, 183, 184, 185, 186, 190, 191, 192,

193, 194, 197, 199, 200, 202, 203, 204, 206, 208, 209, 211, 212, 219, 220, 221, 225, 229, 234, 257, 265, 266, 267, 268, 270, 271, 275, 279, 281, 282, 283, 284, 285, 286, 287, 289, 290, 291, 292, 293, 297, 300, 304, 306, 307, 309, 313, 323, 329, 332, 334, 335, 337, 338, 339, 340, 341, 348, 362
   see also justice, wrongdoing
intellectualism (with regard to emotions), *see* cognitivism
intellectualism (motivational) 37, 44, 105, 153, 174, 182, 183, 196, 199, 205–228, 248, 255–273, 330, 331, 332, 333, 334, 335, 336, 337, 338, 340
intellectualism (virtue) 24–25, 30, 32, 36, 37, 40, 41, 104, 105, 153–178, 197, 204, 255, 260, 300, 315
Ion (Plato's) 47, 146, 174, 224
induction 53, 310, (*epagogē*) 51, 52, 336
irony (*eirōneia*) 92, 108, 109, 243, 266, 301, 315, 317
Irwin, T. 15, 40, 41, 53, 55, 105, 107, 109, 114, 121, 143, 146, 147, 148, 150, 151, 162, 169, 171, 178, 186, 188, 189, 200, 201, 224, 225, 226, 228, 238, 239, 240, 245, 246, 252, 268, 295
Isocrates 58, 350, 351

Jackson, B. 319
Jenks, R. 251
Jirsa, J. 62
Joël, K. 23
Johnson, C. 277, 283, 286, 290, 291, 295
Johnson, D. 23, 39, 41, 43, 44, 347, 363, 364
Johnson, M. 61
Jones, R. 24, 40, 43, 61, 122, 125, 172, 173, 178, 198, 199, 200, 201, 202, 224, 225, 227, 324, 327, 328
Joyal, M. 62
Judet de La Combe, P. 20
justice (*dikaiosunē*) 24, 25, 28, 30, 32, 33, 39, 40, 43, 54, 59, 67, 70, 73, 79, 92, 93, 94, 98, 108, 112, 121, 122, 123, 127, 134, 135, 139, 145, 151, 153–178, 179, 182, 184, 185, 186, 188, 189, 190, 191, 192–194, 199, 200, 201, 202, 203, 204, 259, 262, 264, 266, 267, 268, 275–298, 304, 305, 306, 307, 313, 320, 329, 333, 334, 335, 336, 337, 338, 339, 254, 355

see also craft, injustice, knowledge,
    punishment, virtue(s), wisdom
Justin Martyr 316

Kahn, C. 62, 63, 80–83, 146, 148, 167, 169,
    175, 186, 200, 201, 203, 213, 229,
    230, 236, 243, 273
Kamtekar, R. 210, 211, 212, 222, 223, 224,
    225
Kanavou, N. 20
Kant, I. 198, 244, 247
Kaufmann, W. 316
Kerferd, G. 19
Keuls, E. 18
Kim, A. 282, 284, 286, 287, 296
Klosko, G. 171, 295
knack (*empeiria*) 48, 61, 168, 204
knowledge (*epistēmē*) 23–44, 46, 47, 48, 49,
    51, 52, 53, 54, 55, 58, 59, 66, 68, 69,
    72, 73, 77, 78, 79, 81, 83, 82, 85–125,
    127–151, 153–178, 180, 181, 184,
    185, 186, 189, 191, 195, 198, 199,
    200, 208, 212, 213, 214, 223, 225,
    228, 231, 232, 233, 239, 240, 242,
    243, 259, 262, 263, 265, 273, 275,
    277, 278, 280, 281, 294, 300, 302,
    303, 305, 306, 307, 308, 309, 310,
    311, 312, 319, 320, 323, 324, 325,
    329, 339, 340, 356, 357
    see also craft, ignorance, virtue(s),
    intellectualism (virtue), wisdom
Kolodny, N. 241, 252, 254
Konstan, D. 13, 272, 273
Kosman, A. 248, 252
Kraut, R. 162, 165, 187, 197, 198, 200, 201,
    203, 250, 279, 280, 281, 283, 284,
    286, 287, 290, 294, 295, 296, 297,
    298, 321

LaBarge, S. 59, 60
Laches 6, 280
    see also Laches (Plato's)
Laches (Plato's) 17, 47, 49, 55, 59, 80, 95,
    127, 133, 134, 135, 138, 140, 141,
    143, 146, 147, 148, 149, 153, 156,
    157, 158, 159, 160, 164, 174, 175,
    176, 181, 202, 204, 215, 224, 257,
    260, 261, 306, 338, 339
Lactantius 316
Lamari, A., 19
Lampon 3, 11, 15
Lapatin, K. 17

law/lawful (*nomos, nomimon*) 25, 29, 30, 41,
    99, 168, 275–298, 344
    natural law 320
    obedience to law 191, 193, 203, 275–298
    see also trial (of Socrates)
lawful (*themis*) 308
van Leeuwen J. 21
Lefkowitz, M. 15
Lenfant, D. 14
Lesher, J. 111–112, 131, 147
Lesses, G. 245, 252, 253, 295
Levin, D. 250, 252, 254
Libanius 350, 364
Littman, R. 18
Litz, B. et al. 196
Lloyd, G. 14
Lloyd-Jones, H. 320
Locke, J. 146, 282, 296
Lockwood, T. 251, 252
logos 48, 66, 102, 190, 106, 277, 292, 297,
    298
Long, A. 316
love (*philia*), *see* friend/friendship
    (*erōs*), *see* desire
Lucian 6, 17, 250
luck (*eutuchia*), *see* success
lust, *see* desire(s), sex
Lycon 264, 352, 357
Lycurgus 28
Lysis (Plato's) 52, 55, 59, 61, 80, 93, 127,
    132, 138, 140, 146, 148, 174, 224,
    229–254

MacDowell, D. 14, 17, 360, 363, 365
Mackenzie, M. 235, 237, 238, 239, 240, 244,
    335
McLean, D. 17
McPherran, M. 44, 51, 53, 149, 166, 167,
    171, 176, 178, 200, 297, 298, 316,
    317, 318, 319, 320, 321, 324, 326,
    327, 328, 332, 333, 365
Magna Moralia (Aristotle's) 154, 161, 198,
    213
Magnes 19
Maier, H. 39
Major, W. 15
mantic, *see* divination
Marchant, E. 37, 40, 41, 42, 44, 127
Marshall, C. 17
Marshall, H. 19
Martin, R. 284, 290
Martinez, J. 198, 199, 216, 226

GENERAL INDEX

403

Marzullo, B. 20
mathematics 14, 138
   see also astronomy, geometry
Matthews, G. 55, 122
Maximus of Tyre 364
Meletus 87, 92, 99, 228, 254, 313, 315, 321,
   324, 335, 351, 352, 355, 356, 357,
   360, 361, 363, 364
Memorabilia (Xenophon's), 16, 21, 23–44,
   127, 244, 272, 273, 279, 294, 300,
   306, 307, 309, 310, 311, 312, 313,
   319, 321, 347, 348, 349, 352, 353,
   354, 355, 356, 360, 363
Menedemus 16
Menexenus (Plato's) 269, 319
Meno (Plato's) 14, 46, 47, 55, 56, 59, 62, 68,
   72, 75, 76, 80, 81, 93, 95, 96, 100,
   108, 109, 113, 115, 120, 122, 127,
   132, 133, 134, 137, 138, 139, 140,
   141, 149, 151, 153, 156, 157, 164,
   174, 175, 178, 186, 204, 206, 208,
   209, 210, 211, 224, 225, 304, 352
Metaphysics (Aristotle's) 50, 66, 127, 315
method (*methodos*) 25, 31, 44–62, 72, 122,
   134, 135, 136, 137, 138, 139, 141,
   142, 144, 145, 147, 151, 168, 231,
   242, 250, 263, 296, 299, 300, 301,
   302, 303, 304, 308, 313, 315, 317, 337
   see also elenchus/elenchus
Meynersen, O. 16
Mikalson, J. 317
Miller, M. 1996
misery (*athliotēs*) 10, 181–184, 185, 189,
   191, 197, 199, 200, 201, 202, 204,
   206, 208, 209, 219, 220, 267, 268,
   327, 335
   see also harm, good and bad, happiness,
   suffering
Mitsis, P. 44, 316, 320
Möbus, F. 203, 222, 223
model, *see* paradigm
moderation (*sophrōsunē*) 18, 28, 35, 37, 92,
   132, 134, 135, 143, 153, 175, 182,
   190, 194, 269, 333
   see also self-control
Moline, J. 15
Mondolfo, R. 14
money (*chrēmata*) 4, 5, 10, 17, 26, 35, 54,
   174, 178, 179, 182, 184, 185, 186,
   189, 191, 202, 209, 221, 355
   see also asceticism, poverty, wealth
Montuori, M. 21, 316

Moore, C. 21
Moore, G. 100, 102, 104
moral injury, *see* harm
Moravcsik, J. 382
Morrison, D. 23, 26, 40, 41, 199, 200, 201
Moss, J. 168, 221, 223, 255, 263, 273
Mourelatos, A. 20
Murphy, J. 284, 340
Murray, G. 18
Mysteries 11, 352
myth(s) 260, 300, 302, 313, 323, 330–338,
   358

Nails, D. 18, 21, 46, 363, 365
Napolitano, M. 14
nature (of a thing), *see* essence
   study of 2, 3, 6, 9, 10, 13, 14, 49, 66, 299,
   302, 354, 355, 356
Navia, L. 364
necessity thesis (virtue is necessary for
   happiness) 178, 180, 181, 186, 189,
   194, 197, 202
   see also sufficiency thesis
Nehamas, A. 138–140
Nestle, W. 18
Neu, J. 273
new divinities (*kaina daimonia*) 11, 12, 313,
   314, 315, 344, 347, 348, 354, 356,
   360, 361, 363, 365
Newiger, H.-J. 20, 21
Nichols M. 253
Nicias 280
   see also Laches (Plato's)
Nicomachean Ethics (Aristotle's) 108, 154,
   201, 235, 273, 318
Nightingale, A. 19, 58
North, H. 40
Notomi, N. 19
Nussbaum, M. 18, 287, 297, 316, 317, 319

Obdrzalek, S. 61
obedience/disobedience (*peitheia apeitheia*) to
   divine authority 98, 112, 135, 141,
   290, 291, 298, 308, 310, 311, 312,
   325, 329
   to superiors, law, or legal authorities 98,
   112, 135, 141, 192, 196, 204, 275,
   277, 279, 281, 282, 283–294, 296,
   297, 315, 346, 352, 354
Ober, J. 279, 281, 282, 283, 295, 296, 297,
   298, 363, 364, 365
O'Brien, D. 175

Oeconomicus (Xenophon's) 16, 40
Olson, D. 14, 16, 20
oracle(s) 3, 236, 295, 303, 308, 319, 354
   see also Delphic oracle, divination
oratory, see rhetoric
O'Regan, D. 14
Origen 316
Ostwald, M. 319

pain (ponos) 154, 169, 182, 183, 184, 197,
     203, 214, 215, 216, 219, 220, 222,
     223, 228, 258, 259, 262, 264, 268,
     269, 271, 277, 308, 325, 329, 335,
     336, 337
   see also harm, pleasure
Palamedes 26
Pangle, T. 39
Pantel, 317, 319, 320
Papageorgiou, N. 17
paradeigm (paradeigma) 43, 61, 64, 65, 67,
     71, 72, 74, 77, 79, 83, 84, 92, 162,
     163, 193, 247, 296, 300, 303, 309
   see also form
Parke, H. 319
Parker, R. 317, 320, 321, 345, 346, 352, 363
Parmenides (Plato's) 63, 64, 77, 79, 82
Parry, R. 171, 295
Part/whole (morion/holon) of virtue or other
     craft 24, 47, 51, 59, 77, 121, 135, 140,
     155–166, 168, 171, 172, 175, 176,
     177, 180, 276, 305, 318, 320
   of the soul 154, 179, 183, 256
   of eudaimonia 171, 173, 179, 184,
     189–190, 197, 245
Patzer, A. 13, 15, 16, 17, 20, 21
Peloponnesian War 6, 11–12, 35, 44, 203, 317
   (see also Amphipolis, Delium, Potidaea)
Penner, T. 146, 148, 156, 157, 159, 162, 174,
     199, 209, 210, 211, 213, 215, 216,
     217, 218, 219, 220, 221, 223, 224,
     225, 226, 227, 228, 236, 237, 238,
     239, 240, 244, 245, 246, 248, 251,
     252, 253, 254, 255, 259, 265, 330,
     331, 333, 336
Pericles 3, 44, 187, 201
perplexity (aporia) 46, 49, 55, 56, 57, 93,
     122, 150, 233, 234, 235, 239–240, 252
Peterson, S. 62
Petrarch 316
Phaedo 229 see also Phaedo (Plato's)
Phaedo (Plato's) 4, 15, 16, 20, 21, 48, 55, 56,
     59, 60, 63, 68, 72, 74, 78, 80, 81, 177,

179, 198, 235, 268, 303, 310, 319,
     321, 326, 332, 333, 334
Phaedrus (Plato's), 16, 48, 59, 60, 63, 80, 178,
     249, 250, 307, 309, 310, 319
Philebus (Plato's) 55, 148, 273, 319
Picot, J.-C. 14
Pieters, J. 14
piety (eusebeia) 24, 25, 29, 30, 32, 33, 41,
     64–67, 70, 71, 72, 73, 74, 77–79, 83,
     86, 92, 94, 120, 121, 127, 131, 134,
     135, 138, 139, 141, 145, 148, 153,
     155–158, 159, 161, 164–168, 175,
     176, 177, 194, 195, 228, 259,
     299–321, 343–365
   see also craft, holy, impiety, knowledge,
     religion, virtue(s)
Pindar 17, 20, 301, 314, 318
Piraeus 3, 19, 319
Pirrotta, S. 14
Plataea (battle of, 479 BCE) 135, 141, 143
pleasure (hedonē) 32, 33, 35, 41, 55, 56, 154,
     168, 169, 171, 188, 197, 204, 207,
     214, 215, 216, 218, 222, 223, 223,
     232, 241, 246, 258, 259, 263, 270,
     276, 277, 278, 306, 312, 317, 326,
     327, 328, 330, 333
   see also pain, hedonism
Plato (Comicus) 1, 2, 4, 14
Plato viii, 1, 2, 4, 6, 7, 8, 9, 12, 14, 16, 17,
     19, 20, 21, 23, 24, 25, 29, 40, 41, 42,
     43, 44, 45, 48, 49, 50, 52, 53, 54, 56,
     57, 58, 59, 60, 63, 64, 65, 68, 69, 70,
     71, 72, 73, 74, 75, 76, 77, 78, 79, 80,
     81, 82, 83, 84, 85, 86, 107, 124, 127,
     128, 130, 131, 134, 136, 137, 138,
     139, 140. 145, 146, 148, 149, 151,
     153, 154, 155, 156, 160, 174, 175,
     177, 178, 179, 181, 183, 185, 189,
     190, 193, 194, 195, 197, 198, 204,
     205, 206, 214, 218, 220, 221, 224,
     228, 229, 230, 232, 234, 235, 236,
     238, 239, 240, 242, 244, 246, 247,
     249, 250, 251, 252, 253, 254, 256,
     258, 259, 260, 261, 262, 264, 265,
     266, 267, 268, 269, 271, 272, 273,
     275, 279, 280, 281, 283, 288, 292,
     294, 295, 299, 300, 304, 306, 311,
     315, 316, 318, 319, 320, 321, 323,
     329, 332, 335, 336, 337, 340, 341,
     342, 343, 344, 346, 347, 350, 351,
     352, 354, 355, 356, 357, 358, 360,
     361, 362, 363, 364, 365

GENERAL INDEX

poets/poetry 3, 4, 11, 12, 13, 14, 15, 36, 61, 67, 70, 89, 91, 187, 233, 236, 273, 302, 313, 314, 349, 356, 357, 361, 365
Polansky, R. 48, 49, 50, 146
politics/politicians 1, 24, 25, 27, 35, 36, 37, 38, 39, 44, 59, 60, 89, 91, 115, 168, 203, 209, 210, 250, 266, 275–298, 300, 310, 314, 330, 331, 338, 356, 357, 361
  role of politics in the trial of Socrates 343–365
Politics (Aristotle's) 276, 297
Polus, *see* Gorgias *(Plato's)*
Polycrates 43, 349–351, 365
Popper, K. 279
Potidaea (siege of, 432 BCE) 6, 289, 338
poverty *(penia)* 2, 4, 8, 10, 12, 13, 16
  see also asceticism, money, wealth
power *(dunamis)* cognitive or moral 29, 39, 56, 59, 107, 155, 157, 162–165, 169, 176, 177, 179, 230, 260, 269, 310
  of appearance 169, divine 103, 299, 301, 302, 307, 311, 312, 314, 316
  political 35, 54, 57, 193, 209, 266, 276, 279, 285, 314, 346, 352
prayer *(proseuchē)* 34, 269, 301, 302, 305, 306, 307, 314, 317, 319
Price, A. 232, 248, 251
Prichard, H. 194, 204
Prior, W. 76, 77, 124, 148, 151
Prodicus 11, 16, 88
  see also sophist(s)
product *(ergon)*, *see* craft, cause
prophecy, *see* divination
Protagoras 2, 3, 12, 14, 21, 76, 302, 313
  see also Protagoras (Plato's), sophist(s)
Protagoras (Plato's) 19, 52, 73, 74, 75, 79, 80, 127, 133, 140, 154, 155, 156, 157, 158, 159, 160, 162, 164, 169, 174, 175, 186, 193, 194, 200, 203, 205, 207, 208, 211, 212, 213, 216, 223, 224, 228, 229, 257, 258, 261, 264, 266, 272, 279, 334, 346
protreptic *(protreptikos)* 31, 42, 56, 57, 61, 251, 252, 340
Protrepticus (Aristotle's)
psychology, moral 104, 179–273, 323, 333, 335, 340, 342
  see also intellectualism (motivational), punishment
Pucci, P. 14, 21

punishment *(timōria, kolasis)* 8, 10, 99, 135, 182, 183, 184, 185, 191, 198, 199, 203, 215, 219–223, 228, 264, 286, 297, 323, 330, 331, 332, 334–338, 343, 344
  see also intellectualism (motivational), psychology (moral)
Pythagoras/Pythagoreans 5, 11, 20, 154, 316, 333

Rabinowitz, W. 318
Raines, J. 15
Ralkowski, M. 362, 364
Rau, P. 20
recollection *(anamnēsis)* 68, 69, 70, 72, 96, 137, 148, 249
Redfield, J. 16
Reeve, C. 50, 58, 59, 60, 116–117, 118, 120, 124, 180, 262, 286, 291, 295, 297, 318, 320, 324, 325, 326, 364
refutation, *see elenchus*/elenchus, method
religion viii, 2, 3, 10, 11, 12, 13, 15, 17, 64, 69, 299–342, 344, 345, 348, 352, 353–362, 364, 365
  see also impiety, new divinities, piety
Republic (Plato's) 46, 56, 58, 59, 60, 63, 68, 80, 81, 83, 93, 108, 109, 127, 133, 135, 139, 154, 171, 174, 177, 179, 183, 186, 192, 193, 194, 195, 198, 203, 204, 206, 224, 232, 237, 238, 266, 272, 273, 294, 315, 319, 337
Reshotko, N. 172, 198, 199, 200, 201, 202, 214, 215, 216, 217, 218, 219, 224, 225, 226, 227, 255, 340
respect *(aidōs)*, *see* shame
Revermann, M. 15, 17
rhetoric 2, 8, 10, 11, 12, 49, 54, 59, 61, 127, 131, 140, 147, 153, 168, 276, 277, 293, 299, 346, 347, 348, 350, 351
  see also sophist(s)
Rhetoric (Aristotle's) 273
Riddell, J. 178
Rider, B. 251
right (and wrong), *see* benefit, bad, good, harm, vice, virtue, wrongdoing
Robin, L. 39, 250, 252, 254
Robinson, D. 232, 235, 236, 241, 250, 251, 252
Robinson, R. 50, 51, 52, 53, 55, 134, 145, 147
Roochnik, D. 58, 171, 178, 295, 324, 326, 327, 328

GENERAL INDEX

Rosen, R. 14, 19
Ross, W. 126, 146
Rossetti, L. 16
Roth, M. 238
Rowe, C. 16, 174, 199, 206, 209, 210, 211,
 215, 216, 217, 218, 219, 220, 221,
 223, 224, 225, 226, 227, 228, 236,
 237, 238, 239, 240, 244, 245, 246,
 248, 251, 252, 253, 254, 255, 330,
 334, 335, 336, 337
Rudebusch, G. 160, 162, 166, 169, 170, 171,
 177, 189, 201, 202, 223, 243, 252,
 254, 324, 327, 329
Russell, D. 171, 338
Russo, C. 19
Rusten, J. 14, 17

sacrifice (*thusia*) 34, 300, 301, 302, 305,
 306–308, 313, 314, 317, 319, 344
Saetta Cottone R. 14, 20, 21
Sanderman, D. 255
Santas, G. 147, 149, 150, 174, 175, 177, 178,
 211, 212, 225, 233, 237, 252, 254,
 255, 279, 284, 287, 290
Sarri, F. 21
Schiappa, E. 14
Schofield, M. 56, 162, 298
Schorn, S. 15
schrewdness (*phronēsis*), *see* wisdom
Schuh, G. 201
science (natural), *see* knowledge, nature, wisdom
Scott, D. 62, 151
Scott, G. 60, 146
Sedley, D. 41, 44, 59, 60, 146, 251, 320, 334,
 337, 338
Segal, C. 14, 21
Segoloni, L. 14, 16, 17, 18
Segvic, H. 209, 255, 257
self-control (*enkrateia*) 6, 25, 30, 37, 40, 259,
 260, 266, 331, 355
 see also moderation
separation (of forms) 68, 73, 74, 75, 77, 78,
 79, 80, 81, 82, 83, 84
 separationism (as interpretation of *Crito*)
 292–293, 333
sex 1, 8, 18, 27, 218, 230, 242, 250, 254, 354
Sextus Empiricus 311, 316, 318, 319
shame (*aidos, aischros*) 24, 54, 55, 56, 57, 94,
 98, 130, 131, 132, 135, 136, 148, 211,
 214, 215, 255, 256, 257, 260, 262–264,
 265, 267, 270, 271, 273, 303, 318
 see also emotion(s)

Sharma, R, 24, 40, 43, 176, 199, 200, 201,
 202, 224, 228
Shaw, J. 221, 222, 223, 336, 337, 339
Sheffield, F. 252
Sherman, N. 198
Shorey, P. 80
sign (*semeion* Socrates'), *see daimonion*
Silenus 7, 17, 229
Silk, M. 20
Silverberg, T. 279
Singpurwalla, R. 214, 215, 216, 225, 226,
 255, 257, 272
skill, *see* craft
Slings, S. 19, 42, 324
Smith, A. 124, 125
Smith, N. 15, 16, 18, 43, 45, 46–48, 49, 50,
 51, 52, 53, 55, 58, 62, 77, 78, 86, 91,
 104, 117–121, 122, 123, 125, 140–
 141, 144–145, 146, 147, 148, 149,
 150, 151, 161, 164–166, 171, 173–
 174, 175, 176, 177, 178, 183, 189,
 198, 199, 200, 201, 202, 203, 212,
 213, 215, 216, 217, 218, 219, 221,
 222, 223, 224, 225, 226, 227, 228,
 255, 257, 258, 259, 260, 261, 262,
 265, 266, 267, 270, 272, 273, 279,
 280, 281, 282, 283, 285, 286, 287,
 288, 289, 290, 292, 293, 294, 295,
 317, 318, 319, 320, 324, 325, 326,
 327, 328, 330, 331, 332, 333, 335,
 336, 337, 339, 340, 341, 359, 363,
 364, 365
Snell, B. 15
Socratic Problem 23, 28, 34, 82, 343–365
Solon 200, 314, 327, 346
soothsayer(s), *see* divination
sophist(s) 2, 3, 4, 7, 8, 9, 11, 12, 13, 14, 15,
 26, 29, 57, 61, 88, 127, 133, 266,
 276, 277, 302, 314, 346, 349, 350,
 355, 356
 see also rhetoric, nature (study of)
Sophist (Plato's) 55, 57, 59, 60, 148
soul (*psuchē, psyche*) 12, 13, 19, 21, 36, 37,
 44, 49, 54, 56, 68, 69, 95, 102, 153,
 154, 160, 167, 168, 169, 174, 177,
 179, 181, 182, 183, 188, 191, 193,
 195, 196, 198, 199, 202, 209, 218,
 219, 220, 223, 227, 228, 238, 256,
 257, 259, 263, 267, 268, 269, 271,
 272, 276, 278, 295, 298, 306, 307,
 308, 312, 316, 320, 326, 330, 332,
 333, 334, 335, 336, 337, 340, 355

GENERAL INDEX

see also death and afterlife, emotions, moral psychology, intellectualism (motivational)

sound-mindedness (*sōphrosunē*), *see* moderation

Souto Delibes, F. 13

Sparta (Laconian) 8, 12, 14, 17, 18, 135, 141, 143, 193, 203, 280, 347

Sreenivasan, G. 202

standard, *see* paradigm

Starkie, W. 19, 21

Stavru, A. 16, 17, 21

Stesichorus 3, 4, 5

Stobaeus 267

Stokes, M. 41, 319

Storey, I. 14, 15, 17, 19

Strauss, L. 18, 23, 39, 283, 284, 292

de Stryker, E. 19, 324

success (*eutuchia*) 172–173, 178, 186, 196, 200, 340

suffering (*pathos*) 5, 21, 53, 99, 102, 103, 111, 116, 118, 170, 182, 184, 191, 202, 214, 220, 268, 271, 277, 284, 289, 296, 297, 314, 320, 324, 328, 329, 330, 332, 335, 336, 339, 340

suffiency thesis (virtue is sufficient for happiness) 171, 173, 178, 180, 184, 189, 194, 197, 199, 202

Swanton, C. 189, 202, 204

symposium 3, 5

Symposium (Plato's) 16, 17, 18, 19, 21, 55, 58, 59, 63, 72, 78, 80, 81, 148, 229, 236, 240, 247, 249, 250, 252, 253, 254, 319, 334, 338, 363

Symposium (Xenophon's) 40, 307

Taillardat, J. 14

Tarrant, H. 18, 60, 61

Taylor, A. 13, 279

Taylor, C. 41, 162, 169, 224, 225, 272, 318

teacher/teaching 1, 2, 4, 6, 7, 8, 10, 11, 12, 13, 20, 21, 23–44, 47, 48, 57, 60, 70, 71, 86, 87, 88, 92, 95, 96, 97, 113, 115, 120, 121, 176, 221, 222, 228, 230, 268, 271, 278, 279, 299, 313, 316, 321, 344, 346, 347, 349, 355, 356, 361

Telecleides 1, 2, 3, 4, 5, 9, 13, 15, 16

Tell, H. 13

Telò, M. 17

Teloh, H. 108

temperance (*sophrōsunē*), *see* moderation

Tessatore, A. 240

Tessman, L. 198

Thales 11, 14, 20

Theaetetus (Plato's) 59, 60, 148, 295, 309, 310, 319, 326

Theages (Plato's?) 309, 319

theft (*klepsia*) 4, 5, 16, 21

therapy (*therapeia*) 267, 305

Thrasymachus 8

   see also Republic (Plato's)

Thucydides 44, 201, 203, 302, 303, 317

Tiles, J. 295

Toynbee, A. 316

trial (legal) 12, 14, 20, 21, 99, 203, 280, 286, 297

   (of Socrates) 28, 45, 54, 64, 69, 99, 214, 283, 291, 294, 296, 297, 299, 300, 303, 310, 313–315, 321, 329, 341, 342, 343–365

Trivigno, F. 252

Tsamalikos, P. 21

Tsouna, V. 177

Tuozzo, T. 59

Tertullian 316

Tylawski, E. 19

Tyrtaeus 187, 201

unitarianism 64, 80–83

   see also developmentalism

unity (of virtue), *see* intellectualism (virtue)

Untersteiner M. 14

Vander Waerdt, P. 20, 40

Vasiliou, I., 123, 190, 202, 204, 317

Velleman, J. 247, 254

Vernant, J.-P. 317

Versenyi, L. 108, 236, 238, 239, 252, 254, 317, 318

Versnel, H. 320, 321

Viano, C. 44

vice (*kakia*) 85, 94, 108, 181, 271, 335, 338

   see also ignorance, virtue(s)

Vickers, M. 18

Villa, D. 279, 280, 282, 288, 296

virtue(s) (*aretē*) 23–44, 47, 54, 55, 56, 57, 61, 75, 76, 77, 85, 88, 89, 92, 93, 94, 95, 96, 97, 98, 108, 111, 112, 113, 114, 115, 118, 122, 127, 129, 132, 133, 134, 135, 139, 141, 145, 149, 153–178, 179–204, 220, 230, 238, 241, 245, 246, 249, 253, 255, 259, 260, 262, 263, 271, 275, 277, 278,

279, 280, 295, 299, 300, 302, 304,
305, 306, 307, 308, 309, 311, 315,
317, 318, 320, 323, 329, 331, 332,
337, 338, 339, 340, 342, 348, 355
see also courage, craft, happiness, justice,
knowledge, moderation, piety, vice,
wisdom
Vlastos, G. 28, 29, 41, 50, 51, 52, 53, 61, 64,
69–79, 81, 109–112, 124, 138, 139,
143, 146, 147, 148, 149, 151, 156–158,
162, 169, 170, 171, 173, 175, 176,
178, 179, 180, 181, 184, 189, 198,
200, 201, 202, 230, 231, 232, 238,
240–242, 244, 245, 246, 247, 248, 251,
252, 253, 255, 279, 284, 287, 290,
291, 297, 298, 316, 317, 318, 319,
341, 358, 359, 360, 361, 365
Vogt, K. 207
voice (*phonē*), *see daimonion*
voluntary and involuntary (*hekōn* and *akōn*)
26, 99, 205, 206, 209, 211, 212, 222,
223, 225, 341, 261, 279, 282, 285,
287, 288, 289
see also akrasia, intellectualism
(motivational), moral psychology

Wade, F. 284
Walker, M. 250
Wallace, R. 14
Walsh, J. 255
Walzer, M. 283, 284
Waterfield, R. 350, 351, 352, 353, 363, 364,
365
Watson, L. 317
wealth (*ploutos*) 20, 57, 62, 102, 153, 170,
172, 173, 174, 200, 203, 207, 225,
278, 280, 336, 337
see also asceticism, money, poverty
Weiher, A. 13
Weiss, R. 62, 197, 199, 200, 201, 203, 282,
285, 287, 288, 292, 296, 297
Wenley, R. 316
White, N. 144, 146, 148, 201
Whitman, C. 21
Wilburn, J. 259, 273
Wildberg, C. 15
Willi, A. 17
Williamson, T. 123
willing and unwilling (*hekōn* and *akōn*), *see*
voluntary and involuntary
wine 3, 4, 5, 6, 18, 239, 251, 252, 301, 338
see also drinking/drunkenness, symposium)

Winspear, A. 279
wisdom (*sophia*) 2, 3, 8, 10, 24, 25, 26, 28,
30, 33, 34, 40, 41, 46, 47, 49, 54, 55,
56, 57, 58, 59, 62, 64, 86, 87, 88, 89,
90, 91, 92, 94, 96, 97, 104, 105, 106,
107, 108, 109, 110, 111, 112, 114,
115, 117, 120, 122, 125, 140, 141,
142, 153, 155, 156, 157, 158, 159,
160, 161, 166, 169, 170, 171, 172,
173, 175, 177, 178, 179, 180, 181,
185, 188, 190, 200, 204, 207, 225,
229, 230, 238, 239, 241, 243, 245,
246, 249, 251, 252, 253, 254, 264,
268, 271, 273, 277, 280, 285, 299,
300, 303, 305, 306, 307, 308, 309,
310, 311, 312, 313, 314, 320, 321,
327, 339, 340, 356
(*phronēsis*) 25, 33, 89, 127, 159, 169, 354
see also craft, happiness, ignorance,
knowledge, virtue(s)
wish (*boulēsis*), *see* desire
Wolfsdorf, D. 45, 46, 48, 52, 54, 60, 85, 91,
106, 107, 123, 124, 125, 146, 147,
148, 151, 163, 171, 178, 238, 252,
317
Wood, E. 279
Wood, N. 279
Woodbury L. 21
Woodruff, P. 69, 72–74, 75, 78, 79, 115–117,
118, 120, 146, 147, 149, 150, 161,
165, 201, 202, 203, 255, 262, 264,
273, 289, 295
Woolf, R. 62, 330
Woozley, A. 283, 284, 287, 290
Wormell, D. 319
wretchedness, *see* harm, misery, good and bad,
happiness, suffering
wrongdoing (*adikia*) 35, 87, 154, 180, 181,
182, 183, 206, 211, 212, 219, 220,
221, 222, 223, 224, 225, 228, 264,
268, 289, 290, 297, 349, 362
see also bad, harm, impiety, injustice,
intellectualism (motivational), moral
psychology

Xanthippe 16
Xenophon viii, 1, 4, 7, 12, 16, 21, 23–44,
127, 146, 229, 235, 244, 250, 268,
272, 273, 279, 294, 299, 300, 306,
307, 311, 313, 315, 316, 318, 319,
320, 321, 323, 341, 342, 343, 347,
348, 349, 350, 351, 352, 353, 354,

GENERAL INDEX

355, 356, 357, 358, 360, 362, 363, 364, 365
Xenophanes 11, 14, 20, 312, 314, 318

Yonezawa, S. 285
Young, C. 146

Young, G. 287, 292
Young, R. 273
Yunis, H. 318, 320

Zaidman, 317, 319, 320
Zeyl, D. 78, 169, 201, 276, 328

Printed in the USA
CPSIA information can be obtained
at www.ICGtesting.com
LVHW080832171024
794058LV00005B/172